JOURNEY TO THE

Northern
Rockies

"Much more than a guidebook, *Journey to the Northern Rockies* offers fascinating reading, unparalled in its depth and historical research. A must-read for anyone who plans to visit or live in the Northern Rockies."

—Robyn Griggs, editor, *Mountain Living* magazine

HELP US KEEP THIS GUIDE UP TO DATE

Every effort has been made by the author and editors to make this guide as accurate and useful as possible. However, many things can change after a guide is published—establishments close, phone numbers change, hiking trails are rerouted, facilities come under new management, etc.

We would love to hear from you concerning your experiences with this guide and how you feel it could be made better and be kept up to date. While we may not be able to respond to all comments and suggestions, we'll take them to heart and we'll also make certain to share them with the author. Please send your comments and suggestions to the following address:

The Globe Pequot Press
Reader Response/Editorial Department
P.O. Box 833
Old Saybrook, CT 06475

Or you may e-mail us at:

editorial@globe-pequot.com

Thanks for your input, and happy travels!

JOURNEY TO THE

Northern
Rockies

by

Michael McCoy

The Globe Pequot Press

Old Saybrook, Connecticut

Cover photo by Randy Wells/© Tony Stone Images
Cover design by Nancy Freeborn
Illustrations by Gil Fahey
Text design and maps by Deborah V. Nicolais

Library of Congress Cataloging-in-Publication Data
McCoy, Michael, 1951–
      Journey to the northern Rockies / by Michael McCoy. — 1st ed.
          p. cm.
      Includes bibliographical references (p.   ) and index.
      ISBN 0-7627-0187-0
      1. Rocky Mountains Region—Tours. 2. Wyoming—Tours. 3. Idaho—Tours.
4. Montana—Tours. 5. Yellowstone National Park—Tours. 6. Grand Teton National Park
(Wyo.)—Tours. 7. Automobile travel—Rocky Mountains Region—Guidebooks. I. Title.
F721.M45 1998
917.804'33—dc21
                                        98–17599
                                          CIP

Manufactured in the United States of America
First Edition/First Printing

To Marsha (a.k.a. Swampa), who dragged me kicking and screaming to kindergarten; and to Dodger, who blazed the way back West.

Contents

Acknowledgments   ix
Introduction   xi

I Northwest Wyoming and Adjacent IdaMont: Yellowstone-Teton Country   1
Introduction   3
The Land   6
The First Humans   15
History   22
Seeing Yellowstone-Teton Country   39
Staying There   88

II Western Montana: Glacier-Gold Country   121
Introduction   123
Of Glaciers, Ecosystems, and a Lake Running Through It   127
History   134
Seeing Glacier-Gold Country   150
Staying There   199

III Central Idaho: Sun Valley–Salmon Country   229
Introduction   231
Mobile Continents and Movable Mountains   234
History   240
Seeing Sun Valley–Salmon Country   246
Staying There   283

Practical Hints   303
Bibliography   314
Index   323

Acknowledgments

First, I'd like to thank my wife, Nancy McCullough-McCoy, for joining me on countless adventures . . . and for her support and good humor even at those times when I was face-to-screen with the computer for days on end.

Thanks to the many other friends who've shared experiences with me in the Northern Rockies during the last quarter century, only a few of whose names appear in the book.

I'd like to thank my mother, Mary M. McCoy, for somehow instilling in an inattentive student a love for the written word. An outstanding speller, she would never agree to tell me how to spell a word but, rather, would instruct me to "Look it up." A combination of things—including marriage, World War II, and three children—prevented her from using her journalism degree professionally. Perhaps she can take a bit of professional pride from being largely responsible for this book.

It was my late father, Max McCoy, who persuaded me to return to the state of my birth, Wyoming, to attend college. Had I not ridden out of Iowa and into the sunset toward Laramie on that September day in 1970, I may never have discovered what wonders awaited west of the plains.

Dozens of individuals were invaluable in providing information and support when I was researching and writing this book, including personnel at state travel bureaus, local chambers of commerce, national parks and forests, local and regional museums, and commercial enterprises.

Particularly helpful were Victor Bjornberg at Travel Montana, Georgia Smith at the Idaho Travel Council, Joe Kipphut at the Missoula Ranger District (Lolo National Forest), Karen Connelly at the Jackson Hole Chamber of Commerce, Racene Friede at the Bozeman Chamber of Commerce, Linda Semrow at the Whitefish Chamber of Commerce, Claudia Wade at the Cody Country Visitors Council, Connie Kenney at the Butte Chamber of Commerce, Viki Eggers at the West Yellowstone Chamber of Commerce, and Jack Siback at the Sun Valley Resort.

Thanks go also to Laura Strom at the Globe Pequot Press for inviting me to write this book, to Paula Brisco for gently but firmly reminding me of my deadlines, and to artist Gil Fahey, whose detailed drawings help bring life to the pages that follow. And thanks to Robert L. Casey for blazing the way with his long-running book, *Journey to the High Southwest.*

Finally, thanks to those of you who choose to carry this book along when traveling in the Northern Rockies. If it leads you to pry deeper into the region's nooks and crannies—to discover some of the hundreds of incredible things not even mentioned herein—I will consider my endeavor successful.

"The traveler was active; he went strenuously in search of people, of adventure, of experience. The tourist is passive; he expects interesting things to happen to him. He goes 'sight-seeing.'"

—Daniel J. Boorstin, *The Image*

Introduction

They tell me I was born in Wyoming, and that then my family whisked me away to west-central Iowa only a few weeks after the miraculous event. I really don't remember. I do know, however, that eighteen years later I returned to the Cowboy State, where I attended and graduated from the state university in Laramie. I met my future wife, Nancy, while we were both working at Grand Targhee Ski Resort, nestled high on the west slope of the Teton Range near the Wyoming–Idaho border. We were married in Grand Teton National Park. Then we moved to Montana, where we resided for seventeen years. Now we live in Idaho. I've traveled, for work and for fun—by bicycle, by foot, by skis, and by car—hundreds of thousands of miles throughout the tri-state region.

So, perhaps you can understand why I consider myself a resident not so much of any one of these states, but of the greater Northern Rockies region. I have a problem with state lines, anyway. They interrupt things. They fragment ecosystems, which are nature's more gracious and logical land divisions.

I live in IdaWyoMont, thank you.

Returning to the Rockies coincided with my emergence from the cocoon of adolescence. The timing was right: I was finally ready to start noticing that a universe existed beyond my own realm of self. I was prepared to take an interest in new things, such as the world of nature. And what a stage the Rocky Mountains provided for exploration and discovery!

Now that I have resided in the region continuously for nearly thirty years, I actually consider myself lucky that I did not spend my youth here. I know people who have lived in the Northern Rockies all their lives, and who sadly take for granted the region's incredible scenery and diversity of residents, both human and nonhuman. I'm convinced that growing up in the Midwest, then moving back to the Rockies in my late teens was the ideal way to do it. It has provided me with an auspicious perspective, one which permits me to look at things with the seasoned familiarity of a native *and* the wonder of a newcomer.

My goal in writing this book is to share with you, the reader, some of the magic and beauty I've found to be so richly abundant in the region.

How did I determine what to include and not to include in this book? In some ways it was tough, in other ways easy. Not everyone will agree with the boundaries I have drawn. A geologist, for instance, would tell you that the mountains of Yellowstone and Grand Teton national parks more accurately belong in the Middle Rockies. Technically, the Northern Rockies begin to the north and west of Yellowstone and extend well into Canada. However, going partly on feel, or second sense, and largely on experience, I concluded that a greater "geocultural" Northern Rockies region exists within the United States. For the purpose of this guide, these geocultural boundaries supersede geologic ones. In this book the Northern Rockies region encompasses the Greater Yellowstone Ecosystem, including the Teton Range, an area I have called *Yellowstone-Teton Country*. It also comprises the mountains of

Glacier National Park and the many other ranges of western Montana. This is *Glacier-Gold Country*. Finally, Idaho's contribution to the region, nicknamed *Sun Valley–Salmon Country*, includes the Bitterroots, White Clouds, Sawtooths, Lost Rivers, and other ranges giving rise to the headwaters of the torrential forks of the Snake and Salmon rivers.

Falling outside the Northern Rockies geocultural region (but, admittedly, geologically within the Northern Rockies) are the Purcell Mountains of extreme northwest Montana and the Selkirks and other ranges and adjacent valleys in northern Idaho. The excluded area includes the Libby-Troy area of Montana, and the towns of Sandpoint and Coeur d'Alene, Idaho. Most veteran travelers would agree, I believe, that these areas have more of a Pacific Northwest than a Northern Rockies "feel" to them. Also lying just outside the areas of coverage are Wyoming's Wind River Range and the great city of Boise, Idaho.

Be assured, though, this leaves more than enough to investigate. *Journey to the Northern Rockies* will lead you to some of nature's most gorgeous rivers, mountainscapes, and valley views. The region is rich, too, in unique and surprising accommodations, restaurants, and other attractions of the human-made variety.

To summarize, the area covered extends from Grand Teton National Park north to Montana's Glacier National Park, which straddles the Continental Divide just below the Canadian border. (Brief mention is made of Alberta's Waterton Lakes National Park, which constitutes part of the Waterton-Glacier International Peace Park.) From east to west the region reaches from the winter-summer resort of Red Lodge, Montana, to the winter-summer resort of McCall, Idaho. Falling roughly in the middle of the area of coverage are Butte and Anaconda, Montana. This somehow seems to fit. Butte and Anaconda, hard-edged and hard-earned blue-collar towns, appear sorely neglected at first glance. Yet the countryside surrounding these communities holds wonderful secrets, including some of the most sublime mountains and meadows in the entire chain of Rocky Mountains.

Butte-Anaconda boosters have recently discovered that tourism is a dependable and renewable resource. By building things such as museums, which illuminate the area's colorful past, and the U.S. High Altitude Sports Center, where world-class speed-skating races are contested, the residents are investing in the future. Over time the optimistic among them anticipate accruing riches far greater than those earned in years past, when thousands of workers ripped out the bowels of the earth to make only a handful of men wealthy. In Anaconda, the new Jack Nicklaus–designed Old Works Golf Course was built atop a hazardous

The Northern Rockies region

waste site, a legacy remaining from the greed and ignorance that reigned during the copper-smelting days.

The golf course, paid for largely with U.S. Environmental Protection Agency "Superfund" reclamation monies, might be considered a metaphor for the Butte-Anaconda area. In turn, Butte-Anaconda—a curious mix of past neglect and present foresight—is the entire Northern Rockies region in microcosm.

In the Northern Rockies for more than a century some men and women have struggled with and torn at the land, yet not succeeded in taming its wild spirit or dominating its scenery. Now, echoing a trend seen throughout the Rocky Mountain West, communities in the Northern Rockies are switching from economies based on *ex*traction to ones of *at*traction—attraction of visitors, that is. Many citizens in the region's communities are striving and urging others to live in harmony with the surrounding countryside rather than in strife with it. They are finding out, in contradiction to a timeworn cliché, that one *can* eat the scenery—or make a living from it, anyway. But in order for people to make a living from the scenery, the views and wildlife must be preserved. Over the long term, a slope covered with trees is worth more money to the locals than the trees felled will bring at the mill.

Like the Butte-Anaconda area in particular, and the Rocky Mountain West in general, the Northern Rockies region is a rapidly changing part of the United States. Ironically, in many areas today's number-one threat is not clear-cutting, overgrazing, or destructive mining practices. It is something more insidious. Well-meaning people, many of them former visitors who were seduced into moving to the glorious region, are loving it to death. Large ranches and extensive forest lands are progressively being parceled into subdivisions. This disperses rather than concentrates new residents, transforming former rural areas into tentacles of urban sprawl. It can have many negative side effects, not the least of which is the blocking of traditional and crucial wildlife-migration routes.

You may be surprised by the bustle on the roads surrounding Bozeman, the frantic traffic in the Flathead Valley, or the multimillion-dollar mansions dominating parts of the Jackson Hole and Sun Valley landscapes. Much of the growth

and change, though, is taking place in relatively small pockets such as these. There are other places, deserted and delightful, through which you will travel and where you will wonder, "Growing? Crowded? What's everybody talking about?"

If there is one thing that I implore you to do as you tour the Northern Rockies, it is this: For every expected thing you do—watching Old Faithful erupt, for instance, or driving on the Going-to-the-Sun Road (neither of which you should miss!)—resolve to do something less predictable. Leave the highway now and then, taking time to smell the cows. Tackle a dirt road, by truck or by mountain bike, just to see where it goes. Follow a foot trail to a high-mountain lake. Blast out of the car after a Sunlight Basin rainstorm to inhale the earthy essence of sage. Walk barefoot through a dune field to feel the sand between your toes. Inspect and wonder at how those scraggly lodgepole pines manage to grow out of solid rock at the north end of the Teton Range, along the little-traveled Ashton-Flagg Road. Search for an arrowhead on the hardpan ground that spreads out below Montana's Rocky Mountain Front. Camp in Idaho's marvelous Sawtooth Valley, and listen for the hair-raising, early-morning yipping and yammering of a pack of coyotes. (By the way, the gangly critter's name is pronounced *KIE-oat* in the Northern Rockies, not *kie-O-tee*.) Get yourself stuck in a high-country traffic jam, also known as a cattle drive: Shut off the engine, close your eyes, and hear echoes from the past as cowboys on horseback whistle and whoop to get their mooing, snorting wards a-moving between high country and low.

The tours outlined herein are suggestions only. If you follow them you will not be disappointed, yet you can fashion equally fine "originals" by using information in this book along with a good map. Likewise, no attempt has been made to identify every road, restaurant, accommodation, campground, or shopping opportunity in any of the three sub-regions. To try to do so would require several additional volumes this size, and even then it wouldn't be comprehensive, since things are ever-changing. Nor have I rated facilities relative to their quality. Most of those featured are stores, eateries, lodgings, and campgrounds that I have patronized or at least visited. They are places I would not hesitate to recommend to a friend. The majority are in or near conveniently located communities boasting ample services, towns and resorts where visitors will logically want to stay and spend a greater amount of their time, anyway.

That said, if I've missed a favorite of yours, be it a restaurant, B&B, campground, or whatever, I'd like to hear about it. Send your suggestions in care of the author to The Globe Pequot Press, P.O. Box 833, Old Saybrook, CT 06475, or e-mail your comments to editorial@globe-pequot.com.

Regarding prices, I have used the following categories. For restaurants: inexpensive, up to $24; moderate, $25 to $54; and expensive, $55 and more. These are based on full dinners for two people, excluding tax, gratuities, and cocktails or wine. For accommodations: very inexpensive, $25 to $39; inexpensive, $40 to $59; moderate, $60 to $89; expensive, $90 to $124; and very expensive, $125 and up. The prices of lodgings are those charged for a double room during the high seasons, which generally run from Memorial Day through Labor Day and, where winter snows are an attraction, such as at ski resorts, December through March. During those peak periods, especially in the popular resort areas, you should make advance reservations if you are particular about accommodations. Don't neglect to ask about discounts if you're a member of AAA, AARP, or another organization that may qualify you to save money. It's also important to know that outstanding deals on rooms are often available during the slower shoulder seasons of April–May and September–November. The rates during these months can be half—or even less—of those charged during the high seasons. Autumn, especially, is a splendid time to travel in the Northern Rockies. For those able to slip away during this time of year, I highly recommend doing so.

Most of the campgrounds in the Northern Rockies are one of three types: private, U.S. Forest Service, or National Park Service. The private grounds typically feature more complete services, such as hot showers and hookups for RVs. The National Park Service campgrounds, in particular, fill very early in the day (often before 10:00 A.M.)

during the height of the tourist season. They are typically operated on a first-come, first-served basis. Forest Service campgrounds often are the most pleasant campgrounds to be found in an area, but they are not always well publicized (which is one reason they're so pleasant, after all). Sites at many Forest Service campgrounds can be reserved, for a few dollars extra, by calling (800) 280–CAMP (2267) or the ranger district phone number listed in association with that particular campground. Sites usually can also be reserved at private campgrounds.

Amid this precious land, this cattle- and dude-ranching country, the Old West endures as nowhere else in the United States. As you travel through the Northern Rockies, remember that it is from the land that many livelihoods still are made. From the prehistoric Paleo Indians to the Sheepeater Indians, who in the nineteenth century inhabited high, hard-to-reach mountain places in and around Yellowstone, to the range cowboys and prospectors of the 1800s, to the modern rancher and logger, the land here has provided. Perhaps it has not always provided bountifully, but it has provided nonetheless. In a very real sense, you, as part of the tourism business—the fastest-growing industry in the Northern Rockies—are helping to sustain the residents' time-honored ability to eke out a living from the land.

And what a privilege that is, in a region so beautiful and whose vast expanses of public lands are owned by Americans in common, whoever they are, whatever they do, and wherever they live. During your travels in the Northern Rockies you will bear witness to a land of mountains and wildlife admired and considered sacred by millions of people throughout the world. In view of this, consider yourself not a tourist, but a pilgrim.

Still, be careful not to trespass on private lands and be sure to leave all the gates as you found them—open or closed, that is. Irrigation canals, cattle, and sheep are sacred in the Northern Rockies . . . but so are the wolves, the free-flowing rivers, the grizzly bears, and the old-growth forests of spruce and fir that inhabit high and rarefied, regal places.

Finally, and most important of all: Have fun!

I

Northwest Wyoming and Adjacent IdaMont

YELLOWSTONE-TETON COUNTRY

Yellowstone-Teton Country

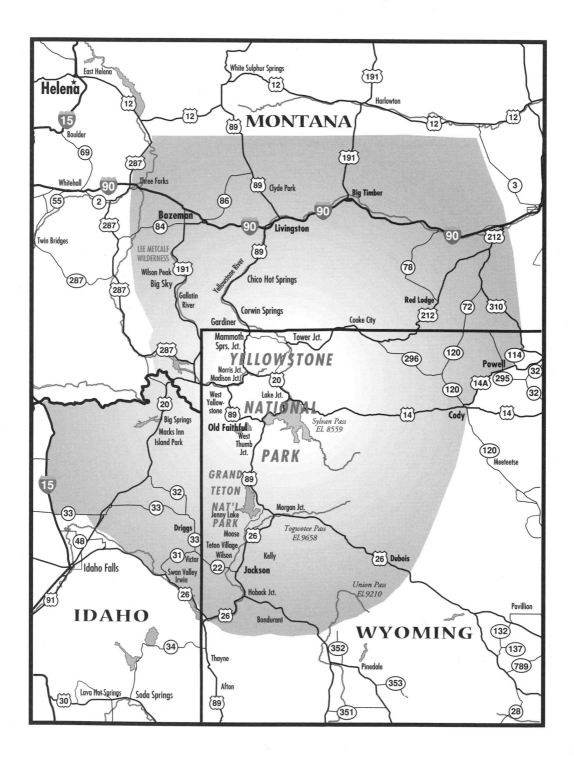

Introduction

A few years ago my wife Nancy and I, while residing in Missoula, Montana, hosted a Japanese student who was attending a summerlong English program at the University of Montana. When asked what she most wanted to see while in Montana, Kaori Kubota didn't miss a beat.

"Yellowstone," our guest said matter-of-factly. The look on her face seemed to inquire why we would even bother asking.

No matter that most of Yellowstone lies in Wyoming and not Montana: For Kaori, as for many of the world's citizens outside the United States, Yellowstone is essentially synonymous with all the northern Rocky Mountain states of Montana, Idaho, and Wyoming. And, really, is there a region of greater concern and intrigue for America's own citizens?

That fascination, among non–Native Americans anyway, began back in 1808 when trapper John Colter returned to Manuel Lisa's fort at the confluence of the Yellowstone and Bighorn rivers. On his solo winter trek Colter had covered at least 500 miles through the heart of the Yellowstone-Teton region. Because of his seemingly tall tales about bubbling, stinking hot pots and other improbable phenomena, Colter was scorned as a lunatic and liar by many of his fellow mountain men. As it turned out, he had witnessed what he claimed to have seen. Now, nearly two centuries later, citizens throughout the United States hear reports at least weekly about the Yellowstone wolves, the killing of the park's bison by wildlife officials, or some other facet of the region. When Old Faithful suddenly turned less predictable a few years ago, it made the headlines in the nation's newspapers. When President Clinton vacationed in Jackson, Wyoming, and subsequently invited that town's high-school band to march in his 1997 inaugural parade, it set off a spat between Jackson and the neighboring community Cody, a town founded by and named for William F. "Buffalo Bill" Cody. The members of Cody's band thought *they* were marching in the parade. The ensuing battle of the bands was followed for days by those watching Tom Brokaw and the other network anchors.

Each year more than three million visitors make the pilgrimage to experience the unique magic of Yellowstone and the greater Yellowstone-Teton region. U.S. citizens and foreigners alike want—almost *need*—to see this legendary land for themselves. They want to feel its weather, watch its wildlife, inhale the sulfur stink of its hot pots, and scan its timeless vistas. Maybe they tell their friends back home that they're heading out to fish in the region's sparkling waters for wild trout or to see how the fires of 1988 altered the landscape. But what they really come for is the magic.

In a planning document recently compiled by the Targhee National Forest, the region known as the Greater Yellowstone Ecosystem (GYE) is described as "an area of 12 million acres and the largest remaining block of relatively undisturbed plant and animal habitat in the contiguous United States." Yellowstone and Grand Teton national parks, while crucial components of the GYE, comprise only part of what makes the region so special. Combined, the parks encompass less than a quarter of those 12 million acres.

Even if somehow, magically and horribly, the pair of legendary national parks were excavated and whisked away, that which remained in the region surrounding the gaping holes would still constitute one of the most magnificent masses of mountains and wildest tangles of terrain in the lower forty-eight states.

Yes, a large share of Yellowstone-Teton Country's premier recreational and leisure opportunities lies "undiscovered" in the broad expanses outside the national parks, and even amid little-visited spots within the park boundaries. These are places typically ignored or glossed over by the media and tourist-promotion bureaus. Consequently, they are bypassed by all but unusually intrepid, lucky, or lost travelers. One of my goals in writing this chapter, indeed the entire book, is to lead the traveler to some of these lesser-known delights. Sure, you'll read about Old Faithful and Yellowstone Lake, but you'll also learn about places whose names won't ring a bell. Have you heard of the Bechler Entrance to Yellowstone, for instance? How about the Grassy Lake Road? Yankee Jim Canyon?

Here's the clincher: On a busy August evening, when the last available campsite at Madison Junction in Yellowstone was claimed at 7:30 that morning, you can probably locate an almost-vacant Forest Service campground just a tent stake's throw from the park boundary. It doesn't make sense, but it's true.

Focusing exclusively on Yellowstone National Park for the moment, consider that during its first century, 1872 through 1972, the park saw some 50 million visitors. By 1993, or twenty-one years later, it had hosted another 50 million. Forecasters say that, at the current rate of growth in tourism, the 150-millionth visitor will pass through the gates in the year 2003, or only ten years since visitation surpassed 100 million. Ten years ago many western congressmen and gateway-community business owners decried the National Park Service's "let-burn" policy, contending that the 1988 Yellowstone wildfires would be the ruination of the region's tourist trade. Instead, the fires seem to have had just the opposite effect: They added fuel to the ever-growing fascination with Yellowstone, and visitation has progressively increased during the decade since the fires.

Yet, even within the bustle of Yellowstone things are not as crowded as they might seem. According to tourism studies, fully 94 percent of visitors to the park stray no farther than 400 feet from their vehicles. In fact, even as total visitation has skyrocketed, the number of backcountry-camping permits has continually declined since the 1970s, when the backpacking boom peaked. The network of roads and adjacent strips of buildings and services covers an extremely small percentage of the park's area. So, even on the sunniest summer day, when traffic is backed up from Old Faithful to West Yellowstone, most of Yellowstone goes unvisited by humans.

Political boundaries such as state lines tend to disregard ecosystems, nature's objective land divisions. Such is the case here, so to some extent I have drawn my own boundaries for the region. Yellowstone-Teton Country includes parts of Wyoming, Montana, and Idaho. If you look at the map on page 2, you'll see that this region includes the mountainous areas of northwest Wyoming; the Montana counties of Carbon, Stillwater, Sweet Grass, Park, and Gallatin; and the portion of southeast Idaho lying east of Interstate 15 and north of U.S. Highway 26. This guidebook takes you no farther south in Wyoming than to the Hoback Rim, a low mountain divide between Jackson Hole and Pinedale. From the rim, waters flow either south into the Green-Colorado river system or north into the Snake-Columbia system. This seems as logical a point as any to draw the line between the Northern and Middle Rockies (although a geologist would tell you that technically the Tetons are part of the Middle and not the Northern Rockies). Regarding the sunrise side of the region, the east slope of the Absaroka (*Ab-SORE-uh-kuh*) Mountains in Wyoming marks the eastern extent of coverage.

No word describes Yellowstone-Teton Country better than *diverse*. The major ranges—the Tetons, Gros Ventres (*Grow-VONTS*), Beartooths, Absarokas, Madisons, and others—rise drastically and grab the moisture out of storms moving from the west. This creates *rainshadow* effects to the east of the mountains. The lofty western slopes of the mountains can receive hundreds of inches of snow in a year. When added to the water that falls during the thundershowers

Cow elk

common in summer, it can equal more than 60 inches of annual precipitation. Meanwhile, some of the dry expanses east of the mountains, such as the Bighorn Basin, are lucky to attract 7 inches of water in a year. This striking contrast in precipitation, along with other factors such as soil types and differences in exposure to the sun, creates a staggering array of environments: alpine tundra, brooding groves of giant Douglas fir and blue spruce, shimmering aspen stands, thirsty desert, and more. You'll see expanses of red rock evocative of southern Utah's canyon country. You will encounter high, sage-covered plains inhabited by far more antelope and wild horses than humans, and irrigated river bottoms as lush as a Midwest farm field. You can hike through high-country tundra that biologically has more in common with areas north of the Arctic Circle than with the deserts lying immediately below.

Yellowstone-Teton Country offers as much adventure as the most intrepid of travelers could possibly crave. Here one can find challenging peaks to scale, rocky roads to explore in a four-wheel-drive rig, and white-water rivers to dance down in a kayak. Wilderness hiking trails beckon, leading to glorious backcountry; so do rugged non-wilderness trails ideal for tackling by mountain bike. In winter and spring, steep ski runs hold

some of the deepest powder snow on earth. Still, if your tastes in travel are more tame, you can view the most sublime splendors imaginable without ever leaving the paved roads (although I do encourage everyone to at least get out of the car occasionally!). In fact, simply driving along some of the region's more precipitous paved roads, such as the Beartooth Highway and Teton Pass, will provide more thrills than many motorists desire.

Yellowstone-Teton Country is big north to south, east to west . . . and down to up. The region's lowest elevation, along the Yellowstone River in Montana, is around 3,000 feet above sea level. The highest, at more than two miles higher, is the 13,771-foot tip of the Grand Teton. (Gannett Peak, Wyoming's tallest mountain and all of 33 feet higher than the Grand Teton, is just outside the geographic scope of this book.) It is truly a land of superlatives, and of firsts. As you can learn more about in the History chapter of this section, the national park idea—perhaps the greatest gift of conservation America or any country has bestowed upon the world—emerged in this region. Yellowstone was the first national park, and the adjacent Shoshone National Forest was our first national forest. This area holds some of the world's most stunning mountains and broadest expanses of public lands. In Yellowstone-Teton Country you can see the biggest herds of wild game in the West, and visit some of its most impressive prehistoric-human finds.

The Rocky Mountain chain runs roughly 3,000 miles, from Canada to New Mexico. Nowhere outside Yellowstone-Teton Country are the forces that created those mountains more evident and, in fact, still abundantly active. The Tetons, at less than 10 million years of age, are the youngest mountain range in the Rockies (most are closer to 50 million years old). This largely explains why they jut up so abruptly from the river flats. The Tetons are still rising, in fact, even as Jackson Hole continues sinking. To the north, in Yellowstone, the time scale is *right now*. Here geology's inner workings are exposed, and you can glimpse the earth as it breathes, belches, steams, and roars.

If there is a heart of the Northern Rockies, it beats in the Yellowstone-Teton Country.

‿‿‿‿‿ The Land

Without learning anything about the "whys" and "hows" of Yellowstone-Teton Country landscapes, you'd still treasure a trip through the region. The plentiful wildlife and incredible scenery are more than enough to keep you in a constant state of wonder. And, anyway, the results of geology can be great to look at, sure, but it's an incredibly dry and complex subject, isn't it?

Well, yes, the concepts behind geology are complex and often difficult to comprehend. But before choosing to ignore the subject altogether, consider that a large share of earth scientists regard the Yellowstone-Teton region as geologically the most compelling place on earth. In this region—and especially in Yellowstone National Park—geology is a far cry from the study of static rock formations. Here the forces that built the earth are in your face and working overtime. Moreover, the geologic past and present are responsible for everything natural you see in the region, from mountains and moose to geysers and geese.

Although it doesn't rise from the sea like a Krakatoa, one of the largest and potentially most dangerous volcanoes on earth occupies Yellowstone's Central Plateau. The volcano, which is of an uncommon variety known as a *resurgent caldera* (a caldera is a basin-shaped volcanic depression that is roughly round in shape), is the most recent of a series of volcanoes that during the past several million years have created the Snake River Plain. The plain extends southwest from Yellowstone, far into Idaho. This resurgent

caldera, part of which forms the bed of Yellowstone Lake, is tough to identify with the naked and untrained eye. This is because after bulging up and releasing immense quantities of rhyolite lava, the caldera collapsed. It then camouflaged itself by filling up with lava in one of the final steps of the eruption.

The story of the "Yellowstone volcano" is actually that of three calderas superimposed atop one another within the Yellowstone volcanic field. Each of the three—the Huckleberry Ridge, Island Park, and Lava Creek calderas—has blown once during the past 2 million years, at intervals of roughly 600,000 years. Disconcertingly, the most recent, the Lava Creek caldera, erupted just over 600,000 years ago. Does that mean it's time for another caldera to erupt? Read on.

No resurgent caldera has erupted on earth since humans began recording history. But the stories told in the rocks reveal that they can have devastating effects over huge regions. The Lava Creek eruption, an explosive event that, like the other two major Yellowstone eruptions, probably lasted only a few hours or days, covered most of the future western United States with ash as much as several feet deep. As far away as Iowa an ash layer 3 inches thick has been identified as coming from the Lava Creek eruption.

Numerous theories have been laid on the table over the years regarding why Yellowstone is volcanically so active. Holding sway at the present time is the "hot spot" theory. This maintains that rhyolite *magma*, the molten rock that is called lava once it exits the earth, is formed by a hot spot

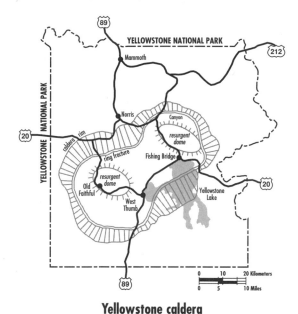

Yellowstone caldera

underlying Yellowstone. Proponents of the theory point out that herculean quantities of lava and ash—some 1,600 cubic *miles* of it—have flowed and erupted from the Yellowstone volcanoes during the past 2 million years. The lava exited at temperatures exceeding 1,500 degrees Fahrenheit. The heat necessary to bring rock to this temperature simply doesn't exist in the vicinity of the earth's crust. So, the heat must have come from much deeper and been fed to the crust by a *thermal mantle plume,* extending from the earth's core through the mantle.

Some forty of these core-to-crust thermal mantle plumes have been identified throughout the world. They supply heat to similar hot spots, including the one responsible for the active volcanism on the island of Hawaii. Most, however, lie hidden on the ocean floor, so the Yellowstone hot spot is unusual in that it occurs on a continent. (Incidentally, the term "hot spot" is a bit misleading, for some measure 700 miles across and a mile high.)

Rhyolite, which flowed from the volcanoes as lava and solidified into the rock that fills Yellowstone's Central Plateau, has a chemical composition similar to that of granite. But it is a much finer-grained rock than granite. This is because rhyolite is an *extrusive igneous* rock. That is, its lava solidifies above ground and at relatively cool temperatures, and therefore more rapidly

than granite, which forms when subterranean magma cools. The faster a molten rock cools, the smaller are the crystals in the resultant material. Occasionally, when rhyolite is cooled exceptionally fast—as, for instance, where it flows as lava into a lake—it forms the dark volcanic glass called *obsidian.* The characteristics of obsidian made it a prized find among Native Americans, who used it to chip high-quality stone tools. Indeed, Yellowstone obsidian was so valued as a trade item that it has been found in prehistoric sites located in the Midwest and Canada, many hundreds of miles from the park.

The youngest rhyolite flows in Yellowstone are approximately 70,000 years old. That's barely over one second in the twenty-four hours of geologic time. (The computation is based on the earth's estimated age of 4.5 billion years.) Put in this time context, it is likely that hot magma still underlies Yellowstone and that the Yellowstone volcanic field is active. There's plenty of evidence supporting the belief that magma still exists. For example, two *resurgent domes* on the floor of the Yellowstone caldera are bulging upward, one near Yellowstone Lake and the other near Old Faithful. This indicates that magma is probably rising below them. This bulging is a classic sign of a volcano about to blow, but don't panic just yet. Before the Yellowstone caldera erupts it will likely provide weeks or even months of warning, in the form of small earthquakes and rapidly growing domes. The eruption might be a year away, it might be 100,000 years in the future, or, say geologists, it's entirely possible that the Yellowstone volcano will never blow again. Instead, the resurgent domes will subside, and the underlying magma thought to exist will slowly crystallize into granite, as the hot spot moves on.

Or, more accurately, as the North American continent moves on. It is accepted that thermal mantle plumes like the one feeding the Yellowstone hot spot remain stationary as the continental plates move across them. Evidence for this in the Yellowstone region comes from additional distinct volcanic fields that through time have joined to create the Snake River Plain. The eastern portion of this progression of volcanic activity delineates a path roughly 50 miles wide between Twin Falls, Idaho, and central Yellowstone. The Picabo (Peek-a-boo, as in ski racer Picabo Street) volcanic field, farthest to the southwest, is the oldest of the three. It is approximately 10 million years of age. Moving toward the northeast, next in the series and in age is the Heise volcanic field. The Yellowstone volcanic field is the northeasternmost of the three and also the youngest. Each of the three fields was active for roughly 2 million years, with a 2-million-year period of "down time" before the next in the series became active. This might indicate that the 2-million-year-old Yellowstone field is at the end of its run—although, as previously noted, the park still could experience another large eruption at some time during the next 100,000 years.

Both the distance separating each of the three volcanic fields from the next and their southwest-to-northeast trend correspond to what is known about the direction and speed of travel of the North American continental plate. The plate moves southwesterly over the hot spot at the rate of between 1 and 2 inches a year. If the hot spot endures—and studies of oceanic hot spots indicate that they have lives of several hundred million years—it is probable that approximately 2 million years from now a new volcanic field will appear in the vicinity of Red Lodge, Montana. Ten million years ago hot pots and geysers, like those that make Yellowstone world famous today, boiled in the vicinity of Pocatello, Idaho (the Picabo volcanic field). Six million years ago they bubbled just outside Idaho Falls (the Heise field). Two million years from now, will tourists, whatever their species and planet of origin, visit the thermal wonders encompassing the former site of the delightful little burg of Red Lodge?

The rock known as *breccia* is composed of angular volcanics lodged in a matrix of fine ash. *Absaroka breccias* make up the Washburn Range in north-central Yellowstone. They also form the Red Mountains, located in the park roughly 40 miles south of the Washburns, and the Absarokas, which spread east from the park's eastern boundary. You can get a good look at the Absaroka breccias by driving the road skirting 10,243-foot Mt. Washburn, between Canyon Village and Tower-Roosevelt. These breccias formed some 50 million years ago, when over a period of several million years muddy mixes of ash and rock repeatedly washed down mountain slopes into what then were lush, low-lying tropical lands.

Geologists have determined that today's Washburn Range is merely a remnant of what once was a much higher and larger range. The ancestral Washburns extended south and eastward unbroken to encompass the Red and Absaroka mountains. Today, viewed from above, the three ranges link to form an arc suggesting a horseshoe that curves around a broad opening to the southwest. Occupying the opening where jagged peaks once dominated is Yellowstone's rhyolite-filled Central Plateau, an undulating, thousand-square-mile upland lying at more than 8,000 feet above sea level. Geologists attribute the plateau's lofty elevation to the fact that the hot spot has caused the continental crust beneath it to expand upward. The Central Plateau will likely subside as the continental plate moves southwestward, transporting the plateau beyond the heat source, even as the terrain to the northeast lifts higher.

The Central Plateau is made up of dozens of rhyolite lava flows far younger than the 50-million-year-old Absaroka breccias. The flows range in age from 500,000 to 70,000 years old. Until the late 1950s geologists believed the Absaroka breccias and these lava flows were part of a geologic continuum. But thesis work published in 1961 by a Harvard graduate student named Francis R. Boyd turned this popular belief on its ear. Boyd demonstrated that the breccias and rhyolites are chemically unrelated, and that they resulted from events separated by millions of years. Although both rocks are volcanic in origin, it is only coincidental that they occupy the same area. Moreover, Boyd found, not even all the younger rhyolite lava flows were what they seemed to be: Underlying and rimming the rhyolite flows are two distinct and older layers of *welded tuff*, a rock that forms when the residual heat in erupted lava and ash causes it to bind back together. Welded tuffs indicate volcanic events that were far more violent and explosive than the slower, flowing action that results in rhyolite.

The pair of welded tuff layers have been dated at approximately 2 million and 600,000 years. The younger of the two offered geologists evidence tying the fate of the massive, ancestral Washburn Range to what is known about the third and most recent eruption of the Yellowstone volcano: It is believed that the mountains exploded and collapsed during this "recent" eruption of 600,000 years ago. The incredibly powerful cataclysm rocked the Yellowstone-Teton region and deposited the lava and ash that became the Lava Creek Tuff, which covers much of the area today. For hundreds of miles around it created a sterile landscape where few things if any could have remained living. As previously mentioned, it spewed ash high into the stratosphere, where much of it was carried hundreds of miles before settling.

To summarize and elaborate, the Yellowstone National Park we see today is not the result of eons of geologic activity that ended millions of years ago. Rather, most of what we see in the park is the result of cataclysmic events of the past 2 million years—the last thirty-eight seconds of our geological twenty-four-hour day. And it is likely that Yellowstone is still volcanically active. The first of the Yellowstone volcano's three eruptions exploded around 2 million years ago. It spewed the lava that solidified into the Huckleberry Ridge Tuff, which can be seen in isolated places throughout the area. These include the Golden Gate near Mammoth Hot Springs, on Signal Mountain in Grand Teton National Park, and in Teton Canyon on the west slope of the range. The second and smallest of the three volcanic explosions produced the Mesa Falls Tuff. It erupted approximately 1.3 million years ago from the Island Park caldera, located in Idaho just west of Yellowstone. The Island Park caldera covered the western arm of the Huckleberry Ridge caldera. Finally, 600,000 years ago the 45-by-28 mile Lava Creek caldera erupted, obliterating much of the Washburn Range and consuming the eastern portions of the Huckleberry Ridge caldera. These all were world-class volcanic events. Few, if any eruptions in the earth's history have exceeded the power of Huckleberry Ridge, the largest of the three. That caldera produced some 600 cubic miles of rock, spewing an incomprehensible *2,400 times* the amount of ash and lava that came from the devastating 1980 Mt. St. Helens eruption. Geologists have determined that violent eruptions such as these require incredibly intense heat sources. This helped lead to the hot spot theory, a theory backed by what is known about the shifting of the continental plate and its relationship to the extinct volcanic fields located southwest of Yellowstone in Idaho.

How do the events covered so far relate to the many mountain ranges that rise beyond the borders of Yellowstone National Park, and which serve to make the greater region so regal—the Beartooths, for example, and the Gallatins, the Madisons, and the Tetons, that most royal range of all?

Assuming that the hot spot hypothesis and the theory of mobile continental plates are valid—and most geologists today subscribe to both—then the moving of the North American plate across the Yellowstone hot spot is also responsible for uplifting major parts of northwest Wyoming, southwest Montana, and southeast Idaho. The same forces are even responsible, albeit less directly, for the fantastic array of plants and animals inhabiting the region's mountains and valleys.

The heating and consequent bulging of the earth's crust has resulted in *faults*, or fractures. Adjacent blocks of the earth's crust along these faults move at angles up or down in relation to one another. Friction along a fault's tilted plane causes tensions to build. Periodically the tensions release as the blocks slip past each other, creating earthquakes. Two major bands of faulting radiate from the Yellowstone hot spot, one of them extending west into central Idaho and the other south into north-central Utah. These are very young and active as fault bands go, and the central parts of both have released many times in recent geologic history, resulting in the steep, high mountain fronts common in the region. A pair of notable temblors occurred in recent memory along the fault band extending into Idaho. The first was the destructive Hebgen Lake earthquake, which on the night of August 17, 1959, caused a landslide that killed twenty-eight campers and dammed the Madison River. The other: the October 1983 Borah Peak earthquake outside Challis, Idaho, a town where masonry falling from a building killed two children on their way to school. Borah Peak, already the loftiest mountain in Idaho, suddenly grew another 6 inches, as the valley below dropped 9 feet.

Let's head south into Jackson Hole along the fault band that reaches toward Utah. One of the best available views of the Teton Range that you can reach in a car comes at the top of Signal Mountain, a solitary, 1,000-foot high topograph-

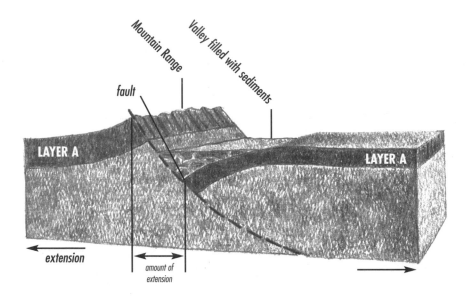

fault

Mountain Range

Valley filled with sediments

LAYER A

LAYER A

extension

amount of extension

How faulting works

ical blip rising above Jackson Lake. Motor up the 5 miles and have a look: It is an arresting, all-encompassing vista. (The best views of the Tetons are available by hiking the short trail to Jackson Point Overlook about a mile before the top, while the rest of Jackson Hole and mountains to the east are best seen from the summit.) The steep angles at which you see the Tetons reposing have been attained only recently, within the past few million years. But the primary rock composing the mountains is ancient. They are Precambrian *basement rocks*, part of the very bowels of the North American continent. The oldest, aged at around 3 billion years, are the layered *gneisses* and *schists* that show up in the northern and southern ends of the range, and less commonly as isolated scatterings amid the lighter-colored granites of the high central Tetons. The granites are approximately 2.5 billion years old.

Rising above the eastern edge of Jackson Hole, in dramatic contrast to the faulted, bereft-of-foothills Tetons, are the Gros Ventre Mountains, a classic *folded* range encompassed by rolling foothills. Why are the nearby Tetons so strikingly steep and raw of rock? At less than 10 million years old, they are the youngest and consequently the least eroded of the Rocky Mountains and the most dramatic example in the Rockies of a steep mountain front created by faulting. Most of the activity along the young Teton Fault, which traces the eastern base of the mountains, has occurred within the past 5 million

years. No discernible earthquake has occurred here in the memory of humans, but based on the fault's record—one major quake approximately every 1,800 years—one should be expected. J.D. Love, the geologist who literally wrote the book on the geological dynamics of the Tetons, has said that a movement along the Teton Fault of as much as 20 vertical feet could happen at virtually any time.

The Tetons and Jackson Hole are both young, tilted blocks of the earth's crust; as the Teton block moves upward along the fault line the Jackson Hole block moves down. This is why the highest peaks of the relatively small range, which is only 40 miles long and 10 to 15 miles wide, rise directly along the eastern front rather than in the center of the range, as is typical with older, more established and eroded mountains. Meanwhile, the terrain on the western slope of the Tetons, as viewed from the Idaho side, is much broader and gentler. The northern reaches of the range lie buried under youthful Yellowstone lava flows.

The Tetons would be a spectacular sight to behold even if they hadn't undergone a final sculpting. Finish work did, however, occur here and throughout the region in very recent geologic times ("finish work" in regard to what we see today, that is, since geologic forces will undoubtedly continue altering the status quo). Even before the Tetons commenced rising and Jackson Hole dropping along the Teton Fault, as volcanoes in Yellowstone exploded and rhyolite lava hot enough to ignite trees oozed over the ground, a force at the other end of the temperature spectrum simultaneously was at work, modifying the landscape. It was ice, in the form of glaciers. Periodically during the past 2 million years glaciers have covered Yellowstone and much of Grand Teton National Park and Jackson Hole, then retreated. In the mountains the glaciers left behind craggy *horns*, sparkling lakes, and steep *cirques* at the head of deep U-shaped valleys. On the slopes and in the valleys below they deposited boulders far from their origins and laid the gravels and rock debris of *terminal moraines* and *lateral moraines*. They also scoured future lake bottoms, built the depressions called *kettles*, and dammed rivers to create lakes, which subsequently collected and deposited deep layers of sediment and occasionally caused formidable flooding.

Stripped to the essentials, a glacier's origin lies in the snowflake, that most delicate and ephemeral piece of nature's art. It is mind-boggling to contemplate how powerful and manipulative of the landscape a glacier, which is nothing more than billions of snowflakes joining forces, can become. When the climate cools enough such that over each of many years it snows in winter more than it melts in summer, snow proceeds to accumulate deeper and deeper. Eventually, in response to temperature and pressure changes, the snow crystals metamorphose and meld together to become ice, the solid form of water. When the layer of ice becomes thick enough—somewhere in the vicinity of 200 feet—its mass responds to gravity, and a newly born glacier begins flowing. It moves at a fraction of a snail's pace, downslope over rock, lubricated by a thin layer of water.

Cyclically and many times during the past 2 million years, atmospheric conditions cooled and became ripe for the creation of glaciers. This was probably due to changes in the earth's rotation around the sun, along with other factors. Immense ice fields piled up and buried much of North America (and other parts of the world), including all of Canada and a large share of the northern United States. The glaciers became self-perpetuating; that is, the higher they rose the more snowstorms they trapped. Then, for whatever reasons, the world re-warmed and the glaciers receded. Massive glaciers most recently covered

the Yellowstone-Teton region during what is called the Pinedale glaciation. Immediately prior to the Pinedale in the sequence was the larger Bull Lake glaciation, which 150,000 years ago extended farther south than did the subsequent Pinedale. The Bull Lake glaciation buried all of Jackson Hole, including the future site of Jackson. Ice filled the scenic little valley approximately to the level of the top of the present ski runs on Snow King Mountain.

More is known about the Pinedale glaciation, whose ice fields began advancing around 70,000 years ago. They reached their maximum extent some 25,000 years ago, and by the time another 10,000 years had passed they were almost gone. Near the Snake River overlook in Grand Teton National Park you can see a series of timber-shrouded terminal moraines known collectively as the Burned Ridge moraine. These moraines, which extend across the Snake River Valley, mark the southernmost advance of the Pinedale glaciation. South of Burned Ridge for some 10 miles extends an unusually flat deposit of gravel. From near the Snake River overlook to Blacktail Butte the main highway runs south along this untimbered *glacial outwash,* which is composed of gravel that was carried and laid down by streams pouring from the edge of the glacier as the Burned Ridge moraine was building. Additional evidence of the ice sheet is found north of Burned Ridge. Here, as the glacier rapidly receded it left behind numerous large masses of stagnant ice. Stream-deposited sediment collected between the ice masses and against their upstream sides; some were buried altogether. They eventually melted to leave kettles, known here as the Potholes.

From its southernmost reaches the Pinedale glaciation extended north more than 100 miles to the approximate location of today's Chico Hot Springs, in Montana's Paradise Valley. At its apex above Yellowstone Lake the ice was 4,000 feet thick. It covered the tops of the Washburn and Red mountains and most of the Absarokas. The glaciers transported rock large and small, depositing it where today it looks, and *is,* entirely out of context. The glaciers even created their own rock debris, as ice ground down through the mountains. The high Tetons, because of their youth and their precipitous nature, were never covered with ice to the extent that the broad-plateaued mountains to the north were, such as the Beartooths and Absarokas. Rather than accumulate and contribute to high-country glaciers, snow in the Tetons tended to avalanche and amass in the valleys below. The prominent moraines rimming Phelps, Taggart, Jenny, and Bradley lakes in Grand Teton National Park are evidence left by Pinedale glaciers that advanced down the canyons above the lakes, carrying rock debris to the floor of Jackson Hole.

In the early stages of the Pinedale glaciation, before ice fields had smothered the Central Plateau of Yellowstone, a tongue of ice flowing south from the Beartooth Plateau entered the Grand Canyon of the Yellowstone River. Here it served as a dam, backing up Hayden Lake. Remaining as testimony to the long-gone lake are the sands and gravels that compose the undulating hills of Hayden Valley. A more vivid reminder of the same glacier is the huge boulder of Beartooth granite perched on the rim of the Grand Canyon of the Yellowstone near Inspiration Point. The glacier transported this boulder, which is as big as a small house, at least 30 miles south before leaving it here.

As the climate warmed and the Pinedale glaciers waned, a tundra-like mix of sagebrush and grasses invaded the newly bared ground. Later, well after the Pinedale glaciation had ended, Engelmann spruce appeared and thrived, thanks to a moist and warmer climate. Still warmer temperatures subsequently made growing conditions good for whitebark and limber pine, as well as for the lodgepole pine that ultimately dominated in the region. Ecologists believe that between 10,000 and 6,000 years ago the average global temperature was substantially higher than today's. The extremely warm and dry summers common then would have resulted in an abundance of wildfires. Lodgepole pine loves fire; for evidence, just look to see what is growing in areas scorched by the 1988 Yellowstone fires. One of the tree's two varieties of seed cones will open and distribute seeds only if it encounters temperatures exceeding 140 degrees Fahrenheit, at which point the resin sealing the cone melts. Moreover, silica, which is the primary component of rhyolite, is a chemical compound in which few things will grow—excepting lodgepole pine, along with fireweed and a few other plants, which thrive in silica-based soil.

Quaking aspen leaves

The lovely quaking aspen so common today also discovered its niche in the Yellowstone-Teton region during this warm period. It is intriguing to consider that some of the aspen groves you see today, sunlight dancing off their trembling leaves, probably are not descendents of those pioneer poplars so much as they are *part* of them. The root system of the aspen, a tree that grows in *clones* rather than as individual trees, can live underground for centuries, even when the aboveground component is destroyed by fire or other means.

Animals arrived with the retreating ice, as well. In addition to many of the critters common today—including black bears, bighorn sheep, bison, and elk—came camels, giant beavers, ground sloths, musk oxen, horses, woolly mammoths, and other large mammals. Skeletal remains of these extinct North American species have not been found directly in the Yellowstone-Teton national parks area, but it is inferred that they lived there, because their fossils have been unearthed in nearby dry plains of the tri-state area. These animals, both today's enduring and extinct species, had lived in North America for millennia, moving south and north with the cyclical glacial advances and retreats.

What about today—do glaciers still grind away at the Yellowstone-Teton landscape? Will they ever return in their full icy force?

A scattering of remnant glaciers, more stagnant ice fields than anything, endures in the Tetons, Beartooths, and elsewhere in the region. But these relatively tiny vestiges occur only in shaded recesses at the highest elevations, and have continued to shrink in recent years. However, as has happened many times in the geologic past—threats of global warming notwithstanding—the climate probably will cool to the point where glaciers spread across the region again.

But of more immediate concern than advancing glaciers are the dynamic features found in Yellowstone, both obvious and not-so-obvious, that result from the underlying hot spot. This is one of the hottest places on earth: On average, over the 965-square-mile Yellowstone caldera the heat flow to the surface is sixty times higher than the global average. It is many times greater than that in the geyser basins proper. Resulting directly from the hot spot are the wonders for which Yellowstone National Park is best known: the geysers and related thermal features, which put on shows that fascinate and astound millions of visitors every year.

Yellowstone encompasses more than 300 geysers distributed among nine basins, or more than half of the active geysers in the world. Geysers and other thermal phenomena result when three things come together: Heat, which is abundant in Yellowstone; water from rain and snowmelt, which there's also no shortage of here; and breaks and fissures in the earth's crust. Cracks are plentiful on the Central Plateau, largely because the heat underlying the caldera has resulted in great crustal pressures. Water percolates down through the cracks to great depth, where high pressure permits it to reach exceedingly hot temperatures without boiling. The superheated waters then rise to the surface through the "plumbing system," emerging slowly and dissipating relatively quietly in hot springs, fumaroles (dry steam vents), and mudpots, similar to hot springs but containing less groundwater.

But in the case of geysers the heat and pressure are not sleepily released. As cold, dense water tries to sink from the surface through the cracks and fissures, water heated at the depths simultaneously seeks higher ground. Periodically, the superheated water turns partly to steam, then rises and expands. Steam bubbles block the plumbing and prevent additional underlying hot water from rising. Ultimately, in releasing the ever-growing pressure, the bubbles blast overlying cooler water out of the vent, which also opens the way in the "pipes" for the release of the underlying superheated water. After emptying, quickly and violently, the chambers begin to refill with water and the process starts anew.

Cone geysers, typified by the world's most famous geyser, Old Faithful, shoot steam and water out of nozzle-shaped extensions. *Fountain geysers*, like Great Fountain Geyser, explode out of hot pools. The latter variety typically sprays a greater quantity of water over a broader area. The

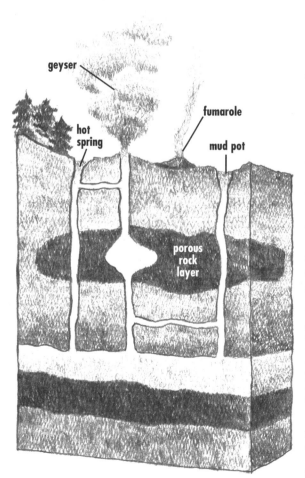

Geothermal Features

chambers underlying geysers range greatly in size, from very small to large, intricate systems of underground caverns, such as those feeding Steamboat Geyser in the Norris Geyser Basin. Steamboat, the world's largest geyser, doesn't erupt very often, but when it does it *really* erupts. It sometimes blasts more than a million gallons of water into the sky.

In closing, let's consider the LeHardy Rapids, a popular place to watch cutthroat trout migrating upstream in June and July, which is located on the Yellowstone River 3 miles north of Fishing Bridge. Underlying heat, and probably bulging magma, has caused the ground surface here to grow 3 feet in the past seventy-five years. In a geological time frame this is a speeding bullet. A volcanic eruption, or another, less destructive sort of right-now release of geothermal energy could happen literally any moment at the rapids.

The forces of geology are alive and doing well in Yellowstone-Teton Country.

The First ～～～～ Humans

At the zenith of the Pinedale glaciation 25,000 years ago, most of the Yellowstone-Teton region lay buried in ice. Ten thousand years later nearly all the ice was gone. As the glaciers retreated, shrubs and grasses reclaimed the newly bared ground, providing an open invitation for birds and animals to return. Eventually, on the trail of large mammals came a species new to the region: *Homo sapiens.*

A collective byproduct of the glaciers was a lowering of global sea levels; this, in turn, exposed large areas of land that today are under water. These included Beringia, a broad plain connecting Alaska and Siberia. Archaeologists contend that approximately 20,000 years ago the first wave of human beings wandered into North America, probably by chance, as they followed animal herds across the expansive plains of Beringia. The timing appears to fit, since the oldest reliably dated archaeological sites in the New World are about 12,500 years old. (Much older sites have been reported, but none verified.) Finds of this age lie as far apart as Wisconsin and Chile. An estimated time of arrival of 20,000 years ago would have permitted plenty of time for such wide dispersal to take place.

When the first known humans poked into the Intermountain West around 11,000 years ago, the average temperature on earth was considerably warmer than today. The Rocky Mountain high country, including Yellowstone's Central Plateau, would have been milder and more hospitable. Game animals presumably were even more abundant than they are now, and there's no question that there was a greater variety of large mammals.

In fact, the appearance of human beings in the western United States coincides with the extinction of several large species, including the camel, long-horned bison, mammoth, and horse. (The forerunner of today's horse appeared much later in history, transported from Europe by Spanish explorers.) It was probably the intense hunting activities of humans, combined with unfavorable changes in the climate, that brought about the animals' demise.

The first hunters in Yellowstone-Teton Country roamed over the high country in summer, then retreated to winter camps at lower elevations along the rivers and in the foothills. Game was pursued by small bands of hunters. The individual bands, probably joined by blood ties, may occasionally have joined with other small bands for large-scale communal hunts. Other early visitors passed through the area by accident or, perhaps, expressly to visit Obsidian Cliff. This immense deposit of dark obsidian is situated in present Yellowstone National Park between Mammoth Hot Springs and Norris Junction. The word—in whatever tongue it was spoken—concerning the rare find surely would have spread among early hunters. At Obsidian Cliff a tool maker could easily obtain exceptionally high-quality volcanic glass with which to fashion projectile points, hide scrapers, and other tools crucial to his band's survival.

Before going further it will help to review some basics of Great Plains–Rocky Mountain archaeology. Stone projectile points—spear points and smaller arrowheads—serve as the archaeologist's chief chronological tool. Distinctive styles of projectile points and arrowheads are regularly uncovered at archaeological excavations throughout the region, often in association with charred wood and bone remaining from ancient fires. The approximate age of the artifacts can be determined by *radiocarbon dating* the charcoal from the associated fires, or by one of several other dating methods. Scientific dating has demonstrated that projectile-point and arrowhead styles are diagnostic of particular time periods. That is, two similar spear points or arrowheads, even if found hundreds of miles from one another, were fashioned at approximately the same time in prehistory.

Particularly revealing are the artifacts unearthed at *stratified* sites, which contain multiple levels of occupation. The rule of stratification, or *superposition,* states simply that in undisturbed sites artifacts found at the lowest level are the oldest, and those at the uppermost level are the youngest. Findings at stratified sites have helped the archaeologist to verify that the accepted chronology of tool types is accurate. A pair of the region's richest stratified sites are Mummy Cave, situated along the North Fork of the Shoshone River a few miles east of Yellowstone, and Medicine Lodge Creek. The latter sprawls below sandstone cliffs in the western foothills of the Bighorn Mountains and enjoys status as a Wyoming state park. An evolution of occupation by humans spanning more than 9,000 years has been documented at both these sites.

By approximately 11,500 years before the present, or 9,500 B.C., the first of several identifiable big-game hunting, or Paleo-Indian "cultures" had emerged along the east front of the Rocky Mountains and on the Great Plains. At that time, with its abundance of large game animals, the plains must have resembled today's game-rich Serengeti. The Paleo-Indian hunters killed large animals with spears that they hurled using the *atlatl,* or throwing stick. The earliest identified Paleo culture is called Clovis. The culture took its name from Clovis, New Mexico, near where the *lanceolate* (lance-shaped) spear point characteristic of the period was first discovered. Mammoth remains are commonly found in association with Clovis points. In fact, hunters of the period seem to have focused almost exclusively on these huge elephant-like animals as their prey. An isolated, partial Clovis point made of obsidian was found

in 1959 during excavations for the post office building in Gardiner, Montana, immediately north of Yellowstone. The find might indicate that its original owner hunted in Yellowstone more than 11,000 years ago. Or, it could have been transported to the site from some distance by a wounded animal or subsequent visitor who found the point elsewhere. Indisputable as well as circumstantial evidence exists, however, that Clovis man did hunt in the general region: at the Anzick Site, north of Livingston, Montana, for example, and at the Colby Site, near the Bighorn Basin town of Worland. These sites provide some of the earliest documentation of humans in the Northern Rockies. Clovis projectiles were discovered at the Colby Site in association with butchered mammoth bones, which were found to be 11,200 years old.

It is likely, then, that more than 11,000 years ago individuals of the Clovis culture became the first geyser gazers in the future Yellowstone National Park. These people, primitive and superstitious by our measure, would have had no basis for comprehending or even guessing at the forces responsible for the fantastic thermal phenomena. We can only imagine how the steaming geysers and bubbling mudpots must have terrified and excited them!

Clovis hunters prevailed for approximately 500 years; then, as the mammoth population dwindled, hunters turned to the long-horned bison, or *Bison antiquus,* a beast ancestral to today's smaller *Bison bison.* The change in quarry was accompanied by a new projectile-point style and associated culture, known as the Folsom. Hunters of the Folsom period (named after yet another town in New Mexico) flourished from approximately 11,000 to 10,000 years before the present. The spear points distinguishing the period are smaller than those used by Clovis hunters, and the lengthwise *fluting* runs the entire length of the point, rather than along only part of it. Moreover, the technologically superior Folsom points were fashioned by applying direct pressure to the stone blank with a flaking tool, which was usually made of rock or antler. Clovis points, in contrast, were crafted by the cruder percussion method, whereby the tool maker simply struck at the blank with another hard object. Folsom points have been excavated at several sites in the

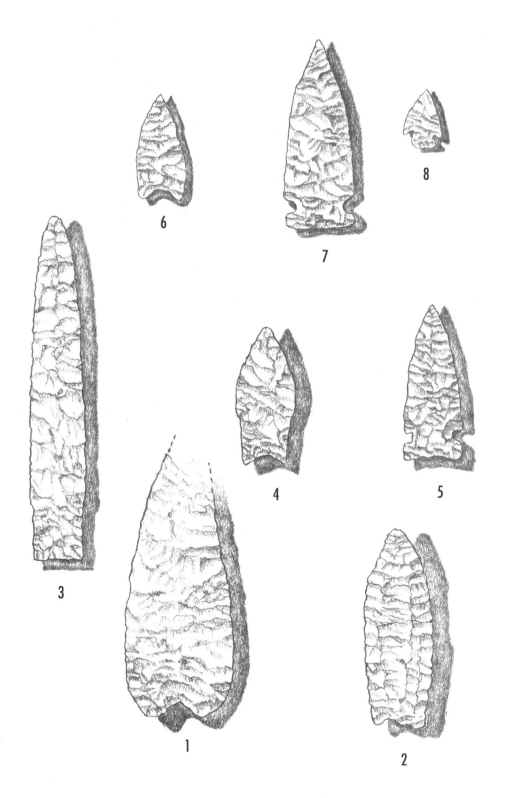

Projectile points: (1) Clovis, (2) Folsom, (3) Eden, (4) Cody, (5) Lookingbill (Altithermal),
(6) McKean (Middle Archaic), (7) Besant (Late Archaic), (8) small corner-notch (Late Prehistoric)

Yellowstone-Teton region, including ones located in the Bighorn Basin, southwest Montana, and Idaho's Snake River Valley.

The Plano Period, which followed Folsom in the progression of people on the plains and in the mountains, extended from about 10,000 to 7,500 years before the present. Projectile points of this period consist of several variations on a theme of refined, nonfluted lanceolates fashioned by an advanced pressure-flaking process. They include points with names like Cody, Hell Gap, Agate Basin, Eden, and Scottsbluff. A large body of evidence from this period has been uncovered and aged at several stratified sites, including Mummy Cave and Medicine Lodge Creek. A 9,500-year-old *bone midden* at Medicine Lodge Creek showed that Plano man was subsisting on a variety of fauna: Bison were still important, but so were smaller animals like deer, bighorn sheep, rabbits, gophers, and wood rats. Evidence of fish and preserved plants being used as food was also excavated at Medicine Lodge Creek. Yellowstone has yielded surface finds of Plano points, and also Cascade points, which are of a similar age but were made by Indians living west of rather than east of the Rockies. The presence of Cascade points indicates that their owners, who hunted primarily in Washington, Oregon, and Idaho, visited the region at roughly the same time as Plano hunters . . . and so begins a long tale of the Yellowstone country serving as a meeting ground of east and west.

The conclusion of the Plano Period 7,500 years ago marks the end of the big-game hunting, or Paleo-Indian age and the beginning of the Archaic Period. The Archaic was characterized by an expanding exploitation of the environment. The climate during the Early Archaic, or Altithermal Period, turned very dry, rendering lower-lying plains like those in the Bighorn Basin uninhabitable. The high country, meanwhile, including Jackson Hole and the Central Plateau of Yellowstone, were fruitful oases where animal life, water, and food plants remained relatively plentiful. Concentrations of Archaic Period winter camps have been discovered along the Yellowstone River north of Yellowstone National Park, in the Gallatin River canyon, and on the Clark's Fork and North Fork of the Shoshone River. Many of the larger mammals by this time

Bighorn sheep

had become extinct, so human hunters, who in ecological terms had been specialists, were forced more and more to become generalists. The taking of small animals became increasingly important, as did the gathering of roots, seeds, and berries. Still, bison, deer, and other large mammals continued to play vital roles in providing food and raw materials for the Native Americans. Side-notched projectile points replaced the lanceolate styles common during Paleo-Indian times. Baskets for gathering nuts and seeds, and *manos* and *metates* for grinding them, began to appear.

Later in the Archaic Period the climate improved, and human activity increased throughout the region. A burgeoning dependency on an ever-growing array of plants, animals, and insects as food is reflected in the archaeological findings. The Archaic Period led into the Late Prehistoric Period, which began shortly after the time of Christ and continued until the arrival of Europeans in North America. It was a time of expanding occupation in the Yellowstone-Teton country. The remains of Late Prehistoric *wickiup* shelters, rock cairns, and log alignments used to drive herd animals for communal hunts have been found at several places in the region, including the Central Plateau and north of Yellowstone in the Yellowstone River Valley.

Horticulture was growing in significance and sophistication in many parts of the country, including the Midwest, the upper Missouri River basin, and the Southwest. This was accompanied by more sedentary lifestyles, the introduction of the bow and arrow, the advancement of pottery, and increasingly complex societies. Horticulture didn't take root in the high, cold Yellowstone-Teton Country, but its effects were felt. Trade among Native American groups increased during the period; for instance, Yellowstone obsidian traded by some means, probably in a village-to-village manner, shows up in the archaeological record at distant sites, such as in the Hopewell burial mounds east of the Mississippi River. The bow and arrow was introduced to natives of Yellowstone-Teton Country by hunters from both the Great Basin to the southwest and the Great Plains to the east. This is evidenced by the smaller projectile points, now called arrowheads, that have been found and dated as old as 2,000 years. Compared to the atlatl, the bow and arrow was more powerful, more accurate, and easier to quickly "load." Cooperation among hunters grew, and communal kills of bison and antelope herds became more common. Flat-bottomed Intermountain pottery showed up in the region for the first time, along with vessels of a similar shape but which, instead of being made of hardened clay, were carved out of soft *serpentine*, or soapstone. This material occurs as outcrops in the Tetons and other ranges.

The distinct Indian tribes whose names we became familiar with in history class and Hollywood movies progressively took shape during the Late Prehistoric Period, which led into the Historic Period. The advent of Europeans on the Great Plains and in the Rocky Mountains began as a trickle but grew to a flood, bringing with it sweeping and ultimately catastrophic changes to the diverse Native American cultures. Change was barely noticeable at first: a glass bead here or a metal arrowhead there, appearing in trade negotiations between two individual Indians, perhaps. But soon the horse, which Spaniards had introduced to the Santa Fe area around A.D. 1600, spread to the north and east, where it rapidly and radically altered the sedentary farming ways that had been adopted by tribes living in the upper Great Lakes and upper Missouri River regions.

Thanks to the newfound mobility provided by the horse, these sedentary tribes—the Sioux, Cheyenne, and Crow are the three we know best—during the 1700s migrated westward. Here they evolved into the nomadic bison hunters and warriors of the Great Plains of legend.

In addition to the horse, the white newcomers brought to the Native Americans a host of other possibilities and problems. Among them: rifles, whiskey, Christianity, commerce, and ravaging disease—namely, smallpox. As an example of just how devastating the disease was, consider that an 1837 smallpox epidemic killed an estimated 6,000 Blackfeet Indians, or roughly two-thirds of the tribe's entire population. And it was just one of three major epidemics to sweep through the Blackfeet tribe.

Most tribes living in the Yellowstone-Teton region eventually adopted the horse, even if they didn't all become as mobile as the Plains Indian tribes. West of the Continental Divide these tribes included the Nez Perce, Flathead, and western Shoshone; to the north and east, the Blackfeet, Crow (or Absarokas), and eastern Shoshone. When John Colter, the first white man known to penetrate Yellowstone-Teton Country, made his epic trek in 1807–8 (*see* History), the fearsome and independent Blackfeet Indians dominated the region north of Yellowstone. The Blackfeet were the only "classic" Plains Indian tribe that had resided on the Great Plains since long before the introduction of the horse. By Colter's time their extensive range reached north across the breadth of Montana into Alberta, and they also frequented areas to the south, in Idaho and even northern Utah. The region to the east of Yellowstone and generally south of the Yellowstone River, where Colter began his sojourn, was Crow country. That to the west, south, and southeast was home to various tribes of the Shoshone language group. Unlike the Plains Indian tribes, who had migrated from eastern Canada and the upper Midwest (including the Blackfeet, although they preceded the other tribes), the Shoshone had moved up from the south and southwest as early as the 1300s. Not surprisingly, their language is closely related to those of the Hopi Indians of Arizona and other tribes in Mexico.

Before the Europeans arrived, all of these tribes and many of their predecessors occasionally traveled to or through the future Yellowstone National Park, Jackson Hole, and Pierre's Hole (Teton Valley, Idaho). There they would hunt in view of the Hoary-Headed Fathers, as the great trio of Teton peaks was known to the Shoshone. The west-slope tribes, particularly branches of the Shoshone and their Bannock allies, made annual late-summer forays through Yellowstone on their way to the buffalo-abundant plains east of the Continental Divide. Other tribes traveled to Yellowstone as a destination, expressly to fish and hunt, obtain obsidian, and/or avail themselves of the healing hot waters that were and are so plentiful in the park. (Today the National Park Service frowns on those who attempt to use them for medicinal purposes!)

Jackson Hole at that time, and well into the late nineteenth century, had far more elk even than it has today; bison, beaver, and bighorn sheep were exceedingly plentiful, too. Moose and deer, however, were less common than they are today: Moose thrived in the wake of fire suppression, which encouraged the growth of subalpine fir, an important winter food for the animal. And mule deer actually benefited from the effects of cattle grazing.

Elk

The harsh winters in Yellowstone and the Tetons, however, discouraged full-time residency. The only tribe living full-time, or close to it, in Yellowstone during the nineteenth century was the somewhat surreptitious Tukarika, literally "Sheepeater." Not a great deal is known about this branch of the Shoshone Indians. In the eyes of fellow Shoshone, the Sheepeaters were what they ate, and that's how they got their name, just as the Shoshone of the plains were called Buffalo Eaters and those living along the Snake River were known as Salmon Eaters. The Sheepeaters moved into Yellowstone and other high-mountain reaches of the region, including Wyoming's Wind River Range, the mountains of central Idaho, and probably Jackson Hole and the Gros Ventre Mountains, possibly as late as 1800. When Captain Bonneville (*see* History) crossed the Wind Rivers in 1835, he encountered a trio of Sheepeaters, describing them as miserably poor, owning no horses, and destitute of every convenience known to the whites. Bonneville's Eurocentric take was countered somewhat by the perspective of the well-read trapper Osborne Russell. He met a group of Sheepeaters in Yellowstone's Lamar Valley, also in 1835: "Here we found a few Snake Indians [a catchall phrase for Shoshone] comprising six men, seven women and eight or ten children who were the only inhabitants of this lonely and secluded spot. They were all neatly clothed in dressed deer and sheepskins of the best quality and seemed to be perfectly happy . . . [they had] about thirty dogs on which they carried their skins, clothing, provisions, etc. on their hunting excursions. They were well armed with bows and arrows pointed with obsidian."

The Sheepeaters never obtained many horses, but they really didn't need to, for they were skilled mountaineers and adept at trapping and driving animals on foot in steep and rugged terrain. The total population of Sheepeaters in Yellowstone probably never exceeded 300 individuals. They were distributed among several groups, each probably tied by blood and marriage. In summer they lived high in the mountains where they fished the streams, sought their favored quarry of bighorn sheep, and moved about with the ripening of various berries and roots. In winter they descended to semipermanent camps along the creeks and river bottoms. They holed up in domed wickiups, which were loose structures of narrow branches bent into an igloo-like shape and covered with bark and animal skins. They dressed in beautiful, brain-tanned skins of elk, sheep, and deer, and crafted exceptional bows by heating and straightening antler and horn, then wrapping it in rawhide. So outstanding were the weapons that it was reported that other Shoshone Indians would trade five or more ponies for just one of them. Sheepeater accoutrements included carved-soapstone vessels and European trade items, such as metal that they formed into knives and other weapons and utensils, and occasional guns and ammunition.

The short-lived and unglamorous "Sheepeater War" of 1879 was set in motion when some Sheepeaters killed five Chinese and two whites near Challis, Idaho. This, along with an 1882 "treaty" banning all Indians from Yellowstone National Park—largely a response to the Nez Perce campaign of 1877 (*see* History)—resulted in the Sheepeaters being rounded up with other Shoshone and moved either to the Fort Hall Reservation in southeast Idaho or to the Wind River Reservation in Wyoming. There they mixed with other Shoshones and disappeared as a distinct people.

History

In 1803 a thirty-something man named John Colter left his home in Virginia and lit out for Kentucky. In the town of Maysville he met and signed on with Meriwether Lewis, who was recruiting expedition members to help execute President Jefferson's ambitious plan to explore the West. The exploratory party's mission: poke through the newly acquired Louisiana Territory, then continue west through the Oregon Territory to the Pacific Ocean.

Mission accomplished, the Lewis and Clark Expedition was wending its way back east down the Missouri River in August 1806, two years and three months after striking out from St. Louis, when Colter requested an early leave. Specimen collection was one of the charges of the party, but by this time the number of beaver being "collected" far exceeded that of other species: Beaver pelts were fast becoming the currency of the Rocky Mountain West and party members were supplementing their meager wages by trapping. Seduced by the possibility of earning far more than his expeditionary stipend of five dollars per month, Colter itched to join a pair of trappers from Illinois, Joseph Dixon and Forrest Hancock, and pursue beaver full-time.

"The example of this man," wrote Nicholas Biddle years later in Philadelphia, as he toiled to condense the journals of Lewis and Clark, "shows how easily men may be weaned from the habits of civilized life to the ruder but scarcely less fascinating manners of the woods . . . just at the moment when he is approaching the frontiers, he is tempted by a hunting scheme to give up those delightful prospects, and go back without the least reluctance

to the solitude of the woods." Lewis and Clark themselves, rather than thinking Colter coldhearted, at the time seemed to consider it nothing more than a speculative and possibly astute career move on his part. His skills as a woodsman and hunter had proved invaluable to the expedition. That he was held in high regard is revealed in this passage from Clark, in response to Colter's request: " . . . as we were disposed to be of service to any of our party who had performed their duty as well as Colter had done, we agreed to allow him the privilege (*sic*) provided no one of the party would ask or expect a similar permission . . ."

On August 17, from the Mandan villages below the confluence of the Missouri and Yellowstone rivers in present North Dakota, the remaining members of the expedition floated out of sight, leaving Colter behind. If he ever kept his own journals they have yet to be found. So, from this point on the record of where Colter was when turns from one of precise documentation into one of conjecture and extrapolation. Evidence indicates that he and his two companions trapped and camped that winter on the Clark's Fork of the Yellowstone, where it exits the canyon from the Absaroka Range. In the spring Colter headed alone down the Missouri toward civilization, only to turn back yet again near today's Omaha, after encountering a band of trappers led by trader Manuel Lisa. The young Spaniard from New Orleans persuaded Colter to guide his party to the confluence of the Bighorn and Yellowstone rivers. Here Lisa would establish Fort Raymond (or Remon), the first in an intended network of trading posts.

In October or November of 1807, employed by Lisa, Colter and a beast of a man called Edward Rose—his forehead was branded and part of his nose had been gnawed off in a brawl—were dispatched on a twofold mission: They were to deploy and survey the country to the southwest for its pelting possibilities and also to spread word to the dispersed camps of Crows and other Indians of the new trading opportunities awaiting at Fort Raymond. Rose's ego apparently got the better of him, and his ceaseless bragging and bullying turned him into a Crow-country laughingstock. His mission failed miserably, making Colter's success shine even brighter by comparison.

During the winter of 1807–8 John Colter tracked a circuitous, 500-mile route through the heart of Yellowstone-Teton Country. He carried on his back thirty or forty pounds of gear and trade items, such as beads, needles, tobacco, and knives. He no doubt packed along snowshoes as well, common at that time among the Missouri River tribes. The trip took him through one of the toughest tangles of terrain on God's own earth. To retrace his steps today—even if it were known precisely where his steps were taken—would be an arduous task, even in midsummer, over improved trails, and with precise maps. What rewards Lisa promised Colter for his toil and risk are unknown; perhaps to prove to himself and others that he could accomplish such a harrowing journey alone, surviving subzero cold and bottomless snows, was reward enough for the intrepid explorer.

Colter left no known maps, but William Clark's *A Map of Lewis and Clark's Track Across the Western Portion of North America From the Mississippi to the Pacific,* published in 1814, includes information Clark gleaned from Colter when the pair met back in St. Louis. Using Clark's map as a guide, it's believed that from Fort Raymond Colter crested the Pryor Mountains to the south, then turned west upstream along Clark's Fork. This river he followed into the Absaroka Range. Into the glorious expanse of crags, swales, and streams now called Sunlight Basin he pressed, over Dead Indian Hill, and down to the Stinking Water River. It was a bubbling and sulfurous stretch along the Stinking Water west of present Cody and not, as many have inferred, the future Yellowstone National Park, where Colter encountered the mudpots and geysers that became known to the mountain men as "Colter's Hell." (Thermal activity is greatly diminished there today, and the Stinking Water was romantically rechristened the "Shoshone" in a turn-of-the-century P.R. move by the town of Cody.)

Colter may have been instructed by Lisa to be on the lookout for a rumored Spanish salt mine as he progressed up the Stinking Water's south fork. (Spanish as far north as Wyoming in 1807? It's possible.) Into the Greybull River drainage he continued, across the low Owl Creek Mountains, over the northern reaches of the wild Wind Rivers at Togwotee (*TOE-guh-tee*) Pass, and into Jackson Hole. At the opposite, south end of the fantastic, unpeopled valley he's believed to have forded the Snake River and persevered over Teton Pass into what became known first as Pierre's Hole and later as Teton Valley. This leg of the journey is backed by the only known physical evidence remaining of Colter's trek. The controversial "Colter Stone" is a 4-inch-thick slab of rhyolite shaped like a man's face and etched on one side with the words "John Colter" and on the opposite with the year "1808." The rock was discovered in 1931 by Teton Valley resident William Beard, as he and his son cleared timber from their land between the north and south forks of Leigh Creek.

Some maintain that the rock was a hoax, but if so, it's a curious one. The Beards swear that in 1931 they'd never heard of Colter, and they didn't even think to mention the rock to anyone until a couple of years later, when they traded it to a neighbor for a pair of boots. Moreover, at that time even those who *had* heard of John Colter believed his entire journey had taken place in 1807, the date indicated on William Clark's map. The Colter Stone, whose etchings have been determined by geologists as sufficiently weathered to be more than a hundred years old, resides under lock and key at the Indian Arts Museum at Colter Bay in Grand Teton National Park. (It can be seen on request.)

Colter returned to Jackson Hole, then traveled north along the west bank of the Snake until wading the river above Jackson Lake (called Lake Biddle on Clark's map). Finally, in what must have been the dead of winter, when snow can lie 15 feet deep in the high country, he entered the future Yellowstone National Park. Apparently

Trumpeter swan

missing most of the area's thermal hot spots, Colter passed Heart Lake and traced the high ridges above Yellowstone Lake. Then he crossed the Yellowstone River at the Bannock Ford below Tower Fall. From there he aimed east on the Bannock Trail, a path worn by west-slope tribes on their yearly forays to the buffalo plains of the Yellowstone Valley. He followed the trail up the Lamar River and Soda Butte Creek, then down to the Clark's Fork. Curiously, before recrossing Pryor's Gap and dropping along Pryor Creek to the Yellowstone, he seems to have detoured south back to the Stinking Water.

Colter made little of his remarkable journey, leaving much to speculation. Perhaps it was reticence, or maybe it was because his hell-on-earth descriptions of the boiling springs near the forks of the Stinking Water had elicited so much laughter and scorn from his peers that he decided he'd said more than enough. Compounding the unknown are probable mistakes in the base maps made by Clark, errors on top of mistakes crafted by his cartographer Samuel Lewis, inaccurate or misleading details provided by Colter, and the fact that the final map incorporated sometimes contradictory information from George Drouillard, the official hunter of the Lewis and Clark Expedition, who also made a couple of trips into the Bighorn River country in 1808. (A sample conundrum: The map depicts Jackson Lake draining into the Wind River, whereas the two

actually lie on opposite sides of the Continental Divide.) Also, many of the meanders and side trips shown on the map seem illogical and excessively dangerous—until one recalls that Colter's goal was not to make a beeline anywhere. Rather, he was there to scout new country and find bands of Indians in their isolated winter camps.

Regardless of the precise route taken, there's no disputing that John Colter made one of the great backpacking trips of all time, in winter-wild country so thoroughly primeval we can only dream of it. In 1810 Colter returned to St. Louis, married, and established a farm. He died from jaundice three years later.

Exploration and enterprise in the Rocky Mountain West temporarily tapered off during and after the War of 1812. Again the Yellowstone-Teton region was largely void of whites until 1818–19, when men working for the North West Company ventured in. The fur trade returned full force after 1822, when Gen. William H. Ashley, on behalf of the Rocky Mountain Fur Company, posted notice in the St. Louis *Missouri Republican.* Ashley sought "one-hundred young men to ascend the Missouri River to its source, there to be employed for one, two, or three years . . . "

Those answering the call of the wild included individuals whose names came to symbolize the very freedom of the frontier, names destined to resound through the crumbling canyons of time like the growl of a grizzly. Jedediah Smith. William Sublette. And David E. Jackson, whose surname would be assumed by the high-country "hole," or valley, that is home to the upper Snake River and from which the Teton Mountains erupt 7,000 vertical feet instantly, and deprived of foothills.

Another who signed with Ashley was an eighteen-year-old former blacksmith's apprentice named James Bridger. During the ensuing forty-five years he spent in the West, Jim Bridger evolved into the king of the mountain men. Utilizing the intimacy he'd earned with great portions of the Rocky Mountains through his trapping travels, he also became the greatest guide the region has known. Author J. Cecil Alter, in his book *Jim Bridger,* listed some Bridger "firsts": He was the first white man to sample the salty waters of the Great Salt Lake, the first to blaze his namesake Bridger's Pass over the Great Divide, and the first to raft the rapids of the lower Bighorn River. More than any early explorer Bridger revealed to the world facts and phenomena of the future Yellowstone National Park. He was the first to report on Two Ocean Creek, a riddling rivulet in the present Teton Wilderness that puddles in swamplands straddling the Continental Divide, then flows both east, down Atlantic Creek, and west, down Pacific Creek (and where, trapper Osborne Russell later wrote, "...a trout of 12 inches in length may cross the mountains in safety").

Bridger was among the relatively few mountain men who, after luck and skill permitted him to survive the multifarious hazards of years in the wilderness, possessed the tenacity and desire to remain in the mountains after beaver pelts lost their luster in the late 1830s, when the beaver fur's role in hat-making was supplanted by silk. After twenty years of negotiating streams swollen with snowmelt and traipsing through country thick with bears and Blackfeet, Bridger "retired" to establish Fort Bridger. The fort, which was actually more of a mercantile and smithy, was located along the Oregon Trail in southwest Wyoming. From his waystation Bridger guided emigrants and explorers alike, including Captain W. F. Raynolds. Bridger led Raynolds's party, which was composed of thirty infantrymen and seven scientists, into and through Jackson Hole and Pierre's Hole in 1859–60. The expedition included a topographer, geologist, botanist, and astronomer. Its mission was to explore "the headwaters of the Yellowstone and Missouri rivers, and . . . the mountains in which they rise."

Raynolds employed Bridger because he wanted the best guide living. Ironically, and uncharacteristically, Bridger never did get the party to its destination. Some speculate that it was by design and not by accident. Because he was getting paid by the day Bridger, now fifty-six, probably was in no hurry to get anywhere, and least of all Yellowstone, which he undoubtedly recalled as a mosquito-filled morass of snowmelt in early June. Instead of bearing north to Yellowstone from the Union Pass area, the party entered Jackson Hole. Here a corporal named Bradley drowned fording the Snake River before the party crossed Teton Pass into Pierre's Hole.

If not dazzled by Bridger's route-finding skills, Raynolds surely was impressed by the mountain man's lively imagination. Aubrey Haines, in *The Yellowstone Story*, tells about one of Bridger's more famous tales, as related by Raynolds: " . . . it was claimed that in some locality [thought to be Specimen Ridge in Yellowstone] . . . a large tract of sage is perfectly petrified, with all the leaves and branches in perfect condition, the general appearance of the plain being unlike that of the rest of the country, *but all is stone*, while the rabbits, sage hens, and other animals usually found in such localities are still there, perfectly petrified, and as natural as when they were living; and more wonderful still, these petrified bushes bear the most wonderful fruit—diamonds, rubies, sapphires, emeralds, etc.etc. as large as black walnuts . . . "

If John Colter had been hesitant to talk about what he had experienced in the Yellowstone country, then Jim Bridger was just the opposite. He was proud to share what he'd seen, and then some. Bridger so elaborated on some of his discoveries and experiences that he became known as the greatest yarn-spinner of his tall-tale ilk. Still, his factual contributions to the geographical knowledge of the region rank as second to none.

The legacy of Benjamin Louis Eulalie de Bonneville, a French-born American and a West Point graduate, was ensured after a fortuitous meeting with author Washington Irving in

**Bridger Creek Canyon,
south of the Yellowstone River**

September of 1835. Bonneville had recently returned from three years in the Rockies, the Utah desert, and the Columbia River Basin when the pair met at the New York City home of John Jacob Astor.

An Army officer by trade, Bonneville had long wanted to go West and participate in the Rocky Mountain fur trade. But he had to wait until age thirty-five to do so, when the Army gave him a leave of absence. Thinking that he'd be returning to open arms, if not a hero's welcome—foolishly perhaps, since he'd stayed nearly two years longer than the leave granted him—Bonneville was ostensibly shocked to find instead that he'd been dropped from the rolls of the Army, " . . . having been absent without leave since October 1833 . . . "

But still Bonneville was convivial, and Irving was captivated by his stories of trappers and Indians, which he found to be no less compelling than the American public had found Irving's legends of Rip Van Winkle and Sleepy Hollow. Of their chance encounter Irving wrote,

> From all that I could learn, his wanderings in the wilderness, though they had gratified his curiosity and his love of adventure, had not much benefited his fortunes. . . . In fact, he was too much of the frank, free-hearted soldier . . . to make a scheming trapper, or a thrifty bargainer. . . .
>
> Being extremely curious, at that time, about everything connected with the Far West, I addressed numerous questions to him. They drew from him a number of extremely striking details, which were given with mingled modesty and frankness; and in a gentleness of manner, and a soft tone of voice, contrasting singularly with the wild and often startling nature of his themes. It was difficult to conceive the mild quiet-looking personage before you, the actual hero of the stirring scenes related.

While waiting in Washington, D.C., for the completion of red-tape negotiations necessary for reinstatement in the Army, Bonneville, spurred by Irving's lively interest, began to condense his journal notes. Soon thereafter Irving took over, transforming Bonneville's rough manuscript into a book filled with true tales more thrilling than fic-

tion, and frequently less believable.

Bonneville had set out from near Independence, Missouri, on May 1, 1832. Following west what would become the Oregon Trail, his party of one-hundred-plus men was the first to drive mule wagons over the South Pass at the tail end of the Wind River Range. Among the stories Bonneville related to Irving of his subsequent time on the frontier was a colorful description of free trappers, who were "free" by virtue of working for themselves (contrasting with the hired trappers who worked for a company or another man). Bonneville first encountered the trappers in the wake of the 1832 Rendezvous of Pierre's Hole—described by mountain man Joe Meek as a "crazy drunk"—and the associated Battle of Pierre's Hole, which pitted hostile Gros Ventre Indians against white trappers and their Nez Perce and Flathead allies. Here are passages from Irving's rendition of what Bonneville told him:

> The wandering whites who mingle for any length of time with the savages have invariably a proneness to adopt savage habitudes; but none more so than the free trappers. It is a matter of vanity and ambition with them to discard everything that may bear the stamp of civilized life, and to adopt the manners, habits, dress, gesture, and even walk of the Indian. You cannot pay a free trapper a greater compliment than to persuade him you have mistaken him for an Indian brave; and in truth the counterfeit is complete. His hair, suffered to attain to a great length, is carefully combed out, and either left to fall carelessly over his shoulders, or plaited neatly and tied up in otter skins of parti-colored ribbons. . . .
>
> They came dashing forward at full speed, firing their fusees and yelling in Indian style. Their dark sunburned faces, and long flowing hair, their leggins, flags, moccasins, and richly-dyed blankets, and their painted horses gaudily caparisoned, gave them so much the air and appearance of Indians that it was difficult to persuade one's self that they were white men, and had been brought up in civilized life.

Irving's book permitted Americans a vivid glimpse of life on the Western frontier. It also made

Prickly pear cactus

Those accompanying him included Omaha photographer William Henry Jackson, whose seminal photos from this trip delivered solid evidence that the stories of fantastic thermal phenomena were more than trappers' tall tales.

Jackson's photos were instrumental in the successful push to create the Yellowstone National Park. Rudiments of the idea for such a park dated to the early 1830s, after artist George Catlin came west aboard the prophetically named *Yellowstone*, the first steamboat on the Missouri to reach the mouth of the Yellowstone River. Captivated by the country and all of its contents, Catlin made a study of the West's aboriginals his life's work. That work led him to propose to the U.S. government that it set aside and manage—in an undetermined but fittingly grand portion of the West—a "Nation's Park, containing man and beast, in all the wildness and freshness of their nature's beauty."

The idea gelled in 1870, when members of that summer's Washburn-Doane-Langford Expedition were camped where the Gibbon and Firehole rivers converge to become the Madison. One of the party's organizers, Nathaniel P. Langford, later wrote about a campfire conversation that took place the evening of September 19, the day after the party had witnessed an incredible, 100-foot column of steam exploding from what later would be called Old Faithful. The fireside chat revolved around ways in which the various expedition members thought the virgin country should be parceled out among them. Dissenting altogether, Cornelius Hedges, a lawyer and correspondent for the *Helena Herald*, "said that he did not approve of any of these plans—that there ought to be no private ownership of any portions of that region, but the whole ought to be set apart as a great National Park, and that each one of us ought to make an effort to have this accomplished."

Langford latched onto the idea which, not incidentally, meshed well with his role as a public relations agent for Jay Cooke and the Northern Pacific Railroad—a post he'd recently assumed after losing both his job as internal-revenue collector for the Montana Territory and his new appointment as governor of the same. Langford, an impetus for and member of the 1871 Hayden Survey, more than any other man led the drive for the new national park. " . . . This new field of

Bonneville famous for the rest of his life, during which he saw further action as a major in the Mexican War, as a lieutenant-colonel in the 1857 Gila River Expedition against the Apaches, and finally as a recruiting officer during the Civil War.

For twenty years following the decline of the fur trade, from 1840 to 1860, the Yellowstone-Teton region again was left to the Indians. Westward-migrating Americans bypassed the region, as they took aim for Oregon, California, or Utah. Then, in the 1860s, in filtered the gold prospectors, optimists wielding little more than a pickaxe and a dream. They generally failed to locate much in the way of glittering riches in the region, but they witnessed incredible things as they poked into its far-removed nooks and crannies. They brought home a mother lode of amazing stories, adding fuel to the flames firing America's collective imagination regarding this area purportedly teeming with boiling mudpots and steaming geysers.

Dr. Ferdinand Vandiveer Hayden, a Civil War medical doctor who had become the head of the U.S. Geological Survey, was sent West in 1871 to explore and document the Yellowstone region.

wonders should at once be withdrawn from occupancy, and set apart as a public National Park for the enjoyment of the American people for all time," asserted the man who would become that park's first superintendent, as he toured and spoke in major cities of the East and Midwest.

The bill to create the park was drafted by Langford and Congressman William Clagget of Minnesota. It included geographic boundaries identified by Hayden's 1871 Survey. The "organic act" passed the Senate on January 30, 1872, and the House on February 27. President Ulysses S. Grant signed into law the bill creating the 3,578-square-mile park on March 1. It marked the first time in world history that wild lands owned by a *federal* government—as opposed to a city, state, or other lesser governing body—were preserved "for the benefit and enjoyment of the people."

The new park encompassed the northwest corner of present Wyoming and small adjacent portions of Montana and Idaho, all still in the territorial stage at the time. Realizing now that much of the wild country in the region, especially to the south, had yet to be explored by an official government party, Congress also appropriated funds for a second Hayden Survey. Its mission: locate and identify watersheds, gather general geographical and scientific knowledge, and map some 9,000 square miles of little-known country. Taking part would be geologists, topographers, naturalists, meteorologists, paleontologists, astronomers, doctors, photographers, and others. The names of many who participated remain today as place names in the region: Joseph Leidy, George Phelps, W. R. Taggart, Gustavus R. Bechler, and Thomas Moran, an artist with the survey's Yellowstone Division whose namesake Mount Moran is one of the most recognizable peaks in the region. Some of Hayden's men even tried to rechristen the Grand Teton in honor of their leader, but the name Mount Hayden tumbled like so much talus off the mountain and into oblivion.

The Yellowstone Division, commanded by Hayden and guided by Jim Bridger, traveled from Corinne, Utah, up the Montana stage road to Fort Ellis, near today's Bozeman. From there they pushed south into the new national park. The second branch, the Snake River Division, was commanded by James Stevenson and guided by

Richard "Beaver Dick" Leigh. Its charge was to explore the upper reaches of the forks of the Snake River on both sides of the Teton Range. Setting out from Ogden, Utah, the party reached Fort Hall, Idaho, in early July, where it was joined by Langford who, coincidentally, had stopped over at Fort Hall en route to his new post as unpaid superintendent of Yellowstone. Stevenson's command, with thirty-seven men on horseback and twenty-five pack mules and horses, survived a long stretch of broiling desert then crossed the Henrys Fork of the Snake and took aim at the Tetons. On spotting the impressive peaks towering in the distance, party members toyed with the idea of ascending the highest among them. But Leigh was quick to discourage them, asserting that the prospect was unlikely. "Beaver Dick told us," Langford wrote, "that though many times attempted, the ascent of the Grand Teton had never been accomplished. And this was the opinion of the Indians."

Once in Teton Valley the survey discovered that the Teton peaks rose 32 miles east of where earlier geographers had positioned them, and so they were in Wyoming and not Idaho. After camping nine miles up the canyon of Teton Creek, on the morning of July 29 fourteen men set out for an attempted climb of the Grand. Due to injury, exhaustion, or other hindrance, just four or five made it over the ice, rock, and snowfields to the last approach, a point roughly 500 feet below the summit. From there only Stevenson and Langford prevailed. "We were amply rewarded," Langford later said, "when, at three o'clock P.M. after the severest labor of my life, we stepped upon the highest point of the Grand Teton."

As the Grand was being scaled, photographer W. H. Jackson and a mule named Old Molly were accomplishing an almost equally formidable feat, hauling tripods, chemicals, and other cumbersome camera gear to the plateau-like summit of 11,106-foot Table Mountain. From there Jackson took the first, and among the finest ever, photographs taken of the high Tetons.

More than twenty years passed before the Grand Teton was summited again. In 1898, William O. Owen, an influential Wyoming official, climbed the mountain with three others, and for thirty years thereafter he devoted great energies to discrediting Stevenson's and Langford's claim of success. Owen said his party had found no evidence that anyone had ever been on the top of the Grand. He asserted that first ascenders almost invariably leave some proof behind, such as a rock cairn. He also pointed out that Langford had mentioned seeing the tracks of mountain sheep and "flowers of beauteous hue and fragrance." Wrote Owen: "There isn't a flower within a thousand feet of the summit, and a mountain sheep would no more be able to climb the last six hundred feet than he would to climb the Washington monument." In his defense, however, Langford did not claim to have seen these things at the summit, but rather *from* the mountaintop when he and Stevenson looked down. Moreover, Langford was known to be a writer who often favored the lyrical over the precise.

Owen, undaunted, managed to convince the Wyoming state legislature in 1929 to declare his the first official party to climb the Grand Teton. But it must be added that Owen enjoyed a less scrupulous record than many men, including one of his companions on that climb, the Reverend Franklin Spalding. (The "Owen-Spalding" remains today a popular route to the top of the Grand.) The Reverend, who was actually the one to lead the others to the summit, said, "I believe that Mr. Langford reached the summit because he says he did, and because the difficulties of the ascent were not great enough to have prevented any good climber from having successfully scaled the peak . . . " The glory-seeking Owen, after whom the second-highest Teton peak was named in 1927, also kept secret the rest of his life a letter written to him in 1899 by Army surgeon Dr. Charles Kieffer. In it Kieffer told Owen that in 1893 he and two companions had climbed the Grand Teton. He even included a map showing their route. Kieffer had thought little enough of the feat, it seems, that receiving credit for it was of minor concern to him.

When Wilson Price Hunt, commander of an 1811 Pacific Fur Company overland expedition, first spotted the Tetons from far-off Union Pass in the Wind River Range, he noted the primary group of peaks as the "Pilot Knobs." This was hardly a suitable title for a trio of the world's most stunning mountains. In 1818 or 1819, a group of French-speaking Iroquois working for the North West Company ventured into the valley gracing the mountains' west slope, a valley later christened Pierre's Hole after Pierre Tivanitagon, a member of this group. The trappers, obviously too long away from home and families, longingly referred to the impressive peaks as *les Trois Tetons*, or "the Three Breasts."

Teton Range

British trappers took to calling them "The Three Paps." Pap, a word defined by *Webster's* as "soft food for infants or invalids," does derive from an archaic term for nipple, but Grand Pap National Park? *Vive les Tetons!*

Yellowstone, meanwhile, could have become known as the Elk National Park. The Crow Indians called the river that rises on the Park's east-slope peaks and lofty plateaus *E-chee-dick-karsh-ah-shay,* or Elk River, because of the large herds of wapiti that migrated through its upper valley on their way to and from winter range. It was down-river Minnetaree Indians who called the river the *Mi tse a-da-zi,* translated by eighteenth-century French explorers to mean *roche jaune,* or "yellow rock." So, the name was inspired not by the vivid formations found in the future national park, but by the yellowish sandstone bluffs that lift along the river's more mundane lower reaches in present eastern Montana. Lewis and Clark, preferring English over the French, on their maps called it the River Yellow Rock, a name that evolved into Yellowstone River. The authors of the organic act of 1872, which established Yellowstone as the world's first national park, referred to the region in question as "The tract of land in the Territories of Montana and Wyoming, lying near the headwaters of the Yellowstone River." In ensuing correspondence the secretary of the interior and the newly appointed park superintendent, Nathaniel P. Langford, took to calling it "the Yellowstone National Park," and the name stuck.

In 1876 Gen. George Armstrong Custer suffered his calamitous defeat at the Little Bighorn. A year later the Indian wars still raged. August of that year was a particularly poor time to be touring the five-year-old Yellowstone National Park, as two unfortunate parties of campers discovered.

The Nez Perce Indians, a tribe that had long enjoyed exemplary relations with the white newcomers, were in a bad way. An 1855 treaty had guaranteed the Indians much of their historical homeland, including portions of northeast Oregon and adjacent parts of Washington and Idaho. That treaty turned to trash, however, after a prospector secretly struck gold on Nez Perce lands in 1860. Whites soon flooded in. By signing off on a revised treaty in 1863 the branch of the Nez

Perce known thereafter as the "Treaty" Indians bargained away much of the reservation. It was a selfish act that proved the undoing of the "non-Treaty" Indians, who continued residing, now illegally, for several years in their traditional territory.

Until 1877, that is, when Gen. Oliver Otis Howard was sent to herd them onto the restricted reservation. In response to this affront, on June 13 a pack of vengeful young Nez Perce slaughtered several white men, women, and children. One of the non-Treaty chiefs, Thunder Coming From the Water up Over the Land—commonly known as Chief Joseph—wanted to surrender immediately to Gen. Howard after this appalling event. But Joseph's will was overruled by the chiefs White Bird, Looking Glass, and Toohoolhoolzote. And so, five warring bands lit out for the buffalo plains of central Montana, where in the past the tribe had enjoyed good hunting and peaceful relations with settlers.

Gen. Howard and his men followed in hot pursuit, striking several blows against the Indians as they trailed through Idaho and western Montana. Among these was a devastating early morning ambush on August 9 in the Big Hole River Valley, on the sunrise side of the Bitterroot Mountains. Led by Poker Joe, a French-Indian who knew the region well, the Nez Perce headed southeast from the Big Hole toward the wilds of Yellowstone. Here they bypassed the well-worn Bannock Trail, opting for a more southerly route along the Madison and the Firehole rivers. Their trail would trace through a tangle of wilderness described by one army scout as "the most outdoors country on earth," and where Gen. Howard would find wagon travel virtually impossible.

After crossing Targhee Pass the Nez Perce entered the park at the present site of West Yellowstone. They established camp the night of August 23 at the juncture of the Firehole River and its east fork (now Nez Perce Creek). Nearby they captured a cool cookie of a prospector named John Shively. By virtue of their force and understandably volatile tempers, the Indians had little trouble pressing Shively into service as a guide, and he proceeded to lead them through Yellowstone for almost two weeks before escaping their company. According to Shively's later account, the Nez Perce totaled approximately 800 individuals, roughly a quarter of them warriors and the rest women and children, and they pushed some 2,000 head of horses. He also contended that no one chief was in command, contradicting the popular idea that Chief Joseph was *the* leader at the time.

Later that evening Indian scouts spied a party of ten whites camped along Tangled Creek in the Lower Geyser Basin, 5 miles south of today's Madison Junction. The group, most of them from Radersburg, Montana, was outfitted with a double-seated carriage, a gear-hauling wagon, and four riding horses. Celebrating what they thought was the last of eight nights in Wonderland, they were gaily staging a makeshift minstrel show and failed to detect the scouts. The next morning they were greeted by several mounted Indians who tried to convince the campers that they were of the Snake (Shoshone) tribe, before admitting they were Nez Perce. As the whites loaded their wagon for what they hoped would be a peaceful departure, one of them, A. J. Arnold, proffered the Indians the coffee and foodstuffs they requested. This infuriated George Cowan, whose wife later said it may have been Cowan's lack of tact in the situation that led to trouble that afternoon.

No sooner had the whites started down the bumpy track leading out of the pine-embraced, steaming, stinking geyser basin, than they were turned back by a group of mounted Indians. The latter ensured the campers that although the Nez Perce were at war with the U.S. Army, they weren't interested in harming civilians; they merely wanted to prevent the party from informing soldiers of the Indians' whereabouts. The campers, having heard previously about these peaceful Indians traveling up the Bitterroot Valley, grudgingly complied.

The party was treated well at first. But annoyance soon turned to terror: Several young bucks, who had been growing more obstinate as the day wore on, ransacked the wagon and carriage at a point where deadfall timber halted the vehicles' further progress. Later in the day, 6 miles beyond the abandoned wagons, Poker Joe informed the captives that the Indians had elected to release them if they would first swap their saddles and rifles for some of the Indians' inferior gear. This they did. Poker Joe said they were free to go, but warned them to move quickly and stay off the main trail

and hidden in the timber. (Poker Joe and the other chiefs, it seemed, were trying but failing to maintain decorum among their young warriors.)

The going was horrible in the woods and after a half-mile of backtracking all but A. J. Arnold and William Dingee had returned to the trail, only to be overtaken and turned back yet again by a group of irate Indians. Anger turned to violence and soon both Albert Oldham and George Cowan had been shot. Cowan's wife, seeing that her husband was hit just above the knee of his right leg, dismounted her horse and attempted to shield him from further harm. An Indian pulled her away. She later recalled, "Wrenching my arm from his grasp, I leaned over my husband, only to be roughly drawn aside. Another Indian stepped up, a pistol shot rang out, my husband's head fell back, and a red stream trickled down his face from beneath his hat. The warm sunshine, the smell of blood, the horror of it all, a faint remembrance of seeing rocks thrown at his head . . . a sick faint feeling, and all was blank."

Frank Carpenter sat on his horse and crossed himself, and his sister Ida Carpenter screamed hysterically. Mrs. Cowan, also a sister to the Carpenters, lay unconscious on the ground. Campers D. L. Meyers, Charles Mann, and William H. Harmon bolted into a brushy marsh, with Indians pursuing and firing at them. Arnold and Dingee, still hidden in the woods, abandoned their mounts and hightailed on foot the 6 miles to the Gibbon River. They didn't dare start a fire. Arnold later said, "as we had neither coats nor blankets, we amused ourselves that night by crawling over fallen trees to keep warm." After four days the pair met up at Henrys Lake with Gen. Howard, whose troops were in the midst of packing to continue the chase. The bullet hitting Albert Oldham had penetrated his left cheek and cut his tongue before exiting beneath his right jaw. He lay suffering in a protected draw for many hours, but was rescued four days later by Gen. Howard's advance scouts.

The three siblings were led to the evening's camp at Mary Lake by a chief, who, after hearing gunfire, had rushed back in hopes of preventing the young hotheads bringing up the rear from wreaking further havoc. Mrs. Cowan later recalled Chief Joseph sitting by the fire that evening, "somber and silent, foreseeing in his gloomy meditations possibly the unhappy ending of his campaign. 'The noble Redman' we read of was more nearly impersonated in this Indian than in any I have ever met. Grave and dignified, he looked a chief."

After crossing the Yellowstone River at the Nez Perce (or Buffalo) Ford the next day, the Nez Perce released Mrs. Cowan and her brother and sister. The Indians gave them food and matches, and the trio headed toward Bozeman. They reached safety near Tower Junction, where they encountered members of the Second Cavalry, recently dispatched from Fort Ellis to help track down the Nez Perce. At the time they believed they were the only survivors of their ordeal. But, miraculously, everyone was alive and all eventually made it home safely—even George Cowan, who had only been knocked unconscious by a weakly propelled shot from a primitive revolver. When he'd finally struggled to his feet he looked up to see another Indian who, adding injury to injury, shot him above the left hip.

Left for dead again, for four days and nights Cowan dragged himself back toward the site where his party had last camped. He was finally retrieved by Howard's column on August 30, when Army doctors found and removed the flattened bullet wedged in place just above his nose. George Cowan, who should have stayed home that summer, arrived in Bozeman on September 25, more than a month after being shot, but only after the ambulance wagon hauling him had spilled over a precipice. "Safe" at last in a hotel room in Bozeman, his bed collapsed and spit the hapless Cowan onto the floor. He persevered, however, and he and his wife made several additional trips to Yellowstone during the ensuing years. Their harrowing tale was told often and Cowan had the bullet from his head turned into a watch fob.

So that his wagons could continue, Gen. Howard was forced to have his men build a makeshift road across Mary Mountain and over the Washburn Range at Dunraven Pass. The wagons arrived at the Lower Falls of the Yellowstone on September 3, after being lowered with snubbing lines down a steep hillside south of Otter Creek. The general's direct command, utilizing pack mules, crossed the Baronett Bridge on September 5, but his wagon train didn't cross

until the twelfth. (Baronett Bridge, which was situated near today's Tower Junction, was constructed in 1871 by Scottish prospector Collins Jack Baronett to serve the mining trade in the Cooke City area. It carried traffic until 1903.)

The Indians were quite dispersed by the time they started filtering out of the Park on September 6. Marauding parties of Nez Perce had roamed as far as north of present Gardiner, where they burned a ranch. They also partially burned the Baronett Bridge prior to Gen. Howard's arrival. Sadly, they also killed two members of the Weikert tourist party, composed of ten men and boys from the Helena area.

Although Howard lagged well behind, he was certain the Indians would be cut off at the mouth of the Clarks Fork canyon by the six companies of the Seventh Infantry, which had been sent down from Fort Ellis. But Nez Perce scouts sniffed out the awaiting ambush, and the Indians made an obvious but false start south toward the Shoshone River. In response, Col. Samuel D. Sturgis moved his troops to where that river exits the mountains. The Nez Perce doubled back and continued unassailed down the Clarks Fork and onto the prairie. By the time Sturgis discovered his blunder he had fallen well behind Gen. Howard, who in turn trailed the Nez Perce by 50 miles. Howard's national reputation as a dogmatic buffoon was ballooning. In fact, even as Howard fought his way through Yellowstone, Gen. William Tecumseh Sherman had sent Lt. Col. C. C. Gilbert to relieve Howard of his command. But Gilbert, no great timber-country soldier himself, failed to find Howard.

On reaching the plains the Nez Perce discovered that they'd fallen from favor with the Crows, former friends from the buffalo-hunting days with whom they'd hoped to find asylum. So, they veered north toward Canada. Their remarkable, 1,200-mile, often valiant and equally tragic trek ended at Snake Creek in the Bear's Paw Mountains on October 5, following six final days of bloody battle. Of the surviving Nez Perce, more than 300 fled the 40 miles to Canada and Chief Joseph surrendered for the rest, who numbered more than 400. The estimated death toll after fifteen skirmishes and nearly four months: 151 Indians and 121 soldiers and civilians.

After eight years on reservations in Kansas

Indian paintbrush flower

and Oklahoma, during which time Joseph evolved into a powerful leader, the Nez Perce were permitted to return to reservations in Washington and north Idaho—but only after Nelson Miles, the general who defeated and yet came to admire them at the Bear's Paw Battlefield, pleaded their case to President Rutherford B. Hayes. They never were permitted to return to Joseph's beloved Wallowa Valley in Oregon. (In 1997, however, in a piece of poetic American justice, their descendents began *buying* back some of the traditional Nez Perce homelands in Oregon.)

In 1883 William O. Owen, a man apparently obsessed with "firsts," with two others from the bicycle club in Laramie, made the first bicycle tour of Yellowstone National Park. It was before the introduction of chain drives and pneumatic tires, and the threesome pedaled primitive, high-wheeled "ordinaries" over rough roads around the park, then west through the Centennial Valley to the railroad depot at Beaver Canyon, Idaho. They, too, had an Indian scare, but it reads more like humor rather than drama. Consider Owen's description of the trio's temerarious, two-wheeled tactics:

> By severe pedaling the top was reached, when, throwing out legs over handles, we began our first coast and flew down the mountain with the speed of the wind. Some distance ahead we observed a large, moving body square in the road, coming our way, but with all our eyes we could not satisfy our minds as to what it might be. At the speed we were going, how-

ever, the distance was soon sufficiently short-ened to explain the matter, and we ascertained that it was a number of Indians traveling west. Here was a predicament indeed, and how to extricate ourselves was the next problem demanding speedy solution. We had no means of knowing whether these Americans were peaceable or on the warpath, and, fearing it might be the latter, it was deemed best to make a rush and frighten them before they could realize what was in the wind. . . .

> In my heart I believe that no men ever moved with greater velocity on a wheel than we did on this occasion. We dashed into their midst at a speed which I dare not even conjecture, and, with the most unearthly yells that ever reached human ears, squaws, chiefs, horses and innumerable dogs scattered in as many directions as there are points to the mariner's compass. It was a desperate charge, but entirely successful, and, passing the Indians, we reached the foot of the hill in safety.

Although Native Americans had been hunting in Jackson Hole and Pierre's Hole for centuries, and non-Indian trappers had taken advantage of the plentiful beaver on both sides of the Tetons since early in the 1800s, there were no permanent white residents in either valley until late in the nineteenth century. The first homesteaders in Jackson Hole consisted of a former trapper named John Holland and his friend, John Carnes. Along with Carnes' Indian wife Millie, in 1884 the pair staked a land claim where Flat Creek flows across today's National Elk Refuge. Others, mostly unmarried men, soon trickled into the remote, long-wintered valley. One was the legendary "Uncle Jack" Davis, who set up housekeeping in virtually lawless Jackson Hole after killing a fellow barroom brawler in Montana. Apparently repentant to an extreme, in his new life Davis transformed into a gentle friend to all things living. Deer ate from his hand and squirrels scampered at will in and out of his open-door cabin; his bunkmates included nesting bluebirds. Davis became a vegetarian, which even in the relatively sensitive 1990s is a rarity in this game-rich corner of the world.

The first population boomlet occurred in late fall 1889, after six wagons filled with five families of Latter-day Saints from Utah crested Teton Pass and literally slid into Jackson Hole. The group of approximately twenty was led by bishop Sylvester Wilson and his brother, Elijah N. Wilson. "Uncle Nick," as the latter became known to his many friends and admirers, never attended school but before turning twenty had experienced adventures that others of any age could only dream of.

Born in Illinois in 1842, Nick Wilson trekked west with his family in 1850 as part of the Mormon migration. At age twelve he was lured away from his family for two years by a group of Shoshone Indians, who offered him a beautiful pinto pony and a promise that he would spend all his hours with them fishing, hunting, and riding. This, he later wrote, "looked better to me than herding a bunch of sheep alone in the sagebrush," and so he went with them. The Indians pulled the risky move of "adopting" a young white boy in order to console the grieving mother of the great Chief Washakie, whose other two sons had been killed in a snowslide and whose only daughter had died after being dragged by a horse. A few years later, after having returned to his white family, Wilson lit out again at age eighteen to ride for the short-lived Pony Express. After that he was known always to wear a hat, even indoors, to cover the scar earned when a flint-tipped arrow fired by an Indian found its mark just above his left eye.

Uncle Nick was nearing fifty by the time he helped drive the wagon train over 8,429-foot Teton Pass. If manhandling the triple-teamed wagons up the roadless route to the summit was an arduous task, then getting them down—at a sane speed, anyway—was nearly impossible. The men switched the front with the rear wheels on each wagon, so that the taller rear wheels would lessen the chances of a forward roll. (Some accounts say they arranged it such that both large wheels were on the downhill side of the wagons, thereby somewhat flattening out the ride on the steep sidehills.) Then they chained the wheels to prevent them from turning. Finally, they tied felled trees to the backs of the wagons to act as drags. Brush and trees were cleared in advance of the wagon train as the Mormons' wagons skidded down the mountain and into Jackson Hole, where even on level ground the group found life to be no picnic.

Having arrived way too late in the season, the

Chuck wagon

newcomers survived the winter only through the grace of God—and the nutritional value of wild elk and antelope meat and the generosity of certain valley bachelors, who permitted them to sit out the season in their cabins. Within a year, however, the Mormons were growing their own hay and living in sod-roofed abodes of their own making. In 1891, the wife of Ervin Wilson, Nick's nephew, gave birth to Effie Jane, the first white child born in Jackson Hole. Uncle Nick Wilson homesteaded along Fish Creek, where the little settlement bearing his surname still thrives. He died there in 1915.

Deserted Mormon Row, in the southeast corner of Grand Teton National Park, sprang up in the mid-1890s when another party of Mormons from Idaho came into Jackson Hole looking for land. Choosing the flats north of the lower Gros Ventre River where tall sagegrass suggested fertile soils, they fully intended the area to serve as home for generations to come. But their plans were foiled several decades later by John D. Rockefeller Jr., who, after visiting Jackson Hole in 1926, began buying land there. Acting anonymously as the Snake River Land Company—he knew he'd be charged madly inflated prices if sellers realized the buyer was one of the richest men in America—Rockefeller spent $1.4 million procuring 35,310 acres, including those encompassing Mormon Row. Most he deeded back to the government for inclusion in Grand Teton National Park. It was a wonderful legacy for the world, but Rockefeller made many enemies in Jackson Hole by virtue of his surreptitious ways and his cost-is-no-concern ability to do as he pleased with "their" lands. Since then, portions of the classic films *Shane* and *Spencer's Mountain* have been shot along Mormon Row, where today only one small private inholding remains.

Now, across the granite and snow of the mighty Tetons to the fertile valley gracing the mountains' west slope. The first group to put down the roots of agriculture in Teton Valley were, again, Mormons branching out from the Salt Lake Valley. Thomas Edward Cheney (a distant relative of Nick Wilson), in *Voices from the Bottom of the Bowl*, writes that four brothers of the Driggs family—Benjamin, Don Carlos, Parley, and Leland—were the valley's original settlers. Don Carlos came in ahead of the rest, in 1888, and staked a 160-acre homestead, which he improved by building the valley's first log cabin. Also early into Teton Valley were Howard and Margaret Wallace, who homesteaded there in 1889. Don Carlos Driggs went on to become the valley's preeminent citizen: He opened the first store where the town called Driggs now sits, where he served "Mormon settlers, trappers, prospectors, and outlaws." He became the town's first postmaster in 1894, and, when it was incorporated a decade later, its first mayor. By the time another decade had passed and the Union Pacific's spur to the head of the valley at Victor was built, Don Carlos Driggs was a state legislator.

One could go back further and argue that Richard "Beaver Dick" Leigh was the original permanent white resident of the Teton Basin. Beaver Dick was a hunter, trapper, and guide; a late-season mountain man . . . not to mention an occasional midwife. Leigh and his first wife Jenny, an Eastern Shoshone of Chief Washakie's people, were the first to build a residence in the basin, but it served primarily as a winter cabin. It was, moreover, closer to the present St. Anthony–Rexburg vicinity than to the upper reaches of the Teton River, the area popularly considered Pierre's Hole, or Teton Valley. Regardless, Dick's life is worth considering, for more than any individual in the Yellowstone-Teton region he bridged the gap between the era of the mountain man and that of the homesteader.

Born in England in 1831, Beaver Dick—possessing a bright-red beard and powerful Cockney-accented voice—used the lower Teton Basin as a base for lengthy wilderness forays throughout the region from the late 1850s until his death. As previously noted, he served as a guide for the Hayden Survey of 1872, whose members honored him when they named Leigh Lake on the east slope of the Tetons, and his wife when they christened nearby Jenny Lake. His name endures on the west slope as well, in the forks of Leigh Creek.

Beaver Dick was ravaged by tragedy in December 1876, when Jenny and all six of their children died of smallpox. After burying his entire family in the frozen ground of Teton Basin, the devastated mountain man took lonesome solace in the splendor of his valley and the high Tetons, which he rhapsodized were "the beautifulest sight in the whole world." He remarried in 1879, to a tiny Indian girl he had helped deliver at birth near Franklin, Idaho, seventeen years earlier. Susan Tadpole, a niece of Bannock Chief Targhee, had been promised to Dick by her grateful parents once she attained a marriageable age—even though Dick had a thirty-one-year head start on her.

Beaver Dick and his new family, as with his first, often took extended hunting and camping trips. On one of these, in September 1891, they probably thought they had the game-abundant Two Ocean Pass country pretty much to themselves, as typically was the case. But this time they ran into the hunting party of one Teddy Roosevelt. Beaver Dick and Roosevelt hit it off immediately, and the pair drank whisky together in the latter's camp. Beaver Dick's ten-year-old daughter Emma even had the distinction of being turned over T. R.'s knee for interrupting their conversations and tripping over his boots. T. R. apologized the next day and gave Emma one of his rifles to ease her shame. "When the party pulled out and we waved goodbye," Emma recalled years later, "I didn't know then that ten years later I would consider it quite an honor to have been spanked by the future President of the United States."

Beaver Dick died in Teton Basin in 1899, fittingly, at the doorstep of the twentieth century.

"Verily a colossal sort of junketing-place!"
Those words were employed by the editor of *Scribner's Monthly* to describe America's new

national park. But the junketeers in large numbers wouldn't arrive at Yellowstone until the train tracks neared and the park's road system was expanded. Colossal numbers would have to wait until the automobile, first permitted in Yellowstone in 1915, provided the masses with a convenient and inexpensive means of traveling long distances. Meanwhile, no more than 500 tourists annually entered the park during its formative years, and those who did suffered long for their rewards. Still, early visitors comprised a diverse lot, ranging from earthy American country folk to the aristocratic likes of England's Earl of Dunraven, who wrote about his 1874 and 1876 visits in a book entitled *The Great Divide.*

Budgetary woes in Yellowstone National Park are nothing new; in fact, they came with the territory. Those who drafted the Yellowstone organic act realized that little, if any, funding to run the new park would be forthcoming from the tight-fisted Forty-second Congress. But they had an ace in the hole: an assured confidence that the Northern Pacific Railroad's tracks would soon reach across Montana, making it a relatively easy matter to haul in the hordes. Thousands of tourists, in turn, would open the doors to private enterprise in Yellowstone. Soon, concessionaires' fees would be pouring in to support the park's upkeep and operation.

As Lord Dunraven pointed out, however, "'When the railway is made' is, in Montana, a sort of equivalent for our phrase, 'When my ship comes home.'"

In 1873 westward progress of the Northern Pacific was halted for six years in Bismarck, Dakota Territory, after Jay Cooke & Company, the railroad's financier, went broke. In the ensuing economic panic all railroad construction in the country came to a standstill. For the time being, then, one of two jumping-off points for the Yellowstone-bound was distant Bismarck, from which point intrepid travelers went by boat up the Missouri River to Fort Benton, Montana. From "the bloodiest block in the West" they left the water behind and proceeded to eat several hundred miles' worth of dust as they endured the stage ride to Yellowstone via one of the Montana Territory's two competing gateway settlements, Bozeman and Virginia City. The second route to the park, shorter but even tougher, began at the Union Pacific's railhead in Corinne, Utah. Here Wells Fargo and Company staged daily departures up the rough-and-tumble miners' road that led ultimately to Virginia City.

Regardless of the route chosen, runaway wagons and turnovers were ever-present possibilities. Plenty of other dangers lurked as well, including Indian attacks, road agents, and fellow passengers who became drunk to ease the tedium then violent from the drink.

The first roads to penetrate Yellowstone, used by those earliest of tourists who made their way to the park unscathed, were built by private concerns. One of the two, a toll road constructed in 1871–74, stretched from Fort Ellis (near Bozeman) to Bottler's Ranch, then up the Yellowstone River to Mammoth Hot Springs via Yankee Jim Canyon. The other connected the

Island Park, Idaho

Lower Geyser Basin with Island Park, Idaho, and, eventually, Virginia City. Gilman Sawtell, an 1860s pioneer Island Park entrepreneur, built the Virginia City Road so that he could transport harvested game, packed on ice, to sell to Virginia City miners. Among Sawtell's bounty were large lake trout harvested with spears in Henrys Lake. With the creation of the national park Sawtell extended the road, along with his business concerns, eastward over Targhee Pass and into the geyser basin. In Island Park he opened an inn, the only hostelry on the road from Virginia City.

Private road-building ended when superintendent Nathaniel P. Langford took over. Langford made it clear from the outset that now only government-built roads were welcome in the national park. That may have been the spark that fired Gilman Sawtell into one of Langford's severest critics. It seems that Sawtell took more interest in the preservation of the park's natural resources than Langford did, and he certainly spent more time there: Langford toured Yellowstone only twice during his five-year stint as superintendent, first with the 1872 Hayden Survey and again on a brief visit in 1874. Langford obviously had less interest in running the park than he'd had in helping to establish it, and Yellowstone suffered during his absentee tenure. It was estimated that in the spring of 1875 the Bottler brothers killed some 2,000 elk up near Mammoth Hot Springs, and other hunters combined slaughtered at least an equal number. Tourists camped where they pleased, killing and dining on elk, swans, and other animals.

Capt. William Ludlow, commanding an 1875 expedition, witnessed tourists poking around, "with shovel and axe, chopping and hacking and prying up great pieces of the most ornamental work they could find. Men and women alike joining in the barbarous pastime." (He failed to mention that geologists with the expeditions did the same under the shelter of science, only often on a grander scale.) Smithsonian Institution collector Philetus W. Norris, tramping alone in the still-warm tracks of Ludlow in 1875, was aghast at the bloodbath. He "found no superintendent or other agent of government" anywhere in the park. Norris proposed to the secretary of the interior that he, Norris, replace Langford as superintendent, and he did—a job, incidentally, that Gilman

Sawtell had vied for, as well.

Until the reign of the ambitious and energetic, bearded and buckskinned Philetus W. Norris, not a penny had been spent by the feds on Yellowstone National Park. He changed that. During his superintendency Norris constructed the first government structures in Yellowstone, and he built some 100 miles of new trails and more than 120 miles of roads. Soldiers could now better negotiate through the wilderness in the case of Indian attack, and tourists could travel by wagon to Tower Fall, Old Faithful, Norris Geyser Basin, and Yellowstone Lake.

Ironically, it was criticisms leveled at the quality, or lack thereof, of Norris's roads that led to his removal in 1882. His demise was decided once the powerful and covetous Northern Pacific Railroad orchestrated a national editorial smear campaign against him. The Northern Pacific, operating under the dictum "Yellowstone Park must be made a summer resort," feared that Norris was about to offer hotel concessions to another company. The railroad had been instrumental in the creation of Yellowstone, and its directors weren't about to let the young park's potential riches slip away.

The railroads neared. In 1879, the year construction resumed on the Northern Pacific, the narrow-gauge Utah & Northern Railway pushed north from Corinne as far as Eagle Rock (Idaho Falls), and soon thereafter to Beaver Canyon (Spencer, Idaho). From there tourists traveled east by wagon through the resplendent Centennial Valley to the West Entrance, where West Yellowstone would emerge 28 years later, after the Union Pacific's Oregon short line reached there in 1907. By September of 1883, meantime, the Northern Pacific had not only reached Clark City (Livingston, Montana), but it had completed its Park Branch south as far as Cinnabar station, just north of Gardiner and the North Entrance.

Those now arriving at Yellowstone's doorstep by train typically traveled through the park in elaborate horse-drawn carriages operated by private companies. They stayed at hotels, which were becoming more common and less rustic. A small hotel was built at the forks of the Firehole during Norris's tenure in 1880, and here Rose Park Marshall entered the wintry world on January 30, 1881, the first white baby born in Yellowstone. In

1883 the original component of the big National Hotel at Mammoth Hot Springs was built, in conspicuous contrast to the shabby McCartney Hotel slapped together there in 1871.

This train-wagon-hotel combination, until the age of the automobile, was the typical way in which the well-to-do got to and through Yellowstone—visitors like an arrogant young Rudyard Kipling, who, when he toured there in 1889, was little impressed by the national park and even less so by the forthright Americans he was forced to travel with. Those of lesser means, often called "sagebrushers," continued to travel through Yellowstone on foot or horseback (or bicycle!). They camped and cooked out on their own, until privately run tent hotels, a happy middle-class medium, popped up near the Grand Canyon of the Yellowstone, in the Upper Geyser Basin, and elsewhere.

After Patrick Henry Conger replaced Norris as superintendent in 1882, vandalism and illegal hunting boomed again. It was Yellowstone's second management crisis, and this time it took the U.S. Army to fix it. Summoned in 1886, soldiers came to patrol the park and protect its resources. They fought man-caused fires, saved geothermal features from wanton and unintentional destruction, and labored long to reduce elk poaching, whose practitioners often kept only the animals'

hides and tongues and left the rest to rot. In winter, when elk, bighorn sheep, and other animals herded up and became easy targets, the soldiers toured on "Norwegian snowshoes," or cross-country skis, to ease the slaughter. Conservationist and hunter Teddy Roosevelt also helped in the effort to reduce poaching, as people in and around the gateway communities grew to appreciate the wisdom in his words: "A deer wild in the woods is worth to the people of the neighborhood many times the value of its carcass, because of the way it attracts sportsmen, who give employment and leave money behind them."

Soon the Army Corps of Engineers had completed the Yellowstone road network, and it looked pretty much as it does today. The chief of the highly skilled Yellowstone Engineers, from 1891 to 1893 and again from 1899 to 1906, was the far-sighted and multitalented Hiram M. Chittenden, who in 1895 authored the essential volume, *The Yellowstone National Park*. The Engineers' work even took them beyond the park's boundaries, as they put the finishing touches on the region's road system. They built a road up to the South Entrance and, after the Chicago, Burlington and Quincy Railroad reached Cody in 1901, a road from that town to the East Entrance. The way was made, if not yet paved, for Yellowstone National Park's future.

Seeing
Yellowstone-Teton
Country

This chapter begins in the wondrous, wildlife-abundant valley known as Jackson Hole, Wyoming. A tour leads north through Grand Teton National Park, then into and around Yellowstone National Park. Spur trips from the various Yellowstone entrances are detailed, too, leading to places such as Cody, Wyoming, and the Montana towns of Red Lodge, Livingston, and Bozeman. Finally, from the community of West Yellowstone, Montana, where you exit Yellowstone at the West Entrance, a narrative account leads southward along the resplendent west slope of the Teton Range and back to Jackson Hole.

Jackson Hole and Grand Teton National Park

Although larger outlying communities, such as Idaho Falls and Bozeman, typically offer more moderately priced accommodations, there is no better place than Jackson Hole to orient yourself to the far-reaching wonders of Yellowstone-Teton Country.

Incidentally, to avoid confusion, keep in mind the distinction between Jackson Hole and Jackson: **Jackson Hole** is the broad, flat expanse of land enclosed by the Teton Mountains on the west; the Yellowstone Plateau on the north; the Absaroka, Washakie, and Gros Ventre mountains on the east; and the Hoback and Snake River ranges on the south. **Jackson**, meanwhile, is the

town sitting at the southern end of Jackson Hole.

Jackson Hole makes a great place for a getaway, winter or summer, as millions—President Clinton and the First Family among them—have discovered. This vacationer's paradise also makes an excellent base from which to launch further travels in the region. In Jackson and surroundings you will find an extensive selection of motels, hotels, B&Bs, all-inclusive resorts, townhouses, and classic dude ranches. A large fleet of rental cars resides at the Jackson Hole Airport, which is served by American, Delta, and United Express airlines.

Huge arches composed of hundreds of elk antlers mark the four corners of the famous Town Square in Jackson. The boardwalks encircling the square resound with the footsteps of visitors from throughout the United States and the world. Horse-drawn stages take on passengers beside the square, and cowboys "shoot it out" here Wild West–style every summer evening, except Sundays, at 6:30—as they have for forty years. In winter, skiers by the thousands arrive to challenge the Jackson Hole Mountain Resort's world-famous steep runs. Many also make the drive over lofty Teton Pass to float through the bottomless powder snows at Grand Targhee Ski Resort, located on the west slope of the Tetons, which consistently attracts some of the most feathery fluff on earth.

Few free-ranging cowboys could afford to live there full-time today, but the breed plays heavily in Jackson Hole's past. The valley's recorded history is a colorful one of cattle ranching, guiding of big-game hunters, and catering to wealthy eastern dudes and dudeens (as female dudes are known).

Town Square, Jackson

In 1869, while still in the territorial stage, Wyoming became the first state or future state to grant women the full rights to vote and hold political office. This earned Wyoming its nickname, the Equality State. So, it seems altogether fitting and fair that Jackson, Wyoming, in 1920 became the first town in the United States governed entirely by a fleet of females. Grace Miller, who had founded the town in 1897, was elected mayor, while fellow females served as city clerk, treasurer, and even town marshal. Women also filled all four town council seats. The situation lasted until 1923.

Already owning a reputation as a wildly beautiful place, Jackson Hole really boomed as a result of three events: the creation of the rudimentary Grand Teton National Park in 1929, the addition to the park of several thousand more acres in 1950, and the establishment of the Jackson Hole Ski Resort in 1965. Now, as the twenty-first century approaches, a lot of the rich or famous, or famous *and* rich, maintain second (or third, or

fourth) homes in Jackson Hole. Real-estate prices have mushroomed beyond the reach of the average family. Jackson does retain a vestige of Old West charm, but even that threatens to disappear as citified boutiques and posh outlet stores progressively crowd out the less-polished establishments of yore.

A lot of Wyomingites from other parts of the state think of Jackson as "artificial," a town fronted with a Wild West facade fashioned to attract tourists and sell them things. But, really, what makes a place "real"? You will certainly see greater ethnic diversity and enjoy more cultural opportunities in Jackson than anywhere else in Wyoming (with the possible exception of Laramie, home to the state university). In some respects, then, perhaps Jackson is more "real" than other towns in Wyoming. Moreover, exceptional though it may be, Jackson Hole is largely responsible for helping to define outsiders' view of the entire state of Wyoming. Parallel situations exist in other communities in the Northern Rockies, such as Sun

Valley, Idaho, and Big Sky, Montana. You can learn more about these later in the book.

To say there is quite a bit to see and do in Jackson is a bit like stating that part-time Yellowstone-Teton Country resident Ted Turner has a little extra spending money. Shopping, sightseeing, and recreational opportunities abound, as you can see by thumbing through the Staying There section. Places to put at the top of your "must-see" list include the **Jackson Hole Historical Society & Museum**. The museum (telephone 307–733–2414), located behind the **Wort Hotel** at the corner of Glenwood and Deloney, is open in summer only. It includes displays on prehistoric Indians, the fur trade, and early dude ranching in Jackson Hole. The society's historical research center (telephone 307–733–9605), open weekdays year-round, is housed a few blocks from the museum in a log cabin at the corner of Glenwood and Mercell. It features a large library, a photo archive, and oral-history recordings, which encompass a bonanza of regional history. During summer the historical society also hosts walking tours of Jackson on Tuesdays, Thursdays, and Saturdays, beginning at 10 A.M. at the museum.

Another mandatory stop is the **National Wildlife Art Museum**, occupying a beautiful new, Southwest-style facility camouflaged on a parched hillside north of town off U.S. Highway 89/191. The museum displays in its 50,000 square feet both classic and new works of wildlife art and photography by deceased masters such as Thomas Moran and Charlie Russell, as well as the work of popular contemporary artists and up-and-comers. It's a museum that Jacksonites are extremely proud of, and rightly so.

From late December through March, hour-long horse-drawn sleigh rides depart just across the highway from the National Wildlife Art Museum, taking visitors on tours of the one-of-a-kind **National Elk Refuge**. The refuge, which covers nearly 25,000 acres, sprawls across the flatlands east of U.S. Highway 89/191, between Jackson and the bucolic settlement of Kelly. Some winters more than 10,000 wapiti migrate to the refuge, chased by deepening snows from Yellowstone National Park and the Tetons and other nearby mountain ranges. Seeing all these majestic animals gathered in one place is a staggering sight. Smaller numbers of other animals live at least part-time on the refuge, too, including moose, bighorn sheep, mule deer, bison, coyotes, and more than 150 species of birds. The rich abundance of species results from the refuge's wide array of habitats: from the grassy meadows and valley marshes along Flat Creek to rocky, sagebrush-covered foothills to the stands of cottonwoods lining the Gros Ventre River.

Before the white settlers arrived, Jackson Hole was already a wintering ground for as many as 25,000 migratory elk. As valley lands began turning to private hands, the wild elk were forced to surrender more and more of their critical winter habitat to the cattle industry. Stories are told of hundreds of desperate, starving elk wandering through the town of Jackson on cold winter nights. Conflicts between elk and settlers, such as when the elk would raid haystacks for food, resulted in severe reductions of the herds. The kill-off/die-off culminated during the extraordinarily tough winters of 1909 through 1911, when thousands of elk died for lack of food. The federal government took action, realizing that sufficient winter range was key to the survival of the elk herds, and, as some locals reminded the feds, that the herds were vital to the economic well-being of Jackson Hole. On August 10, 1912, Congress designated the rudimentary National Elk Refuge in an effort to ensure that the mighty

National Elk Refuge, Jackson Hole

wapiti would always have a safe and food-abundant place to winter in Jackson Hole.

Today, the refuge has grown to nearly ten times its original size. As necessary, when ice or a crust of snow seals off the natural browse, the U.S. Fish and Wildlife Service provides supplemental feed to the animals. During the hardest part of late winter the feeding can exceed thirty tons of pelletized alfalfa hay per day. In late April and May the elk return to the mountains, with the cows giving birth in the higher country between late May and mid-June. But before they leave, beginning in March, tons of antlers are shed by the bulls of the herds. In a unique partnership with the National Elk Refuge, the antlers are gathered by area Boy Scout troops, who sell them at a public auction held each May at the Jackson Town Square. Eighty percent of the money raised goes toward purchasing feed for the elk, thus completing a compelling circle. Most of the antlers are purchased by artists and craftsmen, who utilize them to fashion popular items such as antler chandeliers and belt buckles, and by buyers from Asia, where the antlers are ground into powder or sliced into disks, then used medicinally. Demand has driven the price of antlers higher than $14 per pound on occasion. In 1997 the Boy Scouts raised more than $102,000 by selling a record 11,320 pounds of antlers ($9 per pound).

For more information on the National Elk Refuge, call the headquarters at (307) 733–9212.

To drive across the National Elk Refuge in summer, when the elk are long gone but the terrific scenery remains in place, follow Broadway east out of town to where it turns to gravel and becomes Flat Creek Road. Shortly after curving northward, you'll see a side road turning off to the east. The road, which climbs high into **Curtis Canyon** before dead-ending, winds through a relatively little-visited portion of the Bridger-Teton National Forest. Here you'll discover a pleasant Forest Service campground and also gain a seldom-seen perspective of Jackson Hole and the rough-hewn ridge of the Tetons. The gravel road, in its earlier stages anyway, is hard-surfaced and passenger-car friendly.

Before riding out of Jackson, saddle up, literally, to the **Million Dollar Cowboy Bar** to sip a brew or a soft drink. The house of libation is sit-uated across from the Town Square on North Cache. Inside, astride a leather-saddle barstool, you can watch cue-wielding cowpokes, both real and pretend, shooting pool amid surroundings dominated by burled beams of polished lodgepole pine. Country bands jam at the Cowboy on many evenings, bringing the dance floor to life, and swing-dance lessons for beginners, a time-honored tradition at the Cowboy, are offered every Thursday night beginning at 7:30 P.M.

A Full-Day Auto and Foot Tour of Southern Grand Teton National Park

Five miles north of Jackson you will enter **Grand Teton National Park** (GTNP). It is largely due to the foresight and efforts of some early Jackson Hole residents that much of Jackson Hole and the surrounding mountains are held in common by all Americans. Struthers Burt, an eastern author who established the Bar BC, one of the first dude ranches in the valley, proposed early on that a "museum on the hoof" be created here, with tourism and ranching combining forces to hold encroaching commercialism at bay. The movement crystallized in 1923, when Yellowstone National Park superintendent Horace Albright met with several Jackson Hole locals at the cabin of Maude Noble, located near the present settlement of Moose. The group formulated a plan: They would find and convince a wealthy person to buy up much of the private lands in Jackson Hole and then donate them to the government.

As pie-in-the-sky as the concept sounds, the group did find its benefactor in John D. Rockefeller Jr., who with his wife and three sons came west in 1926 to tour Yellowstone. Superintendent Albright first took them on a tour through Jackson Hole, where Rockefeller was shocked by what he saw littering the gracious landscape: a dance hall at Jenny Lake surrounded by dilapidated cabins and abandoned, rusting cars, for instance, and telephone lines and snack shacks lining the roadway. (Albright no doubt showed him the worst there was to see.) Rockefeller readily bought into the idea and soon his agents began purchasing lands, under the guise of the Snake River Land Company. They eventually acquired more than 35,000 acres for

$1.4 million. Most of the lands Rockefeller deeded back to the government in 1949 for inclusion in GTNP.

As you continue north, ahead and to the left, if clouds don't obscure the view, the world-famous pack of ragged peaks erupts from the floor of Jackson Hole, ripping like the teeth of a colossal saw through the azure sky. The highest, the **Grand Teton**, elevation 13,770 feet, is connected by a saddle to **Mount Owen** to its north. **Teewinot Mountain** rises in front (to the east) of Owen, while south of the Grand and in close proximity are the **Middle Teton** and **South Teton**. North of Owen, above the deep gash of Cascade Canyon, looms the distinctively striated **Mount St. John**. Farther north still, rising above the north end of Leigh Lake, is the massive bulk of **Mount Moran**. (The relative positions of the peaks change, of course, depending on where you are viewing them from. One of the very best places to get an overview is from the top of Signal Mountain, which you'll read about later.)

Teton Range

The mood of the Teton Range changes throughout the day and with the seasons. Early in the morning in summer, as the sun rises in the east over the **Gros Ventre Mountains**, the Tetons are often awash in a soft, pink-purple light. In midday the intense, high-elevation sunlight often makes them appear harsh and somewhat forbidding. But the tones soften again with the arrival of evening light, which turns the mountain front deep blue and inviting. In winter the high peaks and cirques are a mix of deep snow and cold rock. Avalanche accumulations are commonly seen on slopes that are just gentle enough to permit the snow to pile . . . until it gets too deep and/or the weather warms, causing the snow to slide.

GTNP supports four major natural communities, or life zones: the water/wetland communities of lakes, streams, rivers, and ponds, whose residents include trout, beaver, waterfowl, and moose; the extensive sage/grassland community, home to bison, pronghorns, sage grouse, and hosts of songbirds, raptors, rodents, and insects; the seemingly randomly dispersed forest community, which provides vital cover and food for elk, deer, and dozens of birds species; and the uppermost alpine community.

Look up at those alpine heights, where tiny wildflowers bloom late in the summer, long after the colorful floral show on the valley floor has died. It is a high, harsh world; a different world altogether, really, from that of the valley floor. In order to survive amid the brief growing seasons, nutrient-poor soils, summer droughts, and strong winds, alpine plants have evolved many unusual adaptations, such as matting growth and dwarfism, both of which keep the plants low to the ground where conditions are most forgiving, and dark pigments. These help the plants to absorb a greater amount of heat than if they were simply green, as is most vegetation.

The first side road you'll encounter in GTNP leads northeast up the **Gros Ventre River**. The road is well worth exploring, as it continues 40 miles east before running into a dead-end at the historic Horn Ranch. The Gros Ventre Road provides access to a host of hiking and biking trails winding through intriguing and little-visited public lands that are far more arid and "badlands-looking" than most of the terrain in and around Jackson Hole.

Following the Gros Ventre Road, 4.5 miles from the main highway you'll pass the National Park Service's **Gros Ventre Campground**, and at 6 miles you'll skirt **Kelly**, a tiny settlement consisting largely of a scattering of yurts and log cabins. At Kelly the road curves ninety degrees north; 2 miles beyond there you must turn right to stay on the Gros Ventre Road. At 10.5 miles cumulative the road leaves GTNP and enters the Bridger-Teton National Forest.

Three miles after entering the national forest you'll encounter the startling **Gros Ventre Slide Geological Area** overlook. The lake below, which extends east–west for 5 miles and reaches a depth of 200 feet, began filling after the side of Sheep Mountain let loose, probably after an earthquake, on June 23, 1925, and the accumulated debris dammed the Gros Ventre River. The slide's scar—more than a mile long and a half-mile wide—can still be spotted easily from many miles away in Jackson Hole. The earthslide was precipitated by a wet spring that saturated the shale underlying a layer of sandstone. Two years after the earth slid, the temporary earth dam broke, adding injury to insult: The resulting flood obliterated the original town of Kelly, killing six people and destroying every structure except the church and the school, and hydro-hauling trees and houses some 15 miles down to the Snake River confluence.

Upstream from the slide area, at between 14 and 20 miles, you'll pass a trio of pleasant Bridger-Teton National Forest campgrounds. Beyond the string of campgrounds the road is typically so lightly traveled that it's easy to forget just how close you are to busy Jackson Hole. Beware, though, that the upper Gros Ventre Road can be quite rough, and with its gumbo-clay surface it can be a very *un*fun road to be on during and after heavy rains; in fact, it can become impassable. South of the road foot and horse trails penetrate the **Gros Ventre Wilderness**, which, like all federal wilderness areas, is off-limits to bicycles. If you're looking for mountain-biking fun, plan to explore north of the road—up the Horsetail or Cottonwood creek drainages, for examples. Informal, unsigned campsites—the Forest Service calls them "dispersed" sites—are abundant along the quiet upper reaches of the road. (Be aware, though, that back in GTNP camping is permitted only at designated campgrounds.)

On your way back to the main highway, rather than returning south to Kelly, turn north at the T just past **Kelly Warm Springs** (it *is* only warm, not hot). In about a mile you'll pass the right-hand turn onto the road leading northeast to the acclaimed **Teton Science School**. The year-round operation, founded in 1967 by a former Jackson Hole High School teacher, offers courses of varying length, ranging from those aimed at grade-school kids to college-credit courses and elderhostels. The school's headquarters occupies old Elbo Ranch, built in 1932 by the legendary Teton mountaineer Paul Petzoldt. It's worth swinging in just to have a look, in the main building, at the Murie natural-history collection, which comprises stuffed birds, skeletons, and casts of animal tracks. The man who gathered and bequeathed the collection was the noted naturalist and Jackson Hole resident Olaus Murie, whose works include *Peterson's Guide to Animal Tracks,* as well as the volume that is considered the bible on the subject of the North American elk. To call ahead before visiting (a good idea), or to request a course-offering catalog, call the school at (307) 733–4765. Teton Science School's annual fund-raising auction, typically held in late August, in itself is a Jackson Hole institution.

To return to Gros Ventre Junction go north and turn left onto the Antelope Flats Road, proceed west for about 2 miles, then turn south to pass the weather-worn buildings of forsaken **Mormon Row** (*see* History). The timbered hill behind to the west is **Blacktail Butte**, along whose flanks elk can sometimes be seen. This road rejoins the Gros Ventre Road at a point just above the Gros Ventre Campground.

At Gros Ventre Junction turn right onto U.S. Highway 89/191. Keeping to the east side of the Snake River, you'll pass the Jackson Hole Airport (the only commercial airfield within a U.S. national park), then arrive at **Moose Junction**, which is situated 6 miles north of Gros Ventre Junction. Before continuing north on the main road, take the short detour west to Moose, location of the park's headquarters and primary visitor center. Here you can learn about special ranger-led activities taking place in GTNP; pick up a copy of *Teewinot,* the park's newspaper; and also obtain brochures for several short self-guiding trails in the park, including the Menor's Ferry Historic Trail, Cunningham Cabin Trail, Taggart Lake Trail, and Colter Bay Nature Trail. The center is open daily 8:00 A.M. to 7:00 P.M. in summer, and 8:00 A.M. to 4:30 P.M. the rest of the year.

Back on U.S. Highway 89/191, recommended stretch stops as you head north from Moose include the **Glacier View Turnout**, the often-photographed **Snake River Overlook** (shooting locale of one of Ansel Adams's most famous photos), and the **Cunningham Cabin Historic Site**, where rancher Pierce Cunningham, one of the initial sparks that fired the creation of GTNP, homesteaded in 1889. Eighteen miles north of Moose Junction you'll arrive at **Moran Junction**, where you'll want to turn left—but where if you decide to go right instead, you won't be short-changed, either: U.S. Highway 287/26 winds up and over Togwotee (*TOE-guh-tee*) Pass; past the turn to the historic **Brooks Lake Lodge**, a classic Western wayside where the views are stunning and the Yellowstone-bound have been overnighting since 1922; and down to Dubois (*DO-boys*), a cowtown and outfitting center surrounded by dude ranches, brilliant red rock canyons, and wild wapiti and bighorn sheep . . . and a town filled with oversized likenesses of elk, bears, trout, and other wildlife.

After bearing left at Moran Junction, then paying your dues at the Moran Entrance Station, go another 5 miles and turn left at Jackson Lake Junction onto the **Teton Park Road**. Soon you will drive across the **Jackson Lake Dam**, constructed in 1910–11 (and rebuilt in 1988–89) for the purpose of enlarging the smaller natural Jackson Lake, to provide irrigation-water storage for Idaho farmers downstream. South of the dam you'll pass the right-hand turn to the **Chapel of the Sacred Heart**, where, in addition to a charming log Roman Catholic chapel residing in a grove of lodgepole pines, you'll find a pleasant picnic area. South of there, turn right into the **Signal Mountain Lodge** complex. Guests hole up here in a fairly ordinary-looking motel/lodge, or in cabins, some of classic log construction and others more modern, wood-sided structures. Signal Mountain also boasts a boat ramp and a campground. The waterfront here makes an excellent spot from which to watch east-moving thunderstorms boiling over the Teton crest.

A little over a mile farther south along the Teton Park Road is the left-hand turn onto the circuitous blacktopped road leading 5 miles to the summit of **Signal Mountain**. Those pulling trailers are not permitted to drive on this road, those driving large RVs are dissuaded from attempting it, and even those in small vehicles need to proceed slowly and with caution. The drive takes place almost entirely within dense lodgepole forest, so watch not only for other motorists but also for wayward elk and deer.

Not until finally approaching the summit do you understand what it is you came here for: an amazing panorama of the Tetons, Jackson Hole, and the mountains to the east and south; a view that could be surpassed only by taking wing in an aircraft or by scaling the Grand Teton. Far below, a serpentine growth of willows and spruce delineates the course of the Snake River as it braids its way in numerous channels through Jackson Hole, looking more like a prairie rambler than a mountain torrent. The faint green or brown (depending on the time of summer) timberless areas on the valley floor define the *outwash plain*. Here glacial runoff percolated through the layer of quartzite cobbles that fill the valley to a depth of about 2,000 feet. (The cobbles originated from an extinct range that rose to the northwest.) The glacial runoff washed the cobbles clean of clay that would have helped the ground retain water and support plant growth. Now the porous, sterile fill permits water simply to run through, so the

water has little opportunity to feed vegetation; hence, the lack of trees. The porous soil, combined with the harsh climate, is also why cattle ranching has historically been such a marginal undertaking in Jackson Hole.

Depressions on the outwash plain, some filled with water, are the features known as *kettles* (called the Potholes locally), which were created when stream-deposited sediment collected against stagnant remnants of ice. Finally, wherever you see timber growing below, you're looking at glacial moraines, which are younger than the outwash plain. The moraines grew as the ice sheets melted and advanced at roughly the same rate, piling, almost in conveyor-belt fashion, a more-nutritious, clay-rich debris.

Rising above it all to the west, and best seen from below the summit at the Jackson Point Overlook, is the full parade of the Teton peaks, including the poetically named Rolling Thunder Mountain, along with Mount Moran, Mount St. John, and the "Cathedral Group," as the cluster of high peaks including the Grand Teton is known.

Twist back down the long hill, then continue south on the Teton Park Road for a couple of miles to the Mount Moran geologic pullout on the right. Here you can learn the basics of the complex story told in the rocks of the 12,605-foot peak. The massive mountain supports five of the Teton Range's dozen glaciers, all of which were products of the "Little Ice Age" of 500 to 1,000 years ago (rather than remnants of the older

Pleistocene ice sheets). One of the glaciers on Moran, Falling Ice Glacier, is the distinctive ice sheet situated immediately below the dark *dike* that cleaves the top of the mountain like a wedge. The dike is composed of solidified magma intruded subterraneanously long before the Tetons began rising and Jackson Hole sinking.

Now look at the very top of the broad mountain and, unless it's covered with snow, you'll spot a lighter-colored sandstone cap, a remnant of a continuous layer of sandstone that once covered the region. The layer fractured when the Tetons first began building some 9 million years ago, and now the sandstone cap worn by Moran is roughly 6,000 feet above the valley floor. It's believed that the same sandstone layer lies buried some 24,000 feet beneath the ground surface of Jackson Hole, indicating that the valley has sunk *four times* as far as the mountains have risen (also meaning that many thousands of feet of sediment have filled the valley).

The farther south you drive, the closer you will get to the Tetons, until as you veer right at North Jenny Lake Junction the peaks are practically in your face. The view afforded at and around the sumptuous **Jenny Lake Lodge** is nothing if not awesome: Amid the crags and crannies of the Cathedral Group, adjacent pinnacles and sub-peaks angle out and back like successive layers of teeth in the gaping, cavernous mouth of a shark.

The one-way southbound road leading to the South Jenny Lake area is relatively quiet—it's ideal for a bicycle ride—but still, drivers should pull off the road now and then or they'll chance finding themselves gasping at the remarkable mountains more than watching the road. One view definitely worth savoring is that seen across Jenny Lake, into the depths of Cascade Canyon. It's simply stunning.

The **South Jenny Lake** complex includes a campground reserved expressly for tenters, a boat dock, a small visitor center, and the trailhead where you can launch a hike around the lake, meandering through forests of lodgepole pine, subalpine fir, and Engelmann spruce. By following the trail around the south side of the lake for a little over 2 miles you can then make the climb up Cascade Canyon to the popular and aptly named **Inspiration Point**. At the north end of the lake the Jenny Lake Trail links with trails going north to narrow String Lake and Leigh Lake. (As I discovered in early September 1997, this trail around Jenny Lake is an excellent place to catch a glimpse of a bear munching on berries . . . and a good place to get caught in a fall hailstorm, necessitating a ten-minute hunker beneath a great Douglas fir.)

You'll begin distancing yourself from the mighty mountains as you continue south on the Teton Park Road, passing the Teton Glacier Turnout and then the turn to the Climbers' Ranch, where slews of Grand Teton–bound mountaineers bunk overnight in order to get an early jump on the peak. A little over a mile to the south is the right-hand turn to the Taggart Lake Trailhead, where begins a relatively easy, 3- to 4-

Panoramic view of the Teton Range and Jackson Hole from Signal Mountain

mile loop hike visiting **Taggart Lake**. (An informative brochure for the hike can be picked up at one of the park's visitor centers.) The outing is beautiful at almost any time, but particularly so in September, when the crowds have thinned and the aspen groves are aflame in yellows, golds, oranges, and reds. Also at that time of year, especially on the later stretches of the hike along Beaver Creek, listen for the grunting and whistle-like bugling of bull elk; they're hair-raising, quintessentially wild sounds. You may even get to watch a little bull-to-bull sparring action. Give the beasts a wide berth, though, both to avoid upsetting them and to protect your own hide.

From the trailhead you'll begin by crossing sage flats marking a portion of the glacial outwash plain. Here you may notice abandoned irrigation ditches that were excavated by early Jackson Hole homesteaders for the purpose of transporting water to their fields from nearby natural waterways. Taggart Lake is protected—in fact it was created—by a rampart-like moraine that emerged during the late Pleistocene, as debris was laid down from the glacier that moved down Avalanche Canyon, then melted on reaching the valley floor and its warmer temperatures. The size of the rocky litter ranges from small stones to immense boulders of ancient granite and gneiss. The moraine's lodgepole pine forest was consumed by the Beaver Creek wildfire, caused by lightning, in 1985; today the new pines are already 8 to 12 feet high.

The Taggart Lake Trail then climbs steeply over the moraine to the shore of Taggart Lake, where the view into Avalanche Canyon and up at the high Tetons is out of this world. It's *the* lunch stop on the hike. The trail heads south over the lake's lateral moraine, before descending to Beaver Creek and taking aim back at the trailhead.

Back on the main road, south of the Taggart Lake Trailhead you'll approach Moose. Just before

Elk bulls sparring

exiting GTNP at the Moose Entrance Station, a side road heads east to the rustic **Chapel of the Transfiguration**, a popular spot for weddings that was built the year of the Gros Ventre Slide (1925). Also nearby is a reconstruction of the historic, current-propelled **Menors Ferry**. The original cable ferry was built in 1894 by homesteader William D. Menor. William's brother, Holiday Menor, lived across the river on the east shore; ostensibly, though, the two rarely got along and commonly cursed at one another across the roiling waters. In 1918 William D. Menor was bought out by Maude Noble, who ran the ferry until a bridge was built near the present Moose bridge in 1927. Until then the ferry was *the* way in central Jackson Hole to get from one side of the Snake River to the other.

Beyond the visitor center, on the east side of the Snake, is **Dornans'** and an eclectic array of enterprises where you can rent a mountain bike or a canoe, buy groceries, enjoy breakfast or a chuck wagon dinner in an oversized tipi, or choose a good bottle of wine from what is surprisingly one of the best selections in the Northern Rockies. From there, backtrack to Jackson on U.S. Highway 89/191. (Alternatively, from Moose you can follow the narrow, gravel Moose-Wilson Road, which winds for 9 miles to Teton Village before continuing south on pavement to Wilson. The road skirts the Rockefeller family's historic JY Ranch.)

Along the main highway heading south, look up toward the Tetons at about two o'clock and you'll see the red tram towers that identify the **Jackson Hole Mountain Resort**. You can also make out the adjacent ski slopes, although they're not as readily identifiable as the runs straight ahead cut on the face of **Snow King Mountain**, which serves as the backdrop for the town of Jackson. To the right of Snow King you can see the Gros Ventre Buttes and the white gash where State Highway 22 inches its way up Teton Pass. To the east the Sleeping Indian formation on Sheep Mountain is prominent. The Gros Ventre Slide (now out of view) is on the north end of elongated Sheep Mountain, which is also the mountain President Clinton's C-130 support plane, which carried vehicles and other items used by the First Family while vacationing in Jackson Hole, crashed into in summer 1996, killing several Air Force men and women. Between the Sleeping

Indian and Snow King is Jackson Peak, the distinctive mountain rising like a low pyramid against the skyline.

FROM JACKSON LAKE JUNCTION NORTH TO YELLOWSTONE NATIONAL PARK

En route to Yellowstone, about a mile north of Jackson Lake Junction (which is 35 miles north of the town of Jackson) turn left into the Jackson Lake Lodge complex. Take some time to browse around **Jackson Lake Lodge** even if you're not interested in staying there. The elegantly rustic structure, built in the 1950s with the monetary backing of John D. Rockefeller Jr., is fronted by stout concrete pillars molded with a wood-grain effect. Large paintings of wildlife hang high on the walls in the main lobby, off which branch numerous meeting and dining rooms. Square-faced rock adorns the walls, and cast-iron moose silhouettes serve as log holders in the spacious fireplace. Although the architectural merits of the building are debatable—and certainly have been debated—there's no arguing that the view afforded from the immense picture windows in the lobby is top-notch: A broad expanse of willow flats, where moose often browse, leads down to Jackson Lake. On the opposite shore of the lake looms the entire panorama of one of the world's most famous mountain ranges.

Across the road to the east from the Jackson Lake Lodge complex begins the trail leading to **Emma Matilda and Two Ocean lakes**. A loop taking in both lakes makes for a long day hike of approximately 14 miles. Wildlife, particularly waterfowl such as trumpeter swans and pelicans, is richly abundant on the outing. The pair of long lakes are geologically noteworthy in that they are more than three times as old as the dozens of lakes residing high in the Tetons and those nestled against the base of the jutting peaks. Emma Matilda and Two Ocean lakes both formed some 30,000 years ago as glaciers retreated; most other lakes in the park are closer to 8,000 years old. The very highest lakes, turquoise jewels known as *tarns* that wear individuals names such as Surprise, Talus, and Grizzly Bear, were formed in a manner similar to the larger lakes at the foot of the Tetons, which include Phelps, Jenny, and Taggart lakes and others. These newer lakes, all products of the

Tent cabin, Colter Bay Village

latest glacial advance, are identifiable by the young morainal dams backing them up.

Six miles north of Jackson Lake Junction is **Colter Bay Village,** one of GTNP's busiest centers of enterprise and activity. The bay itself is peaceful and beautiful, with massive Mount Moran across the lake serving as a brilliant backdrop. At the marina you can rent a canoe by the hour, to explore the quiet waters of the bay and/or to venture farther into the often wind-whipped waters of Jackson Lake. Hikes possible from Colter Bay Village include the 9-mile round-trip to **Hermitage Point**, a beefy peninsula jutting southwesterly into Jackson Lake, and the mile-long **Colter Bay Nature Trail**.

The attractive rental cabins at Colter Bay are built of dark-stained logs, separated by light-colored chinking and set off with a trim painted dark green. Other amenities at the village include a corral with horse rentals, and tent cabins, those classic national park rental affairs that are sort of a cross between stacked-log cabins and canvas hunting tents. Woodstoves are used for heat, and on a chilly summer morning the rich scent of smoldering pine is powerful amid the tent-cabin village.

By all means, do not miss visiting the museum at Colter Bay, which consists primarily of the **David T. Vernon Indian Arts Collection**. The extensive displays, made more remarkable when you consider that they were the collection of one man, demonstrate graphically and colorfully the extent to which Plains Indians and other Native Americans were able to use naturally occurring products to fashion utilitarian and ceremonial items of remarkable beauty, form, and function. Raw materials utilized ran the gamut from deer bones to buffalo hides, porcupine quills to ermine plews, and eagle feathers to soapstone. Many of the items made in later times also incorporated horsehair, glass beads, silver from melted coins, and other non-native materials that came into play after European contact. Thousands of items are displayed, including moccasins, masks, ceremonial pipes, shirts and dresses, stone tools, and much, much more. One of the more unusual examples: A single bighorn sheep horn, steamed and straightened into a robust, arrow-hurling bow.

Also residing within the museum at Colter Bay is the controversial Colter Stone (*see* History). It is not on display, but it will be retrieved and shown on individual request. The museum is open daily in summer 8:00 A.M. to 7:00 P.M. and in September 8:00 A.M. to 5:00 P.M. It's closed October through mid-May.

Continue north along the shore of Jackson Lake, passing the relatively quiet **Lizard Creek Campground** before leaving GTNP and entering the **John D. Rockefeller Jr., Memorial Parkway**. Management of this 24,000-acre parcel of federal lands was transferred to the National Park Service in 1972, in order to secure protection for the narrow band of lands separating Grand Teton and Yellowstone national parks. Here you'll pass through areas burned by the Huck Fire of 1988, which also torched many thousands of acres in the Teton Wilderness to the east.

About 5 miles after leaving GTNP you'll pass the mega-camping resort known as **Flagg Ranch**. In winter, this is where the road plowing stops and over-the-snow travel begins: either westward travel on snowmobile along the **Grassy Lake Road** (a.k.a. Ashton-Flagg Road and Reclamation Road) or northward into Yellowstone National Park on a snowmobile or in a snowcoach. In summer and fall, the gravel/dirt Grassy Lake Road can readily provide a half day of adventure for those equipped with a high-clearance vehicle and not pulling a trailer or driving a large RV. Along the first 7.5 miles you will pass a string of eight primitive campsites, some more spacious than others, which boast good outhouses and fire rings, but few other amenities. The sites offer a degree of privacy not found at the campgrounds in Yellowstone and GTNP, and they often remain unoccupied even when the national park campgrounds are filled to overflowing. Two and one-half miles west of the westernmost campsite the road leaves the Rockefeller Parkway and becomes rather gnarly, as it crosses the Grassy Lake Reservoir dam, then dances amid a landscape of granite outcrops and scatterings of timber at the northern end of the Teton Range. The road then improves again, exiting the wilds near Ashton, Idaho. From Flagg Ranch to Ashton the distance is approximately 50 miles. This road also offers a shortcut to the largely ignored **Bechler Entrance**, through which you can sneak into the southwest corner of Yellowstone National Park.

Yellowstone National Park and the Gateway Communities

For a century and a quarter the irresistible allure of the world's first national park has attracted travelers from near and far. Some vacationers head straight to Yellowstone and spend as much time as possible inside the national park, while others prefer to dedicate the majority of their time to places outside the park's boundaries, where the scenery and quantity of wildlife are often just as impressive, but the crowds are lacking. Even if you are of the crowd-intolerant type, though, don't miss spending at least two or three days inside Yellowstone. It is with very good reason that this became the world's first national park, and that millions pour through the six entrance stations each year.

If your time in the park is limited—and whose isn't?—you can ward off that that so-much-to-do-and-so-little-time feeling by listing your priorities. For example, are you more interested in seeing wildlife than looking into hot pots? If so, would you rather see a wolf or a bear? By figuring out in advance what you would most like to see and experience while in Yellowstone, you can begin to narrow down the areas where you should spend the majority of your time. Finally, to plan your itinerary, look at the map and figure the best route to follow on the figure-8-with-spurs road system that loops up, down, and around the multitude of wonders in Yellowstone National Park.

FROM THE SOUTH ENTRANCE TO TOWER, THE LAMAR VALLEY, AND COOKE CITY

A couple of miles north of Flagg Ranch you will enter **Yellowstone National Park** at the South Entrance. Proceed north through living forest for a few miles, climbing rather steeply toward the Continental Divide. If it's a sunny day you may find it almost hypnotic, the way the sun flashes through the trees, glancing off their trunks. At about 4 miles from the entrance you'll break out above the canyon of the Lewis River, and gaze out over an implausible expanse of almost entirely scorched forest, stretching to the top of the Red Mountains, roughly 5 miles to the east. This is the first of a great deal of evidence you will see in Yellowstone remaining from the conflagrations of the summer of 1988. Even so, although it's your initial glimpse, it constitutes one of the most impressive fire remains in the entire park.

The summer of 1988 was the driest summer on record in the Greater Yellowstone Ecosystem. Fuel loads, including vast sweeps of dead standing and fallen timber, had been allowed to build to dangerously high levels. This was owing largely to a century of humans toying with the natural scheme of things, suppressing countless fires before they had a chance to do what nature intended them to do—periodically remove the fuel load, that is, and generate new forest growth and encourage new species to take hold. Moreover, that year's exceedingly dry June, July, and August came on the heels of a winter and spring that had seen plenty of moisture, so grass and understory growth was copious. Once this abundant vegetation dried out it turned into tinder, ultimately helping the fires to spread even more readily than they might have otherwise.

The firebox forests of Yellowstone were just waiting for a summer such as this to explode. With the lack of rain, extremely low humidity, and dangerously high fuel loads, the stage was set for fires of unprecedented magnitude. Enter lightning, man-caused fires, inordinately high winds, and the National Park Service's relatively new "let-burn" policy (which was enlightened but a little late in coming), and what we witnessed was the worst fire season in history, battled by the biggest firefighting army in the annals of America. Some 25,000 firefighters' efforts and millions of dollars were spent attempting to suppress the fires, but in the end only nature's September snows could quash the flames. Almost all park buildings were saved, however, and the numbers of wildlife killed by fire were almost negligible—257 elk out of a population of 32,000, for example, and two of 6,000 moose.

In the end, several separate fires had joined forces to burn across nearly a million acres in Yellowstone, or half the park's area, and a total of 1.4 million acres in the Greater Yellowstone Ecosystem. Five of the seven largest fires had begun outside the park but grew in toward it. Only about 25 percent of the park's affected area burned intensively enough to kill a majority of the trees. Far rarer yet was fire so intense that it managed to kill subsurface seeds and roots, which are vital to the regeneration of the forest. Indeed, in most of the burned areas through which you travel today you will see the next generation of lodgepole pine growing strong, already between 3 and 6 feet tall. And most biologists agree that, in terms of wildlife, the fires' long-term effects will be positive, enhancing habitat and increasing the quantity and variety of food sources for vegetarian animals, and, in turn, for carnivores.

As you travel through Yellowstone, you will find some of the roads newly paved and in wonderful shape, some okay, and others in shameful condition. A long-term effort is under way to improve the entire system, but limited funds and a short work season make it a tough row to hoe. Exacerbating the challenge are the heavy traffic, the exceptionally harsh winters, and the fact that most roads, including those composing the 142-mile **Grand Loop**—which is really a figure-8 double loop—follow the routes of the old two-track wagon roads built in the late 1800s. Many miles of these were initially surfaced without benefit of a properly constructed road base.

Eleven miles north of the South Entrance you'll pass the **Lewis Lake Campground** and Lewis Lake. You'll see that fire burned here, but in hodgepodge, skipping fashion, leaving plenty of patches of unburned trees standing. After crossing the Continental Divide, elevation 7,988 feet, you'll descend for a couple of miles through largely unburned forest to **Grant Village**. En route you will pass the trailhead for the 5-mile round-trip hike east to **Riddle Lake**, an easy outing that offers great opportunities to spot moose and waterfowl. It also penetrates spring grizzly habitat, so the trail is typically closed from May 1 until mid-July to protect both bears and humans. Don't miss the visitor center at Grant Village, where an outstanding display on the Yellowstone fires will teach you more about nature's flaming agent of change.

One and one-half miles from Grant Village is the right-hand turn to **West Thumb**, so-named because it's on the shore of Yellowstone Lake's "west thumb." More than a half mile of boardwalks wind through the **West Thumb Geyser Basin**, a relatively small basin containing a great concentration of thermal activity. Notable features include Fishing Cone, which rises like a moon crater above the shallow, close-to-shore waters of Yellowstone Lake. A member of the 1870 Washburn expedition, which passed by here, related the tall-tale-sounding story of catching a fish then accidentally dropping it into this geyser. On retrieving it, the fish was fully cooked! Word spread, and by 1903 a national publication was informing prospective visitors that a trip to Yellowstone was incomplete without the bait-and-boil experience. The practice became so popular—practically a "must," rather like witnessing an eruption of Old Faithful—that the National Park Service was forced to ban fishing in the area in order to protect overly zealous hook-and-cookers from boiling themselves.

The smell emanating from some of the hot pots in the geyser basin is almost overwhelming. The hottest pools are seductively beautiful; seemingly bottomless and pulsating a hue so electrifyingly blue that no word yet invented can do their

Abyss Pool, West Thumb Geyser Basin

color justice. Abyss Pool, one of the park's deepest hot springs, reaches a depth of 53 feet. Depending on the present temperature of its waters, its color will range from shocking turquoise to emerald. The spring is currently dormant, but that could change at any time: In August 1987 Abyss Pool erupted for the first time in recent memory, then it again erupted throughout the winter of 1991–92, several times a day, shooting water 30 to 80 feet high and blowing a plume of steam much higher.

The thermal basin extends out into Yellowstone Lake, too, so in winter when most of the lake is frozen solid, small areas here are kept open by hot waters percolating upward.

From West Thumb you'll begin following the Grand Loop Road's southeasternmost branch. This leg parallels the northwestern shore of **Yellowstone Lake**, which fills a portion of the depression formed when the Lava Creek caldera erupted around 600,000 years ago. The massive body of water is the largest mountain lake in North America, 20 miles long and 14 miles wide, with 110 miles of shoreline and depths reaching almost 400 feet. All in all, it is a captivating scene: On the far shore of the sprawling lake the high Absarokas jut into a crystal, high-elevation sky whose deep azure brilliance occasionally rivals that of Abyss Pool.

At 9 miles, after passing the narrowest part of the lake, you will get a firsthand look at how big Yellowstone Lake truly is. At about 12 miles you can turn right onto **Gull Point Drive**, a quiet road that parallels the Grand Loop for a couple of miles, hugging the shore of Yellowstone Lake as it penetrates a climax forest of Douglas fir and Engelmann spruce. The side road offers good opportunities for picnicking and freshwater beachcombing. The big yellow building to the northeast that you can't help but occasionally noticing is the stately **Lake Yellowstone Hotel**.

Across the road from where Gull Point Drive rejoins the Grand Loop, you'll see the trailhead for the **Natural Bridge Hike and Bike Trail**, an old spur road leading to the feature that gave Bridge Bay its name. Also nearby is the **Bridge Bay Marina and Campground**. At the marina you can rent fishing gear and boats, take an hour-long cruise around Stevenson Island, or, at the vis-

itor station, learn about the ecology of Yellowstone Lake. Described are efforts aimed at reversing a serious situation, in which the (probably illegally) introduced lake trout is outcompeting the native cutthroat trout. This threatens to severely affect the ecology on dry land, too: Creatures such as grizzlies and several bird species are dependent on spawning cutthroat; the lake trout, which, unlike the cutthroat, breeds in deep waters, cannot replace the latter as a food source for these animals.

In another 2 miles you will reach the right-hand turn into **Lake Village**, where you'll find food, lodging, a ranger station, a Hamilton General Store, and a hospital. The main hospital, along with smaller clinics at Old Faithful and Mammoth Hot Springs, boasts a staff of 50 that treats around 12,000 patients per year. The immense Lake Yellowstone Hotel is as bright, lavish, and irresistible inside as it is big, yellow, and boxy on the outside. Its European ambience—made more palpable by the conversations in French and German that you're apt to hear inside—contrasts markedly with Yellowstone's darker and more rustic lodgings at places such as Old Faithful and Roosevelt. Although Continental in tone, Lake Hotel also feels relatively modern, belying the fact that it is Yellowstone's oldest hostelry. The grand hotel, built in 1891, had fallen into serious disrepair before a thorough renovation in the 1980s recaptured the engaging look and feel of its youth.

Windows, windows, then more windows open on the flat expanse of Yellowstone Lake, and plenty of wicker furniture begs visitors to relax amid the light and airy atmosphere of pastel walls, high ceilings, colorful carpeting, steam-heat registers, and hardwood floors. Adding yet more class to the splendid surroundings are a grand piano in the lobby and elaborate wooden balusters and balustrades climbing along the stairways leading to guest rooms above.

Continue to the turn to **Fishing Bridge**, a misnomer since fishing was banned here in 1974 in an effort to help Yellowstone Lake's ailing cutthroat trout population. Although you can no longer fish at the bridge, you are nonetheless welcome to crowd in with other fish fans to watch the congregation of cutthroat trout and low-flying gulls, who *do* still fish. Services at Fishing Bridge include a Hamilton Store, RV campground (no tenting or tent trailers allowed), and museum with outstanding exhibits on the park's bird life. The museum–visitor center is located along the East Entrance Road, a mile off the Grand Loop.

The next segment of the Grand Loop Road crosses Hayden Valley, one of the best places in Yellowstone to spot large mammals such as bison during summer. Particularly along the earlier, forested stretches of the drive you should also watch for elk, moose, and bears. Because this area does provide outstanding habitat for grizzly bears, before striking out on a backcountry hike you should check with a ranger at the Fishing Bridge or Canyon visitor center and inquire about recent bear sightings.

Roughly 3 miles north of Fishing Bridge veer right into the **LeHardy Rapids** turnout, where a stout boardwalk parallels the Yellowstone River for several hundred yards. The ground below the rapids, probably due to underlying heat and bulging magma, has grown an alarming 3 feet in the past seventy-five years (*see* The Land). In June and July a real treat awaits those who tread the wooden trail: a battalion of cutthroat trout, sometimes numbering in the hundreds, jumping through the rapids as they negotiate their way upstream.

If the wind is blowing in the correct direction, you'll probably know that you're approaching the odiferous **Mud Volcano** area, situated 6 miles from Fishing Bridge, before seeing any signs indicating it. Here's how Nathaniel Langford of the 1870 Washburn expedition described the area's phenomena: " . . . the ground beneath us shook and trembled as from successive shocks of an earthquake. . . . [It is] the greatest marvel we have yet met with. . . ."

Today a ⅔-mile boardwalk winds past several caldrons, hot springs, fumaroles, geysers, and mudpots. Impressive Mud Volcano, a cone 30 feet wide and 30 feet high, is filled with thick, bubbling mud; its massive eruptions in the nineteenth century were described in animated terms by pio-

Bison, Hayden Valley

neer explorers, whose awe was apparent. Newer on the scene is Black Dragon's Caldron, which violently exploded into existence in 1948, knocking over nearby trees and blanketing the adjacent forest in mud. Just across the highway to the northeast you will find Sulfur Caldron, whose stinking, roiling, spewing waters, yellow with sulfur, are not only hot but highly acidic.

Once past Mud Volcano you will enter broad, handsome **Hayden Valley**. An arm of ancient Lake Yellowstone once filled the valley, and you can still see the extinct shoreline demarcated by a forested ridge to the east. The lake deposited fine-grained clays and sands—now covered in glacial debris—that inhibit drainage, so much of the valley is quite marshy. Even if devoid of wildlife, Hayden Valley would be one beautiful place; however, the shrubs and grasses thriving here are favored by bison, grizzly bears, and other large mammals, making Hayden Valley one of the great wildlife-viewing areas of the world. There's a constant flapping of waterfowl and raptors, often including Canada geese, mallards, pelicans, trumpeter swans, blue herons, and eagles and ospreys. The valley is also a fine location for watching and photographing fly fishers in action.

Roughly 10 miles from Fishing Bridge you will leave the treeless verdancy of Hayden Valley and re-enter burned-over forest. At 13 miles take the right-hand turn onto **South Rim Drive**, which provides access to overlooks into the Yellowstone River's astounding Grand Canyon. Here, in a matter of miles, the river slices through 1,000 vertical feet of rock. Both the Upper and Lower falls result from the action of water carving across the points where harder and softer volcanic materials abut one another. The canyon's kaleidoscopic colors result from hot mineral water, steam, and gases reacting on the rhyolitic walls.

The **Upper Falls Overlook** trail departs from Uncle Tom's Parking Area, while the much higher, 308-foot Lower Falls can be viewed from a trail beginning at **Artist Point**, located at road's end. You can see it all from the 2-mile-long South Rim Trail, which connects **Artist Point** with the parking area near Chittenden Bridge, which spans the Yellowstone River just off the Grand Loop Road. From Artist Point a trail continues along the South Rim for another 1.25 miles, to **Point Sublime**.

Canyon Village, elevation 7,734 feet, includes camping, lodging, and dining. It is the recommended layover locale if you're interested in becoming well acquainted with the Grand Canyon of the Yellowstone, which extends for some 20 miles and whose present face dates approximately 10,000 years back, from the end of the last glaciation. Here, in addition to the nearby South Rim drive and trail (beginning 3 miles south), starts the one-way, south-bound **North Rim Drive**, which makes a 2.5-mile arc providing access to several additional viewpoints into the colorful canyon. The visitor center at Canyon features a new, informative display on bison. Canyon is also the most centrally located overnight option in all of Yellowstone, with relatively convenient access to Lamar Valley, Mammoth Hot Springs, Old Faithful, and Fishing Bridge–West Thumb.

If you suffer from heart or breathing problems, choose your trail carefully by discussing the options with a ranger. Some of the trails near Canyon feature dizzying, seemingly endless descents down see-through, metal-grate steps. The short **Grandview Point Trail** off the North Rim Drive offers one of the easiest and shortest paths for viewing the Grand Canyon.

From Canyon, continue north on the Grand Loop Road, which immediately turns bumpy and narrow, and remains that way the entire distance to Tower-Roosevelt. This segment of the Grand Loop climbs over the flank of the Washburn Range, the highest and most rugged terrain reachable by car in the park. The road, particularly the segment heading north from Dunraven Pass, provides limitless vistas of what are arguably the most spectacular landscapes in all of Yellowstone. Not surprisingly, the road usually remains closed by snow until early June.

You'll pass the Cascade Lake trailhead on the left at about 1 mile. Two miles later, pull right into the parking area adjacent to the road. The pullout offers a marvelous overview, encompassing the Grand Canyon of the Yellowstone and the mountains beyond. An interpretive sign points out the features defining the skyline as well as those in closer proximity, including the nearby, northern rim of the Yellowstone Caldera; the Absaroka Range to the southeast; and, visible on a clear day, the distant Tetons rising far to the south-southwest. The huge white gash just below, on the near side of the Grand Canyon, is that made by the Washburn Hot Springs complex. No marked trails lead to the springs, where the ground is dangerously unstable.

Five miles into the drive you will crest **Dunraven Pass**, elevation 8,859, where a 3.5-mile hiking trail begins its winding way up **Mount Washburn**. As you begin down the pass you can look back and see a fire lookout perched atop the 10,243-foot peak. After driving through a ghostly forest of scorched skeleton trees, then passing the Chittenden Road at 9.5 miles (which leads, in a mile, to another 3-mile hiking trail up Mount Washburn), you'll come around a left-hand switchback at 10 miles. Pull off the road into the wide area below the switchback, simply to savor the scene: Remains of the 1988 fires blend into a mosaic of grasslands and unburned forests of Douglas fir and aspen, creating a wonderfully appealing vista. The burned-over forest leading up the flanks of Mount Washburn is especially impressive. If you're carrying binoculars—which by all means you should be—spend a while surveying the distant clearings and you may be rewarded by spotting a grizzly bear. Or, along the flanks of Mount Washburn, you might see a herd of bighorn sheep.

Continue bumping down the precipitous road, joining in alongside Antelope Creek as you approach the bottom. Sagebrush clearings beside the creek burst in summer with rainbows of lupine, Indian paintbrush, and dozens of other wildflowers. At **Tower Fall**, 16 miles from Canyon, you'll find a Hamilton General Store, a campground, and a half-mile trail leading to Tower Fall, a 132-foot cataract that catapults earthward from Gothic-like surroundings of tall volcanic spires.

The geology over the next couple of miles is particularly grand, with parallel columnar basalt formations hanging over the road, the aged rock looking as if it were clawed by some giant prehistoric grizzly bear. You'll reach **Tower-Roosevelt**, elevation 6,270 feet, after driving a total of 19 miles from Canyon. As the name Roosevelt might suggest, this is the Old West epicenter of Yellowstone. The rustic **Roosevelt Lodge**, built in the early 1920s and featuring a pair of grand rock fireplaces, was named for the bully Yellowstone supporter Teddy Roosevelt, who camped in the

area around the turn of the century. Horses can be hired at the Roosevelt Corral, and chuck wagon suppers and stagecoach rides in summer are exceedingly popular family activities.

Next up: A 29-mile spur off the Grand Loop from Tower Junction to the Northeast Entrance, which leads first through the Lamar River Valley then up Soda Butte Creek, tracing a landscape quite unlike that found anywhere else in the park. It is also a corner of Yellowstone that is relatively little visited—or was, anyway, until the reintroduction of the gray wolf.

The splendid **Lamar Valley** was chosen as the release point for wolves in Yellowstone for a number of reasons, not the least of which is that it serves as vital winter/spring and fall feeding grounds for hundreds of elk and bison, animals crucial to the wolves' well-being. (In summer the elk and bison are generally enjoying higher pastures, but you'll probably see pronghorns, as well as a host of waterfowl in Lamar Valley.)

Thanks to intensive and highly successful predator-extermination measures taken early in this century, wolves disappeared from Yellowstone in the 1930s, as they did throughout the Western plains and forests. At that time the aggressive canines were feared and considered the enemy by nearly everyone, from stock growers to park managers. But during the ensuing decades a new philosophy emerged, one which recognized that wolves, like all native animals, play a critical role in the ecosystems where they naturally occur.

The culmination of this enlightened outlook occurred early in 1995, when fourteen wolves trapped in Alberta, Canada, were transported to Lamar Valley. They were released in March, after a two-month containment in three large acclimation pens. These wolves have spawned four packs—the Rose Creek, Crystal Creek, and Soda Butte packs, and the new Leopold pack, the first to naturally form in Yellowstone since wolves were eradicated more than six decades ago. Additional individuals, including seventeen brought from Canada in 1996, have also been released, and wolves are again alive and doing well in Yellowstone. Prolific pup production and survival rates the past couple of years have bolstered the numbers, resulting in a wolf population in the Greater Yellowstone Ecosystem numbering approximately one hundred animals.

Columnar basalt near Tower Fall

The benefits and penalties of wolf reintroduction are nearly as intriguing as the animal itself: It appears that wolf kills are aiding the populations of other animals, including scavengers such as eagles, foxes, and grizzly bears. Coyotes, though, for decades the top dog in Yellowstone, seem not to be faring so well. A recent study indicated that the coyote population in the northern ranges of the park has plummeted by 50 percent since the return of the wolf. The coyote is being out-competed by the wolf and, in some cases, even killed by the larger canines. It seems that in Yellowstone, for the time being anyway, the squealing and yip-yammering of the song dog will be supplanted by the lower-pitched howl of the gray wolf.

To the south as you begin up the Lamar River rises **Specimen Ridge**, on whose north slopes shadows are cast by petrified forests of world renown, some of the trees standing upright where they thrived 50 million years ago. Some two dozen successive forests, composed of warm-climate trees like chestnut and magnolia, were buried in volcanic ash over a span of 200 centuries. Later, water percolating through the ash layer gathered silica, which subsequently settled around and replaced

the cells of the subterranean trees, turning them to rock. You can find petrified trees by making the tough hike up Specimen Ridge or, with far less effort, by pulling into the roadside exhibit located not far from Tower Junction.

After passing the left-hand turn to the wonderfully primitive **Slough Creek Campground** you will drive through the narrower Lamar Canyon before opening into the expansive Lamar Valley, whose floor is littered with glacial *erratics*, or rocks and boulders of various sizes carried here by rivers of ice. At about 11 miles you'll pass the old **Buffalo Ranch**, today the location of the headquarters for the Yellowstone Institute, an environmental education organization. Operational until 1952, the Buffalo Ranch was created expressly to enhance bison herds in Yellowstone and beyond, by breeding captive animals, treating them for the most part as if they were cattle. When the ranch began operating in 1907 the population of bison in the American West had dwindled nearly to nothing, and the Bison Ranch served a critical role in bringing the burly, shaggy beasts back from the brink of extinction. Today the park supports a large population of bison that of late has numbered as high as 4,000—too large for the park itself, where winter range is limited. Consequently, hundreds of bison have died in recent winters, both naturally and in controversial public hunts that have been arranged by officials as the animals migrated onto private lands outside the park.

Soon after passing the Buffalo Ranch the road veers northeast, leaving the broad Lamar River and its great sweeps of grass, to follow Soda Butte Creek upstream and take aim at the arresting summits of the volcanic Absaroka Range. On the right at 18 miles you'll pass **Soda Butte**, a terrace composed of calcium carbonate laid down by hot springs water. You'll leave Yellowstone at the Northeast Entrance, 29 miles from Tower-Roosevelt. The classic structure here, erected in 1935, is the best example remaining in the entire national parks system of a log entrance station of that era. After passing through tiny **Silver Gate** you'll enter **Cooke City**, Montana, a mining-turned-tourist town with an eclectic assortment of tourist-related facilities. (A tip: Inquire locally to learn about the drive-and-hike to Grasshopper Glacier, where millions of flash-frozen locusts lie in suspended animation.)

FROM FISHING BRIDGE TO CODY, THEN ON TO RED LODGE: A NARRATIVE ACCOUNT

At Fishing Bridge Nancy and I turn onto the East Entrance Road. It is 6:00 A.M., the very earliest we could possibly get going on this September morning: Due to extensive reconstruction work, the road will be open today only from 6:00 A.M. to 10:00 A.M. and again from 6:00 P.M. to 10:00 P.M. Our crack-of-dawn start is a must if we hope to complete in daylight what is sure to be a very long day. We plan first to drive the 80 slow miles to Cody, Wyoming, then spend several hours at the Buffalo Bill Historical Center before continuing more than 100 miles to Red Lodge, Montana. The twisting, high-elevation back-door route we plan on following to Red Lodge constitutes what I remember as being the most spectacular drive I've ever taken. But it has been twenty-four years since I did the entire thing and I've seen a lot of country since, so we'll see how well my memory serves me.

A mile or two east of Fishing Bridge we enter a wide-open, delta-like marshy area where Pelican Creek flows to meet Yellowstone Lake. Birds—pelicans, ducks, geese, and more—are *everywhere*, it seems. We continue along the lake shore for another 7 or 8 miles before finally commencing the climb toward Sylvan Pass. On the left, shortly after veering away from the lake, we turn left to follow the short spur road leading to **Lake Butte Overlook**. Yellowstone Lake, 615 feet below, stretches far away into the distance. We can see the Washburn Range rising to the northwest and, some 60 miles to the southwest, we can even make out the Tetons on this impeccably clear morning.

As we motor up the pass I think of an old friend in Laramie, who grew up in Casper in the late 1910s and 1920s. He recently told me that he remembers traveling over this road with his family more than once in the 1920s. It was always bumpy and sometimes a sea of mud, he said. On one occasion, he recalled, some of the nails securing the canvas top on their family car shook loose and bounced out onto the ground. The car then rolled over the nails, resulting in two flat tires. On finally arriving at Yellowstone Lake the family set up camp and proceeded to catch dozens of trout at the lake's outlet (the future location of Fishing Bridge, which wasn't built until the mid-1930s). His family wasn't expecting any company in camp that night, so they deposited most of their fish in the large pans sitting right-side-up on the tables in a couple of adjacent campsites. An upturned pan, he told me, signified that the campers occupying that campsite *were* expecting company. Although the fellow campers were complete strangers—or, perhaps more accurately, brand-new friends—it was simply considered the neighborly thing to do, to share one's luck and excess fish with them.

Shining, aptly named Sylvan Lake lies on the south side of the road, surrounded by timber. It is a portrait of calm on this still morning, with Top Notch Peak, a member of the Absaroka Range, serving as a stalwart backdrop. The lake area, 17 miles from Fishing Bridge, includes a rustic picnic ground straddling both sides of the highway.

After cresting 8,541-foot Sylvan Pass the newly widened road narrows, and we follow an antique paved platform that inches its way down a substantially tighter and more heavily timbered canyon, its slopes commonly striped with avalanche-swept clearings. Seven miles from the pass we exit the world's first national park at the East Entrance only to enter the **Shoshone National Forest**, our country's first national forest, which was set aside in 1891 as part of the Yellowstone Park Timberland Reserve. In a couple of miles, on our left we zip by **Pahaska Tepee**, built by William F. "Buffalo Bill" Cody in 1902 to serve as a hunting lodge for him and his friends, and as a wayside stop for others traveling to Yellowstone. Still a going concern, with the original lodge open for tours, the "Pahaska" part of the resort's name derives from Cody's Indian name, which translates to "Long Hair." It is not the last mark made by Buffalo Bill that we will see today, by any means. The very road we are following, in fact, owes its existence largely to Cody's lobbying efforts. In addition to Pahaska Tepee, Cody built another pair of inns along this "Cody Road," which Teddy Roosevelt called "the most scenic 50 miles in America" (or "in the world," depending on which account one reads).

We pass **Threemile Campground**, which lies, not coincidentally, 3 miles from the border of Yellowstone. It is the first of a dozen or so national forest campgrounds we will encounter over the next several miles. Across the road we see the trailhead for the **Pahaska-Sunlight Trail**, which surely must encounter some spectacular country as it traverses the North Absaroka Wilderness en route to its northern terminus in Sunlight Basin. I tuck the trail away in my "Future Places to Visit" mental file. This is the valley of the North Fork of the Shoshone River, nicknamed **Wapiti Valley**. It's a rough-hewn sweep of the West, famous for its abundance of dude ranches—outfits with names like **Crossed Sabres Ranch**, **Elephant Head Lodge**, and **Bill Cody's Ranch Resort**, an enterprise of the grandson of Buffalo Bill. The more than two-dozen dude and guest ranches lining Wapiti Valley typically offer lodging and wilderness horse-packing trips in summer and guided elk hunts come fall.

As we lose elevation along the North Fork the nature of the terrain changes: first from the relatively lush high country of the Absarokas into arid slopes holding sparse timber stands interrupted by bursts of sagebrush, then into an even drier, desert-like landscape of red rock and scant vegetation.

Even so, lofty, dark volcanic peaks loom behind the rocky bottoms and cliffsides, never far away.

We leave the national forest, then, 37 miles from the East Entrance, enter **Buffalo Bill State Park**. The park encompasses a campground, visitor center, and the large Buffalo Bill Reservoir. The reservoir is backed up by the Buffalo Bill Dam (originally Shoshone Dam), which fills the gap between Cedar and Rattlesnake mountains. All of these Buffalo Bill namesakes are not merely honors to the man who served as an ox-team driver at age 11, then went on to become a beaver trapper, gold miner, Pony Express rider, buffalo hunter, Indian scout, showman, statesman, and community founder and booster. No, it was through Cody's efforts, which were greatly aided by his friendship with Teddy Roosevelt, that the dam was begun in 1905 and finished in 1910. Cody was determined to attract farmers to the Bighorn Basin; in order to do that, though, the thirsty, sun-baked desert needed a water supply, and Cody's resolve prevailed. It was an amazing engineering feat, costing seven lives and nearly a million dollars, to build the 328-foot-high dam, which at the time was the tallest dam in the world. Today the reservoir continues supplying irrigation and drinking water; it also generates hydroelectric power and is popular among boaters, anglers, and windsurfers, who come from afar to take advantage of the legendary Wyoming winds that are so common.

On the western outskirts of Cody our olfactory senses make it clear why the Shoshone River was originally known as the Stinking Water; the smell of sulfur hangs heavy in the air, like an invisible greeting sign. Cody, obviously, is another namesake of Buffalo Bill, who helped found the town in 1896. It is said that Cody the man wished to be buried in Cody the town; if so, he's likely been rolling over in his grave now for more than eighty years: Buffalo Bill died in Denver in 1917, and was buried high on Lookout Mountain, in full view of Colorado's capital city.

We're starved, so before going to the museum we drive downtown to the **Irma Hotel**. Buffalo Bill financed construction of the Victorian hostelry, naming it for his youngest daughter, Irma Louise, and opening it in November 1902. The dining room, originally the hotel bar and billiards room, is short on windows and consequently quite dark, as old watering holes are apt to be. But once our eyes adjust we can see that the turn-of-the-century ambience has been well preserved: a fancy antique cash register occupies a spot at the checkout counter; elk, cougar, and moose mounts, along with big old wildlife paintings, decorate the walls; an elk-antler chandelier hangs from the ornate, tin-covered ceiling; small molded bison heads adorn the sides of the dining-booth benches; and flowery carpet covers the floor, no doubt hiding burn stains and maybe even a bullet hole or two. The lavish, French-made cherry-wood back bar leaning against the restaurant's far wall was shipped in 1900 to Buffalo Bill from Queen Victoria, as a gift of her appreciation for his Wild West Show's royal performance.

As is to be expected in small-town Wyoming, we find that the *huevos rancheros* are spicy, the coffee is weak, and the Irma has definitely not been turned into a non-smoking establishment. The local clientele of cowboys and stock growers certainly would rebel if management tried pulling a citified trick like that.

Beyond the Irma's restaurant we find a dozen-plus guest suites, each named for a Cody-area pioneer. Also on the premises are a saloon, private dining/meeting rooms, and a gift shop offering T-shirts and Western-oriented goods and knickknacks.

Adequately fueled for a few hours of being on our feet, we drive back to the **Buffalo Bill Historical Center**. It has been said that William F. Cody at the turn of the century was the most famous man in the world; it seems only right, then, that his museum is regarded as the world's foremost repository of the American West's history and lore. The museum's roots go back to 1917 when, a few weeks after Buffalo Bill died, several Cody residents created the Buffalo Bill Memorial

Stagecoach, Buffalo Bill Historical Center

Association, with a goal to "build, construct and maintain an historical monument of memorial stature in honor of and to perpetuate the memory of our late lamented fellow townsman Hon. William F. Cody."

And what a memorial has evolved! In fact, Cody itself might be considered a memorial to Buffalo Bill, having grown into a bustling agricultural and tourist town of some 10,000 residents. The original Buffalo Bill Museum, which today houses the Cody Chamber of Commerce, is a modest log building that was designed to resemble the ranch house Cody built outside of town. The rudimentary museum opened in 1927. Now, more than seventy years later, the newer Buffalo Bill Historical Center houses four distinct museums under one roof: the Whitney Gallery of Western Art, the Buffalo Bill Museum, the Plains Indian Museum, and the Cody Firearms Museum. Additionally, the Harold McCracken Research Library includes some 15,000 books and manuscripts—including an in-depth collection of Yellowstone National Park papers and publications—along with a quarter-million photographic prints and negatives. The center's 237,000-square-foot size befits its location in broad-shouldered Wyoming, the least populous state in the nation, where there's elbow room aplenty.

Several special gatherings take place annually at the Buffalo Bill Historical Center, including the early April **Cowboy Songs and Range Ballads** event, which celebrates and helps preserve the traditional cowboy songs of the late nineteenth and early twentieth centuries. Nancy and I decide we'd like to return for that one.

I'm a history nut; still, for some reason, I seem unable to spend more than three or four hours in any museum, no matter how fabulous, before my eyes and brain start glazing over. So, we plan our attack carefully, since ideally each of the center's four museums deserves at least a half-day's inspection. We choose to walk rather quickly through the seemingly endless firearms museum, which for gun enthusiasts is a real bonanza but for others seems a bit like overkill. Still, we find that many of the antique weapons—some dating to the sixteenth century—are beautiful, remarkably ornate works of art. At the core of the museum is the Winchester Arms Collection, previously dis-

played at the company's factory in New Haven, Connecticut, but moved to Cody in 1975.

We spend the majority of our time in the centerpiece Buffalo Bill Museum, where old posters vividly and theatrically advertise the Wild West Show and other Buffalo Bill–related happenings. In a wing next to the bright-red Cheyenne & Black Hills Stage wagon that starred in the Wild West Show, we find a Babcock drum-cylinder printing press. Buffalo Bill arranged to have the press shipped to town in 1899, when Cody had all of fifteen residents. The three-ton monster was carried intact by train from Duluth, Minnesota, to Red Lodge, Montana; from there, it was hauled by horse-drawn stage around the foot of the Beartooth Range to Cody. Initially, the press was man-powered, but it was converted to steam soon after a spur of the Chicago, Burlington & Quincy Railroad came to town in 1901—at Buffalo Bill's persuasive beckoning, of course—and delivered a steam generator.

A talented docent dressed in pressman's gear of the day explains, as he puts the press through its paces, how the printing press rivaled the post office as the single most important feature contributing to any frontier town's success. Part newspaper and part promotional flyer, the *Cody Enterprise* greatly assisted Cody in his efforts to seduce farmers to the Bighorn Basin. The newspaper, the docent says, was a "Try Weekly"; that is, they tried to get it out once a week but weren't always successful. Buffalo Bill paid $1,000 for the press, which was used until 1970, so it was "a pretty good investment," the pressman-docent says.

Other exhibits explore the private and public, and the factual and mythical lives of Buffalo Bill, surely one of the most compelling figures in the history of the American West. Displayed are examples of the truth-stretched dime novels in which Cody was the main character, as well as many of Cody's trappings—rifles, saddles, buffalo-hide clothes—and those of others, including a gold-plated .32 caliber Winchester rifle owned by Annie Oakley, the sharpshooter and Wild West Show star.

From there we wander into the Whitney Gallery of Western Art, where we inspect paintings, sculptures, and photographs created by both contemporaries and the legends of the West: Charles M. Russell, for instance, and Frederic

Trail Town, Cody

Remington, George Catlin, Thomas Moran, and the overly realistic art of Albert Bierstadt. Finally, we stroll through the Plains Indian Museum, for which we sorely wish we had allotted additional time. The displays, which delve into the cultural and artistic traditions of tribes such as the Shoshone, Cheyenne, and Blackfeet, are beautiful, evocative, and extensive, ranging from Arapaho Ghost Dance shirts to beautifully beaded baby cradles to highly revered necklaces made of grizzly bear claws.

Back outside on the museum grounds we have a quick look at Buffalo Bill's boyhood home, a bright yellow box that was sawn in half and shipped by train to Cody in 1933 from LeClaire, Iowa. As we motor away I look back at the imposing statue of William F. Cody, standing sentinel in front of his exquisite museum, hat in right hand, lever-action Winchester in the other. Buffalo Bill appears proudly to be surveying the community he built.

Before leaving Cody, we grab a fast-food lunch, then motor back to the west edge of town

to visit **Trail Town**. From the highway it looks as if it might be a tourist trap, but we were informed by a Chamber of Commerce officer that it is much more than that. Indeed, we find it is: Trail Town comprises an eclectic, largely one-man collection of weather-worn cabins, wagons, and pioneer memorabilia; yet another half-day would be required to do it justice. Among the amazing things Trail Town founder Bob Edgar located and brought to these grounds is a cabin used by Butch Cassidy and his gang in Wyoming's Hole-in-the-Wall country. Also, several Western characters have been disinterred elsewhere then reburied here, including John "Liver Eatin'" Johnston, whose life inspired the film classic *Jeremiah Johnson*, which starred Robert Redford.

East of downtown we turn north onto State Highway 120. As we climb above town we can see into the jaws of the North Fork's canyon, through which we drove earlier this morning. Sixteen miles out of Cody we veer left onto State Highway 296, now called the **Chief Joseph**

Scenic Highway, but formerly known as the Sunlight Basin Road or Dead Indian Road. Immediately a sign informs us that for the next 8 miles we'll be traversing the private lands of the Two Dot Ranch, a very old and very large spread. Climbing toward the Absarokas, we skirt grassy swales inhabited by grazing horses and Herefords. In 8 miles, just as the sign said, we leave the Two Dot Ranch and enter the Shoshone National Forest.

What a geological wonderland we have entered! Ahead and to the left rises the volcanic Absaroka Range, a mighty mass of gray silhouetted against a blue-black sky. Behind, red rock formations lend flashes of color to the mostly brown landscape, while far to the east we see the Bighorn Mountains rising from the desolate Bighorn Basin. We can also see Heart Mountain, near which a World War II relocation camp housed some 11,000 Japanese Americans—at the time, the third-largest "city" in Wyoming.

As we climb toward Dead Indian Summit, sparse timber stands grow thicker, claiming more and more of the undulating landscape. I tell Nancy that the last time I drove on this now-paved road, in 1973, it was gravel. I was in the company of my friend Charlie Love, who teaches anthropology and geology at Western Wyoming College in Rock Springs. Moments later, incredibly but as if on cue, we come upon a slow-moving bus painted with the words "Spartans" and "Western Wyoming College." What else would the bus be doing out here, I ask Nancy, but taking students on a geology tour? And if it's a geology tour, who else would be leading it but Charlie?

We gain Dead Indian Summit, elevation 8,060 feet, where the wind is ferocious; apparently a front is blowing in. We're careful not to open both front doors of the car at once, or we'll risk losing everything not bolted down. We feel like we're already on top of the world, so we find it difficult to believe that our continuing drive up and across the Beartooth Plateau will soon take us almost 3,000 feet higher.

The Western Wyoming bus pulls into the turnout and out walks . . . friend Charlie, who not only is leading the tour but is also serving as bus driver. He is dumbfounded to see us. After getting over his surprise he gives his students, now numbering two more than before, a lecture on the

marvel of geology spreading before us in every direction. We can see Sunlight Basin and the North Absaroka Wilderness, and the gash of the canyon of the Clarks Fork River, which Chief Joseph and the Nez Perce Indians followed out of Yellowstone in 1877 (*see* History). Across the canyon looms the ancient Precambrian heights of the Beartooth Plateau. We can also see the road we'll be following down, a path that winds and spirals out of sight, apparently running out of places to go after being consumed by mountains.

We bid Charlie and his students farewell, then dive down to **Dead Indian Campground**, situated a total of 37 miles from Cody. A mile-and-a-half later the gravel Sunlight Road goes left, leading for several miles past classic guest ranches and to the **Sunlight Ranger Station**, which was built by the Civilian Conservation Corps in the mid-1930s. The view from the highway bridge spanning the cleft of Sunlight Gorge is spectacular, but no more so than the late-September explosions of aspens coloring the otherwise autumn-drab mountain slopes. Some of the stands flanking the road appear to glow incandescently, like giant, colored Coleman lantern mantles. All things considered, Sunlight Basin is a geographic splendor worthy of its poetic name.

Having traveled 51 miles so far, we return to evidence of the widespread Yellowstone wildfires of 1988; these particular remains are from of the Clover-Mist Fire. We can't understand how certain buildings, such as those at the **K-Bar-Z Guest Ranch**, can still be standing after the fire came so close. At 56 miles begins a little line of settlement that includes **Squaw Creek Guest Ranch** and **Painter's Store**. In its fire-consumed mountain surroundings the settlement reminds us a bit of Lowman, Idaho (*see* Sun Valley–Salmon Country).

Hunter Peak Campground is on the left at 60 miles, and **Lake Creek Campground** is a mile farther. In the distance we see the constricted pyramid of Pilot Peak, a rocky, volcanic finger pointing skyward. Sixty-two miles from Cody we turn right off the Chief Joseph Scenic Highway, toward Red Lodge onto the **Beartooth National Scenic Byway**. We are only 14 miles southeast of Cooke City at this point, but we won't be taking in that town on this trip.

Immediately the going is second-gear steep. After driving 7.5 miles on the Beartooth Highway we pass a gravel road going left to **Clay Butte Lookout**, which is located 3 miles up the road. In another mile-and-a-half we pass **Beartooth Lake** and its Forest Service campground. Rising in the background is fossil-rich **Beartooth Butte**, whose stratified surface looks markedly different from the surrounding sea of granite, because it *is* different: The butte stands isolated as a rare remnant of the sedimentary layer that once covered the entire Beartooth Plateau. Most of the sedimentary layer was ground down and carried away by the glaciers, which exposed Precambrian basement rocks and scoured out the many depressions now occupied by the plateau's plethora of lakes, many of which teem with cutthroat, rainbow, and brook trout. The jagged erosional promontories on Beartooth Butte's east side, which reminded some early explorer of a row of bear's teeth, gave rise to the name of the entire surrounding Beartooth Range.

Two miles farther along, we pull into the **Top of the World Store & Motel** to pick up an afternoon snack and soft drink. The woman behind the counter says a "big one" is on the way, probably meaning snow at these elevations, this late in the season. The original version of the store was built in 1934 at Beartooth Lake, but the enterprise was moved to its present site in 1966 after the all-important Forest Service lease expired and was not renewed.

In a mile we pass **Island Lake Campground**, elevation 9,518 feet. The relatively gently graded Beartooth High Lake Trail begins here, leading to an array of little lakes dotting the plateau. We continue along the narrow road, passing **Little Bear Lake**, a pretty pond surrounded by boulders of ancient granite. At 14 miles we see a sign pointing right to the **Morrison Jeep Trail**. The rugged dirt road drops several thousand feet to the Clarks Fork, and makes for an outing popular among advanced mountain bikers.

The oxygen-deprived, weather-battered world we have entered is one stripped to the essentials. It is composed of rock, trees, water, sky, and a marginal layer of soil. As we approach timberline, the uppermost elevation at which trees survive, the lopsided growth on scraggly whitebark pines and subalpine firs makes it clear which way the wind usually blows up here. The scant vegetation that does exist is minuscule and ground-hugging, and the abundance of shiny granite boulders and

slabs appear to have been polished by the glaciers. We cannot help but wonder why a road was ever built over this impossible terrain, where the weather permits it to be passable for a maximum of five months each year, from Memorial Day into September or October. Was it for mining? Or was it simply to provide a strong tourism magnet?

(The next day we find the answer in a volume in the **Broadway Bookstore** in Red Lodge: It seems that a group of Red Lodge–vicinity residents, headed by a physician named Dr. J. C. F. Siegfriedt, early in the twentieth century dreamed of creating a new road to Yellowstone, a tourist attraction that would bring in an influx of badly needed dollars. The dream of the doctor and his group came true in 1931, thanks in part to their lobbying, when President Hoover signed into law the Leavitt Bill, which included the "Park Approach Act." Crews from the Civilian Conservation Corps and several private contractors commenced construction, finishing their awesome, $2.5-million task in June 1936. The full run of the Beartooth Highway they built extends 68 miles, from Red Lodge to the Northeast Entrance of Yellowstone.)

After 19.5 miles we crest Beartooth Pass, at the literally breathtaking elevation of 10,947 feet. Realizing that we are tackling the loftiest patch of pavement in the Northern Rockies, we pull off the road and get out of the car to savor the moment and our surroundings. It is an ice-sculpted landscape of dramatic proportions; one which the craziest of mad scientists could never have come up with in his wildest dreams.

Three and one-half miles from the pass we notice the top of a ski lift on our left. We leave the car again, peek over the edge, and see that the chairlift dives precipitously down the headwall of the Twin Lakes cirque. Here bold young skiers with Olympic aspirations, braving the 60-degree pitch of the headwall, train at the Red Lodge International Summer Ski Racing Camp. Next winter is never far away at these heights, and neither is last winter: Along the last couple of miles, in the shadows of the roadside borrow ditch we noticed traces of new snow, remaining from the storm that hit the plateau a couple of weeks ago. Now here, as we look over the headwall, we see that this north-facing slope still holds drifts left over from last winter's snowpack.

At 26 miles we enter Montana and the Custer National Forest. A couple of miles later, we take one glance back at the Beartooth Plateau before commencing the switchbacking drop into the Rock Creek Valley. As we wind down the road, which has turned quite wide, we are confronted by the high Silver Run Plateau across the canyon and, cradling the upper reaches of Rock Creek, a textbook-perfect, glacier-carved U-shaped valley. At 38 miles we arrive at the valley bottom, where a left-hand turn would lead us upstream along the Rock Creek Road to some Forest Service campgrounds. We continue downstream, though, timing it perfectly: At 6:00 P.M. sharp, 44 miles after turning onto the Beartooth Highway, we pull into **Rock Creek Resort**, where we enjoy an excellent European-style feast at the Old Piney Dell Restaurant. The day is still warm and the windows are open, which is great, because as we dine we can hear soothing Rock Creek outside, whispering along below a grove of trees.

Exhausted, but exalted and satiated, we drive the remaining 4 miles to Red Lodge and check into our room at the **Yodeler Motel**. I was right about one thing: The 110-mile outing from Cody to Red Lodge was, and is, the most spectacular drive I've taken anywhere in the United States. And it is a good thing we did it on the Friday that we did. Two days later, on September 28, we pick up a copy of the *Bozeman Chronicle* and open it to this story:

SNOW CLOSES BEARTOOTH

Ground blizzards and 4-foot snowdrifts closed the Beartooth Highway between Red Lodge and Cooke City Saturday morning. Highway crews were plowing the road that provides access to the northeast entrance to Yellowstone National Park, but a dispatcher with the Carbon County sheriff's office said he was not sure whether the road would be reopened. The Beartooth Highway opened for the summer on May 24 this year. It normally closes for the season in October.

FROM RED LODGE TO LIVINGSTON

Victorian, mountain-ringed Red Lodge is a pretty painting; a mining town-turned ski and

Cabin of "Liver Eatin' Johnson"

tourist town of around 2,500 residents. To stroll through the downtown area and into enterprises such as the **Montana Candy Emporium** and the gracious old **Pollard Hotel**, along with Western-decorating specialists like **Elk Ridge** and **Kibler and Kirch**, is to discover a bevy of late-nineteenth-century red brick beauties, well preserved and standing strong. South of downtown you'll find the **Carbon County Historical Museum**, where next to the log main museum is a smaller, nearly windowless cabin once inhabited by mountain man John Johnston. "Liver Eatin' Johnson," as he was known, served a stint as sheriff of Red Lodge. (He's buried at Trail Town in Cody, you'll recall.)

Six miles from town erupts the **Red Lodge Mountain Resort**, a mid-sized but growing ski operation boasting a 2,400-foot vertical drop. Unfortunately, the mountain's geographic location causes it often to suffer from a dearth of snow, but when snow is abundant the skiing is first-class, and new snow-making equipment has recently been installed. On the way up the road leading to the mountain, where not much happens in summer, at 1.5 miles you'll pass the right-hand turn to **Palisades Campground**, which sits in the morning shadow of the Limestone Palisades. The first 2.5 miles of the road leading to the ski area are paved; after that, beyond the junction with the West Fork Rock Creek Road, the road turns to gravel.

Leaving Red Lodge, drive northwest toward Roscoe on State Highway 78, a ribbon of pavement that wraps up and down a progression of ridges and drainages stretching out from the bulk of the Beartooth Range on your left. You'll find your surroundings dominated by cows, farms, fences, horses, willows, wind-whipped grass and cattails, clouds, and ranches large and small. The tiny town of **Roscoe**, located about 20 miles from Red Lodge, is home to a pair of enterprises: **Papa's & Granny's Guest House** (telephone 406–328–6789) and the **Grizzly Bar**. If you arrive in Roscoe at lunchtime, try an enormous Grizzly Burger at the bar and you won't need to sample anything else for hours.

To access a stretch of real Montana outback, where some fairly tricky navigation will be required and where you'll trace sections of the historic **Bozeman Trail**, from Roscoe head northwest along the gravel road leading toward Fishtail. In 6 miles, after crossing West Rosebud Creek, bear right onto pavement. In **Fishtail**, which also is tiny but somewhat larger than Roscoe, you'll find the **Fishtail Store**, open daily. Continue from there to **Absarokee**, located a total of 17 miles from Roscoe, where you'll want to turn left at the **Steak Out Restaurant** onto Route 420, the Stillwater River Road. Be sure you have plenty of gas before leaving Absarokee, in case you take a wrong turn somewhere over the ensuing miles and wind up going farther than anticipated. The roads encountered are generally smooth, but some stretches may be impassable if wet.

Now you're getting into the wide-open. After skirting hayfields and ranches for 6.5 miles, the pavement ends. About a half-mile beyond that point, turn right onto Spring Creek Road, then, in another 1.5 miles, turn left at the T to stay on Spring Creek Road. (North Stillwater Road heads the opposite way.) Next, in less than a mile, turn right onto Stockade Road; if you look closely you'll see that some obliging soul has painted on the signpost an arrow directing you toward Interstate–90. After passing a small ranch house

Hayfield

on the left, the road climbs out of the creek bottom over a crinkling of high, dry hills, exposing grand views of the Beartooths. At just over 6 miles from your most recent turn (approximately 15 miles from Absarokee) continue straight rather than turning right at the deserted, boarded-up building. Two miles from that junction you'll curve right around a couple of private spreads, then begin dropping off the high tableland toward the Yellowstone River, down the canyon of Bridger Creek. For more than 10 miles you'll descend along the rocky, well-protected, and largely deserted canyon, amid a scattered forest of juniper, cottonwood, and ponderosa pine. At 27 miles you'll go by the **Buckin' Horse Bunkhouse** (telephone 406–932–6537), an attractive, flat-sided log cabin offering lodging both by the night and by the week, and with or without breakfast. Finally, 31 miles after leaving Absorakee, you'll pop out at I–90, onto which you'll want to head westbound.

Immediately you will find yourself surrounded by speeding cars and trucks, while you were lucky if you saw a half-dozen rigs in the previous 31 miles. A detour into the bucolic town of **Big Timber** will lead to discoveries such as the historic **Grand Hotel**, an ornate structure of purple brick and dark green trim. The Grand, built in 1890, rents nicely renovated rooms and serves outstanding fare. About 3 miles south of town on State Highway 298 you'll find the **Spring Creek Camp and Trout Ranch**. This road ultimately leads far up the Boulder River, providing another route into the Absaroka-Beartooths, twisting past numerous private dude ranches and Forest Service campgrounds, including **Falls Creek, Big Beaver, Aspen Grove, Chippy Park, Hell's Canyon,** and **Hick's Park**. If you continue, don't miss stopping in at the classic—if not classy—**Road Kill Cafe** ("From your grill to ours") in minuscule McLeod.

The political incorrectness of certain Montana roadside signs is legendary. Consider the one you can find on the outskirts of Big Timber:

THE BONANZA OR BOZEMAN TRAIL

In the early 1860s there wasn't a ranch in this country, from Bismarck to Bozeman, from the Platte River to Canada. To whites it was a land considered fit only to raise Indians. And while some of them were hoping for a crop failure, the majority were indifferent; they didn't care how much the tribes fought among themselves. They were like the old timer whose wife was battling a grizzly bear. He said he never had seen a fight where he took so little interest in the outcome. . . .

As you approach wind-battered **Livingston**, 35 miles west of Big Timber, the bulk of the Absaroka Range hangs nearby to the south, while the Crazy Mountains rise some distance farther away to the north. Although Livingston has been invaded by a degree of the upscale in recent years, it has reached nowhere near the level that other Montana towns such as Bozeman and Missoula have seen. A "Livingston Saturday Night" (as Jimmy Buffett sang about) can still be an Old West experience, particularly if you take in establishments such as the **Livingston Bar and Grill** and the **Owl Cocktail Lounge** and if you stay at the venerable **Murray Hotel** (406–222–1350), which resides on the corner just across West Park Street from the historic railroad depot. The Murray is progressively undergoing renovation, and presently has some nice suites available.

For somewhat more refined pleasures, visit the **Livingston Depot Center**, occupying the grand old Northern Pacific railroad station, which also houses the Chamber of Commerce; **Chatham Fine Art**, purveyors of works that include the moody landscapes of the multitalented Russell Chatham, who even runs a gourmet restaurant next door; and the world headquarters of the **Federation of Fly Fishers**, located in the old Lincoln School.

THROUGH THE PARADISE VALLEY TO MAMMOTH HOT SPRINGS, NORRIS, AND OLD FAITHFUL

Drive south from Livingston on U.S. Highway 89 into the **Paradise Valley**. If you're wondering why it's called that, you won't wonder for long: The free-flowing Yellowstone River tumbles along below the massive peaks of the Absaroka Range, looming on the left, and those of the Gallatin Range, which scratch the western skyline. The valley is broad, turned lush and green with irrigation waters, and graced with homes and ranches, ranging from modest frame houses to mansions that serve as part-time residences of celebrities whose names you'd recognize in an instant.

Four miles from town leave the main road by turning left onto East River Road/State Highway 540. The road crosses the Yellowstone then parallels the river on the opposite, east side from the main highway. After driving 7.5 miles on East River Road, you'll pass the right-hand turn to **Nelson's Spring Creek Ranch**. (The Paradise Valley's spring-fed creeks are known to offer some of the finest private trout-fishing waters in the West.) In another mile you'll pass the right-hand turn to **Jumping Rainbow Ranch**. Soon you'll notice a tall, stout fence paralleling the road, which may make you wonder if the landowners are trying to keep something in or keep something out. At 10.5 miles is the pleasant, shaded spot in the road known as **Pine Creek**, which includes a lodge, store, cafe, and KOA Kampground. After another 10 or 11 miles of motoring amid sublime scenery you'll come to the settlement of **Pray**; 2 miles past there turn left into **Chico Hot Springs**.

CHICO HOT SPRINGS: HISTORICALLY ROMANTIC SINCE 1897 reads the sign greeting you at the entrance to the enterprise, which is back by towering Chico and Emigrant peaks. Whether or not Chico is the foremost hot springs resort in Montana is debatable; few, however, would argue that the food served in the Chico Inn restaurant is not as good as it gets in the Northern Rockies. The main lodge, which holds the restaurant and several guest rooms, is a rather dark place, reportedly still occupied by the ghosts of the original owners, Bill and Percie Knowles. The lobby and restaurant are decorated with antiques and an array of things such as horseshoes, historic photos, and news clippings detailing the literati/artistic/Hollywood connection that is so strong here in the Livingston–Paradise Valley area. (Guests and diners at Chico during its century in operation have included Charlie Russell, Teddy Roosevelt, Steve McQueen, Jim Harrison, Jeff Bridges, Meg Ryan, and many other notables.) Beyond is a saloon, attached to the main lodge in a sort of New England farmhouse style. Rounding out the resort and its activities are the pair of hot springs pools and poolside grill; a beautiful old barn with a river-rock "first story"; guided horseback rides ranging from an hour to a day in duration; hay rides; mountain-bike rentals; and a newer guest lodge with condo units. Dogsled rides are among the wintertime possibilities at Chico.

Back on State Highway 540, a patchwork of pavement and asphalt takes aim at the Gallatin Range. The road becomes so bumpy and in need of further repair that you may wish it had never been paved in the first place. The Yellowstone gradually transforms into a narrower, mountain river, braided and clogged with deposits laid down during floods. Thirteen miles from the Chico junction turn left, returning onto U.S. Highway 89.

After 3 miles on the main highway you'll pass the right-hand turn to Tom Miner Creek Road. Within a few miles the canyon begins to narrow, settlement intensifies, and you'll pass a few guest lodges and bed and breakfasts. At 12 miles, just past a private elk farm, enter **Corwin Springs**, home to the **Cinnabar General Store** and **The Ranch Kitchen**, a restaurant run by the controversial (and reportedly disintegrating) Church Universal and Triumphant.

Seven miles beyond Corwin Springs you will reach **Gardiner**, Montana, where quasi-wild elk love to just hang out. In many ways Gardiner is like a smaller version of West Yellowstone, despite its dry, sparsely timbered setting, which contrasts sharply with West Yellowstone's lodgepole pine–dominated surroundings. Numerous motels, eateries, gift shops, and outfitters line the

two main streets of the town. A sampling: **Jim Bridger Motor Court**, **Yellowstone Inn Bed & Breakfast**, **Yellowstone Raft Company**, and the classic-looking **Cecil's Fine Foods**.

On leaving Gardiner you'll cross the Yellowstone River and proceed into Yellowstone National Park, heading upstream along the tumbling Gardiner River, and leaving the Yellowstone River to the backcountry route it has carved between Tower-Roosevelt and Gardiner.

At 3 miles you'll pass the parking area for the trail leading down to **Boiling River**, where soaking is condoned by the National Park Service—a rare, perhaps even unique situation in Yellowstone. You'll pass a sign marking the 45th parallel and re-enter Wyoming, soon passing a campground on the right, just before entering **Mammoth Hot Springs**, location of the Yellowstone National Park headquarters facilities. On the high ridge above town you can see further evidence of the 1988 fires; you'll also note that there's more aspen growth at this end of the park than you've seen elsewhere. The **Albright Visitor Center** includes excellent displays on park wildlife, a movie presentation, and exhibits of historic Thomas Moran paintings and W. H. Jackson photos, two men who were involved in the early park expeditions. Elk can often be seen up close and personal on the lawns of Mammoth, strolling about like so many tourists. In September the big bulls bugle, dig at the ground with their antlers, and work hard to gather and keep harems intact. They're also mad, so remember: These are potentially dangerous animals—keep your distance!

Additional things to investigate in the Mammoth area include the amazing travertine steps of the **Upper and Lower Mammoth Terraces**, both of which feature self-guiding boardwalk/asphalt trails, and the old **Fort Yellowstone** complex. The U.S. Army was summoned in 1886 to patrol Yellowstone, on the lookout for vandals and poachers (*see* History). The soldiers-as-park-protectors scenario was intended to be short-lived, but it wound up lasting more than thirty years, during which tenure several structures were built to serve as permanent quarters. Buildings still standing from the era include seven stout beauties built in 1909 by skilled Scottish masons, using locally quarried sandstone. One of these houses the Albright Visitor Center, originally built to serve as the bachelor officers' quarters, while others today hold various park administrative offices.

MOUNTAIN BIKING THROUGH YANKEE JIM CANYON: A NARRATIVE ACCOUNT

Longtime friend Ramon and I plan to pedal our mountain bikes north some 25 miles, beginning at Mammoth Hot Springs and following a series of dirt roads depicted on our Gallatin National Forest visitors map. Meanwhile, Nancy will drive down to the anticipated ending point, then ride south to meet us along the way. We've been told that this is a relatively easy ride, suitable for nearly any level of rider.

It's only May 1, but at this relatively low-lying northern portion of Yellowstone winter's snows are but a memory. It's hard to imagine all the snow still burying the Yellowstone Plateau, where an even harder winter than usual dumped several dozen feet of snow. It's also unseasonably warm. The air temperature makes it feel more like the Fourth of July than May Day.

After parking the Jeep in front of the visitor center, we lift two of the three mountain bikes down off the roof rack and set them on their sides on the green lawn. Then—helmets on, nuts and bolts checked and tightened, and snacks, rain gear, and emergency tools packed—Ramon and I spin onto the one-way gravel road signed GARDINER 5 MILES that heads uphill immediately behind the grand old **Mammoth Hot Springs Hotel**. After only a half-mile of climbing, the road begins descending across an exposed, sage-covered hillside. Below we see cars buzzing along the main highway and waters formed of recent snowmelt glancing along within the banks of the Gardiner River.

After approximately four miles, at the bottom of a long hill, Ramon and I turn onto the highway. After a half-mile of northbound riding, we pass under the famous **Roosevelt Arch** and leave Yellowstone at the North Entrance. On a tablet at the top of the arch, which Teddy Roosevelt dedicated in 1903, we see inscribed the words, FOR THE BENEFIT AND ENJOYMENT OF THE PEOPLE.

Once past the arch we turn left, leaving the highway. We now are paralleling the Yellowstone River, into which the Gardiner River empties at Gardiner. As I ride a short distance in front, I hear Ramon laughing behind me. I look back and he points to his right. There, not 100 yards away, four pronghorn bucks graze between the goalposts on the Gardiner High School football field. Where else, but in Yellowstone Country?

A short distance past the football field/antelope fast-food joint we re-enter Yellowstone. Then, after riding a total of 9 miles, we again leave the park and begin skirting the Royal Teton Ranch, home to the Church Universal and Triumphant. CUT, widely known in the region for its apocalyptic prophecies and occasional taboo activities, such as gunrunning, has bought up vast acreages adjacent to Yellowstone and in other parts of Park County, Montana. Of late, however, owing to financial problems, they have been trying to unload some of those lands.

Ramon and I hear a rumbling of thunder in the distance, and we see that a wall of black clouds is rapidly moving our way. We know that soon we'll be drenched if we don't act quickly. We locate some trees for cover not far from the base of **Devil's Slide**, a startlingly colorful formation of sedimentary rock layers that are tilted almost straight up and down on edge. Ramon, a geologist by training, consults his geological map, then informs me that the bright red layer in the Devil's Slide is of the Chugwater formation, a mudstone that formed some 200 million years ago during the Triassic Period of the Mesozoic era. Not one to argue about such things, I take his word for it.

Explosive thunder is preceded by lightning strikes as close as a half mile away. ("One thousand one, one thousand two, one thousand BOOM!") The storm appears to be directed higher on the mountain front, though, so we don't feel in immediate peril. The rain hits hard for about ten minutes. Then, as quickly as it appeared, the storm gives way to clearing skies and the return of sunshine.

Back on our bikes, the warming, evaporative action of the sun's rays fills the air with the pungency of sage. There's no other smell like it; for me the scent of sage after a summer rainstorm is the defining essence of the basin and foothills country of the Northern Rockies.

After 13 miles of bicycling we bear right along the Yellowstone River, rather than going left toward

Devil's Slide, Paradise Valley

CUT's headquarters. The road narrows. We pass tiny Cutler Lake then, at 17 miles, descend onto the floodplain of the river and into the heart of **Yankee Jim Canyon**. The road turns even rougher, becoming more like a trail than a road in places. If I were searching for a pleasant, out-of-the-way campsite, this spot in the Gallatin National Forest is a place I would definitely consider returning to. Immense walls of yellow and iron-rich red rock rise on the west, and a protective grove of cottonwood trees hugs the bank of the Yellowstone to the east. Nancy, coming from the north, rides in as Ramon and I meditate here on nature's own music: Wind whispering through the cottonwoods harmonizes with the river, whose singing waters hiss across rocks and against dirt banks.

Just past 18 miles the three of us stop to investigate an old, intricately constructed rock retaining wall that supports a stretch of road crossing a steep sidehill. Perhaps, we speculate, it's a component of the original toll road that Jim George erected through this canyon. According to the history guide I've toted along, George, or "Yankee Jim" as he was known, in the 1800s hacked out a makeshift wagon toll road over these cliffs, opening the upper Yellowstone Valley to travel by gold prospectors for the first time. For many years thereafter Yankee Jim earned his living by charging travelers a fee to pass through, and also by providing overnight accommodations at a roadhouse he constructed. Yankee Jim was the only game in the canyon until the Northern Pacific Railroad built its National Park Branch up-valley from Livingston in 1883. Although Jim and the railroad finally did reach a right-of-way agreement, after long and often heated negotiations, he was said never to forgive the intrusion of the iron horse into his domain. It's reported that well into the twentieth century Yankee Jim could be spotted by Yellowstone-bound passengers on the train, his white hair and beard flapping in the wind and his fist shaking violently in the air . . . no doubt accompanied by some choice words.

In another half mile the three of us roll past Sphinx, where a structure built as a section house in 1910 remains. At 21 miles we veer right onto an improved road rather than turning left toward Tom Miner Basin. The path not taken looks intriguing, but it'll have to wait for a subsequent visit. According to our Forest Service map, at the end of the road, about 12 miles to our southwest, lies the **Tom Miner Campground**. The map also depicts a hiking trail roughly 2 miles in length leading from the campground to the **Gallatin Petrified Forest**. "Now *that* sounds like old-growth timber," Ramon jokes to Nancy and me. "I wonder if any petrified spotted owls live there?"

At 25 miles we top out, after a rather steep climb, on what the map tells us is Point of Rocks. From here it's a quick 1-mile zip back to the highway and the car. Well exercised, we figure we deserve a good meal and a soak in some soothing waters. Unsurpassable Chico Hot Springs is only 16 miles away, so the decision of where to go next is a no-brainer.

CONTINUING FROM MAMMOTH TO OLD FAITHFUL

Leaving Mammoth Hot Springs, drive south toward Norris on the Grand Loop Road. In 2 miles you'll pass the right-hand turn leading to **Upper Terraces Loop Drive**. About 2 miles farther you'll pass an unusual sight known as **The Hoodoos**, which are made up of a mad jumble of jagged pieces of old travertine terraces that broke apart and covered the mountainside during colossal landslides.

Continue climbing up the canyon through the pass known as **Golden Gate**, surrounded by yellow and orange walls of Huckleberry Ridge Tuff, which was spewed by the first of Yellowstone's three big eruptions (*see* The Land). South of Golden Gate you'll see, on the left, the southwestern terminus of the old **Bunsen Peak Road**, now a bicycling route that wraps around Bunsen Peak and re-emerges at the Grand Loop Road in 5.2 miles, not far south of Mammoth. The lofty, grass-filled **Swan Lake Flat** you have entered is like a bowl, rimmed with low, burned-over mountains. Higher peaks rise far in the distance.

Eight miles from Mammoth you'll pass the left-hand turn leading to **Sheepeater Cliffs**, once home to some of the only Native Americans that lived year-round in Yellowstone (*see* The First

Humans). At 11 miles you'll pass **Apollinaris Springs Picnic Area**, then, in another mile, **Obsidian Cliff**. Native Americans, some from very far away, would make pilgrimages here to obtain the highly prized black volcanic glass, out of which they would fashion projectile points and other implements. As different as it looks, the obsidian resulted from the same lava flows that makes up the tuff of Golden Gate—the difference being that the obsidian was super-cooled, probably by flowing into a lake, so the crystals that formed are microscopic.

At 16 miles stop to inspect **Roaring Mountain**, a rather ungainly white thing largely devoid of vegetation. Until the mid-1920s one of the mountain's many fumaroles emitted a loud howling noise, which travelers could hear and which lent the mountain its name. It looks as if fire raged intensely through this area, where you can see hundreds of downed trees shining brightly under the intense midday sun.

At 20 miles turn in toward the **Norris Campground** to visit the **Museum of the National Park Ranger**. Inside the cozy old log cabin, built in 1908 as one of sixteen soldier outposts in Yellowstone, you'll discover a collection of uniforms, badges (including several from other countries), and other items tracing the history of park rangers, from the era of the U.S. Army to modern times. Don't neglect to stroll out onto the front porch and take a load off, just to feel the afternoon sun on your face and admire the mellow Gibbon River shimmering past. You may not want to leave.

At 21.5 miles you'll reach **Norris Junction**. The nearby **Norris Geyser Basin,** where inner earth bares all, is generally considered the most impressive concentration of hot springs and geysers in Yellowstone. A little more than 2 miles of trail wind through the pair of basins here, which hold the park's hottest and oldest (more than 100,000 years old), yet most dynamic thermal features. These include **Steamboat Geyser**, the tallest active geyser in the world. Steamboat can send steaming water plumes as high as 400 feet . . . or just as likely lie dormant for months at a time. Other features with intriguing and descriptive names include **Green Diamond Spring**, **Whale's Mouth**, **Whirligig Geysers**, and **Black Growler Steam Vent**. Between Back Basin and

Porcelain Basin is the **Norris Geyser Basin Museum**, which is *the* interpretive stop to visit if you'd like to better understand the workings behind—make that *underneath*—Yellowstone's geothermal wonders.

At Norris Junction continue southwest toward Madison Junction, rather than turning left toward Canyon Village. In a couple of miles you'll enter fire-rimmed **Elk Park**, through which the Gibbon River gently meanders. In another 2 miles, after passing the trailhead for the half-mile trail to the delightful and colorful **Artists' Paint Pots**, the terrain changes dramatically as you enter the pinched recesses of Gibbon Canyon. At 5.5 miles from the junction stop to have a look at **Beryl Spring**, one of the hottest and prettiest springs in Yellowstone. You'll understand why its name was borrowed from a brilliant, blue-green gemstone. Below the blast of **Gibbon Falls**, where the river tumbles 84 feet over the wall of the Yellowstone Caldera (the wall of rock on the opposite side of the road is part of the inner rim of the caldera), is the **Gibbon Falls Picnic Area**. Obviously, the site occupies a spot that once was well-shaded, but now appears quite naked since the fires ripped through. As you continue toward Madison Junction, the river keeps foaming along beneath burned-over forest; the river, too, is far more visible than it was prior to the summer of 1988.

At 13 miles you'll come to **Madison Junction**. Before driving the 14 miles to West Yellowstone, continue for 16 miles south on the Grand Loop Road to visit Yellowstone's most famous feature, **Old Faithful Geyser**. A half mile south of the junction veer right onto the one-way, 2-mile long **Firehole River Drive**, where you'll earn intensely close-up looks at the river on your right and of the impressive canyon wall of rhyolite on the left. There's even a designated swimming area just off the road. A few miles after rejoining the main road you'll cross Nez Perce Creek, then enter **Lower Geyser Basin**. At 8.5 miles is the turn into **Fountain Paint Pots** on the right and, on the left, the northern terminus of the **Firehole Lake Drive** (it's one-way northbound, so you access it a little over a mile south of here). From Lower Geyser Basin continue through a world of steam, burned trees, and living forests, first passing through **Midway Geyser Basin** then entering **Upper**

Inn at Old Faithful

Geyser Basin. Together, these three basins encompass the majority of the world's active geysers.

At 16 miles is the turn, reminiscent of an interstate cloverleaf, into **Old Faithful**, the name of both the entire visitor services area and its world-famous geyser. Set aside plenty of time to stroll along the boardwalks, to watch Old Faithful erupt (her expected schedule, along with those of other nearby geysers, are posted at the visitor center), and to absorb the Old West meets Old World atmosphere of the **Inn at Old Faithful**, where you will mingle with visitors from across the globe.

THE INN AT OLD FAITHFUL: A NARRATIVE ACCOUNT

Looking good would present a formidable challenge for any man-made structure if it sat smack in the middle of the glorious Firehole River Valley, surrounded by country loved throughout the world for its wildlife and scenic grandeur, and where the powerful Snake and Yellowstone rivers rise and where the forces that built the earth are available for viewing.

The Inn at Old Faithful rises to the challenge. I think of it as our country's nondenominational National Cathedral.

Nancy and I and our friends, Tom, Denise, and seventeen-month-old Turner finish supper at the inn's good restaurant. Then we sink into the irresistible couches gracing the second-story balcony that encircles the lobby below. Nearby writing tables feature copper cutouts and green stained glass. It is solid furniture, lacking the adornment of cowboys and bison, but of Western flair nevertheless. Maybe because it's the last day of operation for the lodge this year, October 21, or maybe because it's snowing outside, or maybe both: But, in spite of its open, sprawling floor plan—six stories of balconies, beams, and braces—the Old Faithful Inn tonight is deliciously warm and intimate. Everyone seems in an uncommonly good mood. Smiles abound. The employees are fired up, moving on tomorrow to whatever else it is they do and wherever they do it.

I stand in the lobby and look around, taking things in. Somewhat surprisingly, no stuffed animal heads grace the walls. Gazing up I find the straight lines provided by lodgepole pines that grew up healthy, interrupted by the twisted angles of malformed limbs and trunks serving as braces and staircase uprights. They support a structure proud of its body, exposed right up to its catwalk-surrounded ceiling of unpeeled logs for all the world to see just how it was assembled during the tough winter of 1903–4. In some respects the skeletal maze looks like a Rube Goldberg joke. It seems there's no way the place could stand. But stand it does, and stand it has for almost a century, so it seems that architect Robert C. Reamer indeed must have known what he was doing (although the highest levels of the inn have been closed to the public since 1959, when that summer's earthquake caused damage).

Suddenly everyone's out the front door and so am I. "It's going off!" screams a little girl. Just across the way Old Faithful, despite being less faithful than she once was, is right on schedule tonight. Steam rises high into the void, backlit by parting skies awash with moonlight and stars. Turner squeals. The eruption fades to a fizzle. The air has turned colder and the snow, right at freezing when it fell, has crusted up. Our big family crunches back to the inn, strangers as one on this singular, autumn-becoming-winter evening.

Back on the second-story balcony I walk through the hole in the wall opposite the piano player, which opens onto a small deck overlooking the dining room. Fellow fall arrivals, surrounded by millions of acres of wilderness, dine on succulent prime rib and veal Parmesan, made of Midwest beef. They wash it down with good California and French wines. I wonder what will be done with leftover supplies. Will the employees enjoy a two-day bash before departing?

People, hundreds of them, of nearly every color, age, fashion, and nationality sit around or stroll about. A chattering of Japanese, point-and-click necklaces still hanging about their necks after supper, laugh and drink and sing Beatles tunes and wrap arms around one another's shoulders in the Bear's Den Tavern. Near the lobby's gargantuan rock fireplace, which incorporates more than 500 tons of stone, sits a young couple speaking Dutch and wearing baggy clothes and matching nose rings. A pair of recent retirees, sitting on a bench close to the pianist, are no doubt responsible for the entertainer's mellow rendition of "The Tennessee Waltz." Knee-slapping and grinning ear to ear, the gray-haired owner of a Tennessee country store tells me in his folksy manner about being forced to stop the van today in Lamar Valley to let several bison cross the road. "And we saw a wolf!" he exclaims, eyes asparkle like a child's. The kids, now adults, are minding the store and Daddy hasn't a worry in the world. This is the first time they've been out of Tennessee since the 1970s, and it's their first time ever in Wonderland. They absolutely love it. It's way better even than they'd expected.

Friend Tom, who years ago worked in Yellowstone, leads us onto one of the inn's several outdoor decks. The snow has resumed, and it's piling up. The lone stranger sharing our perch points to two young boys below playing in the snow in the dark and asks rhetorically, with a Scandinavian accent, "We should have a snowball fight, yah?" So we all start fashioning snowballs out of the perfect-for-that-purpose wet snow. Battle ensues.

"Hey mister, you really pack 'em good!" one of the kids offers. What's this "mister" stuff?, I wonder. Oh yeah, I'm in my mid-forties. I forgot there for a second. "Years of practice!" I yell, whizzing one just over his head.

As we walk back through the lobby en route to our rooms in the recently remodeled west wing, we encounter a pair of rangers who are busily spreading the word that all park roads are closed. Road crews will attempt to have them opened by mid-morning tomorrow.

Not that anyone here was planning to go anywhere at this late hour anyway, but still the mood turns even more festive and friendly as the news of our captivity circulates. All of us—three hundred or so guests and several dozen employees—are snowed in at Old Faithful. We can't think of anyplace we'd rather be. Not even celebrating the victory or mourning the loss of our team in tonight's final game of the World Series. Bereft of television and radio, no one here seems to know or even care how the game came out. I never hear the topic mentioned.

At eleven-thirty the next morning, after the roads are finally plowed and covered with a thick layer of sand—the National Park Service isn't taking any chances with all of these snow tire–less cars and motor homes—everyone departs simultaneously, captives released, bumper-to-bumper buddies dispersing to every corner of the globe.

Today they'll board up the Inn at Old Faithful, and the occasional maintenance worker will have it to himself or herself for the next six months.

AT THE WEST ENTRANCE: WEST YELLOWSTONE

Leave the wonders of Wonderland behind by driving from Madison Junction to the West Entrance. Prepare to be shocked by the sudden explosion of commercialism running rampant just beyond the boundaries of our nation's most beloved natural area. At first glance, with its overabundance of T-shirt and curio shops, ragtag buildings, and snack stands, **West Yellowstone** seems a rather tacky town. A closer inspection, though, reveals signs of a maturing service community, with accommodations and activities to suit nearly any personality and pocketbook.

West Yellowstone can be a lively place, especially at the height of summer and during the long, snowy winters, when temperatures often drop to the minus-twenties and lower. During those frigid months herds of snowmobilers roam free at all hours, driving their machines nearly anywhere in town that they please. But West Yellowstone, though wild in its own way today, did not begin life like a lot of Wild West towns, which were built on shaky foundations of prospecting or cattle-ranching. Rather, it emerged as a center to serve tourists, and a tourist town it remains. In fact, West Yellowstone just may be the quintessential

tourist town of the Northern Rockies.

For more than 30 years visitors had been entering and exiting Yellowstone where the Madison River leaves the national park, when the town of West Yellowstone popped up at the site in 1908. The impetus was the Union Pacific Railroad. A year earlier the U.P. had completed construction of a spur line up from Ashton, Idaho, crossing the Continental Divide at Reas Pass, making it possible to ride the rails all the way from Utah to Yellowstone.

West Yellowstone grew first as a strip town, with businesses paralleling the railroad tracks on the opposite side of Yellowstone Avenue. A trio of early structures that remain today includes **Eagle's Store**, situated at the corner of Yellowstone Avenue and Canyon Street (established in 1908 as the town's first commercial business and still in the Eagle family); the **Canyon Hotel**, located just west of that corner on Yellowstone Avenue; and the Oregon Short Line/Union Pacific depot, at 124 Yellowstone Avenue. The depot, designed by architect Gilbert Underwood, was built in a rustic fashion utilizing native materials, echoing the look and style of National Park Service buildings in Yellowstone. Now listed on the National Register of Historic Places, the depot houses the intriguing **Museum of the Yellowstone**. Within are exhibits on Native Americans, mountain men, wildlife, wildfires, and more. The building set the tone for many additional business and residential structures in West Yellowstone, as you will discover if you drive or wander the back streets of town. Often these are tucked amid collections of more modern and less attractive trailers and slap-shacks.

As time progressed the commercial district shifted north along Canyon Street, where today you will find the majority of retail businesses. More recently the town began spreading south of where the railroad tracks formerly ran. Here, in the Grizzly Park addition you can visit the popular **Grizzly Discovery Center** and the **National Geographic IMAX Theatre**. There's also a growing number of motels and fast-food restaurants in this part of town. At the Grizzly Discovery Center—nicknamed "Grrrassic Park" by locals—you can watch several grizzly bears in action (or, just as often, in inaction). Most are orphans from north of the U.S.–Canada border. A pack of captive wolves also resides at the center.

Grizzly

In a sense wolves, recent returnees to the Greater Yellowstone Ecosystem, have replaced bears as *the* animal to spot while in the park. During the 1960s and earlier, it was common for visitors to encounter several bears a day in Yellowstone (on a trip in 1963 with my family, we recorded seeing 23 bears in two days). It was when Yogi the Bear was at his most popular, both literally and symbolically. Today's visitor is lucky to see even one bruin. This is due largely to measures enacted in the 1970s by the National Park Service to dissuade tourists from feeding the bears, a practice that is dangerous for humans and unhealthful for the animals.

The IMAX Theatre, adjacent to the Grizzly Discovery Center, shows dramatically produced films on a six-story-high screen. Productions include the arresting film *Yellowstone*. The show is spectacular, but be forewarned: Its action is so realistic and *lifelike* that it may give you motion sickness. Both the Grizzly Discovery Center and the National Geographic IMAX Theatre are open year-round.

New attractions such as these, along with an ever-growing reputation for world-class fly-fishing in summer and fall, and equally great snowmobiling and cross-country skiing in winter, are responsible for the community's growth into more than just a jumping-off point for tourists headed to Yellowstone National Park. Indeed, West Yellowstone is evolving into a destination in its own right.

SKIING THE WEST YELLOWSTONE RENDEZVOUS: A NARRATIVE ACCOUNT

Cross-country skiing alone, or with one or two companions, amid a hushed and deserted winter mountainscape can be exhilarating. It is one of my favorite ways to while away spare time during the long Northern Rockies winters.

Solitude is wonderful, absolutely, yet there is nothing quite comparable to whizzing through a lodgepole forest over roller-coaster terrain on cross-country skis in the company of 600 like-minded Nordic nuts. This is what I am typically found doing on the morning of the second Saturday of each March, because that is when the annual West Yellowstone Rendezvous ski race happens. Being part of this flood of humanity, sliding on skis through the woods, is intoxicating: Everybody is traveling under their own power, although enjoying the occasional, and hard-earned boost from gravity. So, just about the only sounds heard are those of labored breathing, skis hissing over snow, and a sporadic "Hup, hup, hup!," shouted Norwegian-style by spectators hugging the trails.

The Rendezvous is one of a handful of events of the annual American Ski Marathon Series, the foremost race series for cross-country ski enthusiasts across the United States. The community of West Yellowstone is rightfully proud to host such a prestigious event. Nordic skiers of nearly every skill level, and from throughout North America, participate in the Rendezvous, from near-neophytes just getting their ski legs to past and potential Olympians. Participants choose one of several distance options, ranging from 2 kilometers for the kids all the way up to 50 kilometers (31 miles) for the truly dedicated.

It is past 9:00 A.M. and the adrenaline is almost palpable in the air. Skiers clad in colorful, skin-tight Lycra suits, and others wearing less flashy outfits all chatter nervously. Many old friends and acquaintances haven't seen each other since last year, same place, same time. But suddenly the cannon sounds, sending shock waves through the thin, high-country air and scaring everyone. We are off, in a frenzy of poling and skating motions, across the flat meadows that feed into the hills traced by the Rendezvous Trail System.

The trails begin directly on the south edge of town, then meander for several miles over Gallatin National Forest lands. Construction of the trails started back in the 1970s as a project of the Neal Swanson family. Now the network is groomed throughout the long winters by the community of West Yellowstone for the enjoyment of its residents and its visitors.

I'm participating in the 25-kilometer event, which I consider far enough to be a true test of skill and endurance, but not so long that it becomes a survival outing. Moreover, I will get to see and ski all of the race course, since 50-kilometer skiers simply go twice around the 25-kilometer loop.

As I pole along a flat stretch of trail my mind wanders back to an article about West Yellowstone I read several years ago in *Montana* magazine. Before the snowmobiles, and before Yellowstone National Park remained open in winter, West Yellowstone pretty much boarded up once the snow started falling. By the 1930s, though, several families were staying on. The roads leading to town and those winding around it went unplowed and simply filled in with the white stuff. Cars, sitting wherever they were last parked, became bumps in the snow. In particularly snowy winters even the bumps disappeared. Children walking to school created tunnels through the snow, which often led there via the house of a friend, in one door and out another. Those paths, in turn, would dictate the circuitous routes followed by adults later in the day. I wonder what those pre-1960s residents would think today, if they could see and hear the hundreds of snowmobiles whining around on the town's plowed roads, and witness the grooming machines that head out in the morning to pack trails for cross-country skiers. After all, for the early residents skis and snowshoes were means for traveling through deep snows. They were utilitarian, not recreational tools.

My event started fifteen or twenty minutes after the 50-kilometer race, so I soon begin catching and passing dozens of slower skiers doing the longer distance. "Passing on your left . . . thanks!" becomes my mantra. The flat and downhill stretches along Windy Ridge, the high point of the race course, are exhilarating. They are definitely worth the effort they took to reach. After passing

the cabin sitting near the crest of the steepest and longest downhill, I tuck and schuss, probably accelerating to 25 miles per hour. "Yippee!" I think but don't say. At this high speed I need to concentrate to keep my skis bottom-side down.

We take a hard left at the biathlon range. Here Olympic hopefuls can often be seen practicing the target-shooting component of their unusual sport, which combines cross-country skiing and marksmanship. Long-time race director Drew Barney told me yesterday that the course had been changed this year, so I have an idea of what lies ahead. In years past when we reached the biathlon range we had only three relatively flat kilometers to go. Today five hilly kilometers remain.

Cross-country skiing, Rendezvous Trail, West Yellowstone

I'm getting really tired and starting to lock up, so I put nearly as much effort into trying to relax as to skiing hard. Finally the finish line comes into view. Even though I'm spent and winded, I try to speed up and look fresh as I ski across it. But after skidding to a parallel stop I fall over, exhausted. I'm glad I did the race, but awfully happy that I'm not setting out on a second loop, as a lot of my friends are.

After standing up and catching my breath, I start greeting those who finished ahead of me and those coming in behind. I've completed my annual reaffirmation of love for cross-country skiing and the Rendezvous Trails, which I consider to be one of the finest venues on earth to practice the world's greatest sport. Now it's time to practice the cross-country camaraderie that comes so naturally to those sharing the special experience of skiing with hundreds of others through the West Yellowstone outback.

FROM WEST YELLOWSTONE TO BOZEMAN

This excursion leads from West Yellowstone to Bozeman by way of Big Sky. The direct route is less than 100 miles, but there are plenty of opportunities for off-route exploring.

Head north from West Yellowstone on U.S. Highway 191/287, passing the **Hebgen Lake Ranger Station** on the edge of town, **Baker's Hole Campground** three miles north of town, then, in another half-mile, the left-hand turn to **Madison Arm Campground and Resort**. At a distance of 8 miles from town you'll emerge from dense lodgepole pine forest into a broad opening, which proffers good views of the high Madison Range and Henrys Lake Mountains to the west. Bison—escapees from Yellowstone, actually—can sometimes be seen in the vicinity, grazing about as if they own the place. At the junction located here, U.S. Highway 191 continues north toward Bozeman, and U.S. Highway 287 goes west toward Ennis, skirting the shore of sparkling Hebgen Lake for several miles.

After 16 miles, the side trip past Hebgen Lake leads to **Quake Lake**. The lake is one reminder of the night of August 17, 1959, when the earth cracked open and the Madison Range rose higher into the sky as the valley below subsided. The 7.1-magnitude earthquake caused a mammoth portion of mountainside to break loose, and the ensuing landslide killed 28 of 250 campers sleeping below. It also dammed the Madison River with rock and debris, which resulted in the formation of Quake Lake. Today, skeletal trees rise eerily out of the water, a massive scar remains on the mountainside, and rubble jumbles the terrain below. The Cabin Creek fault scarp, seen north of the highway between Hebgen and Quake lakes, although made less obvious with the passage of four decades, still shows clearly just how severely the earth ripped apart that night. The total displacement between mountains and valley was 15 feet. The **Madison Canyon Earthquake Area** visitor center, open daily through the summer, tells the story in greater detail. A pair of pleasant Forest Service campgrounds are also found in the area.

Back at the junction where U.S. Highways 287 and 191 part ways, continue north toward Bozeman on Highway 191, which immediately climbs along Grayling Creek back into a forested area. Two and one-half miles from the junction you will enter Yellowstone National Park and pass through yet more evidence of the big fires of 1988. After cresting Fawn Pass, 22 miles from West Yellowstone, the road begins paralleling the Gallatin River as the river snakes through a wide-open landscape embraced by timbered hills. Before leaving Yellowstone and entering the Gallatin National Forest at 31 miles north of West Yellowstone, you'll pass several trailheads, where trails set out and poke into some of Yellowstone's less-frequented niches. A pair of these include the **Specimen Creek Trail** (4.5 miles from the pass) and the **Black Butte Trail** (approximately 6.5 miles).

Steep rock walls close in as you proceed downstream along the Gallatin, which transforms from a high-meadow meanderer into a frothing canyon torrent. If the season is right, expect to see plenty of anglers and river-runners taking advantage of the river's acclaimed waters. The Gallatin is not only a sublime river but also an experienced actor, having played the part of the Big Blackfoot River in Robert Redford's memorable screen adaptation of *A River Runs through It*. The actual Blackfoot, a less photogenic river, flows east of Missoula, the town where the novella's author, Norman Maclean, grew up. (Livingston, Montana, landed the role of Missoula in the movie.)

Rafting on the Gallatin

As you approach the entrance to Big Sky, you'll note a growing number of Western-flair accommodations and restaurants, Forest Service campgrounds, commercial river-running outfits, and large, elaborate homes. Sagebrush blankets the flats, while pine and fir trees miraculously grow from the steep, rocky mountain slopes.

Surrounding the entrance to **Big Sky Ski and Summer Resort**, located 48 miles north of West Yellowstone, is an island of enterprise, replete with gas stations, realty offices, a mini-market/deli, a bookstore, and more. Turn west at the entrance and drive the 9 miles to the resort's Mountain Village, to enjoy an overnight, grab a bite, or just have a look. Big Sky is the dream come true of the late, Montana-born newsman, Chet Huntley. (He's buried at the cemetery in Bozeman.) The "town" of Big Sky is actually a community composed largely of part-time residents, with homes and businesses dispersed over a large area. Big Sky has no long history of concentrated settlement, contrasting with several of the other major ski towns in the Northern Rockies—Jackson Hole, Ketchum, and Whitefish, for example, all of which boast historic downtown districts. The whereabouts of Big Sky accommodations, eateries, and other enterprises are generally identified as being in one of three locations: Mountain Village, where the alpine skiing begins; Meadow Village, the lower-elevation area between Mountain Village and the main highway; and Canyon, which can indicate either north or south of the entrance to Big Sky, in the Gallatin River Canyon.

On the way to the ski resort you'll go through Meadow Village and past the local golf course, which doubles as a cross-country ski center in winter. Glorious Lone Peak, the ski area's 11,166-foot apex, stands sentinel above it all. Not far north of the road is the southern boundary of the Spanish Peaks Unit of the Lee Metcalf Wilderness Area. Combined, the four units of the Lee Metcalf—named in honor of a popular U.S. senator from Montana who was active in conservation legislation—cover more than 250,000 acres of the surrounding Madison Range. It's a rugged labyrinth of land, ranging from peaks higher than 11,000 feet in elevation to a whitewater stretch of the Madison River running through lower, desert-like country.

Approximately 180 lakes are found within the wilderness, and nearly 300 miles of trails beckon backpackers and explorers on horseback.

The most striking feature of Big Sky, other than its grand mountain backdrop, is its *newness*. Ski development didn't begin on what formerly was the Crail Ranch until the early 1970s. Although a few dude ranches had been established early on, including several that are still operational, previous to the 1970s the area was largely the haunt of cowboys, cattle, and even wilder critters. Several older establishments do line the banks of the Gallatin, but nearly everything in Mountain Village and Meadow Village is modernistic, lending Big Sky a somewhat fabricated feel. Moreover, in summer, after the snow melts, the ski runs look rather barren and eroded, and many of the distant slopes show scars where they've been cleared of their timber. If you find the combination unsettling and/or undesirable, continue on to Bozeman, a town of historic substance.

If it doesn't bother you, by all means stay awhile in Big Sky, because it's a fun place, rich with recreational opportunities. Summer activities include hiking, riding the gondola up the ski mountain, fishing and floating on the Gallatin River, horseback riding, golfing on the eighteen-hole course lacing through Meadow Village, and mountain biking on surrounding national forest lands.

But it is in winter that Big Sky really comes into its own. Some of the Northern Rockies' best downhill and cross-country skiing and other snow sports attract visitors from throughout the United States and the world. Big Sky's vertical rise of 4,180 feet from bottom to top is the greatest of any ski area in the United States, topping Wyoming's Jackson Hole Mountain Resort by all of 41 feet. Not surprisingly, a not-too-subtle and rather humorous competition exists between the two resorts. After Big Sky constructed its new, often wind-tossed (and consequently often closed) Lone Mountain Tram—in large part, apparently, so that management could claim the biggest vertical in the country—Jackson Hole altered its description from "the greatest vertical rise in the United States" to the "greatest *continuous* vertical rise . . . " The careful wording alludes to the fact that skiers are obliged to do some lift-hopping to gain the summit at Big Sky, whereas a single tramway goes from bottom to top at Jackson Hole.

Back along U.S. Highway 191, the paralleling Gallatin River continues its down-slope dance toward Bozeman, mellowing for 3 or 4 miles until the steepening, narrowing, talus-sloped canyon pinches it into a repetition of white-water rapids that churn, foam, and whirlpool along. Watch for the bobbing head and whirligig arms of the occasional kayaker, brilliantly colorful against the drab backdrop of murky water and brown rock. An interesting side trip can be made by turning west onto the Spanish Creek Road, just before the highway emerges from Gallatin Canyon. En route to a dead end at the Lee Metcalf Wilderness Area's Spanish Creek trailhead, the road passes through Ted Turner's Flying D Ranch, where segments of Turner's bison herds can often be seen.

At approximately 23 miles north of Big Sky you squeeze out of the Gallatin Canyon and, just like that, pop into Big Sky farming country. The river, meantime, turns westward before ever reaching Bozeman, taking aim at its confluence with the Jefferson and Madison near Three Forks, where the trio of mountain rivers collectively become known as the Missouri River.

There's not a great deal to the town of Gallatin Gateway, 29 miles north of Big Sky (and west off the highway), other than the grand **Gallatin Gateway Inn**. The inn's bright red tile roof is hard to miss, and its expansive, well-manicured grounds beg passersby to get out of their cars and amble about. The hotel was built in 1927 by the Chicago, Milwaukee and St. Paul Railway, better known as the Milwaukee Road. The railroad intended it to house Yellowstone-bound tourists, who would arrive by train from Three Forks then be bused the remainder of the way to West Yellowstone. But the railroad's timing was poor, for it coincided with the burgeoning popularity of auto travel and related decline of rail travel. Consequently, the inn failed in its first life, falling into serious disrepair in the 1950s. But now, in the wake of an extensive renovation in the 1980s, the twenty-five-room inn is attracting overnighters as never before. And its large lounge and lavish ballroom have become a fashionable spot for weddings and other celebrations.

At **Four Corners**, where U.S. Highway 191 and State Highways 84 and 85 converge, turn east toward **Bozeman**. An attractive town of around 30,000 residents (60,000 in the county), Bozeman claims eight designated historical districts and more than forty properties listed on the National Register of Historic Places. Back in 1892 Bozeman was among the seven cities vying for the title of capital of Montana in a statewide popular election. The public vote for the capital site had been mandated under the terms of statehood, which was granted Montana on November 8, 1889. Although Helena ultimately won out, Bozeman did land the state's agricultural school, today's **Montana State University**.

The highway takes you first through the strip portion of town, lined largely with the same car dealers, superstores, and fast-food outlets that you'll see in Anytown, U.S.A. There are some diamonds to be mined amid this rough however, so keep your eyes wide open. The **Montana Woolen Shop**, on the outskirts of town, is one of them. Here you'll find piles and racks full of high-quality woolens—sweaters, blankets, fabric, rugs—from Hudson Bay, Woolrich, and many other companies, all priced to sell. A mile farther east, just north of U.S. Highway 191 on 19th Avenue, is the **Spanish Peaks Brewery and Italian Caffe**. The microbrewery makes a great lunch stop, with its beers and brick-fired pizza and other dishes, all served under the watchful eye of pictures of the enterprise's Black Labrador mascot. (Black Dog Ale is the establishment's best-known brew.)

U.S. Highway 191/Main Street leads directly into Bozeman's historic downtown area. The **Baxter Hotel**, at the corner of Willson and Main, and the **Bozeman Hotel**, at the corner of Rouse and Main, are a pair of the more venerable and memorable structures in downtown. Ongoing renovations have updated and transformed many of the apothecaries and hardware stores of yore into fine-art galleries, stylish clothing and furniture stores, and other sorts of high-end enterprises. The **Downtown Bozeman Visitor Center** is located at 224 East Main. A block south of there, at 234 East Babcock, is the compact **American Computer Museum**, a truly unexpected and rewarding find. On display are a host of computing devices ranging from the ancient abacus of the Babylonians to punch card devices to modern microcomputers. Graphic evidence of just how far technology has advanced is presented in items such as a 1950 IBM electronic computer, which weighs in at over a ton and comprises more than 1,200 vacuum tubes.

Stock up on picnic makings after browsing through downtown Bozeman's well-rounded selection of stores. Then continue east on Main Street a few blocks and take the right-hand turn onto Cypress to lovely **Lindley Park**. (If visiting in winter, forget about the picnic and plan a cross-country ski outing instead. Trails at Lindley are groomed for residents and visitors alike.)

Next, hunger satisfied, head south on Willson Avenue toward the campus of Montana State University. There you'll find the outstanding **Museum of the Rockies**, located at 600 West Kagy Boulevard. It is one of the two or three best repositories of things old in the entire Northern Rockies. Although there's a great deal more than ancient beasts to inspect at the facility, where the theme is *One Place Through All of Time*, the museum is best known for its Phyllis B. Berger Dinosaur Hall. The *One Day 80 Million Years Ago* display features finds from the renowned Egg Mountain dinosaur nesting colonies near Choteau, Montana. And don't miss *Maiasaura peeblesorum*, Montana's official state fossil. Also on

chainlink horse sculpture, Museum of the Rockies

site is the Taylor Planetarium, which offers special tours of the night sky on Friday evenings. Outside the planetarium an enormous mural entitled *The Big Sky* helps visitors find their place in the universe. Other features at the Museum of the Rockies include excellent exhibits on Native American cultures, the Corps of Discovery, the mountain men, and the pioneer miners, railroaders, and sod-busters who settled Montana. Finally, the interactive Martin Discovery Room is a bonanza for kids who have trouble keeping their hands off things (and for parents weary of reprimanding them for it).

If you're interested in finding out even more about the area's past, but on a more local level, before moseying out of Bozeman find the **Gallatin County Pioneer Museum**, housed downtown in the old jail facility at 317 West Main. Particularly compelling and telling are the photographic archives and written family histories detailing the settlement of the area.

A TOUR TO A PAIR OF STATE PARKS: A NARRATIVE ACCOUNT

Up with the sun, which is way too early at this latitude during the week of the summer solstice, we're out of our room at Bozeman's **Fairfield Inn** even before the motel begins serving its complimentary continental breakfast. That's okay, though, because we plan to return here tonight, so we'll eat twice as much at tomorrow's sitting. We slip instead before leaving town into **The Leaf and Bean,** located downtown on West Main. The strong coffee is a real eye-opener, and the warm muffins are scrumpdelicious.

Rather than driving northwest along Interstate–90, we take the frontage road that parallels I–90 along its north side. There's very little traffic, so we drive slowly, taking time to look things over. In 8 miles we pass through **Belgrade**. Bozeman's airport is located just outside of this small town, so Belgrade effectively is part of Bozeman. On the east edge of town, at Lewis and Clark Park, we see folks setting up for the Saturday morning farmers market, which according to a sign is set to open at nine o'clock. Flowers and locally grown produce galore magically appear from trailers and covered pickup trucks. Belgrade's small downtown area also looks interesting; maybe we'll browse around there on the way back to Bozeman, time permitting.

We pass under the interstate in Belgrade, and drive onto Highway 347. This is rolling agricultural land, pleasing to the eye, with occasional farm and ranch homes gracing the landscape. It could be Iowa but for the mountains, which are never far away or out of sight, as is the case throughout the western half of Montana. Dutch emigrants were some of the first Europeans to settle in this area, and their influence can still be felt, particularly in the names of some of the small, quaint towns (Amsterdam comes to mind). It's simply a wonderful country drive, lending support to our dictum that getting off the interstate is the only way to really see an area.

At Churchill we turn north onto Highway 288, return to the north side of I–90, and enter the lazy burg of Manhattan, which is the antithesis of its counterpart in New York state. A store we've been wanting to visit is located here, but it's not open this early in the morning. **Big Sky Carvers Outlet Gallery** proffers a host of fascinating items. Some are of little practical use but are wonderfully whimsical—chainsaw-carved bears holding various poses, for instance. Other products, such as cleverly worded signs, are equally whimsical and could even serve a utilitarian purpose.

At Logan, after passing the **Land of Magic Dinner Club**—reputed to serve some of the best steaks in Big Sky Country—we turn left to again pass under the interstate. Immediately on the left we pass a new-looking angling business, standing alone on the roadside. The dirt road we're traveling along heads south into a rather bleak-looking landscape, with brown hills lifting out of arid grasslands. It's easy to imagine an endless herd of bison stretching across this landscape, farther than the eye can see. And the bison certainly were here at one time, as evidenced by the finds unearthed at **Madison Buffalo Jump State Park**.

Park signs inform us that bone deposits as thick as five feet were excavated at this former buffalo jump, or *pishkun*. The styles of projectile points found in association with the slaughtered animals indicated that Native Americans were hunting at this spot at least 2,000 years ago. The bison—probably both lone individual animals and small groups—would be herded by one com-

ponent of a hunting party westward along the plateau to our east, then driven off the cliff that rises away from today's observation deck. Some bison probably died from the fall, while those only injured would be finished off by additional hunters waiting below. After the animals were all dead, the women of the tribe would commence the butchering process. Native Americans obtained not only food supplies to last many months from these communal bison kills, but also raw materials for fashioning clothing, tipi skins, bone tools, and more.

This method of hunting bison predated the 1700s arrival of the horse on the Great Plains and Rocky Mountains. Horses gave the Indians a new freedom of mobility and led to an altogether different method of procuring bison.

Although we know to leave everything as we find it, even seemingly unimportant stone chippings, we can't resist climbing up on the plateau to look for evidence of prehistoric people. My college education is in anthropology, and both Nancy and I spent much of the 1970s doing archaeological surveys in Wyoming and Montana. In fact, for us—owing to the hundreds of hours spent searching for artifacts—looking down at the ground often seems more natural than looking up and ahead.

We stumble across a faint depression, which I allow may have once served as an eagle-catch pit. As improbable as it sounds, an Indian would crouch down in an excavation such as this, cover himself with brush, and put a dead rabbit or other animal on top of the whole affair. And there he would wait, certainly for countless hours on occa-

Projectile point in situ

sion, hoping that an eagle would swoop down to retrieve the offered snack. If and when the eagle did, the Indian would attempt to grab it by the talons and kill it. If successful, the brave owned a new supply of highly valued eagle feathers.

Two hours slip away before we know it, and it's past eleven o'clock. We get into the car, drive back to Logan, then turn west to continue on the frontage road. In 3 miles we pass the right-hand turn to **Missouri Headwaters State Park**, which we plan to visit this afternoon. First, though, we want to grab lunch, and we know from previous trips through the area that there's no better lunch-grabbing place than the **Willow Creek Inn** in tiny Willow Creek. We enter **Three Forks**, drive pass the stately **Sacajawea Inn**, and continue south for 7 miles to Willow Creek. We learn that the restaurant has changed hands since the last time we were here, but the attention to preparing great food remains constant.

Now it's on to Missouri Headwaters State Park, located 3 miles east of Three Forks then 1.5 miles north on Highway 286. The Corps of Discovery found the spot while traveling from a different direction on July 25, 1805. Meriwether Lewis was quite taken by this place where three rivers converge to become the Missouri, writing: " . . . the beds of all these streams are formed of smooth pebble and gravel, and their waters are perfectly transparent; in short they are three noble streams." Lewis and Clark named the "three noble streams" the Madison, Gallatin, and Jefferson. Prior to their arrival, the area was of paramount importance to the Blackfeet, Gros Ventre, and other Indian tribes, serving as a prolific big-game hunting ground. Later, after the Corps of Discovery visited and party members spread the word concerning the area's abundance of fur-bearing animals, the Headwaters quickly became a vital crossroads for the mountain men and others involved in the trapping trade.

Today the confluence is at the heart of a 560-acre state park. It seems to us that the scenery must be little changed since that day nearly 200 years ago when the Corps of Discovery arrived. For its size, less than a mile square, the park encompasses a surprising diversity of terrain and habitat types. The three rivers spawn adjacent wetlands, while farther out spread grassy bottoms. Above those are rocky, desert-like uplands. We read that more than ninety species of birds can be seen at the park at various times of the year.

We hike along an interpretive trail leading high onto a tableland. Among the sparse vegetation growing on the dry mesa is an abundance of prickly pear cactus. Then we amble down to the banks of the Gallatin, where we watch a pair of anglers wading midriff-deep, whipping their magic wands over sparkling waters in hopes of casting a spell on one of the river's copious cutthroat or brown trout.

We wish we were outfitted for camping, after finding that the park features an extremely pleasant campground. Surprisingly, it's only about half full despite that it's the weekend, it's getting late in the day, and the calendar tells us the tourist season should be in full bloom. We have our motel room reserved back in Bozeman, though, where we return after a wonderful day afield. But not before sampling a pair of those sizzling sirloins at the Land of Magic Dinner Club. They are, we find, all they're cracked up to be.

THE "OTHER SIDE" OF THE TETONS AND YELLOWSTONE

Back in West Yellowstone, U.S. Highway 20 leads west out of town, over 7,072-foot Targhee Pass and into Idaho, then drops into the high caldera valley known as **Island Park**. It is hard to guess which is more popular in this recreational paradise: snowmobiling in winter, or fly fishing in summer. The opportunities for both are world-class and, not surprisingly, each activity draws thousands of its respective enthusiasts from near and far. The powder snow can lie 10 feet deep in Island Park in the dead of winter. And here originates the Henrys Fork of the Snake, a legendary river whose very name can send an avid angler into his or her own dream world. Some profess that the Henrys Fork is *the* finishing school for fly fishers. The river's trout are huge, smart, and notoriously tough to tempt with an artificial fly.

WEST YELLOWSTONE TO JACKSON: A NARRATIVE ACCOUNT

At around six o'clock yesterday afternoon Nancy and I drove into West Yellowstone, where we joined friend Connie for a good supper at the

Stage Coach Inn. We stayed the night at her house in anticipation of spending the next three on the ground, camping, as we meander back toward our home in Teton Valley, Idaho. The direct-route distance is only a little over 100 miles, but there's a lot to see off the main highway. This trip is a bit unusual for us: It seems that the last places we ever think of visiting are those closest to home. We plan to stay at Forest Service campgrounds, which, because it is midweek, should have sites available. The same campgrounds will probably be full to overflowing next weekend, as they are most weekends in July and August.

Dropping out of the timber from Targhee Pass, we look out across **Island Park** and see lofty **Sawtell Peak**, snowcapped and satellite-tower-tipped, rising on the other side of the flats. The mountain, an isolated remnant of the rim that once encircled the Island Park Caldera, was named for Gilman Sawtell, a pioneer Island Park stock grower and entrepreneur. Sawtell was the first white man to live along Henrys Lake, where he settled in the late 1860s.

On the state road map Island Park is represented by a small circle, the symbol for a distinct town, but everyone I know refers to the entire valley as Island Park. The "town" of Island Park is more like a 30-mile-long string of enterprises—from fishing outfitters and pottery shops to cabin accommodations and convenience stores—lining the highway. It is an area of rather unsettling contrast, where natural beauty mixes with human-made havoc. We drive across the bridge spanning the Henrys Fork, and look out to see anglers in float boats and others walking in waders. Not far from the fishermen in the pristine, window-clear water bob Canada geese, several kinds of ducks, and a pair of stunning white trumpeter swans. Meanwhile, much of the surrounding commercial development looks just the opposite of pristine; it is disheveled and obviously not part of any organized plan.

Nancy reads aloud from a roadside-history guide, informing me that the name Island Park dates back to the 1890s, when the Yellowstone stage made a regular rest stop here, within a timber-surrounded opening that reminded someone of an island. At the **Sawtell Resort** we turn east onto Forest Road 059 toward Big Springs, zip past the local golf course, and cross a bridge spanning

what a sign informs us is the Henrys Lake outlet. From the bridge two young girls and three boys with spinning rods make casts with varying degrees of skill and success. They stand so close together that we wonder how, or if, they're managing not to catch each other before their hooks and lures find the water. In another couple of miles we pull into the **Big Springs Campground**, where we have no trouble finding a pleasant, pine-protected campsite. Almost before I shut off the engine of the Jeep a gray-haired campground host is there to welcome us, and to warn us of recent black bear problems. Just last night, she says, a modern-day Yogi ripped apart a picnic basket left outside by some campers. She asks us to please be sure to keep a clean camp, wash the dishes after supper, and store food in the car overnight.

Although the day was sunny and warm, probably 80 degrees, by six o'clock the air is already bracing. We can feel that it is going to get chilly tonight, maybe even below freezing. The soothing scent of pine is rich in the cool high-country air. After setting up the tent we follow the short hiking trail to **Big Springs**, which is adjacent to the campground. The deep water is absolutely clear. We read that the springs, which form the headwaters of the Henrys Fork, flow out of the Yellowstone aquifer. Daily, more than 400 million gallons emerge at a reliable 52 degrees Fahrenheit, an ideal temperature for trout to thrive. As if on cue, some of the largest rainbow trout we've ever seen swim about below the bridge. Maybe the key to their size and longevity is that they can read: A nearby sign informs us that the area is closed to fishing.

The log cabin once resided in by Johnny Sack sits on the far side of the springs; to its right, looking like a leprechaun's lodge, is a miniature version of the cabin. The smaller structure is a pump house, and beside it, at water's level, is a water wheel. Johnny Sack, who might have *been* a leprechaun—he stood barely 5 feet tall—was an early-twentieth-century Island Park oxymoron, an ebullient and sociable hermit who loved to host company. Sack built his home by hand here at Big Springs in 1932. After he died in 1957, the Forest Service planned to destroy the sound, picturesque structures, but a local outcry led to intervention by U.S. Senator James McClure of Idaho. The upshot: Not only does Sack's cabin still stand proudly at

Big Springs today, but it resides on the National Register of Historic Places, as well.

As twilight nears, Nancy and I stroll down the boardwalk leading along the springs' outlet. Lining the banks of the glimmering, transparent stream are several sturdy-looking vacation cabins of classic log construction, backed by huge conifers. It's about as pretty a setting as we can imagine.

Morning has arrived, and we had no bear problems last night. I should know, because I laid awake most of the night worrying and waiting for the bruin's visit. The springs and the campground are so pleasant that we almost decide to linger for another day. But instead, we break camp and load up. After a good country breakfast at the **Island Park Lodge**, we're ready for a long, hard day of sight-seeing. We drive south for a few miles then turn off the highway into **Harriman State Park**. From the parking area/trailhead at the end of the park's lone road, we follow a flat, wide hiking trail that leads for several hundred yards to the historic structures of the Railroad Ranch. The meadow lying between us and the nearby Henrys Fork practically explodes with wildflowers. A bald eagle soars overhead. Off to our right we watch as a cow moose, standing in shallow water, submerges her entire head and then brings it out again. Her face is wringing wet and she's chewing on a mouthful of something. We think she looks ridiculous, but we're not getting any closer to tell her so.

Among the several old cabins and buildings gracing the expansive lawns of the ranch is an old cookhouse, which today is being used by a Mormon Church youth group from Rexburg. A pair of women on horses canter by and say howdy. We inspect a sign that describes the park's hiking and equestrian trails, and also depicts several miles of trails that are groomed in winter for cross-country skiing.

It is an unusually peaceful spot. Harriman State Park is the namesake of the family of Averell Harriman, who was a primary owner of the Union Pacific Railroad and whose Idaho legacy also includes the Sun Valley Resort. At the turn of the century the wealthy Guggenheim family was the majority owner of what at that time was called the Island Park Land and Cattle Company. Harriman and Charles Jones, of the Atlantic Richfield Company, were minor shareholders in the enterprise. Guests of the time included the

conservationist John Muir, who spent a relaxing ten days at the ranch in 1913. The Harrimans eventually garnered all the shares in the ranch, which progressively became less of a cattle ranch and more of a nature retreat. Reluctant to think of their beloved ranch someday falling into the hands of developers, Averell, Gladys, and Roland Harriman in 1961 willed their Railroad Ranch to the state of Idaho. The gift was contingent on several stipulations, including that the state agree to permanently preserve habitat here for trumpeter swans. The ranch was finally deeded to the state in 1977 and opened to the public as Harriman State Park in the early 1980s.

The bustling highway is too much to bear after our quiet interlude at Harriman, so we head back north for a short way on the main road then turn east onto the pothole-abundant **Mesa Falls Scenic Byway**. The traffic immediately dwindles to nothing. It strikes me how odd it is that people will bypass fascinating back roads such as this in their mad scramble to get to where everyone else is going. Vacations really should be about slowing down, not hurrying around. Anyway, that's what I think.

We pull into the **Upper Mesa Falls** overlook. Adjacent to the parking area stands a 1907 lodge undergoing renovation. Nancy muses about how grand it must have been to overnight here, while traveling to Yellowstone in a horse-drawn stage. In the parking lot a young woman on a touring bicycle asks us, in a heavy French accent, how far it is to Yellowstone. (About 50 miles.) A hard-surfaced trail leads us on a short walk to an observation deck. Here the Henrys Fork storms violently over a drop of more than 100 feet. We can feel the mist. The falls reminds us of how deceptively innocuous millions of gallons of water can seem when flowing at a low gradient, like that which the Henrys Fork maintains through Island Park. Add a simple break in the geology and some gravity, and you've got raw power unleashed.

Late afternoon surprises us by arriving so soon. A few miles before rejoining the main highway, we pull into the **Warm River Campground**. It's one of the nicest Forest Service campgrounds we've visited. There's even a large covered canopy in the adjacent picnic area, probably used for gatherings such as family reunions. Kids splash in the shallow water of the river, which runs directly in front of some of the sites. The river is anything but warm, we soon find out.

They really must train their campground hosts to be vigilant in these parts, because again we're immediately greeted. The older gentleman eyes the mountain bikes resting on our car rack, and asks if we've ridden the old Union Pacific Railroad grade, which he says is accessible here. We haven't, but we do. The tracks are gone, and the gentle grade leads us on a dirt surface upstream along the Warm River, which becomes a jumble of whitewater as the canyon narrows. After 3 miles we pedal through a quarter-mile long, timber-supported tunnel, where the temperature feels at least twenty degrees cooler than out in the hot sun. After another 3 miles of uphill travel we arrive at a closed gate and decide to turn around, even though the host told us the rail-trail continues all the way to West Yellowstone. First, though, we inspect a wall of volcanic rock where a cut was made for the railroad tracks. Names accompanied by dates as old as 1909 are etched in the stone, no doubt the handiwork of pioneer Yellowstone-bound tourists.

The next morning we ascend from the rugged canyon where the Warm River meets the Henrys Fork and, just like that, we're in green, rolling farm country. We pass the left-hand turn that leads to the isolated **Bechler Entrance** in the southwest corner of Yellowstone. Then we cross the **Ashton-Flagg Road**, which cuts between Yellowstone and Grand Teton national parks to emerge at the Flagg Ranch.

The community of **Ashton** reminds us of a small Midwest farm town that has seen better days. A filling station attendant tells us that they serve a great burger at the restaurant west of the railroad tracks; after verifying his claim, we follow the signs leading south and east to the **Aspen Acres** golf course. The trip takes us on a dizzying maze of rural gravel roads. Just as we start suspecting we've been wild-goose chased, we come upon the golf course. What a find! It's a short, rustic eighteen-hole course that looks as if it may have materialized soon after a potato farmer, enduring one too many bad years, decided his land would be better suited to golfing than tilling. Aspen Acres also incorporates a very pleasant campground/RV park, with broad aspens providing a surplus of shade. By the settled-in looks of

Barleyfields, outside Driggs, Idaho

many of the recreational vehicles parked in the sites, we guess that retired folks must spend their summers here at this laid-back spot, then head south before the snow flies. This is a place we definitely plan to return to, golf clubs and camping gear in tow.

The road heading south from Ashton toward Driggs is a sports-car driver's dream: left and right it twists, and up and down, like a roller coaster. We serpentine through fields of barley and wheat that are green-turning-golden in early August, and which undulate in the wind like ocean waves. The road passes through the ghostly remains of former settlements, whose stores and post offices were vital to early settlers in this hard-winter country before the advent of modern transportation and communications. In the distance we see the unmistakable Teton peaks, rising above **Teton Valley**.

There is a quiet but persistent debate between the residents of Jackson Hole and Teton Valley, regarding which is the "front" side of the Tetons. Wyomingites claim the east side is the front: After all, Jackson Hole is where most of Grand Teton

National Park is located, so it is far more heavily visited than Teton Valley. And the mountains do jut more dramatically into the sky along the east front. Teton Valley residents—of which I am one (but entirely unbiased, of course)—counter, accurately, that it was the view from the west side, the perspective Nancy and I enjoy as we drive along, that gave the mountains their name. The mountains were called *les Trois Tetons* by early-nineteenth-century French-Iroquois trappers traveling through Teton Valley, obviously because the peaks reminded them of something. They look like something altogether different when viewed from the east side. In fact, an earlier name, the Pilots Knobs, was given the peaks when they were seen from that side. (*See* History for more details.)

It seems simple to me: the mountains are known as the Tetons and not the Pilots Knobs, so the west side is the front of the Tetons.

We drive through **Driggs**, a once-simple farm community now making the stressful transition into a ski town. **Grand Targhee Ski Resort** is 12 miles east from here, back across the Wyoming border. Nancy and I discuss heading up there for supper, but instead opt to continue to Jackson Hole before ending our trip. From the friendly village of **Victor** we wind into the pine and fir stands of the Targhee National Forest and begin the steep pull up Teton Pass. At the top I gear down for the even steeper descent into tiny Wilson. Here we swing into the **Otto Brothers Brewing Company**, which occupies a cozy old log cabin nestled between the hardware store and the fire station. Nancy samples a small glass of Old Faithful Ale, and I opt for the poetically named Moose Juice Stout. Then we continue toward Jackson, watching as the late-afternoon sun illuminates the **Sleeping Indian** formation of distant Sheep Mountain, which rises just above the top of the much closer West Gros Ventre Butte. We turn left onto Spring Gulch Road and wind for two miles up East Gros Ventre Butte to the **Spring Creek** resort, where we enjoy a gorgeous sunset and a memorable dinner at **The Granary** restaurant.

The view of the back side of the Tetons from here is stunning.

⸻⌁⌁⌁⌁⌁ Staying There

Jackson Hole and Teton National Park

Jackson Hole is a convenient and logical place to begin your wanderings through Yellowstone-Teton Country. The valley overflows with dining, lodging, shopping, and sight-seeing opportunities, it claims an airport with car-rental outlets, and it is in close proximity to Grand Teton and Yellowstone national parks. (In fact, Grand Teton National Park covers a fair share of Jackson Hole. A re-reminder: Jackson is the town and Jackson Hole the larger valley containing the town.)

Jackson Hole boasts at least fifty motels, fifteen bed and breakfast establishments, twenty guest ranches, and countless townhouse and condominium rentals. Even so, unclaimed rooms can be rare during the busy summer and ski seasons. Advance room reservations should be secured if you'll be visiting between June and Labor Day or between mid-December and late March. Plenty of rooms go vacant at other times of the year, when the cost of renting them also drops—by more than half in some cases. Regardless of the time of year, don't forget to inquire about discounts if you're a member of AAA, AARP, or another organization that may qualify you for a room-rate reduction.

Restaurants, likewise, sprout throughout Jackson Hole, with particular concentrations in Jackson, Wilson, and Teton Village. Eateries come and go, but most of those listed here have been in operation long enough to qualify as old standbys.

LODGING

In Jackson

The Alpine House Bed & Breakfast. 285 North Glenwood. This Scandinavian-style lodge of timber-frame construction is located in a quiet corner of Jackson, close to the Jackson Hole Historical Society's research center, yet it is very convenient to the Town Square. Radiant floor heat, down comforters, and rugged country-style furniture are among the niceties. Each of seven airy rooms claims French doors opening onto an exterior balcony. Breakfast consists of fresh breads, waffles and pancakes, yogurt, fresh fruit, and bracing black coffee. The living room, where guests are urged to dawdle, includes a library brimming with books on adventure and mountaineering. If one of those books inspires you, hosts Hans and Nancy Johnstone also arrange and guide winter and summer backcountry trips. Both are both former Olympic Nordic skiers for the U.S. Ski Team, and Hans leads climbs for Exum Mountain Guides. Telephone: (307) 739–1570 or, toll-free in the United States, (800) 753–1421. Expensive.

Angler's Inn. 265 North Millward, two blocks from the Town Square. The Angler's twenty-eight units are decorated in "Rocky Mountain fishing camp" style, with lodgepole furniture and wrought-iron lamps, and they also include refrigerators and microwaves. Telephone: (307) 733–3682 or, toll–free in the United States, (800) 867–4667. Moderate to expensive.

Cowboy Village Resort. Just off West Broadway at 120 South Flat Creek Drive. Individual log cabins situated in the middle of Jackson, within walking distance of the Town Square. The cabins feature kitchenettes and covered outdoor decks, with picnic tables and grills. The small resort also has Jacuzzis and a pavilion perfect for reunions, parties, and small meetings. Telephone: (307) 733-3121 or, toll-free in the United States, (800) 962-4988. Expensive to very expensive.

Davy Jackson Inn. 85 Perry Avenue. Mountain man Davy Jackson never had it so good, at least not while trapping in his namesake valley of Jackson Hole. A full country breakfast and afternoon tea are two of the indulgences designed to spoil guests to the maximum. This luxurious country inn is within a short walk of the Town Square. Telephone: (307) 739-2294 or, toll-free in the United States, (800) 584-0532. Very expensive.

Flat Creek Motel. 1935 North Highway 89. A rather plain motel and consequently a reasonably priced one, by Jackson Hole standards anyway, located just north of the bustle of town, near the National Elk Refuge and the National Museum of Wildlife Art. Rooms feature fully equipped kitchens and the motel has a hot tub and sauna room. Telephone: (307) 733-5276 or, toll-free in the United States, (800) 438-9338. Very inexpensive to moderate.

Huff House Inn Bed and Breakfast. 240 East Deloney, two blocks east of the Town Square. Built in 1917 for Charles W. Huff, one of the valley's fist doctors, the Huff House is now an inn boasting five guest rooms; with private baths, and four guest cottages. The cost of renting a room or cottage includes a family-style breakfast and use of the inn's hot tub. Telephone: (307) 733-4164. Expensive to very expensive.

The Lodge at Jackson Hole. 80 Scott Lane, just off West Broadway and adjacent to the Gun Barrel Steak and Game House. Known for its whimsical carved bears, which are found in the most unexpected places, this new Best Western motel features 154 mini-suites, some replete with fireplaces and oversize jetted baths. Telephone:

(307) 739-9703 or, toll-free in the United States, (800) 458-3866. Expensive to very expensive.

Motel 6. 1370 West Broadway. Not all of the accommodations in Jackson Hole are exquisite and expensive. The economy-room franchises have found their niche in the valley, too, as evidenced by this motel, where they keep the lights on and you know exactly what to expect when you walk into your room. Telephone: (307) 733-1620 or, toll-free in the United States, (800) 466-8356. Very inexpensive to inexpensive.

Painted Buffalo Inn. 400 West Broadway. Good, clean accommodations located convenient to downtown Jackson. Kids stay for free. Telephone: (307) 733-4340 or, toll-free in the United States, (800) 288-3866. Inexpensive to expensive.

Parkway Inn Best Western. 125 North Jackson. Country elegance, with Victorian suites available, nestled in a quiet niche just 3 blocks from the Town Square. The inn includes an extensive spa and exercise facility, with hot tubs, sauna, swimming pool, and gym. Telephone: (307) 733-3143 or, toll-free in the United States, (800) 528-1234. Expensive to very expensive.

Snow King Resort. 400 East Snow King Avenue. Conference resort situated at the foot of Snow King Mountain. Two restaurants reside within the hotel: Gourmet dinners are served at Rafferty's, and all three meals are dished out informally in The Atrium. The Shady Lady, with its regular live-music performances, is one of Jackson's kickin'-est night spots. Telephone: (307) 733-5200 or, toll-free in the United States, (800) 522-KING (5464). Expensive to very expensive.

Super 8 Motel. Located on U.S. Highway 89, three blocks south of the State Highway 22 junction. Another old reliable. Telephone: (307) 733-6833 or, toll-free in the United States, (800) 800-8000. Inexpensive to expensive.

The Virginian Lodge. 750 West Broadway. The spread-out Virginian encompasses 170 deluxe rooms with a 104-site RV park to boot. Rooms vary from hotel rooms to cozy Jacuzzi suites and larger two-room suites with kitchenettes. Also on-site are the Virginian Saloon, Smoky's Restaurant, a full liquor store, a beauty salon, a 5,000-square-foot conference center, and an office of Old Faithful Snowmobile Tours. The ample grounds fronting the lodge host various events throughout the summer, ranging from canoe and outdoor-gear sales to vintage auto shows. Telephone: (307) 733–2792 or, toll-free in the United States, (800) 262–4999. Inexpensive to expensive.

Wort Hotel. Located downtown at the corner of Glenwood and Broadway. The landmark Wort Hotel, built in the early 1940s, is to Jackson as the Stage Coach Inn is to West Yellowstone; in fact, they were designed by the same Idaho Falls architect. After a fire destroyed much of the hotel in 1980, the Wort rose like a phoenix. The hotel's tavern, a hopping nightspot popular with both visitors and out-on-the-town locals, features 2,032 uncirculated 1921 silver dollars inlaid into the aptly named Silver Dollar Bar. All three meals of the day can be taken in JJ's Silverdollar Grill, with some of Jackson's best prime rib a dinner specialty. Telephone: (307) 733–2190 or, toll-free in the United States, (800) 322–2727. Very expensive.

Red Lion Wyoming Inn. 930 West Broadway. Country-style lodge with a distinct Western flair. A large share of the seventy-three deluxe rooms have gas fireplaces, Jacuzzi baths, and/or fully equipped kitchenettes. Extra touches include wool blankets, feather pillows, and continental breakfast served in the light and airy breakfast room. Telephone: (307) 734–0035 or, toll-free in the United States, (800) 844–0035. Moderate to very expensive.

Out of Town in Jackson Hole

Alpenhof Lodge. Nestled at the base of the tram in Teton Village. Bavarian-style hotel encompassing the popular, four-star Alpenhof Dining Room and the more laid-back Alpenhof Bistro. Deluxe rooms boast hand-built furnishings from Bavaria; some have fireplaces. If your primary purpose for visiting is to ski at the Jackson Hole Mountain Resort, the convenient location of the Alpenhof Lodge is unsurpassed. Telephone: (307) 733–3242 or, toll-free in the United States, (800) 732–3244. Expensive to very expensive.

Cowboy Village Resort at Togwotee. Located an hour from Jackson, east of Moran Junction on U.S. Highway 287. More than fifty new log cabins hug the woods surrounding the main lodge, which holds a dining room, the Red Fox Saloon, and three dozen guest rooms. Hiking, mountain biking, horseback riding, and fishing opportunities abound in the surrounding Bridger-Teton National Forest. The resort is a popular spot in winter for snowmobilers, who know that some of the best "sledding" terrain in the Northern Rockies is found on and around nearby Togwotee Pass. Snowmobile rentals are available, and dogsled outings can also be arranged. Telephone: (307) 733–8800 or, toll-free in the United States, (800) 543–2847. Expensive to very expensive (prices are all-inclusive, including three meals per day).

Grand Teton Lodge Company. Established by park benefactor John D. Rockefeller Jr., the Grand Teton Lodge Company maintains the three following lodging complexes in Grand Teton National Park. In keeping with national park tradition, all rooms lack television. The lodges are open mid-May through mid-October. Telephone: (307) 543–2855 or, toll-free in the United States, (800) 628–9988.

Jackson Lake Lodge. Historic full-service resort residing on a bluff above Jackson Lake and in view of the full run of the Teton Range. The main lodge has three dozen guest rooms, and more than 300 cottage rooms are located on the surrounding grounds. Rocky Mountain cuisine is served in the Mural Room, with lighter meals available in the Pioneer Grill. Among the activities and amenities: horseback riding, Snake River float trips, Western clothing shops, and an outdoor swimming pool. Conference facilities can host up to 500, May–June and September–October. Expensive to very expensive.

Jenny Lake Lodge. Centrally located in the park near Jenny Lake. This rustic, yet luxurious and exclusive hideaway is worthy of the rare double it has scored, earning both the Mobil Four Star and the AAA Four-Diamond rating. Three dozen cabins surrounding the log-cabin main lodge are tucked into peaceful glades in view of the Tetons. Included in the price of renting one of Jenny Lake Lodge's Old West–style cabins are breakfast, a six-course gourmet dinner served in the lodge, and the use of horses and bicycles. Very expensive.

Colter Bay Village. Located near the shores of Jackson Lake, Colter Bay Village has it all—almost, anyway. The array of accommodations includes economical canvas-and-log tent cabins, which make their occupants feel like pioneer Yellowstone-Teton Country sagebrushers. Also at the village: a full-service marina with boat rentals, guided fishing trips, and scenic cruises; a pair of family-style restaurants (the Chuckwagon and the John Colter Cafe Court); a grocery store; gift shops; horses for hire; and a big RV park and campground, with a special section reserved for tenters. At Colter Bay Village you will also find a National Park Service visitor center/Indian Arts Museum and an amphitheater. Very inexpensive to expensive.

The Inn at Jackson Hole. Situated in Teton Village at 3345 West McCollister Drive. This Best Western facility with ski-in convenience from the aerial tram at the Jackson Hole Mountain Resort, features eighty-three guest rooms, many including kitchenettes, fireplaces, and loft suites. Ski lockers and a tuning shop, conference facilities, and sauna and hot tubs are also on-site. Expensive to very expensive. Telephone: (307) 733–2311 or, toll-free in the United States, (800) 842–7666.

Spring Creek. Located two miles above Spring Gulch Road, north off State Highway 22. This full-service, high-end resort offers a choice of hotel rooms or spacious, fully equipped condominiums with rock fireplaces. The four-star Granary restaurant also is located here. Horseback riding, tennis, and swimming are available at the resort in summer; popular winter activities include sleigh rides and skiing on groomed cross-country trails. Telephone: (307) 733–8833 or, toll-free in the United States, (800) 443–6139. Very expensive (as much as $1,200 a night during high season for the most lavish of lodgings—but that does include breakfast!).

Teton Pines. West off Teton Village Road at 3450 North Clubhouse Drive. Luxury country club suites located on the Teton Pines Golf Course. Tennis and swimming, along with fly-fishing lessons from the illustrious angler Jack Dennis, are available in summer; in winter the golf course transforms into a cross-country skiing center. Located only five minutes from the Jackson Hole Mountain Resort. A bar and the Grille at the Pines, a good restaurant serving fresh seafood daily, are situated within the sumptuous clubhouse. Telephone: (307) 733–1005 or, toll-free in the United States, (800) 238–2223. Very expensive.

Colter Bay

Vacation Rentals. A veritable city of Jackson Hole houses and condominiums, many of them part-time residences of the owners, are available to rent by the night or week. Locations include Teton Shadows, the Aspens/Racquet Club, Teton Village, and within the city limits of Jackson. Call Black Diamond Vacation Rentals at (800) 325–8605, Jackson Hole Property Management at (800) 443–8613, or Teton Village Property Management at (800) 443–6840. Prices vary widely.

Guest Ranches. Jackson Hole's vacation trade is built on a foundation of dude ranches, and several classics are still going strong. Single overnights are sometimes available, but most guest ranches operate on the all-inclusive, multi-day basis, with group meals served in a main lodge. Horseback riding, wrangling, float trips, backcountry outings, Dutch-oven cookouts, fishing, photography, and fireside sing-alongs are common activities. Most also offer guided elk hunts in the autumn. Rates typically are in the very expensive range. Among the ranches:

Darwin Ranch. Nestled on the upper reaches of the Gros Ventre River east of Jackson Hole. This one of the most isolated and hard-to-reach guest ranches in the lower forty-eight states, in one of the most glorious settings you'll ever work hard to find. A maximum of eighteen guests at a time share the remote mountain valley with elk, bear, and other animals. Telephone: (307) 733–5588.

Heart Six Ranch. Located 35 miles northeast of Jackson in the Buffalo River Valley. Extensive children's program, and plenty for adults to do, too. The five-day backcountry fishing trips are popular. Telephone: (307) 543–2477.

Lost Creek Ranch. Located outside Moose. Tastefully furnished deluxe cabins, celebrated cuisine, and sumptuous main lodge. Attention to detail is Lost Creek's trademark. Telephone: (307) 733–3435.

Moose Head Ranch. Family-run outfit within Grand Teton National Park. Modern cabins, delectable fare, and fly-fishing ponds; maximum of forty guests at a time. (307) 733–3141.

Red Rock Ranch. Situated 30 miles northeast of Jackson in the Gros Ventre River drainage. Dudes can even take part in the ranch's fall cattle roundups. Telephone: (307) 733–6288.

Triangle X Ranch. Working cattle and dude ranch located 26 miles northeast of Jackson, within Grand Teton National Park. The Triangle X has been run by the same family for more than six decades. Telephone: (307) 733–2183.

Turpin Meadow Ranch. Nestled in the Buffalo River Valley, east of Moran Junction. Covered-wagon cowboy cookouts are a special highlight for guests here. Telephone: (307) 543–2496 or, toll-free in the United States, (800) 743–2496.

Housekeeping Cabins. Here's another popular way to "do the Hole thing." These housekeeping cabins might be considered a cross between a guest ranch and standard motel. The settings are rural and the cabins Old West rustic, but guests find their own entertainment and prepare their own grub.

Mad Dog Ranch Cabins. Six miles northwest of Jackson. Two-bedroom cabins, with an outdoor hot tub on the premises. Telephone: (307) 733–3729 or, toll-free in the United States, (800) 992–2246. Expensive to very expensive.

Spur Ranch Log Cabins. Located adjacent to and operated by Dornan's in Moose. There's never a shortage of activity at Dornan's; among the possibilities are hootenannies, chuck wagon meals, canoe rentals, horseback riding, shopping, and a great selection of wines. Cabins are available with one or two bedrooms. Telephone: (307) 733–2522. Expensive.

Twin Creek Cabins. Quietly located northeast of Jackson across the National Elk Refuge. Seven log cabins of various sizes, sleeping between two and eight persons. Cabins include kitchens and wood stoves. Recreation area includes grills, volleyball, horseshoe pits, and a playground. Available by the week. Telephone: (307) 733–3927. Moderate to expensive.

CAMPGROUNDS AND RV PARKS
Private

A-1 Campground. Located in the town of Jackson at 125 South Virginian. Telephone: (307) 733–2697.

Flagg Ranch Resort. Situated just south of the South Entrance of Yellowstone National Park, this is the granddaddy of Yellowstone-Teton Country camping resorts. Flagg Ranch includes RV and tent sites, cabin rentals, and an impressive new lodge containing a grocery, restaurant, pub, and espresso bar. The enterprise even offers shuttles to and from Jackson and the Jackson Hole Airport. Come winter, it serves as a launching point for snowmobile tours in and around Yellowstone National Park. Open June 1 through October 15 and December 20 through March 15. Telephone: (307) 543–2861 or, toll-free in the United States, (800) 443–2311.

Grand Teton Park KOA. Located east of Moran Junction on U.S. Highway 287. Telephone: (307) 733–1980.

Jackson Hole Campground. Located south of town on U.S. Highway 89 South. Open year-round. Telephone: (307) 733–2927.

Teton Village KOA. Located north of State Highway 22 on Teton Village Road. In addition to the RV and tent sites, the campground includes several economical KOA Kamping Kabins outfitted to sleep from four to six. Telephone: (307) 733–5354.

Virginian RV Park. Located in the thick of things, beside the Virginian Lodge at 750 West Broadway in Jackson. Telephone: (307) 733–2792.

Wagon Wheel Campground. 525 North Cache in Jackson. Telephone: (307) 733–4588.

U.S. Forest Service

Call the Bridger-Teton National Forest at (307) 739–5500 for campground information or 800–280–CAMP [2267] for information on reservations:

Curtis Canyon. Delightfully isolated campground sitting high above Jackson Hole, seven miles northeast of Jackson on gravel roads. The surrounding area is tops for mountain biking, hiking, and "wildflowering."

Atherton Creek. On the Gros Ventre Road, 20 miles northeast of Jackson.

Hatchet. East of Moran Junction on U.S. Highway 287, 40 miles from Jackson.

Cabin Creek. West of Hoback Junction on U.S. Highway 89, near Astoria Hot Springs, 19 miles from Jackson.

Granite Creek. Adjacent to Granite Hot Springs, 35 miles southeast of Jackson (10 miles on gravel).

National Park Service

Call Grand Teton National Park at (307) 739–3603 for information:

Jenny Lake. Twenty miles north of Jackson. Tents only.

Signal Mountain. On Jackson Lake, 32 miles north of Jackson. Includes tenter-only sites.

Colter Bay. On Jackson Lake, 40 miles north of Jackson. Tenters, RVers, and trailer campers are segregated.

Lizard Creek. On Jackson Lake, 48 miles north of Jackson. This quiet campground resembles area Forest Service campgrounds more than it does the somewhat crowded camping conditions you'll find at places such as Colter Bay and Signal Mountain.

John D. Rockefeller Jr. Parkway. Eight primitive, relatively little-used camping sites are distributed along the first seven miles of the Ashton-Flagg Road, a dirt byway heading west from Flagg Ranch.

FOOD

Some restaurants close or operate on reduced schedules during the shoulder seasons, so call ahead if visiting at those times.

Billy's Burgers. Billy's, an adjunct to the Cadillac Grille, is located across from the Town Square on North Cache. Telephone: (307) 733–3279. Betcha can't—or shouldn't, anyway—eat more than one of the monster half-pound burgers served here. Plain or with cheese, and with all the trimmings, the scrumptious burgers are served alongside a mountain of custom-cut French fries. Lunch and dinner. Inexpensive.

The Bunnery. Located in the Hole-in-the-Wall Mall at 130 North Cache Street. Telephone: (307) 733–5474. A bakery-restaurant combination that's long been a breakfast tradition in Jackson. The Glory Bowl, named for a famous avalanche zone near Teton Pass, is a mouth-watering mix of homefries topped with fried eggs, which in turn is smothered with mushrooms and Swiss cheese, then broiled. The Gros Ventre Slide is another popular breakfast dish that slides down easy and is named after another famous slide area (this one a landslide). Light dinner in summer only; breakfast and lunch year-round. Inexpensive.

Bubba's Bar-B-Que. 515 West Broadway. Telephone: (307) 733–2288. Very popular family-oriented eatery that makes a good place to grab a quick bite that will stay with you during a long day of sight-seeing. House specialties are traditional Texas-style barbecue beef and hickory-smoked ribs and chicken. Breakfast, lunch, and dinner. Inexpensive.

Cadillac Grille. Across from the Town Square at 55 North Cache. Telephone: (307) 733–3279. Good food served in a relaxed, 1940s art deco atmosphere. The Cadillac features elegantly crafted creations involving seafood, pasta, steaks, and wild game. To name a trio: red chili roasted caribou, T-bone steak with roasted garlic and peppercorn sauce, and stuffed Dakota pheasant breast in a boysenberry-Merlot sauce. Lunch and dinner. Moderate to expensive.

Calico Italian Restaurant. North of State Highway 22 on Teton Village Road, across from the Teton Pines resort. Telephone: (307) 733–2460. This longtime valley establishment specializes in custom pizzas and other things Italian, including spaghetti Bolognese, veal scallopini, and linguine with fresh spinach. Pre- or post-meal, adults can enjoy the full bar with pool table while the kids romp on the restaurant's expansive grounds. Dinner only. Inexpensive to moderate.

The Granary. Located at the Spring Creek resort, north of State Highway 22 off Spring Gulch Road. Telephone: (307) 733-8833. The good food served at the Granary—buffalo tenderloin, Colorado lamb, and much more—is surpassed only by the restaurant's view, which is stupendous from its setting atop East Gros Ventre Butte. Because of the view, the Granary is also a popular cocktail stop for sunset-gazers. (Spring Creek also operates the Rising Sage Cafe, located within the National Museum of Wildlife Art complex.) Breakfast, lunch, and dinner. Expensive.

The Gun Barrel Steak and Game House. 862 West Broadway. Telephone: (307) 733–EATS (3287). Wild game, fresh fish, and tender steaks are grilled to perfection over an open river-rock mesquite grill. The Western ambience is palpable within the fishing and hunting lodge-like setting, which is filled with wood, rock, and stuffed animals. Extensive selection of draft beers. Dinner only. Moderate to expensive.

Jedediah's House of Sourdough. On Broadway 1 block east of the Town Square. Telephone: (307) 733–5671. This popular breakfast stop, occupying an old log cabin adorned with historic photos and trapping artifacts, specializes in sourdough pancakes. Dinner in summer only; breakfast and lunch year-round. Inexpensive to moderate.

Jenny Leigh's. Located in Teton Village at the Inn at Jackson Hole. Telephone: (307) 733–7102. Jenny Leigh's is the namesake of the first Indian wife of mountain man and guide Richard "Beaver Dick" Leigh. Appropriately, the restaurant specializes in wild-vittle dishes, such as bison steak with fried onions, and elk steak with lignonberries in green peppercorn sauce. Breakfast, lunch, and dinner. Moderate to expensive.

Lame Duck Chinese Restaurant. 680 East Broadway. Telephone: (307) 733–4311. Here, at one of Jackson's most popular ethnic restaurants, a host of poetically named dishes are prepared: Eggs in a Cloud, for instance, and Saigon Surprise, and Five Stars Around the Moon.

Among the establishment's specialties are Thai food and several varieties of sushi; super mai-tais and hot sake are some of the sipping possibilities. Private tearooms are available by reservation. Dinner only. Inexpensive to moderate.

Merry Piglets. On North Cache, 1½ blocks north of the town square. Telephone: (307) 733–2966. This popular hangout for locals and visitors has been serving handmade Mexican and Tex-Mex fare for nearly three decades. Mesquite-grilled fajitas are a house favorite. Eat in or carry out. Lunch and dinner. Inexpensive.

Million Dollar Cowboy Steakhouse. Across from the Town Square on North Cache in the basement of the Million Dollar Cowboy Bar. Telephone: (307) 733–4790. Choice cuts of Midwest beef are served in a setting highlighted by Western art and burled lodgepole pine. Other menu items include salmon, lobster, elk, and pheasant, and the bar specializes in microbrews and single-malt scotches. Dinner only. Moderate to expensive.

Mountain High Pizza Pie. Located 1 block west of the Town Square at 120 West Broadway. Telephone: (307)733–3646. Terrific pizza made with fresh dough, real cheese, and some out-of-the-ordinary toppings. Pizza lovers can pick from traditional, whole-wheat, or deep-dish crusts; pizzaphobics can choose from a more extensive menu featuring Italian-style goodies like calzone, stromboli, and subs. Lunch and dinner. Inexpensive.

Nora's Fish Creek Inn. Located in Wilson on the south side of State Highway 22. Telephone: (307) 733–8288. Nora's, a rustic and relaxing restaurant in slow-paced Wilson, vies with one or two others for the title of "most popular breakfast spot in Jackson Hole." Steaks, seafood, pasta, and other favorites are prepared for supper. Breakfast, lunch, and dinner. Inexpensive to moderate.

The Range. 225 North Cache, 2 blocks north of the Town Square. Telephone: (307) 733–5481. One of a handful of Jackson's true gourmet restaurants, the Range is a good choice for a romantic and/or unhurried dinner. Regional specialties are prepared before your eyes in an exhibition-style kitchen. A pair of menu samplers: roasted loin of elk in a huck-leberry glaze with wild rice pancakes, and roasted duck breast with sun-dried berries and jalapeño spaetzle. Mmmmmm. Dinner only. Expensive.

Snake River Grill. On the town square. Telephone: (307) 733–0557. *Snow Country* magazine included this intimate restaurant in an article entitled "Beyond Buffalo Burgers" and subtitled, "These eight ski-town restaurants rival Manhattan's best." Whether you choose the spicy grilled swordfish, free-range veal, grilled loin lamb chops, antelope braised with pearl onions and anchovies—or one of a host of other options—you're guaranteed a memorable dining experience at the Snake River Grill. Dinner only. Expensive.

Sweetwater Grill. Located in Jackson at the corner of King and Pearl. Telephone: (307) 733–3553. Come summertime, the Sweetwater is one of the most popular and enjoyable lunch and early dinner stops in town. There's ample outdoor seating, with shade provided by umbrellas. Sandwiches and salads for lunch, and mesquite-grilled trout, salmon, and red meats for supper. Lunch and dinner. Inexpensive to moderate.

Vista Grande. North of State Highway 22 on Teton Village Road. Telephone: (307) 733–6964. For twenty years this popular restaurant has dished out traditional Mexican specialties such as enchiladas and burritos. Grilled delights are also popular, including pollo asado, blackened tuna, and charbroiled beef, chicken, or shrimp fajitas. Dinner only. Inexpensive to moderate.

MICROBREWERIES

Jackson Hole Pub & Brewery. 265 South Millward. Telephone: (307) 739–BEER (2337). Jackson's original brewpub serves English-style ales, porters, and stouts, and European-style lagers. The food served to accompany the hearty brews includes sandwiches, pasta, and wonderful wood-fired pizzas, with surprising toppings available.

Otto Brothers' Brewing Company. Nestled in a tiny, 1930s-era log cabin in Wilson, between the hardware store and the fire station. Telephone: (307) 733–9000. Handmade beers brewed here include Old Faithful Ale and Teton Pass Ale. Otto

Brothers recently opened a brew pub on the other side of Teton Pass in Victor, Idaho.

BICYCLING

Along with a handful of other Western locales, Jackson Hole has evolved into a heralded destination for fat-tire mountain bikers from just about everywhere. The Cache Creek–Game Creek loop is the choice for a classic ride right out of town, but dozens of equally great outings web the outlying areas. Also, a growing network of paved pathways in and around Jackson provides cyclists, in-line skaters, and walkers an alternative to the valley's busy roads.

Grand Teton National Park. During late March and most or all of April, interior roads in Grand Teton National Park are closed to vehicle traffic, when they become de facto bike paths. Because they're permitted to fill in with snow in winter, and no sanding or graveling takes place, when the roads are plowed in spring they're debris-free. Open to cyclists, in-line skaters, and other self-propelled recreationists are the Teton Park Road, from the Taggart Lake parking area to Signal Mountain Lodge (15 miles), and the inside loop running past Jenny Lake and String Lake. The National Park Service stresses that pets are permitted only if leashed.

Teton Cyclery. 175 North Glenwood Street. Teton Cyclery is a good place to get your bearings, and to get your bearings greased. It is one of several establishments in town where you can procure a copy of *Mountain Biking in the Jackson Hole Area*, a map brochure produced by the Adventure Cycling Association in cooperation with the Bridger-Teton National Forest. Telephone: (307) 733–4386.

Teton Mountain Bike Tours. This company offers guided rides in the Bridger-Teton National Forest, on the National Elk Refuge, and in Grand Teton and Yellowstone national parks. Lunch and transportation from Jackson are included. Telephone: (307) 733–0712 or, toll-free in the United States, (800) 733–0788.

FAIRS, FESTIVALS, AND EVENTS

Grand Teton Music Festival. "One of the world's great orchestras is hidden in a small town in Wyoming." Those words were attributed to Zubin Mehta, who was referring to Jackson Hole's Festival Orchestra, which has been making music for nearly four decades. Throughout July and August the musicians stage orchestral and chamber music concerts at the acoustically acclaimed Walk Festival Hall in Teton Village. From baroque to Beethoven and ragtime to Romantic, the Tetons reverberate with the sounds of the classics. Very popular and highly recommended for classical music fans. Telephone (Walk Festival Hall Box Office): (307) 733–1128.

Pole, Pedal, Paddle. Held the first Saturday in April, this rite of spring marks the end of the ski season and the beginning of the rest of the year. The four-leg race combines downhill skiing, cross-country skiing, bicycling, and canoeing. It is one of the most popular all-comers competitions in the entire Northern Rockies region. Competition is divided into several categories, including mixed male-female teams, single-gender teams, and soloists. Telephone (Jackson Hole Motors): (307) 733–2351.

HORSEBACK RIDING

Nowhere does surveying the surrounding countryside from the back of a steed feel more natural than it does in Jackson Hole. Fortunately, several enterprises make it possible, including these.

Mountain biking, Teton Range, Wyoming

Jackson Hole Trail Rides. Outings ranging from an hour to all day in duration depart from Teton Village. Telephone: (307) 733–6992, (307) 733–5047.

Snow King Stables. Located behind the Snow King Resort in Jackson. Hourly trail rides are available, as are evening and breakfast chuck wagon outings. Telephone: (307) 733–5781.

HOT SPRINGS

Granite Hot Springs. The relaxing pools at Granite Hot Springs are open in summer and in winter, when the 10-mile access road is accessible only by cross-country skis, snowmobile, or dogsled. The trailhead is located east of U.S. Highway 191, south of Hoback Junction, at the foot of the sandstone ramparts known as Battle Mountain. Telephone: (307) 733–6318.

Astoria Hot Springs. Located west of Hoback Junction on U.S. Highway 89. Found at Astoria are a 40-by-80-foot soaking pool (temperature 95 degrees), a separate kiddies' pool, a snack bar and grocery, and a pleasant campground with more than 100 RV and tent sites. The popular family spot also boasts a sand volleyball court, horseshoe pits, a basketball court, and an extensive playground. Telephone: (307) 733–2659.

RIVER FLOATING

Barker-Ewing Jackson Hole River Trips. Since 1963 Barker-Ewing has been thrilling clients by guiding them through Snake River rapids. Trips of various lengths, including overnighters, are available by reservation. If tackling white water isn't your idea of fun, mellower trips can be arranged, on which the thrills come from spotting osprey, bald eagles, moose, and other wildlife. Telephone: (307) 733–1000 or, toll-free in the United States, (800) 448–4202.

Triangle X Ranch Float Trips. These folks offer several different trips, including a mellow "osprey float," a good choice to get your river-floating feet wet. It takes only about an hour to cover this par-ticular 5-mile stretch of the Snake in Grand Teton National Park. Telephone: (307) 733–5500.

Jackson Hole Kayak School. An alternative for those who would rather negotiate the Snake River solo. Located at Rendezvous River Sports, across from McDonald's at 1035 West Broadway. Telephone: (307) 733–2471.

SKIING

Jackson Hole Mountain Resort. Located at Teton Village, 12 miles northwest of Jackson on State Highway 22 and Teton Village Road. Best known for its steep, challenging runs and monster vertical rise of 4,139 feet, the Jackson Hole Mountain Resort is a full-service, year-round resort. The aerial tram leading to the summit and eight additional chairlifts serve a total of 22 miles of groomed runs. The tram also runs in summer, providing access to some fabulous hiking and sightseeing. The Jackson Hole Nordic Center (telephone 307–739–2710), located at the base of the alpine mountain in Teton Village, grooms for both skate and classic cross-country skiing on 15 kilometers (9.3 miles) of trails twisting through aspen-studded hillsides and across open flats. The Teton views are spectacular, and lessons, rentals, and guided natural history tours are available. Teton Village brims with accommodations, shopping opportunities, and restaurants, including on-slope eateries. At the unique and very popular Mangy Moose Saloon (telephone 307–733–4913) in Teton Village, the strange and interesting things hanging from the ceiling include a full-sized stuffed moose. The Alpenhof Bistro (307–733–3242) is another popular après-ski stop. For detailed information on lift tickets and other services, call the ski area at (307) 733–2292. To purchase or rent downhill ski gear, go to Pepi Stiegler Sports (307–733–4505) or Teton Village Sports (307–733–2181). Both are located in Teton Village.

Snow King Mountain. 400 East Snow King Avenue. Jackson's "town hill" offers steep, cheap, no-frills skiing and snowboarding for locals and other dedicated alpine enthusiasts. There's also a tow-served tubing hill. In summer, Snow King continues providing gravity-induced thrills to kids of all ages, by way of its alpine slide. Telephone: (307) 733–5200.

Spring Creek Touring Center. Three miles north of State Highway 22 on Spring Gulch Road. The Spring Creek resort grooms 20 kilometers (12.4 miles) of trails for skating and classic skiing, mostly over terrain suitable for beginners. Includes rentals, ski school, and optional guided ski tours in Grand Teton National Park; snowshoe tours are also available. Telephone: (307) 733–1004.

Teton Pines. Three miles north of State Highway 22 on Teton Village Road. This high-end golf resort transforms into a full-service Nordic touring center in winter, making it a rarity: an Arnold Palmer-designed ski course! Teton Pines maintains 13 kilometers (8 miles) of tracks for skating and classic skiing, and the lavish clubhouse includes a bar and restaurant. Telephone: (307) 733–1005.

Teton Pass. Located just "up the hill" west of Wilson. Teton Pass is one of the most popular backcountry-skiing destinations in the Northern Rockies. The slopes surrounding the pass hold powder or corn snow from December well into spring and even summer. No one will charge you to ski here, but you have to get to the top of the slopes under your own power. However, a few outfitters—including Rendezvous Ski Tours of Teton Valley (telephone 208–787–2906)—offer guided tours around the pass. For rentals and route information visit Wilson Backcountry Sports in Wilson, telephone (307) 733–5228. To obtain information on current avalanche conditions—a must when skiing on Teton Pass or anywhere in the mountainous outback surrounding Jackson Hole—call the Bridger-Teton National Forest's twenty-four-hour avalanche hotline at (307) 733–2664.

Skinny Skis. Located at 65 West Deloney Avenue in Jackson. For a quarter century Skinny Skis has been providing Jacksonites and visitors to town the best in high-performance Nordic racing and backcountry skis. The business also specializes in running gear and leisure wear. Telephone: (307) 733–6094.

High Mountain Heli-Skiing. To experience the ultimate in "lifts" and to float through some of the deepest untracked snows in the region, helicopter skiing is the way to go. The skiing is centered south of Jackson in the Snake River and Hoback ranges. Group size is small, with only three or four clients per outing. Guides are trained in avalanche safety and rescue. If your skiing skills are only moderate, don't despair: A new generation of parabolic "fat-boy" skis has made it possible for intermediates to handle deep-powder conditions that until recently were the domain of experts only. Telephone: (307) 733–3274.

WINTER TOURS

Jackson Hole Iditarod Sled Dog Tours. There's nothing quite like zipping through the snow-filled wilds on a sled pulled by a team of high-energy hounds. It's great fun. With this company you can enjoy a full-day outing to Granite Hot Springs or a shorter half-day tour. After a short orientation you can even try your own hand at mushing. Hosted by six-time Alaskan Iditarod competitor Frank Teasley, who also organizes the International Rocky Mountain Stage Stop Race, Wyoming's premier doggy-team dash. Teasley co-founded this business not only to share his love of dogsledding with others, but also to serve both as a retirement activity for his veteran Alaskan sled dogs and as a training school for future competitors. Offered daily by reservation only. Telephone: (307) 733–7388.

National Elk Refuge. Horse-drawn sleigh rides leave between 10 A.M. and 4 P.M. daily in winter. Park your car and purchase tickets at the National Wildlife Art Museum, located 3 miles north of Jackson on U.S. Highway 191. Telephone: (307) 733–0277; reservations for groups of twenty and more should be made by calling (307) 733–3534.

Snowmobile Rentals and Tours. Plenty of outfitters can point you to or guide you along the Continental Divide Snowmobile Trail and other popular destinations in and around Jackson Hole. Try Grand Teton Snowmobile Rentals, located at Grand Teton Park KOA near Moran Junction, or

Flagg Ranch Resort. (For information on both, *see* Campgrounds and RV Parks.)

Solitude Cabin Dinner Sleigh Rides. Telephone: (307) 733–6657. Sleighs depart from Nick Wilson's, located in the Clock Tower Building at Teton Village, at 5:30 P.M. and 7:30 P.M. every Monday through Saturday in winter. Lap robes aplenty will keep you warm during the horse-drawn sleigh ride, which ends at the Solitude Cabin, where passengers transform into diners and partake of a four-course meal. The choice of entrees includes prime rib and filet of salmon. Live entertainment is included and reservations are required. Dinner in winters only. Expensive.

Spring Creek Sleigh Rides. Horse-drawn sleigh ride only, or sleigh ride with gourmet meal, beginning at Spring Creek's Granary restaurant. Telephone: (307) 733–8833.

OTHER ACTIVITIES

Billiards. Good pool tables, and lots of them, are found within the Rancher Spirits & Billiards, located on the south side of the town square, above the Coldwater Creek store. Telephone: (307) 733–3886.

Covered Wagon Tours

The Bar-T-Five Covered Wagon Cookout and Wild West Show. Begins 1 mile east of the Town Square on Cache Creek Road. Hungry diners are hauled in horse-drawn covered wagons up scenic Cache Creek Canyon every summer evening to an outdoor dining room. Appetites are appeased with hearty, Western-style Dutch oven fare, and the Bar-T-Five Cowboys cook up tunes as tasty as the grub. Reservations required. Telephone: (307) 733–5386.

Grand Teton Covered Wagon Cookouts. The Box K Ranch runs these grub-fests, which begin east of Moran Junction along the Buffalo Valley Road. A twenty-minute wagon ride leads to a protected aspen grove, where vittles are dished up. Breakfast rides ($15) feature country flapjacks, scrambled eggs, hash browns, and bacon and sausage. The evening outing ($25) includes lip-smackin' rib-eye steak and classic cowboy entertainment. Kids

age four and under eat for free. Reservations required. Telephone: (307) 543–2407.

Four-Wheel Drive Outings. You can bounce along some of the area's most scenic back roads with Wild West Jeep Tours. Trained guides drive the convertible-top Jeeps and share their knowledge of the flora, fauna, and history of Jackson Hole. Telephone: (307) 733–9036.

Golf. A pair of top-notch, top-dollar golf courses grace Jackson Hole: The Arnold Palmer-designed Teton Pines (off Teton Village Road at 3450 North Clubhouse Drive; telephone 307–733–1005); and the older, Robert Trent Jones Jr.–designed Jackson Hole Golf & Tennis Club (just off U.S. Highway 89, 8 miles north of Jackson; telephone 307–733–3111). Both feature first-class dining and lodging facilities; the latter is operated by the Grand Teton Lodge Company.

Hot-Air Balloon Rides. Not to be outdone by the river rats, the Wyoming Balloon Company claims that their excursion is Jackson Hole's "ultimate float trip." An hour ride in one of these quiet, colorful giants—from which you can survey the Tetons and surroundings as in no other fashion—begins early in the morning on calm days only. Call to make reservations and to obtain directions to the launch site. Telephone: (307) 739–0900.

Ice Skating. Free skating in winter is available at the Snow King Outdoor Rink, located at the base of the Snow King Mountain in Jackson, and at the Wilson Outdoor Rink, in Owen Bircher Park in Wilson. Call (307) 733–5056 for information on hours at both rinks. Skating for a fee, with rentals available, can be enjoyed indoors at the Snow King Center. Hours vary; call the hotline at (307) 734–3000.

Mountaineering. A growing number of visitors feel they haven't really seen Yellowstone-Teton Country unless they've looked down on it from the region's apex, the summit of the Grand Teton. For information on guided climbs up the Grand and other peaks, contact Exum Mountain Guides (telephone 307–733–2297) or Jackson Hole Mountain Guides (telephone 307–733–4979).

Indian paintbrush flowers

Theater. The Grand Teton Mainstage Theatre, located at 50 West Broadway in Jackson's Pink Garter Plaza, offers Broadway-style entertainment every evening in summer. The box office opens daily at 10 A.M. Telephone: (307) 733–3670.

SHOPPING

Make certain your credit-card slate is relatively clean before visiting Jackson Hole, for there's a wealth of opportunities to rack up purchases—from cowboy hats and Western wear to works of wildlife art and outdoor gear. Here's a tiny sampling of the possibilities at hand.

Coldwater Creek. 10 East Broadway. Telephone: (307) 734–7771. This large new addition to the Town Square is a retail outlet of the popular

Sandpoint, Idaho-based mail-order clothing company.

Fighting Bear Antiques. 35 East Simpson Avenue. Telephone: (307) 733–2669. One of several antiques shops in town specializing in Old West/dude ranch accoutrements.

Hide Out Leather Apparel. 40 Center Street. Telephone: (307) 733–2422. A longtime Jackson establishment with a good selection of high-quality leather items.

Mangy Moose Emporium. In the Broadway Shops on West Broadway. Telephone: (307) 739–2166. Anything goes here, as long as it is moose-related, from chandeliers to earrings to clothing.

The Roundup. 115 West Broadway. Telephone: (307) 733–3405. Established in 1947 and one of the few surviving classic tourist shops in Jackson. Stetson hats, boots, T-shirts, and all sorts of curios are sold.

Trailside Americana Fine Art Gallery. 105 Center (corner of Center and East Deloney). Telephone: (307) 733–3186. A large facility displaying a staggering array of Western and wildlife art. Several additional galleries are located nearby, in this area just north and east of the Town Square.

TELEPHONE NUMBERS

Jackson Hole Area Chamber of Commerce and Visitor Center. (307) 733–3316.

Jackson Hole Airport. (307) 733–7682.

Car Rentals. Alamo, (307) 733–0671; Budget, (307) 733–2206; Eagle, (307) 739–9999; Hertz, (307) 733–2272; Thrifty, (307) 739–9300.

Public Transportation. S.T.A.R.T. Bus (runs between Jackson and Teton Village), (307) 733–4521. Targhee Express (ski bus running between Jackson and Grand Targhee), (307) 733–3101. All Star Taxi, (307) 733–2888. Buckboard Cab, (307) 733–1112.

Yellowstone National Park

LODGING

Opportunities for indoor lodging in Yellowstone are fairly limited and straightforward. For information and reservations for any of the following call AmFac Parks & Resorts, the park concessionnaire, at (307) 344–7311. Six months in advance is not too soon to secure reservations for your stay in the park.

Mammoth Hot Springs Hotel and Cabins. Located at the park headquarters settlement of Mammoth Hot Springs. One wing of the hotel was built in 1911, with the others you see today added in 1937. The colorful terraces of the springs are situated nearby; in fall, bull elk herd their harems within view of the hotel rooms. Open summer and winter, with cross-country skiing in winter and horseback riding and hiking in summer. Very inexpensive to very expensive. Dinner reservations required; call (307) 344–5314.

Old Faithful Inn. If you have only one night to spend indoors in Yellowstone, make the Old Faithful Inn your choice. Said to be the largest log structure in the world, the Inn was designed by architect Robert C. Reamer to look as if it grows naturally from its surroundings, with the interior an extension of the wilderness-embraced exterior. The core of the landmark hotel was built in 1903–4, with wings added in 1913 and 1928. The inn features a rustic tavern, good restaurant, and cafeteria. The on-site gift shop is filled with enough Yellowstone books and postcards, toy bears and wolves, and T-shirts to keep the most curio-curious occupied for a long while. Summer and fall only. Inexpensive to very expensive. Dinner reservations required; call (307) 545–4999.

Old Faithful Snow Lodge and Old Faithful Lodge Cabins. Less expensive than the Old Faithful Inn, the access to Old Faithful and the surrounding countryside is equally great from the rock-and-log Old Faithful Lodge, which was built in 1928 and has nearby cabins for rent in summer. The Old Faithful Snow Lodge, recently replaced by a new structure, offers a unique winter getaway for snowmobilers and cross-country skiers. Very inexpensive to expensive.

Grant Village. TW Recreational Services calls the motel/cabins at Grant Village "a conventional motel in a very unconventional setting." That unconventional setting includes Yellowstone Lake and its wild backdrop, the Absaroka Mountains. Two restaurants are located here, too, at the southernmost lodging option in Yellowstone. Summer only. Moderate to expensive. Dinner reservations required; call (307) 242–3499.

Lake Yellowstone Hotel & Cabins. Built in 1889–91 by the Northern Pacific Railroad, then radically renovated in the early 1900s by Robert C. Reamer (the architect responsible for the Old Faithful Inn), Lake Hotel is the oldest hostelry in the entire national parks system. It is also the Yellowstone's most refined hotel, where string quartets are often found entertaining in the expansive Sun Room. Lakeside dining room, deli, gift shop, and Frontier Cabins. Summer only. Moderate to very expensive. Dinner reservations required; call (307) 242–3899.

Lake Lodge Cabins. Rustic accommodations located close to the Lake Yellowstone Hotel. The lodge has a cafeteria, lounge, and gift shop. Inexpensive to expensive.

Canyon Lodge Cabins. Situated close to the Grand Canyon of the Yellowstone. The main lodge, which offers hotel-style rooms, includes a dining room and cafeteria. The majority of accommodations consist of single-story cabins, each containing four or more guest units. Horseback riding is available. Summer only. Inexpensive to expensive. Dinner reservations required; call (307) 242–3999.

Roosevelt Lodge Cabins. Located near Tower Junction in the northeast quadrant of the park, west of the spectacular Lamar Valley. As the name Roosevelt indicates, this is the most Old West–oriented of Yellowstone accommodations. The Rough Rider and Rustic Shelter cabins available here are heated with wood-burning stoves.

Horseback riding and Old West Dinner Cookouts are available, and so is family-style dining in the lodge. Very inexpensive to moderate.

CAMPGROUNDS AND RV PARKS

Of the eleven campgrounds within Yellowstone, four are operated by park concessionnaire AmFac and the others by the National Park Service. Only the campground at Mammoth is open year-round; the others generally open in May or June and close in September or October. Sites at seven of the campgrounds are available only on a first-come, first-served basis (get there first thing in the morning in summer!). Reservations at the other four may be secured by calling AmFac at (307) 344–7311. RV hookups are available at AmFac's Fishing Bridge RV Park, which is not open to tents or tent trailers. Reservations can also be made for these sites by calling the above-listed number.

The NPS first-come, first-served campgrounds are located at Mammoth (elevation 6,239 feet), Tower Fall (6,600 feet), Slough Creek (in Lamar Valley; 6,250 feet), Pebble Creek (northeast of Lamar Valley; 6,900 feet), Indian Creek (south of Mammoth; 7,300 feet), Norris Junction (7,484 feet), and Lewis Lake (7,779 feet). The campgrounds at which reservations can be made by calling AmFac are located at Bridge Bay (7,784 feet), Grant Village (7,773 feet), Canyon (7,734 feet), and Madison (6,806 feet).

BICYCLING

A few short bicycle paths are located in the vicinity of Mammoth Hot Springs and in the Lower and Upper geyser basins, near Old Faithful. Mountain bicycling on backcountry trails is prohibited in Yellowstone, as it is in almost all of the national parks. Road riding is generally not a pleasant experience, unless you visit during the shoulder seasons when the vehicle traffic diminishes, or—in summer—ride very early in the morning, before traffic picks up. As park management progressively upgrades the roads they are adding provisions for bicycling such as shoulders, so the situation should improve.

TELEPHONE NUMBERS

Superintendent's Office of Yellowstone National Park, (307) 344–2386 or 344–7381. Call for information on organized activities, both winter and summer—including fishing rules, hiking trails, cross-country skiing and snowmobiling opportunities, and ranger-led activities.

Cody

LODGING

In addition to accommodations listed for the town of Cody, a string of some two dozen guest and dude ranches can be found in the Wapiti Valley, between Cody and Yellowstone's East Entrance. Among them: **Pahaska Tepee** (307–527–7701 or 800–628–7791), 2 miles east of Yellowstone's East Entrance; **Shoshone Lodge** (307–587–4044), 4 miles east of Yellowstone; **Crossed Sabres Ranch** (307–587–3750), 9 miles east of Yellowstone; and **Elephant Head Lodge** (307–587–3980), situated 11 miles east of the park.

Burl Inn. 1213 17th Street. Forty-room motel that looks rather plain on the outside, but which inside is appointed with Western furnishings reminiscent of those crafted by the master, Thomas Molesworth. Telephone: (307) 587–3031 or, toll-free in the United States, (800) 388–2084. Inexpensive to moderate.

Chapel House Bed & Breakfast. 1241 Wyoming Avenue. Unique accommodations in a 1930s church are either in the Outdoor Adventure suite or the smaller Antique Room. Telephone: (307) 527–5711. Moderate.

Cody Guest Houses. 1401 Rumsey Avenue. Eight individual properties for rent, each richly appointed in antiques and historic artwork. The houses, cottages, and suites available range from one to four bedrooms in size. Fully equipped kitchens, living rooms, and daily housekeeping come with the deal. Telephone: (307) 587–6000 or, toll-free in the United States, (800) 587–6560. Prices vary greatly.

Days Inn. 524 Yellowstone Avenue. Features fifty deluxe rooms and two spa suites. Pool, Continental breakfast. Telephone: (307) 527–6604 or, toll-free in the United States, (800) 329–7166. Inexpensive to moderate.

The Irma. 1192 Sheridan Avenue. The Irma, the symbolic and actual hub of downtown Cody, was built by Buffalo Bill in 1902. In addition to several historic, renovated guest rooms, you'll find the Buffalo Bill Bar, Silver Saddle Lounge, and Irma Grill. Telephone: Toll-free in the United States, (800) 745–IRMA (4762). Inexpensive.

Super 8. 730 Yellowstone Avenue, 5 blocks from the Buffalo Bill Historical Center. Telephone: (307) 527–6214 or, toll-free in the United States, (800) 800–8000. Inexpensive.

CAMPGROUNDS AND RV PARKS

Private

KOA Kampground. 5561 Greybull Highway. Telephone: (307) 587–2369 or, toll-free in the United States, (800) 562–8507. Campground featuring an abundance of grassy sites, free Cody Nite Rodeo Shuttle, and western chuck wagon dinner and show.

Ponderosa Campground. 1815 Yellowstone Highway. Large campground, with plenty of RV and tenting sites, located just 3 blocks from the Buffalo Bill Historical Center. Telephone: (307) 587–9203.

State Park

Buffalo Bill State Park. Located 15 miles west of Cody. This large park, which encompasses the Buffalo Bill Reservoir, includes a pair of campgrounds (North Fork and North Shore Bay). Telephone: (307) 527–6057.

FOOD

The Irma. 1192 Sheridan Avenue. Telephone: (307) 587–4221. The Irma Grill serves all three meals daily in the hotel's old bar-billiards room. Prime rib and buffalo cuts are the dinner specialties. Moderate.

La Comida. 1385 Sheridan Avenue. Telephone: (307) 587–9556. Good south-of-the-border fare, including the specialty spinach enchiladas, served indoors or, in summer, on the patio. Inexpensive to moderate.

Maxwell's. 937 Sheridan Avenue. Telephone: (307) 527–7749. Looking more like residential property than eatery, Maxwell's specializes in sandwiches, steaks, and pasta dishes served in a relaxed setting. Lunch and dinner. Inexpensive.

Olive Glenn Golf & Country Club. 802 Meadow Lane. Telephone: (307) 587–5688. Good choice for something a bit fancier, featuring fine fare and an extensive wine list. Moderate.

FAIRS, FESTIVALS, AND EVENTS

Cody Nite Rodeo. Held at the Stampede Park grandstand west of town. America's longest-running buckfest takes place every night at 8:30 P.M. during June, July, and August. Telephone: (307) 587–2922.

Western Design Conference. Slated for several days in late September. Cody has earned a far-ranging reputation for its Western-oriented festivals and art shows. This one is a world-class event, where only a few dozen top-notch craftspeople are invited to exhibit, showcasing Western architecture, furnishings, and fashions. The show takes place at the Cody Auditorium, while related lectures, art auctions, and other activities happen at the Chamber of Commerce building and the Buffalo Bill Historical Center. Telephone: (307) 587–2297.

Yellowstone Jazz Festival. Takes place in Cody and nearby Powell in July. This festival, something a little different for cowboy- and cowgirl-oriented Cody, has been happening for over a decade. Telephone: (307) 587–3898.

SHOPPING

Cody's most unusual shopping opportunities focus on—not surprisingly—things Western, both old and new. There's a whole slate of saddleries, Western-design specialty stores, and

Western/wildlife art galleries, most of them centered downtown along Sheridan Avenue. Here's a tiny sample of the options:

Big Horn Galleries. 1167 Sheridan Avenue. Telephone: (307) 527–7587. Proffers fine contemporary Western and wildlife art, including entertaining works by Donna Howell-Sickles and Buckeye Blake.

Cody Rodeo Company. 1291 Sheridan Avenue. You'll find lots of interesting things in this store, including a good selection of cowboy lids, and a unique photo opportunity that'll have you atop a (stuffed) raging bull.

Prairie Rose. 1356 Sheridan Avenue. Telephone: (307) 587–8181. Offers silverwork, blankets, pottery, bead and quill work, and other items reflecting traditions of the Northern Plains Indians. Also sells New Age and Native American music, and unusual craft supplies, such as beaver and fox teeth.

Wyoming Buffalo Company. Downtown Cody at 1276 Sheridan. Telephone: (307) 587–8708 or, toll-free in the United States, (800) 453–0636. All sorts of buffalo cuts can be bought here and shipped home. The business also offers smoked trout, elk and venison specialties, and nearly a dozen varieties of jerky.

TELEPHONE NUMBERS

Park County Travel Council. (307) 587–2297.

Buffalo Bill Historical Center. (307) 587–5714.

Big Sky–Bozeman

LODGING

In and Near Big Sky

320 Guest Ranch. Trail riding, and sleigh and hayride dinners are among the many options at this Western retreat, located 12 miles south of the entrance to Big Sky off U.S. Highway 191. Full-service resort with fishing shop, saloon, indoor horse arena, and fine dining; restaurant is open for all three meals, to non-guests as well as guests. Features private log cabins with fireplaces, some with kitchen facilities. Open year-round. Telephone: (406) 995–4283 or, toll-free in the United States, (800) 243–0320. Some cabins available by the night; others on a multi-day basis only. Expensive to very expensive.

Best Western Buck's T-4 Lodge. Located 1.5 miles south of the entrance to Big Sky. Room rates include full continental breakfast. Telephone: (406) 995–4111 or, toll-free in the United States, (800) 822–4484. Expensive to very expensive.

Golden Eagle Lodge. Located in Meadow Village. Economical lodging in rooms and suites with private baths. Also offers property management, renting condominiums and houses to match a range of budgets. Telephone: (406) 995–4800 or, toll-free in the United States, (800) 548–4488.

Huntley Lodge and Shoshone Condominium Hotel. Located in Mountain Village, at the base of the ski runs. The ski-in, ski-out centerpiece of the Big Sky Resort offers a variety of room types. Adjacent to the Yellowstone Conference Center, which comprises some 40,000 square feet of meeting space. In the surrounding area are several other complexes, including the Beaverhead, Arrowhead, Lake, Stillwater, and Big Horn condominiums. Telephone: (406) 995–5000 or, toll-free in the United States, (800) 548–4486. Very expensive.

Lone Mountain Ranch. Located 4 miles west of the entrance to Big Sky, at the base of the hill leading to the ski area. Specializing in multi-day stays in log-cabin lodgings; cross-country skiing in winter and horseback riding and fly fishing in summer. Telephone: (406) 995–4644 or, toll-free in the United States, (800) 514–4644. Very expensive.

Rainbow Ranch Lodge. Located 5 miles south of the entrance to Big Sky, along the west bank of the Gallatin River. Beautiful lodge appointed in the finest of rustic Western furnishings, and featuring outdoor hot tub and bonfire pit. The staff bends over backward to please, and will arrange guest activities including snowmobiling, rafting, nature hikes, and tennis. Also serves gourmet dinners for guests and non-guests. Telephone: (406) 995–4132 or, toll-free in the United States, (800) 937–4132. Expensive to very expensive.

In and Near Bozeman

Best Western City Center. 507 West Main. Conveniently located on the west edge of downtown, across the street from Bangtail Bicycles. Telephone: (406) 587–3158. Moderate to expensive.

Fairfield Inn by Marriott. 828 Wheat Drive. Good choice among the several franchise motels situated off 7th Avenue close to Interstate 90. Free continental breakfast, indoor pool and spa, and several nearby restaurants. Telephone: (406) 587–2222. Moderate to expensive.

Gallatin Gateway Inn. Located in Gallatin Gateway, 12 miles southwest of Bozeman. Resplendent old railroad hotel, renovated in the late 1980s. The Spanish Colonial Revival–style inn, stuccoed on the exterior and owning a bright red tile roof, was built by the Milwaukee Road in 1927, at what was then called Salesville, at the southern terminus of the branch line from Three Forks. Accommodations are available in one- and two-room suites, and the on-site dining room serves seasonal menus popular with both locals and those passing through. Outside is a pool and hot tub, and fly-casting pond. Telephone: (406) 763–4672. Expensive.

Holiday Inn. 5 Baxter Lane, near where North 7th meets I–90. 179 rooms, including an executive suite and a pair of Jacuzzi suites. Complimentary airport transportation, full-service restaurant, indoor pool, and banquet and convention facilities. Telephone: (406) 587–4561 or, toll-free in the United States (800) 366–5101. Expensive.

Lehrkind Mansion Bed & Breakfast. Located at the corner of East Aspen and North Wallace in the Brewery Historic District. Julius Lehrkind, a brewmaster's apprentice who stowed away at age seventeen on an America-bound ship in 1860 to avoid compulsory military service in his native Germany, established a brewery in Bozeman in 1895 and built this Queen Anne–style mansion three years later. Rooms range from one room to a two-room suite with a tower! Telephone: (406) 585–6932. Moderate to expensive.

Lindley House Bed & Breakfast. 202 Lindley Place. Elegantly restored 1889 Victorian situated close to downtown. Hot tub, with niceties that include ginger cookies, brandy nightcap, and full gourmet breakfast. Telephone: (406) 587–8403 or, toll-free in the United States, (800) 787–8404. Moderate to very expensive.

Voss Inn. Located at 319 South Willson, between downtown and the university campus. Brick Victorian built in the mid-1880s has six guest rooms, each with private bath and phone. Breakfasts are served in the private rooms. Telephone: (406) 587–0982. Moderate to expensive.

Gallatin National Forest Recreational Cabins. Two dozen rustic cabins, some close to Bozeman and others farther out, at locations such as Hebgen Lake and the Livingston–Big Timber area, are available by reservation at $25 per night. Most are outfitted with woodstoves, cots or bunks, and cooking utensils. Some sit high on mountaintops; others front rushing streams. Food and water are generally BYO (water from nearby streams or lakes can be ingested if filtered). Some of the cabins are available in winter only, others in summer only, and some year-round. For an informational brochure and/or reservations, which are accepted six months ahead of time, call the Bozeman Ranger District at (406) 587–6920.

CAMPGROUNDS AND RV PARKS

Private

Bear Canyon RV Park & Campground. Located at 4000 Bear Canyon Road (take exit 313 off I–90, four miles east of Bozeman). Playground, pool, 100 RV sites, and fifty tenting sites. Telephone: (406) 587–1575.

Lehrkind Mansion Bed and Breakfast, Bozeman

Bozeman KOA. Located on U.S. Highway 191, just south of Four Corners and next to Simpson's Hot Springs. Tent sites, hookups, and KOA Kamping Kabins. Open year-round. Telephone: (406) 587–3030.

Sunrise Campground. Just east of Bozeman, off I–90 at exit 309. Laundry, hookups, leashed pets welcome. Telephone: (406) 587–4797.

U.S. Forest Service

Some campgrounds are available by reservation; call the Gallatin National Forest at (406) 587–9054 for information:

Red Cliff. In Gallatin Canyon, 6 miles south of the entrance to Big Sky.

Moose Creek Flat. In Gallatin Canyon, 8.5 miles north of the entrance to Big Sky.

Swan Creek. In Gallatin Canyon, 9.5 miles north of the entrance to Big Sky.

Greek Creek. In Gallatin Canyon, 10.5 miles north of the entrance to Big Sky.

Langohr, Hood Creek, and Chisholm. Located, respectively, 11, 17, and 18 miles south of Bozeman on Hyalite Canyon Road #62. Great hiking, and good fishing and boating on Hyalite Reservoir.

Battleridge. 22 miles north of Bozeman on State Highway 86.

Fairy Lake. 22.5 miles north of Bozeman on State Highway 86, then 5 miles west on Fairy Lake Road. A high-clearance/four-wheel-drive vehicle is recommended for negotiating the Fairy Lake Road.

FOOD

In Big Sky

Buck's T-4. Located 1.5 miles north of the entrance to Big Sky, on the west side of U.S. Highway 191. Telephone: (406) 995–4111. A surprise wrapped in a plain brown package, this restaurant has garnered a reputation as one of the best in the region. Great Plains Bison, New Zealand Red Deer, and Yellowfin Tuna are among the choices. Breakfast and dinner. Moderate to expensive.

Edelweiss. Located in Meadow Village. Telephone: (406) 995–4665. European-style restaurant specializing in veal, lamb, fish, and seafood. Moderate to expensive.

In Bozeman

Azteca. 134 East Main. Telephone: (406) 586–5181. Hole-in-the-wall Mexican cantina that's hard to miss, with its bright red chili pepper sign extending over the sidewalk. House specialties include Steak Picado, Chili Colorado, and Chili Cheese Enchiladas. Open for lunch and supper (closed Sunday); take out or dine in. Inexpensive.

The Baxter. 105 West Main. Telephone: (406) 586–1314. The Bacchus Pub portion of the restaurant serves dinner, lunch, and perhaps the most heralded breakfast in town. The adjacent Rocky Mountain Pasta Company dishes up Italian cuisine for supper. Open daily. Moderate.

Casa Sanchez. In the university area at 719 South 9th. Telephone: (406) 586–4516. Dine-in or take-out Mexican specialties, including vegetarian dishes. Inexpensive to moderate.

Fred's Mesquite Grill. Northwest corner of Church and Main. Telephone: (406) 585–8558. Converted filling station popular for lunch and dinner, with ample outside seating in summer. Inexpensive.

John Bozeman's Bistro. 242 East Main. Telephone: (406) 587–4100. Known for robust coffee, great desserts, and seafood that tastes too good to be this far from the ocean. Lunch, dinner, and locally acclaimed Sunday brunch. Closed Monday. Moderate to expensive.

MacKenzie River Pizza Co. 232 East Main. Telephone: (406) 587–0055. Gourmet pizza topped with all kinds of things, as well as good salads and sandwiches. Delivery available to area lodgings. Inexpensive to moderate.

Pickle Barrel. Two locations: downtown on East Main next to the Rockin' R Bar and in the university area at 809 West College. Telephone: (406) 587–2411. A long-popular Bozeman sandwich shop, serving traditional submarines. Inexpensive.

Great Harvest Bread Company. Located in a classic old brick building at the corner of 7th and Main, adjacent to Rocky Mountain Roasting (coffee). Telephone: (406) 582–8369. Great Harvest, a Dillon, Montana–based company with several franchisees throughout the region, bakes the best loaves between St. Paul and San Francisco. Drop in and try one of their free samples to see if you don't agree.

Fred's Mesquite Grill, Bozeman

MICROBREWERIES

Spanish Peaks Brewery and Italian Caffe. 120 North 19th Avenue, just north of Main. Telephone: (406) 585–2296. An ideal lunch or dinner stop, serving microbrews and brick-fired pizza and other dishes seven days a week.

BICYCLING

Grizzly Outfitters. Located 1.7 miles west of the entrance to Big Sky, on the south side of road. Offers mountain-bike and camping-gear rentals and bicycle sales, maps, and tips on where to ride in the area. Telephone: (406) 995–2939.

The Bozeman area hides miles of rides, from paved farm roads to mountain-biking trails in gorgeous spots that include Hyalite, Bear, and Sourdough canyons. Go to **Bangtail Bicycles** (406–587–4905), at 508 West Main, which rents bikes for $20 per day. **Backcountry** (406–586–3556) is a company based in Bozeman that operates first-class bicycling and

hiking adventures in many regions of the Rocky Mountains, including around their hometown area.

FISHING

Gallatin Riverguides. Located a half mile south of the entrance to Big Sky on U.S. Highway 191. Telephone: (406) 995–2290. Year-round guided fly-fishing trips on the Gallatin, Madison, Yellowstone, and Missouri rivers. Also offers casting clinics and is an authorized dealer of several brands of equipment, including Montana-made Winston rods.

Montana Troutfitters. Located in the Beaver Pond Plaza at 1716 West Main in Bozeman. Telephone: (406) 587–4707. Instruction, guided outings, licenses, and expert tips on what flies to use where.

R J Cain and Company Outfitters. 24 East Main in Bozeman. Telephone: (406) 587–9111. Classy downtown enterprise offering Stetson hats, fly-fishing gear and literature, Montana-made gifts, and more. Guided trips on the Madison, Gallatin, and Yellowstone.

Fish Technology Center. Located outside Bozeman at 4050 Bridger Canyon Road. Telephone: (406) 587–9265. In addition to fishing the legendary waters surrounding Bozeman, avid anglers may want to visit this facility of the U.S. Fish and Wildlife Service. Research on diseases, reproduction, management, threatened species, and more is conducted at the facility, open to visitors daily from 8:00 A.M. to 4:00 P.M.

Fairs, Festivals, and Events

Sweet Pea Festival. This gathering, held the first weekend of August in Lindley Park and elsewhere about town, is Bozeman's major event and one of the biggest summerfests in the Northern Rockies. The huge "family reunion" celebrates the arts and recreation, with a footrace, dancing, art displays, a parade, and much more. Information: (406) 586–4003.

National Parks Postcard and Antique Show. Held at the Gallatin County Fairgrounds, typically the third weekend in May. An irresistible event for those drawn to old postcards, books, posters, and other memorabilia associated with America's national parks and the West in general. You're guaranteed to find and purchase something you didn't know you needed, and which you'll wonder how you ever got along without. Buyers and sellers come from throughout the West and beyond. Telephone: (406) 582–3270.

Montana Shakespeare in the Parks. Traveling summer troupe that stages periodic performances in The Grove at Montana State University. Information: (406) 994–5885.

Golf

Golfers may find it necessary to gear down a club at Big Sky, where the balls fly farther at the 6,500-foot elevation. The resort's scenic eighteen holer is a sprawling, links-style course designed by Arnold

Palmer, which winds along the west fork of the Gallatin River. Located in Meadow Village, 2 miles west of the entrance to Big Sky.

Bozeman claims two eighteen-hole public courses, from which stunning views of the Gallatin and Bridger ranges are par for the course. **Cottonwood Hills Golf Course** (406–587–1118) is located 7 miles west of town near Four Corners; **Bridger Creek Golf Course** (406–586–2333) is found at 1071 Storymill Road.

Horseback Riding

Dalton's Big Sky Stables. On the way to Mountain Village, 5.5 miles west of the entrance to Big Sky. Horses for riders of all experience levels; outings are from an hour to a day in duration. Telephone: (406) 995–2972.

River Floating

Geyser Whitewater Expeditions. One mile south of the entrance to Big Sky in Gallatin Canyon. Mellow scenic floats, thrilling whitewater outings, and horseback ride-float combinations. Most popular is a half-day trip on the Gallatin, which leaves three times a day during the floating season. Telephone: (406) 995–4989 or, toll-free in the United States, (800) 922–7238.

Skiing

Big Sky Ski & Summer Resort. Montana's biggest and most glittery ski area boasts the greatest vertical rise of any ski area in the United States, and features 80 miles of designated runs spread over two mountains and 3,500 acres. Official slope-difficulty percentages: 10 percent beginner, 47 percent intermediate, and 43 percent expert. The area typically opens for skiing in mid-November and closes in mid-April, then re-opens in summer for hiking, gondola rides, mountain biking, and high-country relaxing. A host of eateries, shops, and taverns/nightclubs are located in Mountain Village, at the base of the ski slopes. For detailed information on lift tickets and other services, call the ski area at (800) 548–4486.

Lone Mountain Ranch. Nordic-skiing center and guest ranch located 4 miles west of the entrance to Big Sky. Excellent grooming on an extensive, 65-kilometer (40-mile) trail system (but less interesting terrain than that traced by the Rendezvous Trails, found 50 miles south in West Yellowstone). Telephone: (406) 995–4734 or, toll-free in the United States, (800) 514–4644.

Bridger Bowl Ski Area. Located 16 miles north of Bozeman on State Highway 86. This alpine gem offers first-rate skiing and snowboarding at uncommonly reasonable prices. For more than four decades Bridger Bowl has served Bozeman's locals, and increasingly those from beyond the area are discovering what's been one of the best-kept downhill skiing secrets in the Northern Rockies. Operated as a nonprofit (Montana State University is the designated benefactor, should the area ever sell), all excess revenues return to the area for improvements. Although it's a community-based business, Bridger Bowl's statistics are anything but small-town. The area boasts 1,200 acres of skiable terrain and 2,000 feet of vertical rise, and an average of 350 inches of snow per year falls on the immense bowls that loom above runs cut through the trees. Most out-of-towners stay in Bozeman in order to enjoy the good restaurants and lively night life, although slopeside accommodations are available, in the form of condominium, chalet, and lodge rooms. Telephone: (406) 586–1518 or, toll-free in the United States, (800) 223–9609.

Bohart Ranch Cross-Country Ski Center. Located just north of Bridger Bowl. Day-use area featuring 25 kilometers (15.5 miles) of trails groomed for both diagonal and skate skiing. The network comprises 30 percent easy/beginner trails, 40 percent moderate, and 30 percent more difficult. Bohart also rents equipment, offers lessons, and has a warming cabin. The trails are open to the public in the summer, too, for walking, jogging, mountain biking, and horseback riding. Bohart also hosts Summer Biathlon competitions combining running and target shooting, and features an eighteen-hole Frisbee Golf Course. Telephone: (406) 586–9070.

TOURS

Northern Rockies Natural History. Telephone: (406) 586–1155. Safari-style outings originating in Bozeman, but conducted throughout Yellowstone-Teton Country. Led by a trained wildlife biologist. Tours include river-drift birding and alpine hiking in summer, and skiing and snowshoeing in winter. Half-, full-, and multi-day trips are available, for singles or entire families.

Walking Stick Tours. Telephone: (406) 995–4265. Specializing in hiking and auto tours in the Big Sky area and in Yellowstone National Park. Lunch, shuttles, and knowledgeable guides are part of the package. Tipi cookouts are another possibility.

OTHER ACTIVITIES

Birding. The lower forty-eight's largest concentration of migrating golden eagles can be viewed in autumn—usually during the first two weeks of October—from two locations in the Bridger Mountains: (1) At the top of Bridger Bowl (reached by hiking 2,100 vertical feet up the chairlift slope); and (2) Sacajawea Park, also accessible by hiking from Fairy Lake. For an informational brochure, call the Gallatin National Forest at (406) 587–6752.

Hiking. From easy strolls around town on tamed paths such as the Highland Ridge Trail and the Gallagator Linear, which follows the old Milwaukee Road railroad grade, to challenging mountain treks in the Gallatin Range, Hyalite Canyon, Madisons, and elsewhere, the Bozeman–Big Sky hiking is first-rate. Information on the surrounding mountain trails can be obtained through the Bozeman Ranger District.

SHOPPING

Country Bookshelf. Located at 28 West Main Street. Telephone: (406) 587–0166. One of the best bookstores in the region, with an extensive selection of Yellowstone-Teton Country reading material.

Great Rocky Mountain Toy Company. 233 East Main in the historic Bozeman Hotel (also has a branch at Big Sky in the Snowcrest Lodge). Telephone: (406) 585–3322. Kids of all ages will be tempted to spend too much time browsing here. Great selection of toys, both ordinary and unusual.

Montana Trails Gallery. 219 East Main Street. Telephone: (406) 586–2166. Western, wildlife, and sporting themes, all evocative of Montana. Paintings, sculptures, limited-edition prints, and jewelry.

Northern Lights Trading Company. 1716 West Babcock (there is also a branch in Big Sky). Telephone: (406) 586–2225. Bozeman is one of the premier outdoor recreation meccas in America, so it should be no surprise that it's also home to one of the finest outdoor equipment stores you'll ever visit. Northern Lights Trading Company, occupying a large, wide-open timber frame building, specializes in summer sports such as backpacking, climbing, and river-running, and in winter sports including cross-country skiing and snowboarding. Good selection of year-round outer and inner wear.

Petunia's by Cindy Owings. Corner of Main and Willson in the Baxter Hotel. Telephone: (406) 585–3404. Purveyor of striking, custom-designed, hand-dyed wool coats.

Poor Richard's News. 33 West Main. Telephone: (406) 586–9041. Old-style news and tobacco shop, hawking fine cigars, a good selection of periodicals and local-interest books, and, on Sundays, the *New York Times.*

T. Charbonneau's Trading Company. Southeast corner of Rouse and Main. Telephone: (406) 587–9198. "Rustic reminders of our Montana heritage" in the form of clothing, furniture, and gifts are sold at this business, apparently named for the husband of Sacajawea.

Thomas Nygard Gallery. 127 East Main. Telephone: (406) 586–3636. Western-oriented art of the nineteenth and twentieth centuries. Classics by Albert Bierstadt, Charlie Russell, O. C. Seltzer, and others, as well as works by contemporary artists.

AIRPORT

Gallatin Field Airport is located 8 miles northwest of Bozeman, outside the small town of Belgrade. The airport is served by Delta, Northwest, and Horizon airlines.

TELEPHONE NUMBERS

Big Sky Chamber of Commerce. (406) 995–3000.

Bozeman Ranger District. 3710 Fallon Street. (406) 587–6920 or, for the twenty-four-hour recreation line, 587–9784.

Central Reservations. (800) 548–4486.

Car Rentals. Budget, (406) 388–4091; Rent-A-Wreck, (406) 587–4551; Avis, (406) 388–6414; Hertz, (406) 388–6939; National, (406) 388–6694.

Public Transportation. City Taxi, (406) 586–2341. Provides transportation between Gallatin Field and Bozeman.

West Yellowstone and Island Park

LODGING

Comfort Inn. 638 Madison Avenue. Located in a quiet West Yellowstone neighborhood 6 blocks west of Canyon Street, this chain motel boasts a pool/spa and several specialty suites. Continental breakfast is included with the price of a room. Telephone: (406) 646–4212. Expensive to very expensive.

Firehole Ranch. Situated northwest of town on the southwest side of Hebgen Lake. All-inclusive establishment that's also an Orvis-endorsed fly-fishing ranch. Located adjacent to the Madison River, which offers outstanding dry-fly fishing for rainbow and brown trout. Guides are available by the day for float- and/or wade-fishing in the Madison and other nearby rivers. The food and accommodations are first-rate; in addition to fishing, ranch pursuits include canoeing, hiking, horseback riding, and mountain biking. Telephone: (406) 646–7294. Very expensive (rates include three meals, open bar, and all ranch activities).

Grey Wolf Retreat. East of U.S. Highway 20 in Island Park. Another gem hidden off the beaten track, Grey Wolf Retreat specializes in accommodating groups as large as twenty-six persons. Three cabins are available; the smallest sleeps two to four, the mid-sized cabin four to six, and the largest as many as sixteen. No dining facilities are located on the premises, but the big cabin has a fully equipped kitchen and meals also can be catered by Mack's Inn or a couple of other nearby restaurants. Telephone: (801) 547–0130 (Utah) or, toll-free in the United States, (800) 705–2178. Inexpensive to moderate.

Hibernation Station. 212 Gray Wolf Avenue, in West Yellowstone's Grizzly Park addition. The delightfully intimate individual log cabins here are dressed in Western "rustic elegance," an apparent oxymoron that you will appreciate once you step inside. Queen-size lodgepole beds covered with fluffy down comforters make sleep come easy. Fireplaces and kitchenettes are available in some cabins, atop all of which reside wooden bears, fishermen, geysers, and other whimsical characters. Telephone: (406) 646–4200 or, toll-free in the United States, (800) 580–3557. Expensive to very expensive.

Jacob's Island Park Ranch. Located west off U.S. Highway 20 in Island Park. This ranch, a bit hard to find but well worth the search, rents variously sized cabins nightly or by the week. Some sleep up to eight. Highlights include horseback riding, weekend rodeoing, and a popular weekend dinner deal. Telephone: (800) 230–9530. Moderate.

Sleepy Hollow. This collection of small cabins is representative of the several cabin camps tucked amid residential areas in West Yellowstone. The cabins are rustic, but clean and thoroughly enjoyable. Many include kitchens. Telephone: (406) 646–7707. Inexpensive to moderate.

Stage Coach Inn. 209 Madison Avenue. If there is one gathering place that blends the feel of the present with that of an earlier day in West Yellowstone, it is the Stage Coach Inn. This half-century-old community cornerstone occupies much of the entire block fronted on the south by Madison Avenue and the east by Dunraven Street. The original portion of the full-service inn, which opened in 1948, was built by J. L. Grimmett of Idaho Falls, who earlier had built the Wort Hotel in Jackson. The Inn's dormered exterior is of a style aptly described as "Western Swiss." Rooms, including those in the new wing, which opened in 1990, feature a Western motif, rich with icons like bison and arrowheads. The lobby boasts a fireplace and irresistible lodgepole furniture that is easy to sink into but not so easy to get out of. Above, a broad staircase leads to an overlooking balcony gracing the second floor. Adorning the lobby's walls of varnished knotty pine are stuffed animal heads, including one of the most lifelike jackelope mounts you'll find. Also on display: historic photographs and maps, and the vivid works of Gary Carter, an acclaimed Western artist who calls West Yellowstone home. The inn's spa, particularly hard to resist during the cold of winter, features a warm hot tub and an adjacent *hot* hot tub, and the on-site gift shop proffers books and clothing thematic of Yellowstone-Teton Country. The Stage Coach features a lively bar, with an adjacent poker room and dance bands playing on most weekends. Telephone: (406) 646–7381 or, toll-free in the United States, (800) 842–2882. Inexpensive to expensive.

Three Bear Lodge. 217 Yellowstone Avenue. Conveniently located to downtown and to Grizzly Park, the Three Bear Lodge includes an outdoor pool (summer) and four indoor whirlpools. Complete winter packages, including snowcoach and snowmobile tours in Yellowstone can be arranged. Telephone: (406) 646–7353 or, toll-free in the United States, (800) 646–7353. Inexpensive to moderate.

West Yellowstone Conference Hotel. 315 Yellowstone Avenue. As the name suggests, this relatively new Holiday Inn franchisee features the most extensive meeting facilities in town. Among the hotel's 123 rooms are king spa suites and two-room family units. The Oregon Short Line Restaurant and adjacent Iron Horse Saloon (which features Montana microbrews) recall earlier days when the railroad ran to town. The railroading ambience is amplified by an immaculately refurbished 1903 Oregon Short Line luxury car residing within the building just outside the restaurant. The hotel also features a year-round Jacuzzi-exercise-sauna room. Telephone: (406) 646–7365 or, toll-free in the United States, (800) 646–7365. Expensive to very expensive.

Yellowstone Townhouses. 15 Madison Avenue. These furnished, fireplace- and kitchen-equipped rentals are dispersed around West Yellowstone in several locations. They offer a great option for families preferring to "cook at home." Telephone: (406) 646–9523 or, toll-free in the United States, (800) 438–5263. Rates vary.

CAMPGROUNDS AND RV PARKS

Private

Grizzly RV Park. 210 South Electric Street. This 152-space park is located just 4 blocks from the West Entrance to Yellowstone, within walking distance of all West Yellowstone services and attractions. Telephone: (406) 646–4466.

Madison Arm Resort. Located northwest of town on the south side of Hebgen Lake. The establishment's ninety-site campground includes both RV and tent sites nestled amid groves of pine. Also on-site are a general store, cabins, and a marina, with boat rentals available. Telephone: (406) 646–9328.

Valley View at Henry's Lake. Situated 14 miles from West Yellowstone in Island Park. RV park open year-round; includes a grocery and fifty-five pull-through spaces. Telephone: (208) 558–7443.

U.S. Forest Service

(call the Hebgen Lake Ranger District at 406-646-7369 or the Island Park Ranger District at 208-558-7301 for information).

Baker's Hole. Located 3 miles north of West Yellowstone on U.S. Highway 191. Hard-sided

camping only, due to potential presence of grizzly bears.

Rainbow Point. On Hebgen Lake's Grayling Arm, 5 miles north of West Yellowstone on U.S. Highway 191 then 5 miles northwest on forest roads.

Cabin Creek. Near Quake Lake, 8 miles north of West Yellowstone on U.S. Highway 191 then 13 miles west on U.S. Highway 287.

Beaver Creek. Near Quake Lake, 8 miles north of West Yellowstone on U.S. Highway 191 then 14 miles west on U.S. Highway 287.

Lonesomehurst. Located on Hebgen Lake, 8 miles west of West Yellowstone on U.S. Highway 20 then 4 miles north on Hebgen Lake Road.

Big Springs. U.S. Forest Service campground located in Island Park adjacent to the bubbling headwaters of the spring-fed Henrys Fork of the Snake River.

State Park

Henrys Lake State Park. Situated on the southern shore of Henrys Lake in Island Park. Fishing, boating, water skiing, and bird watching are popular activities.

FOOD

Few if any West Yellowstone restaurants have headlined *Gourmet* magazine recently, but the situation is improving and good fare can be found. Along with the recent arrival of McDonald's and other purveyors of fast food, a handful of non-chain eateries have popped up, too.

The Gusher Pizza and Sandwich Shoppe. Corner of Madison and Dunraven. Telephone: (406) 646–9050. Venerable West Yellowstone establishment dishing up pizza, steak, shrimp, and other goodies. Inexpensive.

Nancy P's Baking Company. Canyon Street. Telephone: (406) 646–9737. The best coffee and baked goods this side of the Firehole River, served in a simple and friendly atmosphere. Nancy P's also operates the espresso and baked-goods bar at Freeheel & Wheel (*see* Bicycling). Light breakfast and lunch. Inexpensive.

Old Town Cafe. Located not far from the Stagecoach Inn. Also known as "Cafe Eat," this small diner is big on quality food and low prices. It is a particularly popular spot for breakfast, but also serves lunch and dinner. Inexpensive.

Oregon Short Line Restaurant. Located in the West Yellowstone Conference Hotel, 315 Yellowstone Avenue. Telephone: (406) 646–7365 or, toll-free in the United States, (800) 646–7365. Good food is served throughout the day in a relaxed and cozy setting. Inexpensive to moderate.

Stage Coach Inn. 209 Madison Avenue. Telephone: (406) 646–7381 or, toll-free in the United States, (800) 842–2882. The Stage Coach makes a good choice for a quick breakfast or lunch, and for a casual or semiformal dinner. Inexpensive to moderate.

Three Bear Restaurant. 205 Yellowstone Avenue, adjacent to the Three Bear Lodge. Telephone: (406) 646–7811. Favorite family stop for West Yellowstone locals and visitors for forty years. Steaks, chicken, and homemade apple brown betty are among the house specialties. Inexpensive to moderate.

BICYCLING

Freeheel & Wheel. 40 Yellowstone Avenue. Telephone: (406) 646–7744. Full-service bike shop graced with a feminine touch, a relative rarity in the male-dominated bike business. The pair of lady proprietors offers a good selection of mountain and road bikes, rentals, repairs, and crucial "where-to-go" information. (A couple of great places to mountain bike include the Rendezvous Ski Trails—after the snow melts—and the old Union Pacific grade, which can be taken all the way from West Yellowstone to the Warm River Campground outside Ashton.) In winter the business switches gears and turns into a Nordic-ski specialty shop. An on-site espresso and bake-goods bar make a visit worthwhile even if you're not shopping for a bike or skis.

FISHING

The Madison River runs adjacent to West Yellowstone, just across the Idaho border meanders the legendary Henrys Fork, and the Firehole and other acclaimed rivers flow through nearby Yellowstone. Not surprisingly, West Yellowstone has garnered a reputation as a fly-fishing paradise. For licenses, information on where to go, and/or to recruit the services of a guide, visit one of the shops listed below.

Bud Lilly's Trout Shop. 39 Madison Avenue. Telephone: (406) 646–7801. Some say Bud Lilly is to fly-fishing what Babe Ruth is to baseball. Although the legendary angler no longer runs his namesake enterprise, the shop still features an excellent choice of gear and a dedication to responsible use of the resources.

Madison River Outfitters. 117 Canyon Street. Telephone: (406) 646–9644. Pro shop specializing in guided trips on the Madison, Gallatin, and other trout-rich rivers of the region.

HORSEBACK RIDING

Diamond "P" Ranch. Located 7 miles west of West Yellowstone on U.S. Highway 20. Individuals of any age, all the way down to young children, can be accommodated with a horse to fit one's size and experience. Telephone: (406) 646–7246.

Parade Rest Guest Ranch. Ten miles north of town on U.S. Highway 191. Rides of two, four, or six hours in duration can be arranged. Especially popular are the Monday and Friday evening outings, which culminate in a cookout under the stars. Telephone: (406) 646–7217.

SKIING

Rendezvous Trail System. West Yellowstone's acclaimed Rendezvous Trail System is one of the premier Nordic-skiing venues in America. Throughout winter Olympians, college racers, and casual ski enthusiasts come to enjoy early consistent snows, great skiing, and camaraderie. In early March the West Yellowstone Rendezvous attracts some 600 skiers. For more information call the West Yellowstone Chamber of Commerce at (406) 646–7701.

WINTER TOURS

There are more outfitters in West Yellowstone and Island Park offering winter snowmobile rentals and tours than you can shake a ski pole at. Another popular activity originating in West Yellowstone are the snowcoach outings that tour Yellowstone National Park. Arrangements for snowmobile and snowcoach tours can be made individually through outfitters or through many of the lodgings in town, including the Stage Coach Inn, the West Yellowstone Conference Hotel, and the Three Bear Lodge. Contact the West Yellowstone Chamber of Commerce at (406) 646–7701.

SHOPPING

The Book Peddler. Canyon Street. Telephone: (406) 646–9358. A relaxed bookstore stocked with a good selection of regional and Western titles, and an adjacent coffee and sandwich bar.

Madison Crossing. 121 Madison Avenue. A mandatory stop for shop-till-you-droppers. When the new high school was completed and occupied in the mid-1990s, the old school building was converted into this retail complex. Specialty shops, where you can buy clothing, Western furnishings, and much more, include the Cabin Kitchen, the Homeroom, Treetop Toys, and the fascinating Yellowstone Apothecary.

Eagle's Store. 3 Canyon Street. Telephone: (406) 646–9300. A West Yellowstone institution since 1908, Eagle's features fishing and hiking gear, T-shirts, jewelry, souvenirs, and a good choice of Western-style Stetson hats.

Smith & Chandler. 121 Yellowstone Avenue. Telephone: (406) 646–7841. Here you'll find Western and outdoor clothing, Indian jewelry, postcards, and much more. Serving West Yellowstone since 1925.

Christmas in Montana. 29 Canyon Street. Telephone: (406) 646–9347. The store specializes in holiday gifts and decorations with a regional twist.

Twin Bear Gift Shop. 3 Yellowstone Avenue. Telephone: (406) 646–9378. The Twin Bear, established in 1931, is one of West Yellowstone's original curio shops. The enterprise owns the distinction of being closer than any business to the West Entrance of Yellowstone National Park. Videos, jewelry, jackelope mounts, and more.

TELEPHONE NUMBERS

West Yellowstone Chamber of Commerce. Canyon Street and Yellowstone Avenue. (406) 646–7701.

Hebgen Lake Ranger District (Gallatin National Forest). (406) 646–7369.

Island Park Ranger District (Targhee National Forest). (208) 558–7301.

Teton Valley

The services on the "quiet side" of the Tetons are far more limited than in Jackson Hole. That is a major reason, after all, that it is the quiet side. Those passing through or preferring to distance themselves from the bustle of Jackson, however, are not without possibilities.

LODGING

Grand Valley Lodging. Offers a variety of fully equipped Teton Valley cabins and houses for rent, typically for three nights or longer (single overnights are occasionally available, depending on the length of breaks between other reservations). Telephone: (208) 354–8890 or, toll-free in the United States, (800) 746–5518. Expensive to very expensive.

Pines Motel and Guest Haus. 105 South Main Street in Driggs. Lodge offering various sorts of relaxed accommodations. Telephone: (208) 354–2774. Inexpensive.

Super 8 Teton West. Located north of Driggs on State Highway 33. Good, clean rooms with refrigerators and microwaves. Large hot tub. Telephone: (208) 354–8888 or, toll-free in the United States, (800) 888–8000. Moderate.

Teton Teepee Lodge. East of Driggs in Alta, Wyoming. The goal of the hosts at this unique, highly recommended lodge is to do everything possible to permit guests to worry only about skiing. (In summer the lodge runs a mountain-biking program, with rentals and guided trips available.) Shuttles to and from Grand Targhee, prepaid lift tickets, hearty family-style breakfasts and suppers, and much more are included. Accommodations range from small, European-style sleeping rooms with private baths, to a large dormitory with bunk beds for the kids (and for the adults, if desired). The huge circular, open-pit fireplace in the middle of the common room, with comfortable seating surrounding it, fosters socializing and getting acquainted with one's fellow guests. Ideal for families, ski clubs, and other groups. Telephone: (307) 353–8176 or, toll-free in the United States, (800) 353–8176. Moderate to expensive.

CAMPGROUNDS AND RV PARKS

Private

Teton Valley Campground. Just west of Victor on State Highway 31. Pleasant tent and RV sites and clean, modern bathroom facilities. Telephone: (208) 787–2647.

U.S. Forest Service

Call the Teton Basin Ranger District at 208–354–2312 for information:

Trail Creek. Located east of Victor on the Teton Pass Road.

Mike Harris. East of Victor on the Teton Pass Road.

Pine Creek. Located west of Victor on State Highway 31.

Teton Canyon. Situated 10 miles east of Driggs up Teton Canyon.

FOOD

The Breakfast Shoppe. 95 South Main in Driggs. Telephone: (208) 354–8294. Good place to grab a hearty breakfast before a day on the slopes at Grand Targhee. Breakfast and lunch. Inexpensive.

Lost Horizon Dinner Club. Located in Alta, Wyoming, 6 miles east of Driggs on the Grand Targhee Road. Telephone: (307) 353–8226. The Lost Horizon offers a decidedly one-of-a-kind dining experience. Plan on four hours to make your way through the ten-course meal, which consists of "half Japanese and half Chinese" food. For more than twenty years the enterprise has been owned and operated by Chuck Irwin, a retired Air Force man and brother of the late Apollo 15 astronaut Jim Irwin. Chuck's wife, Shigeko, is the chef. The dinner club features a full liquor license and a superlative view of the Cathedral Group of the Teton Range. It seats a maximum of twelve persons on Friday, Saturday, and Sunday evenings. Reservations required. Dinner only. Expensive.

Mike's Eats. 10 North Main in Driggs (just look for the bison gracing the building top). Telephone: (208) 354–2797. Buffalo burgers and buffalo hot dogs, soups, salads, and more are served at this popular lunch stop, whose decor evokes the 1950s rock-and-roll era. Often closed in winter. Breakfast, lunch, and dinner. Inexpensive.

Tony's Pizza & Pasta. Located at 364 North Main in Driggs. Telephone: (208) 354–8829. Tony's serves good pizza and other Italian dishes, and features a selection of more than fifty microbrews. Relaxed, ski-lodge ambience. Lunch and dinner. Inexpensive to moderate.

Knotty Pine. 58 South Main in Victor. Telephone: (208) 787–2866. The Pine is considered by Teton Valley locals as the place to go for a quality dining experience. The beef and lamb served are as tender and tasty as any you'll find in Yellowstone-Teton Country. The establishment boasts one of Teton County, Idaho's rare full-service bars (Mormon influences remain strong), and good dance bands

Mike's Eats, Driggs

get things moving and keep them kicking on most weekend evenings. Breakfast, lunch, and dinner. Moderate to expensive.

Victor Emporium. Located in Victor at 45 North Main Street, "the widest street in the smallest town in the West." Telephone: (208) 787–2221. This is *the* daytime hangout in Victor, where tourists, fishing guides from "over the hill" in Jackson, and locals converge to eat and gossip. Lunch consists of simple daily specials, such as burritos and burgers, typically chased by one of the Emporium's deservedly famous huckleberry milkshakes. (Folks who have sampled them include former president Ronald Reagan, and a photo of the Gipper hangs above the soda fountain.) Fishing supplies and licenses are sold at the Emporium, which also offers Teton Valley's largest selection of T-shirts. Lunch only. Inexpensive.

SKIING

Grand Targhee Ski & Summer Resort. Located 12 miles east of Driggs on the west slope of the Teton Range. Grand Targhee resides in Wyoming, but you cannot drive there without passing through Idaho, so both states claim the resort as theirs. It is a fun, relatively relaxed resort frequent-ed in winter by local farmers and ranchers, groups from Idaho Falls, and Jackson Hole destination skiers who drive over Teton Pass to sample Targhee's famous snow. A stay at Grand Targhee is much more of a "mountain getaway" experience than is a stay at the more commercial Jackson Hole Mountain Resort. Families love it. The resort owns a well-deserved reputation as the powder-snow capital of the Northern Rockies; more than 500 inches per winter is the norm. After a good storm the white stuff can be so deep that skiers not only lose sight of their skis, but often their knees and even their waists, as well. The Dreamcatcher detachable quad lift, installed in the winter of 1996–97, whisks schussers in only eight minutes to the top of Fred's Mountain, where they're faced with more than 2,000 vertical feet of downhill possibilities leading through open glades and down untimbered slopes. Additional winter activities include sled-dog rides and cross-country skiing on 15 kilometers (9.3 miles) of groomed trails. Come summer, Targhee is popular for mountain-bike and horseback riding, hiking, practicing one's mountaineering moves on the climbing wall, and simply hanging out in an exhilarating high-mountain setting. The Targhee Institute offers various programs, including a Science Explorers Day Camp for kids ages six to twelve. The annual bluegrass festival, held in August, is fast growing in reputation and attendance. Regular performers include Alison Krauss, David Grisman, and Peter Rowan. The restaurants, lodgings, and Trap Bar remain open most of the year. Telephone: (307) 353–2300 or, toll-free in the United States, (800) TARGHEE (827–4433).

WINTER TOURS

Rendezvous Ski Tours & Guest House. Located at the mouth of Fox Creek Canyon, east off State Highway 33 between Driggs and Victor. The enterprise offers guided backcountry ski tours, including instruction, in Grand Teton National Park and on Teton Pass. Rendezvous maintains three yurts at remote locations, high on the west slope of the Tetons in Plummer Canyon and on Baldy Knoll and Commissary Ridge, where many clients spend one or more nights. They also offer multi-day backpacking instructional trips in summer. Telephone: (208) 787–2906.

Grand Targhee Ski Resort

THEATER

Spud Drive-In. You can't miss this Teton Valley landmark, located two miles south of Driggs on State Highway 33. Probably the biggest "potato" you'll ever see resides here, sitting on a flatbed truck between the highway and the movie screen. The Spud shows first-run movies Monday through Saturday from Memorial Day through Labor Day. Movies begin just after dark. Telephone: (208) 354–2727.

Pierre's Playhouse. Located on Main Street in Victor. A delicious frontier Dutch-oven chicken dinner precedes entertaining, traditional hiss-and-boo melodramas. A Victor mainstay, Pierre's has been operating for more than three decades. The shows start at 7:00 P.M. Wednesday through Saturday evenings from mid-June through August. Telephone: (208) 787–2249.

OTHER ACTIVITIES

Bicycling. Big Hole Mountain Bikes, 20 West Little Avenue in Driggs (telephone 208–354–2209), or Peaked Sports (208–354–2354), located on East Little, are the places to go for information. Skinny-tire riding is popular on the low-traffic paved roads winding around Teton Valley and on the hard-surfaced rail-trail, new in 1997, that connects Driggs

and Victor. Top-notch mountain-bike rides are found outside the wilderness areas in the Tetons (the Aspen Trail is a local favorite) and, on the west side of the valley, in the lower and somewhat easier to access Big Hole Mountains.

Golf. The laid-back and inexpensive Targhee Village Golf Course (telephone 208–354–8577) occupies former farm fields east of Driggs, just over the Wyoming border. It is the antithesis of the high-end courses on the opposite side of the Tetons in Jackson Hole. (Additional courses are under development or on the drawing board in Teton Valley.)

Green Canyon Hot Springs. Located south off State Highway 33, 21 miles west of Driggs. Telephone: (208) 456–4666. At this establishment, tucked way off the beaten track, you will find an outdoor Jacuzzi pool as well as a naturally heated Olympic-size pool. A snack bar and indoor picnic area are also located on the premises.

Hiking. Popular hikes on the west side of the Tetons, where you will typically find the trails less crowded than on the east side, include the tough but rewarding climb up 11,106-foot Table Mountain. From the mountain's plateau-like summit, the commanding Grand Teton seems almost within grasp. The 12-mile round-trip hike begins at the end of the Teton Canyon Road near Teton Canyon Campground, about 10 miles east of Driggs. A popular two- or three-day backpack outing begins at the same trailhead, leading southeast through Alaska Basin and skirting Buck Mountain before descending Death Canyon to Phelps Lake and Jackson Hole.

Soaring. Grand Valley Aviation (telephone 208–354–8131) offers reasonably priced glider rides—a quiet, exhilarating, and unusual way to view the high Tetons. They begin at the airport just north of Driggs.

SHOPPING

Dark Horse Books. North Main in Driggs. Telephone: (208) 354–8882. A top-notch little bookstore that serves as the literary epicenter of Teton Valley.

Mountaineering Outfitters. 62 North Main in Driggs. Telephone: (208) 354–2222. This shop, which appears to be in total disarray (the proprietors *claim* they know where everything is), is an outdoors lover's dream world. Gold-panning supplies, USGS and county maps, water purifiers, snowshoes, and rugged outdoor wear are only a few of the items found amid the jumbled inventory.

RU Outside. Located just south of downtown Driggs. Telephone: (208) 354–3457. Retail outlet of a mail-order company specializing in hard-to-find outdoor gear, aimed particularly at snowmobile and mountain-bike enthusiasts. Great store with unusual stuff.

Yostmark Mountain Equipment. 12 East Little Avenue in Driggs. Telephone: (208) 354–2828. Purveyors of backpacks, tents, climbing gear, backcountry skis (including a model called the Mountain Noodle, which was designed by proprietor Clair Yost), boots and clothing, and Orvis brand fly-fishing gear.

TELEPHONE NUMBERS

Teton Valley Chamber of Commerce. The Outfitters building, on North Main in Driggs. (208) 354–2500.

Teton Basin Ranger District. Ranger station located on South Main in Driggs. (208) 354–2312.

II

Western Montana

GLACIER-GOLD COUNTRY

Glacier–Gold Country

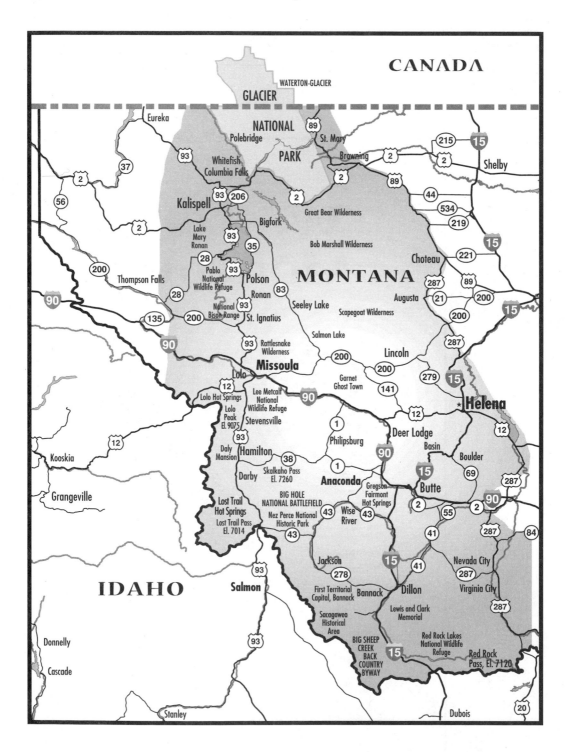

Introduction

In his book *Travels with Charley*, John Steinbeck called Montana's mountainous west "a great splash of grandeur." Amen, Mr. Steinbeck. In the time that has passed since Steinbeck and his big poodle partner passed through, western Montana has been discovered by travelers in a very big way, with Glacier National Park and the nearby Flathead Valley as its headlining attractions. In a rush evocative of the 1860s stampede of gold prospectors, an ever-growing stream of visitors is pouring into Montana. Folks want to see for themselves the bonanza of scenery and wildlife rumored to be so abundant. After discovering the truth behind the rumors, more than a few meet with real estate agents and stake their own claim in Big Sky Country.

This chafes at some longtime residents. They lament that Missoula, for example, has become overstocked with espresso stands and fancily outfitted fly-fishers. They curse the flood of vehicles that in July and August sometimes dams the flow of traffic around Flathead Lake. They bemoan that golfers and ten-acre ranchettes are increasingly supplanting Herefords and historic spreads in the rolling meadows separating Whitefish and Kalispell. (Golf-playing residents and visitors, though, celebrate the area's copious collection of top-notch courses.)

These longtimers yearn for the Montana of an earlier day, when big skies prevailed and forthright men and women fished in tennis shoes (and when the coffee was only slightly darker than water, although they don't necessarily long for that aspect of an earlier Montana).

The thing is, and most of those longtime residents secretly know it, that the Montana of the imagination endures. One simply has to know where to look for it. Try driving north from Yellowstone to Glacier National Park, following the back roads that rise like ramps to the sky along the Rockies' resplendent east slope. The drive leads through dusty old cow towns like Augusta, and it provides sweeping views of splendiferous terrain, such as that lifting toward the mountains west of Choteau, where A. B. Guthrie, author of *The Big Sky*, lived and wrote. If the time is right, it even permits the traveler to partake of the St. Patrick's Day Wild Game Feed in tiny Wolf Creek. There one can join other revelers feeding on uncommon delicacies such as breaded rattlesnake and roasted beaver tail.

The real Montana remains amid the wind-whipped stands of stunted aspen spilling off the eastern flanks of the Continental Divide. It endures outside the Blackfeet Indian tribal center of Browning, where the countryside teems with open-range cattle that are nearly as likely to be eaten by a wild grizzly bear as to wind up on the barbecue spit. You can get acquainted with a more traditional Montana by becoming engaged in a game of eight-ball, or in a "friendly discussion" about wolf reintroduction, in a smoky tavern in any Rocky Mountain Front settlement big enough to own a stop sign.

Alternatively, you might consider tackling the motor trip leading through the sublime and sparsely populated Big Hole River Valley. Here, verdant bottomlands sprawl in conspicuous contrast to surrounding hillsides baked brown by the sun. Haystacks in countless shapes cast dark shadows under broad, blue skies. A dust trail rises on the horizon, probably kicked up by a herd of racing antelope. The wind blows hard, determining the lean of trees and old barns. Amid these basins and ranges, where real cowboys still cowboy (it is a commonly used verb in these parts), you can discover what it means to be truly alone, and experience just how fine that can be.

In other words, to discover western Montana you must leave the beaten track and head for the hills and deserted valleys, advisably on dirt roads at least occasionally. But by no means bypass the well-known destinations altogether. Their acclaim is generally well deserved, and it would be a shame to miss them. Moreover, "crowded" is a relative term, so you may find few real crowds in Montana. Except, perhaps, in Glacier National Park, to which the "Glacier" in the phrase Glacier-Gold refers.

In a typical year Glacier National Park hosts more than 2 million visitors. By far the majority visit between mid-June and Labor Day. Just one, 53-mile through road bisects the park, and it is an exceptionally snaking, precipitous, and slow road. So you can see why Glacier National Park's visitor services do become a bit overwhelmed in summer. This is the chief reason that the shoulder seasons of April–May and September–October are growing in popularity. Fall, in particular, can be a sterling time to visit. There is nothing quite like hiking through a deserted western larch forest in Glacier National Park on a sunny October day, the aroma of crackling dry leaves and organic decay rich in the air and golden larch needles drifting earthward like fairy dust . . . or bicycling up the Going-to-the-Sun Road, with an exhilarating breeze blowing and sunlight dancing off the kaleidoscope of autumn-burnt deciduous brush.

The "Gold" in the phrase relates to two distinct aspects of the region: one, the fields of grain that undulate in the wind like ocean waves; the other, the crumbling and compelling ghost towns littering the hills, where gold and other precious metals once were sought.

Glacier-Gold Country covers roughly the western one-third of the state. It encompasses all of the Montana Rockies lying north and west of the five counties included in Yellowstone-Teton

Country. This is an immense and greatly disparate region. East of the Continental Divide, where the views are infinite, you will see farmers and cattle ranchers working their fields and fences. West of the Divide, steep-sided valleys and thick timber stands create settings that are more closed and intimate. Here loggers fell monster trees, and in summer lookouts occupy fire towers that are perched atop lofty, wind-buffeted peaks. Theirs is the quintessential room with a view, a view taking in millions of acres of national forest lands. Visit one if you can (but don't leave town without the equipment necessary to change a flat tire!).

Fittingly, Glacier National Park presides above it all, in regard to its location at the top of the map, anyway. The Continental Divide wears Glacier like a bejeweled crown.

But if you consider for a moment nothing but the elevations of the highest peaks in Glacier, you might conclude that they are rather mundane mountains. How wrong you would be! It is true that the highest peak in Glacier National Park is not much over 10,000 feet in elevation. That's nearly 4,000 feet lower than the apex of Yellowstone-Teton Country, the 13,771-foot Grand Teton. Only after learning that the valley floors below are proportionately lower—3,000 to 4,000 feet above sea level, compared to 6,000 to 7,000 feet in Yellowstone-Teton Country—can you appreciate just how high into the sky those Glacier mountains jut. This is because the Rocky Mountains and adjacent intermontane basins reach their highest in Colorado, then slope ever-downward as they extend to the north. Some valley floors in the heart of the Colorado Rockies actually sit at elevations higher than many of Glacier's stunning, ice-clad peaks. But even the heralded "fourteeners" rising from those Colorado valleys are no more remarkable, and are often less so, than the crystal mountains giving Glacier National Park its sparkle.

Even excluding the magnificent mountains of Glacier, try counting on your fingers and toes the number of Rocky Mountain sub-ranges contained in Glacier-Gold Country and eventually you'll need to borrow digits from a friend. If you get tired of looking at the multitude of mountains from afar—as if one ever could—then go into them and see them from the inside out. Penetrate the high country in your vehicle where car travel is both permissible and possible. Travel by foot, mountain bike, or horseback where cars are impractical and/or off-limits. In winter you can go into the ranges on skis, by snowmobile, or even aboard a sled pulled by high-energy huskies. These mountains hide secrets that are a joy to learn: secrets such as old-growth forests of Douglas fir and Engelmann spruce, cold lakes inhabited by hungry trout, and isolated campsites where you can listen for the howl of a gray wolf.

Or, keep to the valleys and the mountain flanks in your search for natural wonders. You won't have to look far wherever you are, because Mother Nature was uncommonly generous to western Montana when handing out her gifts. Because of the surplus of natural phenomena, and because so many of them lie on lands owned by and open to the public, Glacier-Gold Country rivals any area in North America regarding the outdoor recreation possibilities close at hand. How about a backpacking or llama-packing trip into the Bob Marshall Wilderness Area? "The Bob" adjoins with the Great Bear and Scapegoat wilderness areas to create an unbroken chain of wildlands that covers a mind-boggling 1.5-million acres. An outing here can provide the backcountry trip of a lifetime. For something shorter and tamer, simply tackle a day hike in one of the national forests described in Seeing Glacier-Gold Country. Or go "rock-hounding" for garnets, or digging for amethyst crystals in the Pioneer Mountains. Or enjoy an altogether relaxing evening dip in a natural outdoor hot spring. So submerged, you can tilt back your head and gaze into a night sky containing far more stars than you ever knew existed.

Wherever you are and whatever activity you are enjoying, keep an eye out for wild birds and animals. Both are richly abundant throughout Glacier-Gold Country. You might see Rocky Mountain goats (shaggy white creatures with pointed black horns), bighorn sheep (darker and stockier, with curled horns), black bears, or grizzly bears. You may encounter moose, mule and white-tailed deer, elk, pine marten, mountain lions, swans, or one of a countless number of other species, both big and small.

Glacier-Gold Country features a host of other alluring aspects, as well, including an incredible array of wild waters. Rivers rising in Montana's

Rocky Mountain goat

mountains drain in three directions and empty into three oceans. The waters west of the Continental Divide flow to the Pacific Ocean, via the Clark Fork–Columbia system. The waters of most streams east of the Divide end up in the Gulf of Mexico, via the Missouri-Mississippi system. Rivers arising on the east side of Glacier National Park, however, flow into the Belly and St. Mary's rivers and into Canada, then northeast via the Saskatchewan River system into Hudson Bay. Eventually those waters wind up in the Arctic Ocean.

Also of compelling interest in Glacier-Gold Country are the Native American cultures that are so evident. Possibly in no area outside the Navajo and Pueblo Indian regions of Arizona and New Mexico do Native Americans retain closer ties to their past than they do in western Montana. See if you don't agree after attending the North American Indian Days, celebrated in Browning each July, or after visiting the People's Center in the village of Pablo, where the lifeways of the Salish, Kootenai, and Pend d'Oreille Indians are explained and illuminated.

In closing, let's reconsider Missoula, a town that a lot of folks grumble has been "ruined" by publicity and population growth. I lived in that city for fifteen years, so I have a pretty good sense for its pulses. Bared to the essence, Missoula is a vibrant, cosmopolitan, and idea-rich community. There are plenty of vibrant, idea-rich cities in the United States, of course. But from how many of them can you spot a herd of wild elk grazing on the side of a mountain while you're sitting in the bleachers, cheering on your team in a college football game? Or watch a bald eagle fishing over waters flowing through the middle of the business district? Or fly-fish for trout in a river that runs behind the offices of the city's chamber of commerce? All of these are possible in Missoula. It is an exceptional place, indeed.

And so is the greater Glacier-Gold Country. This is an enticing, exciting region, with diversions, scenic splendor, and elbow room to spare. It is changing in some very real ways, sure, as are all areas of the Rocky Mountain West. Change is inevitable. But western Montana remains an inviting and incredible place to visit . . . time and time again.

Of Glaciers, Ecosystems, and a Lake Running ∿∿∿∿∿ Through It

Throughout Glacier-Gold Country; indeed, in all of the Northern Rockies, elevation, relative exposure to the sun and weather, soil type, and other environmental factors combine to help determine what plants and animals reside in a given area. Nowhere in the region in such a small area, though, are the differences more pronounced, and easier to view, than in Glacier National Park. And nowhere within Glacier can one more readily observe the changing life zones than by traveling on the Going-to-the-Sun Road, which extends from just over 3,000 to 6,646 feet above sea level in a matter of a few miles.

Most of what you learn in Glacier National Park can be adapted to other parts of the region. Think of Glacier as a university, its mountains and pinnacles lofty ivory towers, then take what you learn there and apply it elsewhere. By acquainting yourself with some of the basics regarding the life zones in Glacier—how to identify them, why they prevail where they do, and so forth—you will open new windows on your explorations beyond the park. If you find one familiar plant growing in another place, you'll be able to predict with some degree of certainty what other plants and animals you might expect to encounter. This familiarity can help breed a real sense of feeling "at home" in the mountains, forests, and meadows of the Northern Rockies.

Glacier National Park comprises one of the widest ranges of habitats of any compact geographic area in North America, meaning that it boasts one of the greatest diversities of plants and animals, too. More than 1,000 species of plants inhabit the park's 1 million acres. Sixty native mammals live in Glacier (two additional natives, the woodland caribou and mountain bison, are no longer found in the park), along with more than 200 species of birds, two non-venomous snake species, five types of amphibians, and twenty-two species of fish, six of them introduced and the rest native to the park.

The most important factors determining life zones are elevation and latitude, with changes in one mimicking changes in the other. By climbing 6,000 feet in Glacier National Park you will encounter life zones similar to those you would observe by walking at a constant elevation from Glacier to a point 1,800 miles north.

We tend to think of geology and biology in separate terms, as more or less unrelated subjects. However, geologic forces set the stage for everything inhabiting a given area, a fact that becomes particularly clear in Glacier National Park, where the topsy-turvy terrain offers amazing elevation differentials, all within a relatively small area.

The mountains in Glacier are so steep and abrupt that, in some instances, in order to cover a linear mile, one must climb vertically for *more* than a mile. This tremendous topographic relief, of course, is the result of geologic forces; namely, glaciers moving across an enormous slab of sedimentary rock. Over a period of many millions of years, Precambrian Belt rocks of limestone and mudstone, which had been deposited as sediments on the floors of ancient seas, were pushed upward along the Lewis overthrust fault. This resulted in ancient Precambrian rocks becoming superimposed atop much younger Cretaceous rocks, which is the opposite of how it usually works (that is, with younger rocks overlying older ones). The slab, hundreds of miles long and thousands of feet thick, moved eastward at least 35 miles, beginning at a point west of today's Glacier National Park.

The break between the underlying Cretaceous and overlying Precambrian sedimentary rocks can clearly be recognized on the eastern front of the Rockies in Glacier. The younger, softer Cretaceous rocks, which are between 65 million and 100 million years old, form the rolling hills that lie beneath the billion-year-old Precambrians. The latter, which are much more resistant to erosion, have formed steep cliffs and mountain walls.

As the rudimentary Rocky Mountains formed, the erosional forces of water and wind simultaneously battered them, knocking down the high plateau even as it grew. The resulting rounded, lowered mountainous plateau east of the Lewis overthrust fault was intermittently invaded by glaciers over a period of more than 2 million years. Late in the Pleistocene epoch of the Cenozoic era, glaciers flowing and growing south from Canada engulfed the low-lying areas of northern Washington, northern Idaho, and western Montana. But the high-mountain reaches such as the future Glacier National Park were not covered by these icy extensions from the north. Rather, the mountains actually grew their own glaciers as the climate cooled during the Ice Age, causing high alpine snowfields to grow ever larger.

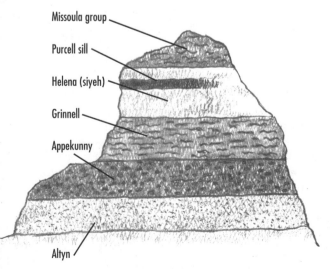

Precambrian rock layers

Ice was the primary sculptor responsible for creating the impressive terrain we see in the park today. But Glacier might more accurately be called De-Glaciered National Park, because the few surviving ice sheets are little more than glorified snowbanks compared to the groaning, frozen oceans that moved across the landscape during the Pleistocene. (In fact, the glaciers today cover only about 25 percent of the area they encompassed as recently as the 1800s.) Imagine a sea of ice, 3,000 feet thick in places, unbroken but by a few tips of the very highest mountains sticking out like pointed islands, and you'll have a vague image of what the area in and around Glacier looked like 20,000 years ago.

Glaciers chopped, chiseled, scraped, scoured, shaped, and polished the landscape. Moving in response to their own mass being pulled by gravity, the glaciers dragged boulders, stones, pebbles, and sediment as they moved across Precambrian rocks. Slowly, but sometimes advancing much more rapidly than at other times, the glaciers carved bedrock into a jumble of jagged, angular peaks; they gouged immense, straight-running *U-shaped valleys*; and like conveyor belts they deposited materials into moraines, which today dam lakes such as McDonald and St. Mary. Moving ice sculpted the serrated skyline, leaving behind *cirques, horns, hanging valleys*, and other features including the knife-edge ridges called *arêtes* (ah-RETS).

The changes wrought by the rivers of ice are directly or indirectly responsible for the staggering array of habitats and animals—every nook and cranny, animal and flower—found in Glacier today. Glacier is a meeting ground where flora and fauna common in the Northern Rockies thrive in close proximity to plants and animals found in the Arctic, as well as close to others native to the wind-buffeted Great Plains, the rain-soaked Pacific Coast, and the arid Great Basin. Certain plants in Glacier grow no farther south than there; others reach the easternmost limits of their ranges in the park; others still, their westernmost. Glacier National Park is an island of sorts, unique in the world.

As a rule, for every 300 feet gained in elevation, the mean temperature drops approximately 1 degree Fahrenheit. On a sunny July afternoon the temperature can be a sweltering 90 degrees in

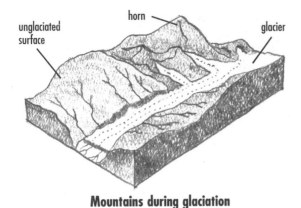

Mountains during glaciation

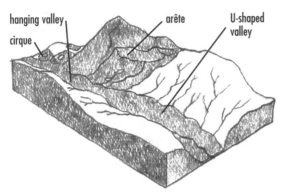

Mountains after glaciation

the valley of the North Fork of the Flathead River, but a pleasant 70 degrees in one of the park's high-elevation meadows. And it could readily drop to below freezing at the uppermost elevations that night. (Even this is an oversimplification: For example, in winter, cold air often settles in the valleys or in the mid-elevation cirques. When these *temperature inversions* occur, the warmest spots of all are often the highest, wind-blown ridgetops.)

Another result of going higher in elevation is an ever-increasing quantity of precipitation. High mountains in general are moisture magnets, and those in Glacier National Park are so to an extreme. No place in the U.S. Rocky Mountains can claim more precipitation. At lofty altitudes on the west slope of the Rockies in Glacier, more than 100 inches of moisture can fall in a year, most of it in the form of snow—as much as 700 inches per winter. Meanwhile, at the low valley elevations on both the east and west slopes of the Continental Divide, just miles away, annual precipitation is often less than 30 inches.

Even at constant elevations and precipitation levels, though, different life zones persist. Glaring evidence of this can be seen by comparing north-facing and south-facing mountain slopes. Shaded north slopes hold rain and snow much longer than sun-battered south-facing slopes; consequently, you will generally see far more timber growing on a north-facing slope. A more specific example: The lower elevation landscapes on the east side of Glacier—where great sweeps of grass lean with the wind, growing to the edge of drought-resistant groves of timber—appear to be much drier than those on the west, where brooding forests of hemlock, cedar, and Douglas fir thrive. Yet the lower eastern portions often receive as much annual precipitation as the lower western elevations. What's going on?

On the west side of the mountains the influence of Pacific maritime weather is strong and, consequently, the conditions in general are relatively moderate and stable. The east slope, meanwhile, which is greatly affected by the continental air masses, endures some of the harshest weather in the United States. The national record for the greatest temperature fluctuation in one day was set in Browning, just east of Glacier National Park. There, within a twenty-four-hour period in January 1916 the temperature dropped from 44 degrees Fahrenheit to –56, after a warm *chinook* (an Athabascan Indian word meaning "snow eater") was chased out by a frigid Arctic front. That's a 100-degree difference in one day! Also, desiccating winds are an almost constant companion to those living along the eastern front: Cold, frigidly bitter winds in winter, along with the occasional warm, melting chinook, whose winds can reach 100 miles per hour; and hot, dry winds in summer. The resolute winds serve to dramatically dry up the soil and the plant life.

Another factor contributing to micro-habitats is subtle contours in the land, even in terrain that would appear to receive the same exposure to sun and weather. Yet another is wildfire, which historically and prehistorically was a regular phenomenon in the heavily wooded portions of Glacier. And it still is, although large-scale suppression efforts have diminished the role fire plays.

Complicating and oftentimes contradictory situations create an ever-changing mosaic of habitats in Glacier National Park, including the occasional uncommon communities of *sphagnum fen, dry meadow, wet meadow,* and *fellfield,* which often grows near glacial moraines and on talus slopes. Still, it is possible to generalize and discuss Glacier's four primary life zones that predominate at different elevations.

Grassland/parkland community.

Prairie communities maintained by periodic fires are located in Glacier National Park at elevations lower than 4,500 feet on both sides of the Continental Divide. The grasslands east of the Divide are generally an extension of those found in southern Alberta. In addition to a rich mix of grasses they support dense groves of gnarled aspen, clinging to wind-whipped morainal hills and protected crannies. Brushy thickets of buffalo berry, serviceberry, snowberry, wolf willow, and wild rose are common, too, along with summer wildflowers, including wild geranium and Indian paintbrush. The most extensive grasslands are located beyond the park's boundaries on the Blackfeet Indian Reservation, but these extend, finger-like, into the park's coniferous stands. They're particularly evident in the Belly River, Many Glacier, and St. Mary areas. Douglas fir, lodgepole pine, limber pine, and Engelmann spruce incessantly invade and attempt to crowd out the shade-intolerant aspens. But then fire hits again, spawning new growth of the aspens' root suckers, while burning out the conifers. Ponderosa pine, a drought-resistant, fire-loving tree that would appear to fit right in amid the east slope's grasslands, is not part of this community. Apparently it is too sensitive to the harsh, windy winters to thrive there.

West of the Divide grasslands are found along the relatively arid valley of the North Fork of the Flathead River, which serves as the national park's western boundary. Here lightning-caused fires periodically clear away invading forests, maintaining a prairie that's closely related to the Palouse grass communities of western Idaho and eastern Washington. The west-side prairies typically abut dry-country forests composed of Douglas fir and ponderosa pine.

In the grasslands on both sides of the Continental Divide watch for burrowing animals such as badgers and ground squirrels. Mule deer and elk are part-time residents, particularly in the

spring, when they are attracted by the new growth of grasses. Consequently, itinerant residents also include the scavengers and hunters that follow these large mammals: grizzly and black bears, coyotes, cougars, and wolves, which returned to Glacier in the 1980s after a fifty-year hiatus. The eastern grasslands in particular support a prolific mix of bird species, thanks to the rich diversity of habitats provided by the mix of prairie, aspen stands, and coniferous forests. Beavers, whose favorite food and building material is aspen, are abundant in and along the streams of the eastern grasslands.

Low- to mid-elevation forest community.

More than 60 percent of Glacier National Park is blanketed in forests, which comprise nineteen tree species. Thriving at just above the 3,000-foot level in one particularly warm, moist area west of the Continental Divide—namely the Lake McDonald–Avalanche Creek vicinity—is a temperate forest supporting stands of old-growth western red cedar and western hemlock. Some of the ancient giants of this forest are more than 400 years old. Prior to the massive fires of 1910, which consumed woodlands and settlements throughout western Montana and northern Idaho, the cedar-hemlock community prevailed in other low-lying areas of Glacier. The community did not, however, occur above 3,500 feet, which is the highest elevation in Glacier at which these temperature-sensitive species can survive before the climate turns too harsh.

Living amid the old-growth forests is a host of birds, such as swifts, chickadees, thrushes, crossbills, and woodpeckers, including the large pileated woodpecker (just think "Woody"). The rarely viewed pine marten and even rarer fisher, both elusive members of the weasel family, are predators in the community. Understory growth includes bracken ferns, devil's club, mosses, mushrooms, lichens, and other shade-tolerant flora you'd more reasonably expect to find in the rain forests of the Pacific Northwest than in the Northern Rockies.

The western larch, a tree that grows tall and broad, with a wonderfully straight grain, is an enigma: It is a deciduous conifer, whose needles turn yellow and drop in the fall, glimmering in the sun and coloring the forest floor below. Stands of western larch are often found growing on the west slope between 3,000 and 3,500 feet, where the cedar-hemlock forests of an earlier day thrived. In fact, you can see the dead snags of some of those earlier trees still standing amid the mixed forests of larch and lodgepole pine, looking much like weathered ghosts from the past.

Above the grasslands and low-lying forests on both sides of the Continental Divide is the transitional Douglas fir forest. Higher yet, from 4,000 to around 6,000 feet above sea level, forests of Engelmann spruce and subalpine fir dominate. These extend to near the tree line, where scattered forests of subalpine fir grow. Berry-filled shrubs are common in the understory of the spruce-fir forests. Slicing through these forests you will see avalanche chutes, those timber-cleared swaths that are so common on the steep mountainsides of Glacier. (Incidentally, it's not the sliding snow that typically takes out the trees; rather, it is the powerful winds that blow in front of the avalanches.) Bears regularly dine within avalanche chutes, and they also use them as travel corridors. Huckleberries, a favorite food of black and grizzly bears, grow abundantly in slide chutes near the forest edge. With binoculars in hand, watch one of the vegetation-choked openings for awhile— higher up the later it is in the season, because berries ripen as the snow line recedes. If you do this, you'll have a good chance of spotting a grizzly bear from a distance . . . which is the only way you want to see a griz!

Huckleberry

Bird and animal life is more varied in these forests than in the other life zones. The forest floor, the low shrubs, the smaller tree understory, and the high canopies of the mature timber each serve as a rich ecological niche, replete with a variety of full- and part-time residents. For instance, animals common to the forest floor include insects, weasels, grouse, and snowshoe hares, along with the hare's chief predator, the Canada lynx. The low shrubs, meantime, provide a haven for nesting birds, including nuthatches, waxwings, and dozens of others. Higher still, squirrels and woodpeckers are drawn to the food and shelter provided by the tall trees.

Subalpine community.

Pockets of stunted, gnarled subalpine firs grow beyond the upper limits of the spruce-fir community but below the arctic zone, generally between 6,000 and 7,000 feet above sea level. Trees living near the tree line, where the growing season is only about six weeks long, also include whitebark pine, Engelmann spruce, and limber pine. The trees here typically grow in islands, or dense groups, a biological strategy that permits trees to help others survive by providing a degree of protection from the cold, blasting winds. The trees surviving at the highest, windiest areas, where the growing season is the shortest, assume the stunted form known as *krummholz* (literally "crooked wood"). These trees resemble shrubs and rarely grow taller than 2 feet high. A second species of larch, the subalpine larch, also occurs occasionally in Glacier at the upper limits of treeline, far higher than where the western larch can be found.

Alpine community.

The highest, harshest reaches are above the tree line, which generally occurs at an elevation of about 7,000 feet in Glacier, but can occur even below 6,000 feet. The elevation of the tree line is primarily a function of the length of the growing season, which can change markedly at similar elevations, depending on local topography, exposure, and other factors.

More than 20 percent of Glacier is included within the alpine life zone. But the plant communities found above the tree line can vary dramatically, changing with the different ground surfaces, exposures to sun and wind, and moisture levels. Vegetation typically consists of low-growing perennials and shrubs, including the dwarf willow, which spreads across the ground like a thick carpet. Dense growth such as this is a survival strategy, maximizing water retention in the harsh, moisture-sucking climate. On lofty slopes covered with the loose rock known as *talus,* hardy alpine plants such as sky pilot, limestone columbine, and alpine buttercup flourish during the brief summer. Even where snow persists all summer long you can see living things thriving, in the form of oil-containing algae that color the snow where they grow densely enough.

Animals found in the arctic extremes include bighorn sheep, which migrate there in summer, and mountain goats, year-round residents of the high, rarefied places. The shaggy white beasts—which are not true goats, but relatives of the European chamois—in winter survive on mosses and lichens, which they scratch from the high ridges that are kept relatively snow-free by high winds. Other animals common in the alpine zone include pikas, hoary marmots, and white-tailed ptarmigans, a grouse that is the sole permanent bird resident of this community.

Now, for quite a different geological tale, let's travel 130 miles south from Glacier. Approximately 15,000 years before the late Norman Maclean wrote *A River Runs Through It,* his memorable coming-of-age story about fly-fishing in the Missoula area, a lot more

than a river ran through the Missoula Valley.

The first geologist to visit the Missoula Valley in the 1870s noticed several horizontal lines etched on the hillside bordering the valley on the east. He correctly assumed that the parallel lines could have been created only by a now-extinct lake, whose shoreline level had changed over the decades. Those lines can still be seen today, particularly well when there's just a dusting of snow on Mount Sentinel, which looms above the University of Montana campus in Missoula.

Here's how it happened: As the ice sheets of the Pinedale glaciation reached toward their maximum size in the late Pleistocene, a tongue of ice extending from British Columbia's Purcell Valley grew southward into the Clark Fork River Valley, in the area of today's Lake Pend Oreille near Sandpoint, Idaho. The huge ice flow acted as a dam, eventually backing up the waters of the Clark Fork all the way to the Missoula Valley, and also damming the Kootenai River to the north. Glacial Lake Missoula, as we now call the reservoir that formed behind the ice-dammed Clark Fork, at its highest level may have joined with the lake formed by the Kootenai, creating one very big pond covering much of northwest Montana. (It is believed that the same phenomenon, but on an even larger scale, occurred during the earlier Bull Lake glaciation. For more on the Bull Lake and Pinedale glaciations, *see* The Land, Yellowstone-Teton Country.)

With the river outlet entirely blocked, the lake continued to grow larger and larger, backing up into the drainages feeding the Clark Fork. It's estimated that at its maximum size, Glacial Lake Missoula was as big as the present Lake Ontario. At the ice dam the lake was roughly 2,000 feet deep; in the Missoula Valley, more than 1,000 feet deep. But it couldn't last forever: Ice floats, so before the water reached the level where it would spill over the top, the ice dam began floating, then breaking up. This set off the first in a series of floods that are the most dramatic recorded in the geologic record of the world's rocks.

The process repeated itself—as the ice continually grew south from British Columbia—nearly forty times, spanning a period of approximately 1,000 years. Geologists have determined, by inspecting the sediment layers put down during the various stages in Lake Missoula's life, that the

Hoary marmot

first and longest filling of the lake persisted about sixty years, while the last and shortest lasted only nine years. Each time the dam floated and broke, the magnitude of flooding downstream was inconceivable. Water poured to the west and southwest, inundating the valleys and many of the hills of eastern Oregon and Washington, including the present site of Spokane. Evidence of the floods can be seen today in the form of boulders of Precambrian sedimentary rocks from western Montana's Belt formation, lying out of context in the Columbia River Gorge between Oregon and Washington, 1,000 feet above water level. Similar boulders are scattered about the floor of the valley of the Willamette River near Salem, Oregon.

History

On December 20, 1803, the Stars and Stripes were raised over New Orleans, and the size of the United States instantly doubled.

The Louisiana Territory had become a troublesome wilderness for Napoleonic France, which consented to sell it to the United States for the modest sum of $15 million. The somewhat vaguely defined area included the lands between the Gulf of Mexico and British North America, from the Mississippi River west to the (at that time, hypothetical) Continental Divide. Excluded were those Spanish-claimed lands lying east of the Continental Divide, west of the 100th meridian, and south of the Arkansas River.

As we know now, the Louisiana Territory's 828,000 square miles—purchased for less than three cents an acre—turned out to contain some of the most productive farmlands and fantastic landscapes on earth. President Thomas Jefferson wasted no time in dispatching an expedition to investigate the new frontier. He christened his exploratory party the "Corps of Discovery," naming as party organizer and leader his personal secretary, a serious and seriously bowlegged twenty-nine-year-old Army captain from Virginia named Meriwether Lewis. The president admired Lewis for his "firmness of constitution and character, prudence, habits adapted to the woods, and a familiarity with the Indian manners and character."

As his co-leader Lewis chose the tall, redheaded William Clark, an amiable and outgoing officer four years Lewis's elder, whom he had served under in the militia. The expedition's chief mission: scout for a possible water route to the Pacific Ocean via the Missouri and Columbia rivers, while strengthening the U.S. claim on the Oregon Territory. Secondary charges included the tasks of collecting and cataloging flora and fauna found in the unexplored lands, recording the weather, and fostering peaceful relations with the Native Americans encountered. Jefferson expected this to pay future dividends, by setting the stage for luring fur-trade business away from the British North West Company.

In May of 1804, aboard canoes and a keelboat, the Corps of Discovery headed upstream on the Missouri River from near its mouth at Wood River, Illinois. Two dozen men accompanied the co-leaders; among them: colorful characters like George Drouillard, a French-Shawnee whose fluency in sign language would prove indispensable to the expedition; Meriwether Lewis's black slave, a powerfully built man named York; willowy and one-eyed Pete Cruzatte, whose fiddling talent would often serve to elevate low spirits; and the stocky Irishman Patrick Gass, an expert boatbuilder and woodsman.

The men spent the winter of 1804–5 regrouping in the Mandan Indian villages located 40 miles upstream from today's Bismarck, North Dakota. Here they took on a French trader named Toussaint Charbonneau. Accompanying Charbonneau were his fifteen-year-old Shoshone wife, Sacajawea, and the couple's infant son, Jean Baptiste. Lewis and Clark believed that Charbonneau's inclusion would benefit the expedition, since he had traveled and traded in the upper Missouri country and ostensibly was conversant in several Indian languages. And Sacajawea, the leaders correctly believed, would be able to aid them in horse-trading negotiations with other Native Americans.

The corps continued traveling upstream, arriving on April 26, 1805, at the confluence of the Yellowstone and Missouri rivers, where they entered the future Montana. As they pushed, poled, and paddled deep into Big Sky Country they encountered increasing numbers of wildlife—bison, bighorns, mule deer, elk, rattlesnakes, prairie dogs, beaver, otter, and much more. Lewis and/or Clark was the first to describe several species, including the western meadowlark, the sage grouse, and the cutthroat trout, whose Latin name, *Salmo clarki*, honors the older captain. The party traveled more miles and spent more time in Montana than in any other future state of the Union, and left behind a larger legacy of place names here than anywhere else. Fittingly, to a greater degree than the residents of any state, today's Montanans relate to and claim as "theirs" the Corps of Discovery.

The expedition spent several weeks traveling upstream through the drylands of eastern Montana, passing through the phantasmagoric terrain known as the Missouri Breaks. Subsequently, an advance party spent nearly a week of June mapping an 18-mile portage around the Great Falls of the Missouri, where the city of Great Falls now resides. (The series of five falls, described by Lewis as "the grandest sight I ever beheld," has since been obliterated by hydroelectric works.) Meanwhile, other party members built makeshift wagons to carry the watercraft over the harrowing portage, which wound up taking the group thirteen days to accomplish. Intense heat and "our trio of pests"—mosquitoes, gnats, and prickly pear cactus—combined to make the slow going particularly miserable. Lewis noted that he saw "not less than 10,000 buffaloe within a circle of 2 miles . . . " in the vicinity of the Great Falls. He also encountered grizzly bears; in fact, on one occasion he was chased into the river by a charging griz. He called the experience a "curious adventure," which can only be called a world-class understatement by anyone who has seen a grizzly bear up close and personal.

Once above the Great Falls the men and Sacajawea continued upstream, heading southwest. Approximately 70 miles beyond the falls they entered a spectacular canyon, described by Meriwether Lewis in these words:

[The] river appears to have woarn a passage just the width of its channel over 150 yds. It is deep from side to side nor is there in the 1st 3 Miles of this distance a spot except one of a few yards in extent on which a man could rest the soal of his foot....This rock is a black grannite below and appears to be of a much lighter color above and from the fragments I take it to be flint of a yellowish brown and light creem-coloured yellow. From the singular appearance of this place I called it gates of the Rocky Mountains.

Waters backed up by Holter Dam give the canyon a very different look today from 1805, but still the Gates of the Mountains is an extraordinarily scenic place. Cliffs rise 1,200 feet above the river, and the abundant wildlife includes bighorn sheep and mountain goats. The canyon is best viewed by boarding one of the tour boats that depart daily in summer from the Gates of the Mountains Recreational Area marina, located 3 miles east of Interstate 15 from a point 17 miles north of Helena.

From the Gates the expedition persevered upstream, becoming on July 25 the first white Americans to reach the headwaters region, where three rivers merge to become the Missouri. Concluding that none of the three was adequately larger than the other two to justify calling it

Mountain bluebird

the Missouri, they named those "three noble streams" the Madison, Gallatin, and Jefferson. The names honored the U.S. secretary of state, the secretary of the treasury, and "the author of our enterprize," President Jefferson. Indian tribes including the Blackfeet, Gros Ventre, and Flatheads had frequented this game-abundant headwaters region during the eighteenth century, but by the time the Corps of Discovery arrived the Blackfeet dominated, though none were encountered here. Soon thereafter, the headwaters evolved into one of the premier beaver-trapping regions of the West, playing an important role in the era of the mountain man.

Today's bucolic Headwaters State Park, located just outside the town of Three Forks, provides camping, picnicking, fishing, and interpretive hikes highlighting the area's pivotal role in the exploration and settlement of Montana. There's even an on-site ghost town in the remains of Gallatin City, which was established here in 1864.

Next, in an effort to locate the absolute origin of the waters that become the Missouri, while also looking for a relatively easy way over the Continental Divide, the party pushed into southwest Montana. They followed the Jefferson River to where it is formed by the convergence of the Big Hole, Beaverhead, and Ruby rivers near present Twin Bridges. (Lewis and Clark called those rivers the Wisdom, Philanthropy, and Philosophy, but their conceptual names didn't stick.) From there they traveled south up the Beaverhead, establishing Camp Fortunate at a spot now covered by the waters of the Clark Canyon Reservoir.

They knew that a nasty tangle of terrain loomed ahead. While the others waited at Camp Fortunate, Lewis led an advance party over 7,373-foot Lemhi Pass, crossing the invisible line separating the Atlantic and Pacific watersheds. Here they also passed from Montana and the Louisiana Purchase territory into the future Idaho. At Lemhi Pass, which today can be reached by following a rough and narrow, summer-only Forest Service road, a jubilant Lewis found a spring he thought to be the "most distant fountain of the waters of the Mighty Missouri . . . . I had accomplished one of those great objectives on which my mind had been unalterably fixed for many years." However, Lewis would be disappointed to learn that the

truly "most distant fountain" was later found to lie some 100 miles to the southeast, in the Centennial Valley. His spring still trickles, though, at the Sacajawea Historical Area, located on the Montana side of Lemhi Pass. The site includes a small campground/picnic area.

On the western side of the pass Lewis and his companions encountered a band of Shoshone Indians. At the Indians' camp, located north of present Tendoy, Idaho, the men met with Chief Cameahwait. After spending a couple of nights there, Lewis and his companions, with Cameahwait and several other Shoshone accompanying them, crossed the Continental Divide back into Montana, where they rejoined the rest of the Corps of Discovery. In the Headwaters Region Sacajawea had begun recognizing the surroundings as the country of her childhood, where she'd lived before being kidnapped at age ten by Minataree Indians. Incredibly, now she recognized Chief Cameahwait as her long-lost brother. The journals relate that upon recognizing her sibling, Sacajawea "instantly jumped up, and ran and embraced him, throwing over him her blanket and weeping profusely . . . ."

Oddly, these Shoshone were the first Indians the corps had encountered in all of Montana—and they were first encountered in Idaho. Trade negotiations with them must have taken a while: Sacajawea translated her brother's Shoshone words to Charbonneau in the Minataree language, which the couple both spoke. Charbonneau passed along the information in French to another member of the expedition. Finally that fellow–French speaker translated it into English so that Lewis and Clark could understand and respond. So it went, back and forth. But the dealings were successful and the party obtained the horses they needed to penetrate the rough-country mountains that lay ahead.

Subsequently, the entire party traveled over Lemhi Pass. The corps had finally reached the Pacific side of the Continental Divide and they knew it. However, they discovered the nearby Salmon River's canyons too precipitous and its waters too turbulent to consider even trying to negotiate. So, instead, on September 4 they crossed Lost Trail Pass back into Montana, still remaining on the west slope. Today's traveler driving through the picturesque Bitterroot Valley, which extends from the base of Lost Trail Pass north 90 miles to Missoula, will see that the expedition's journey down the valley is well documented by historic markers.

About a dozen miles north of the pass, near present Sula along the East Fork of the Bitterroot, is the site where the expedition met a group of approximately 400 Flatheads. Despite speaking a language that sounded extremely weird to Clark's ears, the explorer described these Indians as "the likelyest and honnestst Savages we have ever yet Seen." The friendly meeting culminated in the acquisition of additional horses by the Corps. Charlie Russell's famous work *Lewis and Clark Meeting the Flathead Indians at Ross' Hole* re-creates the event. The very large painting hangs in the state capitol in Helena, on the front wall of the floor of the House of Representatives. (The broad riverside opening was named Ross' Hole after Alexander Ross of the Hudson's Bay Company, who camped here the winter of 1824.)

For three days the Corps of Discovery traveled north down the Bitterroot Valley, where they found plant life abundant but game scarce. On September 11, after laying over for a couple of days at Travelers' Rest (the site of the town of Lolo), they left the Bitterroot River and headed west up Lolo Creek. This marked the beginning of probably the toughest stretch of their entire journey. It was an eleven-day struggle, leading past Lolo Hot Springs and over the Bitterroot Mountains, along a trail of sorts used by the Nez Perce Indians in yearly forays to the buffalo plains east of the Rockies. The explorers found it necessary to maneuver over and around a constant maze of deadfall timber and thick brush, making route-finding nearly impossible. The going was painfully slow, and food was so scarce that the men killed horses for sustenance.

On cresting Lolo Pass the Corps left Montana and re-entered Idaho, then followed the Clearwater, Snake, and Columbia rivers to the Pacific. After wintering at Fort Clatsop, near present Astoria, Oregon, they re-crossed Montana on their return trip to St. Louis. After camping at Travelers' Rest late in June of 1806, the party split into two contingents. Lewis and his group proceeded down the Bitterroot to the location of today's Missoula, camping at the confluence of Rattlesnake Creek and the Clark Fork

River. From there they headed northeast through the Hellgate Canyon, up the Blackfoot River, and over the Continental Divide into the drainage of the Marias River. Lewis named that river in honor of his cousin, Maria Wood (although it is pronounced *mah-RYE-us* and not *mah-REE-ahs*). The river runs through what was then the heart of Blackfeet country, so Lewis took extra measures to "avoid an interview" with those Indians. Still, it was here that the corps experienced the only white–Native American clash of their entire trip. The skirmish took the lives of two Blackfeet and left expedition members running for theirs. Clark's contingent, meantime, headed south and east through the Big Hole and Gallatin valleys. Eventually they gained the Yellowstone River, following it downstream to its juncture with the Missouri. The two parties met as planned at the confluence on August 12, where they emulated the two rivers by again forming one party. Calling it "a judicious position for the purpose of trade," Clark prophesied that whatever country gained control of this confluence would eventually control the fur trade of the entire Northwest.

The Corps of Discovery continued downstream along the Missouri, reclaiming St. Louis on September 23, 1806. The entire expedition had been given up as lost by most of those back east. But, in fact, only one member had died, and he from what Clark called a "bilious Chorlick," thought to mean a burst appendix. It happened in the wilds near present-day Sioux City, Iowa, but a ruptured appendix in that day would have killed Sgt. Charles Floyd regardless of where he'd been—even if he was sitting in the doctor's office in St. Louis—because it wasn't until 1887 that an appendectomy was successfully performed in the United States. Lewis and Clark's meticulously kept journals provided detailed information of all sorts concerning what until then had been largely *terra incognita*. Although they failed to find an all-water route to the Northwest, the explorers, who had covered some 7,000 miles and been gone nearly two-and-a-half years, still were triumphant beyond anyone's wildest dreams. The expedition's resounding success was due to a number of factors, including first-class leadership, excellent preparation, careful choice of members . . . and lots of good luck.

To better understand the subsequent history of Glacier-Gold Country, let's consider what was going on far outside the region, as well as in adjacent areas that fed the mountainous west of the future state of Montana.

For the five decades following the Corps of Discovery's extensive travels through Montana, the territory remained largely a wild frontier. Its population consisted primarily of big-game animals, nomadic Indians, and a few white fur trappers and traders. The latter were lured by fabulous tales of abundant wildlife—particularly those of fur-bearing breeds—which had been brought back east by members of the corps. In Europe, a distant 5,000 miles from Montana, beaver fur hats had become all the rage; indeed, they were a mark of affluence: The higher the hat the wealthier its wearer. So those stories of the upper Missouri's bounteous beaver populations had fired the imagination of the adventurous and money-hungry.

Within a year of Lewis and Clark's return to St. Louis, Fort Remon became the first "permanent" structure constructed by whites in Montana. The fort, established by a Spaniard from New Orleans named Manuel Lisa, was built of cottonwood logs at the juncture of the Bighorn and Yellowstone rivers. It was from there that John Colter was dispatched on his legendary 1807–8 scouting mission (*see* History, Yellowstone-Teton Country).

But Fort Remon was abandoned in 1811, largely because Lisa had been unable to draft the friendly Crow Indians into service as trappers and traders. Moreover, the dominant and potentially dangerous Blackfeet Indians had prevented the white entrepreneur from effectively expanding his range into beaver-abundant regions like the Missouri River headwaters and the Rocky Mountain Front (as the east slope of the Continental Divide in Montana is known).

Meanwhile, others poked into the mountainous reaches of Montana from other directions. To combat the growing threat of competition from Americans, in 1807 David Thompson of the British North West Company built Kootenae House, a post located at the foot of Lake Windermere in southeast British Columbia. From there he sent an employee, Finian McDonald, down the Kootenai River to establish a post near today's Libby, Montana. They soon built a second post near present-day Bonner's Ferry, Idaho (Kullyspell House), then a third near Thompson Falls, Montana (Saleesh House). From these, Thompson and others pushed farther into Montana. In 1812 Thompson himself traveled through the fair valley now home to the city of Missoula.

The American fur trade slowed during the War of 1812 but rebounded with a vengeance in the war's wake. By the time another twenty years had passed the Northern Rockies had been so intensively trapped that the beaver was nearing depletion. Simultaneously, changing tastes brought about a new fashion era in Europe, in which the silk of a worm replaced the fur of a rodent as the material of choice. By 1834 the heyday of the mountain man was over. The solitary beaver trappers, although they had generally kept few records and built nothing of lasting value, had explored nearly every nook and cranny of the Rocky Mountain West. They went on to serve as guides or otherwise pass along knowledge that made the going far easier than it otherwise would have been for the hordes of emigrants who followed in their footsteps. In 1847, in the midst of the flurry of westward migration, George Frederick Ruxton wrote these words regarding the trappers in his *Adventures in Mexico and the Rocky Mountains*:

> *From the Mississippi to the mouth of the Colorado of the West, from the frozen regions of the North to the Gila in Mexico, the beaver-hunter has set his traps in every creek and stream. All this vast country, but for the daring and enterprise of these men, would be even now a* terra incognita *to geographers. . . .*

As the beaver industry waned, an interest in buffalo robes waxed. This drew the interest of the Crow Indians, who had had little time for trapping and preparing beaver and other small fur-bearing mammals. Now the Crow were suddenly intrigued at the prospect of becoming partners in commerce with the white man. In 1829 John Jacob Astor, a German emigrant living in New York City, built his flagship post, Fort Union, near the juncture of the Missouri and Yellowstone rivers. This, of course, was the confluence

William Clark had predicted would become so vital to the fur trade. But to get to that fort the Crow had to travel through country quite possibly inhabited by Blackfeet, so they requested that a post be built nearer to their homeland, farther up the valley of the Yellowstone River. In response, Astor's American Fur Company began building smaller forts upstream, deeper in Montana. Among these were Fort Cass, built in 1833 at the mouth of the Bighorn River, and Fort Van Buren, constructed in 1835 near where Rosebud Creek empties into the Yellowstone.

At these and other satellite forts whites traded with, lived among, and even "married" Indians. These unions between white men and Native American women helped to cement the vital ties between the traders and tribes; the downside was that they resulted in the Indian men treating their women as items of trade, much like furs. But in all it was a mutually beneficial arrangement: Crows and members of other tribes brought bison robes to trade and also helped protect the forts from invaders. In return, the Indians were treated well by the white traders. Commerce and the making of a profit, rather than the stealing of Indian lands, was the foremost interest of the purveyors of the fur trade. Making that profit hinged on establishing and maintaining good relations with the Indians. The whites could not simply view the Indians as obstacles to their progress, as future settlers would. These white men *needed* to be friendly and generous with the Native Americans; it was only good business practice. Consequently, the traders learned to recognize and appreciate the vast differences setting apart the dozen or so tribes they traded with. They found, indeed, that great distinctions existed between individuals of the same tribe.

Sadly, though, the Crows unwittingly helped to bring about the demise of the Plains Indian cultures, their own included. They taught their white companions where to find the bison herds, how to dress the animals, and how to prepare the hides. This precipitated large-scale massacres, in which both greedy white and Indian hunters took part. In Montana and elsewhere on the Great Plains, the 1860s, 1870s, and 1880s witnessed, almost to the point of extinction, the decimation of the once seemingly infinite bison herds. The slaughter culminated between 1877 and 1884,

when a new and inexpensive tanning process caused buffalo hides to become even more valuable on the market. The U.S. government exacerbated the bloodbath by promoting it. The feds believed, correctly, that the extermination of the bison would speed the destruction of the Indians' way of life. This would—and did—cause them to succumb to domination and lead more quickly to their "civilizing."

Granville Stuart was a pioneer Montanan who seems to have popped up just about everywhere in the state at one time or another. Regarding his travels through the Yellowstone Valley in 1880, Stuart reported that " . . . the [river] bottoms are literally sprinkled with carcasses of dead buffalo. In many places they lie thick on the ground, fat and the meat not yet spoiled, all murdered for their hides which are piled like cordwood all along the way. . . . 'Tis an awful sight." Stuart believed that approximately 10,000 bison had been killed in the area that winter, but his guess was probably a conservative one: It was later estimated that between 1881 and 1883 the Northern Pacific Railroad shipped some 300,000 buffalo hides to eastern markets from its railhead at Miles City, Montana. Only the bones, left to lie bleaching in the sun, remained as reminders of the once great herds. And eventually even those were shipped east—hundreds of thousands of pounds of them—to be ground up and used as fertilizer.

Back for the moment to earlier times, when trappers seeking fur-bearing mammals first ventured into the upstream reaches of the Yellowstone and Missouri rivers. Their explorations led to the common belief that large boats should be able to negotiate the Missouri River as far as present Fort Benton; even above there—perhaps all the way to the headwaters—it was recognized that the river would be intermittently navigable by smaller craft. These realizations helped seal the fate of the territory.

In 1830 Kenneth McKenzie, the American Fur Company's administrator at Fort Union, sent employee Jacob Berger west to try to convince the uncooperative Blackfeet and Atsina Indians to travel to Fort Union to trade. Berger built Fort Piegan in 1831 at the mouth of the Marias River, ten miles downstream from present Fort Benton. The short-lived post, abandoned and burned to the ground after an Indian attack, was replaced in

1832 by Fort McKenzie. The attack apparently was instigated by the rival Hudson's Bay Company—an enterprise that had been around so long that its initials HBC were often said to stand for "Here Before Christ." In fact, though, the company wasn't chartered by the English crown until 1670.

For the next decade Fort McKenzie served as the epicenter of the northern Montana fur trade. Here, in 1837, occurred an event that was a turning point in the history of western Montana. Passengers aboard the keelboat *St. Peter*, traveling from Fort Union, brought to Fort McKenzie the devastating disease smallpox. The ensuing epidemic wiped out some 6,000 Blackfeet Indians, or nearly two-thirds of the tribe's population. Never again would the Blackfeet be the formidable foe they had been. Still, remaining Blackfeet did cause the abandonment of Fort McKenzie in the mid-1840s, which led to the 1846 construction of Fort Lewis to replace it. Friendly Indians didn't like the location of this fort, because getting to it necessitated a dangerous river crossing. So, in 1847 the cottonwood-log fort was moved 3 miles downstream and named Fort Clay. Soon it was renamed Fort Benton, in honor of Senator Thomas Hart Benton, a Democratic senator from Missouri who was active in promoting western expansion.

Of a dozen major fur-trading posts established in Montana between 1808 and 1847 by the numerous American, English, and Canadian fur companies working the region, only the American Fur Company's Fort Benton endured. That was due primarily to its fortuitous geographic position, which saw the fort become the upstream terminus of steamboat traffic on the Missouri River.

A new breed of broad-bottom boats introduced around 1860 permitted steamboats to travel on formerly unnavigable waters, including the stretch of the Missouri between Fort Union and Fort Benton. By the mid-1860s Fort Benton had evolved into a major port, serving as the center of trade between the Eastern markets and the booming gold-mining regions of southwest Montana. From the waterfront at Fort Benton, bullwhackers driving teams of oxen took over. At times, a thousand oxen could be seen filling the streets of town, readying for the dusty trip to the mining outposts. In 1867 alone some 10,000 prospectors jumped

off boats in Fort Benton, and more than 8,000 tons of supplies were unloaded. Warehouses lining the river were full to overflowing with necessities . . . and luxuries, as well, for life on the frontier was not entirely composed of eating hardpan bread and sleeping on the hard ground. For the return trip downriver, the steamboats took on tons of gold dust. One steamer in one trip that year reportedly carried $1.25 million in raw gold back to St. Louis.

The fact that Fort Benton earned so many nicknames—among them, "the Birthplace of Montana," "Chicago of the Plains," "the world's most inland port," and "the bloodiest block in the West"—attests that here was a place of significance and great activity. Fort Benton had become the most important settlement in northern Montana, a status it enjoyed until the railroads pushed through late in the 1800s.

Since before the nineteenth century Indians of the Iroquois Confederacy had been employed as trappers and canoemen by the British and Canadian fur-trading companies. In the process, in Montreal and elsewhere, many Indians were exposed and converted to Catholicism. When they traveled into the Northern Rockies of the United States to help the fur companies teach other Indians the tricks of the trader and trapper, they also shared their Jesuit learnings. In some cases Iroquois men settled with natives of this new land, such as four individuals who moved in with the Flathead Indians in the 1820s. One of these Iroquois, Big Ignace, spoke often to the Flatheads of the Black Robes, or Jesuit priests, and of the powers of their teachings.

Big Ignace obviously was a devout convert and an effective proselytizer. Curiosity concerning the Black Robes among the peaceable Flatheads grew to wonderment; wonder to obsession. The consuming fascination culminated in four separate journeys to the Midwest taken by Flathead delegations between 1831 and 1839. The purpose of the trips: to compel and persuade one or more priests to travel back west with the Indians to "save" their people. The first trip resulted in several Methodist and Presbyterian missionaries heading west, but the Protestant teachings held little interest for the Flatheads; they wanted only the words of the Black Robes. The second delegation, led by Big Ignace, was likewise unsuccessful in luring the Black Robes. The entire third party, of which Big Ignace again was a member, was killed by Sioux warriors.

Finally, the fourth delegation, sent east in 1839, was successful. Delegates Peter Gaucher and Young Ignace received a promise from a bishop named Rosati that he would send to their people a Black Robe. Rosati chose for the mission Father Pierre-Jean De Smet, a stocky and muscular priest who the following year traveled with an American Fur Company party to the upper Green River in Wyoming, where he was greeted by a group of Flatheads. Here, a few miles south of the Hoback Rim, on July 25, 1840, Father De Smet offered the first Holy Mass heard in the Northern Rockies. The Flatheads then led the priest to Pierre's Hole (Teton Valley, Idaho), where nearly the entire Flathead tribe, along with many Nez Perce, awaited his arrival. From there the large group traveled into Montana. At summer's end De Smet returned to St. Louis to meet with his superiors and discuss how to proceed.

Because they had no money available to build a mission for the Flatheads, the priest was permitted to travel widely that winter to try to raise funds on his own. Father De Smet proved to be an adept fund-raiser, and in the spring of 1841 he headed back to Montana with a pair of fellow priests and a trio of laymen. In September they arrived in the Bitterroot Valley and immediately began constructing the St. Mary's Mission at the site of today's Stevensville. The mission consisted of a cottonwood-log chapel and two log cabins.

For nearly five years all went well, with the instruction of religion and agriculture continuing nearly nonstop. On one occasion, after Father De Smet lamented that across the Atlantic Ocean fellow Catholics were suffering persecution, Chief Victor of the Flatheads even suggested that Pope Gregory XVI should come and live in safety with his people!

When the Flatheads returned from buffalo hunting in fall 1846, though, the situation deteriorated. Father De Smet earlier had headed back to St. Louis; the new mission leader, Father Ravalli, suddenly heard war cries and witnessed "savage obscenity and shameless excesses of the flesh." What had gone wrong?

It seems that what the Jesuits had believed to be devotion to God was actually more of a desire among the Flatheads to gain an advantage over the hated Blackfeet, the tribe most responsible for driving the Flatheads into the mountains (they would have preferred to live on the plains). The Indians were not "true believers" so much as believers that the cross and Christianity were powerful medicines, or tools to be used to their advantage. The Indians' cultural traditions inherently made it difficult for them to abide by rigid dictums such as one wife, one God, no alcohol, and the practicing of farming instead of hunting. The last straw was issued when they heard Father De Smet, before leaving for St. Louis, talking about stepping up his efforts to deliver Christianity to the Blackfeet. How could he even consider offering the powerful medicine to the worst enemy of the Flatheads? It was more than the Indians could take, and they rebelled.

Relations subsequently improved slightly for a while, but by 1850 they had disintegrated altogether. The white Catholics, sensing the futility of further preaching, headed back to St. Louis, not to return to the Northern Rockies for more than fifteen years.

Except for the occasional missionary and a continuing trickle of trapper-traders, western Montana saw little white activity during the 1840s and 1850s. But the cry of "Gold!" cracked the quiet.

A number of strikes were reported prior to 1860, including a find at Gold Creek in the Deer Lodge Valley in 1858, by the brothers Granville and James Stuart. But the three primary gold rushes in Montana—at Bannack, Alder Gulch (Virginia City), and Last Chance Gulch (Helena)—happened only after several factors coalesced. One, the mad mining scrambles in California, Nevada, and the Pierce City–Orofino area of Idaho had tapered off by 1862, and most of those who had rushed in had ambled away still empty-handed. Their itch to get rich was unscratched, so these men were easily seduced to nearly any location that held even the glint of a promise. Two, Indian dangers in Montana's mountainous west had greatly diminished with the smallpox decimation of the Blackfeet. Three, the first low-displacement steamboat reached Fort Benton during the high water of spring in 1860 (and between two and thirty-nine of them arrived each spring during the ensuing decade). And, four, new overland roads and trails had been approaching Montana, and by the early 1860s the heart of the state was readily penetrable from the west, east, and south.

The Mullan Road, a military wagon road linking Fort Benton and Fort Walla Walla, Washington Territory, was completed in 1863. It created an overland/over-river route from the East and the Midwest to the Pacific Northwest—that is, the Missouri River from St. Louis to Fort Benton, then the Mullan Road from Fort Benton to the Northwest. This provided a much shorter and cheaper alternative to the long boat trip around Cape Horn. At about the same time John Bozeman, in spite of constant harassment by Sioux and Cheyenne Indians, had finished plotting the Bozeman Trail. The "bloody Bozeman," which linked the Yellowstone Valley with the heavily traveled Oregon Trail, began accommodating heavy use in 1864. And, finally, a stage road was completed that connected Virginia City with the Union Pacific railhead at Corinne, Utah.

Montana, formerly a sparsely populated wilderness, was suddenly in the thick of things. Prospectors flooded in. The first major gold strike,

discovered by John White and his Colorado companions, occurred along Grasshopper Creek near the Big Hole River Valley on July 28, 1862. The town of Bannack, where today a state park encompasses the town's well-preserved remains, quickly materialized. Some $5 million in gold was removed from area streams during the next twelve months.

The glitter of gold attracted not only miners, of course, but also those interested in garnering, by both legal and illegal means, some of the riches of the newly rich. Saloons, doctors' offices, bakeries, a blacksmith shop, mercantiles, and even a bowling alley soon popped up along the streets of Bannack, whose population had exploded to nearly 3,000 by the summer of 1863. As the easiest placer pickings were picked, miners fanned out farther and farther, and a second large strike occurred at Alder Gulch, in the Ruby River Valley. Virginia City, Nevada City, and other "cities" emerged.

In the hills surrounding the towns, cutthroat road agents honed their "trade." Although the accuracy of it has recently been questioned by some historians, the story of one Henry Plummer is a compelling one.

The territorial court of Montana determined that the settlements of Bannack and Virginia City,

Corral, Big Hole River Valley, Montana

separated by 70 miles of rough road, required only one sheriff. A charming and smooth, but psychopathic character named Henry Plummer got himself elected to the position. In his eight months as sheriff, during which he was responsible for protecting the citizens of the region, Plummer and his gang of road agents, known as the "Innocents," worked the wagon road connecting Bannack and Virginia City. It is estimated that they killed at least a hundred individuals and relieved hundreds more of their weighty burdens of gold. Thomas Dimsdale, who was there at the time, wrote this about the thieves:

The usual arms of a road agent were a pair of revolvers, a double-barrelled shotgun of large bore, with the barrels cut down short, and to this they invariably added a knife or dagger. Thus armed and mounted on fleet, well-trained horses, and being disguised with blankets and masks, the robbers awaited their prey in ambush.

In response to the activities of Plummer and his men, late in 1863 the Vigilantes Committee was organized by a group of citizens determined to take the law into their own hands. Their frontier justice prevailed a few months later, when they hanged Plummer from the gallows he himself had erected not long before. The two dozen or so principal Innocents were likewise hanged, and the vigilantes' unexplained sign of "3-7-77" was pinned to many of their corpses. The graves of Plummer and some of his ilk can be visited today at Boot Hill, high on the hillside behind Virginia City. (It is worth noting that previously Plummer had served a short stint as sheriff of Nevada City, California, until he was jailed for murdering the husband of a woman with whom he was having an affair. After his release he murdered another man and spent a few more months in jail, before bribing his way out and hightailing to Montana.)

The vigilantes' actions against Plummer and company appear to have been justified. In fact, they were probably about the only remedy for a situation like this in such a lawless territory. But overzealousness among some of the vigilance committee members later resulted in acts more heinous than the crimes they were designed to punish. Nevertheless, many of the vigilantes grew

into leaders of territorial and state government in Montana.

Rumors of superior strikes elsewhere were persistent in the boomtowns, in some cases probably fabricated by prospectors who wanted to see the crowds thin. Word of a strike in northwest Montana on the Kootenai River—which turned out to be *only* a rumor—lured a group of men who came to be known as the Four Georgians. Before reaching the Kootenai the men encountered several discouraged miners who had already been there and found nothing, so the Four Georgians prospected instead on the Little Blackfoot River, in the vicinity of the Marias River, and in the Prickly Pear Valley, just west of the Missouri River. Here, in what they called Last Chance Gulch, on July 14, 1864, they located enough color to justify a supply trip back to Virginia City by one of the men. Apparently recognizing that the man, John Cowan, was up to something big, a drove of others accompanied him from Virginia City back to Last Chance Gulch, around which the rudiments of Helena emerged.

Bannack, Virginia City, and Helena all began as ragtag assortments of tents, wickiup shelters, and cave habitations. Hand-hewn log cabins soon appeared; then, with the establishment of mills, structures of unplaned lumber were built. Paint was a rare luxury, so the buildings looked worn out as soon as they were erected. Piles of gravel, flumes, and sluice boxes littered and bisected the unplanned towns, which grew in whatever directions the gulches branched. The streets turned to mud in the spring and fall, and in the dry of summer they became deep repositories of powdery dust. Most early residents were men, of course, although more women arrived early on than is commonly thought. A large percentage of the residents were southerners or Confederate sympathizers; consider that Virginia City was originally known as Varina, a name honoring Jefferson Davis' wife.

The population of the territory in the winter of 1862–63 was estimated at just under 7,000 (excluding Chinese, who were considered lower than second-class citizens at the time and weren't even counted); of those about 10 percent were "respectable" females. After 1865 women starting arriving in even larger numbers, and by 1870 the

Montana Territory's population had grown to more than 20,000.

Scratch the ragged veneer of the early gold camps and you can see that a society of substance was emerging. Gambling, drinking, prostitution, violence, and other dubious pursuits were ever-present, but so were less-reported and more respectable activities and residents. Those accomplishing the majority of the building and commerce gathered not in gaming parlors or taverns, but in stores, churches, and Masonic Temples. Boxing matches and horse races were commonplace, but so were literary societies, French study groups, theatre, and church choirs.

By 1866 the mad gold rush was over. Some former boomtowns languished and some disappeared altogether, though their contribution to the beginnings of modern society in western Montana were substantial. As a direct spin-off from the mining activities agriculture and cattle-growing took root. Other towns, like Helena, flourished. Here simple placer mining, an activity carried out by lone individuals or informal groups of miners, was replaced by the mining of hard-rock quartz lodes. This required far more than running water and a gold pan or simple sluice; it called for capital, cooperation, and long-range planning. Roads were built for transporting equipment, corporations formed, and banks emerged. Helena suddenly found itself a center of trade, and by 1867 several substantial stone buildings stood along the streets of the burgeoning young city. In 1876, the year of Custer's undoing along the Little Bighorn River in the southeast of Montana, Helena's population stood at around 4,000, with another 2,000 populating the nearby rural surroundings.

In 1883 the narrow-gauge Utah Northern Railroad, a branch of the Union Pacific promoted by the son of Brigham Young, had reached north into Montana as far as Garrison Junction (45 miles west of Helena, and between Butte and Missoula). At this point it met the standard-gauge Northern Pacific, which had come in from the Dakota Territory then up the Yellowstone Valley. The Great Northern Railway extended across northern Montana and to the Pacific Ocean a few years later, in the early 1890s. The trains carried with them the end of the need for navigation on the Missouri River. The day of stage companies and bullwhackers was over. Bustling Fort Benton went to sleep, even as the mountainous west of Montana awoke to the industrial age.

Before Montana was alternately whittled down and expanded to its present size and shape, various portions of the state served as components of several different territories. That portion of Montana lying east of the Continental Divide and south of the Missouri River was included in the original Louisiana Purchase territory. Montana west of the Continental Divide became part of the Oregon Territory in 1848, then part of the Washington Territory from 1853 until 1863. Montana east of the Divide during those years was included in the Nebraska Territory, before being made part of the Dakota Territory. Confused yet?

On March 4, 1863, President Abraham Lincoln declared the Idaho Territory a separate entity. Composed of former portions of the Washington and Dakota territories, it included all of present Montana, all of Idaho, and most of Wyoming. Serving as capitol of this immense, sparsely populated region was Lewiston, which is in western Idaho (and is not to be confused with the central-Montana community of Lewis*town*).

Bannack ghost town

Separating Lewiston and the burgeoning gold camps of Montana were some 300 mountainous, rough-and-tumble, tough-to-travel miles.

In 1863 the only representative of organized government in the entire tri-state area was Sidney Edgerton, who had been appointed chief justice of the Idaho Territory by President Lincoln. Comprehension of Western geography in the nation's capital was rudimentary at best, and Edgerton was assigned to Bannack instead of Lewiston, where he should have been sent. Once he arrived and came to understand the scope of the country he was to administer, Edgerton concluded that the territory lying east of the Bitterroot Mountains could never be effectively managed from distant Lewiston. The violence and lawlessness in Bannack and Virginia City exacerbated and underscored the problem, convincing Edgerton and others that there was a pressing need for a more compact, self-governing territory. Miners and merchants collected $2,500 and sent Edgerton to Washington to lobby Congress. He left for the capital in mid-January of 1864.

Originally from Ohio, Edgerton had served that state in the U.S. House of Representatives from 1859 to 1863, so he knew the ropes and had connections in Washington. A friend and fellow Buckeye Stater, James M. Ashley, happened to be chairman of the House Committee on Territories at the time. Ashley, coached by Edgerton, drafted a bill creating the Montana Territory, with the Bitterroot Divide serving as the western boundary. It breezed through both houses of Congress. It would be intriguing to know what went on behind the scenes; according to Edgerton, Montana's rich gold deposits contributed to the quick passing of the bill "in a mercenary age such as ours." On May 26, 1864, President Lincoln signed the legislation and named Edgerton the first governor of the territory.

Fifteen years later, in 1879, when Montana's population stood at almost 40,000, the territorial legislature petitioned the Congress to grant statehood. The request was ignored for six years then held up by politics for another four. The Republicans, who in 1885 controlled the Senate but not the House, did not want an additional Democratic state—which Montana would be—added to the Union. But in the 1888 elections

Bitterroot, Montana's state flower

Republican Benjamin Harrison was elected president and the Republicans gained control of the Senate *and* the House. With total control they would be able to create what states they wanted, and when. The Democrats realized they'd better act quickly, before the new administration took office and while the Democrats still controlled the House. They introduced an omnibus bill, readying Montana, Washington, North Dakota, and South Dakota all for statehood.

The proposed new states were split between Democratic and Republican, so the balance would be maintained and the Republicans appeased, or so hoped the Democrats. (New Mexico was originally included, but it was dropped like a hot spud when the Congress learned that, besides being Democratic, it contained 100,000 individuals who could not read or write English. New Mexico and Arizona were finally admitted as the last two states in the contiguous United States in 1912.)

When the bill came up for discussion in Congress in January of 1889, Montana delegate Joseph K. Toole pleaded the case for his new state: The territory had a surplus of funds in its treasury, he said, and the majority of its residents were born in America. Moreover, its progress was being stunted by the restrictions imposed by territorial government. In February of 1889, President Cleveland signed the omnibus bill, and on November 8, 1889, President Harrison declared Montana the forty-first state. The following year, Idaho—a Republican state—had little trouble gaining statehood.

Until the bounty of its beauty was realized, the cold and forbidding area encompassed by today's Glacier National Park was largely a no-man's land. The Kootenai, Salish, and other west-slope Indian tribes had long utilized mile-high Marias Pass, which lies immediately south of the park, to reach their buffalo-hunting grounds along the Rocky Mountain Front. Occasionally they did venture into the mountains of the future national park to hunt, as did Cree and Blood Indians from north of the border in Canada. And through the eastern foothills of Glacier ran a trail worn bare by the various sub-tribes of the Blackfeet. Known as the Old North Trail, the path remained just far enough east of the Rockies to stay clear of the heavy timber. It's thought to have extended as far north as Calgary, Alberta, and south into New Mexico and perhaps even old Mexico. En route it ran close to the present site of Helena. Occasional vestiges of the timeworn trail can still be seen in places, where horses dragging *travois* carved ruts or where the Blackfeet built cairns of stone.

The first white man known to scratch the surface of Glacier National Park was Peter Fidler of the Hudson's Bay Company, who was guided to the eastern foot of the mountains by Blackfeet warriors in 1792. Meriwether Lewis probably saw the park's Chief Mountain from a distance of 25 miles or so, and other trappers and explorers occasionally traveled in the park during the first half of the nineteenth century. Among them was Finian McDonald of the British North West Company, who traveled through the future park in 1810.

In 1883 a professor named Raphael Pumpelly walked through the future national park from west to east, in the company of a pair of companions. One of them, W. R. Logan, who worked for the Indian Bureau (now the Bureau of Indian Affairs), was destined to become the first superin-

tendent of Glacier. Pumpelly, an eminent naturalist and outdoorsman of the day, wrote this about what they saw:

Among these limestone mountains—from lofty crest and in cirques—you will see the grandest scenery in the United States; and the best time to see it is when, from high-lying snow fields water falls are plunging 2,000 feet down the almost vertical steps.

Pumpelly's glowing report, and others equally passionate, piqued the interest of a young conservationist and hunter named George Bird Grinnell. The curious Easterner decided he'd better see it for himself, so he traveled there on a hunting trip in 1885. His odyssey of getting to Glacier involved riding the Northern Pacific Railroad as far west as Helena, continuing by stage 120 miles to Fort Benton, then riding in a wagon to the old Piegan Agency on Badger Creek, nearly 100 miles from Fort Benton. From there he traveled by horse into the high country.

Grinnell found the hard-to-access mountains full of game, recording that during the eight days he spent hunting with a party of Kootenai Indians they killed more than seventy beavers, "many" bighorn sheep and mountain goats, and at least two or three each of elk and moose. On this trip he climbed what became one of his namesakes in the park, Grinnell Glacier. (The ice field, which is nestled against the east side of the Garden Wall, is accessible today by a round-trip hike of approximately 11 miles, gaining 1,700 feet in elevation, beginning near the Many Glacier Hotel.)

Grinnell was one of a rare breed of educated, turn-of-the-century Easterners who became so fascinated with the West that they dedicated their lives to its welfare. He became altruistically and enthusiastically involved in protecting the wildlife and forests of the region; ultimately Grinnell was instrumental in the creation of two still-potent conservation organizations, the Audubon Society and the Boone and Crockett Club (headquartered in Missoula since the early 1990s). He became Teddy Roosevelt's chief conservation adviser, and also a leading authority on and advocate for the Plains Indians, particularly the Blackfeet.

Ironically, Grinnell had been a member of George Armstrong Custer's 1874 foray into the western Dakotas. It was on this trip that gold was discovered in the Black Hills. The resultant rush of prospecting was largely responsible for creating the friction with the Sioux Indians that precipitated the Battle of the Little Bighorn. Fortunately, Grinnell was too busy with his studies at Yale to accept Custer's invitation to accompany him and his Seventh Cavalry on a similar exploratory outing into southeast Montana in 1876. Had he participated, Grinnell might well have died at the Little Bighorn, along with Custer's 200-plus soldiers, at the hands of Sioux and Cheyenne warriors. (It might be added that Grinnell was none too impressed by Custer's baseless braggadocio on the earlier trip, which may also have affected his decision not to join him again.) And Glacier National Park may never have been born, for George Bird Grinnell was the engine that powered the park's creation.

As natural history editor of *Forest and Stream* magazine, Grinnell used his post as a pulpit, preaching for the protection of the unique and unusually delicate world of mountains, ice, and timber residing at the top of Montana. Beginning in 1887 Grinnell visited the region every summer for many years to hunt, explore, and learn more about the Blackfeet. In the process he visited and named many features in Glacier. Often he preserved the Blackfeet names or named the features after Blackfeet friends, as probably few of his time would have done.

Meanwhile, something new was transpiring that also would contribute to the creation of Glacier National Park. James J. Hill, president of the Great Northern Railroad and a proponent of dryland farming, wanted to extend his railroad west from Minot, Dakota Territory, which it had reached in 1886, across Montana. There was a little problem, though: Most of northern Montana east of the Rockies had been set aside by the government as reservations for the Indians.

Relentless pressure, however, persuaded President Cleveland and the Congress to appropriate the Great Northern a 75-foot right-of-way through the Indian lands, further granting that the railroad could use resources on adjacent lands for construction needs. Helping to apply that pressure were Marcus Daly and Hill's friend, Paris Gibson. Daly, one of the legendary copper kings of the Butte-Anaconda area, believed that a second, more northerly rail line across Montana would provide the Union Pacific competition and drive down the cost of shipping copper. Gibson,

Great Northern Railway locomotive, Whitefish, Montana

founder of the city of Great Falls, was convinced that a railroad would attract settlers all across northern Montana and help turn his fledgling city into another Minneapolis.

And so, by the autumn of 1887 the Great Northern Railroad had reached across the Hi-Line as far as Great Falls. (The term Hi-Line refers to the route of the Great Northern and also to the surrounding region of Montana lying north of the Missouri River and east of the Continental Divide.) Hill's plan called for the railroad to extend all the way to the West Coast, but it wasn't until the winter of 1889 that his engineer, John F. Stevens, managed to locate the long-looked-for Marias Pass, which lies along the southern boundary of Glacier National Park. The pass had been used in earlier days by the Salish, Blackfeet, and other Indians, and even by white trappers. But somehow its location had been forgotten, and previous railroad surveys had been unsuccessful in locating it, despite it being one of the lowest and most accessible routes over the Continental Divide in all the Northern Rockies.

The Great Northern's tracks subsequently pushed over Marias Pass in 1891 and reached Puget Sound in the summer of 1893. Built entirely without federal assistance, the completion of the Great Northern is regarded as one of the greatest railroading success stories in history.

In the fall of 1891 George Bird Grinnell, a great visionary, first suggested that the government should obtain the land of glaciers and mountains and turn it into a national preserve. Precedents existed, including the 1872 establishment of Yellowstone and the recent designation of California's Yosemite in 1890. At this time the park belonged to the Blackfeet as part of their hunting grounds and reservation. In truth, though, they were primarily a plains people and had little interest in the difficult mountain reaches. In negotiations led by Grinnell, whom the Blackfeet knew and respected—in fact he was considered one of their own, and had been given the name Pinut-u-ye-is-tsim-o-kan, the Fisher Hat—the government in 1896 purchased the mountain portions of the Blackfeet Reservation.

The region was opened to prospecting two years later, in 1898, and miners poured in. Little or no gold or silver was discovered, although some

fair copper and oil deposits were found. Forecasts that the area would become a "bigger camp than Old Butte" proved unfounded, though, and most of the disillusioned miners soon moved on.

But by the dawn of the twentieth century there still was no national preserve encompassing the region. As the mining boomlet fizzled, Grinnell sensed that the time was right for what he'd been waiting to do. In the September 1901 issue of *Century Magazine* Grinnell wrote a persuasive article entitled "The Crown of the Continent" (a nickname Glacier National Park still wears). And he and some friends in Montana independently worked on T. H. Carter, convincing the Montana senator to introduce a bill creating a new national park. It passed the Senate but foundered for lack of interest in the House. But in the meantime Grinnell was joined by a newfound fellow proponent—James J. Hill, who recognized a tremendous opportunity for promoting tourism where his Great Northern Railroad skirted the potential national park. He took it on himself to lobby Representative Pray of Montana, who carried the ball in the House. Grinnell's and Hill's labors came to fruition on May 11, 1910, when President William H. Taft signed into law legislation creating Glacier National Park.

Grinnell had been working for nineteen long years to make it happen, and finally his work paid off handsomely, in the establishment of one of the crown jewels of the national park system.

Little government funding was forthcoming, but Hill's railroad had soon invested more than a million dollars in park improvements. Starting out by fashioning trails and backcountry tent camps, they eventually built the high chalets and grand hotels that still grace the park. The Many Glacier Hotel, the Glacier Park Hotel, and the Sperry and Granite Park chalets were all built by the Great Northern in the 1910s and today all are listed on the National Register of Historic Places.

The tourist-hauling monopoly enjoyed by the Great Northern Railroad came to a screeching halt in 1933. The previous year the Civilian Conservation Corps had completed the engineering feat known as the Going-to-the-Sun Road, an incredible byway whose high reaches wind precipitously along a ledge carved in the ancient rock of untimbered mountainsides, and whose construction had begun way back in 1911. Now the park was opened to the private automobile, and visitation skyrocketed. During the mid-1920s approximately 40,000 people per year had visited the park; ten years later, with the advent of the auto, the number had grown to more than 200,000.

But in general the later visitors earned a more superficial look at Glacier, and this remains true of the majority of today's visitors: Most simply drive the Going-to-the-Sun Road, stopping in at the visitor center at Logan Pass and maybe spending a night or two at one of the historic lodgings. Then they look outside the park for new things to see and do. In contrast, those arriving by railroad prior to 1933 were provided with suggested itineraries that kept them in Glacier National Park for a full week of hiking, fishing, and riding on horseback to distant backcountry destinations.

To the north, Canada's Waterton Lakes Forest Preserve (now Waterton Lakes National Park) was established in 1895, fifteen years before Glacier National Park. Through the combined efforts of Rotarians in Alberta and Montana, legislation passed in both the U.S. Congress and the Canadian Parliament in 1932 establishing the Waterton-Glacier International Peace Park. This park, the first of its kind in the world, celebrates the friendship and cooperation long shared by the two countries. It serves as a sparkling model of joining together to protect an interrelated and fragile ecosystem that knows no political boundaries. The adjacent pair of parks remain separate jurisdictions, but their overseers share a goal: to preserve one of the world's most compelling and marvelous mountain regions.

Seeing Glacier-
Gold Country

This section of the book begins by leading you on a driving tour through the remote, sparsely populated Centennial Valley, home to the Red Rock Lakes National Wildlife Refuge. Then, after arriving at and driving north on Interstate 15, you will motor through the Big Hole River Valley, a broad basin filled with sprawling ranches, where you may gain a new appreciation for the phrase "Big Sky Country." From the big empty of the Big Hole the tour leads to and through the more heavily settled Bitterroot, Missoula, and Flathead valleys. Also detailed is an alternative route north through the tall-timber environs of the Seeley-Swan Valley.

An appropriately large share of the chapter subsequently is devoted to the outstanding resort community of Whitefish, and to the immense national park constituting that town's "back yard." From Glacier National Park the narrative leads to the Blackfeet Indian capital of Browning, then south along the resplendent east slope of the Rockies, known regionally as the Rocky Mountain Front. After touring the "mining core" of Montana—which includes the engaging cities of Helena and Butte—the text describes a loop beginning in Butte and leading to historic Virginia City, to the picturesque settlement of Pony, and to Lewis and Clark Caverns State Park.

Continental Divide Corner: The Centennial and Big Hole Valleys

From Island Park, Idaho, on the western fringe of Yellowstone-Teton Country, follow State Highway 87 as it wraps around the northeastern shore of Henrys Lake. If you turn west onto Forest Road 055, a high-grade gravel road that initially hugs the shore of the lake, in a few miles you will arrive at a low crossing of the Continental Divide at **Red Rock Pass**. If you look at a map and think too hard about the situation, you'll undoubtedly find it perplexing that, although you're driving westward, you're proceeding from the west to the east slope of the Continental Divide—and from Idaho into Montana, a state generally thought of as lying east of Idaho. Such are the geographic tricks played by the twisting line traced by the Continental Divide.

From the summit, which is generally snow-free from May through October, the road descends into Montana's **Centennial Valley**, one of my favorite hidden corners of the Northern

Rockies. The basin is a bit of a paradox in the rapidly growing Northern Rockies region, in the sense that far fewer folks live in the scenic, mountain-rimmed valley today than lived there sixty-five years ago.

As you motor westward from the pass, the impressive **Centennial Mountains** are on your left. Even well into the summer you'll see patches of snow remaining from last winter, hidden in the north-facing crevices of 9,855-foot Taylor Mountain and other high peaks. You'll also notice the light green leaves of aspen trees flittering in the breeze. Their gnarled, black-on-white trunks often grow out of the damper, shadier creases in slopesides predominantly blanketed in the darker green of pine and fir trees.

Aspens can and do multiply by dispersing seeds, but their seeds are uncommonly sensitive, and they remain productive for only a few days after dropping to the ground. Unless the temperature and moisture conditions are absolutely ideal during the short window of opportunity, the seeds simply die. More often aspens regenerate by sprouting suckers from the roots of existing trees, a process that is fostered when living trees are cut down or burned. Because of this mode of reproduction, new and old trees within a grove are actually part of the same organism; technically, they are genetic clones of one another. Another way of putting it: All of the trees in a grove sharing a root system are effectively part of a single plant. Consequently, you'll see that the trees within a given stand resemble one another in their configuration. And if you drive through the Centennial Valley or another aspen-abundant high place in autumn, after their leaves have begun changing color, you'll notice that the trees within a grove share a similar hue of orange or yellow. That color will often differ dramatically from the aspens residing in an adjacent, genetically distinct grove.

After dropping from Red Rock Pass, to your right sprawls the wide, flat basin of Red Rock Creek. You'll cross Hell Roaring Creek, the most distant headwaters stream of the Missouri River, then, 7 miles from the pass, you'll come upon broad, shallow Upper Red Rock Lake, with its primitive **Upper Lake Campground**. Those who prefer peace and quiet over an abundance of human-made services and/or diversions would be

hard pressed to find a better spot than this low-use campground to spend a few days. Canoeing, fishing, mountain biking, hiking, and wildlife-viewing opportunities are all right at hand, and the sunrises and sunsets are something to behold. Another dividend: The cold water flowing from a captured spring at the campground is tastier than any bottled water you'll pay good money for at a grocery store.

Not far from the lake is the site of the old **Shambo Station** of the Yellowstone & Monida Stageline. By 1915 this large operation's horse-powered wagons were hauling more than forty percent of all Yellowstone-bound tourists, of which there were approximately 20,000 annually at that time. It was a long, one-day ride to cover the 70 miles from the Oregon Shortline's Monida railhead to Dwells, located near the western boundary of the park.

Farther down the road is lake number two, Lower Red Rock Lake. Far to the north erupt the foothills of the **Gravelly Range,** putting an abrupt end to the all the flatness. The two lakes and the surrounding wetlands constitute the **Red Rock Lakes National Wildlife Refuge**, the majority of which enjoys double protection as a designated federal wilderness area. The wilderness designation means, among other things, that motorboats are not permitted on the waters of the wilderness portions of the refuge.

If you're carrying the indispensable Southwest Montana Interagency Visitor Map (available at Forest Service offices and elsewhere in the region), notice how the Centennial Valley appears as a virtual rainbow of colors on the map. The colors indicate which agency oversees which acreages, and you can see that it's a real hodgepodge here. Dark blue on the map represents the National Wildlife Refuge lands. Those are surrounded by the light blue of Montana State Lands, the white of privately owned acreages, the bright yellow of federal Bureau of Land Management lands, and the light green of lands administered by the U.S. Forest Service. Also popping out a couple of miles south of the refuge is the olive green of lands administered by the Agricultural Research Service, which maintains its Sheep Experiment Station in the Centennial Mountains.

Now nearly devoid of human settlement outside the spot in the road called **Lakeview** (population ten, plus or minus), the Centennial Valley once was a thriving ranching basin and home to several hundred people. Monida, the virtual ghost town where soon you will meet Interstate 15, was a busy settlement of more than 100 residents in the 1920s, when the town served as an important stock-shipping railhead. The human population there and in the Centennial Valley declined dramatically after 1935, when the creation of the Red Rock Lakes National Wildlife Refuge took thousands of productive acres out of the hands of cattle and sheep growers.

The refuge was established primarily to protect vital nesting and breeding habitat for the rare trumpeter swan, whose population in the Greater Yellowstone Ecosystem had plummeted, due to hunting and the draining of wetlands, to fewer than 100 birds—and this was the last remaining viable flock in the U.S. The move paid a hand-

some reward: Today between 300 and 500 trumpeters are full-time breeding residents of the refuge, and the arrival of migratory birds from the north, drawn to the region's unfrozen waters, brings the number closer to 2,000 in winter.

Moreover, even with parts of the Centennial Valley having been taken out of grazing commission, the sheep and cattle populations in the Northern Rockies are doing just fine, too!

Anticipate seeing and hearing the unmistakable honking of the big, white trumpeters on the waters of Upper Red Rock Lake; Upper Lake Campground is one of the best potential viewing sites. To avoid disturbing the sensitive birds, try watching them from a distance of no closer than 400 yards, using binoculars to "get close." The sheer size of the swans is as startling as is their pure-white plumage. When fully grown, a trumpeter's wingspan can exceed 8 feet, they can measure 4 feet in length, and they can weigh as much as thirty pounds.

The needs of trumpeter swans may have been the impetus for creating the 42,525-acre refuge, but dozens of other wildlife species have benefited from the protection provided, as well. The refuge and adjacent public lands are home, either part- or full-time, to a host of waterfowl species and other birds, including bald eagles, great gray owls, American avocets, willets, long-billed curlews, great blue herons, white pelicans, and terns. You can also see and hear a medley of songbirds, and an army of raptors, including redtail hawks and peregrine falcons. Bigger and hairier creatures, too, are common on and around the refuge, including moose, elk, deer, and pronghorns.

In Lakeview the U.S. Fish and Wildlife Service maintains a small headquarters station, along with an adjacent grounds perfect for a picnic. West of Lakeview the landscape suddenly opens up and dries out, and the views are infinite from the bumpy dirt road. After climbing over an immense hill, you'll begin the descent into **Monida**, situated just off Interstate 15 at Exit 0. Although located in Montana, Monida almost straddles the Montana–Idaho state line, hence the town's name. Turn north here onto Interstate 15, and in 14 miles pass the exit to **Lima**, where you should go if your car's tank is low on gas. In another 9 miles is the exit to **Dell**, where you

Yellowheaded blackbird

should visit if your personal tank is low on fuel. For that matter, stop even if you're not hungry.

Yesterday's Calf-A, occupying a converted schoolhouse in Dell, is a one-of-a-kind eatery-museum, serving homestyle cooking at its lip-smackingest. This is the real thing, and you will encounter no prefabricated pies or mashed potatoes out of a box at Calf-A. The tiny old school, which discontinued its life of education in 1963, opened in 1978 as a restaurant. But you can still learn plenty here, because the interior and the grounds outside the restaurant teem with a non-stop collection of pioneer Montana paraphernalia and memorabilia. Items on display run the gamut from crosscut saws and bison skulls to kerosene lanterns, old magazines and sheet music, windmills, wagon wheels, and yellowed photographs depicting things you're guaranteed never to have seen. The daily menu appears written in chalk on the schoolroom's blackboard and your fellow diners will probably include long-haul truckers and ranchers from surrounding spreads in Montana and Idaho. Guaranteed: You cannot go wrong at Yesterday's Calf-A for breakfast, lunch, or dinner.

If the dirt-road drive through the Centennial Valley only whetted your appetite for Montana's outback, from Dell drive under the interstate and follow the signs leading to the **Big Sheep Creek Back Country Byway**. This and other Back Country Byways are designated by the Bureau of Land Management as that agency's counterpart to the U.S. Forest Service's National Scenic Byways. Back Country Byways, including the Big Sheep Creek, usually incorporate dirt roads, whereas National Scenic Byways are typically paved.

The Big Sheep Creek Back Country Byway recontacts pavement 60 miles to the northwest, where a right-hand turn will lead you back to Interstate 15 by way of Clark Canyon Reservoir. By going left rather than right at the junction with pavement, you can follow paved, gravel, and rough dirt roads up and over 7,373-foot Lemhi Pass, where Lewis and Clark and the Corps of Discovery first surmounted the Continental Divide. (*See* History.)

You'll find the Big Sheep Creek Back Country Byway to be rough and probably muddy in places—perhaps even impassable—so a high-clearance vehicle is advised. Don't tackle the trip unless you're equipped with a spare tire and tire-changing tools, a full tank of gas, a good map, and an adequate supply of food and water. It's prudent also to inquire about the road's condition ahead of time by calling the BLM's Butte District Office at (406) 494–5059.

Anglers in particular will find the roiling waters of Big Sheep Creek inviting, while history buffs will thrill at tracing segments of the 1860s wagon supply road that connected the Bannack mining camp with the Union Pacific railhead in Corinne, Utah. Pronghorns, mule deer, and golden eagles are all regulars, and the drive is heralded for its brilliant wildflower displays in early summer. Bighorn sheep can often be seen, too, especially in the evenings in the tighter portions of Big Sheep Creek's canyon. Undeveloped camping sites abound, particularly along the first 20 miles of the route.

After leaving the relatively narrow canyon of Big Sheep Creek the road shoots through a broad swath of emptiness bordered on the west by the barren Beaverhead Mountains, whose ridgeline defines the Continental Divide and the border of Montana and Idaho. In early summer, after the road is generally passable but before the mountain snows have all melted, the landscape is surprisingly evocative of backcountry Alaska, with a parade of imposing, bald white peaks marching along the limits of a treeless, tundra-like basin.

If, on the other hand, you would prefer remaining on pavement for a while, after filling up at Yesterday's Cafe continue north on Interstate 15. Twenty miles north of Dell is **Clark Canyon Reservoir**, popular with anglers the year around and with boaters after the ice melts. The Bureau of Reclamation maintains several campgrounds on the shore of the lake; however, if you're not particularly trout-crazy you may find the stark setting, probable wind, and often less-than-full reservoir not a particularly appealing combination.

If that's the case, continue to **Dillon**, a typical ranch town except that it's home to the small, charming campus of **Western Montana College** of the University of Montana. Since the 1890s the private-sized public college has served as the state university system's teacher-education branch. An average of just over 1,000 students enroll at Western each year. Another, even less expected find in the classic cow town: a **Patagonia Outlet**, located downtown at 34 North Idaho Street.

Some good deals on Patagonia's high-quality and ordinarily high-priced outdoor wear can often be found at the outlet. This is particularly true on Labor Day weekend, when blowout sales are conducted, attracting polyester pile-philes from throughout the tri-state region.

Another place not to miss while prowling through downtown Dillon is the **Beaverhead County Museum**, which inhabits an old log structure at 15 South Montana Street. The better-than-average small-town repository of lore features excellent exhibits on the area's Native American and pioneering Anglo cultures. Some 1,700 cattle brands, both discontinued and current, are displayed along the exterior boardwalk of the museum, and a homesteader's cabin is another interesting find. Also worth seeing is the 20-foot-long **Lewis & Clark Diorama**, located at the Beaverhead Chamber of Commerce visitor center in the old Union Pacific depot, south of the museum at 125 South Montana Street.

Dillon, population 4,000-plus, is just large enough to hold a handful of motels and fast-food and slow-food restaurants, but small enough that you may find little reason to linger . . . unless the small-town allure, abundance of parks, and unexpected mix of vintage architectural styles lull you into a mosey-around mood. Or, unless it is Labor Day weekend, when typically quiet Dillon turns loud and boisterous, thanks, in addition to the Patagonia sale, to the town's annual rodeo and related festivities.

But in Dillon, as in the Northern Rockies in general, it is the countryside beyond town and what it encompasses that is the real attraction. There's that mountain creek teeming with trout, the ghost town just on the other side of the next ridge, and the see-forever basin green with growing alfalfa and dotted white and off-red with lowing cattle. And there is no direction you can travel from Dillon without shortly encountering some of each. To the west, for instance, State Highway 278 (which meets I-15 3 miles south of Dillon) crests Badger Pass then Big Hole Pass, before descending into the **Big Hole River Valley**, one of the most sublime basins in all of Montana, enclosed by some of the Treasure State's grandest mountain ranges. It's the highest, widest, and emptiest major valley in western Montana.

If there were nothing to see in this lonely corner of Glacier-Gold Country but the endless views, it would still be a highly recommended tour. But there is much more to see; in fact, two of the most evocative historic sites in the entire Northern Rockies lie along this route following State Highways 278 and 43: **Bannack State Park** and **Big Hole National Battlefield**.

Three miles-plus after cresting 6,760-foot Badger Pass, which is approximately 14 miles west of the interstate, take the left-hand turn leading 4 miles to Bannack State Park. It seems that the earth is trying hard to reclaim the old mining town, where sagebrush higher than your head lines the dusty main street. But Bannack endures. The ghostly remains of Montana's original territorial capital comprise some five dozen buildings, well preserved in a state of "arrested decay." Among the structures you can visit: the Graves House, built in 1867 as the first frame house in the Montana Territory; the Meade Hotel, originally built to serve as the Beaverhead County Courthouse; an 1877 Methodist Church; and the Renois Cabin, one of the oldest structures in town.

Bannack exploded out of nothingness after gold was discovered on Grasshopper Creek on July 28, 1862. The White's Bar placer discovery—

Pack mule

named for prospector John White, who led a group of fellow "Pike's Peakers" from Colorado—was the first recorded mining claim in the Montana Territory, and it ignited Montana's first big gold boom. The Grasshopper diggings suddenly became a magnet, attracting prospectors who poured in along trails from all directions. Within a year of the strike, Bannack's population had mushroomed to a ragtag assortment of more than 3,000, which included miners as well as entrepreneurs posed to suck whatever gold they could out of successful prospectors. Blacksmith shops, a billiard hall, saloons, stables, a Chinese restaurant, houses of ill repute, a bowling alley, and much more quickly materialized.

In 1864, when the Montana Territory was split off from the year-old Idaho Territory, newly appointed governor Sidney Edgerton declared Bannack the capital of the territory. Bannack's luster quickly tarnished, though, after an even bigger strike was made in the Alder Gulch–Virginia City area. Hundreds of Bannack prospectors hit the trail for Virginia City, taking with them the designation of capital, which Virginia City assumed in 1865. Still, although the big boom fizzled after only a couple of years, Bannack continued as a viable mining settlement for many years afterward. In 1895 the "F. L. Graves" that fired up in Bannack was the first electric dredge operation in the U.S., and it wasn't until the 1940s that almost all mining activity had quieted.

A visit to Bannack is largely self-guided. A pleasant, although often mosquito-filled campground is also located within the park. A particularly good time to visit (not to avoid the crowds, though) is the third weekend in July, when the Bannack Days celebration revives the nineteenth century, with black-powder shooting, horse-drawn buggy rides, buffalo barbecues, and more.

West of its junction with the Bannack Road, State Highway 278 becomes part of the **Lewis and Clark National Historic Trail**. In 7.5 miles you'll pass the turn to the **Pioneer Mountains National Scenic Byway**, which leads north to the settlement of Wise River. The road, which is paved for the northernmost 29 of its 46 miles, cuts between the east and west units of the Pioneer Mountains, reaching an elevation of 7,782 feet before dropping to 5,600 feet at Wise River. As you'll see, the two components of the Pioneers look dramatically different from one another. Some 70 million years ago the western mountains subsided a half-mile in relation to the eastern range, along the fault running through the valley separating them. The higher, more rugged East Pioneers, consequently, have weathered far more erosion, which has exposed the underlying granites. The West Pioneers by comparison are rolling, subdued mountains, blanketed in dark timber.

BICYCLING THE PIONEER MOUNTAINS NATIONAL SCENIC BYWAY: A NARRATIVE ACCOUNT

The Pioneer Mountains National Scenic Byway connects the settlements—I hesitate to call them towns—of Wise River and Polaris, Montana. The byway makes for an outstanding drive and, when the weather is favorable, an even better bicycle ride.

Nancy and I drove this scenic road five or six times during the years we lived in Montana, but for some reason we never got around to bicycling on it . . . until now. From our perspective, one experiences much more, via all the senses—and experiences everything with much more clarity—when on a bicycle than when enclosed in a fast-moving car. So we bicycle almost any time the opportunity comes our way.

We've seen so few other cars and trucks on this road in the past that it has reminded us of a beautiful, paved bike path, carrying only the occasional wayward motor vehicle, whose driver seems to have lost his way and inadvertently driven onto the bikeway. If it were ten years ago, we would have hauled along our mountain bikes as the vehicles of choice for this outing. Since that time, however, pavement has been extended to a point within 17 miles of the byway's southern terminus. So, it is narrow-tired road bikes that grace our car-top today.

Twenty-five miles west of Dillon on State Highway 278 we turn north onto the national scenic byway, a designation given the road by the U.S. Forest Service. Brown grasses blanket the late-summer foothills, which are mere lumps compared to the bare-rock peaks of the East Pioneer Mountains rising behind. We drive past a rangy old rancher on a tractor, busy cutting his alfalfa hay. He waves, and we wave back. The green fields, with stacks of freshly cut and baled hay standing about, reach to meet the brown hillsides. Under the angles of early morning sun, it's an altogether arresting scene.

Four and one-half miles after leaving the highway we pass the tiny, vintage Polaris School. In another 2 miles we drive through **Polaris**, which comprises just a house or two, a post office, and the unique, self-serve Polar Bar. A hand-lettered sign scribbled on the door informs us of the basics: B.Y.O.B CLUB ONLY. HOURS: WHEN YOU CAN FIND WALT. Farther along, after passing **Ma Barnes Country Market** ("If You Forgot It Ma's Got It") on the right and the **Grasshopper Inn** motel and restaurant on the left, the road narrows to twist amid a collection of timber-embraced, canyon cabins before it enters the Beaverhead National Forest. Still driving on gravel, we pass the left-hand turn to **Maverick Mountain**, a small ski area that, I'm told, come winter attracts prodigious amounts of both snow and Dillon-area schussers.

Thirteen miles after leaving the highway we pass the entrance to **Elkhorn Hot Springs**, where we intend to return after our ride and after setting up camp at one of the string of Forest Service campgrounds located above. The rustic resort has a large warm pool, a limited-menu restaurant, and primitive, sans-plumbing cabins and lodge-room accommodations. In fact, we would simply begin bicycling here if not for the steep uphill 4-mile stretch of gravel lying just ahead. (Bicycling and hot springs go together like shoes and laces, and with the wealth of hot springs found in western Montana the combination of riding and soaking is a very popular one.)

We were told back in Dillon that plans are on the drawing board to pave the rest of this road. If it's true, we hope it doesn't happen soon. And if it does happen, we hope it won't mean the lazy byway will turn into a major thoroughfare.

At the top of the climb, where we encounter pavement, we pull off the road, park, and prepare for the ride. Now begins the fun.

The ribbon of blacktop cuts a swath through a seemingly impenetrable forest of lodgepole pine. A tangle of gray deadfall litters the forest floor, and sun rays glance off the rusty brown trunks of standing trees. Where the slopes aren't covered in timber they're often covered in dark, blackish scree. What

a difference a 1,500-foot elevation gain can make! It's a startlingly different setting from the grasslands we passed through just a few miles back. It stays cooler at this altitude, and to some extent the mountains make their own weather, so in both summer and winter the precipitation is substantially greater here than at the lower elevations.

We zip effortlessly down the road; too effortlessly, we know, because it means that riding in the opposite direction, uphill, will not be such a breeze. The first designated site we pass—and, it turns out, by far the busiest—is the **Crystal Park Picnic Area**. Judging by the number of cars and trucks occupying the parking area we guess that a family of Smiths, Wilsons, or Andersons must be staging a reunion. But then we pull over and ask a dark-haired, middle-aged woman just what is going on. She's hauling a shovel over her right shoulder and carrying a small screening box in her left hand. "Crystals" is what it's all about, she tells us. Quartz crystals are abundant in the decomposed granite soil here, we are told; crystals of both smoky, or brown quartz and amethyst, or purplish quartz. The crystals generally range in size from about an inch up to 6 inches long.

We learn more by reading a sign posted in the parking area: It seems that the Butte Mineral & Gem Club maintains mining claims at the location. In partnership with the Forest Service, the club keeps the claims open to the public, which is permitted to dig crystals using hand tools only. The word has obviously spread far beyond Butte, for among the vehicles in the parking lot are cars from as far away as Maine and South Carolina. A new- and inviting-looking picnic area, featuring blacktopped pull-ins, picnic tables, and fire grates sits adjacent to the digging hills.

Back on the bikes, after joining in alongside Mono Creek we pass a couple of campgrounds, where we slow our pace and eye them carefully. Our map indicates that at least five Forest Service campgrounds line the road between Elkhorn Hot Springs and Wise River, and we want to choose the best one for our night's campsite.

Much of the terrain we pedal through, although encompassed by the Pioneer Mountains, is quite flat. A trail shooting off from a roadside trailhead in the opening called Harrison Park looks as if it would offer fun and relatively easy hiking or mountain biking. In Harrison and Moose parks we're surprised to see thousands of rocks and boulders littering the ground. They range in size from tiny to enormous. A roadside sign informs us that they're *glacial erratics*, composed of the same rock as the high East Pioneer peaks in the distance, which broke off thousands of years ago and were transported to these open meadows by ice- and mudflows.

After pedaling a total of 15 or 16 miles, we pass several campgrounds in short order, including **Willow Campground** and **Lodgepole Campground**. We decide we preferred one of those we zipped by earlier, the one called **Little Joe**. Longtime fans of the *Bonanza* television show, we definitely like the name best of all.

As we lose elevation we enter the broad, unforested valley of the Wise River. The valley is flanked by dark timbered mountains, with fluffy cotton clouds flirting high above their summits. Drier-looking mountains lie ahead to the north. A slight headwind carries the delicious scent of sage. We pass the Wise River Airport, recognizing it only because of the fluorescent-orange wind sock pointing at us as we approach. Then we ride through a progression of rural homes, and even past a couple of tipis. As we cross a bridge spanning the Wise River we look to our right to see a man fishing, as his female companion sits nearby, sketching.

As we continue downstream, the hillside timber stands thin and the terrain turns rocky and dry. On this hot and sunny day we enjoyed the cool shade of the forest far more than this open country. Not to worry, though, because soon we'll be riding back the 29 miles the way we came. In **Wise River,** a scattering of cabins, trailers, outfitters, bars, and sheep and cattle, we head directly into the **Wise River Club**, an antiques- and stuffed-animal-filled bar that reeks rural Montana. After downing a burger, all that's left to do is pedal back to the car, then set up the tent at Little Joe Campground. The soothing waters at Elkhorn Hot Springs may be more than 30 miles and two hours away, but we can already feel the steam and smell the minerals.

INTO THE BIG HOLE

On descending westward from Big Hole Pass along State Highway 278—if you can ignore the occasional motorized vehicle, farm machinery, and satellite dish—you might start thinking you've entered a nineteenth-century time warp. The broad Big Hole River Valley, more commonly known simply as the Big Hole, is home to some of the least cut-up-and-parceled spreads of ranchlands remaining in the Northern Rockies. Like Jackson Hole in Wyoming, the valley's name recalls frontier times, when a broad basin was referred to as a "hole." Collections of hay adorn the valley floor, assuming countless configurations—small bales, big bales, pinwheel rolls, bread-loaf shaped stacks, big piles held together by fencing, and others—earning the Big Hole its long-time nickname, "the valley of 10,000 haystacks."

Several other features commonly seen in the valley also help cement the Big Hole's ties to its past ranching traditions. Among them: long stretches of buck-and-rail fences delineating property lines and the tall, wooden structures that look rather like angled baseball backstops. You may have seen them elsewhere in the tri-state area, but they're particularly plentiful here. The pseudo-backstops are actually beaverslide haystackers, a model designed in the Big Hole and patented in 1910 as the Sunny Slope Slide Hay Stacker. The ingenious contraption permitted ranchers to stack their hay much higher than they previously could, utilizing teams of horses to run the belts that lifted the hay to the top of the inclined slide before dropping it onto the stack. Many beaverslides are

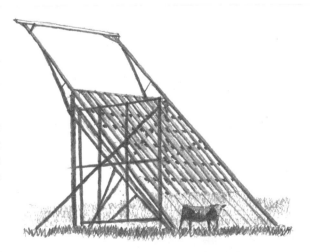

Beaverslide haystacker, Big Hole Valley

still in use, although in most instances motors have replaced horse power.

The valley floor stretches to mountains in every direction of the compass: the Bitterroots and Beaverheads lie to the south and west, the Anaconda-Pintlers to the north, and the Pioneers to the east. Amid all this stunning scenery you'll soon arrive in bucolic **Jackson**, which is almost, but not quite small enough to throw a rock from one end to the other. It would be easy to barely slow down and simply continue past the little cow town, but to do so would represent an error in judgment.

As it was in 1805 when the Corps of Discovery visited the site of the future Jackson, the local hot springs remains *the* attraction here. At **Jackson Hot Springs** resort you'll find a main lodge with a bar and immense dance floor encircled by animal mounts; lodge and cabin rooms for rent; and a good restaurant. The irresistible, 30-by-75-foot indoor hot pool at the lodge became an outdoor pool a few years back, after the proprietors tore off the overhead roof. Across the street from the lodge is a second good eatery, in the form of **Rose's Cantina**.

South and southwest of Jackson on gravel roads you can find the Beaverhead National Forest's **North Van Houten**, **South Van Houten**, and **Miner Lake** campgrounds settled against the Beaverhead Mountains. Way off the beaten track, they're excellent places to go to enjoy a woodsy reprieve.

Continuing north along the Big Hole River, in 19 miles you'll come to **Wisdom**, home to the **Nez Perce Motel**, a couple of restaurants including the good **Big Hole Crossing**, the **Wisdom Ranger Station** of the Beaverhead National Forest, and the decidedly one-of-a-kind **Conover's Trading Post**. In typical rural Montana, politically incorrect fashion, the enterprise features an immense likeness of an Indian maiden lying seductively over the entrance, and an equally tacky inventory inside that includes trophy mounts of jackalope and a "rearwolf." (Don't ask, just go see it.) Conover's sells fishing gear, elk ivory teeth, candy bars, and other goods and goodies, too.

If you think you've heard of Wisdom before but can't remember why, chances are you've listened to the weatherman in winter saying it's the coldest spot in the contiguous United States. And if you need help keeping your head warm while visiting the potentially frigid area, no problem: Wisdom's **Kirkpatrick Custom Hat Company** hand-fashions some of the finest lids in the West.

A Side Trip from Wisdom to Wise River

The Big Hole continues flowing northeast from Wise River, then, in approximately 30 miles, leaves the broad valley that gave it its name. Several pull-offs provide access for anglers, who come from afar to pursue the renowned lower river's trophy brown and rainbow trout. The river defines a huge, backward S, wrapping to the east to flow past the town of Wise River, then south, back east, and, finally, to the north again before contributing to the Jefferson River near Twin Bridges.

Heading north on State Highway 43, at a point several miles out of Wisdom you'll pull in alongside Big Hole, still a mellow river slicing through an open basin. The spectacular peaks of the Anaconda-Pintler Wilderness to the north provide a thrilling backdrop to an otherwise hushed scene.

After crossing the Big Hole River and entering Deer Lodge County, you'll commence hugging the left-hand bank of the river. A few miles later you'll cross LaMarche Creek then pass, on the left, the **Sundance Lodge** saloon and restaurant. The gradually tapering valley is still rather wide, offering occasional peeks at the mountains to the north. Plenty of fishing-access and dispersed camping sites line the highway. At roughly 28 miles you'll pass the left-hand turn onto State Highway 274. En route to Anaconda, 25 miles away, this road leads over the Continental Divide and past the popular **Mount Haggin Recreation Area**, where Butte's Mile Hi Nordic Ski Club maintains well-groomed cross-country ski trails in winter.

As you continue on State Highway 43 the valley narrows considerably, its high slopes putting an end to the long-range views. At 31 miles you'll see the riverside **Dickey Bridge Recreation Area**, which includes a Bureau of Land Management campground. At 37 miles is the **Troutfitters** fly shop, a business offering river shuttles and guided fishing trips on the Big Hole. A mile later you'll reach tiny **Wise River**, home to enterprises such as the **H & J Saloon and Cafe** and the **Gnose**

Mercantile. From Wise River you can access the northern end of the Pioneer Mountains National Scenic Byway, or continue following State Highway 43 and the Big Hole River for 12 miles to Divide, where you'll meet Interstate 15.

On the Trail of Lewis & Clark and Chief Joseph: From the Big Hole to the Bitterroot Valley

From Wisdom leave the Big Hole River by veering west onto State Highway 43 to begin the gentle ascent toward the Bitterroot Mountains. You'll motor by the mini-city known as the Spokane Ranch, then, at approximately 4 miles, pass the left-hand turn to the Gibbonsville Road, which leads over the Continental Divide into Idaho.

At approximately 10 miles turn right toward **Big Hole National Battlefield**, a primary component of the multi-state Nez Perce National Historical Park. The site occupies stunning surroundings, with fingers of mountain timber reaching down toward the confluence flats where Trail and Ruby creeks come together to form the North Fork of the Big Hole River. The bucolic setting belies the turbulence that erupted here early on the morning of August 9, 1877.

Five bands of "non-Treaty" Nez Perce Indians, numbering approximately 800 individuals, had set up camp here in the Big Hole on August 7, probably looking forward to some badly needed rest. The Indians were midway on their epic 1,200-mile journey, as they fled their beloved northeastern Oregon homeland. For two months the Nez Perce, who were herding approximately 2,000 horses, had outsmarted and largely eluded their intended captors, until they were ambushed here in the Big Hole. The surprise attack, led by Col. John Gibbon and carried out by both civilian volunteers and soldiers of the seventh U.S. Infantry, culminated in the death of 89 Nez Perce. It was far from the end of the trail for the Indians, though: They eventually repelled their attackers in

the Big Hole, even capturing the Army's Model 1863 Mountain Howitzer. It was another two months before the Nez Perce were quelled, when they surrendered in the Bear's Paw Mountains, just 40 miles shy of their destination of Canada.

In the wake of the ultimately tragic trek of the Nez Perce, Gen. William Tecumseh Sherman's respectful words summed up the feelings of many: " . . . The Indians displayed a courage and skill that elicited universal praise; they abstained from scalping, let captive women go free, did not commit indiscriminate murder of peaceful families . . . and fought with almost scientific skill. . . ."

The National Park Service visitor center at the Battlefield, open daily year-round, presents a film and includes exhibits interpreting the events precipitating and those transpiring on that sad summer morning. Among the exhibits you'll find vivid, evocative profiles, accompanied by photos, of several of the men who took part in the battle, including all three: Indians, soldiers, and civilians. Also displayed are findings from the 1991 archaeological excavations conducted at the site. A brochure entitled "Guide to the Trails at Big Hole National Battlefield" can be procured at the visi-

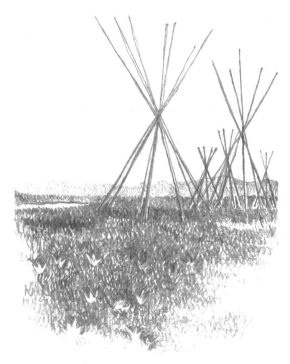

Nez Perce camp, Big Hole Battlefield

tor center, too. Trails beginning at the lower parking area lead to the hillside Howitzer capture site, through the main siege area, to memorials honoring the men buried on the battlefield grounds, and to the site of the Nez Perce encampment. At the encampment site you'll find skeletal tipi frames, looking like ghosts devoid of skin, silhouetted against the Big Hole's backdrop of big sky and broad-shouldered mountains. (*See* History, Yellowstone-Teton Country for more information on the Nez Perce trek, including an account of the Indians' subsequent travels through Yellowstone National Park.)

Continue driving west on State Highway 43, a low-traffic ribbon of a road embraced by forests of spindly lodgepole pine. The occasional meadows interrupting the timber stands are often lined with zigzagging buck-and-rail fences and alive with grazing cattle; low mountains hover beyond. You'll pass the left-hand turn to the Beaverhead National Forest's **May Creek Campground** at 16.5 miles from Wisdom, then, 2 miles later, pass the right-hand turn to Trail Creek Road 106. This generally good gravel road follows both the Lewis and Clark National Historic Trail and the Nez Perce (Nee-Me-Poo) National Historic Trail. It crests the Continental Divide at Gibbons Pass before descending into Montana's Bitterroot Valley, meeting U.S. Highway 93 just south of the Sula Ranger Station. If you follow the route, you'll pass picturesque **Hogan Cabin**, which graces the wildflower-filled Trail Creek Meadows not far off the road. The cabin, which goes to work in summer housing Forest Service employees, is available to rent by the public during the snowy parts of the year, from December 1 through March 31. (Call the Wisdom Ranger District at 406–689–3243 for information and reservations.)

Alternatively, continue climbing gradually on pavement along State Highway 43, topping out at **Chief Joseph Pass** and the Continental Divide. The slopes and flats surrounding the 7,264-foot pass consistently attract some of the lightest and deepest powder snow in western Montana; not surprisingly, both snowmobilers and cross-country skiers by the dozens are drawn to the lofty locale come winter. The Bitterroot Ski Club, headquartered in Hamilton, maintains a network of ski trails radiating from the parking area at the pass.

From Chief Joseph Pass descend through a mile of Idaho before turning right to crest Lost Trail Pass and re-enter Montana. You can't miss seeing the nearby cleared slopes of **Lost Trail Powder Mountain**. The small ski area, which has garnered a large reputation for its abundance of deep powder, is popular with skiers from both the Salmon, Idaho, area and from the Bitterroot Valley all the way to Missoula. The area straddles the state line, so downhillers enjoy the unusual opportunity to ski in two states in one day.

Considering the long descent required to reach the valley bottoms going either south or north from Lost Trail Pass on U.S. Highway 93, the surrounding terrain is rather subdued: No really impressive peaks loom nearby, and many of the timbered slopes show signs of overzealous logging practices. After dropping from the pass heading north, at 6.5 miles you'll pass **Lost Trail Hot Springs** (telephone 406–821–3574) on the left. Swing in to have a look and maybe enjoy a soak or even an overnight at the peaceful getaway. In addition to its hot mineral pool, hot tub, and sauna, the resort offers a bar-restaurant, lodging in cabins of various configurations, camping, and trail rides. The rustic rental cabins, thick green moss covering portions of their roofs, sit amid deep, dark woods. The exterior surfaces of some of the buildings match almost exactly the rich, weathered brown trunks of the surrounding ponderosa pines.

Nine miles north of Lost Trail Pass you'll pass **Camp Creek Inn B&B** (telephone 406–821–3508), an attractive, big old brown-and-white box sitting well off the highway on the right. Good horseback-riding trails branch out from the ranch grounds. A couple of miles later on the right, just beyond the northwest terminus of the Gibbons Pass Road, you'll see the **Sula Ranger Station,** where you can pick up a copy of the visitor map of the Bitterroot National Forest. Thirteen miles from the pass, adjacent to the point where the East Fork Road meets the highway, is the unique **Sula Store**, which also features a campground/RV park. The store occupies a charming little log building, whose dark-brown stained logs are highlighted with light-colored chinking and butt ends painted white. The Sula Store's diminutive size is inversely proportionate to that of its inventory; the extensive array of things crammed into the little enterprise includes turquoise-and-silver jewelry, wool shirts and jackets, Minnetonka moccasins, Montana-theme T-shirts, and a good selection of food items. A wooden Indian out front greets all those who enter.

If you head east here from on the paved **East Fork Road**, which opens onto a pastureland that contrasts markedly with the tight, timbered canyon traced by the main highway, in 5.5 miles you'll reach **Broad Axe Lodge**. There you can sit in the comfort of the resort's restaurant while watching the bighorn sheep that frequent the adjacent steep hillsides. The restaurant (telephone 406–821–3878) opens for dinner Wednesday through Sunday in summer and Friday through Sunday in winter. Cabins are also available to rent.

Back on U.S. Highway 93, you'll soon pass **Spring Gulch Campground**, where you can make camp at a spot where Lewis and Clark did the same. The canyon you're traveling through is narrow, with dry slopes on the east supporting grasses and ponderosa pine, while darker forests of Douglas fir and other species thrive on the west side. Seventeen miles from Lost Trail Pass you'll pass **Rocky Knob Lodge** (telephone 406–821–3520), a solitary enterprise offering lodging and good steak and hickory-smoked rib dinners.

At roughly 21 miles on the right is a pull-out adjacent to the easy-to-miss **Medicine Tree**. From the branches of the tall, dead-topped ponderosa pine hangs a rainbow of Native American offerings, in the form of bright streamers, colorful scarves, and other items. The ancient pine is the cultural property of the Confederated Salish and Kootenai tribes, to whom it is sacred, and it is protected by federal and tribal law. (Take only photos, please.)

Soon the valley widens and the Bitterroot Range pops into view on the left. You'll pass the left-hand turn onto Route 473, the West Fork Road, which leads 23 miles southwest to **Painted Rocks Reservoir**, whose name derives from prehistoric Native American rock art in the area. En route to the lake you'll pass the trailhead for a trail providing a surprisingly non-technical route up glacier-carved Trapper Peak, elevation 10,157 feet. It's the distinctive crag you can see from the main highway, hanging high above the valley of the Bitterroot River. Trapper is the tallest peak in the entire run of the Bitterroots, whose ridgeline defines some 200 miles of the Montana–Idaho border.

At the reservoir, a long, narrow body of water created by the damming of the Bitterroot River's

Trapper Peak, Bitterroot Range

West Fork, you'll find **Painted Rocks State Park**, which includes a campground. Continue approximately a mile south from there and you'll come across the surprising **West Fork Meadows Ranch** (406–349–2468), a cattle and guest ranch run by a pair of transplanted Europeans. Exceptional continental cuisine is served in the dining room, located in the lavish main lodge. Available to rent are a suite in the main lodge and private log cabins, whose sumptuous, wilderness-embraced ambience is anything but rustic.

Thirty miles north of Lost Trail Pass you'll enter **Darby**, "The Best Kept Secret in Montana," or so claims the sign at the edge of town. Before getting into the heart of the small downtown area you'll pass the **Wilderness Motel**, where the marquee frequently proffers words to live by, such as FISHING ISN'T A MATTER OF LIFE OR DEATH—IT'S MORE IMPORTANT. Darby historically has thrived on the logging industry, but increasingly it is an Old West aura the town is assuming. Among Darby's handful of businesses is **Bud & Shirley's Restaurant** (telephone 406-821-3401), a few-frills eatery located in Bud & Shirley's Mall, next to Bud & Shirley's Motel. The restaurant fries up what may be the best hash browns this side of the Idaho border.

A couple of other spots you may want to check out include the **Darby Trading Post**, which sells antler art and other neat Western-oriented stuff, and the colorful **Lone Wolf Saloon**. You should also swing into the **Darby Historic Center of the Forest Service**, which resides in the original Darby Ranger Station, located on the grounds of the Bitterroot National Forest's Darby Ranger District. In addition to finding maps and other information there, you can visit a room made up to resemble a pioneer ranger outpost. You'll also find displays and implements relating to the earlier days of wildfire-fighting.

Somewhere between Darby and Hamilton the Bitterroot transforms from a tumbling mountain stream into a tamed, meandering river, embraced by cottonwoods and surrounded by the pastures and crop fields of a widening valley. The high Bitterroots to the west continue commanding your attention. The mountains' lower slopes and gentler high slopes are blanketed in extremely dense timber stands, while the precipitous upper reaches are exposed to their rocky core. The upper slopes are included in the 1.3-million-acre **Selway-Bitterroot Wilderness**, a tangle of primeval terrain laced with trails and graced with cold alpine lakes. Most of the wilderness lies in Idaho, but nearly a quarter-million acres of it extend onto the Montana side of the mountains.

Occasionally, the Bitterroot front is cleft by deep, steep-sided canyons, such as **Blodgett Canyon** west of Hamilton. The trail leading up Blodgett offers a ready route into the heart of the Bitterroots; it's a surprisingly gentle path for one leading through such dramatic terrain. Putting a halt to the east side of the Bitterroot Valley are the Sapphire Mountains, a low-slung, deceptively modest range that in its own right hides plenty of wild country and wildlife.

As you approach the hum of **Hamilton** you may start getting the feeling that, yes, okay, Montana *is* mushrooming in population. Newcomers settling "up the Bitterroot," to use the local jargon (remember, the Bitterroot River flows from south to north), include ultra-conservative back-to-the landers, retirees from southern California and other areas of dense population, and folks who work in Missoula but prefer living in a slightly more rustic setting.

Largely as a result of this third category of "Bitterrooter," U.S. Highway 93 between Hamilton and Missoula often carries heavy traffic, particularly during weekday commuting hours. Here's a way to bypass several miles of the busy road and enjoy a wonderful rural drive: At the stoplight at the main intersection adjacent to downtown Hamilton, turn east onto the Eastside Highway, which will lead you toward the challenging, eighteen-hole **Hamilton Golf Club**.

On the outskirts of town you'll find a real treasure in the **Daly Mansion**, which was the part-time residence of Marcus Daly, the most famous of Butte's late-nineteenth-century "copper kings." Daly, an immigrant from Ireland who made a vast fortune mining and smelting copper, lived many summers here at his Riverside Mansion, which he had built on his Bitterroot Stock Farm in the 1890s. Daly, apparently thinking he needed a town to go with his summer home, also conceived and planned Hamilton.

For more than four decades following the 1941 death of Daly's widow the mansion sat boarded up, looking altogether like a haunted house sitting at the end of its long drive, which is framed by deciduous trees. (They lend a delightful and uncommon burst of color to the countryside in fall.) Fortunately, in 1987 the state of Montana purchased the grand old place and opened it to the public. The three-story, 24,000-square-foot Georgian Revival–style residence recalls an earlier day, with its forty-two rooms, seven marble fireplaces, and impressive collection of period furnishings. It's widely considered the most baronial of Montana's trio of grand mansions (Kalispell's Conrad Mansion and the Moss Mansion in Billings are the other two). The manicured grounds surrounding the home—highlighted with a tennis court, swimming pool, and dozens of shade trees—make it easy to imagine seeing a young Cary Grant and Katharine Hepburn come strolling around the corner, arm in arm.

The Eastside Road undulates through a rural terrain of truck farms, horse ranches, and ranchettes inhabited by city workers and retirees. The first town of any size you'll encounter is **Stevensville**, where Father Pierre-Jean De Smet and his party arrived from the Midwest in 1841, at the urging of the Flathead Indians (*see* History). Here, just thirty-six years after the Corps of Discovery had passed through the Bitterroot Valley, the Jesuits built the **St. Mary's Mission**, which consisted of a cottonwood-log chapel and two log cabins. Today at the site you'll find a new information center, the renovated chapel and study, Father Anthony Ravalli's log house, an old Native American graveyard, and the home of Chief Victor, which houses a small museum.

Continuing north on the Eastside Highway, just outside Stevensville you will skirt the **Lee Metcalf National Wildlife Refuge**. By turning onto the road looping through the riparian refuge you're likely to spot white-tailed deer, as well as a host of waterfowl and "fisher birds" that can include ospreys and bald eagles. Gentle hiking trails lead through the refuge's woods, and you'll have little trouble finding a private, shaded spot beside the hissing Bitterroot River to enjoy a picnic or afternoon snooze.

The Lee Metcalf is one third of the threesome known as **The Watchable Wildlife Triangle**, the other two being the Willoughby Environmental Education Area and the Charles Waters Nature Trail. Within a 30-mile route you can visit a marvelous diversity of wildlife habitats, including wetlands, sagebrush benches, and old-growth timber stands. (You can obtain a map and informational brochure on the Watchable Wildlife

Osprey

Triangle by calling 406–777–5552.) The Charles Waters Nature Trail begins at the **Charles Waters Campground**, located 4 miles north of Stevensville on U.S. Highway 93, then 3 miles west on Bass Creek Road. The pleasant site is one of the closest public campgrounds to the Missoula urban area.

The Eastside Highway rejoins U.S. Highway 93 at Florence, where you'll be remiss if you don't stop in at **Glen's Cafe** to sample the justifiably famous homemade pies. Nine miles north of Florence you'll pass through the bedroom community of **Lolo**. Here you can continue straight toward Missoula, located 10 miles to the northeast, or turn left onto U.S. Highway 12, which leads 33 miles to the Idaho border and **Lolo Pass**. The snow-buried winter sports area at Lolo Pass is exceedingly popular with snowmobilers and cross-country skiers, and the mountain bicycling and wildflower viewing in summer are likewise first-rate. Seven miles before the summit you'll pass the **Lolo Hot Springs Resort**, whose beckoning waters are *just* right.

A Visit to Missoula

Plain and simple, Missoula is a great town. The "Garden City," vibrant and buzzing, boasts a diversity of residents few communities even two or three times its size can rival. The University of Montana is known not only as the state's chief liberal arts school but also as Montana's most *liberal* school. The university brings to town all sorts of interesting folks, both from Montana and from outside the state. U.M.'s creative writing, forestry, wildlife, law, and journalism departments all are among the best found in the United States.

Some of the most recognized corporate names in the timber industry have mills and/or offices in Missoula. Not surprisingly, perhaps, some of the country's best-known anti-logging organizations have established offices here, too. These include the Alliance for the Wild Rockies and Wilderness Watch. Caught in the middle is the USDA Forest Service, which maintains a slate of local, regional, and national offices in Missoula, making the agency one of the city's primary employers. Several nonprofit organizations of national scope are headquartered in Missoula, as well. These

attract a lot of pilgrims to town, and also help often to draw the national spotlight on the city.

Finally, the arts are alive and kicking in Missoula, and the abundance of nearby outdoor recreational activities is second to none.

A Summer's Day in Missoula: A Narrative Account

As a challenge during this free day in Missoula, I plan to stay active from sunup to sundown, enjoying some of the things I miss most about my former hometown of fifteen years. I'll also take in several of the city's more popular attractions, some of which I rarely visited while living here. It is June 25, only four days after the summer solstice, and at this latitude I'll have plenty of daylight hours to fill.

Missoula is nothing if not a city of trails, so I begin the day by celebrating that fact. At 5:15 A.M. sharp I meet friend Robin at the base of the **M** trail, located just across Campus Drive from the University of Montana's football field. The steep path switchbacks up the lower flanks of **Mount Sentinel**, which, as its names suggests, stands watch over the Missoula Valley. Unceremoniously, and only half awake, we are off, alone on our trek at this early hour, walking or jogging as the grade permits. Despite that July is right around the corner, the morning air is chilly, so we're both wearing sweatshirts.

In about fifteen minutes we reach the immense, whitewashed concrete **M** (for Montana) that can be seen from just about anywhere in Missoula—and from where we look down on most of the city. At this point the designated trail ends, and several ragged, makeshift trails lead the rest of the way to the summit of Sentinel. Sweatshirts now tied around our waists, we take the steep, straight-up trail hugging the rim of **Hellgate Canyon**. The barren, west-facing slope we're following is grass- and weed-covered; just below the rim, however, the north-facing slope drops off into stands of big Douglas fir.

In 40 minutes—but only after scaring a small herd of mule deer—we arrive at the rock cairn marking the summit of Mount Sentinel. The view is sublime: Missoula spreads out before us, 2,000 feet below, its structures filling the big floodplain basin and also making their way up the nearby hillsides to the south. Out toward Fort Missoula we can see snaking groves of cottonwoods converging toward the point where the Bitterroot River meets the Clark Fork of the Columbia. Large expanses of green mark the city's many parks and golf courses. In every direction mountains put an end to the flatness. To the north rises the Rattlesnake Range. Farther to the left, snow-tipped Squaw Peak stands above the Ninemile Valley. To the southwest, far on the other side of the Interstate 90 corridor, the white, 9,075-foot bulk of the Bitterroot Range's Lolo Peak dominates the skyline.

After savoring the view and having a drink of water, we continue down the backside of the mountain and onto the newer **Smokejumper Trail**. We follow the well-engineered footpath down into Hellgate Canyon, through which the Clark Fork River makes its entrance into Missoula. The old Milwaukee Road railroad grade paralleling the river, now known as the **Kim Williams Nature Trail**, leads us back to the university campus. The rail-trail was named in memory of the raspy voiced, Eastern-accented Missoula woman who became a popular National Public Radio commentator.

The hike-and-jog took almost two hours, and it left us starved. So, after showers, at 8:00 A.M. we meet Nancy and Peggy and five-year-old Ian at **The Shack**, a venerable Missoula eating establishment whose breakfasts, in my estimation, are the best in town. I chow down on my old favorite, the breakfast burrito (which for a couple of hours afterward doesn't let me forget that it was plenty spicy).

After breakfast Nancy and I drive west from downtown on Broadway to the national headquarters of the **Rocky Mountain Elk Foundation**. This very successful organization, which began up in tiny Troy, Montana, in the early 1980s, exists to enhance populations of wild elk and other animals, largely by raising funds to acquire and improve habitat lands. The foundation's large membership, dispersed throughout North America and beyond, is made up of hunters and others concerned about maintaining viable populations of what is arguably North America's most regal animal.

At the headquarters, situated at 2291 West Broadway, the foundation maintains its Wildlife Visitor Center. Here we inspect taxidermy mounts of elk and other animals, including grizzly bears, mountain goats, and mule deer, along with an outstanding array of wildlife art. After browsing for a while, then taking in a wildlife video in the center's main theater, we continue west on Broadway to the **Smokejumpers Base and Aerial Fire Depot Visitor Center**, located adjacent to Missoula International Airport. Here we take a guided tour of the nation's largest base and training center for the U.S. Forest Service's airborne, first-strike wildfire-fighters. The tour highlights various aspects in the professional life of a smokejumper, and includes a visit to the large parachute-repair room, which is stocked with stout, industrial-strength sewing machines. The tour guide talks some about the rigorous testing and training that potential smokejumpers must go through in order to qualify for the elite jumping corps. Murals, video presentations, and historic photos add to our knowledge of these intrepid men and women who jump out of airplanes into our Western forests, in efforts to keep fires from spreading.

We have time for one more stop before lunch, so we drive back downtown, then go south on Higgins Street across the Clark Fork River. A block south of the stoplight in front of Hellgate High School we angle right onto Blaine Street and pull into a parking spot just across the street from **Rockin Rudy's**. The singular enterprise, which occupies a large, ex-bread-baking facility, offers the greatest and most eclectic selection of music of any record store I've visited—from mainstream rock to jazz, world beat, country, folk, Irish, and many other styles. In addition to the endless racks of new and used compact disks, audiotapes, and vinyl albums, several mini-businesses within the main business hawk coffee, humorous greeting cards, T-shirts, unusual gift items, and more.

I could spend the rest of the day browsing at Rockin Rudy's, but the time comes to leave. It's about fifteen minutes before noon when we go out the front door, so we decide to remain parked where we are and simply walk back the 6 blocks north to **Caras Park**. The park sits along the Clark Fork's north bank, west of the Higgins Street Bridge. Today is Wednesday, which in summer means **Lunch in the Park**, and we're guessing that we wouldn't be able to locate a parking space closer than 6 blocks, anyway. The gathering, which happens weekly from June through August, is *the* midweek social event during summer in Missoula.

As we stroll across the bridge we look down on Caras Park, which overflows with a kaleidoscopic mix of people, several thousand strong. Some are simply standing and chatting or listening to the live music, others are strolling about, and many are sitting on the park's bleachers and grassy slopes. We see businessmen and women dressed in business attire; what might be called middle-aged hippies, hundreds of whom migrated to Missoula in the late 1960s and early '70s and found little reason to leave; college-age kids making it appear as if the '90s have brought a new surge of hippie-ness, with their long hair, tie-dyed shirts, sandals, and baggy pants; grandmotherly and grandfatherly older folks; shiny young mothers cradling newborns; and many, many more.

Up front near the bandstand fifty or sixty people dance to the Texas-swing band, some with partners, some on their own. Food booths representing numerous Missoula restaurants arc around much of the park's perimeter. The lines at some of the stands are much longer than those at others. We follow the flight of stairs adjacent to the Wilma Theatre down to the park, and choose a medium-length line to stand in. After gathering and paying for our Greek *gyros*, we eat them as we wander through the crowd, greeting old friends we haven't seen for some time.

By one-thirty everything has pretty well wound down. Before leaving the park, though, we walk over to the building housing **A Carousel for Missoula**, a very special addition to town finished in the mid-1990s. Led by Missoulian Chuck Kaparich, who as a kid played on the carousel at the now-defunct Columbia Gardens in Butte, and fueled by the monetary donations of thousands of businesses, individuals, and school classes, a spate of volunteers organized to carve the carousel's thirty-eight ponies and perform related tasks. Each of the carousel's gorgeous ponies, all of them unique in name and personality, took literally hundreds of hours to carve. The volunteers toiled under the tutelage of Kaparich, a woodworker by trade, in his garage workshop.

Kids of all ages now can pay a small fee to ride the horses, but be forewarned: They move pretty fast! We opt just to watch the carousel, which today is full of actual kids, go around and around to the accompaniment of music blaring from the largest military band organ in America, which the Carousel for Missoula Foundation purchased for $65,000. We find the carousel to be not only a beautiful tribute to horses and to the enduring essence of youth, but also a testimonial to the spirit of community that is so strong in this Montana city.

Before leaving downtown we walk north along Higgins for four blocks, then go a block east on Pine Street to the world headquarters of the **Adventure Cycling Association**. (It's located immediately north across the street from the **Art Museum of Missoula**, housed in the old Carnegie Library, and kitty-corner from the Forest Service Northern Region headquarters, where you can find a good selection of maps and other information.) From their offices here, situated in the city's old Christian Science Church, the not-for-profit Adventure Cycling Association serves some 35,000 members, making it the largest cycling organization in the United States. A staff of twenty-plus puts together a periodical and other publications for its members, organizes road and mountain-bike tours which are run throughout the country, and produces bicycling maps considered state of the art in the field. Several antique/historic bicycles are displayed at the office, where there's also a retail outlet selling maps and guidebooks, camping gear, and cycling accessories.

Speaking of bicycling, it's time to get a little more exercise. From East Broadway we drive roughly 3 miles north, first following Van Buren, then Rattlesnake Drive, before taking the left-hand turn toward the **Rattlesnake National Recreation Area and Wilderness**. This expanse of federally protected wildlands puts a sudden end to Missoula's northward expansion, and to have the RNRAW in such close proximity is truly one of the city's outstanding attributes. It's not uncommon for residents here in the northeastern reaches of Missoula to be paid visits by black bears or mountain lions. Gray wolves have passed through the area on occasion, too.

At the trailhead we meet friends Joe and Clarisse, who, like us, have mountain bicycles mounted atop their car. After retrieving the bikes and getting ourselves ready, we pedal north along

Beargrass

the old dirt road following Rattlesnake Creek upstream. The road corridor, although largely surrounded by designated wilderness, actually lies outside the wilderness area, and that is why bicycles are permitted. The road is no longer open to motorized traffic, but we pass plenty of walkers and joggers going our way and, heading the other way, a group of seven horseback riders. We're careful to slow down and greet the equestrians, so that we don't spook their horses with our bikes. We spin past a couple of old homesteads, where just about the only evidences remaining are a scattering of apple trees and some unnatural-looking rock piles. The riding is gently uphill, but the surrounding, timber-covered slopes are exceptionally steep. As we roll along, Joe points overhead and the rest of us look up to see a bald eagle perched on the very tip of a tall western larch tree.

As much as we'd like to continue to the road's terminus, which lies at the wilderness boundary at Wrangell Bridge, roughly 15 miles from the trailhead, we opt to turn around at Franklin Bridge, just 8 miles out. It took us more than an hour to

get to the turnaround point, but we zip back to the cars in only 40 minutes.

Although the sun is still high in the sky, dinnertime has arrived already. The four of us retreat to the Hobnob Cafe, located downtown at 208 East Main, inside the **Union Club Bar**. After a scrumptious supper we drive a few blocks south and west from the university campus to **Bonner Park**. In a long-standing summer tradition, on Wednesday nights the Missoula City Band performs at the Bonner Park bandshell, playing patriotic John Philip Sousa marching songs and similarly rousing tunes. I have several friends in their late forties who remember attending the Bonner Park performances as young children. In fact, I run into a couple of them tonight, with a new generation of concert-goers in tow.

There's one more mandatory stop before we call it a day. Our small motorcade of two cars pulls off South Higgins onto Pattee Canyon Drive, then onto Whitaker Drive, which we ascend to **Shadow's Keep**. Here we rejoin Peggy and Robin, who await our arrival on the deck. The restaurant-lounge-clubhouse sits above the hilly, nine-hole **Highlands Golf Club**, occupying an attractive new timber-frame structure that was built to replace the historic Greenough Mansion, which was destroyed in a tragic fire in the early 1990s. (The 1897 mansion had been hauled in pieces in the 1960s to its hillside perch from its original location, north of the Clark Fork River where **Greenough Park** is found today.) We sip a drink on the deck as we watch the sun dipping below the mountains to the west, turning the sky and clouds into a mass of flame red. More and more lights pop on across the valley below, making it clear that Missoula is beginning to resemble a large city.

It's been a very long day, but a successful one. The only item that didn't get checked off my to-do list is **The Historical Museum at Fort Missoula**. On past visits I've really enjoyed the rambling, indoor-outdoor museum, which graces the grounds of the old Army post established in 1877, during the days of the Indian wars. I hear that currently there's a good display—entitled *A Long and Dusty Road: Fort Missoula's 25th Infantry*—focusing on a piece of history that particularly fascinates me: the 1897 bicycle ride accomplished by the black soldiers of the Twenty-fifth Infantry. The soldiers, along with their white leader, Lt. James Moss, pedaled 1,900 miles from Fort Missoula to St. Louis, experimenting with the bicycle as a means of troop transport.

But Fort Missoula and the Twenty-fifth Infantry will have to wait until tomorrow.

From Missoula to the Seeley-Swan Valley

From Missoula, travel 5 miles east on Interstate 90 to the Bonner exit, then proceed east on State Highway 200. After traveling through the tight, timbered valley of the lower Big Blackfoot River, at a point approximately 17 miles from Missoula you will break into the open Potomac Valley. Plenty of logging activity is evident on the slopes of the low Garnet Range bordering the valley on the south. At 21 miles on the left you'll pass the **Potomac Country Store**, purveyors of the infamous "Awful Burger." Six miles later you will see the right-hand turn to the **Garnet Range Road**, an 11-mile detour leading to **Garnet Ghost Town**.

Back in 1898, after a rich gold vein was discovered at the Nancy Hanks mine, Garnet became home to roughly 1,000 persons, including both hardy miners and their equally hardy families. The federal Bureau of Land Management and the nonprofit Garnet Preservation Association have worked hand in hand to save and renovate several structures here, including the hundred-year-old J. K. Wells Hotel, a three-story structure built on a foundation of wooden posts. Several somewhat newer buildings at the site include a couple of cabins that rent in winter to parties of snowmobilers and cross-country skiers. (The road you followed to Garnet is groomed for over-snow travel between January 1 and March 31. Call the BLM in Missoula at 406–329–3914 for more information and cabin reservations.)

Back on the main highway, at a point one-half mile past the Garnet Range Road you'll pass the right-hand turn into **Lubrecht State Experimental Forest**. Roughly 7.5 miles farther, just before

Clearwater Junction, you'll see **Clearwater Crossing** on the left, a primitive campground and fishing-access site maintained by the Montana Department of Fish, Wildlife and Parks. Turn left at Clearwater Junction, where you'll see a small general store, to leave the Blackfoot River and commence traveling up the Clearwater River drainage, first passing through the **Blackfoot-Clearwater Game Range**.

In 5 miles you'll come to timber-surrounded Salmon Lake, a long, narrow, and typically calm lake that's terrific for exploring by canoe. **Salmon Lake State Park**, which includes camping and picnicking sites, hugs the east bank, while the west shore is bordered by Lolo National Forest lands. A mile past the north end of Salmon Lake you'll pass the left-hand turn leading 3 miles to **Placid Lake**, where there's yet another campground that is low on frills but high on privacy.

Twelve miles after turning at Clearwater Junction, as you come into the outskirts of the town of Seeley Lake, on the right you'll pass the **Double Arrow**. The fun resort rents cabins in both summer and winter and serves good food in the main lodge. Double Arrow encompasses a challenging nine-hole golf course, where cross-country trails are groomed once the snow begins falling. There's also a pool, tennis, and horseback riding.

Seeley Lake, a settlement lining the eastern shores of the lake of the same name, is a timber and tourist town that's a fine place to hang out regardless of the season. In summer, water sports reign supreme, and in winter they do, too; sports conducted on and in *frozen* water, that is: ice fishing, snowmobiling, and cross-country skiing. Skiers head for the extensive Seeley Creek trail system, which offers some of the best Nordic skiing in the state, on wide, roller-coaster trails groomed by the Seeley Lake and Missoula Nordic ski clubs. The trails, which trace Forest Service lands, are also great for mountain biking in summer. The trailhead is located about a mile east of town on Morrell Creek Road.

A trio of Forest Service campgrounds graces the shores of Seeley Lake, including **Big Larch**, found a mile north of town just off the highway. Three miles north of Seeley Lake you'll pass the Lolo National Forest's Seeley Lake Ranger Station, then, a mile farther, the road going left down to the **Clearwater Canoe Trail**.

FLOATING ALONG THE CLEARWATER CANOE TRAIL: A NARRATIVE ACCOUNT

After turning west off State Highway 83 at a point 4 miles north of the community of Seeley Lake, we begin bumping down the track that leads to the put-in for the Clearwater Canoe Trail. A mile back we'd stopped in at the Seeley Lake Ranger Station, where a knowledgeable ranger had guaranteed us that this river "trail" is suitable for any level of canoeist. In fact, he told us, the Forest Service designated it for precisely that quality: The agency wanted to promote a stretch of river that nearly anyone can safely and enjoyably navigate. Unlike many streams in the region, the channel on this stretch of the Clearwater River is deep enough that beavers haven't managed to close it off by constructing dams, and log jams don't commonly block the river's flow as they do on many area streams.

We were very pleased to hear from an official that the Clearwater Canoe Trail is negotiable by neophytes, because that's certainly what we are. At the parking area, three quarters of a mile from the highway, we wrestle the bright red canoe, generously lent to us by a friend in Missoula, off the top of the Jeep. We gently set it down close to the launching point while we retrieve lunch, binoculars, spare clothing, and other necessities from the car. Then, after we don our life jackets, Nancy crawls into the bow and I push us adrift, jumping into the stern just before the water deepens dramatically.

We paddle from the brackish backwaters put-in area into the main channel. Even there the water is so placid that we can hardly detect a current. Our efforts at synchronized paddling fall far short of Olympic perfection; in fact, it takes a while before we stop spinning down the river like a top turning counterclockwise circles. I decide to try simply using the paddle as a rudder to steer and keep us in the channel, while Nancy paddles. It works. Our canoe slices smoothly through the mirror surface of the water, cutting a V that ultimately spreads the width of the stream behind us.

Finally the river widens and we gain sufficient distance from the embracing willows that we can see our surroundings. It's a flawless fall day: Probably 65 degrees and not a cloud in the sky, whose blue brilliance is rivaled and simultaneously complemented by the rich colors of early October. Amid blanketing stands of Douglas fir

tower thick-trunked western larch trees, their needles burned gold by the season. Occasionally a breeze blows some loose, and they drift earthward, sparkling in the sun's rays like gold dust. Far to our east looms the **Swan Range**, one of several mountain ranges contributing to a 1.5-million-acre wilderness complex that includes the **Scapegoat, Bob Marshall,** and **Great Bear** wilderness areas. Add to these the nearly 1 million acres of Glacier National Park, which is separated from the Great Bear only by a road corridor, and you've got a wildlands continuum larger than Yellowstone National Park.

The treeless tops of the Swan Range's highest peaks are dusted with white. We guess that the snow fell yesterday, while we were enduring hours of rain in the valley. To the west, and much closer than the Swans, hang the bulky peaks of the **Mission Mountains Wilderness**. I spot an osprey high overhead in dead snag some 50 feet off the river, apparently surveying all that happens in her domain. Unfortunately, our intrusion spooks her; we can actually hear the large bird's wings whipping through the crisp fall air as she flaps into flight.

It seems that each bend in the madly meandering stream is followed by a turn. We begin wondering if there's a straight stretch on the entire river trail. A flock of coots scoots away, flying just above water level, as we round one bend. Then, there they are, waiting for us at the next, where they repeat their short flight for safety. In some places the river twists through willow thickets so high and tight that they block out the sun and surrounding mountains, causing us to lose all sense of direction. It doesn't matter, though, because there's really no way to become truly lost here. With the mountains obscured, the marsh environment makes it easy to imagine that we're in Minnesota rather than Montana.

After about an hour on the water, we hear a strange "wobbly" noise. We round a left-hand bend and encounter the source of the sound: a common loon, bobbing along close to the starboard bank. (For you fellow landlubbers, that's the right side—as Nancy, who grew up in a Seattle seafaring family, informs me.) According to the canoe-trail brochure we obtained at the ranger station, the bird is anything but common here in the Northern Rockies. The brochure also informed us that in spring, songbirds like thrushes, finches, and warblers are common along these waters. A host of other animal life hangs out in, on, and around the canoe trail, too: Part- and full-time residents include fish such as perch and land-locked kokanee salmon (whose fall spawning helps explain the presence of ospreys), painted turtles, muskrat, moose, and white-tailed deer. Even the occasional elk and mountain lion have been spotted by alert paddlers.

Shortly we pull up to a clearing and step onto dry land. It's a heavenly spot for a picnic. Peanut-butter sandwiches, potato chips, and orange pop have never tasted so good. I lie down on the grass face-up, while Nancy tries her hand at tempting a trout by casting a fly. Ah, autumn in the Rockies: intense sunshine, very few bugs, and the hearty scent of decaying leaves rich in the air. Absolute peace and quiet.

We push off again, and all too soon the Clearwater empties into Seeley Lake, taking us along for the ride. In contrast to the intimacy enjoyed on the canoe trail, we suddenly feel overly exposed. Mellow waters yield to a surface shattered by a gusty breeze. The final half mile to the take-out at the ranger station is our first real test at making forward progress. But we do get there, where we pull the canoe up onto the sprawling lawn.

Underscoring just how wildly the 4-mile canoe trail twists and turns, we find that the hiking trail that parallels the river and leads us back to our car is only 1 mile long. Though merely a few hundred feet from the river, it penetrates an altogether different world, a forest of old-growth spruce, larch, and pine, where the geese and ducks of the waterway are replaced by goshawks and owls. On this fall day the crackling forest seems as desiccated as the canoe trail was waterlogged.

Exactly four hours after setting afloat we reclaim our car. Our only wish is that the outing had taken twice that long.

From Missoula to the Flathead via the Mission Valley

Back in Missoula, head west on Interstate 90, passing the turn to U.S. Highway 93 North at 8

miles out. Eventually you'll want to go north on that road; before doing so, though, consider visiting a very special corner of Glacier-Gold Country by continuing on I–90 for another 12 miles before taking exit 82. After traveling 1.5 miles on the paved road winding northwestward from the exit, turn right onto Remount Road just before the **Nine Mile House** restaurant.

In another 1.5 miles you'll see, on the left, the quaint, brightly painted **Schoohouse and Teacherage Bed and Breakfast** (telephone 406–626–5879). In 1975 Les and Hanneke Ippisch purchased the old schoolgrounds and buildings here, which discontinued their educational roles in the mid-1930s. The school had been built early in the twentieth century by the Anaconda Company for the purpose of educating the children of loggers who felled timber to stoke the fires at the Butte-Anaconda smelters.

The Ippisches are somewhat of a local institution, having for years offered their popular Christmas and Easter markets, where they sell hand-made wooden toys, decorations, and novelties. More recently Hanneke has garnered a degree of notoriety extending beyond the Missoula area, since the 1996 publication of her book for young readers, entitled *Sky*. It's the heartfelt and thrilling story of Hanneke's own role as a teenage girl in the Dutch resistance movement against Hitler's Nazi forces.

Even without the compelling and magical stories you're bound to hear from Hanneke in her heavily accented English, a stay at the whimsically appointed bed and breakfast would be a joy. But add to the formula Hanneke's elfish presence and Les's unassuming ways—both of them seem constantly to have sly sparkles in their eyes—and an overnight at this inn is a bit like entering a fairyland. The inn's Dutch, Swedish, Montana, and Amish rooms feature handmade quilts, down comforters, and plenty of antiques and folk art.

Now, if you're at all intrigued by the history of fire-fighting in the Northern Rockies, and/or you are an animal lover, continue up Remount Road from the Schoolhouse and Teacherage. In a mile you'll arrive at the gracious grounds of the **Ninemile Remount Depot**. The depot—located adjacent to the still-active Ninemile Ranger District of the Lolo National Forest, which was added here in 1962— was built in the 1930s by workers of the Civilian

Conservation Corps. The three 200-man companies stationed at Ninemile constituted the largest group of CCC workers in the country.

Conceived and designed by Evan Kelley, regional forester at the time, the depot was built in response to the massive wildfires the region had repeatedly suffered in the 1910s and 1920s, and to the Forest Service's dearth of manpower and other fire-fighting resources. The centralized depot at Ninemile, so envisioned Kelley (and accurately), would serve as a vital training and dispatching center for crews and mule teams, which would be utilized to haul fire-fighting gear to remote mountain locations. Kelley wanted the utilitarian facility also to be a showpiece, so rather than simply slapping together another rustic backwoods ranger outpost he designed the buildings to resemble a well-kept Kentucky horse farm. For two decades, until the advent of smokejumpers and an expanding network of backcountry roads, the Remount depot served as a major hub of fire-fighting activities for a large portion of the Northern Rockies.

Today the renovated Cape Cod–style buildings are in sound shape and listed on the National Register of Historic Places. Displays in the visitor center will guide you through the depot's intriguing past. In addition to maintaining its Ninemile Ranger District here, the Forest Service recently added the Arthur Carhart National Wilderness Training Center to the Ninemile complex. Forest Service employees as well as land managers working for other agencies from throughout the country arrive for training in the arts of mule packing, wilderness skills, and using hand tools, which are utilized to build trails, bridges, and other amenities in wilderness areas, where power tools are not permitted.

Last but definitely not least, the facility is home to the Forest Service mule pack train, which by a large measure constitutes (I would argue) the federal agency's most astute and loveable public relations move. The mules travel in a big, hard-to-miss, Forest Service-green trailer, with each of the mule's names painted on the outside, opposite its stall. The long-eared galoots perform trail work, march in parades, and occasionally even appear on national television. They've paid a visit to the *Today Show*, for instance, and marched in the Tournament of Roses Parade.

Return to Interstate 90, backtrack east for 12 miles, and then turn north onto U.S. Highway 93. After pulling up Evaro Hill and entering the Jocko Valley and the **Flathead Indian Reservation**, behind to the south you will see the steep wall of the heavily glaciated Rattlesnake Mountains' "back side" (according to Missoulians, anyway). To the east rise the gentler Jocko Hills and, to the west, the mountains of the Reservation Divide. The gentle, rolling character of those ranges clashes with that of

Pack mule train

the precipitous Rattlesnakes, revealing that the former were bypassed by the Pleistocene rivers of ice. As dramatically different as they appear from one another, though, all of the mountains are composed of similar Precambrian Belt rocks.

Arlee is a small and ordinarily quiet reservation town residing in the Jocko River Valley. But it bursts at the seams for several days around Independence Day, during the **Arlee Pow Wow**, when a sea of tipis, tents, and trailers fills the Arlee flats and uncommon scents and sounds fill the air. If you're interested in adding a powwow to your itinerary while in Montana, and if the date fits, make this the one. (There are several others to choose from, including the smaller powwow held later in July at nearby Elmo, on the west shore of Flathead Lake.)

A century in the running, the Arlee Pow Wow is the Confederated Salish and Kootenai tribes' foremost celebration. It attracts Indians from throughout North America for singing, drumming, and dancing, both ceremonial and competitive in nature. If you've never experienced in person the ancient power of Native American drumming and high-pitched singing, prepare to be spellbound. Also on tap are food booths, arts-and-crafts displays, and gambling opportunities that include traditional stick games as well as less complicated contests. Non-Indians are more than welcome at the celebration, but they're expected to know and abide by powwow rules and etiquette, which, among other things, forbid the use of drugs and alcohol.

Even the rugged Rattlesnake Range, which soon you will leave behind, is merely a teaser compared to the sky-ripping peaks of the **Mission Mountains**, which you'll see on the right as you crest the big hill north of Ravalli Junction. The new visitor station sitting beside the highway at the hilltop was built in a partnership involving the Confederated Salish and Kootenai tribes, chambers of commerce, Boy Scout troops, and other local groups. Here you'll find picnic shelters, rest rooms, and some of the most sublime mountain views in Montana, along with information interpreting just what it is you're looking at.

In appearance, composition, and the way in which they were made and modified, the Missions are kin to the mountains of Glacier National Park. They're also home to a fair-sized population of grizzly bears, another trait they share with Glacier's wild mountains. Much of the west slope of the Missions is encompassed by the Mission Mountains Tribal Wilderness, and to legally hike and camp there you must obtain a tribal use permit at the tribal complex in Pablo or at one of several sporting goods stores on the reservation.

The Mission Mountains were named for the **St. Ignatius Mission**. The namesake peaks have provided a thrilling backdrop to the church since it was constructed in 1891 by Native Americans who worked under the direction of Jesuit missionaries. Any day of the week you can visit the splendid, still-active house of worship, which is located just east off the highway in the town of St. Ignatius. (Locally, by the way, even the town is known as "Mission.") Inside the church, on the walls and ceiling you'll see stories from the Old and New testaments interpreted through strikingly beautiful murals and frescoes. They're the handiwork of an Italian Jesuit named Joseph Carignano. The works are made all the more marvelous when you consider that Brother Carignano, who was the mission cook and handyman, had no formal training in art.

Those interested in Western and Native American art and artifacts will want to stop both at **Doug Allard's Flathead Indian Museum**, located on U.S. Highway 93 near St. Ignatius, and at the **Four Winds Trading Post**, situated 3 miles farther north. Among the Indian-made goods for sale at Allard's is an exceptional array of beadwork items. At Four Winds, where a number of pre-statehood (pre-1889, that is) buildings lend an aura of authenticity, you'll likewise find Indian items on display and/or for sale, as well as a museum devoted to toy trains and railroading memorabilia. Components of this enterprise's extensive collection have appeared in several popular movies, including Kevin Costner's *Dances With Wolves.*

For a rewarding side loop, at a point 1 mile north of **Allentown**, which is 8 miles north of St. Ignatius, turn left onto Route 212. The road continues west for 2.5 miles through the waterfowl-filled **Ninepipe National Wildlife Refuge**, which includes a large reservoir surrounded by marshes occupying dozens of glacier-scoured potholes. After passing through the village of Charlo, whose name recalls a revered late-nineteenth-century chief of the Salish-speaking Flatheads, the road meanders to Moiese (*Moy-EESE*), where you'll want to turn into the **National Bison Range**. This unit of the National Wildlife Refuge System comprises more than 18,000 acres of grasslands and timber stands, all enclosed by a high, bison-resistant fence.

Stop first at the visitor center (telephone 406–644–2211), open daily year-round, where you'll find displays and film presentations illuminating the past and present of the refuge, and the vital role it played in the comeback of the "monarch of the plains." In the early 1800s as many as fifty million bison inhabited the West, roaming the plains from Canada to Mexico. In some instances the herds blanketed the broad landscape as far as one could see in every direction. Fewer than a hundred years later the seemingly endless herds had been decimated, almost unbelievably, to the brink of extinction. By 1900 only twenty known free-ranging individuals survived.

Fortunately, though, several private herds also remained. Dr. William D. Hornaday of the American Bison Society spearheaded the 1908 creation of the National Bison Range, which was one of the world's first refuges established for the sake of a big-game species. Under Hornaday's leadership the society raised funds to purchase three dozen bison from the private Conrad herd in Kalispell. Those bison, augmented with several other donated animals, were released on the newly fenced range in 1909. Today, a healthy herd of between 300 and 500 bison thrives on the refuge.

Knowledgeable staff at the visitor center can orient you and tell you where you'll be most apt to encounter herds of bison. They'll point you to the one-way Red Sleep Mountain Drive, which threads through the refuge, first climbing over the top of Red Sleep Mountain and then descending Antelope Ridge. Along the road's 19-mile length you may have opportunities to see not only bison, but also elk, deer, pronghorns, black bears, bighorn sheep, Rocky Mountain goats, and a host of smaller mammals and winged things. Allow a couple of hours to negotiate the mountainous road, which is passable in summer and fall, during daylight hours only. (Staff at the visitor center can also provide information on the optimum times to watch waterfowl back at Ninepipe National Wildlife Refuge, which you can re-visit on the way north to Flathead Lake.)

After returning to Moiese, follow Route 212 south for 5 miles to its junction with State Highway 200. From there, it is 6 miles east back to Ravalli Junction, where you'll turn north. In case you didn't notice on your first trip up Ravalli Hill, for more than a mile this highway skirts the southeastern extremity of the National Bison Range.

Alternatively, rather than returning to Ravalli, go west on State Highway 200 and loop around to Polson and Flathead Lake by following either Route 382 north from Perma or State Highway 28 northeast from Plains. Here's a recommended spur tacked onto a side loop: Three miles before reaching Paradise on State Highway 200, follow State Highway 135 for a couple of miles to **Quinn's Paradise Resort** (telephone 406–826–3150). The delightful hot springs resort, located in the valley of the Clark Fork River, boasts a large hot pool, a smaller and hotter Jacuzzi, rustic rental cabins, a campground, and a cozy bar-restaurant.

Back along U.S. Highway 93, 5 miles north of the junction with Route 212 you'll pass through the attractive small town of **Ronan**. Golf enthusiasts should investigate the outstanding, public-welcome links at the **Mission Mountain Country Club**, situated west of town on Round Butte Road. As anyone who's tried the game knows, golf can be an irritating sport. But regardless of how poorly one is hitting the ball, it would be difficult to have a bad time in this spectacular setting, dominated by the Mission Mountains. You may not score an eagle on the Mission Mountain course, but you've as good a chance as any golf pro of seeing one soaring overhead.

Five miles north of Ronan you'll arrive in the reservation headquarters town of **Pablo**, home to **The People's Center**. The center, whose "people" refers to the Salish, Kootenai, and Pend d'Oreille Indians, is a museum and more. Visitors can take part in various activities, including half-day ("History, Heritage and Culture") and full-day ("A Walk Through Time") Native Ed-Venture Tours, on which participants learn about the Indians' lifeways and worldviews. Individuals, families, and groups can also arrange for customized tours, which can include being hosted in a Native American home. (For details call toll-free, 800–883–5344.)

On reaching the apex of the morainal hill just

south of Polson you'll catch your first glimpse of remarkable **Flathead Lake**, the largest freshwater lake west of the Mississippi River. The lake is 27 miles long, between 8 and 15 miles wide, nearly 400 feet at its deepest, and surrounded by 124 miles of shoreline. Five state recreation areas, each including a campground, grace its banks.

Polson is a lovely resort community wrapped around the southernmost shore of Flathead Lake. Sites you should see while in town include the decidedly one-of-a-kind **Miracle of America Museum**, whose vast collection comprises more than 100,000 pieces of neat and unexpected stuff. It's located a mile south of town—just watch for the *Paul Bunyan,* a 65-foot logging tug. Other attractions include the **Polson-Flathead Historical Museum**, a more traditional pioneer museum located at the corner of 8th and Main, and the Best Western **KwaTaqNuk Resort**, a hotel complex opened in 1992 by the Confederated Salish and Kootenai tribes. In addition to boasting more than 100 rooms for rent, along with a good restaurant, KwaTaqNuk includes a marina offering boat rentals and a gallery filled with Western and Native American art and photographic works.

Recreational possibilities in Polson include golfing on the community's heralded eighteen-hole course, enjoying a picnic and a swim at **Riverside Park** (located next to the highway bridge at the lake outlet), touring town in a horse-drawn wagon of the **Forest Davis Freight & Carriage Co.**, and hopping aboard the 50-passenger *Port Polson Princess*, which thrice daily plies the waters of Flathead Lake, beginning at a dock at KwaTaqNuk Resort.

At Polson you must decide whether to follow State Highway 35 around the forested east side of Flathead Lake, or the busier and wider U.S. Highway 93 around the west shore, where you'll discover a greater number of services and attractions, including several antiques shops. Three of the lake's five state recreation area campgrounds are found on the east shore: **Finley Point**, **Yellow Bay**, and, just outside Bigfork, **Wayfarers**.

Especially on the east side you'll find that in many places the native forests have been cleared only to make room for more trees—but they're cherry trees, rather than pines and firs. It's a toss-up as to which is more popular in this area:

Flathead cherries or the wild huckleberry, which grows in abundance on many of the high mountain slopes in northwest Montana. The purple berry, a delectable and juicy relative of the blueberry, has resisted repeated attempts at domestication by humans. To locate a dependably productive patch is truly a marvelous find, and their locations are often closely guarded secrets passed down through the generations like family heirlooms.

Heading north along the west shore on U.S. Highway 93, you can't miss the large, water-encircled mountain rising from Big Arm Bay. Apparently the resistant rock of **Wild Horse Island** prevented its being ground down by the glacier that hollowed out the depression now occupied by Flathead Lake. Since 1977 most of the island has been a state park, although some fifty privately held lots remain along the shoreline. The park, open for day use only, is an outstanding place to spend a day exploring. A large herd of bighorn sheep populates the 2,163-acre island, and so do smaller numbers of black bears and mule deer. Also calling the area home—appropriately so, given the island's name—are several wild horses captured and released through the Bureau of Land Management's adopt-a-horse program. Birds are richly abundant, too, including redtail hawks, bald eagles, and numerous species of songbirds. To arrange transportation, visit the Indian-owned-and-operated **Eagle Fishing Charters** in Big Arm. Or, call the Montana Department of Fish, Wildlife and Parks in Kalispell (telephone 406–752–5501) for additional tips on getting to and from Wild Horse Island.

At Dayton you'll pass the left-hand turn to **Lake Mary Ronan**, a popular fishing spot featuring a state park campground, located 7 miles off the highway. Kokanee salmon, which in recent years have been outcompeted in Flathead Lake by the tiny mysis shrimp, are still a plentiful catch in Lake Mary Ronan. That goes for summer and for winter, for those dedicated anglers who enjoy chopping holes in the ice and then standing around trying to keep warm. The lake was named for the wife of Peter Ronan, a Flathead Reservation superintendent in the late 1800s. Peter Ronan is rumored to have dumped three barrels of fish into the lake in 1892, thereby initiating the great fishery found there today. Commercial facilities on the quiet lake include

Camp Tuffit (telephone 406–849–5220), which rents larch-log cabins and offers RV sites with electric and water hookups. The Crawdad Cafe is also part of the complex.

Here's a great way to precipitate a picnic: Swing in to the **Mission Mountain Winery**, located just outside Dayton, and buy a bottle of good wine. Next, pick up sandwich makings, condiments, and other fixings at **M&S Meats**, located 5 miles north of the winery. (Adjacent to the store, which specializes in buffalo meats and sausages, there's also an RV park and a snack stand proferring ready-made buffalo burgers.) From there, continue north past picturesque Rollins Bay and pull down into the **West Shore** component of Flathead Lake State Park. Pleasant picnicking sites sit right along the water's edge. Tall, broad-canopied Douglas firs provide a surplus of shade, most welcome on a hot afternoon.

Hunger abated, as you continue north toward Lakeside you'll roll through stands of tall timber and catch occasional glimpses of cabins and charming homes nestled in clearings along the lake to the right. You'll pass through the small resort settlement of **Lakeside**, which boasts a handful of cafes and accommodations, including rental cabins perched along the shoreline. At **Somers**, 6 miles north of Lakeside, go east on State Highway 82 toward Bigfork, rather than continuing along U.S. Highway 93 toward Kalispell.

Bigfork, like a California coastal community transported to Montana, brims with galleries, good restaurants, boutiques, and real estate offices. It's a fun place to spend a summer's day shopping in the afternoon, then enjoying a good dinner and taking in a Broadway-style performance at the very popular **Bigfork Summer Playhouse**.

The countryside surrounding Bigfork is one of striking contrasts: In close proximity to the arresting village in one direction or another are Flathead Lake; the wild timberlands of the Flathead National Forest; dozens of hillside cherry orchards; flat agricultural lands planted in grains, mint, and other crops; and rolling terrain trimmed with Christmas tree farms, some of them abandoned and gone feral, looking more like forests than farms. As you drive north from Bigfork on State Highway 35, on the right you can see the slopes of the **Jewel Basin Hiking Area**, a lake-filled, foot-traffic-only parcel of Flathead National Forest lands nestled at the north end of the Swan Range. On the other side of that ridge—beyond sight, of course—stretches Hungry Horse Reservoir, a 34-mile-long lake formed by the damming of the South Fork of the Flathead River.

The unbelievable explosion of summer color on the left just before Creston (10 miles north of Bigfork) is the **Gatiss Gardens**, a privately owned and tended garden of perennials and other plants that includes a mile-long, self-guiding foot trail open to the public. On the opposite side of the highway from the gardens you'll see Fish Hatchery Road. By following it for a mile north you'll come to the **Creston Fish Hatchery**, location of the rearing waters for thousands of rainbow and cutthroat trout that one day will end up in Montana's lakes and rivers. A picnic ground sits adjacent to the hatchery.

As you continue north through the pastoral upper Flathead Valley, notice the obvious ski runs cut into the face of the distant mountain ahead. They're the slopes of The Big Mountain ski area, hanging high behind the town of Whitefish. At the junction approximately 4 miles north of Creston you can either bear right onto Route 206 and take the backroad way into Columbia Falls and Whitefish, or continue west on State Route 35, following it into bustling **Kalispell**. If you take the latter route, don't miss visiting the resplendent **Conrad Mansion**, located on 4th Street East in Kalispell. Guided tours of the twenty-three-room beauty (telephone 406–755–2166), built in 1895, are available in summer and fall.

Whitefish and Beyond

Whitefish is a terrific place to visit regardless of the season. In the great sprawling out-of-doors surrounding the town of 5,000 there's always something to do and, it seems, someone to do it with, for this recreational paradise attracts hundreds of outdoor enthusiasts as both residents and visitors. For summer and fall fun, hundreds of miles of mountain trails await exploration by foot, by mountain bike, on horseback, or in an all-ter-rain vehicle. Boaters, swimmers, windsurfers, and water skiers head to Whitefish Lake, while anglers wet their lines there or in any of dozens of additional lakes, rivers, and streams watering this wet region. Canoeing and kayaking are wildly popular, as well, and so are golf, tennis, and big-game hunting. Camping is big, too, with both designated campgrounds and dispersed camping sites plentiful on the surrounding state-forest and national forest lands. Another big-time diversion for locals, if not for visitors: firewood-cutting, that time-honored activity that ultimately warms a person at least twice.

In winter, snow sports rule, naturally, including downhill skiing and snowboarding at **The Big Mountain**, and cross-country skiing on groomed trails at The Big Mountain's Nordic center and on the Whitefish Lake Golf Course. In winter, and in early spring, too, there's no shortage of backcoun-

"Snow ghosts," The Big Mountain

try skiing and snowmobiling opportunities awaiting in the mountains that radiate in every direction from town.

The Big Mountain, which recently entered the second half of its first century of commercial operation, started life as a locals' hill. The beginnings of the area date to the 1930s. That's when members of the loosely organized Hell Roaring Ski Club began trudging up the slopes of one of the highest mountains in the Whitefish Range, typically outfitted in woolies and 8-foot-long, solid-wood skis with climbing skins or ropes attached to the bottoms. When they got to where they wanted to be, they turned around, removed the climbing skins, and pointed their ungainly boards straight down the mountain, employing controlled—or uncontrolled—falls as their primary means of stopping and changing direction.

Club members eventually built a couple of cabins high on the mountain for warming and overnighting, then convinced the Forest Service in 1939 to extend the road that already went part way up the mountain to a mining claim. While insiders knew the real reason for the road extension—to enhance access for skiers, that is—the 2 miles of road were ostensibly built for the purpose of fire control.

Dozens of Whitefish residents learned to ski in this setting, which set the stage for the sport to blossom locally into a business. That it did after World War II, when a group of investors on March 31, 1947, formed Winter Sports, Inc. (WSI), which is still the name of the company operating The Big Mountain. The "money people" involved rejected the proposed name of Hell Roaring Ski Corporation, fearing it would scare off potential visitors. (Hell Roaring was and is the name of a creek drainage creasing the face of The Big Mountain.) On December 14 of that year The Big Mountain opened to paying customers, offering a short list of amenities that included a warming hut, T-bar, and rope tow. But the price was right: $2 for a lift ticket and 25 cents for a hamburger.

The Big Mountain has evolved into a first-class winter destination resort, while the greater Whitefish area continues drawing folks the year around. Even so, Whitefish retains an authentic and friendly small-town atmosphere. The monied are moving in, including a growing number of celebrities, but for the most part even they have realized that Whitefish is no Aspen—which is one reason, after all, that they have chosen Whitefish as their home-away-from-Hollywood. Longtime locals hope those following in their tracks will likewise leave their flamboyant ways behind, and help Whitefish sustain its laid-back, unassuming character.

Whitefish generally lacks the wind and extreme cold that you'll experience in Montana east of the Continental Divide, but it makes up for it with more than its share of cloudy and wet weather. If you're unfortunate enough to visit during the inevitable winter, spring, or summer rains, the choices in activities are more limited, but definitely not nonexistent. You can visit the **Stumptown Historical Museum**, located in the 1927, chalet-style Great Northern (now Amtrak) depot, downstairs from the Chamber of Commerce office. There the timbering and railroading past of old Stumptown, as frontier Whitefish was nicknamed, are well documented in photos and other displays. You'll also find some outstanding shopping opportunities in downtown Whitefish. For a jolt of java that'll get your head above the clouds, drive just south of town to the tasting room of the **Montana Coffee Traders**. A large share of the best coffee brewed throughout the Northwest emanates from this Whitefish-based roasting company.

Alternatively, there could be worse things to do than simply curling up with a book beside the fireplace in your condominium or cabin and sitting out the rains. Don't forget, though, that in winter valley rain often translates to snow on the slopes of The Big Mountain.

The winding, often-chuckhole-filled 5-mile road leading to The Big Mountain begins at a point 2 miles north of downtown. The purpose for negotiating the road in winter is obvious; less clear is why one would want to drive on it in summer. But good reasons exist: Like at alpine areas throughout North America, summer visitation is rapidly growing at The Big Mountain. Management is scrambling to keep up with the growth, even as they work to provide ever more reasons for warm-weather visitors to make the climb from Whitefish. A growing network of segregated mountain biking, hiking, and equestrian trails web The Big Mountain, including the popular **Danny On National Recreation Trail**, a 5.6-mile hiking trail

connecting the base and the summit. There's also a 7.2-mile single-track mountain-biking trail, new in 1997, that similarly links the mountain's top with its bottom. Fully suspended mountain bikes can be rented at the mountain, and cyclists can choose to ride up and/or down the undulating, well-designed trail, whose grade rarely exceeds 5 percent, making it negotiable in either direction even by riders of moderate riding skills and fitness.

Good accommodations and dining facilities still run strong during the summer season, too. Winter or summer, the vistas from the top of the ski area are arguably the best, readily accessible views in all of northwest Montana. The silvery peaks of Glacier National Park shine to the near east, while on the far side of the U.S. Highway 2 corridor 7,234-foot Columbia Mountain is a dark hulk dominating the skyline. Below, in close proximity, are Whitefish and Whitefish Lake; farther in the distance you'll see the sprawl of Kalispell, backed by the flashing waters of Flathead Lake. You can also see the Swan and Mission ranges far to the south, the Cabinet Mountains to the west, and, to the north, the Canadian Rockies.

If you can tear yourself away from the views, walk inside the Summit House to the lower level, where in summer the U.S. Forest Service maintains its **Big Mountain Environmental Education Center**. Bird mounts, mammal furs, and other floral and faunal displays are on exhibit. And, in case you forgot your binoculars, staffers typically have loaners on hand, which you can employ to earn a close-up look at the peaks of Glacier National Park, by aiming them through the windows of the center. (*See* Staying There for additional information on winter and summer activities in Whitefish and at The Big Mountain.)

DRIVING TO POLEBRIDGE AND GLACIER NATIONAL PARK THROUGH THE BACK DOOR: A NARRATIVE ACCOUNT

Nancy and I arise at 6:00 A.M. at the **Garden Wall Inn** to be greeted by a three-course breakfast too good to be real. The feast is served by Rhonda Fitzgerald, the inn's ebullient owner and hostess. I'm too sleepy to try to guess what time she must have gotten out of bed to begin preparing the meal, which includes elegantly presented fruit, scones, juice, ham, crepes, eye-popping coffee, and more.

Well fed and then some, we bid Rhonda *adieu* and drive north from downtown across the high railroad overpass. After zipping past the right-hand turn to The Big Mountain, we continue on the paved road that runs above the east shore of Whitefish Lake. At just over a mile past the Big Mountain junction we pull left off the pavement onto gravel and drive for a third of a mile down to the parking area of **Les Mason Park**, just to have a look. A friend told us that this low-use park is a favorite place for locals to head when wanting to avoid the crowds at the much larger City Beach. From the parking area a short trail leads us down to a brush-surrounded beach, which we find is as peaceful and private as our friend raved.

Approximately 8 miles after leaving downtown Whitefish the main road turns to gravel. The somewhat ravaged Stillwater State Forest lands we're traveling through are riddled with unnamed roads, apparently the legacy of recent logging activities. We encounter a confusing intersection, and another after that. Still, we manage to stay on track, thanks chiefly to the Flathead National Forest visitor map that we're carrying.

After passing a road heading uphill to the right toward Werner Peak Lookout, we see another road going left toward U.S. Highway 93. The road we're driving on seems to turn bumpier the deeper into the wilds we go. At just under 25 miles we arrive at **Upper Whitefish Lake**, where we see two or three groups of campers occupying campsites adjacent to the water. We park, get out of the car, and walk not down to the water, but up onto a brushy, sparsely timbered slope opposite the lake. It just happens that it is early August, the heart of what we've heard this year is an exceptional huckleberry season. Back in Whitefish we were told that a huckleberry hound can't go wrong in the vicinity of Upper Whitefish Lake.

We were not misled. Nancy and I, each carrying a three-pound-size coffee can, proceed to pick the plump, deep-purple explosions of flavor, and plopping them into the cans. We know that huckleberries are a favorite food of black and grizzly bears (they're no dummies), so as we browse we make plenty of noise, hoping to notify any bears within hearing distance that we're in the area. It takes about an hour to fill the cans, and it probably would have taken half that long if we hadn't

continually sampled as we picked. But no person could possibly exercise that much restraint.

Hands and lips dyed purple, after cresting the Whitefish Divide we continue past **Red Meadow Lake**, an unusually beautiful little lake gracing a wilderness setting that reminds us of places in British Columbia we've visited. Great, steep slopes rise high above the lake, their stands of dense, dark timber interrupted in many places by swaths cleared by winter snowslides. Way up toward the top of one of the precipitous slide areas, maybe a half-mile away, Nancy sees a suspicious-looking golden-brown spot. After stopping the car, I retrieve the binoculars, focus in, and—sure enough—make out the unmistakable, humped-neck profile of a grizzly bear. We hand the binoculars back and forth to watch the bear, who's obviously busy dining, for at least a half hour before pressing on.

We haven't been through this area since the big Red Bench Fire blew up in 1988—it was the same dry summer of the Yellowstone fires—and the formerly lush landscape appears strangely nude. After following Forest Road 115 downstream along Red Meadow Creek to the North Fork Road junction, we take a right and drive 5 miles into **Polebridge**, a north woods settlement straight out of an earlier era. We immediately head for the **North Fork Hostel** to say hello to a longtime friend who owns and operates the rustic lodge. The hostel lacks indoor toilets, but it does boast lights and hot running water. However, power is provided by propane and a gas-fired generator: Even today, at the threshold of the twenty-first century, the electric lines haven't made it to Polebridge.

John tells us we should drive up to see the old **Hornet Peak Lookout**, which he and the North Fork Preservation Association, along with the Flathead National Forest, have been renovating over the past few summers.

That we do. We follow the North Fork Road 10 miles north to the Ford Station of the Flathead National Forest. At this point, just 10 miles south of the Canadian border crossing, we turn west, continuing for 8.5 miles up Forest Roads 318 and 9805. Both of the old logging roads have good, hard gravel surfaces. At a ridgetop pull-out we park and leave the car, cross the road, and walk onto the obvious foot trail. After a mile or so of steep climbing we reach the top of 6,744-foot **Hornet Peak**.

The old lookout cabin is right there, but what initially grabs our attention is the view to the east, opening onto Glacier National Park. Several long, narrow glacial lakes, separated by steep, timbered ridges, glisten like watery fingers, their eastward ends reaching toward crystal mountains topped with ice and snow. As best we can tell from our map, we think it's Kintla, Bowman, and Quartz lakes that we're gazing at. What a view!

Hornet Lookout is not perched on a tower as many lookouts are; rather, it's simply a log cabin topped with an aerie-like cupola. We've read that the lookout was built in 1922, and that it's the only D-1 Standard model still standing. Pioneer Forest Service workers built the structure from native materials, using crosscut saws to down on-site timber. It really is a beauty, and the recent restoration work has the seventy-five-year-old building looking almost like new.

After hoofing it down to the car, Nancy and I loop back through seemingly virgin stands of tall western larch and Douglas fir lining Forest Road 907, which follows Tepee Creek to the North Fork Road. On regaining Polebridge, before leaving town we swing in for a sandwich and bowl of soup at the **Northern Lights**, the only dining option in "town." It's situated close to the historic **Polebridge Mercantile**, which is—you guessed it—the only store in town.

We drive over the new bridge spanning the wide North Fork of the Flathead River (the Red Bench Fire took out the previous one), driving into **Glacier National Park** at an entrance relatively few park visitors have encountered. Somewhat pressed for time, we opt not to take the 14-mile drive north to **Kintla Lake** or even the shorter, but bumpier drive to **Bowman Lake**. Instead, we head south along the **Inside North Fork Road**. Despite that it's a narrow, little-traveled gravel byway, the Inside Road is the oldest road in the park. It dates to early in the twentieth century, when it was built after oil was discovered near Kintla Lake. We follow its winding way past **Winona Lake** and **Quartz Creek Campground**. Generally, because of the heavy timber cover in these western bottoms of the park, the views are close-ups of streams, leaves, wildflowers, and other portraits of nature, rather than the exalted mountain vistas for which Glacier is best known.

Twenty-five miles after leaving Polebridge we emerge from the roaded wilds at **Fish Creek Campground**, where we locate a site, set up camp, cook and eat supper, and have a half hour of daylight to spare. It's an uncommonly beautiful evening on the southwest shore of Lake McDonald—making it hard to imagine a better place to be.

FOLLOWING THE MAIN ROUTE FROM WHITEFISH TO GLACIER NATIONAL PARK

If exploring the wild hinterlands of northwest Montana isn't quite your style, from Whitefish

Lake McDonald, Glacier National Park

you can still take a quiet route as far as Columbia Falls before pulling onto the busy main highway. The drive traverses a pleasing countryside filled with rural homes and small farms. A labyrinth of dirt roads webs the area, though, so follow these directions carefully: Immediately north of the railroad overpass in downtown Whitefish, turn east onto Edgewood Place. At just over 2.5 miles the road curves right and turns to gravel; then, in another 2 miles pavement resumes. After driving 1 mile on pavement (a total of 5.5 miles from Whitefish), just beyond a right-hand curve turn left onto the unsigned paved road. A mile later turn right at the T. In another mile you'll pass **Meadow Lake,** a four-season resort that includes an excellent eighteen-hole golf course. A mile and a half past Meadow Lake you'll want to turn right at the four-way junction. Next, after crossing the series of railroad tracks a little less than a mile farther along (10 miles since leaving Whitefish), turn right onto Railroad Street.

A left turn onto Nucleus Avenue will lead you through downtown **Columbia Falls** and to the intersection with U.S. Highway 2, where you'll want to turn left. From this point to West Glacier the highway is lined with an eclectic assortment of things of the sort that seem to pop up outside many of our national parks: a waterslide, for instance, along with fruit and beef jerky stands, a go-cart track, RV parks, cabin rentals, wildlife museums, a miniature golf course, helicopter tours, river-running outfits, and much, much

more. There's even the **Glacier Maze**, where you might arrange literally to lose your kids for a while if they're feeling a bit too rambunctious.

Diamonds sparkling amid the rough include the **Hungry Horse Dam Visitor Center**, located 4 miles south of the town of Hungry Horse on Forest Road 895. Farther up that road—which, together with Forest Road 38 ultimately encircles the reservoir—you'll come across a progression of Flathead National Forest campgrounds, pleasantly sited on the shores of colossal Hungry Horse Reservoir.

Glacier National Park

It's almost a relief to reach **West Glacier**, where the park-style architecture makes things feel more in line with the national park way. Oddly, though, the most impressive attraction in town is the visitor center maintained by the Canadian province of Alberta. In town you'll also find the Glacier Natural History Association's bookstore, which sells a good selection of maps and books focusing on the region. The facility (telephone 406–888–5756) is situated at the main highway junction in the Belton Depot. Tucked away on a side road a short distance west of town is the **Glacier View Golf Club**. A number of accommodations, ranging from rustic to

Hungry Horse News, Columbia Falls, Montana

A scenic overlook in Glacier National Park

quite luxurious, also hide amid the wooded nooks and meadowed crannies of the immediately surrounding private lands.

Drive north from West Glacier across the Middle Fork of the Flathead River, and presently you'll arrive at the West Entrance of **Glacier National Park**. Soon after entering the park you'll come to a stop sign: A right turn leads to Logan Pass via Going-to-the-Sun Road, while a left turn will take you to **Apgar Village**, where you'll find a visitor center, motel accommodations, and other visitor services. Apgar is also the launching point for a pair of the park's less-frequented motorways: the paved **Camas Creek Road**, which leads 12 miles northwest to the park's Camas Creek Entrance and the North Fork Road; and the Inside North Fork Road, leading 25 miles northwest to Polebridge. (The latter is previously described in Driving to Polebridge and Glacier National Park through the Back Door.)

TACKLING GOING-TO-THE-SUN ROAD . . . AND A BRIEF VISIT TO CANADA: A NARRATIVE ACCOUNT

Mid-morning on a brilliant day in early July, Nancy and I pull up at the West Entrance station of Glacier National Park, where I hand my Golden Eagle Passport to the young female National Park Service ranger on duty. I always try to be extra friendly to entrance-station rangers such as her, because I know well how boring their work can be: Years ago I spent most of a summer in a similar booth, outfitted in a similar uniform, at Devil's Tower National Monument in northeast Wyoming.

Just north of the entrance station we turn right at the stop sign onto the celebrated **Going-to-the-Sun Road**, which begins modestly enough, just a platform of pavement stretching through an enclosure of lodgepole pine. But in less than a mile we emerge in a clearing above the shore of Lake McDonald, where it's revealed that our surroundings are anything but commonplace: The upper, northeastern end of the lake is wrapped in high, stratified peaks. The waters of Lake McDonald appear strikingly blue against the dark-green mountainsides . . . but not as blue as the turquoise sky that envelops the entire scene in its fold. The water- and sky-framed mountains are a picture we've seen a hundred times, in magazines, in books, on television, and even on tourism-booster billboards.

Whereas Glacier National Park encompasses only approximately 100 miles of roads, including both paved and gravel, I've read that it is laced with more than 700 miles of horse and foot paths. These statistics make it obvious that one can see relatively little of the park through the windows of a car. That's one reason we plan to drive today only as far as Lake McDonald Lodge, where we have reservations for the night. We intend to spend most of this crystal day in the out-of-doors, beyond sight of cars and roadways.

At 8 miles, just past the Lincoln Lake trailhead, on our left we see the **Sprague Creek Campground**, which, according to the sign posted at the entrance, permits no towed trailers. A mile farther along we turn left and pull into a parking space at the **Lake McDonald Complex**, where aside from the main lodge we see that there's also a general store, an art gallery, some rather plain-looking cabins for rent, a post office, and several other buildings. On the drive fronting the main lodge six bright red touring cars line up as if in formation, waiting to take on passengers. One of our park brochures informed us that the motor coaches were built by the White Motor Company in the mid- to late-1930s, making them nearly as old as the Going-to-the-Sun Road itself. Their drivers, called Jammers—short for "gear jammers"—haul visitors throughout the park in these classic beauties, relating the geology, lore, and tall tales of Glacier as they go.

"In keeping with the era in which the Complex was built, televisions, elevators, kitchens

"Jammers"

and air conditioning are NOT available." These are the words employed in another brochure, describing our rooming situation at Lake McDonald. That's fine with us. We hadn't counted on sitting around watching *Hart to Hart* reruns, anyway. Lake McDonald Lodge was built by John Lewis in 1913, using spruce and fir logs that were felled up Snyder Creek then transported to Lake McDonald during the floods of spring runoff. Early guests who sat around the lodge's immense rock fireplace included senators, writers, artists, entertainers such as Will Rogers, and artist-entertainers: in particular, Charlie Russell, a frequent visitor who was often called on to amuse other guests with his wry, sometimes tall tales of life in the West. Today's visitors generally enter the lodge through what was originally designed as the back of the building: Until cars came onto the scene in 1929, guests arrived via boat, then climbed from the lakeshore up a winding path to the front entrance.

After checking into our room on the third floor of the lodge, we change into hiking clothes and stuff a rucksack with food, spare clothes, and a few other items. Then we walk out the front door of the lodge to cross Going-to-the-Sun Road and locate the **Gunsight Pass–Sperry Chalet Trail**. The bear bells attached to my rucksack make a continual jingling sound that is slightly annoying but simultaneously comforting, assuming they accomplish the intended purpose: that is, scaring away bears before we get close enough for them to see us and us them. Still, for insurance I've packed along a canister of pepper spray, which I carry in a holster attached to my belt.

We climb steeply along Snyder Creek through thick forest for approximately 1.5 miles before coming to the junction with the **Mount Brown Lookout Trail**, where we bear left. If we were to continue straight, approximately 5 miles from this point we would reach the historic **Sperry Chalet**. Sperry and its sister, **Granite Park Chalet**, are classic backcountry hotels that were built early in the century by the Great Northern Railroad. Both were ordered closed by the state in 1992 because of faulty sewage systems. After extensive renovation work, Granite Park (telephone toll-free 800–521–7238) is now back in business as a hiker hut, and Sperry is expected to reopen in 1999.

After veering onto the lookout trail, we begin zigzagging up a seemingly endless procession of switchbacks that zipper their way toward the fire lookout, climbing through forests of white pine and Douglas fir. As we approach the top we break into a clearing, from which we finally can see the lookout perched above us, appearing a bit like a Japanese pagoda occupying a marvelous alpine setting. Five switchbacks later and we gain the ridgetop that leads us right up to the lookout. I counted a total of 30 switchbacks to get here; Nancy stopped at 29. Either way, it was a lot. I discover by inspecting our map that the fire lookout doesn't sit on Mount Brown, but rather atop a knob roughly a thousand feet below and a mile southwest of the mountain's summit. Our elevation at the lookout is 7,478 feet, precisely 4,325 feet above the water level of Lake McDonald, which we can see below in the distance, stretching away from the Apgar Range. As our tired legs remind us, that's a lot of altitude to gain in the course of barely more than 5 miles. But every step was worth it, considering the incredible views we have earned of Heaven's Peak, the valley of the North Fork, Lake McDonald, and other features in and out of the park.

Hunkering on the leeward side of the lookout, we pull on our spare clothes before gobbling a snack and each drinking a quart bottle of water. Neither of us is particularly thirsty, but we know that at high, dry elevations such as this water is every bit as important as protein, fat, or carbohydrate—and also that lack of thirst is no indicator of fluid needs.

We then begin retracing our footsteps, taking a look at the back side of everything we saw on the way up. We reach Lake McDonald Lodge six hours and more than 10 miles after setting out. Pounding back down to the lake, we agree, was even harder on our legs than was climbing up to the fire lookout. So, after a delicious steak dinner in the Cedar Dining Room, we relax our legs, along with the rest of our bodies, on the lodge's second-story veranda. Lake McDonald and its mountain backdrop sprawl before us.

On hitting the road early the next morning we find, remarkably, that the quality of the scenery increases almost exponentially after we pass the head of Lake McDonald and continue up McDonald Creek. We see that some of the avalanche chutes high above are still packed with deep snow, despite that today is the Fourth of July—a day that few persons in the United States associate with snow. After pulling over briefly to marvel at the frothing waters of **Upper McDonald Falls**, 2 miles later we pass the **Avalanche Campground**, then the **Trail of the Cedars** nature trail. Even before seeing the sign marking the trail we'd been noticing that the woods had been changing in character, into a lush drooping of timber suggestive of a Pacific Northwest rain forest. Now we can see luxuriant carpets of moss spreading over the forest floor, which is also punctuated with occasional growths of ferns and other plants. Otherwise, though, the damp ground lying in the constant shadows cast by the broad canopy of ancient western red cedar and mountain hemlock appears strangely open and void of vegetation.

Ten miles from the lodge we reach Logan Creek and begin to climb in earnest, passing through a large brushy clearing, which a roadside sign informs us was fashioned by the 1967 Garden Wall wildfire. After creeping through an unnervingly narrow tunnel blasted through solid rock, at just under 14 miles from Lake McDonald Lodge we reach **the Loop**, where the really thrilling part of the road begins. Before continuing, though, we pull into the parking area to take advantage of a world-class photo opportunity that encompasses Heaven's Peak and its far-flung, celestial surroundings. Here we also see the trailhead for a trail leading to the Granite Park Chalet. (A tip: There's a better route to take if you'd like to visit the chalet on a day outing. Beginning at Logan Pass, hike the spectacular, wildflower-lined **Highline Trail** along the Garden Wall to the chalet, then drop down the 4 miles to the Loop. After finishing the 12-mile hike, you can catch a ride back to Logan Pass on a shuttle bus. The route also provides access to a tough, 1.5-mile round-trip to the lofty **Grinnell Glacier Overlook**, which you can tack on to your hike if time and energy permit.)

Between the Loop and Logan Pass, Going-to-the-Sun Road is nothing but a shelf chiseled from a cliff of solid limestone. The road was designed for smaller vehicles—and smaller *numbers* of vehicles—than it carries today. So, driving on it in the thick of summer can be a near bumper-to-bumper experience, as we find it is today.

Bicycling, a pollution-free and exhilarating way to view the surreal surroundings, may be a better way for the fit and ready to traverse Going-to-the-Sun Road. There's no disputing that it constitutes a climb, but it's neither as steep nor as tough as it appears on first sight. Cycling up the west side of Going to the Sun Road should be on the "must do" list of any serious cyclist who hasn't done it. In fact, the adventure has been commemorated in a very popular poster created by Missoula artist Monte Dolack for the Adventure Cycling Association.

Nevertheless, the National Park Service sees fit to continue prohibiting bicycles on two stretches of the road between 11:00 A.M. and 4:00 P.M., from June 15 through Labor Day. One of the stretches is the spectacular 11.5-mile climb from Logan Creek to Logan Pass. Personally, I tell Nancy, I'd prefer that they temporarily ban cars and motor homes and leave the road open to bicycles, but I doubt that it will happen any time soon. (The wider and less harrowing Going-to-the-Sun Road east of the Continental Divide, between Logan Pass and St. Mary, remains open in its entirety to bicycles.)

As we inch up the winding road, Nancy reads aloud from a history booklet we purchased in West Glacier. She tells me that the rudimentary, westernmost stretch of Going-to-the-Sun Road, originally called the Transmountain Highway, was built in 1911, soon after the park's creation. They were a hard-earned 2.5 miles for William R. Logan, Glacier's first superintendent, whose goal was to construct a road through the "pleasuring ground," as he referred to the national park, "from some one of the mountain passes from the east to the west side."

But 2.5 miles was as far as Logan got, and further funding for the roadway was not forthcoming until 1921, when Congress appropriated $100,000. The money permitted Logan's successors to award a contract for a 3.5-mile stretch of road reaching farther up Lake McDonald. From there, surveyors decided, a route by way of Logan Pass was the way to go. It would keep the west-slope portion of the road mostly in the sun and out of the shadows, a vital concern in an area that is so steep and endures such prolific snow accumulations. Planners proclaimed that the road would be 16 feet wide and would maintain an average grade of 6 percent, as it first skirted below the Garden Wall and then rose along the mountainside, fully exposed to the warming rays of the sun, to the Continental Divide at Logan Pass.

Nancy continues reading, informing me that during the construction of Going-to-the-Sun Road west of the Continental Divide, dozens of construction workers, many of them veterans of the first World War, were stationed in several camps dispersed along the way. Implements of removal, grading, and rebuilding included dynamite, tractors, crowbars, crosscut saws, snowplows, and steam shovels. Three men lost their lives while building the road, two of them from falls and one from a being struck by a rock.

By October 1928 the road ran uninterrupted from the West Entrance to Logan Pass, and construction of the less-challenging east side was finished three years later. After that it took two additional years to complete the road's gravel surface and to install guardrails. On July 15, 1933, with great pomp and circumstance—which included a Blackfeet band playing "The Star-Spangled Banner" and the passing of the peace pipe among government officials and Blackfeet, Kootenai, and Flathead Indians—Going-to-the-Sun Road, one of the most beautiful and amazing engineering feats in history, opened its full length to motor traffic. Thousands were on hand to enjoy the revelry and listen to speeches, including one by Horace Albright, the newly appointed director of the National Park Service. " . . . Let there be no competition of other roads with the Going-to-the-Sun Highway," Albright proclaimed. "It should stand supreme and alone."

Three miles from the Loop Nancy and I pull briefly into the **Bird Woman Falls Overlook**, then, 2 miles later, drive beneath the **Weeping Wall**, where the spray provides our car with a brief washing. As we round an outside bend we can see cars ascending and descending above, looking from our perspective as if they're flying along next to the cliff rather than negotiating a road. The view into the glacier-carved valley below, and at the glacier-sculpted mountains towering above, is almost beyond belief: A medley of greens of lush summer meld with the cold, blue-white ice of never-summer mountains, all of it bejeweled in a mix of shining rock, sparkling sky, and tumbling falls of snowmelt water.

Any time I try to steal a glance, though, Nancy scolds me; she seriously thinks I should keep my eyes on the road. She's probably right. On some curves there's scarcely enough room for two cars to squeeze by between the jutting cliffside and the old rock guardrails. Indeed, at a couple of such locations we see that the jagged cliff rock is decorated in paint scrapings of numerous colors, no doubt left behind by many years' worth of nervous motorists.

At 21 miles we negotiate a final switchback, then take direct aim at the slot in the mountains that is Logan Pass, a narrow ridge of land remaining where a pair of glaciers back-cut their cirques to meet at the Continental Divide. A half mile later we crest the 6,680-foot summit and pull into the large parking lot. When we set out early this morning at Lake McDonald the air was already quite warm, obviously a scorcher of a day in the making. But here it is, noon, and, even though there's not a single cloud marring the blue sky, the air temperature feels much colder than it did at 7:00 A.M. at Lake McDonald.

Deep snows still bury some of the flatter terrain surrounding the pass. The breeze coming across those snowfields is absolutely cold. We see a couple of dozen cross-country skiers, both young and old, walking in heavy boots and carrying their skis and poles between the parking lot and the trail that begins behind the visitor center. Others are standing around slathering sunscreen onto their arms, necks, and faces. They all seem to be wearing uniforms of bright colors and dark sunglasses. Skiing on the Fourth of July—marvelous!

We're pleased to find a fire roaring in the open fireplace inside the visitor center. After hugging the fire and watching it snap and dance for a few minutes we turn to inspecting the center's wildlife displays and extensive selection of maps, books, and brochures for sale. Then we stroll out the back door and onto the **Hidden Lake Trail**. It begins as a beefy raised boardwalk, built to protect the sensitive, wildflower-filled **Hanging Gardens** from potential harm inflicted by thousands of waffle-soled boots. We see skiers propelling themselves across long snow fields, using smooth skating motions. Higher up in the distance, over toward prominent **Raynolds Mountain**, we see several other skiers carving classic, graceful telemark turns.

Near the base of Clements Mountain, where the boardwalk ends, we join in with a half dozen other shutter-snappers to capture images of a trio of shaggy, shedding, dirty-white mountain goats. Considering how closely they permit us to approach, it is clear that we're not the first human beings these semi-wild beasts have encountered.

We turn around at the **Hidden Lake Overlook**, roughly 1.5 miles out, and walk back to the visitor center. From there we leave the parking lot and begin driving down the east slope of the Continental Divide, where we're greeted by awesome peaks of bare rock wearing names like **Heavy Runner** and **Going-to-the-Sun**. Instantly, the landscape appears substantially drier and more weather-battered than the terrain we traversed on the west slope. Five miles from the pass we pull into the **Jackson Glacier Overlook**, where a 6.3-mile-long trail to **Gunsight Lake** begins. The hike is both a favorite day outing and the first leg of a popular 20-mile hike linking St. Mary Lake with Lake McDonald, by way of Sperry Chalet.

St. Mary Lake, narrow and deep, stretches before us for 10 miles. We can tell by the white-caps on the water, and also by the flapping jackets worn by a trio of roadside point-and-clickers photographing **Wild Goose Island**, that the wind is blowing hard. Moreover, clumps of short, twisted aspens and pines lean with the wind like tight little fists, their gnarled configurations disclosing the fact that the raging wind is not a rare phenomenon over here.

Soon we pass the **Rising Sun Campground**, where the road levels out along the shore of St. Mary Lake. Fourteen miles after leaving Logan Pass we pull into the viewpoint overlooking **Triple Divide Peak**, a triangular mountain that is unique on the North American continent. A snowflake landing on the tip of Triple Divide Peak might melt, depending on the whims of the wind and other factors, to wind up in one of three oceans: either the Pacific, the Atlantic, or the Arctic. In another 4 miles we go by the **St. Mary Campground**, then exit the park at the St. Mary Entrance Station. After passing the turn to the 1913 ranger station historic site we arrive at **St. Mary Village**, situated 18.5 miles from Logan Pass, where we grab a quick but tasty lunch at the **Park Cafe**.

We've found that when touring Glacier National Park it is nearly impossible to ignore the proximity of Alberta's much smaller Waterton Lakes National Park. Geographically the parks are a continuum, and Waterton is even depicted on the National Park Service map we received when entering Glacier. The pair of national parks constitutes the **Waterton-Glacier International Peace Park**, created in 1932 as the first of its kind in the world (*see* History). So, at St. Mary Nancy and I head north, determined to visit our Canadian neighbor—but with a hidden agenda: We intend to slip back into Glacier National Park later today from the north, via watercraft. It's not an altogether spontaneous decision, either. Knowing that competition would be keen for rooms, I've secured advance reservations to stay the night at the Prince of Wales Hotel in Waterton Townsite.

After following U.S. Highway 89 along the east shore of Lower St. Mary Lake, at **Babb** we opt not to drive west into the marvelous **Many Glacier** area of Glacier National Park. Instead, we vow to visit there in a couple of days, on our return trip south. We continue north through an open, undulating terrain flanked by stands of stunted aspen; country conceived by the marriage of mountains and plains. It's so different compared to where we were only six hours ago that we feel as if we've traveled 5,000 miles rather than just 50.

Four and one-half miles out of Babb we veer northwest onto the **Chief Mountain International Highway**, then, 11 miles later, re-enter Glacier National Park. In another 3.5 miles we arrive at the Port of Chief Mountain (open mid-May to mid-September only). With little fanfare other than a question from the border guard regarding the amount of cash we're carrying, we cross into the country of Canada, the province of Alberta, and **Waterton Lakes National Park**.

In 2.5 miles we pass the left-hand turn to the **Belly River Campground**. After crossing the Belly River we temporarily leave Waterton to traverse lands of the **Blood Indian Forest Reserve**. Fourteen miles from the international border we turn left onto Highway 5 East then, a half mile later, cross the Waterton River and turn left toward **Waterton Townsite**. Just past there we pull up to pay our park fee at the Waterton Lakes National Park entrance station.

Before long it strikes us that simply because Glacier and Waterton share mountains, valleys, and national park status, not everything is necessarily the same. For one thing, we pass a rolling eighteen-hole golf course, a feature definitely not found in Glacier or Yellowstone national park. In many ways Canada is more Continental or British than the United States, a quality their showpiece national parks seem to reflect by melding the rustic diversions of the wild outback with the more civilized pleasures. In this spirit it seems appropriate that the park was created, soon after the turn of the century, at the urging of John George "Kootenai" Brown, a well-read pioneer who was part mountain man and part Rennaissance man.

Waterton Townsite, we find, is indeed a small town with most of the expected things a town would have, including a smattering of year-round residents. On pulling up to the stunning **Prince of Wales Hotel**, a seven-story chalet perched atop a glacial ridge high above mountain-embraced **Upper Waterton Lake**, we immediately partake of afternoon tea. Nancy calls it "high tea in the high country." We learn from talking to a pair of young Swiss men that several hiking trails in the park are open also to mountain biking. This is another feature distinguishing Waterton from its neighbor to the south: All hiking trails in Glacier are off-limits to bicycling. Nancy and I agree that tomorrow morning we will look into renting bicycles and sampling one or two of those trails.

But it is still today, the Fourth of July. Temporary expatriates on our country's birthday, we know that shortly we'll be back in the good old U.S. of A. The "tea"—which comprised much more than just tea—leaves us feeling as if eating supper would be superfluous. So we retire to our room for a while. In contrast to the spacious, open nature of the lobby and other common rooms below, the room is rather cramped, with only two small windows. Apparently, when the hotel was built in 1927, rooms were designed for sleeping, and one did one's gazing at the scenery in a more social setting.

We grab our wind clothes then head outside and down to the dock to jump aboard the MV *International*, a touring boat that's been negotiating the waters of Upper Waterton Lake since the year the Prince of Wales Hotel was built. The sunset cruise, which is scheduled to last two or three hours, takes us southward up the long lake, deep into wilderness and into the United States and Glacier National Park. As we leave Canada we can see the international border clearly delineated, in the form of a clearing sliced through timber covering steep slopes.

After arriving at the upper end of the lake we dock at the **Goat Haunt Ranger Station** of Glacier National Park. Throughout the summer dozens of backpackers hop off the boat here, then ground-pound their way through some of Glacier's most remote backcountry. Destinations include Logan Pass via the Granite Park Chalet, and Kintla Lake, by way of Boulder Pass. The latter is a trek of approximately 31 miles, with one significant logistical snag: When hikers reach the roadhead at Kintla Lake, their car, if it remains back at Waterton Townsite, is 140 miles away by road.

On the return boat ride, just before we float back into Canada, a middle-aged man—obviously a fellow Yank—yells, at the top of his lungs, "Happy Birthday, America!" Nancy and I second the motion, albeit much more quietly than our countryman's loud proclamation.

South from St. Mary

If you drive south from St. Mary, after a few miles you'll emerge onto open prairie, capped by a big sky stretching endlessly eastward. Closer to the mountains, high buttes rise above bursts of wind-distorted timber. Approximately 11 miles from town the hilly, wildly winding road leads down to cross the South Fork of the Milk River. Four miles from there you'll see a gravel road going right; it penetrates the valley of the meandering North Fork of Cut Bank Creek. If you drive west into the valley you'll be confronted by a rampart of mountains owning compelling, Blackfeet-derived names like **Bad Marriage** and **Mad Wolf**. After leading for 4 miles across Blackfeet tribal pasturelands, the road enters Glacier National Park, then ends a mile later at the primitive **Cut Bank Campground** (trailers and large RVs not recommended). Here, too, you'll find the trailhead for the 14.2-mile there-and-back hike to **Triple Divide Pass**.

Back on the main road, you'll reach Kiowa at 19 miles, where a deli/store and a campground front the highway. By bearing left you can continue for 12 miles along U.S. Highway 89 to the Blackfeet Indian capital of **Browning**, location of the excellent **Museum of the Plains Indian**. A rich array of Blackfeet art and artifacts are displayed, as well as arts and crafts of other Plains tribes, including the Northern Cheyenne, Sioux, and Crow Indians, all historic enemies of the once-fearsome Blackfeet. Contemporary as well as historic works are displayed, with many of them offered for sale in a shop operated by the Northern Plains Indian Crafts Association. The museum (telephone 406–338–2230), located just west of town, is open daily June through September and weekdays the rest of the year.

For four days each July the multifarious and colorful sights, sounds, and scents of **North American Indian Days** fill and spill out from the Blackfeet Tribal Fairgrounds, situated next to the museum. Native Americans from throughout the United States and Canada gather at the celebration (telephone 406–338–7276) for singing, dancing, and games. Non-Indians are welcome, too, and they arrive in droves. While in Browning be sure also to take in the **Bob Scriver Museum of Montana Wildlife**, a place that's alive with the sculptures of the talented Scriver, along with the creations of other artists, a mad mix of taxidermy mounts, and other finds.

Back at Kiowa, a right-hand turn onto State Highway 49 leads the 12 miles to East Glacier, along an astoundingly twisting, hilly, bumpy, and narrow road. En route, you will pass the right-hand turn onto Two Medicine Road, which leads to Glacier National Park's **Lower Two Medicine and Two Medicine lakes**. One of the most gorgeous niches in the park, the Two Medicine area has no indoor accommodations, but it does boast a large campground, a general store and snack stand, and tour-boat and boat-rental concessions. The easy, half-mile round-trip hike to **Running Eagle Falls** is considered a must-do for anyone visiting the Two Medicine area.

Even if you don't follow the Two Medicine Road westward, the views overlooking the area are stupendous, encompassing the lakes and high peaks of Glacier National Park's southern reaches. The main highway soon leads to **East Glacier Park**, a collection of motels, cabins, restaurants, and other tourist services lying just outside the park. **Glacier Park Lodge**, another of the old Great Northern Railroad hotels, is a 154-room knockout gracing a grand splash of grounds that include a nine-hole golf course. So immaculately kept is the entire spread that it's rather hard to tell where the golf course ends and the rest of the lawns begin. There's also swimming, horseback riding, and good Western dining at Glacier Park Lodge. The princely setting practically demands that you get out of your car and wander around, even if you've no intention of spending the night.

Also in East Glacier: the **John L. Clarke Western Art Gallery and Memorial Museum**. Clarke, whose Blackfeet name was *Cutapuis*, or "The-Man-Who-Talks-Not," was a Blackfeet Indian born in 1881. A bout of scarlet fever at age two left Clarke deaf and unable to speak—through his mouth, anyway. But speak he did, by way of his beautifully crafted sculptures, paintings, and wood carvings—particularly through his detailed cottonwood carvings of bears, mountain goats, and other wildlife thriving in his home territory. Clarke, who died in 1970, became exceedingly popular during his lifetime; for instance, the mountain goat mascot of the Great Northern Railroad was based on one of his carvings. At the memorial museum—which his adopted daughter, Joyce, started in 1977—Western creations by numerous artists are available for sale, as are limited editions of Clarke's own works.

Leaving East Glacier, U.S. Highway 2 wraps for some 50 miles along the southern boundary of Glacier National Park, first heading southwestward then bending northwestward. At 2.5 miles from East Glacier you'll pass the **Bison Creek Ranch Bed & Breakfast**; then, a mile later, you'll leave the Blackfeet Indian Reservation and enter the Flathead National Forest. Eleven miles from town you'll crest the Continental Divide at **Marias Pass**, despite that you may not even have noticed the gentle climb preceding the summit. The Forest Service's **Summit Campground** is situated nearby, and the popular **Bear Creek Guest Ranch** is on the right at about 18 miles. Soon you'll pass **Devil Creek Campground** and follow Bear Creek into its steep-sided canyon. At 29 miles you'll arrive at the left-hand turn into **Essex**—but only after passing **Goat Lick** a couple of miles before, where dozens of mountain goats often congregate to take advantage of natural salt licks.

In Essex, hidden well off the highway, the buzzing **Izaak Walton Inn** serves as one of the most popular getaways in Glacier-Gold Country, both in summer and in winter, when the enterprise maintains an outstanding network of groomed cross-country ski trails. The inn, sitting beside the railroad tracks, was built in the late 1930s chiefly to serve as a home away from home for Great Northern Railroad employees assigned to work through the long winters clearing snow from the tracks on and around storm-battered Marias Pass. But the lodge was built bigger than needed if that was its sole purpose, which it wasn't: At the time it was believed that the inn occupied a spot in close proximity to what would eventually become a central entrance into Glacier National Park—an idea that never materialized.

For the final 27 miles back to West Glacier, the road traces the canyon of the Middle Fork of the Flathead River. The lower stretches are particularly popular with independent and commercial river runners; keep your eyes peeled if the season is right, and you're sure to see plenty of rafts full of adrenaline-pumped whitewater screamers.

A DRIVING TOUR ALONG THE ROCKY MOUNTAIN FRONT

The following drive is striking in its beauty and startling in its broad, wide-open character, especially when compared to the timber-shrouded recesses so common in Montana west of the Continental Divide. To begin, head south from Browning on U.S. Highway 89. Alternatively, if beginning in East Glacier you can take the scenic Heart Butte Cutoff to the Heart Butte Road, then follow the Birch Creek (a.k.a. Arrowhead) Road. This meets U.S. Highway 89 a few miles north of Dupuyer (*Duh-POOH-yer*), not far from the site of the only confrontation that exploded between Native Americans and the Corps of Discovery (*see* History). A caveat, however: If taking this backroads route you should

have on hand detailed maps of the area, such as those found in DeLorme Mapping's *Montana Atlas & Gazetteer.*

Whichever route you take, initially you'll travel across Blackfeet tribal lands. After leaving the reservation the roads followed to Helena traverse private lands almost exclusively, but they're roads that offer full-force views of the Rocky Mountain Front and the public lands of the Lewis and Clark National Forest. From Dupuyer a side road leads roughly 20 miles west to **Swift Reservoir** and its public campground and picnic grounds. Even closer to town, just to the southwest: **Theodore Roosevelt Ranch**, owned and operated by the Missoula-based Boone & Crockett Club, where hiking and wildlife viewing are available to the public, except between October 15 and December 1.

From tiny Dupuyer continue south to similarly tiny Bynum, before pushing on to the relative metropolis of **Choteau**, an attractive settlement that may remind you of a bucolic Midwest farm town. At a point 5 miles north of Choteau, Teton Canyon Road departs from U.S. Highway 89, following the Teton River upstream. It leads west toward a number of interesting discoveries, including the intimate, family-friendly **Teton Pass** ski area (telephone 406–799–6833). Before that, roughly 15 miles from the main highway, you'll pass the left-hand turn to **Pine Butte Swamp Preserve**, an 18,000-acre Nature Conservancy holding that protects important habitat for grizzlies and other wildlife species. Access is strictly managed on the wildlife preserve, so call the headquarters (telephone 406–466–5526) to arrange either solo or organized hikes up Pine Butte and to other destinations. Weeklong stays in summer, and daily stays in May and September, can be arranged at the **Pine Butte Guest Ranch**, the former private Circle 8 Ranch now run by the Nature Conservancy.

This country that is home today to bears, elk, and countless other animals apparently was once a good dinosaur habitat, as well. Nearby is **Egg Mountain**, the now-famous site where Bynum rock-shop owners John and Marian Brandvold in the late 1970s first discovered the fossilized nests of duck-billed dinosaurs. Jack Horner, paleontologist at Montana State University and the Museum of the Rockies, proceeded to find many additional nests of *Maiasaura* (Good Mother Lizard), which was proclaimed Montana's state fossil. At Choteau's **Old Trail Museum** you can learn more about the findings and sign up for paleontological field trips and camps. The museum (telephone 406–466–5332) also features displays on early white settlers and the even earlier Old North Trail, a Blackfeet Indian path that ran through the area.

Another reason to negotiate the canyon of the Teton River is simply to see the plains transform, almost imperceptibly, into mountains, as more and more of the open range is claimed by pockets, then groves of limber pine. Much of the high mountain front looming ahead and above is contained within the immense **Bob Marshall Wilderness**, whose other side you saw if you made the trip through the Seeley-Swan Valley.

From Choteau, in order to continue skirting the front of the Northern Rockies rather than spilling onto the Great Plains, veer southwest onto U.S. Highway 287. Over the course of 26 wide-open miles the road leads to **Augusta**, one of the best examples of cow town ambience surviving in Montana. East of Augusta, home to a rodeo known as The Wildest One Day Show on Earth, good gravel roads lead to high and handsome hideaways, such as **Gibson Reservoir** and the nearby **Mortimer Gulch National Recreation Trail**; the pine-studded, grizzly- and elk-inhabited rolling hills of the **Sun River Wildlife Management Area**; and **Beaver Creek Canyon**, whose stunning drama of folded rock will remain with you for years to come, should you choose to investigate it.

A tip for those hauling along their mountain bicycles: Sun River W.M.A. is crisscrossed with dirt roads that are perfect for exploring by bike. Likewise, several irrigation canals running between the mountains and the highway feature parallel roads that are open to the public. Travel to **Pishkun Reservoir**, for instance, by driving southwest from Choteau on signed county roads. (Again, the *Montana Atlas & Gazetteer* will prove indispensable.) From the reservoir you can follow either Pishkun Canal west toward Gibson Reservoir, or the Sun River Slope Canal southeasterly to U.S. Highway 287. These canal roads, snaking through the middle of nowhere, will lead

you through corners of Glacier-Gold Country visited by very few pilgrims.

From Augusta, wind your way up and down U.S. Highway 287, past big ranches and Hutterite farms, to Bowmans Corners, where State Highway 200 bisects the U.S. highway. After approximately 19 miles, as you approach Interstate 15, a rutted ranch road veering right leads a mile-plus to **The Bungalow** (telephone 406–235–4276), one of the more out-of-the-ordinary inns in a region teeming with unique overnighting options. The structure was designed by Robert C. Reamer, architect of the Inn at Old Faithful. It dates to 1913, when it was completed as a summer residence for Helena-area entrepreneur Charles C. Power. The cedar logs of The Bungalow—which, not surprisingly, looks a bit like a miniature Old Faithful Inn—were hauled by train to Wolf Creek from the big-timber country of Sandpoint, Idaho. Fly-fishers take note: The dessicated, rocky terrain surrounding The Bungalow belies the fact that merely minutes away are some of the Missouri River's most trout-prolific riffles and holes.

From Wolf Creek it's 34 miles via Interstate 15 to **Helena**. Midway between Wolf Creek and Montana's capital city you'll pass the exit for the road leading to the Missouri River's **Gates of the Mountains Recreation Area**, which is 3 miles east of the interstate. The limestone-walled canyon is best viewed by boarding one of the private, open-air tour boats (telephone 406–458–5241) that depart from the recreation area's marina several times daily in summer. The cruise leads through a deep gorge named by the Corps of Discovery in 1805 (*see* History). Wildlife viewing opportunities are rife along the river, with potential spottings that include bighorn sheep, mountain goats, and mule deer. Bald eagles, ospreys, and redtail hawks are also commonly seen, perched in trees or soaring overhead.

Arrangements can be made to hop off at the Meriwether Picnic Area, then hike one or more of the trails branching from there before boarding a later-arriving boat. Potential destinations include Mann Gulch, site of a 1949 forest fire that killed 13 firefighters. The event is the subject of *Young Men and Fire*, a book by the late Norman Maclean.

Brief Visits to Helena and Butte

Missoula, Bozeman, and the Flathead Valley receive—and, assuredly, deserve—a large share of the travel-press ink that is devoted to Montana. Less publicized, though, and in many regards underappreciated, are Helena and Butte. The pair of old mining towns are two of Montana's most compelling cities, each mixing a colorful history with a contemporary vigor and optimistic outlook for the future.

If you stop at only one place in **Helena**, make it the museum of the **Montana Historical Society**, located across from the state capitol at 225 North Roberts Street. The museum encompasses several wings, including the 10,000 square-foot Montana Homeland exhibit, which could stand on its own as one mighty fine museum. More than 2,000 artifacts trace the trail of humankind through Montana, beginning with the Native Americans who came into the country at least 11,500 years ago, and continuing through World War II. Along the way, the distinctive lives led by the mountain men, miners, homesteaders, and pioneer ranchers are explored. Displays focus on the tools and lifestyles of those who arrived in Montana largely to avail themselves of the wealth and diversity of natural resources, but who often grew to appreciate the territory for its natural beauty, as well.

Another wing displays the works of F. Jay Haynes, official photographer for the Northern Pacific Railroad from 1884 to 1904, and for Yellowstone National Park from 1887 to 1916. The exhibit includes images exposed and photographic equipment used by Haynes, along with an array of railroading and national park artifacts. Still another museum wing houses the Mackay Gallery of Charles M. Russell Art, which claims more than sixty original oils, watercolors, sculptures, pen-and-ink drawings, and unique illustrated correspondences created by the undisputed head wrangler of cowboy artists. The gallery's centerpiece is the large, lifelike *When the Land Belonged to God*, which spectacularly depicts a herd of bison on a rise overlooking an east slope, dry-country river. The backs of the beasts are lit by the slanted rays of the sun, while steam emanating from their nostrils appears to be puffing off the canvas and into the gallery.

The Montana Historical Society museum (telephone 406–444–2694) is open daily Memorial Day through Labor Day, and Monday through Saturday the rest of the year. Another property of the society is located a bit farther afield at 304 North Ewing: the **Original Governor's Mansion**. Built in 1888 as the private residence of William A. Chessman, the mansion was purchased by the state in 1913, then commenced housing nearly a half-century's worth of Montana governors and their families. To arrange to visit the grand mansion on a guided tour, call (406) 444–4789.

If you'd like to have a look at art that's newer and typically less realistic than that of Charlie Russell's—the contemporary artists intended it that way, no doubt—visit the **Holter Museum of Art** at 12 East Lawrence Street and/or the **Archie Bray Foundation for the Ceramic Arts**, located on the western fringe of town at the former brickyards of the Western Clay Manufacturing Company. The latter, a nationally renowned ceramic-arts school, is surrounded by an extensive grounds filled with fun and unexpected ceramic creatures and other creations of clay.

For historic lodgings while in town, consider bunking at the **Sanders Bed and Breakfast**, located close to the Original Governor's Mansion at 328 North Ewing. The house was constructed in 1875 as a residence for the family of Wilbur Sanders, who arrived in Bannack early on, with the wagon train of Sidney Edgerton. Edgerton, who was Sanders's uncle, had traveled to Bannack in 1863 to assume the post of chief justice of the Idaho Territory; a year later he became the first governor of the whittled-down Montana Territory (*see* History). Wilbur Sanders, meantime, was a force in organizing the Vigilantes Committe, which led to a political career that saw him become one of Montana's original U.S. senators when statehood was achieved in 1889.

Today the comfortable, seven-room Sanders Bed and Breakfast (telephone 406–442–3309) remains filled with many of the furnishings of the original residents. It's owned and operated by the husband-and-wife team of Rock Ringling and Bobbi Uecker. Rock, a member of the famous

Ringling Brothers Circus family, can spin some humorous tales about life as a young boy at the family ranch in Ringling, Montana, where visitors were as likely to see an elephant as a cow.

Last Chance Gulch, where gold was struck by a group of Georgians in 1864, today is a closed-to-cars pedestrian mall packed with offices and businesses. It's fun simply to stroll along the main walk and look for intriguing things decorating the exterior of many of the old buildings, such as garish gargoyles and giant lizards. One enterprise you should see the *inside* of is the one-of-a-kind **Parrot Confectionery**. For three quarters of a century the Parrot has been fashioning and selling handmade chocolates, today utilizing the same recipes they used in 1922, when the shop began life at 22 North Last Chance Gulch. (It moved to its "new" location at 42 North Last Chance Gulch in 1935.) In addition to scrumptious chocolates, the Parrot also dishes out regionally lusted-after chili, ice cream, and other goodies.

To learn more about Last Chance Gulch and other aspects of historic Helena, jump on board the **Last Chance Tour Train** (telephone 406–442–1023). Sites visited on the hour-long tour include the restored brick miners' shanties lining **Reeder's Alley**, the plethora of opulent Victorian homes in the "millionaires' district," and **St. Helena Cathedral**, a spectacular Catholic church adorned with 230-foot-high spires, which was patterned after the Votive Church in Vienna, Austria. Trains depart from the Montana Historical Society museum several times daily between May 15 and September 30. Special tours can be arranged, too, between April 15 and May 14 and from October 1 through October 15.

As intriguing as the history of Helena is, many veteran visitors would contend that the lakes and hills beyond town constitute the best reason to go there. Excellent hiking is as close as **Mount Helena**, which holds a 900-acre city park bordering the west side of town. Immense **Canyon Ferry Lake,** and smaller **Hauser and Holter lakes**—wide spots in the Missouri River, actually, backed up by a trio of dams—are highly developed recreation areas popular for camping, boating, fishing, and windsurfing. The string of lakes is located a few miles outside Helena to the southeast, east, and northeast.

Heading south from town, Interstate 15

meanders along Prickly Pear Creek to the Peace Valley, an undulation of mountains and broad openings littered with dozens of old framed-in mines, piles of tailings, and vanishing ghost towns. Best known—and least vanished—is **Elkhorn**, a once-flourishing silver town whose steeply slanting streets hold some of the best, and best-kept, examples of frontier architecture in Glacier-Gold Country. One particularly attractive structure is the two-story Greek Revival–style Fraternity Hall. It could be considered the mascot for Montana ghost towns, so often has its likeness appeared on the printed page. Through the decades the building hosted boxing matches, parties, plays, and who-knows-what other events. To track down Elkhorn, leave the interstate at **Boulder**, drive 7 miles south on State Highway 69 (passing **Boulder Hot Springs** on the right at roughly the halfway point), then go 12 miles east and north on the gravel Elkhorn Road.

Another good backcountry drive that will take you past ample evidence of early mining activities: Forest Road 175, heading north from the settlement of **Basin** up aptly named Cataract Creek. An out-and-back trip on the gravel, oftentimes narrow road will lead you along the tumbling stream as it cuts through Deerlodge National Forest lands, and past old mines with names such as Morning Glory and Hattie Ferguson.

Several dead mines in the Boulder-Basin area have been resurrected as destinations where folks come expressly to descend underground to breathe and absorb low levels of radon gas. One of them: **The Free Enterprise Health Mine** (telephone toll-free 800–474–8657; also has an RV campground). The gas is rumored to relieve all sorts of ailments, from allergies to arthritis. Never mind that thousands of people throughout the Northern Rockies region have spent hundreds of dollars to rid their basements of radon, which others say is a health hazard!

From Basin, for a fun mini-adventure you might choose to drive under the interstate, then go west on what becomes a signed "non-maintained cattle access trail." Typically in passenger-car-friendly condition, the path closely parallels Interstate 15 through the canyon of the Boulder River. Five miles from Basin it passes under I–15, leading from the south to the north side of the interstate. After going through a tunnel approximately 5 miles from that point, the road skirts several pleasant, informal campsites, then empties onto a paved road. At a point 22.5 miles from Basin you'll want to drive onto Interstate 15, Butte-bound.

The choppy land-ownership patterns surrounding **Butte**—patterns you can see represented by a maze of white-against-green on the Deerlodge National Forest visitor map—are indicative of a mining region. (In non-mining areas property divisions tend to follow section lines, so right angles are the norm.) Butte fills part of a sloping, mile-high bowl defined by an erratic, 180-degree curve in the Continental Divide. The city spreads west and south over the surface of what remains of the "Richest Hill on Earth." Appearing tarnished and neglected at first glance, Butte is like an East-Coast blue-collar town that has seen better days, and which somehow and for some reason was deposited amid the high hills of Montana.

But the timeworn buildings and mining scars cloak a unique allure, one that grows on people as they become better acquainted with Butte. The point being: Don't bypass Butte because of what you may have heard about it, and don't leave too quickly simply because you don't think you like the way it looks. Think it over for a while first. Drive to **Joe's Pasty Shop**, located at Harrison and Grand. There you can sample one or two of the hard-crusted meat-and-potato pies that early Welsh and Cornish miners carried in their lunch buckets deep into the Butte mines. Pasties (*PASS-tees*) are as symbolic of Butte as is the **Berkeley Pit**, the hole that remains after a large share of the Richest Hill on Earth was dug up, beginning in 1955, and hauled to Anaconda to be smelted for copper. The 7,000-foot long, 5,600-foot wide, and 1,600-foot deep pit displaced entire mini-towns on Butte's east side, after the Anaconda Company bought up hundreds of working-class homes, along with businesses, schools, boardinghouses, and even the lavish Columbia Gardens amusement park to make way for their open-pit mine.

When mining operations ceased in 1982, the pumping of water also stopped. Groundwater, rising through hundreds of miles of tunnels webbing Butte Hill, began seeping into the pit. The resultant toxic soup that you see today, splashing against the scarred banks of a disemboweled earth,

Berkeley Pit, Butte, Montana

is a tremendously ugly legacy remaining from years of abuse. It's also extremely fascinating, and one of the city's biggest attractions.

For a little contrast, and to preview how Butte plans to enter the twenty-first century with a tourist-attracting vengeance, drive to the large, new **Butte–Silver Bow Chamber of Commerce Visitor Center** at 1000 George Street. (It's located next to the KOA Kampground off Montana Street, north of Interstate 90 at exit 126.) Staffers will direct you to at least a dozen additional sites they'll say you shouldn't miss—and they're probably right. Among them is the hard-to-find **Granite Mountain Mine Memorial**, located off North Main near the neighborhood/village of Walkerville. The memorial commemorates the 1917 Speculator Mine fire, which took 168 miners' lives, making it the worst hard-rock mining disaster in American history. Nearby, head frames remaining from three defunct mines stand hard against the skyline, looking like timber skeletons. In the southern distance, though, spread the living forests of the Highland Mountains, along whose ridgeline runs the Continental Divide. The Highlands are vivid reminders that, even in industrial-strength Butte, the beckoning backcountry is never far from reach when you're in western Montana.

Easier to locate than the mine memorial is the volunteer-built **World Museum of Mining & Hell Roarin' Gulch**. The sprawling indoor-outdoor museum and artificial town occupy the twelve-acre grounds of the old Orphan Girl silver and zinc mine. Hell Roarin' Gulch is a "town" of 1899, replete with dozens of artifact- and antiques-packed enterprises. These include a lawyer's office, sauerkraut factory (really!), millinery shop, general store, funeral and embalming parlor, and Chinese laundry. The museum continues onto the two floors of the Orphan Girl's old hoist house, where you'll find more old photos and historic paraphernalia than you'll have time to investigate. The museum (telephone 406–723–7211), located at the west end of Granite Street, is open from mid-June through Labor Day seven days a week from 9:00 A.M. to 9:00 P.M. Spring and fall hours are 10:00 A.M. to 5:00 P.M. Tuesday through Sunday. It's closed during the long, bitter Butte winters, from November through March.

The World Museum of Mining is one stop on the route of **Old Number 1**, a gas-powered replica of the electric trolley cars that ran through the streets of a younger Butte. Ninety-minute tours depart from the visitor center (telephone 406–723–3177) several times daily from June through September. Other stops along the way include the Berkeley Pit overlook, the **Mineral Museum** at Montana Tech, and the **Mai Wah**, a former noodle parlor housing displays that focus on the Asian heritage of Butte and the Northern Rockies.

Other features in Butte worthy of a visit include a slew of antiques, collectible, and junk stores, where you're guaranteed to find things you never knew were invented. One of the more interesting shops—in regard to its earlier life if not its present inventory—is the **Dumas Red Light Antique Mall**, situated at 45 East Mercury. The Dumas was the longest-running of the numerous two-story brothels that graced the stretch of East Mercury known as Venus Alley. In fact, the Dumas was built in 1890 for that purpose, and it continued filling the role until 1982. Another recommended stop: the **Copper King Mansion**, former home of mining magnate William Andrews Clark, which is located at 219 West Granite. The national historic site is open daily for tours from May 1 through October 31, from 9:00 A.M. to 4:00 P.M., and by appointment the rest of the year (telephone 406–782–7580). The mansion also serves year-round as a bed and breakfast, letting five grand rooms each night to a few fortunate overnighters.

The home of Charles Clark, son of William A. Clark, is another place you should take a gander at. Known today as the **Arts Chateau**, the lavish, castle-like structure is located at 321 West Broadway. It encompasses an art gallery, with period furnishings on loan from The University of Montana. (All three of the previously described attractions are briefly visited on the Old Number 1 tour.)

Individuals representing dozens of ethnic groups migrated to Butte in the late 1800s, when the city was growing into the leading copper producer in the world. By 1917 the city's bloated population of 100,000 comprised former residents of Poland, China, Italy, Croatia, Finland, Serbia, Sweden, Lebanon, Austria, Mexico, Germany, and many other countries, including Ireland. For a literal taste of Butte's colorful past-

Copper King Mansion, Butte

meets-present, wind down the day at the **Irish Times Pub**, situated in Uptown at 2 East Galena in the old Butte *Daily Post* newspaper building. Per capita, few towns or cities in America can rival Butte's population of smilin' Irish folks—a fact you're sure to hear more about at this popular meeting place. The pub features both furnishings and brews imported from Ireland.

If daylight remains, spend some time just wandering around the old Uptown area. (A good "Walking Tour of Historic Butte" is outlined in the visitor guide available at the visitor center.)

Although much of the wealth produced during the heyday of the mining era seeped beyond the borders of Montana and into the pockets of investors living far away, a good deal of it was invested in a youthful Butte, as well. As you will see, if Butte ever manages to pull off a major urban renewal effort, the lavish old buildings residing in the historic business district will compose a downtown area rivaled by few, if any, in the Northern Rockies. It would take millions of dollars to make it happen but, considering the can-do attitude of the city's hardy residents, some day it probably will.

SCENIC DRIVES OUT OF OLD BUTTE

If you've grown fond of the dirt and gravel roads so commonly found threading the outback of Montana, here's another to add to your been-there-done-that list. For this one be sure your tires are good and that you're carrying a detailed map, such as the Deerlodge National Forest visitor map.

Head south from the east edge of Butte on Continental Drive, crossing over Interstate 90

and, just over a mile later, passing the **U.S. High Altitude Sports Center** speed-skating facility. At a point 5.5 miles from the interstate turn left onto State Highway 2, where you'll enter Thompson Park and pass the **Lion's Den Campground**. After driving a little more than 2 miles on the state highway, turn right onto Forest Road 84/Roosevelt Drive. Approximately 3 miles later, at an intersection located in an area of rural homes, continue straight rather than bearing right. Soon you'll enter the Butte watershed-protection area, where you'll earn spectacular views of the Berkeley Pit and its mountainous backdrop as you climb toward the Continental Divide.

On cresting the Divide, continue straight rather than turning left toward Highland Lookout. The road dips into a rolling, open park, adorned with sagebrush thickets and stands of aspen, and offering views in the direction of the distant Pioneer Mountains. Five miles from the Divide you'll want to bear right at the intersection where a sign points you toward Interstate 15 (and BUTTE—15 MILES). In another 6.5 miles, at the bottom of a precipitous dive the road passes under

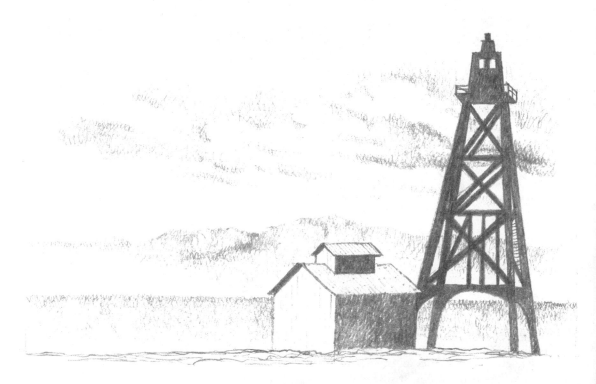

Butte Skyline

Interstate 15, at a point roughly 10 miles south of the Interstate 90 junction. Go a mile north on the frontage road and you'll come to an interchange where you can get on the interstate. Alternatively, by heading west from this point on Divide Creek Road, in 6 miles you'll come to the timber-protected **Beaver Dam Campground**. From there the road continues upward, deteriorating in quality as it climbs into the resplendent high country flanking 9,436-foot **Mount Fleecer**.

Scenery- and history-rich driving possibilities from Butte that are paved include an outstanding 170-mile loop to the southeast. To begin, head south and east on State Highway 2, passing through Whitehall en route to the intriguing **Lewis and Clark Caverns State Park**. From there the route heads south along U.S. Highway 287. A short, highly recommended spur from the community of Harrison climbs to pretty **Pony**, an old mining settlement perched on the sloping flank of the Tobacco Root Mountains. By traveling roughly 7 miles from Pony on dirt roads leading through the Beaverhead National Forest, if you're lucky, you can find **The Lodge at Potosi** (telephone, toll-free 800–770–0088), at once one of the most remote and most sumptuous hot springs resorts in Glacier-Gold Country.

The main route continues to the Madison River fly-fishing epicenter of **Ennis**. From there you'll want to go east on State Highway 287 to the well-preserved Old West settlement of **Virginia City**. Virginia City, which in its entirety is listed as a National Historic Landmark, is the present seat of Madison County and the past capital of the Montana Territory. Until recently, most of Virginia City's sites were privately owned and operated . . . and on the auction block. Fortunately, the state of Montana has purchased the town, securing its future as a place for visitors to continue earning vivid impressions of the nineteenth-century gold rush days.

From Virginia City–Nevada City, return to Butte via State Highways 287, 41, and 2. On the way you'll visit the quaint town of **Twin Bridges**, near which the Ruby, Beaverhead, and Big Hole rivers merge to become the Jefferson River. The short-run Jefferson, in turn, contributes to the Missouri River only 60 miles to the northeast at Headwaters State Park.

A drive of an almost equal distance—160

miles—makes for a great loop on the opposite, northwest side of Butte. Begin by heading northwest on Interstate 90. Seven miles past the Interstate 15 junction you'll want to leave I–90 at the **Gregson Fairmont Hot Springs** exit. A low-traffic road winds west past the popular resort—where there are golf, hot pools, fine lodging, and other amenities—then curves north to meet State Highway 1. A left turn onto that road leads into **Anaconda**, surely one of the longest, narrowest towns in America.

Anaconda was founded to serve as a dumping ground of sorts. Because of Butte's worsening air-pollution problems in the early 1880s—the air was turning poisoned and thick with sulfur smoke—Marcus Daly's Anaconda Company built its huge Washoe Smelter and Reduction Works in neighboring Anaconda, to where ore was subsequently hauled from the Butte mines. The **Anaconda Smelter Stack**, an idle giant nearly 600 feet high, remains as testimony to those times. So do surrounding hillsides largely denuded of trees and other vegetation, a result of nearly a century's worth of toxic smoke belching from the stack.

A much newer addition to town, but one built on a foundation of history: the **Old Works Golf Course**, which opened to the public in 1997. When the Atlantic Richfield Company (ARCO) bought out the Anaconda Company in 1977, one of the "assets" acquired was the severely contaminated earth surrounding the old smelter works, where the ground was toxic with arsenic and other heavy metals. In 1983 the U.S. Environmental Protection Agency granted the area the dubious distinction of Superfund site, leaving ARCO with two options: They could remove tons of tailings and slag—but put it where, and at what cost?—or somehow reclaim the area, sealing off the poisoned grounds.

The creative solution was to build a golf course, a feat accomplished through a unique partnership involving ARCO, the EPA, the community of Anaconda, the state of Montana, and golf pro Jack Nicklaus. "I think it's kind of fun to take something that people think is not pretty and make something pretty of it," Nicklaus said in 1992, as plans materialized. Plenty of people scoffed at the idea of Anaconda infamously tarnished, ailing, and winter-battered—becoming another Pebble

Beach. Naysayers were ignored, though, and, almost miraculously, a piece of trashed countryside has successfully been transformed into a prestigious Jack Nicklaus Signature Design golf course, the first of its kind in Montana.

The world-class 18-hole facility is surprisingly affordable to play, thanks to its city-county ownership and ARCO subsidization. The course winds along Warm Springs Creek, incorporating old brick walls, smokestack flues, and other features that were either left in place or added as reminders of the mining heritage. Bunkers, instead of holding the usual white sand, are filled with fine black slag, a by-product of the smelting process. A layer of limestone underlying the sod of the golf course serves as a cap that is expected to seal off the contaminates below from the possibility of water percolating through, picking up toxins, and contaminating the groundwater. Though some environmentalists consider the whole affair nothing but sleight of hand on the part of ARCO—covering up the waste, that is, to avoid the cost of removing it—there's no arguing that the resultant golf course is now a true asset for Anaconda, one that is attracting a lot of curious folks to the old blue-collar company town.

Not far from Anaconda hides gorgeous **Lost Creek State Park**. Bighorn sheep and mountain goats can often be spotted on the 1,200-foot-high cliffs of the canyon of Lost Creek, while lower down a pair of campgrounds totaling a couple of dozen sites await human beings who take the trouble to find the place. To be one of them, travel east 1.5 miles from Anaconda on State Highway 1, then 2 miles north on State Highway 273, and, finally, 6 miles west on the park road.

From Anaconda follow State Highway 1 to **Georgetown Lake**, passing the right-hand turn to **Discovery Basin**. The mid-sized alpine ski area offers 1,300 feet of vertical drop and a good bargain for the skier's buck. During the snowless months a string of Deerlodge National Forest campgrounds surrounding the shore of Georgetown Lake provides a host of agreeable overnighting options for those equipped to camp.

After descending Flint Creek Hill continue downstream past Philipsburg, home to the **Ghost Town Hall of Fame**, then to Drummond, where you'll want to head eastbound onto Interstate 90. (At this point, incidentally, you're only 50 miles east of Missoula.) Continue past Garrison Junction to Deer Lodge, whose attractions have been succinctly summarized on a billboard that boasts "Cowboys, Cars, and Cons." The "Cons" refers to the operational state penitentiary and to the **Old Montana Prison**, the first territorial prison built in the Western United States and in use until 1979. Within the old prison complex is the **Montana Law Enforcement Museum**, which commemorates, among other things, the more than one hundred Montana officers who have been killed while on duty; and the **Frontier Montana Museum**, displaying artifacts from the Old West, with a focus on firearms and antique booze bottles.

"Cars" relates to the **Towe Ford Museum**, located adjacent to the prison complex. More than a hundred classic Ford models, all shining like new, are on exhibit. The automobiles are the legacy of Mr. Edward Towe, a Ford man with few peers.

Finally, the "Cowboys" in the phrase celebrates not only cowhands currently residing in and around Deer Lodge, but also the **Grant-Kohrs Ranch National Historic Site**. Located at the north end of town just off Main, the ranch's roots reach back to the late 1850s, when a Canadian mountain man named Johnny Grant settled in the Deer Lodge Valley, establishing one of the first cattle spreads in the future state of Montana. He moved the operation closer to the town's location in 1862, then sold out four years later to Conrad Kohrs, a German immigrant who was a butcher by trade. Kohrs married a woman named Augusta Kruse in 1868, then took his half-brother John Bielenberg on as a partner. Together they grew the operation to the point where their cattle grazed on not only vast portions of the Deer Lodge Valley, but also on more than a million acres stretching across four states and into Canada.

Today the ranch is the only National Park Service site dedicated exclusively to the lifeways of the nineteenth-century cowboy and cattleman. Covering 1,500 acres, the park contains a bonanza of old buildings and implements, while exhibits and living-history demonstrations trace the long history of the Northern Rockies cattle industry. Grant-Kohrs Ranch National Historic Site (telephone 406–846–2070) is open daily year-round.

From Deer Lodge, a 40-mile drive south and east on Interstate 90 will deliver you back to Butte.

⎯⎯⎯⎯〰〰 Staying There

Dozens of small and medium-sized towns, many with motels, bed and breakfasts, and/or nearby guest ranches, grace western Montana's towns and rural areas. Bowing to space limitations and personal preferences, this section focuses primarily on the communities of Dillon, Hamilton, Missoula, Bigfork, Whitefish/Glacier National Park, Helena, and Butte, with occasional inclusions of particularly enticing or unusual lodgings, campgrounds, and restaurants in the outlying areas (and with others mentioned sporadically in Seeing Glacier-Gold Country).

To receive a comprehensive, bare-bones listing of accommodations for the entire state, call Travel Montana at (800) 847–4868 (within Montana call 406–444–2654) and request the annually updated *Montana Travel Planner*. For detailed information on a network of lodgings in northwest Montana, spanning the region from Polson to Glacier National Park, you can call Montana Reservation Central at (406) 862–7589 or, toll-free in the United States, (888) 224–4759.

Dillon and the Big Hole Valley

LODGING

In Dillon

Best Western Paradise Inn. 650 North Montana Street. Dillon's full-service accommodation, with restaurant, lounge, and pool on the premises. Telephone: (406) 683–4214. Inexpensive to moderate.

Centennial Inn. 122 South Washington. Comfortable bed-and-breakfast inn doubling as a quality dining house. Telephone: (406) 683–4454 or, toll-free in the United States, (800) 483–4454. Moderate.

Comfort Inn. 450 North Interchange. Telephone: (406) 683–6831 or, toll-free in the United States, (800) 442–INNS (4667). Inexpensive to moderate.

Creston Motel. 335 South Atlantic. Economy lodgings also boasting the "Best Montana T-Shirt Shop in Town." Telephone: (406) 683–2341. Very inexpensive to inexpensive.

Super 8 Motel. 550 North Montana. Some units include microwaves and refrigerators. Telephone: (406) 683–4288 or, toll-free in the United States, (800) 800–8000. Inexpensive.

Out of Dillon

Beaverhead National Forest Recreational Cabins. Three rustic cabins located in the forests above the Big Hole Valley—the May Creek, Twin Lakes, and Hogan cabins—are available to rent in winter for those traveling by snowmobile or cross-country skis. Reservations are accepted for the following winter beginning October 15; bookings, particularly for weekends, go quickly after that date. Call the Wisdom Ranger District at (406)

689–3243 to make reservations or to request additional information.

Hildreth Livestock Ranch. Located off the Big Sheep Creek Back Country Byway, 23 miles south of Route 324 (which meets Interstate 15 at the north end of Clark Canyon Reservoir). Working cattle ranch in a wonderfully remote location, offering accommodations in kitchen-equipped cabins or in a new guest house. Includes private fishing pond and family-style meals. Telephone: (406) 681–3111. Call for rates, which vary.

Red Rock Inn. Located in Dell, 40 miles south of Dillon on Interstate 15. Recently renovated, century-old inn that provides ready access to the Centennial Valley and the Big Sheep Creek Back Country Byway. Rents seven cozy rooms, including one with a hot tub. Also features a good restaurant serving dinner Wednesday through Sunday. Telephone: (406) 276–3501. Moderate.

Rush's Lakeview Guest Ranch. Located in Lakeview, near the headquarters of Red Rock Lakes National Wildlife Refuge. Offers weeklong summer stays, fall hunting, and winter snowmobiling and skiing; wildlife photography is a year-round option. Rush's also trains guides through their professional outfitters school. Telephone: (406) 276–3300 summer, 494–2585 winter. Expensive.

CAMPGROUNDS AND RV PARKS

Private

Dillon KOA. 735 East Park. Large campground located on the Beaverhead River, with tent and RV sites, pool, Kamping Kabins, and gift shop. Telephone: toll-free, (800) 562–2751.

Maverick Mountain RV Park. Located on the Pioneer Mountains National Scenic Byway, near Maverick Mountain ski area. Open year-round;

Melrose still life

also has cabins and bed and breakfast service available. Telephone: (406) 834–3452.

U.S. Forest Service

Call the Wisdom Ranger District at 406–689–3243 for additional campground information.

Miner Lake. From Jackson, 10 miles west on county and Forest Service roads.

Pioneer Mountains National Scenic Byway. Several exceptionally pleasant Forest Service campgrounds are found along this road, which connects Route 278 and State Highway 43. Among them: **Grasshopper**, **Mono Creek**, **Little Joe**, **Willow**, and **Fourth of July**.

Twin Lakes. Seven miles south of Wisdom on Route 278, then 13 miles southwest on county and Forest Service roads.

Montana Department of Fish, Wildlife and Parks

Bannack State Park. From 5 miles south of Dillon, 21 miles west on Route 278 and then 4 miles south on park road. Campground, adjacent to historic ghost town, is open year-round. Legendary for its mosquitoes in summer, so go prepared! Telephone: (406) 834–3413.

U.S. Bureau of Reclamation

Clark Canyon Reservoir. Twenty miles south of Dillon on Interstate 15. Several campgrounds, each featuring tent and trailer sites, surround the shore of this large reservoir. Open year-round.

FOOD

In Dillon

Anna's Oven. 120 South Montana. Telephone: (406) 683–5766. Specializing in fresh-baked bread, soups, salads, and sandwiches. Breakfast and lunch. Inexpensive.

Longhorn Saloon & Grill. 8 North Montana. Telephone: (406) 683–6839. Comfortable

restaurant offering daily lunch and dinner specials. Breakfast, lunch, and dinner. Inexpensive to moderate.

Out of Dillon

Big Hole Crossing Restaurant. Located in Wisdom. Telephone: (406) 689–3800. A surprising find in this small Big Hole outpost, serving Western fare for breakfast, lunch, and dinner. Inexpensive.

Yesterday's Calf-A. Located in Dell, 40 miles south of Dillon on Interstate 15. Telephone: (406) 276–3308. One-of-a-kind schoolhouse turned eatery/museum, serving down-home food prepared from scratch. Also encompasses the Little Red Schoolhouse gift shop. Breakfast, lunch, and dinner. Inexpensive.

BICYCLING

As in all of Glacier-Gold Country, excellent mountain and road biking routes lace the hills and valleys surrounding Dillon. For specific route information, go to **Backcountry Bike & Boards** (telephone 406–683–9696), located at 35 East Bannack.

FISHING

Good trout waters are found in every direction from Dillon. They include the Big Hole River, Red Rock River, Beaverhead River, Blacktail Deer Creek, and Lima and Clark Canyon reservoirs. For information, equipment, and/or to hire a guide, visit **Frontier Anglers** (telephone 406–683–5276), located in Dillon at 680 North Montana.

HORSEBACK RIDING

Diamond Hitch Outfitters. 3405 Ten Mile Road. Telephone: toll-free (800) 368–5494. Specializing in horseback rides to surrounding high lakes for fishing and camping. Also arranges fishing and scenic floats on the Big Hole and Beaverhead rivers.

HOT SPRINGS

Elkhorn Hot Springs. Located toward the south end of the Pioneer Mountains National Scenic Byway, 13 miles north of Route 278. Interesting woodsy resort with restaurant, and lodging in very primitive cabins. Close to Maverick Mountain ski area. Telephone: (406) 834–3434.

Jackson Hot Springs Lodge. Located in tiny Jackson, population 50. Great hot pool and bar, good dining, and comfortable cabin accommodations. Telephone: (406) 834–3151.

SKIING

Maverick Mountain. Located west of Dillon on Route 278, then north on the Pioneer Mountains National Scenic Byway. Telephone: (406) 834–3454. Despite its remote location, this day-use area attracts plenty of skiers in winter, thanks to its prodigious snowfall and more-than-respectable vertical drop of 2,100 feet. Lodging is available nearby.

SHOPPING

Johnson Saddlery. Located in Dillon across from the old Metlen Hotel at 125 West Bannack. Telephone: (406) 683–4452. Traditional saddlery also selling belt buckles, jewelry, and other quality Western items of potential interest even to nonequestrians.

Kirkpatrick Custom Hat Co. Occupies a small, false-front building near the main highway in the town of Wisdom. Telephone: (406) 689–3630. Producers and purveyors of fine Western-style hats; also offers cleaning, blocking, and renovation services.

Old West Cinema Gallery and Gifts. 23 North Idaho in Dillon. Telephone: (406) 683–4600. This place is packed full of great gift items, most of them made in Montana: Monte Dolack prints, huckleberry candy and jams, and much more.

Patagonia Outlet Store. 34 North Idaho. Telephone: (406) 683–2580. Good deals on high-end Patagonia outdoor wear can often be procured at this unexpected Dillon find.

TELEPHONE NUMBERS

Beaverhead Chamber of Commerce. 125 South Montana, Dillon. (406) 683–5511.

Dillon Ranger District (Beaverhead National Forest). 420 Barrett Street. (406) 683–3900.

Bureau of Land Management's Dillon Resource Area. 1005 Selway Drive. (406) 683–2337.

Hamilton and the Bitterroot Valley

LODGING

In Hamilton

Best Western Hamilton Inn. 409 South 1st Street. Telephone: (406) 363–2142 or, toll-free in the United States, (800) 426–4586. Inexpensive to moderate.

Comfort Inn. 1113 North 1st Street. Motel featuring sixty-four rooms, hot tub and sauna, and a Lucky Lil's Casino. Telephone: (406) 363–6600 or, toll-free in the United States, (800) 442–INNS (4667). Inexpensive to moderate.

Sportsman Motel. 410 North 1st Street. Sixteen rooms, most with a double and a queen. Close to shopping and restaurants. Telephone: (406) 363–2411. Very inexpensive to inexpensive.

Out Of Hamilton

Guest ranches, bed and breakfasts, resort lodges, and vacation-home rentals all abound in the Bitterroot Valley. For a comprehensive listing, call the Bitterroot Valley Chamber of Commerce at (406) 363–2400. Here's just a quartet of possibilities.

Broad Axe Lodge. Located 5.5 miles east of Sula up the East Fork Road. Fully furnished cabins with kitchens and baths; also features restaurant and lounge. Bighorn sheep can often be seen from the lodge. Telephone: (406) 821–3878. Moderate.

Camp Creek Inn B&B Guest Ranch. Located 9 miles north of Lost Trail Pass on U.S. Highway 93 (38 miles south of Hamilton). Great old main lodge and cabins, with breakfasts sized for a hard-working wrangler. Trail rides and backcountry pack trips in summer, and special Lost Trail Powder Mountain ski packages in winter. Telephone: (406) 821–3508. Inexpensive to moderate.

Deer Crossing Bed & Breakfast. Outside Hamilton at 396 Hayes Creek Road. Pleasant inn situated on twenty-five scenic acres. Three guest rooms, bunkhouse, and two suites for rent. Telephone: (406) 363–2232 or, toll-free in the United States, (800) 763–2232. Moderate to expensive.

West Fork Meadows Ranch. Twenty-four miles southwest of Conner on West Fork Road/Route 473 (a mile past Painted Rocks Reservoir). Unexpectedly sumptuous lodgings and enticing, European-flair dining deep in the wilderness. Trail rides, jeep outings, fishing, snowmobiling, and other activities await. Telephone: (406) 349–2468 or, toll-free in the United States, (800) 800–1437. Expensive to very expensive.

CAMPGROUNDS AND RV PARKS

Private

Angler's Roost. Three miles south of Hamilton on U.S. Highway 93. Also rents cabins and provides river shuttles for floaters and anglers. Telephone: (406) 363–1268.

Lick Creek Campground. Ten miles south of Hamilton on U.S. Highway 93. The name of this enterprise has a catchy rhyme to it, so long as you pronounce "creek" like a good Montanan *(crik).* Pleasant tent and RV sites close to great fishing. Telephone: (406) 821–3840.

St. Mary's Motel & RV Park. Situated at 3889 U.S. Highway 93 in Stevensville. Spaces for tents, trailers, and motor homes. Convenience store and bowling alley nearby. Telephone: (406) 777–2838.

Sula Store and Campground. Located at Sula,

35 miles south of Hamilton on U.S. Highway 93. Telephone: (406) 821–3364.

Montana Fish, Wildlife and Parks

Painted Rocks State Park. Located 23 miles southwest of Conner on Route 473.

U.S. Forest Service

Call the Bitterroot National Forest supervisor's office at 406–363–3131 for additional campground information.

Black Bear. From 3 miles south of Hamilton, 13 miles east on State Highway 38. Several miles farther east this road, also known as the Skalkaho Road, ties in with the Rock Creek Road, which meets Interstate 90 at a point 22 miles east of Missoula. Highly recommended backcountry driving loop.

Blodgett Canyon. Located 5 miles northwest of Hamilton.

Charles Waters. Located 4 miles north of Stevensville on U.S. Highway 93, then 3 miles west on Bass Creek Road.

Spring Gulch. Located 5 miles northwest of Sula on U.S. Highway 93. One mile southwest of here on a forest road is **Indian Trees Campground**; 3 miles farther yet is **Crazy Creek Horse Camp**.

FOOD

Cantina la Cocina. Located on U.S. Highway 93 in the town of Victor, 12 miles north of Hamilton. Telephone: (406) 642–3192. Good homemade Mexican food and "almost famous" margaritas. Also features cocktail lounge and casino. Dinner only. Inexpensive to moderate.

The Hamilton, A Public House. 104 Main Street in Victor. Telephone: (406) 642–6644. In the spirit of an English pub, the Hamilton specializes in fish and chips and imported beers. Lunch and dinner (closed Sundays). Inexpensive.

La Trattoria Italian Restaurant. 315 South 3rd

Street in Hamilton. Telephone: (406) 363–5030. Meals prepared from scratch daily, served in the fireside ambience of a Victorian home. Dinner only. Inexpensive to moderate.

Morning Glory Coffee House. 111 South 4th Street in Hamilton. Telephone: (406) 363–7500. Cozy meeting place occupying a sumptuous Victorian house. In addition to fine coffees, Morning Glory serves muffins, scones, croissants, and sandwiches. Open "early to latte," meaning to 9:00 P.M. or later.

FISHING

The main Bitterroot, as well as its upper forks, offers good fishing for trout. For information visit the **Fishaus** (telephone 406–363–6158), a fly-fishing specialty shop located at 702 North 1st Street in Hamilton.

HOT SPRINGS

Lost Trail Hot Springs Resort. Located at the northern foot of Lost Trail Pass, west off U.S. Highway 93. Features cabins, condos with lofts, teepees, campground, dining room and lounge, and natural hot-mineral pool and hot tub. Telephone: (406) 821–3574 or, toll-free in the United States, (800) 825–3574. Inexpensive to moderate.

SKIING

Lost Trail Powder Mountain. Rises above Lost Trail Pass, 45 miles south of Hamilton on U.S. Highway 93. Telephone: (406) 821–3211. By no means is Lost Trail the largest ski area in Montana—the vertical drop is only 1,200 feet—but this day-use area consistently attracts deep accumulations of light powder snow that are the envy of bigger operations, such as The Big Mountain and Montana Snowbowl. Lodging is located just to the north in the Bitterroot Valley. Outstanding cross-country skiing can be found at nearby Chief Joseph Pass, where the Bitterroot Ski Club maintains groomed trails.

TELEPHONE NUMBERS

Bitterroot Valley Chamber of Commerce. 105 East Main, Hamilton. (406) 363–2400.

Bitterroot National Forest supervisor's office. 1801 North 1st Street. (406) 363–3131.

Missoula

LODGING

The following are all located relatively close to downtown Missoula and the campus of The University of Montana, where most travelers desiring to become acquainted with the city will naturally want to stay. Many additional options are located on South Brooks, at the I–90 Reserve Street interchange, in the bedroom community of Lolo, and at other locations.

Best Western Executive Inn. 201 East Main. Unbeatable downtown location, close to the Clark Fork River greenway. Telephone: (406) 543–7221 or, toll-free in the United States, (800) 528–1234. Moderate to expensive.

Birchwood Hostel. 600 South Orange. The trees that gave this hostel its name have recently been reduced to tall stumps, but the cordial hospitality remains the same as it's been for more than twenty years. Intrepid low-budget travelers from throughout the world recognize the Birchwood as a "must-stay" when visiting the Northern Rockies, and hundreds of them consider high-spirited host Ernie Franceschi a friend. The hostel features twenty-two beds divided among four rooms, one private room, a fully equipped kitchen, and a lounge–dining room. Telephone: (406) 728–9799. Very inexpensive.

Campus Inn. 744 East Broadway, just across the river from the university campus. Motel featuring eighty-two rooms, some with kitchenettes, and a heated pool, meeting room, and nearby restaurants. Telephone: (406) 549–5134 or, toll-free in the United States, (800) 232–8013. Inexpensive.

Creekside Inn. 630 East Broadway. "Rooms with Running Water" (the waters of Rattlesnake Creek, that is) are available at this motel, which also boasts a twenty-four-hour restaurant. Telephone: (406) 549–2387 or, toll-free in the United States, (800) 551–2387. Moderate.

Goldsmith's Inn. Located at 809 East Front, adjacent to the chamber of commerce building and to the footbridge leading to the university campus. Bed-and-breakfast inn associated with popular Missoula ice cream vendor, featuring rooms with private baths. Includes a honeymoon suite. Telephone: (406) 721–6732. Expensive to very expensive.

Holiday Inn Missoula Parkside. 200 South Pattee. Beautifully located along the Clark Fork River, this Holiday Inn features some 200 rooms, an indoor pool and spa complex, and a restaurant and lounge. Telephone: (406) 721–8550 or, toll-free in the United States, (800) 399–0408. Moderate to expensive.

Rock Creek Cabin

Hubbard's Ponderosa Lodge. 800 East Broadway. Conveniently located near The University of Montana campus. Telephone: (406) 543–3102 or, toll-free in the United States, (800) 341–8000. Inexpensive.

CAMPGROUNDS AND RV PARKS

Private

Ekstrom's Stage Station. Located 22 miles east of Missoula (I–90 exit 126), then a mile south on Rock Creek Road. Tent and RV sites located along Rock Creek, a nationally famous, blue-ribbon trout stream with few peers. Resort also features a cozy restaurant housed in a 110-year-old stage station. Telephone: (406) 825–3183.

Elkhorn RV Ranch. Located 22 miles east of Missoula (I–90 exit 126), then 4 miles south on Rock Creek Road. This resort enjoys an enviable mile of private frontage on Rock Creek. More than one-hundred sites, including pleasant, wooded tent sites right along the creek. Also offers fully furnished cabins with kitchens and baths. If you tire of fishing, there's also hiking in the Welcome Creek Wilderness, as well as nearby horseback riding and mountain biking. Telephone: (406) 825–3220.

KOA El-Mar Kampground. Tucked away in a secluded corner of Missoula at 3695 Tina Avenue. Full-service franchisee of the Billings, Montana–based KOA chain, featuring a swimming pool and plenty of trailer and tent sites. Open year-round. Telephone: (406) 549–0881.

Outpost Campground. North of I–90 exit 96 at 11600 North Highway 93, on the way to the Flathead Valley. En route to this one you'll also pass the **Jellystone RV Park**. Telephone: (406) 549–2016.

U.S. Forest Service

Call the Missoula Ranger District at 406–329–3814 for additional information.

Lewis & Clark. Located 15 miles west of Lolo on U.S. Highway 12.

Lee Creek. Located at the foot of Lolo Pass, 26 miles west of Lolo on U.S. Highway 12.

Montana Department of Fish, Wildlife and Parks

For more information call the agency's Missoula office at 406–542–5500.

Beavertail Hill. Located 26 miles southeast of Missoula, just off Interstate 90.

Chief Looking Glass. From 5 miles south of Lolo on U.S. Highway 93, 1 mile east.

FOOD

4-B's. Several locations, including a centrally located facility at 301 East Broadway. Telephone: (406) 543–7366. This Missoula-based chain, which opened its doors more than forty years ago, is a favorite of families and retirees. Open twenty-four hours. Inexpensive.

Bagels on Broadway. 223 West Broadway. Telephone: (406) 728–8900. Surprisingly good, New York-style bagels in a variety of flavors and with a host of spreads to adorn them. Also serves salads, sandwiches, and espresso. Inexpensive.

Bernice's Bakery. 190 South 3rd West (south of downtown, across the Clark Fork River). Telephone: (406) 728–1358. Serving scrumptious baked goods such as scones, muffins, and mini-pizzas, and a bold jolt of coffee that practically stands on its own.

The Bridge. Located upstairs at 515 South Higgins, just south of the Higgins Street Bridge. Telephone: (406) 542–0002. Italian and other specialties served in a cozy room that long ago served as a dance hall. Dinner only. Inexpensive to moderate.

Curley's Broiler. Located at 2915 Brooks. Telephone: (406) 728–9868. This low-profile restaurant seems to try to do its best to remain a secret. But the word is out, thanks to accolades such as those coming from the Montana Beef Council, which voted Curley's the best beef restaurant in Montana—and that's no mean feat in beef-abundant Big Sky Country. Curley's serves only U.S.D.A. Prime beef, aged for twenty-eight days and hand cut daily into 1¾-inch thicknesses. Dinner only. Expensive.

The Depot. Corner of Ryman and Railroad in downtown Missoula. Telephone: (406) 728–7007. For twenty-five years The Depot has been serving good dinners, making it one of Missoulians' three or four favorites for a special night out. "The Deck" (enclosed and heated in winter) is a casual addition popular with the after-work crowd for drinks and appetizers. Dinner only. Expensive.

Food for Thought. Located across the street from The University of Montana campus at 540 Daly Avenue. Telephone: (406) 721–6033. Hip college hangout, serving good food and coffee. Food for Thought has spawned related businesses in town, including the Second Thought News & Deli, located downtown at 529 South Higgins. Inexpensive. Breakfast, lunch, and dinner.

The Golden Pheasant. Downtown at 316 North Higgins. Telephone: (406) 728–9953. Established in 1941, this is one of Missoula's longest-running restaurants. The recently remodeled establishment features outstanding Chinese cuisine and a full-service bar. Lunch and dinner. Inexpensive to moderate.

Hob Nob Cafe. Located in the Union Club, downtown at 208 East Main. Telephone: (406) 542–3188. Out-of-the-ordinary specials served daily for lunch and supper on weekdays only. Moderate.

Loco's Burrito Bus. Changing locations around downtown. Homemade burritos with healthful ingredients and great flavor. Telephone: (406) 240–5050.

MacKenzie River Pizza Co. 137 West Front Street. Telephone: (406) 721–0077. Purveyors of pizza topped with things you never would think of putting on a pie. Also serves good salads and sandwiches. Lunch and dinner. Inexpensive.

The Mustard Seed. Located downtown at 419 West Front and also in Southgate Mall. Telephone: (406) 728–7825. Contemporary Oriental cuisine, with vegetarian options and special desserts made daily. Lunch and dinner. Inexpensive to moderate.

The Old Post Pub. Located downtown at 103 West Spruce. Telephone: (406) 721–7399. Microbrews, spirits, Southwest cuisine, and pasta specials are served at this pub located behind Worden's Market and across the street from the Iron Horse Brew Pub. Live jazz often livens the place up on evenings. Lunch and dinner. Inexpensive to moderate.

The Oxford. 337 North Higgins. Telephone: (406) 549–0117. You may or may not care to sample the house specialty of brains and eggs, but this is the place to go in downtown Missoula to witness an amazing array of humanity. Open twenty-four hours; also features a bar and gambling.

Paul's Pancake Parlor & Cafe. Located at 2305 Brooks in Trempers Shopping Center. Telephone: (406) 728–9071. A down-home diner that should not be missed if you like your sourdough pancakes *sour*. Breakfast, lunch, and dinner. Inexpensive.

Perugia. 1106 West Broadway. Telephone: (406) 543–3757. Relatively new restaurant run by a long-time Missoula chef and restaurateur. Perugia specializes in Mediterranean cuisine, whether it be Italian, Greek, Spanish, or Middle Eastern. Dinner only. Moderate to expensive.

The Shack. Located downtown at 222 West Main. Telephone: (406) 549–9903. The Shack—which originally *did* occupy a shack but today resides in much nicer digs—serves, arguably, the best breakfasts in Missoula. You can order breakfast for lunch or dinner, too, but a host of other dishes gracing the menu will tempt you at those times. Inexpensive to moderate.

Shadows Keep. Located at 102 Ben Hogan Drive, at the top of Whitaker Drive in Missoula's South Hills. Telephone: (406) 728–5132. Outstanding dinner restaurant whose spectacular predecessor, The Mansion, burned to the ground in a fire in the early 1990s. Shadows Keep, which also serves as the clubhouse for the Highlands Golf Club, specializes in fine steak, seafood, international cuisine, and the best views of Missoula in Missoula. Popular for banquets and parties. Dinner only. Expensive.

BICYCLING

Missoula is regularly heralded in the bicycling press as one of the premier cycling cities in America. Several good bike shops are located in town, including **Open Road Bicycles & Nordic Equipment** (telephone 406–549–2453), located at 517 South Orange.

The city's eminence in the two-wheeled world is largely due to the fact that it is home to the 35,000-member Adventure Cycling Association (telephone 406–721–1776), America's largest recreational bicycling organization. Visitors are welcome at the organization's office, headquartered downtown in the city's former Christian Science Church building at 150 East Pine. Among the highlights of a visit is an exhibit of vintage bicycles. Detailed information on local, regional, and nationwide road and mountain-bike rides can be obtained at Adventure Cycling, as well.

The local bike club sponsors the annual Tour of the Swan River Valley (TOSRV), a two-day, 221-mile ride in May. The event's several hundred spots consistently fill rapidly after registration opens. For information call the Chamber of Commerce at (406) 543–6623.

FAIRS, FESTIVALS, AND EVENTS

International Chorale Festival. Held several days in July at various venues in Missoula, every other year only. Incredibly beautiful and diverse musical menu, with all performances free. Telephone: (406) 728–4294.

International Wildlife Film Festival. This heralded event of national renown celebrated its twentieth anniversary in 1997, making it the world's longest-running juried wildlife-film competition. Begun by University of Montana bear researcher Charles Jonkel, the early April event draws some 200 film entries from the United States, Canada, Great Britain, and elsewhere. Festivities include public film viewings, a WildNight costume ball, and the very popular WildWalk Parade through downtown Missoula, in which kids of every age portray all sorts of critters. Telephone: (406) 728–9380.

Rock Creek Testicle Festival. Held annually in late September at the Rock Creek Lodge, 22 miles east of Missoula. That the same area can support events as disparate as the refined International Chorale Festival and a raucous celebration such as this, speaks volumes for its diversity of characters and interests. Not for the squeamish or shy, the Rock Creek Testicle Festival has been described as the "last best party in the last best place." It includes dancing, games (such as cowpie tossing), beer swilling, and dining on that most Western of delicacies—Rocky Mountain oysters, a.k.a. the testicles of bulls, calves, sheep, and/or lambs. The slippery little devils, which are typically battered and fried, taste—depending on who's doing the tasting and on the age of the animal when castrated—like chicken, liver, gizzard, or rubber bands dipped in castor oil. Telephone: (406) 825–4868.

Western Montana Fair. Held annually during the third week of August. If you like rain, visit Missoula during the fair, for old-timers swear that the skies never fail to open that week. This is a good, old-fashioned regional fair, with rodeos, horse racing, country-music acts, rides, games of chance, and buildings packed full of judged animals, baked goods, and arts and crafts. Telephone: (406) 721–FAIR (3247).

FISHING

Missoula-area trout fishing is exceptional, particularly on Rock Creek and along certain stretches of the Clarks Fork and Bitterroot rivers. To find out where and what the fish are biting, and/or to procure the services of a guide, visit **Grizzly Hackle** at 215 West Front (telephone 406–721–8996) or **Streamside Anglers** at 317

South Orange (telephone 406–728–1085), an enterprise owned by professional golfer Miller Barber. Staff at either shop can also provide information on local river runners, who offer thrilling white-water trips through Alberton Gorge on the Clark Fork River, down the Lochsa River (on the other side of Lolo Pass in Idaho), and elsewhere.

GOLF

If it has to do with the outdoors—from softball to hang-gliding—it probably has its legions of devotees in Missoula. Golf is no exception. An outstanding selection of public courses in and around town includes the nine-hole **University Golf Course**, located at 515 South Avenue East (telephone 406–728–8629); the community-owned, eighteen-hole **Larchmont Golf Course**, located at 3200 Old Fort Road (telephone 406–721–4416); the short, nine-hole **Linda Vista Golf Course**, found at 4915 Lower Miller Creek Road (telephone 406–251–3655); and the nine-hole **Highlands Golf Club**, located at 102 Ben Hogan Drive (telephone 406–728–7360). A bit farther afield, but only minutes away: the **King Ranch Golf Course**, located 15 miles west of Missoula in Frenchtown, at 17775 Mullan Road. King Ranch (telephone 406–626–4000) also boasts a good restaurant.

HOT SPRINGS

Lolo Hot Springs. Located on U.S. Highway 12, en route to the Lolo Pass Winter Sports Area. Open year-round, this spot is particularly popular with snowmobilers and cross-country skiers, who enjoy thawing out in the resort's indoor and outdoor hot pools after a cold day afield. In addition to the pools, the resort encompasses lodging, a restaurant, and a saloon. Telephone: (406) 273–2290.

SKIING

Marshall Mountain. Telephone: (406) 258–6000. Located 7 miles east of Missoula, north off State Highway 200. A locals' hill featuring a 1,500-foot vertical drop, night skiing, a snack bar, and a pub. Marshall often suffers from its low elevation and relatively warm temperatures, making it tough even to manufacture man-made snow. But when the snow is good, the skiing is great.

Montana Snowbowl. Located at 1700 Snowbowl Road, 12 miles from town off the I-90 Reserve Street exit. Telephone: (406) 549-9777 or, toll-free in the United States, (800) 728-2695. Snowbowl, boasting an impressive vertical drop of 2,600 feet, is adored by those who like their skiing steep and challenging. However, radical terrain and often icy conditions toward the bottom can make things worse than challenging for beginner and intermediate skiers, but the resort is striving to improve those conditions. For years a day-use area only, Snowbowl recently added the Gelendesprung Lodge, making overnighting an option.

Lolo Pass Winter Sports Area. Located 45 miles southwest of Missoula on U.S. Highway 93 and U.S. Highway 12. Telephone: (406) 329-3814 (Missoula Ranger District's visitor information line). Lolo Pass, sitting a mile high along the Bitterroot Divide, is a snow magnet; dozens of feet of the white stuff bury the ground here each winter, typically from late November through April. The roads and slopes surrounding the pass are popular with backcountry skiers and with snowmobilers, as well.

Pattee Canyon Recreation Area. Five miles southeast of town on Pattee Canyon Drive. Outstanding cross-country skiing, snow conditions permitting, on trails groomed for skating and classic skiing by the Missoula Nordic Ski Club. The club also hosts races, waxing clinics, and learn-to-ski events periodically through the winter. For a report on ski conditions in Pattee Canyon, call the Missoula Ranger District's visitor information line at (406) 329-3814.

Seeley Creek Trails. Located just outside the town of Seeley Lake, 50 miles northeast of Missoula on State Highway 200 and State Highway 83. One of the best cross-country systems in Montana, rivaling West Yellowstone's Rendezvous Trails for its variety of twisting, roller-coaster trails. (Call the Seeley Lake Ranger District at 406-677-2233 for a snow report.) The ski trails—and the foot trails and logging roads webbing the surrounding Lolo National Forest lands—provide outstanding mountain biking come summer. Seeley Lake and surroundings

offer an array of lodging opportunities, from the luxurious likes of the **Emily A. Bed and Breakfast** (telephone 406-677-FISH) to more inexpensive, cabins-on-the-lake-style accommodations. For a real wilderness treat, there's the quintessentially Western **Holland Lake Lodge** (telephone 406-754-2282), located 20 miles north of Seeley Lake, then 4 miles east. The lodge and corrals occupy a stunning lakeside location adjacent to the west slope of the Bob Marshall Wilderness.

SHOPPING

Obviously, you'll find more than a few shopping opportunities in a burgeoning city such as Missoula. Here are just a few of the author's favorites.

Freddy's Feed & Read. 1221 Helen Avenue. Telephone: (406) 549-2127. Top-notch neighborhood bookstore located close to the university campus. Also features health/gourmet groceries and a deli bar.

Missoula Pendleton Shop. 127 North Higgins. Telephone: (406) 543-2803. High-quality, warm and colorful clothes and blankets from the famous Oregon mills.

Monte Dolack Gallery. 139 West Front. Telephone: (406) 549-3248 or, toll-free in the United States, (800) 825-7613. Dolack's posters and prints, depicting gloriously colorful mountainscapes and whimsical subjects—such as wild animals taking over human abodes—can be seen adorning walls throughout western Montana and the Northern Rockies. The works of other artists can be viewed and purchased at the gallery, too, including those of Mary Beth Percival, a talented landscape artist.

Rockin' Rudy's. Located at 237 Blaine, just south of downtown. Telephone: (406) 542-0077. Simply the best record/CD store in the Northern Rockies. Also features cards, posters, jewelry, T-shirts, toys, and an assortment of unusual, often humorous gift items.

Stringed Instrument Division. 123 West Alder. Telephone: (406) 549–1502. Tucked away in the pawnshop district on the proverbial wrong side of the tracks (even though it's on the south side of the tracks, along with the rest of downtown Missoula), this delightful shop features a surprisingly large inventory of high-end guitars, both new and vintage, by Gibson, Alvarez, and other companies. Fiddles, banjos, and other instruments are also offered for sale.

THEATER

Missoula Children's Theatre. 200 North Adams. Headquarters of the largest and most-heralded touring children's theater in the country. MCT Community Theatre annually presents several productions in the Missoula area. Telephone: (406) 728–1911.

TELEPHONE NUMBERS

Missoula International Airport. Served by Delta, Northwest, Horizon Air, and Alaska airlines. (406) 728–4381.

Missoula Chamber of Commerce. Van Buren and Front, near the east edge of town south of Broadway. (406) 543–6623.

Missoula Ranger District (Lolo National Forest). (406) 329–3814. Office is located at Fort Missoula, off Fort Road (west of Reserve Street at a point just south of South Avenue).

Car Rentals. Budget, (406) 543–5830; Dollar, (406) 542–2311; Enterprise, (406) 721–1888; Hertz, (406) 549–9511; National, (406) 543–3131; Payless, (406) 728–5475; Rent-A-Wreck, (406) 721–3838.

Public Transportation. The Mountain Line city bus service. (406) 721–3333.

Bigfork and Area

LODGING

Averill's Flathead Lake Lodge. Just south of Bigfork off State Highway 35. This all-out dude ranch continues a proud tradition the Averill family began more than a half century ago. The ranch encompasses more than 2,000 acres, including a long, sandy stretch of Flathead Lake shoreline (which is rather like a western Montana gold standard). A pair of lodges, several smaller cabins, a rodeo arena, a swimming pool, and tennis courts also grace the expansive grounds. Relaxing is per-

Old machinery

mitted, but it's hard to find the time to do it with all the activities at hand. They include mountain biking, sailing, cookouts, water skiing, horseback riding, and volleyball. Telephone: (406) 837–4391. Very expensive (weeklong stays only; the lodge operates on the American plan, with all meals and activities included).

Bayshore Resort Motel. 616 Lakeside Boulevard in Lakeside. Units housing as many as six are available at this motel on Flathead Lake. Kitchenettes, boat slips, and charter fishing trips are also available. Telephone: (406) 844–3131 or, toll-free in the United States, (800) 844–3132. Inexpensive to moderate.

Bigfork Rental Agency. This enterprise manages vacation rentals, which come in a variety of houses, condominiums, and cabins—both tucked in the woods and perched on the shore of expansive Flathead Lake. Each property has a name alluding to its ambience or surroundings: Hermit's Hideaway, for example, and Orchard Estate. Telephone: (406) 837–6424.

Creston Country Inn Bed & Breakfast. 70 Creston Road (off State Highway 35 between Bigfork and Kalispell). Captivating two-story farmhouse built in the 1920s, now featuring four antiques-appointed guest rooms with private baths. The house has a great porch for relaxing, along with several acres of lawns full of barns, willow trees, and good mountain views. Telephone: (406) 755–7517 or, toll-free in the United States, (800) 257–7517. Moderate to expensive.

Marina Cay Resort. 180 Vista Lane on Bigfork Bay. Luxurious resort nestled at the north end of Flathead Lake, offering condominiums in one-, two-, and three-bedroom options. Also has restaurant, lounge, pontoon and ski-boat rentals, and meeting facilities. Telephone: (406) 837–5861 or toll-free in the United States, (800) 433–6516. Moderate to expensive.

O'Duachain Country Inn. Located outside Bigfork at 675 Ferndale Drive. Unique log bed-and-breakfast accommodations nestled on private, five acre grounds and offering well-appoint-

ed suites, a common living room, outdoor hot tub, and the chance to rub elbows (wings?) with the proprietors' peafowl. Telephone: (406) 837–6851 or, toll-free in the United States, (800) 837–7460.

Food

Bigfork Inn. This Swiss chalet–style restaurant is a defining landmark of downtown Bigfork, and the food served is as delicious as the building is attractive. Dinner only. Telephone: (406) 837–6680. Moderate to expensive.

Coyote Roadhouse. 602 Three Eagle Lane near Ferndale. Telephone: (406) 837–4250. One of the finest restaurants in Montana, as verified by *Travel & Leisure* and other publications promoting the good life. Also encompasses the Coyote Riverhouse Cabins. Reservations required; dinner only (closed in winter). Expensive.

Swan River Inn Cafe and Dinner House. Located at 360 Grand Avenue, overlooking Bigfork Bay. Telephone: (406) 837–2220. Fine meals, served either in the dining room or on the exterior deck. The business expanded in 1996, adding three elegant inn suites. Breakfast, lunch, and dinner. Moderate to expensive.

Festivals, Events, and Theater

Bigfork Festival of the Arts. This large art fair is held in early August on and around Electric Avenue in downtown Bigfork. Several additional events are held in conjunction with the fair. Telephone: (406) 837–6397.

Bigfork Summer Playhouse. 526 Electric Avenue. For some forty years one of the finest repertory theaters in the Northern Rockies has been staging Broadway plays in Bigfork. The playhouse is open from late May through August, with shows on Monday through Saturday. The box office phone number is (406) 837–4886.

Golf

See information on Eagle Bend and the Flathead Valley Golf Association, under Whitefish.

Tours

Pointer Scenic Cruises. Located at the bay in downtown Bigfork. Private Flathead Lake charters, replete with captain, heading to destinations that include Wild Horse Island. Telephone: (406) 837–5617.

Whitefish, Glacier National Park, and the North Fork

Kalispell, a bustling service community, is the largest town in the upper Flathead Valley. In addition to its trio of good golf courses—which, combined, constitute the primary attraction that would persuade many vacationers to spend more than a few hours in town—Kalispell has plenty of lodging and dining options, which are not highlighted here. The city is very close to the resort community of Whitefish and to Glacier National Park, which most folks will find to be superior to Kalispell as bases to use for exploring the region.

LODGING

In Whitefish and Area

All Pro Rental Agency. Kalispell-based agency that manages rentals of a variety of vacation properties, with locales including Kalispell, Lake Blaine (east of Kalispell), and Flathead Lake. Telephone: (406) 755–1332.

Bay Point Estates. Lakefront accommodations on Whitefish Lake, offering special summer golf and winter ski packages. The accommodations, available in both one bedroom–one bath and two bedroom–two bath units, include fully equipped kitchens, decks, barbecues, and fireplaces (in most units). A stay here includes unbeatable lake access, along with use of the indoor pool and sauna. Telephone: (406) 862–2331 or, toll-free in the United States, (800) 327–2108. Moderate to very expensive.

Best Western Rocky Mountain Lodge. 6510 Highway 93 South in Whitefish. New motel featuring seventy-nine rooms, including both standard rooms and mini-suites with Jacuzzi, fireplace, and sofa bed. A stay includes a European-style breakfast and use of the exercise room, heated outdoor pool, and shuttle service. Meeting and banquet facilities are also available. Telephone: (406) 862–2569 or, toll-free in the United States, (800) 327–2108. Moderate to expensive.

The Big Mountain Ski and Summer Resort. This destination ski resort just outside Whitefish encompasses several lodging options, ranging from the inexpensive/moderate **Hibernation House**, to the very expensive mini-village of condominiums and chalets collectively known as **Annapurna Properties**. Between these on the price scale are the **Alpinglow Inn**, the outstanding **Kandahar Lodge**, and others. For information and reservations call The Big Mountain Central Reservations at (406) 862–1900 or, toll-free in the United States, (800) 858–5439.

Comfort Inn. 6390 South U.S. Highway 93. Located on the commercial strip south of downtown Whitefish. Sixty-five rooms, indoor heated pool with a 90-foot spiraling water slide, Jacuzzi, and two outdoor hot tubs. Telephone: (406) 862–4020 or, toll-free in the United States, (800) 700–7934. Moderate to expensive.

Duck Inn. Perched on the banks of the Whitefish River at 1305 Columbia Avenue. Spacious, ten-room cedar lodge with a European flair; each room has its own fireplace, balcony, and large bathroom with deep soaking tub. Telephone: (406) 862–3825 or, toll-free in the United States, (800) 344–2377. Moderate to expensive.

Flathead National Forest Rental Cabins. Four forest cabins, ranging from modern to rustic, are available to rent for the night. They include the lofty, hike-to Hornet Peak Lookout in the North Fork Flathead Valley. Reservations are handled by the Hungry Horse Ranger District. Telephone: (406) 387–3800.

Garden Wall Inn. 504 Spokane Avenue. Whitefish's premier bed and breakfast inn, owned and operated by the town's preeminent cross-country skiing family. Any one of five antiques-appointed rooms in the house, which was built in the 1920s, will provide a private and comfortable retreat just two blocks from downtown. Afternoon/evening sherry in front of the fireplace is one Garden Wall tradition; another is celebrated in the morning, when guests come fork to face with an amazing multicourse breakfast. Telephone: (406) 862–3440 or, toll-free in the United States, (888) 530–1700. Moderate to expensive.

Grouse Mountain Lodge. Located at 2 Fairway Drive (west of downtown off U.S. Highway 93). At the other end of the spectrum from the cozy Garden Wall is this major resort hotel, centered on a spacious lobby, gourmet restaurant (Logan's Grill), and bar, all replete with fireplaces faced in natural river rock. Some rooms include Jacuzzis, kitchens, and loft bedrooms, and the lodge can accommodate meeting groups of up to 300. Grouse Mountain is located adjacent to the Whitefish Lake Golf Course, where in winter trails are groomed for cross-country skiing. The hotel also operates the sumptuous Kandahar Lodge on The Big Mountain, and special ski-lodging packages are available at both properties. Free shuttles to and from Glacier Park International Airport and The Big Mountain Resort. Telephone: (406) 862–3000 or, toll-free in the United States and Canada, (800) 321–8822. Moderate to very expensive.

Hargrave Cattle & Guest Ranch. Located in the Thompson River Valley near Marion (southwest of Kalispell on U.S. Highway 2). As have many cattle ranchers in the West, the Hargraves have found that by adding "Guest" to the name of their spread they can more readily afford to keep the "Cattle," too. A maximum of fifteen guests at a time, holed up in the ranch house or in log cabins, take part in spring and summer herding and fall roundups. Fishing, canoeing, swimming, campouts, hiking, four-wheel-driving, and other diversions are right at hand. Telephone: (406) 858–2284. Expensive.

La Villa Montana. Situated on ten private acres off State Highway 40, between Whitefish and Columbia Falls. The chalets of Italy's Tyrol region

inspired this charming bed and breakfast, where guests choose from four guest rooms, each with a bath. Telephone: (406) 892–0689 or, toll-free in the United States, (800) 652–8455. Moderate to expensive.

Loon's Echo Resort and Fish Farm. 1 Fish Lake Road, at the base of Stryker Peak (approximately 30 miles northwest of Whitefish on U.S. Highway 93, then 4 miles east on gravel). This retreat is hard to find, but it a makes a great getaway for those who manage to locate it. With the flexible rooming situation made possible by the combination of a five-room lodge and a variety of houses and cabins, it's particularly suited for family reunions and other small groups. Fishing, hiking, skiing, snowmobiling, and other outdoor pursuits start right outside the door. Telephone: (406) 882–4791 or, toll-free in the United States, (800) 956–6632. Moderate to expensive.

Meadow Lake. Outside Columbia Falls at 100 St. Andrews Drive. Four-season vacation and time-share resort located close to Glacier National Park, boasting an eighteen-hole golf course that's earning quite a name for itself. Nearly 200 guest rooms are available for rent, including luxury villas and town homes ranging in size from one to five bedrooms. Meadow Lake also features tennis, pools, a restaurant-lounge, and shuttles to The Big Mountain Resort. Telephone: (406) 892–7601 or, toll-free in the United States, (800) 321–GOLF (4653). Moderate to expensive.

North Forty Resort. 3765 Highway 40 West between Whitefish and Columbia Falls. Deluxe log cabins—two of which accommodate up to five and the third up to eight—settled in the woods at the North Forty include fireplaces and kitchens. A sauna and hot tubs are available for use. The ample grounds and flexibility afforded by the cabins' sleeping arrangements make the North Forty another getaway well suited for gatherings such as family reunions. Telephone: (406) 862–7740 or, toll-free in the United States, (800) 775–1740. Very expensive.

Quality Inn Pine Lodge. 920 Spokane Avenue. The Pine Lodge features swimming pools, a Jacuzzi-exercise room, and rooms richly appointed with Montana-made furniture. The larger suites include spas, mini-kitchens, and fireplaces. Continental breakfast is included with the price of a room. Telephone: (406) 862–7600 or, toll-free in the United States, (800) 305–7463. Expensive to very expensive.

Whitefish Lake Lodge Resort. On the shores of Whitefish Lake at 1399 Wisconsin Avenue. One-, two-, and three- bedroom condominium units at this four-season resort include full-sized kitchens and comfortable living rooms with fireplaces. In summer there's a marina and outdoor pool-spa. Telephone: (406) 862–2929 or, toll-free in the United States, (800) 735–8869. Expensive to very expensive.

Whitefish Property Management. 128 Central Avenue. A full slate of vacation rentals are available, including condominiums and houses on Whitefish Lake. Telephone: (406) 863-4651. Prices vary widely.

In Glacier National Park and Area

Apgar Village Lodge. Located in Apgar Village. This is the only motel/hotel within Glacier National Park not operated by Glacier Park, Inc. Apgar Village Lodge has forty-eight units, half of which include kitchenettes. Telephone: (406) 888-5484. Moderate to expensive.

Izaak Walton Inn. Located in Essex, 29 miles southeast of West Glacier on U.S. Highway 2. This historic Great Northern Railroad hotel, which still serves as a flag stop on Amtrak's Empire Builder line, is a terrific place to stay in summer or in winter, when the inn grooms 30 kilometers (18.5 miles) of cross-country ski trails, partially on surrounding Flathead National Forest lands. A rich lore of railroading memorabilia fills the lodge and spills right out the door—to the extent that guests can hole up in a renovated caboose, complete with modern plumbing and kitchen. Telephone: (406) 888–5700. Moderate to very expensive.

Mountain Timbers Wilderness Lodge. A mile outside Glacier National Park near West Glacier. Impressive lodge constructed of enormous logs,

with hiking trails—and, in winter, groomed cross-country ski trails—right outside the door. Separate game and audio-video rooms, and a great Jacuzzi. Telephone: (406) 387–5830 or, toll-free in the United States, (800) 841–3835. Moderate to expensive.

North Fork Hostel and Square Peg Ranch. Located in Polebridge, a backwoods settlement accessible via dirt roads from Whitefish, Columbia Falls, or Lake McDonald in Glacier National Park. The electric wires still haven't reached Polebridge . . . and they won't, if the like-it-like-that residents have their way. So, the lights, hot-water heater, and other power-requiring amenities at the hostel are run either by gas-powered generator or propane. Bathroom facilities are of the old-fashioned, outside, two-holer variety. A variety of rooming options are available at the rustic hostelry, including bunk beds in the main building and, out back, primitive cabins. A kitchen is available for cook-it-yourself dining. Despite its far-removed location, the North Fork Hostel is part of a worldwide network of low-cost accommodations, so don't be surprised to hear a conversation in French or German at the northwoods hideout. The associated Square Peg Ranch, which includes rental log cabins, is located just up the road. Telephone: (406) 888–5241. Very inexpensive.

The following properties are all operated by Glacier Park, Inc. In an effort to remain in touch with the lodgings' historic pasts—and/or to save enormous retrofitting expenses—most facilities lack television, air conditioning, and elevators. If you're interested in staying at one of these facilities, make reservations as soon as you know the dates you'll be visiting. For the latest information on rates, dates of operation, and services available at the various park lodgings, call Glacier Park, Inc. Central Reservations at (602) 207–6000 (in Phoenix, Arizona).

Village Inn. Located at Apgar Village, 3 miles inside the west entrance. Lake-view rooms are available with one or two bedrooms, some with kitchens and some with living-room suites. Several other visitor services are located in Apgar and nearby West Glacier, including a variety of restaurants/snack stands and shops. Moderate to expensive.

"Longhorn tavern"

Glacier Park Lodge. Located near the southeast edge of the park in East Glacier Park, across from the East Glacier Park Amtrak station. Blackfeet Indians—purportedly wowed by the immense, 800-year-old Douglas-fir pillars used in the lobby of the grand 1914 Great Northern Railroad hotel—called Glacier Park Lodge Oom-Coo-la-Mush-Waw, or "Big Tree Lodge." The lodge and annex encompass 154 rooms, in versions that accommodate two, four, or six persons. On-premises restaurants include the casual Great Northern Steak and Rib House (open for all three meals) and the Country Mercantile, where snacks and groceries are available. A regulation nine-hole golf course is adjacent to the grounds, while a nine-hole pitch-and-putt course weaves around the landscaped gardens in front. Horseback riding is another option. Expensive to very expensive.

Lake McDonald Lodge Complex. Located on the shore of Lake McDonald, 10 miles east of the west entrance, in the largest glacier-carved, water-filled basin in Glacier National Park. Rooms in the original 1913 lodge, small and large cottage rooms, and rooms in an adjacent motor inn are all options. Dining facilities include the Cedar Dining Room and adjacent Stockade Lounge, and Russell's Trails End Family Restaurant. Both serve breakfast, lunch, and dinner. A gift shop and camp store are also located at the complex, where launch cruises, fishing, hiking, and horseback riding are popular pastimes. Moderate to expensive.

Many Glacier Hotel. Located in the northeast corner of the park, 11 miles west of Babb, Montana. This five-story, 208-room Swiss chalet–style hotel was built on the shores of Swiftcurrent Lake by the Great Northern Railroad in 1915. The hotel serves as a major hiking hub, with five valleys radiating up and out toward sprawling glaciers, high passes, and sparkling mountain lakes. Options in the lodge run the gamut from value rooms to suites, with a trio of others between those two (standard, lakeside, and family rooms). Dining options include the casual Ptarmigan Dining Room, dishing up all three meals, and Heidi's, which serves hot dogs, baked goods, and other snacks. Also on the premises: the Swiss Room and Interlake Lounge, specializing in Montana-made microbrews. Launch cruises on Swiftcurrent Lake, ranger-naturalist presentations, and horseback riding are among the popular pursuits at Many Glacier; another, in July and August, is attending a performance of the American Cabaret Theatre. Moderate to very expensive.

Rising Sun Motor Inn. Located 6 miles west of the St. Mary visitor center. Cottage or motor-inn rooms. Two Dog Flats Mesquite Grill, located in the main registration building, serves all three meals daily. Boat tours and a camp store and gift shop are also located at Rising Sun. Moderate.

Swiftcurrent Motor Inn. Located about 1 mile from the Many Glacier Hotel. The Swiftcurrent Motor Inn was added to round out Glacier's tourist facilities after car travel began growing in popularity in the 1930s. Rooming options include no-frills, no-bath, one- and two-bedroom cottages, and motor-inn rooms. The Italian Gardens Ristorante serves breakfast, lunch, and dinner. Very inexpensive to moderate.

Prince of Wales Hotel. Located at Waterton Townsite in Waterton Lakes National Park, Alberta. At this seven-story Canadian gem, built in 1927 on a knoll overlooking Upper Waterton Lake, guests enjoy refined digs amid a rough-hewn landscape. Golfing, horseback riding, cruises on Upper Waterton Lake, and canoeing on nearby Cameron Lake are among the outdoor activities popular here. The Garden Court Dining Room serves all three meals in English and Continental styles, while Valerie's Tea Room serves Continental breakfast and afternoon tea from 2:00 to 5:00 P.M. Very expensive.

CAMPGROUNDS AND RV PARKS

Private

La Salle R.V. Park & Campground. Located 3 miles west of Columbia Falls (7 miles east of Whitefish) on Highway 2 West. Full-service campground with hookups, tent sites, laundry, and playground. Telephone: (406) 892–4668.

Whitefish KOA. 5121 Highway 93 South. Large campground in a pleasant, wooded setting and with a playground for the kids. Telephone: (406) 862–4242 or, toll-free in the United States and Canada, (800) 562–8734.

Montana Department of Fish, Wildlife, and Parks

Whitefish Lake State Park. Located about a mile north off U.S. Highway 93 from a mile west of downtown. Good, but quite often very busy campground on the shore of Whitefish Lake. Also located here are a good beach, a boat launch . . . and a set of operational railroad tracks, so be prepared for the ground to shake occasionally during the night. Telephone: (406) 862–3991.

U.S. Forest Service

Call the Tally Lake Ranger District at (406) 862–2508 for additional campground information.

Big Creek. Pleasant, private campground located 21 miles north of Columbia Falls, along the North Fork of the Flathead River.

Red Meadow Lake. Located 30 miles north of Whitefish on gravel roads (use the Flathead National Forest visitor map for navigation). Primitive, "dispersed" camping is available at this high-mountain gem.

Tally Lake. Located several miles west of Whitefish on U.S. Highway 93 and Forest Service roads (use the Flathead National Forest visitor map for navigation). Also features boat ramp, boat rentals, and a beach.

Tuchuck. Located 24 miles northwest of Polebridge on Forest Road 486 (North Fork Road) and Forest Road 114. Remote and primitive campground nestled in the heart of the wild Review Mountains. Drive to the watershed divide 5.5 miles west of the campground and you'll earn a view straight out of Alaska. Watch for grizzly bears!

National Park Service

Call Glacier National Park at 406–888–7800, or Waterton Lakes National Park at 403–859–2224, for additional information.

The following developed campgrounds in Glacier are all accessible by paved road. They include fire pits, picnic tables, washrooms, and cold running water: **Apgar, Avalanche Creek, Fish Creek, Many Glacier, Rising Sun, St. Mary, Two Medicine,** and **Sprague Creek.** All include facilities for trailers, except Sprague Creek, which is closed to towed vehicles. See Waterton-Glacier map for locations.

The following primitive campgrounds in Glacier feature fire pits, tables, and pit toilets. They are accessible only via gravel roads, which can be narrow and rough: **Cut Bank, Kintla Lake, Bowman Lake, Quartz Creek,** and **Logging Creek.** See Waterton-Glacier map for locations.

Campgrounds in Waterton Lakes National Park include **Townsite, Crandell,** and **Belly River.** See Waterton-Glacier map for locations.

FOOD

Buffalo Cafe. 514 3rd Street. Telephone: (406) 862–2833. This is a favorite breakfast hangout of Whitefish locals; not surprisingly, the servings are ample and tasty. Breakfast and lunch. Inexpensive.

Cafe Kandahar. Located at The Big Mountain. Telephone: (406) 862–6247. Regarded as one of the finest restaurants in the area, Cafe Kandahar specializes in French Provincial cuisine. The intimate Snug Bar is located adjacent to the restaurant in the lobby of the lodge. Breakfast and dinner; reservations required for dinner. Moderate to expensive.

Diamond K Chuckwagon. Located south of Whitefish off Highway 93. Telephone: (406) 862–8828. Fun Western meal and Branson-style entertainment, aimed at the whole family. Closed in the winter. Inexpensive to moderate.

Great Northern Bar & Grill. 128 Central Avenue. Telephone: (406) 862–2816. Longtime downtown establishment dishing up great hamburgers and good times. Lunch and dinner. Inexpensive.

Hellroaring Saloon and Eatery. Located in the Chalet at The Big Mountain. Telephone: (406) 862–6364. Ostensibly named for a nearby creek drainage, and not for the house ambience, Hellroaring nevertheless is a good-times bar and eatery, where diners can sample the best south-of-the-border fare in the Whitefish area. This is where the Northern Rockies meets Old Mexico. Lunch and dinner. Moderate.

Montana Coffee Traders. 5810 Highway 93 South. Telephone: (406) 862–7633. Not exactly a restaurant, but a must-stop for anyone craving a hit of java. This Whitefish establishment is said to have started after the founder had "a cup of the world's worst coffee in the all-night railroad cafe." Today the enterprise, still headquartered in Whitefish, also maintains roasting facilities in Austin, Texas; Moscow, Russia; and Monteverde, Costa Rica. Coffee-related gifts are offered for sale in the tasting room.

Northern Lights Saloon. Nestled in the north woods settlement of Polebridge, an hour north of Columbia Falls or Lake McDonald on gravel. Homesteader's cabin turned bar and eatery that serves as the social epicenter of Polebridge. Don't be surprised to find yourself involved in a game of pickup volleyball if you visit during daylight hours in the summer.

Truby's. 115 Central Avenue. Telephone: (406) 862–4979. Downtown Whitefish establishment dishing up outstanding wood-fired pizzas, either inside or out, on the covered patio. Lunch and dinner. Inexpensive to moderate.

Tupelo Grille. 17 Central Avenue. Telephone: (406) 862–6136. Good Cajun grub and Lousiana-style seafood served in a relaxed atmosphere. Lunch and dinner. Inexpensive to moderate.

Whitefish Lake Restaurant. Telephone: (406) 862 5285. Located west of downtown in a Depression-era log clubhouse on the Whitefish Lake Golf Course. *The* dress-up-and-go-out place in Whitefish, serving traditional steak, fowl, and seafood dishes of the highest quality. Moderate to expensive. Dinner only.

MICROBREWERIES

Great Northern Brewing Company. Located at 2 Central Avenue in the heart of downtown Whitefish. Telephone: (406) 863–1000. Great Northern, best known for their Black Star Premium Lager, is a sort of a maxi-microbrewery: The enterprise was begun by Minott Wessinger, grandson of the well-known beer crafter Henry Weinhard. In addition to the widely distributed Black Star, the tasting room offers samples of smaller productions such as Wild Huckleberry Wheat Lager and Big Fog Amber Lager. The tasting room is open daily in summer from 1:00 to 6:00 P.M. and during the winter Wednesday through Sunday from 3:00 to 7:00 P.M. It has quickly become the early-hours place to go for après-ski fun in downtown Whitefish.

BICYCLING

The Missoula-based Adventure Cycling Association's Great Divide Mountain Bike Route, which follows the Continental Divide from Canada to Mexico, runs directly through Whitefish. For map-ordering information call (800) 721–8719. For bike rentals and for information on the abundance of additional good roads and mountain-bike rides in the Whitefish area, visit the friendly folks at **Glacier Cyclery**, located at 336 2nd Street (telephone 406–862–6446).

Glacier National Park's Going-to-the-Sun Road offers a once-in-a-lifetime road cycling experience. But be forewarned: The National Park Service closes to bicycles the narrower western

Black Star truck, Great Northern Brewery

portions of the road during peak traffic hours (11:00 A.M. to 4:00 P.M.) from June 15 through Labor Day. Recommended off-pavement rides in Glacier include the Inside North Fork Road, a gravel road going northwest from the Fish Creek Campground to Polebridge. Once at Polebridge, outstanding rides in the park lead to destinations including Bowman Lake and Kintla Lake. West of the North Fork of the Flathead River, outside Glacier but within the Flathead National Forest, good rides out of Polebridge include those up to the Hornet Peak Lookout and to Whitefish, via Red Meadows and Upper Whitefish lakes. For additional ride recommendations around Polebridge, visit with the staff at the North Fork Hostel. (*Note:* Hiking trails in Glacier National Park, as in other U.S. national parks, are off-limits to bicycles. In Canadian national parks, however, the policy is different, and several trails in Waterton Lakes National Park are open to mountain bikes.)

FAIRS, FESTIVALS, AND EVENTS

Like most resort towns, Whitefish has its share of festivals, in both winter and summer; the following four are merely a teasing. For information on others, call the chamber of commerce at (406) 862–3501.

Flathead Music Festival. Three weeks of music in late July and early August, held at different venues around the valley. Varied menu of sounds, from big band to country to jazz. Past performers have included (How's this for a diverse range of styles?) local resident Jim Nabors (a.k.a. Gomer Pyle), John Mayall, Crash Test Dummies, and the Paris Opera Boys Choir. For a schedule, call (406) 257–0787.

Whitefish Arts Festival. Held for a two-day period in early July at the Central School, located at Second Street and Spokane Avenue. Artists and craftspeople from throughout the Northwest display their creations. Telephone: (406) 862–3501.

Whitefish Lake Run. Long one of the most popular events in Montana for everyday athletes. The main event, a 10-kilometer (6.2 mile) run, begins north of town above Whitefish Lake. Telephone: (406) 862–3501.

Winter Carnival. This three-day February series of events constitutes northwest Montana's premier winterfest. Events include a torchlight parade, fireworks, and many ski-related festivities. Telephone: (406) 862–3501.

GOLF

Flathead Valley Golf Association. The upper Flathead Valley—generally, the area from Bigfork north to Whitefish—has evolved into something of a mecca for golfers. Courses involved in the association include Bigfork's **Eagle Bend Golf Club**, the top-rated course in Montana; the beautiful, thirty-six-hole **Whitefish Lake Golf Club** in Whitefish; the **Meadow Lake Golf Resort** in Columbia Falls; and three courses in Kalispell: the twenty-seven-hole **Buffalo Hill Golf Club**, the Scottish-links-like **Northern Pines Golf Club**, and the **Village Greens**. For information on rates or to make tee times at any of the courses call, toll-free in the United States, (800) 392–9795.

HIKING

Waterton-Glacier International Peace Park and the Flathead National Forest lands surrounding Whitefish—including the stellar Jewel Basin Hiking Area—together offer a staggering network of trails that few locales in the United States can begin to rival. Glacier alone has 730 miles of trails, and another 114 wind through the adjacent Waterton Lakes National Park. (Backcountry permits are required if you plan to camp at one of Glacier's backcountry campsites; the permits are issued at the various ranger stations on a first-come, first-served basis, but no more than twenty-four hours in advance.) Popular and scenic trails within Glacier include the **Highline Trail**, which begins at Logan Pass and traverses the spectacular Garden Wall; the **Sperry Chalet Trail**, a tough climb beginning at Lake McDonald Lodge and leading through a medley of Glacier's life zones; and the **Swiftcurrent Lake Trail**, a short and easy, but incredibly scenic hike beginning at the Many Glacier Hotel.

A unique and fun footpath located outside the park and close to Whitefish: the **Danny On National Recreation Trail**, which connects The Big Mountain's base area and summit. On was a well-liked Forest Service silviculturist and acclaimed nature photographer who died in a skiing accident on The Big Mountain in 1979. His namesake 5.6-mile-long nature trail can be accompanied by a good interpretive brochure available at the resort. You can hike the trail both up and down the mountain, or hike it in just one direction and ride the chairlift the other.

HORSEBACK RIDING

Two-Medicine River Outfitters. Located across from the Glacier Park Lodge in East Glacier Park. One of several horseback outfitters in the Whitefish–Glacier Park region, this one specializes in trail rides, pack trips, and fishing trips on Blackfeet Indian tribal lands adjacent to the national park. Telephone: (406) 226–4408 or, toll-free in the United States and Canada, (800) 569–0857.

RIVER FLOATING

Great Northern Whitewater. Located in West Glacier, a mile from the west entrance of Glacier National Park. The meat and potatoes of this popular outfitter is outings on the Middle Fork of the Flathead, where segments of *The River Wild,* starring Meryl Streep and Kevin Bacon, were filmed. The splash fest includes rides up and over—or so one hopes—rapids with intimidating names such as Jaws and Bonecrusher. Telephone: (406) 387–5340 or, toll-free in the United States, (800) 735–7897.

Montana Raft Company. Located in West Glacier. Offers floats on the Middle Fork and also the North Fork of the Flathead. Telephone: (406) 387–5555 or, toll-free in the United States, (800) 521–7238.

RODEO

In summer, the **Glacier Gateway Rodeo** gets under way every Wednesday at 7:30 P.M. The grounds are located 2 miles east of East Glacier on U.S. Highway 2. Telephone: (406) 338–7767.

SKIING

The Big Mountain Ski & Summer Resort. Located 5 miles up the big hill north of Whitefish. Telephone: (406) 862–2900 or, toll-free in the United States, (800) 859–3526. This aptly named ski area boasts a merely respectable vertical rise of 2,300 feet, but an enviable expanse of 3,000 skiable acres. It's one of a pair of Montana's premier winter–and–summer destination resorts, the other being Big Sky, located south of Bozeman. Three factors coalesce to make the weather conditions here rather mild: a geographic location relatively close to the Pacific Coast, a rather low elevation (The Big Mountain's summit is 7,000 feet), and the proximity to Flathead Lake, a body of water that is large enough to make its own weather. Consequently, the temperatures are often warmer here than at other ski resorts in the Northern Rockies. The downside is that The Big Mountain tends to have a wetter, heavier snow compared to resorts farther south, which are higher in elevation and less

affected by coastal weather. Still, although it may not be the fluffy stuff of a powder hound's dreams, in a typical winter The Big Mountain gets buried under 300 inches of snow, and the mountain's sixty-three signed runs offer something for all levels of skiers. Come summer, music festivals, hiking, flycasting, tennis, and sight-seeing opportunities keep things kicking. Mountain biking, especially, has mushroomed in popularity in recent years: In addition to offering bike rentals, the mountain maintains some 20 miles of single-track trail expressly for mountain biking, including a new, bottom-to-top (or top-to-bottom, for those preferring to let gravity do the work) 7.2-mile trail. Simply to ride the Glacier Chaser gondola or an open chairlift up the mountain and back down, leaving the hiking and cycling to others, is to earn some of the finest views in the region: the peaks of Glacier National Park loom to the east, while Whitefish Lake, the Flathead Valley, and even the Canadian Rockies sprawl in other directions. A special highlight, especially for kids, is the U.S. Forest Service's Environmental Education Center, maintained on the lower level of the Summit House in summer. Stuffed animals, along with skulls, furs, and other fun things relating to the local flora and fauna are on display at the hands-on center, which is open daily in summer from 10:00 A.M. to 5:00 P.M.; call (406) 862–1972.

Cross-Country Skiing. For cross-country skiing on groomed trails, head for the extremely hilly trails that radiate around the base of The Big Mountain, the more forgiving trails webbing the Whitefish Lake Golf Course, or—a bit farther afield—the fun trails that wind amid the implausibly scenic valleys surrounding the Izaak Walton Inn in Essex.

TOURS

Dog Sled Adventures. Located northwest of Whitefish in the Olney area. This company runs thrilling dog-powered tours, which lead through the winter stillness of the Stillwater State Forest. Clients keep warm by wrapping themselves up in elk-fur robes. Their irresistible phone number: (406) 881–BARK (2275).

Going-to-the-Sun (Natos'i At'apoo) Sun Tours. Van tours of Going-to-the-Sun Road guided by Native Americans from the Browning area. On these unique tours you'll hear the Blackfeet Indians' interpretation of the sacred landscape of Glacier National Park, which differs markedly from the often nuts-and-bolts, scientific outlook common among Anglos. Arrangements can be made for pickup in either East Glacier or St. Mary. Sun Tours is an authorized concessioner of the National Park Service. Telephone: (406) 226–9220 or, toll-free in the United States, (800) 786–9220.

The Great Montana Adventure Company. Offices located at 1205 Highway 93 West in Whitefish. This adventure broker in summer arranges tours in Glacier National Park by foot, by boat, and aboard the red Jammer touring cars. They also offer white-water raft trips, chuck-wagon dinner rides, horseback rides, fly-fishing outings, and tours of the Blackfeet Indian Reservation. Come winter, the Great Montana Adventure Company can help plan and arrange cross-country ski, snowmobile, sled-dog, and horse-drawn sleigh adventures. Telephone: (406) 862–8166.

Historical Walking Tour. A compelling stroll about old Whitefish begins at the Stumptown Historical Society Museum, located below the Chamber of Commerce in the old Burlington Northern Depot on North Central Avenue. You can pick up a guide brochure at the museum, which is open 11:00 A.M. to 7:00 P.M. Monday through Friday and 11:00 A.M. to 3:00 P.M. on Saturday. For more details call the historical society at (406) 862–0067.

Burlington Northern Depot, Whitefish, Montana

Ride the Reds. Driver-guides, also known as "jammers" (for "gear jammers"), operate these vintage red, canvas-top, fifteen-passenger motor coaches that were built by the White Motor Company in the late 1930s, and which have a long-standing relationship with the Going-to-the-Sun Road. Tours of various lengths link all hotels within Glacier, as well as the Prince of Wales Hotel in Waterton Lakes National Park. This is the ideal way to travel on the park's legendarily precipitous main road for those whose vehicles are too large (maximum size allowed on Going-to-the-Sun Road is 21 feet long and 8 feet wide), or for those whose nerves aren't quite up to it even if their vehicles are. Telephone: (406) 226–9311.

SHOPPING

Opportunities are so plentiful that it can be tough to know where to begin. Here are a couple of less-obvious suggestions.

Antiquing. Some two-dozen antiques stores are scattered about the Flathead Valley. To obtain the brochure, "Antique Guide for the Flathead Valley," call the Whitefish Chamber of Commerce at (406) 862–3501.

Polebridge Mercantile. Located in "downtown" Polebridge, an hour north of Columbia Falls mostly on gravel. A 1914 backwoods general store, heated by a potbelly stove and appointed with furs, antiques, and memorabilia. Very primitive rental cabins are also available. Telephone: (406) 888–5105.

WATER SPORTS

Public beaches fronting Whitefish Lake include **City Beach**, site of the local scene in summer (canoe rentals are available at the site), and **Les Mason Park** (406–862–7633; donation-supported), which is much more secluded and far less frequented (*see* Seeing Glacier-Gold Country for driving directions). The Whitefish Lake Lodge (telephone 406–862–9283) maintains a public marina at 1399 Wisconsin Avenue, where they rent ski boats, sailboats, canoes, and other watercraft by the hour, half-day, full-day, or week. They also offer twilight cruises aboard the historic *Red Eagle*,

departing from the marina at 6:00 P.M. Kids age five and under board free . . . so long as they inquire about the Whitefish Lake Monster.

In Glacier National Park, the Glacier Park Boat Company (telephone 406–888–5727) operates scenic cruises on Lake McDonald, St. Mary Lake, Two Medicine Lake, and, in the Many Glacier area, on Swiftcurrent and Josephine Lakes. Most cruises include the option to hop off, take a hike, and board a later arrival for the return trip. In Waterton, the Shoreline Cruise Company's MV *International* plies the water of Waterton Lake, heading south into the U.S. and docking at the Goat Haunt Ranger Station in Glacier. Call (403) 859–2362 for further information.

TELEPHONE NUMBERS

Whitefish Chamber of Commerce. Downtown, in the old Great Northern Railroad Depot. (406) 862–3501.

Tally Lake Ranger District (Flathead National Forest). 1335 Highway 93 West, in Whitefish. (406) 862–2508.

Glacier Park International Airport. Located just outside Kalispell, ten minutes from downtown Whitefish. The airport is served by Delta, Northwest, and Horizon Air. (406) 257–5994.

Amtrak. (406) 862–2268 or, toll-free in the United States and Canada, (800) 872–7245. The Chicago-to-Seattle Empire Builder stops daily at depots in East Glacier, Essex, West Glacier (Belton Station), and Whitefish.

Glacier National Park information. (406) 888–7800.

Car Rentals. Budget, (406) 862–8170; Dollar, (406) 892–0009; Hertz, (406) 863–1210; Payless, (406) 755–4022.

Helena

LODGING

Bed & Breakfast Inns. Helena includes a good selection of historic—and not-so-historic—bed-

and-breakfast inns, ranging in price from moderate to very expensive. Among the choices: the **Appleton Inn**, located at 1999 Euclid Avenue (telephone 406–449–7492); **The Barrister**, at 416 North Ewing (telephone 406–443–7330); and **The Sanders**, situated at 328 North Ewing (telephone 406–442–3309).

Best Western Colonial Inn. 2301 Colonial Drive. Large facility with 150 rooms, a pool, and a restaurant. Telephone: (406) 443–2100 or, toll-free in the United States, (800) 422–1002. Moderate to expensive.

Jorgenson's Holiday Motel. Located at 1714 11th Avenue. Longtime Helena family-run establishment, featuring restaurant, lounge, and pool. Telephone: (406) 442–1770 or, toll-free in the United States, (800) 272–1770. Inexpensive to moderate.

Motel 6. Located at 800 North Oregon. Telephone: (406) 442–9990. Inexpensive.

Park Plaza Hotel. 22 North Last Chance Gulch. Of all the accommodations in town, this quality hotel is the most conveniently located to the Last Chance Gulch pedestrian mall. Includes a restaurant and lounge on the premises. Telephone: (406) 443–2200 or, toll-free in the United States, (800) 332–2290. Moderate to expensive.

CAMPGROUNDS AND RV PARKS

Private

Helena Campground and RV Park. Three miles north of Helena at 5820 North Montana Avenue. Full-service campground that even offers bingo and free movies in July and August. Open year-round. Telephone: (406) 458–4714 or 458–5110.

U.S. Forest Service

Telephone (406) 449–5490; and Montana Department of Fish, Wildlife and Parks (telephone 406–444–3750)

Canyon Ferry Lake. A slew of campgrounds—with names like Chinaman Gulch, Hellgate, and Confederate Gulch—line the shores of massive Canyon Ferry Lake. There are some twenty campgrounds in all, including several accessible only by boat. Hauser and Holter lakes each feature state-park campgrounds. The trio of lakes are southeast, east, and northeast of Helena.

MacDonald Pass. Forest Service campground located 15 miles west of Helena on U.S. Highway 12, near the Continental Divide.

Park Lake. Nineteen miles south of Helena on forest roads.

FOOD

Carriage House Bistro. 234-½ East Lyndale. Telephone: (406) 449–6949. Special gourmet entrees served to a small seating each night except Sundays. Dinner only. Moderate to expensive.

No Sweat Cafe. 427 North Last Chance Gulch. Telephone: (406) 442–6954. Best breakfasts in town. Breakfast and lunch.

On Broadway. 106 Broadway. Telephone: (406) 443–1929. Intimate Italian-style restaurant specializing in homemade pasta. Dinner only. Moderate.

Park Avenue Bakery. 44 South Park Avenue. Telephone: (406) 449–8424. Brick-oven bakery where you'll find Old World–style breads, pastries, and specialty desserts.

Stonehouse Restaurant. 120 Reeder's Alley. Telephone: (406) 449–2552. Fine dining in an old building in the historic miners' section of town. Lunch and dinner weekdays, dinner only on Saturdays, and closed Sundays. Moderate.

Windbag Saloon and Grill. 19 South Last Chance Gulch. Telephone: (406) 443–9669. This is the place that Helena residents gather for a fun meal in a social, relaxed atmosphere. Good meat and fish dishes, and a large selection of beers. Housed in an old stone building that in a former life was a house of prostitution, until urban renewal hit Last Chance Gulch in the early 1960s. Lunch and dinner. Inexpensive to moderate.

BICYCLING

Helena is one of very few large towns visited by the Great Divide Mountain Bike Route, an off-pavement cycling route running along the Continental Divide from Canada to Mexico. By following the route southward into the Helena National Forest you can visit pretty Park Lake, then ride into the Deerlodge National Forest and past fascinating old mines before reaching Basin. Likewise to the north, the route skirts a wealth of mining remains en route to the town of Lincoln (former hideout of the convicted Unabomber). For more information or to order maps, call Adventure Cycling in Missoula at (800) 721–8719. For additional information on Helena-area road and mountain-bike rides, visit **Great Divide Cyclery** (406–443–5188), located at 336 North Jackson.

FAIRS, FESTIVALS, AND EVENTS

Governor's Cup. First Saturday in June. The largest and most prestigious gathering of runners, walkers, and wheelchair athletes in the Northern Rockies. The Governor's Cup includes a marathon run of 26.2 miles, and shorter races of 20, 10, and 5 kilometers (12.4, 6.2, and 3.1 miles respectively). The marathon begins high in the hills at Marysville, a historic mining town. Telephone: (406) 442–6451, 442–4120, or, toll-free in the United States, (800) 7–HELENA (743–5362).

Montana Traditional Jazz Festival. Held several days in late June at various venues around Helena. Festival showcases some twenty jazz acts from around the western United States. Telephone: toll-free, (800) 851–9980.

Race to the Sky Sled Dog Race. Contested in February. This multi-day sled-dog race begins in Helena before heading for the mountains of western Montana and looping back to end in the capital city. The route features several scenic, relatively easily accessible places for spectators to hang out and watch the action. Telephone: (406) 442–4120 or, toll-free in the United States, (800) 7–HELENA (743–5362).

Gold Panning. To learn about Helena-area opportunities to pan for gold or search for sapphires, call the Spokane Bar Sapphire Mine at (406) 227–8989 or the Helena National Forest at (406) 449–5201.

FISHING

The big Missouri River reservoirs, and stretches of the Missouri below the Hauser Dam, are heralded for their trophy brown trout, which sometimes exceed fifteen pounds. For information on regulations and where to go, call the Montana Department of Fish, Wildlife and Parks at (406) 444–2535.

SKIING

Great Divide Ski Area. Located near Marysville, approximately 20 miles northwest of Helena. Telephone: (406) 449–3746. Day-use area—but with night skiing, too—featuring a 1,300-foot vertical drop and more than 700 acres of skiable terrain encompassing seventy runs. The area, known for its low lift-ticket prices and family-friendly atmosphere, includes a restaurant and bar.

MacDonald Pass. Located 15 miles west of Helena on U.S. Highway 12. Telephone: (406) 443–5360. Cross-country trails are periodically groomed by the Last Chance Nordic Club on Helena National Forest lands surrounding the pass.

SHOPPING

The Base Camp. 333 North Last Chance Gulch. Telephone: (406) 443–5360. Exceptional outdoor store specializing in most gravity- and self-propelled sports.

Days of Yore. Located next to the Windbag Saloon at 25 South Last Chance Gulch. Telephone: (406) 443–7947. A fun and varied collection of antiques and re-creations are for sale.

Holton's of Helena. 1219 11th Avenue. Telephone: (406) 442–3688. Gift shop specializing in Montana-made goods. Operated by a retired fisheries biologist who's active in the local Audubon Society, so this is a great place to go to procure fishing and bird-watching tips.

The Parrot Confectionery. 42 North Last Chance Gulch. Telephone: (406) 442–1470. For more than three quarters of a century the Parrot has been providing shoppers with lip-smacking, handmade chocolates.

TELEPHONE NUMBERS

Helena Area Chamber of Commerce & Visitor Center, (406) 442–4120 or, toll-free in the United States, (800) 7–HELENA (743–5362). The main office is located downtown at 225 Cruse Avenue, Suite A; the Visitor Information Center, open June through August, is located off I–15 at the Cedar Street exit 193.

Helena Regional Airport. The airport is served by Delta/Sky West and Horizon airlines. (406) 442–2821.

Helena Ranger District (Helena National Forest). 2001 Poplar Street. 406–449–5490.

Car Rentals. Avis, (406) 442–4440; Hertz, (406) 449–4167; Rent-a-Wreck, (406) 443–3635.

Butte

LODGING

Best Western Copper King Park Hotel. 4655 Harrison Avenue South. Large, full-service hotel located close to the airport. Features pool and Jacuzzi, indoor tennis courts, sports bar, restaurant, and convention facilities. Telephone: (406) 494–6666 or, toll-free in the United States, (800) 332–8600. Moderate to expensive.

Comfort Inn. 2777 Harrison Avenue. Centrally located motel featuring 150 guest rooms and an adjacent 4B's family restaurant. The inn has a spa-sauna and fitness center, and some rooms are available with kitchenettes and/or whirlpool baths. Telephone: (406) 494–8850 or, toll-free in the United States, (800) 442–INNS (4667). Inexpensive to moderate.

Copper King Mansion. 219 West Granite. Thirty-four-room former residence of copper king and U.S. Senator William A. Clark, whose income at the apex of his mining activity was said to be $17 million monthly. Not surprisingly, this is considered by many the most unusual and impressive bed-and-breakfast accommodation in the Northern Rockies. The mansion was purchased in 1953 by Anna Coté, who at the time found little evidence within of its original splendor. Renovation was, and is, an all-consuming task. Today owners Erin Sigl and John Thompson—Coté's grandchildren, who moved into the 10,000-square-foot house with their family in 1957—let five antiques-appointed rooms, including the Master Suite that was used by Clark. Telephone: (406) 782–7580. Moderate to expensive.

Scott Bed & Breakfast Inn. 15 West Copper. Restored 1897 red brick inn located at the base of the hill below Walkerville. The gorgeous old place features seven rooms, each with private bath and telephone, and a large lounge area Telephone: (406) 723–7030 or, toll-free in the United States, (800) 844–2952. Moderate to expensive.

Super 8 Motel. 2929 Harrison Avenue. Old reliable motel featuring 104 rooms and situated close to shopping and restaurants. Telephone: (406) 494–6000 or, toll-free in the United States, (800) 800–8000. Inexpensive.

Victoria Joy's Bed & Breakfast and Tea House. 627 North Main. "Victorian elegance in a crude historic West" is how this establishment describes its offerings. Eight rooms, three with private bath. Telephone: (406) 723–6161 or, toll-free in the United States, (888) 272–6002. Moderate to expensive.

CAMPGROUNDS AND RV PARKS

Private

KOA Butte. 1601 Kaw Avenue. Full-service campground conveniently located behind the new Butte–Silver Bow Chamber of Commerce Visitor Center. Telephone: (406) 782–0663.

U.S. Forest Service

Call the Butte Ranger District at 406–494–2147 for additional campground information.

Basin Canyon. Five miles northwest of Basin on Forest Road 172. (Basin is 27 miles north of Butte on Interstate 15.)

Mormon Gulch. Located 23 miles north of Butte on Interstate 15, then 2 miles west on Forest Road 82. Two miles farther west is **Ladysmith Campground**; another 4 miles west of that is **Whitehouse Campground**.

FOOD

Doreen's Family Restaurant. 138 West Park in Uptown Butte. Telephone: (406) 782–7625. Doreen's vows to serve homemade food only, and that includes their pies, soups, and halibut fish and chips. Breakfast, lunch, and dinner (closed Sunday). Inexpensive.

Joe's Pasty Shop. A block south of the Civic Center at Harrison and Grand. Telephone: (406) 723–9071. Since 1947 Joe's has been serving the traditional meat-and-potato pies known as pasties. Also includes a full-service bar. Breakfast, lunch, and dinner (closed Sundays). Inexpensive.

Lydia's Supper Club. Located at 4915 Harrison. Telephone: (406) 494–2000. For more than a half century Lydia's has been serving some of the best dinners in Butte. Their homemade ravioli borders on legendary. Dinner only. Expensive.

Pekin Noodle Parlor. Located at 117 South Main. Telephone: (406) 782–2217. Butte's oldest Chinese restaurant, specializing in Cantonese and spicy Szechwan dishes. Dinner only (closed Tuesdays). Inexpensive to moderate.

Pork Chop John's. Two locations: 2400 Harrison and Uptown at 8 West Mercury. Telephone: (406) 782–1783. Long-standing Butte establishment serving regionally renowned pork-chop sandwiches and other goodies. Lunch and dinner (the Uptown restaurant is closed Sundays). Inexpensive.

Rancho Los Arcos. 815 East Front. Telephone: (406) 782–8421. Mexican-food restaurant popular with families. Lunch and dinner. Inexpensive.

Uptown Cafe. 47 East Broadway. Telephone: (406) 723–4735. Surprising restaurant earning recommendations from *Bon Appetit, Gourmet,* and other food and travel publications. "Civilized dining in the Wild, Wild West" is the proud slogan of the Uptown, which serves unique French, Cajun, Italian, and other specialties. Lunch on weekdays only and dinner seven days a week. Moderate to expensive.

BICYCLING

The dirt and gravel roads in the hills surrounding Butte provide some outstanding bicycle rides. For where-to-go information, visit **Great Divide Cyclery** (telephone 406–782–4726) at 827 South Montana.

Barn

Fairs, Festivals, and Events

St. Patrick's Day. Most of Butte and a large share of western Montana turns Irish and turns out for this Katy-bar-the-doors celebration. The festivities include a major parade, and corned beef and cabbage can be procured in nearly every eatery and saloon in Uptown. Telephone: (406) 723–3177 (Butte–Silver Bow Chamber of Commerce).

Winternational Sports Festival. Annual multisport festival held during February and March, incorporating all-comer competitions that range from speed-skating to skiing . . . to wrestling! Telephone: (406) 723–3177 (Butte–Silver Bow Chamber of Commerce).

Hot Springs

Fairmont Hot Springs Resort. Located 15 miles west of Butte (take I–90 exit 211). Beautifully sited, full-service resort with eighteen-hole golf course, RV park, two Olympic-sized pools and two mineral soaking pools, dining, and lodging. Telephone: (406) 797–3241 or, toll-free in the United States, (800) 322–3272.

Skiing

Discovery Basin. Located west of Anaconda off the Pintler Scenic Route (State Highway 1). Telephone: (406) 563–2184. Intimate day-use ski area with great skiing. Features a 1,300-foot vertical drop and four chairlifts. Lodging facilities are found nearby on Georgetown Lake and elsewhere.

Mount Haggin Nordic Ski Area. Located 15 miles southwest of Anaconda on Route 274. Telephone: (406) 494–4235. As you climb out of Anaconda through a toxic-waste moonscape, it's tough to believe that a place as beautiful as the Mount Haggin Recreation Area is so close. Butte's Mile Hi Nordic Ski Club does an outstanding job of keeping trails groomed at this high-elevation locale, where the high snowbanks and low temperatures are legendary. Luckily, the club also maintains a warming hut. The views of the Pintler Mountains from the trails are stunning.

Shopping

Butte brims with shops hawking quality antiques and other fascinating stuff of more dubious worth. Among these: **Antiques on Broadway**, located at 45 West Broadway; **Debris L.T.D.**, at 123 North Main; **Someplace Else**, found at 117 North Main; the **Donut Seed**, at 120 North Main; **All Star Collectibles**, at 1822 Harrison Avenue; **Dublin Gulch Antiques**, situated at 606 South Montana; and the **Dumas Old Time Photography Antique Mall**, located at 45 East Mercury.

Butte Copper Co. Located at 3015 Harrison Avenue, next to McDonald's. Telephone: (406) 494–2070. Reflective of the mineral that made Butte what it is—and what it isn't, considering how much of the city was hauled away to smelter at Anaconda—this enterprise offers "Anything & Everything in Copper."

Main Stope Gallery of Original Art. 126 South Main. Telephone: (406) 723–9195 or, toll-free in the United States, (800) 406–9199. Pottery, wood carvings, paintings, sculpture, and jewelry, most of it embodying the spirit of Butte and/or the Northern Rockies.

Pipestone Mountaineering, Inc. 829 South Montana. Telephone: (406) 782–4994. Outfitting enterprise specializing in quality climbing, backpacking, river-running, and cross-country skiing gear.

Theater

Mother Lode Theater. Finished in 1923, when Butte was the cultural hub of the Northern Rockies, the Mother Lode recently underwent renovation, bringing it up to and beyond its original beauty. Events taking place here include regular performances by the Butte Symphony Orchestra, the community concert series, and a classic movie series. For information call the theater at (406) 723–3602.

TOURS

Our Lady of the Rockies Bus Tours. Daily tours, beginning at the Plaza Mall Gift Shop at 3100 Harrison Avenue, climb high above town to visit one of Butte's most amazing attractions: Our Lady of the Rockies, a 90-foot-high statue composed of concrete and metal. Our Lady is said to symbolize all women, regardless of religion. The tour takes about two and one-half hours. The statue can be seen from miles away at night, when it's brilliantly illuminated. Telephone: (406) 782–1221 or, toll-free in the United States, (800) 800–5239.

TELEPHONE NUMBERS

Butte–Silver Bow Chamber of Commerce Visitor and Transportation Center, (406) 723–3177 or, toll-free in the United States, (800) 735–6814. Facility is located at 1000 George Street, just north of Interstate 90 at exit 126.

Butte Ranger District (Deerlodge National Forest). In Butte, just off Harrison Avenue at 1820 Meadowlark Lane. (406) 494–2147.

Bert Mooney Airport. 101 Airport Road. Served by Delta/Sky West and Horizon airlines. (406) 494–3771.

Car Rentals. Avis, (406) 494–3131; Hertz, (406) 782–1054; Payless, (406) 723–4366.

III

Central Idaho

SUN VALLEY–SALMON COUNTRY

Sun Valley–Salmon Country

~~~~ Introduction

Idaho is an oddly boot-shaped state that suffers a bit of an identity problem, both internally and beyond its borders, at least when compared to the other states of the Northern Rockies. For example, even those living outside the region generally have a pretty good idea of what Montana is: It's Big Sky Country, a vast spread of mountains and grasslands teeming with wildlife and spectacular vistas. Similarly, Wyoming is known to almost everyone, romantically and rightfully, as the Cowboy State. Idaho, meanwhile—a state containing country and characters every bit as colorful as those found in Montana and Wyoming—is known first and foremost for its potatoes. Not for its wildlife-filled mountains, not for its hundreds of miles of wild, frothing rivers, but for its starch-filled tubers.

Suppose you knew these things, and nothing else, regarding the three states of the Northern Rockies. Then suppose you were given a chance to visit just one of them. Where would *you* choose to go on vacation? Probably not Idaho, unless you happen to be an avid student of agriculture.

Consequently, for those Americans who do have an image of Idaho, it is often something like a cross between Iowa and Ohio (two great states, but not exactly brimming with mountains). And as long as the farm lobby remains the powerhouse that it is, "Famous Potatoes" will probably continue gracing Gem State license plates, and spuds will continue filling the role of the state's primary public relations agent.

Maybe that's a good thing, after all; perhaps it will help keep the sparsely peopled Idaho outback free of crowds. Because a rich abundance of wonderful secrets hides behind the state's mundane slogan. For instance, Idaho is home to more miles of white-water rivers than any state in the Union. The Salmon River—the legendary River of No Return; the longest undammed, free-flowing river in the United States—runs from beginning to end within the state. The equally legendary Snake River, excepting its uppermost and lowest stretches, is also at home in Idaho.

Idaho truly is a land of superlatives. Where the Snake River forms the border between Idaho and Oregon it carves Hells Canyon, the deepest river gorge in North America. Hells Canyon reaches as deep as 7,900 feet, or half again as deep as the Grand Canyon of the Colorado. Idaho, the most heavily forested of the Rocky Mountain states, is home to millions of acres of wilderness, including the 2.2-million-acre Frank Church–River of No Return Wilderness, the largest wilderness area in the contiguous forty-eight states. The only thing separating the Frank Church–River of No Return from its neighbor to the north, the 1.3-million-acre Selway-Bitterroot Wilderness (a small percentage of which lops over into Montana), is the Magruder Corridor, a narrow, backcountry road that ultimately links Elk City, Idaho, and Montana's Bitterroot Valley. Combined, these wilderness areas comprise some 3.5 million acres. How big is that? Big enough to hold the state of Connecticut, with room to spare.

Idaho's farm fields, deserts, and northern timbered hills, along with the east front of the Bitterroot Range in Montana, are like an ever-changing buffer zone that cordons off Sun River–Salmon Country, a region holding some of the richest wild-country treasures in America. The buffer surrounds a grand stand of mountains that for the most part are composed of the granites of the Idaho *batholith*. (A batholith is any large expanse of granite covering approximately 50 square miles or more.) Much of the area within the batholith, even outside the wilderness areas, remains unroaded, owing to its rugged nature . . . and to the fact that much of its timber resources were destroyed in the great wildfire of 1910.

Whether you go by foot, skis, horseback, small aircraft, or a combination of modes, a sojourn into the unroaded heart of central Idaho should be on the "to-do" list of anyone who considers him- or herself a fan of the Rocky Mountain West.

Ironically, it may be that Idaho's dizzying geographic diversity contributes to the blurry perception of the state held by outsiders. It's true that the Wyoming landscape also changes quite a bit from east to west; less so, however, than Montana, where the differences are striking. But even Montana's broad range of landscapes falls short of that which you'll find spread across the length and breadth of Idaho. The Gem State is part Rocky Mountains, part Pacific Northwest, part Great Basin, and part high desert, with occasional sand dunes, frozen lava flows, and cities of rock thrown in for good measure.

These vast differences greatly affect the lifeways and political leanings of the residents. Those living in Coeur d'Alene and the surrounding big-timber country up north often feel more closely aligned with Spokane, Washington, or even with Seattle than with their own capital city. Meanwhile, many of those living in the southern farming areas of Idaho go to Wyoming to buy their groceries, to Nevada to spend their spare change, or to Salt Lake City to get married. Boise? Where's that? Somewhere over near Oregon, isn't it?

Generally, Sun Valley–Salmon Country is defined as the region lying south of the U.S. Highway 12 corridor, north of the Snake River Plain (or north of U.S. Highway 20), and east of U.S. Highway 95 and State Highway 55. Not included in the realm of this guide is the capital city of Boise, a beautiful and thriving community nestled in the desert just beyond the foothills of the Rocky Mountains. Also excluded is the northern panhandle of the state, which in my view culturally belongs to the Pacific Northwest more than to the Northern Rockies.

Sun Valley–Salmon Country teems with mountains: relatively well-known ranges like the Sawtooths, Pioneers, and Salmon Rivers; lesser-known ranges such as the Lost Rivers, White Clouds, and Clearwaters; and mountain ranges with obscure names, like the Yellowjackets, White Knobs, and Bighorn Crags.

At the bottom and center of the region, like a foundation, sits Sun Valley and the nearby Sawtooth National Recreation Area. It seems that even many of those who don't have a clear idea of where or what Idaho is can conjure images of Sun Valley. Their notions of North America's preeminent ski resort include fur coats, diamonds, movie stars, trophy homes, fancy cars, and flashy skiers. These stereotypes, while true to an extent, are merely part of the picture. More surprising, and usually more impressive to the first-time visitor is the tremendous array of mountainscapes surrounding Sun Valley—mountains that can provide some of the best and least crowded backpacking, horse packing, mountain biking, fishing, and hunting in the entire run of the Rocky Mountains.

It was that fishing and hunting, in part, that kept Ernest Hemingway returning time after time to the Sun Valley area after he first visited in the late 1930s. His initial trip came at the invitation of Averell Harriman, who had spearheaded the Union Pacific Railroad's creation of the Sun Valley Resort. The railroad's manager believed, correctly, that an appearance by the popular writer would attract other luminaries and tourists to the burgeoning resort. Another factor contributing to Hemingway's coming back for more than twenty years—on top of the great trout fishing in Silver Creek and pheasant hunting on the Picabo desert—was the unpretentious farmers and other locals he grew to know. These folks seem to have impressed Hemingway more than the Hollywood celebrities did, and among them he made some of his best friends ever.

Some of the finest, most down-to-earth people in America continue inhabiting the Idaho heartland. Not surprisingly, country as remote and hard to penetrate as some of that found in Sun Valley–Salmon Country has also attracted and/or bred its share of out-of-the-ordinary characters. Consider Sylvan Hart, for instance, whose life is documented in Harold Peterson's 1969 book *The Last of the Mountain Men.*

Hart, a.k.a. "Buckskin Billy," moved to the banks of the Salmon River in 1929, in an attempt to find security amid the failing economy of the Great Depression. He later said that in the early days he'd gotten by on roughly $50 a year, which he'd spent to procure what little he needed that he couldn't shoot, find, or fabricate. Hart ended up staying on the Salmon for more than forty years, spending his days hand-crafting items such as flintlock rifles, knives, copper pots, furniture, and deer- and elk-hide clothes. He also hunted, tended a 10,000 square-foot garden, and showed off his place and his creations to hundreds of river floaters who stopped by at his Five Mile Bar homestead. By his own measure Hart was not a hermit; he simply enjoyed living the self-sufficient life in the wilderness. In fact, he put his master's degree in engineering to professional use during World War II, when he left Idaho to work as a toolmaker at an airplane factory in Kansas. But when he died in 1980, it was at his beloved Five Mile Bar that Hart was buried.

The list of pursuits to keep the intrepid and/or energetic visitor occupied during a Sun Valley–Salmon Country visit is nearly inexhaustible. You can ski, camp, or fish; you can skate on blacktop, ice, or snow; and you can shop, ride horses into the wilderness, or take a scenic plane ride. Out of the scores of possibilities that exist, though, a trip to central Idaho is perhaps most incomplete without a dip in a natural hot springs, those serendipitous dividends arising as a result of the region's geology. Idaho has more hot springs than any other state, and most of them are in Sun Valley–Salmon Country. Dozens of opportunities to soak in nature's own hot waters await the visitor: from developed resorts built around natural springs, such as Zim's near New Meadows and Challis Hot Springs near Challis, to primitive backwoods pools, such as Weir Creek Hot Springs near Powell and Sunbeam Hot Springs outside Stanley.

Try it—you'll like it. Oh yes, and one other thing. Few potatoes are raised commercially in Sun Valley–Salmon Country. What agriculture is successfully carried out tends to be in the form of the same hay crops characteristic of high valleys throughout the Northern Rockies. Nevertheless, don't neglect to sample the spuds when visiting anywhere in Idaho. Fried, baked, scalloped, or mashed, they're the best you'll find in the world.

Moose

Mobile Continents and Movable Mountains

Y ou'll probably not be shocked to discover that the geology of Sun Valley–Salmon Country is closely related to that of western Montana. You may, however, be surprised to learn that a large share of the mountains in Glacier-Gold Country actually originated in western Idaho, before fracturing off and literally sliding into Big Sky Country.

Similarly, the inner workings of the mountains of central Idaho are tied to that which bubbles beneath Yellowstone-Teton Country, as residents of the Challis, Idaho, area were rudely reminded on an October morning in 1983. An earthquake measuring 7.3 on the Richter scale—severe enough to cause widespread disaster had it struck in a heavily populated area—was centered on nearby Borah Peak. The earthquake occurred along a band of faulting that radiates from the Yellowstone hot spot, the same band along which the Hebgen Lake earthquake shook and shattered things in August 1959.

The Borah Peak earthquake was felt throughout the region. It had far-flung effects, including that of altering the previously dependable schedule of Old Faithful. It also added a crack to the plastered dining-room ceiling of the author's home at the time in Missoula. Much closer to the epicenter, a pair of children en route to school in Challis were killed, as the tremor shook loose masonry from the Main Street building they were walking beside. New springs gushing groundwater appeared, while others dried up. The Big Lost River Range—including Borah Peak, already the highest mountain in Idaho—rose nearly a foot as the valley below to the west subsided several feet.

A high, impressive scarp line extending some 20 miles at the western base of the Lost Rivers marks the break along which the valley and mountains moved in opposition to one another. You can visit a scarp interpretive site by turning east off U.S. Highway 93 at a point 28 miles south of Challis, and driving 2.5 miles. Watch for a highway sign marking the turn.

Let's travel back in time a few years before the Borah Peak earthquake—say, 200 million years, to the beginning of the Jurassic Period of the Mesozoic era. A lot of what follows sounds like good, or maybe even bad science fiction; to accept it as truth requires great faith in geological science. In fact, much of it is in the theoretical stage and subject to change, as geologists dig deeper, then decipher, debate, and determine their findings.

The theory of *plate tectonics* states, generally, that the earth is surrounded by a relatively rigid outer layer called the *lithosphere*, made up of roughly a dozen immense *lithospheric plates*. The plates, which average about 60 miles in thickness, consist of the outermost portion of the earth's mantle topped with either oceanic or continental crust. Continental crust is composed of light igneous and metamorphic rocks. Oceanic crust, in contrast, typically consists of heavier basalts, which originate deeper within the mantle. Oceanic crust forms after basaltic lava erupts into the gap of an oceanic ridge, which is the zone where two plates are pulling apart from one another.

Lithospheric plates move independently of each other, atop a mass of partially melted rocks. This hot, slippery zone of the mantle is called the *asthenosphere.* Over time, as the plates slide around they collide with or move away from one another, fashioning new ocean floors and destroying old ones . . . and breaking apart existing continents while also creating new ones.

Geologists tell us that at the beginning of the Jurassic Period the western edge of the North American continent was located approximately where Idaho now borders Oregon and Washington. The future locations of towns such as Orofino were beachfront property, or close to it. In fact, the edge of the continent that existed during Jurassic times, when dinosaurs roamed the earth, can be seen at locations near Orofino, such as in the area of the visitor center at the Dworshak Dam. (Orofino is located 30 miles northwest of Kooskia on U.S. Highway 12; the dam is just north of town.) Geologists refer to this as the western Idaho *mylonite*, a zone of dramatically sheared rock approximately a mile wide. They believe the mylonite formed where friction from the sinking Pacific oceanic plate sheared the edge of the continental plate. East of the mylonite zone the rocks are continental granites representative of the Idaho batholith; west of the zone many of the rocks are dark gray diorites that suggest ancestral ties to the ocean.

As alluded to above, during the Jurassic Period the North American continental plate, moving west, encountered the plate of the Pacific Ocean floor. The ultra-slow-motion collision fractured the oceanic plate, which then began diving below the continental plate. This is the way it always works. A lithospheric plate covered with oceanic crust is denser than a plate covered with continental crust; any time the two collide, the oceanic plate is the one to sink. As an oceanic plate dives below a continental plate, its rock is consumed by the heat of the mantle and recycled into magma, the building material of future crust.

The collision of the plates caused a monumental crumpling and buckling of the edge of the continental crust, greatly thickening the western margin of the continent. Continental crust piling up along *thrust faults* created a broad band of rudimentary mountains. It was the first stage in the creation of the Northern Rockies. A deep *trench* formed where the sinking Pacific plate was overridden by the North American continental plate. The trench accumulated massive quantities

of sediment, which also contributed to the growth of mountains. For millions of years crust and sediment continued rising, eventually forming mountains that geologists say may have resembled today's Andes, a towering South American range similarly made up of thrust faults along a continent's western edge.

As the continent continued moving west at the rate of approximately 2 inches per year, overtaking the floor of the Pacific, two huge remnants of continental crust lying at sea, along with numerous groups of islands, approached closer and closer to the mainland. These land masses ultimately nestled against North America. Composed of rock too light to sink with the oceanic plate, they proceeded to stack up against the continent in the area of the trench. The twisted rocks of the Seven Devils complex, which you can see between Riggins and White Bird (they're largely contained in the Hells Canyon Wilderness and National Recreation Area), are the compressed remains of an assemblage of former Pacific islands that docked against the continent in this manner during the Cretaceous Period, around 100 million years ago. Geologists, after analyzing fossils embedded in sediment of the Seven Devils, speculate that the islands destined to become mountains in Idaho may have begun their lives in the ocean somewhere between Peru and Guatemala.

The process continued for a period of approximately 100 million years, with North America accumulating more and more real estate, continually chasing the west coast farther west. Enough land piled up against the continent that it finally covered and killed the oceanic trench. Still, westward movement of the continent continued, so something had to give: The oceanic plate fractured in a new place, forming another trench farther to the west. Finally, by roughly 40 million years ago the West Coast as we know it had taken shape. Today the oceanic trench, the third in the series, is located off the coast of Oregon and Washington, where it continues swallowing the ocean floor and bringing land lying at sea closer and closer to North America.

Back to the rudimentary Northern Rockies of Jurassic times. Unfathomable amounts of heat were produced as the oceanic slab sank, scraping down against the mantle. For many millions of

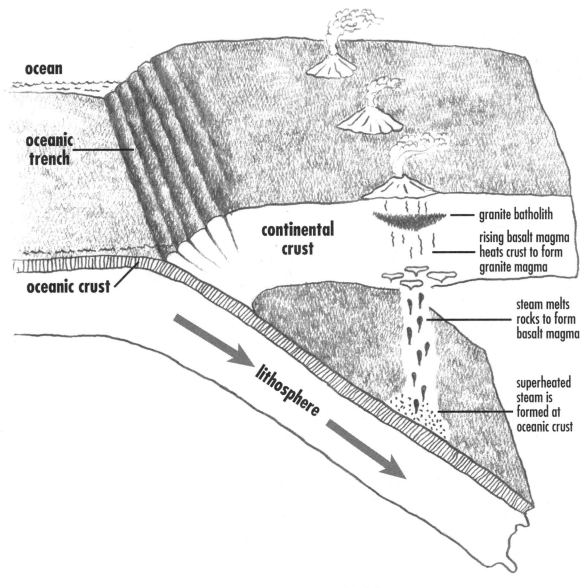

How granite magma is formed

years water escaping in the form of steam blasted at the mantle above the descending slab, forming basalt magma. Heat rising from the basalt magma, in turn, soaked the lower continental crust, causing it to melt into granite magmas. These bubbled upward, ever higher into the crust.

By late Cretaceous times, approximately 70 million years ago, tremendous quantities of magma had intruded into the rudimentary mountains lining the former western edge of the continent. The hot magma had weakened and softened

the mountains, with the eventual effect of breaking off gargantuan slabs, which slid down to the east along a slick layer of granite magma into east-central Idaho and southwestern Montana. One of the suspected results of this is the Boulder batholith, the source of the ore that made Butte, Montana, the "richest hill on earth."

The ancient mountains, having attained elevations of perhaps 20,000 feet, were now reduced into a lower and broader outline of mountains. Those transported mountains, along with the sheared-off mountains they left behind, were the building blocks—or, perhaps more accurately, the tearing-down blocks—of much of the Northern Rockies as we know them.

As it approached the earth's surface, the magma responsible for weakening and fracturing the mountains crystallized into granite, creating the Idaho batholith. The Idaho batholith, which encompasses most of the rock seen in central Idaho today, is actually two very large spreads of Cretaceous granite—the Bitterroot batholith to the northeast and Atlanta batholith to the southwest. The two are separated by an arc of ancient basement rocks that follows the course of the Salmon River. Complicating things, though, is the fact that not all granite in central Idaho belongs to the Idaho batholith: Additional igneous events occurred in Eocene times, roughly 50 million years ago, in many areas intruding younger granites into older ones, and also spitting out tons of rhyolite ash. The latter can clearly be seen in places such as the Challis volcanic rocks, just south of the town of Challis.

South and east of the Idaho batholith the mountains are more characteristically the result of *basin and range faulting*. The ranges running from the Challis and Salmon areas southeasterly to the Snake River Plain—the Lost Rivers, Lemhis, Pahsimerois and others—and the valleys between them are distinct crustal blocks that have fractured apart from an earlier version of the Rocky Mountains. As these blocks pull away from each other, some move up to fashion mountains as others move down to make valleys. The southeast-to-northwest trend of the basins and ranges can readily be discerned by looking at a state road map of Idaho: Just notice the paralleling roads running through the valleys that separate the main ranges in that part of the state.

Basin and range faulting apparently began at about the same time the Snake River Plain, and the Columbia Plateau farther west, began building. It is thought that these all were set in motion approximately 17 million years ago by a fantastic geologic event of celestial proportions, when a giant meteorite crashed to earth in southeast Oregon. The resultant explosion set off earthquakes which, among other things, created deep cracks extending through the mantle and crust. This created escape routes for pressurized magma,

which began flooding out to fashion the Columbia Plateau. The outpouring of hot lava was so massive that it turned the climate of the region—perhaps that of the entire planet—warm and wet.

Basin and range faulting began shortly after the meteorite's impact, first fracturing the crust in northern Nevada and western Idaho, areas close to the site of the explosion, then migrating eastward. Some geologists contend that the earthshattering force of the meteorite's impact is also what gave birth to the Yellowstone hot spot. Evidence seems to back it up.

The Snake River Plain is composed primarily of 15 million years' worth of rhyolitic volcanic eruptions, similar to those that most recently have smothered Yellowstone's Central Plateau. The volcanoes get progressively older the farther west you travel down the Snake River from the active Yellowstone volcano. The Plain's westernmost, and oldest volcanoes are located in southwestern Idaho, not far from where the Oregon meteorite landed. What this means is that the Snake River Plain defines the swath of the continent that has passed over the hot spot. By tracking the age of features of the Snake River Plain, it appears that the continent has traveled roughly 350 miles in 15 million years—or just under 2 inches a year, which backs up other findings. (For more information on the Yellowstone hot spot, *see* The Land, Yellowstone-Teton Country.)

The eastern Snake River Plain has seen two stages of volcanism, which is typical of an area associated with a heat source like the Yellowstone hot spot. The first poured forth deep rhyolitic lava flows; the second, much more recent stage resulted in shallow basaltic flows. Basaltic lavas form relatively deep in the earth, where the bottom of the crust meets the mantle; rhyolitic lava, in contrast, forms from crustal material closer to the earth's surface. Rhyolite contains a great deal of silica, so it doesn't readily permit trapped gases to escape. Consequently, rhyolite volcanoes, like uncorked bottles of shaken-up champagne, explode with great violence. They release incredible amounts of ash and thick, pasty lava.

The plain's older, much thicker rhyolite flows, which underlie the basaltic flows, emerged directly as a result of the intense heat provided by the Yellowstone hot spot. The rhyolite volcanoes died out as the continent moved over the hot spot. The younger basaltic flows resulted from residual heat in the mantle and crust, which continued to produce an upswelling of magma long after the hot spot was far away. As it moved upward, the basaltic lava collected in magma chambers, where it built enough pressure to finally escape through cracks and fissures.

Some of Sun Valley–Salmon Country's most recently laid-down landscapes are those at Craters of the Moon National Monument, where basaltic lava flows as young as 2,000 years bake black in the sun. The monument abuts the mountains at the northern margin of the Snake River Plain, 20 miles southwest of the town of Arco.

It appears that this area of the Snake River Plain is in the early stages of basin and range faulting—stretching apart, breaking into blocks, and growing new mountains and valleys—and that the event responsible for cracking the earth in the area of Craters of the Moon was the formation of a volcanic *rift zone*. The *Great Rift*, along which Craters of the Moon lies, is a line of short, deep clefts in the earth's crust approximately 60 miles long and 1.5 to 5 miles wide, dotted with craters and cones. Its northwesterly trend mimics that of the basin and range faulting both north and south of the Snake River Plain. It was through cracks provided by the Great Rift that basaltic lava found its way to the surface here.

More than sixty distinct lava flows along the Great Rift—flowing from two dozen vents and during eight major periods of eruption—have contributed to the lava fields at Craters of the Moon during the past 15,000 years. Each eruption, or release of pent-up pressure, lasted approximately 1,000 years before it was followed by a roughly equal time of calm, during which the pressures within the crust resumed building. Based on the time record in the rocks and in unearthed, charred vegetation, the next period of activity could be right around the corner.

Basaltic lava contains less silica than rhyolite, making it more fluid and less gas-filled. It tends to ooze onto the scene, rather as molasses would, rather than explode in the mode of a rhyolite eruption. You can detect this by investigating the results at Craters of the Moon National Monument, where much of the basalt looks like lava that simply froze in its tracks. The taffy-like, black billows

Pahoehoe lava

of basalt called *pahoehoe* resulted from eruptions of lava that contained adequate quantities of water to make them quite fluid. *Aa* flows, in contrast, are rough, craggy, masses of boot-eating basalt filled with little gas bubbles. (*Pahoehoe* and *aa* are both words of Hawaiian derivation.) While chemically similar to pahoehoe, the lava of aa flows contained very little water when erupting—just enough that heated steam trying to escape was trapped as bubbles—resulting in angular blocks with sharp edges and rough surfaces.

In closing, let's travel from deep rifts lying beneath Craters of the Moon National Monument to lofty mountains located just a few dozen miles northwest of there. The most popular and spectacular mountains of central Idaho, the Sawtooths, rise like a wall against the western edge of the Stanley Basin. Crustal movement along the Sawtooth fault resulted in the Stanley Basin dropping even as the Sawtooth Range moved skyward. The pinkish granite you'll see in the mountains is that of the Sawtooth batholith, which was intruded during the Eocene, some 20 million years after the mountains' paler granites of the Idaho batholith crystallized.

In subsequent, relatively recent geologic times the Sawtooths were dramatically altered by Pleistocene glaciers. Rivers of ice obviously traveled down the mountains' drainages to just beyond the valley mouths, where they deposited the moraines that impound lakes such as Redfish and Alturas. The Sawtooths weathered far more glacial sculpting than did the White Cloud Mountains, which rim the opposite, eastern side of the Stanley Basin. Only the very highest reaches of the White Clouds are glaciated, yet the peaks of those mountains reach elevations as high as or even higher than those of the Sawtooths.

Why were the Sawtooths so heavily invaded by glaciers, whereas the nearby White Clouds went almost untouched?

It's presumed that the Sawtooths snatched more than their share of snow from eastward-moving storms, thereby shortchanging the White Clouds. It's another reminder that the shapes assumed by landscapes are often related to phenomena occurring far beyond the innards of the earth—from the jet stream to meteorites.

History

When they crested the Continental Divide at Lemhi Pass on an August morning in 1805, Meriwether Lewis and three companions became the first non-Indians known to step into the future Idaho.

Triumphant, the party descended the steep west side of the pass to find, Lewis later wrote, "a handsome bold running Creek of Cold Clear water . . . [where] I first tasted the water of the great Columbia river." Soon Lewis and his companions encountered a band of Shoshone Indians, who were initially frightened by the white men, but within moments were showering them in a greeting that surpassed any expectations or desires. "We were all carressed and besmeared with their grease and paint," wrote Lewis, "till I was heartily tired of the national hugg."

At the Shoshone's camp, located north of present Tendoy, Idaho, the men met with the chief Cameahwait. Through Lewis's interpreter, the French-Shawnee George Drouillard, Lewis learned that the river they were camped on, the Lemhi, fed nearby into the much larger Salmon River. Cameahwait allowed as that river's waters and canyon were altogether impassable by any means, including foot, horse, or watercraft.

After spending a couple of nights at the Shoshone encampment, Lewis and his companions, with Cameahwait and several other Shoshone accompanying them, crossed the Continental Divide back into Montana, where they rejoined the rest of the Corps of Discovery at Camp Fortunate. It was at this meeting where it was learned that Cameahwait and Sacajawea were long-separated siblings, a fact that didn't at all hinder the horse-trading negotiations to follow.

The next day William Clark set out with several others on a scouting trip, to see for himself if Cameahwait's appraisal was accurate, regarding the impassable nature of the Salmon River and its canyon. After crossing Lemhi Pass the party followed the Lemhi River northwest to its confluence with the Salmon, at the present site of Salmon City. Clark proclaimed the bigger of the two streams "Lewis's River," a name that obviously did not stick. The group proceeded to travel down that river for roughly 35 miles, until Clark looked ahead at the treacherous Pine Creek Rapids and into one of the roughest tangles of terrain in the Rocky Mountains. His Shoshone guide told him that what they'd floated at this point was nothing, compared to the torrent the river became downstream. In his journals Clark wrote that the river " . . . runs with great violence from one rock to the other on each side foaming & roreing thro rocks in every direction, So as to render the passage of any thing impossible . . . " and that the embracing mountains were "like the Side of a tree Streight up . . . "

Clark sent one of his companions, John Colter, back to meet with Lewis, carrying word that the party should move north to locate another, less tortured fork of the Columbia to descend. That they did, after regrouping, by traveling up the Salmon's north fork and over Lost Trail Pass, down the Bitterroot River, then up Lolo Creek to Lolo Pass. From there, on the Bitterroot Divide, they traveled along the ridges north of the Lochsa River to reach the Clearwater River, which they subsequently followed to its confluence with the

Snake. Clark correctly surmised that this river, the Snake, carried the waters of the river he had earlier scouted (the Salmon, that is). Again he tried honoring his friend and fellow captain by naming this waterway "Lewis's River."

The Lewis and Clark expedition had given America only a loose handhold on the Oregon country, which included present Idaho. The future Gem State remained disputed territory for another forty years. By 1825 Spain and Russia had given up their claims to parts of the country, leaving Great Britain and the United States to duke it out regarding who owned what. Explorers representing both nations penetrated the nooks and crannies of the mountainous outback of Idaho, trapping the beaver out of one drainage, then moving on to find another where beaver still thrived. As they webbed the countryside, both Americans and Englishmen attempted to befriend Indians, whom they hoped would later be used as allies in the struggle against the other country's claims.

During the winter of 1832–33, twenty-seven years after the Corps of Discovery had camped not far from the site of Salmon, both American and British fur trappers congregated at the confluence of the Lemhi and Salmon rivers, holing up with encampments of friendly Indians. Kit Carson was there, and so were Thomas Fitzpatrick, Joe Meek, Captain Bonneville, and Jim Bridger, who wore a recently acquired Blackfeet arrowhead in his back.

But the days of beaver-trapping were rapidly winding down, and the mountain man was soon supplanted by the missionary. The first whites to settle in Idaho were the Presbyterians Henry and Eliza Spalding, who established a mission in 1836 up north in Nez Perce country, at Lapwai. Despite Henry Spalding's distasteful, contentious personality, the mission putted along for more than a decade. It was closed in 1847, however, after Marcus and Narcissa Whitman, with whom the Spaldings had first come west, and twelve others were killed by Indians at the Whitmans' mission near present-day Walla Walla, Washington.

In 1855 a contingent of Brigham Young's Latter-day Saints established Fort Limhi, named for a king in the Book of Mormon, not far from the point where Meriwether Lewis had entered Idaho fifty years earlier. (Gentiles misspelled it

"Lemhi." The name stuck, and it was later lent to the nearby river, mountain range, and Indian tribe.) A Bannock chief had persuaded the Mormons to settle on the Lemhi, pointing out that here they would enjoy ready access in summer to Flatheads, Shoshone, Nez Perce, and Bannocks, all of whom met in the area to trade and catch spawning salmon.

In 1857 it was looking as if Fort Lemhi would become Idaho's first permanent white settlement. The settlers had baptized more than a hundred Indians, and after paying a visit that year and liking what he saw, Brigham Young had even sent in additional settlers. But the entire thing fell apart that winter, owing to brewing unrest between the Mormons and the U.S. government, which opposed the Mormons' polygamous ways and feared an attempt at succession by them. Related problems also flared between the Mormons and Indians. Realizing that the U.S. Army was probably more on their side than that of the Mormons, in February 1858 several Shoshone and Bannocks took advantage of the situation by attacking Fort Lemhi, killing two and wounding several others, and making off with more than 200 head of cattle. The Saints had all headed south for the Salt Lake Valley before spring arrived.

So, for more than fifty years after Lewis and Clark passed through, the future Idaho remained primarily a place where whites only visited—to find beaver, find their way to Oregon, or try to help the Indians find Jesus. In 1860 two events coincided that precipitated permanent white settlement both in the south and the north of the state. One: In April, five companies of Mormon colonizers, which Brigham Young had dispatched from the Salt Lake Valley, founded the permanent community of Franklin in the extreme southeast of present Idaho on the Cub River, in what was then the Washington Territory. The settlement demands an asterisk, though, since the founders believed they still were inside Utah, and, in fact, in 1868 the Utah legislature incorporated the town. Four years later a survey revealed the boo-boo.

Two: In September 1860 Irish immigrant E. D. Pierce and a group of fellow prospectors, surreptitiously working the forks of the Clearwater River on the Nez Perce reservation, found gold in Orofino Creek, not far from where the Corps of

Discovery had exited the wilds of the Bitterroot and Clearwater mountains on their trip west. A nearby townsite was platted, and Pierce City began to explode as word got out and the gold-hungry came in.

By the next spring, Lewiston, located roughly 75 miles west of Pierce at the mouth of the Clearwater on the navigable Snake River, had evolved into a primary supply center. Henry Plummer, of Bannack-Virginia City, Montana, infamy, spent a spell in and around Lewiston, honing his trade of relieving miners of their gold. As thousands of Union and Confederate soldiers fought for their lives and countries on the battle-fields of the South, hundreds of their fellow coun-trymen—both Northerners and Southerners—ran through the hills of Idaho selfishly looking to make a quick buck. Additional strikes in the region came quickly as the prospectors fanned out—first at Elk City, then at Florence near the Salmon River, then at Warren (northeast of present McCall), and then in the Boise Basin, which proved the most productive area of all.

Most of the earlier gold strikes occurred on the Nez Perce reservation. Never mind the fact that the Treaty of 1855 had promised the Nez Perce, Yakima, and Umatilla that the tribes "would never again be disturbed while the sun shone or water ran." Lewiston, nicknamed "Ragtown," started life as a city of canvas tents, chiefly because it was on Nez Perce lands, and Indian agent A. J. Cain had threatened to rip down any permanent-looking structures built there by white squatters.

Relations between whites and the Nez Perce, which to this point in history had generally been positive, took a turn for the worse, and then kept turning. The branch of the Nez Perce known thereafter as the "Treaty" Indians in 1863 signed away 90 percent of the reservation, at less than a dime an acre, which angered and alienated the non-Treaty branch of the tribe. Festering tensions exploded in June 1877, when a group of young Nez Perce murdered several white settlers. This culminated in the flight of the non-Treaty Nez Perce from the region that year. (*See* History, Yellowstone-Teton Country.)

For the most part—other than the short-lived Mormon experiment up the Lemhi River—things had remained pretty much as they'd been at and

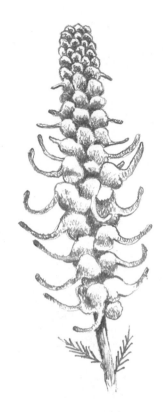

Elephant head flower

around the confluence of the Lemhi and Salmon for the six decades following Lewis and Clark's visit. The quiet came to a screaming halt in 1866, when the cry of "Gold!" was heard in nearby Leesburg. Salmon City quickly mushroomed as a supply cen-ter, after being platted by George Shoup, a mer-chant from Virginia City, Montana. Shoup made a fortune through his mercantile and land-and-cattle businesses in the Salmon area, then continued on to become Idaho's last territorial governor, then its first state governor, and, finally, one of its first U.S. senators, serving from 1891 to 1901.

On March 4, 1863, President Lincoln signed into law the Idaho Organic Act, creating the Idaho Territory. The bill cleaved the future state of Idaho from the Washington Territory, and added most of the future Montana and Wyoming to the newly formed territory. Lewiston was named as capital (illegally, since it was on Nez Perce lands). In the following year, 1864, things changed again, when most of Wyoming was attached to the new Dakota Territory and Montana was split into a separate territory. Idaho almost as we know it had taken shape, although a bit of the future western Wyoming was still attached.

It was to the chagrin of many in northern Idaho and the new northwest Montana that the dividing line between the Idaho and Montana territories was determined to be the Bitterroot Divide, rather than the Continental Divide. The new borders in many ways ignored natural boundaries, and created the strangely skinny panhandle of Idaho. Had those unhappy folks up north gotten their way, today Missoula, Butte, Flathead Lake, and most of Glacier National Park would all be in Idaho instead of Montana.

As some men struck it rich in the new territory's gold diggings and stayed, and many more remained poor and moved on, others, like Lloyd Magruder, died. Seven months after the creation of the Idaho Territory, on October 3, 1863, Magruder, a native of Maryland, left Bannack on a return journey to Lewiston, following a fruitful business trip to the Montana goldfields. With him he carried several thousand dollars worth of cash and gold dust, which he had earned by selling a load of supplies he'd wrangled from Lewiston aboard a pack train of five dozen mules.

In Magruder's company were David Renton, James Romain, Christopher Lower, and Billy Page, men whom Magruder had met in Virginia City, Montana (at that time part of the Idaho Territory). After gaining Magruder's confidence, the men had requested and gained permission to accompany him across the Bitterroots and back to Lewiston. Four others joined the party, too, including Charles Allen, two brothers from Missouri named Chalmers, and Bill Phillips, a man whom Magruder had known earlier when both were working the gold country of California.

From the Bitterroot Valley Magruder and company followed the South Nez Perce Trail into the mountains, a route long used by Nez Perce Indians to access the bison-abundant plains of Montana. En route, late on the night of October 11, the men who had first joined Magruder in Virginia City murdered him and the four others in cold blood, as well as killing their horses and mules. They employed axes and shotguns to perform the grisly deeds.

After bypassing Elk City then leaving the mountains, the foursome caught a stage to Walla Walla, then hightailed it with Magruder's booty to San Francisco. A friend of Magruder's named Hill Beachy, working on a hunch and an assumption, tirelessly tracked the culprits through California. Beachy, the generous, garrulous, and good-natured proprietor of the Luna House hotel in Lewiston, managed to find the murderers and bring them back to Lewiston to stand trial.

Found guilty of the murders, Renton, Romain, and Lower were put to death by hanging on March 4, 1864, a year to the day after the creation of the Idaho Territory. Theirs were the first legal executions in the territory. Page, whose testimony had helped to convict the other three—and who apparently was innocent of murder, although his attitude toward the entire affair seemed rather cavalier—was spared.

Today a marker found along the rough-and-tumble Magruder Corridor, which links Elk City and Montana's Bitterroot Valley, memorializes the dark night of the Magruder Massacre.

As it turned out, contrary to what William Clark had concluded, the Salmon River was not unrunnable. But it was not until more than ninety years after Clark had scouted the river that anyone proved it.

In 1896 one Harry Guleke captained a flat-bottomed scow all the way from Salmon City to Riggins. The monster of a boat that Guleke and first mate Dave Sandiland rode through dozens of miles of rapids was 32 feet long and 8 feet wide, and it had ponderously long and heavy sweeps, with blades 6 feet long, 18 inches wide, and 2 inches thick. An elevated platform in the middle of the boat offered the captain a relatively auspicious perch from which to check out what lay ahead, and the boat's bottom was doubly covered in lumber to enhance buoyancy and durability. Fully loaded, the scow weighed more than four tons. Owing largely to the abundance of green lumber used, however, it floated like a cork, displacing only approximately 6 inches of water.

After his maiden voyage, Guleke proceeded to make a commercial success of one-way trips down the River of No Return, rocketing through the rapids carrying food, sluice boxes, farming implements, and other supplies, which he delivered to homesteaders and prospectors working the gravel bars and mountain slopes separating Riggins and

Salmon City. He served as the outback residents' primary means of communication both to and from the world beyond.

Word spread of Guleke's temerity and skill, and he soon evolved into the Salmon River's earliest commercial outfitter, as joyriders signed on to take the trip with him. Those floating on the Salmon with Guleke included numerous luminaries, and even an expedition of the National Geographic Society went downriver with him in 1935.

Still, hauling freight, and not thrill-seekers, remained Guleke's primary motive for continuing to tackle the Main Fork of the Salmon. For each trip he would build a new scow in Salmon, sell the boat in Riggins or Lewiston, then find his long and circuitous way back to Salmon by intermodal means that often included foot, stage, and train. During four decades of floating, Guleke never lost a life, although more than a little freight took a soaking ride in the river.

Ketchum was established in 1880 as a smelting center for the Warm Springs mining district, where lead and silver were being extracted from the hills. The town was initially labeled "Leadville," but the postal department quickly suggested that a more original name be chosen, since several Leadvilles already dotted the maps of the West. So the town was re-christened in honor of David Ketchum, who had staked a claim and constructed a cabin in the Big Wood River Valley in 1879.

The lead-and-silver boom in the mountains surrounding Ketchum lasted only about a decade, when it shriveled due to descending mineral prices and ascending labor unrest. Fortunately for Ketchum's future, the abundant mineral resources had attracted the Wood River Branch of the Oregon Short Line, a subsidiary of the Union Pacific, which reached town in 1884. Those staying on in the area after the mining activity died down typically turned to raising sheep or cattle. Thanks to those railroad tracks running to town from the main line in Shoshone, tiny Ketchum in the first part of the twentieth century grew into the biggest sheep-shipping center in the West, and reportedly second in the world only to Sydney, Australia. But even then things in Ketchum were ordinarily pretty quiet, turning loud only in the

Mining ruins

fall, when thousands of bleating sheep flocked to town from the surrounding hills and basins.

Ultimately, more important to Ketchum's future than that which the Wood River Branch hauled out of town—minerals and livestock, that is—was what it hauled *into* town. On a January day in 1936 Count Felix Schaffgotsch, a young Austrian in the employ of the Union Pacific Railroad, stepped off the train in the upper Wood River Valley. Approximately a mile east of Ketchum he located what he had been dispatched to find; that which he had traveled thousands of miles searching for, and the sleepy valley awoke to a new and entirely unexpected reality.

W. Averell Harriman, chairman of the board of the Union Pacific, at the onset of the Great Depression had resolved to build a ski resort in the Western United States that would measure up to those in Europe where he had skied. The 1932 Winter Olympic Games in Lake Placid, New York, which Harriman had attended and greatly enjoyed, had further bolstered his interest in the gravity-fed sport of skiing. Of course, it wasn't an altogether altruistic plan on the part of Harriman and the railroad: By offering travelers a sizzling new destination, Harriman knew he could punch up the U.P.'s sagging ticket sales.

Harriman talked the railroad's president into footing the bill for Schaffgotsch's extended travels, on which he combed the mountains of the West, searching for promising locations for Harriman's dream resort. Schaffgotsch toured Washington, Oregon, California, Utah, Colorado, and

Wyoming. He encountered places that looked good, some of them very good, but none of them *just right*. It seemed that either they had too much wind, or too little snow; or they were too far from a railhead, or too close to a city.

Then Schaffgotsch happened into the sheep-shipping center of Ketchum, Idaho. Reporting to Harriman on his discovery, he said: "It contains more delightful features for a winter sports center than any other place I have seen in the United States, Switzerland or Austria." Later he would refer to the area surrounding Ketchum as "God's own choice for a ski resort."

Within days of receiving word that Schaffgotsch had found *the* place, Harriman traveled to Ketchum and on behalf of the U.P. snapped up the 4,000-acre Brass Ranch for $39,000. Almost immediately construction began on the Sun Valley Lodge, a 220-room beauty boasting a pair of immense, V-shaped wings. Largely as a fire precaution, much of the lodge was constructed of dense concrete, which was poured into rough-sawn lumber forms, lending pillars and other features a faux wood grain appearance.

Remarkably, the Sun Valley Lodge opened on December 31, 1936, the last day of the same year that Schaffgotsch had first steamed into town. Not long after the resort's gala opening, *Life* magazine ran an article and pictorial entitled "East Goes West to Idaho's Sun Valley, Society's Newest Playground." And in came the celebrities. However, wanting to beckon regular folks as well as the rich and fancy, the railroad also built the Challenger Inn, named for the U.P.'s economy-class luxury trains. The name "Sun Valley" was chosen by Steve Hannagan, the P.R. whiz hired by Harriman who had helped transform Miami Beach from a stretch of deserted sand into a world-famous destination resort. The first chair-lifts in Sun Valley—and in the nation—were constructed on Dollar and Proctor mountains. Designed by a U.P. engineer named James Curran, they were modifications of a machine Curran had designed for loading bananas onto ships; he simply substituted chairs where formerly there had been banana hooks.

(Meanwhile, other events in the 1930s were transpiring to blaze the way for outdoor pursuits in Sun Valley–Salmon Country. At about the same time the Sun Valley Resort began attracting its first skiers, President Roosevelt's New Deal was investing soundly in Idaho's recreational future, by way of the Civilian Conservation Corps. An army of young men invaded Idaho's forests, where they built trails, roads, and fire lookouts; constructed scores of public facilities; and fought fires and cleared timber to prevent future fires. The CCC's legacy in Idaho, while often seamless and transparent, is profound.)

Roughing it in luxury was the Sun Valley Resort's dictum from day one. The tradition, which continues today, stopped only once for a hiatus between 1943 and 1946, when the resort served as a convalescent center for members of the Navy returning from World War II. In 1964, the board of directors of the Union Pacific, concluding that operating a resort and managing a railroad shared little in common, sold the Sun Valley Resort to the Janss Corporation. Since 1977 it has been owned by R. Earl Holding, proprietor of the Little America chain of hotels.

Seeing Sun Valley–Salmon Country

Lolo Pass to McCall

This section of the book begins at Lolo Pass, sitting a mile high at the Idaho–Montana border. From there the text leads to Grangeville, through the wet and wild spread of mountains fashioned by the sculpting action of the Lochsa and Selway rivers and countless lesser streams. From White Bird, located a few miles southwest of Grangeville, the narrative leads along the lower Salmon River to Riggins. (The span of country separating Lolo Pass and Riggins is the only area covered in this book that is within the Pacific Time Zone; everywhere else is in the Mountain Time Zone.)

From Riggins the route climbs back to the high country at New Meadows by way of the Little Salmon River. After exploring the year-round resort of McCall and the countryside surrounding it, you'll dive headlong through miles of mountain fastness to the glorious Stanley Basin; from there it's on to Sun Valley, the essential North American destination ski resort. (Know, however, that the Stanley–Sun Valley area makes a great place for a vacation even during those times of year when no snow covers the mountains and valleys!) From Sun Valley you'll continue into east-central Idaho, a big, empty, and often overlooked region defined by rivers like the Big Lost, Little Lost, Pahsimeroi, and Salmon, and the mountains around and through which they flow.

TRACING LEWIS AND CLARK THROUGH IDAHO: THE LOCHSA-SELWAY OUTBACK

At **Lolo Pass**, straddling the Bitterroot Divide, you'll find the parking area for the Lolo Pass Winter Sports Area, a favorite playground of cross-country skiers and snowmobilers who head from the parking area across Packer Meadows before climbing onto the slopes above. The parking lot, as well as the Lolo Pass Visitor Center fronting it, are in Idaho, but it is Montana-licensed cars and trucks that you'll see filling the lot on a snowy winter weekend. Metropolitan Missoula is just 45 miles away, whereas the nearest Idaho community of any size is well over 100 winding miles in the distance. The same roads and trails used for over-snow travel in winter offer terrific hiking and mountain biking in summer, when the camas and bear grass often present unusually beautiful displays in Packer Meadows and surroundings.

From Lolo Pass, continue southwest into Idaho along U.S. Highway 12, the **Lewis and Clark Highway**, and soon you'll come to the **DeVoto Memorial Grove**, a stately stand of wet woods cloaked in western red cedar and footed in ferns. The grove's name honors the Western scholar and conservationist Bernard DeVoto, best known for his work on editing the journals of Lewis and Clark. The historian asked that when he died his ashes be spread in this grove, a place where he often camped while researching the route of the Corps of Discovery. And so it was done, when DeVoto died in 1955.

Near **Powell**, situated 13 miles into the Gem State near milepost 162, White Sand Creek and the Crooked Fork merge to become the Lochsa (*LOCK-saw*), a quintessentially clear and tumultuous, north woods river that is a component of the officially designated **Middle Fork Clearwater Wild and Scenic River**. Avid kayakers and river runners using other sorts of watercraft come from the world around to challenge the Lochsa, as well as to tackle its wild-country comrade, the Selway River.

At Powell swing into the **Powell Ranger District** (telephone 208–942–3113), where you can acquire an almost-essential visitor map of the Clearwater National Forest. (Consider picking up the map for the adjacent Nez Perce National Forest while you're at it.) Secrets revealed by this map—ones which may be elaborated on by the ranger on duty, if you can persuade him or her to divulge additional information—include a pair of nearby, *au naturel* hot springs. **Jerry Johnson Hot Springs** is located south off the highway from a point approximately 10 miles west of Powell, where you'll cross a footbridge spanning the Lochsa then hike for about a mile up the trail following Warm Springs Creek. **Weir Creek Hot Springs** is found another 9 miles down the road, then a short hike to the north. Weir, the less publicized of the pair, is ordinarily the lesser used, as well.

West of Powell U.S. Highway 12 snakes crazily alongside the Lochsa, which swirls and splashes through steep-sloped surroundings of rock and timber. Look high into the seemingly impenetrable tangle of wooded terrain to the south. In places you're peering at the northern margin of the immense wildlands complex consisting of the large Selway-Bitterroot Wilderness and the even larger Frank Church–River of No Return Wilderness. Their trails and untrailed wilds are legally accessible only by going on foot, on horseback, or on skis (although several grandfathered-in landing strips do remain). The next road to the south, a dirt byway known as the Magruder Corridor, is roughly 50 miles away as the raven flies—but much farther than that if you were to attempt to walk along the twisting and mountainous route from here to there. The next *paved* road you would hit if you were able to stroll from U.S. Highway 12 in a beeline due south—that being State Highway 75 at a point east of Stanley—is approximately 160 miles away.

You would see some incredible and magnificent things between the two swaths of pavement. And, in fact, a trail has been blazed: the **Idaho State Centennial Trail**, which links existing trails to run the north-to-south length of the state. The trail crosses U.S. Highway 12 not far east of the Lochsa Historical Ranger Station, located roughly 40 miles southwest of Powell. To follow the trail from U.S. Highway 12 to State Highway 75 would be much farther than 160 miles, of course, since undulations in terrain preclude beeline travel. Obviously, this is a jaunt that would require extensive planning and good fitness.

Now, look to the north. It was up there, somewhere, through a jungle of rocks and downfall timber, that late in 1805 the Lewis and Clark expedition fought their way across the west slope of the Bitterroot Range. They more or less followed a trail that had been used for decades by west-slope Nez Perce Indians, who had traced it en route to hunting expeditions on the plains to the east, where bountiful bison herds grazed. Khusahna Ishkit, or "buffalo trail," as the Nez Perce called the trail, was oppositely followed by early Salish Indians living east of the Bitterroots, who used the trail westbound to avail themselves of the Lochsa River's fruitful spawning runs of salmon and steelhead trout.

The **Lolo Trail**, as the path came to be called, was perhaps the most arduous leg of the Corps of Discovery's entire journey. The going and route-finding were extremely difficult, and game was so scarce that expedition members were reduced to killing horses for food. On finally breaking out of the mountains and encountering friendly Indians, the party traded for dogs to eat—even though the Native Americans had offered them salmon. Fish, it seems, was not a fashionable food among the expedition, whose members had become accustomed to eating as much as nine pounds of red meat per day back in buffalo country.

Seventy-two years later, in 1877, Chief Joseph and the Nez Perce crossed the trail heading east as they fled from General Oliver O. Howard and his U.S. Army troops. The going by then was easier: In 1865 Congress had appropriated $50,000 to widen the trail into a wagon road, making it possible for supply wagons to travel between the port of Lewiston, Idaho, and Montana's mushrooming gold camps. Then, more than fifty years later the trail was upgraded again. During several summers in the early 1930s, Civilian Conservation Corps workers, toiling from both ends, constructed a rough road through that tortuous terrain traced by the Lolo Trail. They met somewhere near the middle in 1934.

You can follow this winding, gnarly track of history if your vehicle is up to it. The byway is known variously as the **Lolo Motorway**, the High Road, and Forest Road 500, with any of them often preceded by an expletive or two by those who have chosen to challenge it. Along the way several Lewis and Clark campsites and other Corps of Discovery locations of significance are marked—places wearing evocative names like **Bears Oil & Roots**, **Indian Post Office**, and **Horse Sweat Pass**. The roller-coastering road, which seems to go with the terrain rather than through it, contrasts sharply with the wide, over-engineered, consistently graded Forest Service roads you'll find elsewhere in the Clearwater and other national forests.

Bald eagle

Ralph S. Space, an early Clearwater National Forest supervisor who first crossed the Lolo Trail on horseback in 1924, when it *was* just a trail, years later guided numerous parties along the new motorway. For their benefit he wrote this rhyme, which still very much applies:

> *This road is winding, crooked and rough,*
> *But you can make it, if you are tough,*
> *God help your tires, God help your load,*
> *God bless the men who built this road.*

You can gain access to the Lolo Motorway by driving up Forest Road 569 from Powell or, at a point several miles northeast of there, by driving onto Forest Road 109 where it meets U.S. Highway 12. Many miles later you will emerge—depending on which forks are followed—at Kooskia, Kamiah, Weippe, or Pierce. For detailed directions and an opinion as to whether or not your vehicle is suited to the rough-and-tumble ride, check in at the Powell Ranger Station. (A lot of history buffs wanting to take their time choose to follow the Lolo Trail by horseback or mountain bike. Inquire at the Powell Ranger Station for leads on outfitters.)

Between Powell and Lowell U.S. Highway 12 cuts a wilderness swath that you may begin thinking is never going to end—but end it does, after *only* 65 miles. Except for the occasional Forest Service campground and beckoning trailhead, there are no services along the stretch. At either end, however, you'll find backwoods retreats worthy of a visit and maybe even an overnight. At Powell is the **Lochsa Lodge** (telephone 208–942–3405), an especially popular getaway in winter for Missoula-area cross-country skiers. The lodge offers cozy cabins and a restaurant/bar. At Lowell, where the Selway and Lochsa rivers flow together to form the Middle Fork of the Clearwater, the **Three Rivers Resort** (telephone 208–926–4430) likewise features cabins and a restaurant. The resort's prime location makes it a natural as headquarters for several commercial river floaters, as well as a popular hangout for free-agent river rats.

Among the few human-made diversions lying between Powell and Lowell is the **Lochsa Historical Ranger Station**, where a good collection of early-day rangering, logging, and fire-fighting paraphernalia is displayed. The wilderness outpost, built in the 1920s, narrowly escaped burning during an intense 1934 wildfire. The station was accessible only by trail until 1956, when the gravel Lewis and Clark Highway reached it at last.

For a real treat, from the recreation-outfitting center of Lowell take a side trip southeast up the Selway River along Forest Road 223. A string of more than ten Nez Perce National Forest campgrounds lines the road, which dead-ends after approximately 20 miles near the Selway-Bitterroot Wilderness boundary. Highlights toward road's end include spectacular **Selway Falls** and the 1912 Selway Falls Guard Station. At Selway Falls, steelhead trout and chinook salmon can sometimes be seen in spring and summer, fighting and leaping their way upstream toward spawning beds.

Back on the main highway, after passing through tiny **Syringa** (also the name of Idaho's state flower), you'll leave the national forest then, several miles later, enter the **Nez Perce Indian Reservation** and the town of Kooskia (*KOOS-key*). Here you'll want to turn left onto State Highway 13.

Alternatively, by veering north to continue along U.S. Highway 12 you soon will arrive at **Orofino**, location of the headquarters of the Clearwater National Forest (telephone 208–476–4541). Staffers there can provide information on several cabins and lookout towers available to rent in the region. A night in a lookout tower will provide an overnight you'll never forget, particularly if a lightning storm hits. Also, if you're especially interested in geology, in the vicinity of Orofino you can take a gander at what once was the western edge of the North American continent. (*See* Mobile Continents and Movable Mountains, Sun Valley–Salmon Country.)

Back along State Highway 13, you'll find that the forks and feeder streams of the Clearwater have made a maze of the countryside; you'll wind up, down, and around chopped mountains en route to the high, surprisingly flat **Camas Prairie**. On the way there, at a point 2 miles north of Harpster, you'll pass the left-hand turn leading to the extremely rugged **Elk City Wagon Road**, which you can access by taking Sally Ann Creek Road/County Road 284. If you'd like to visit the Wild West wilderness jump-off settlement of **Elk City**, but you're not interested in tackling the historic wagon road, alternatively you can simply follow State Highway 14, which continues along the Clearwater's South Fork for 50 miles, skirting woods, meadows, and Forest Service campgrounds en route to that hermit of a hamlet.

Elk City was Idaho's bridesmaid of a gold camp, second only to Pierce City. By the peak of its brief boom in 1861 Elk City boasted a ragtag population of around a thousand individuals. Today the outpost serves as a center for fishermen, backpackers, and other wilderness users; it's also the launching point for further driving adventures. These include the relatively tamed drive to **Red River Hot Springs**, a commercial enterprise offering rustic rental cabins, and the decidedly untamed, wild-country sojourn along the **Magruder Corridor**. The Magruder crests the Bitterroot Range at Nez Perce Pass before dropping into the Bitterroot Valley and re-contacting civilization near the town of Darby, Montana.

The Magruder Road, along with the Elk City Wagon Road, began as yet another trail blazed by bison-seeking Nez Perce in the 1700s and 1800s, and evolved into a route followed by gold prospectors and mining-camp suppliers. Today the Magruder's narrow, serpentine right-of-way is the only swath of non-wilderness lands preventing the Selway-Bitterroot Wilderness and Frank Church–River of No Return Wilderness from being an unbroken continuum. To follow the 100-plus miles of the corridor is still an adventure; the narrow, rocky, often single-lane road can be littered with downfall timber, mired in mud, or even smothered in snow virtually any time in the summer or fall. Before heading out, check on current conditions by visiting the Nez Perce National Forest's **Elk City Ranger District** (telephone 208–842–2245).

Back along State Highway 13 you soon will pull into **Grangeville**. The attractive farming, logging, and outfitting town comes as a bit of a surprise after the woodsy, tight-canyoned trip it took to get there. For those who like their landscapes broad, to spiral out of the Clearwater River bottoms and up onto the Camas Prairie will be like grabbing a breath of fresh air. Enjoy it, because more deep canyons follow after you cross these highlands separating the drainages of the Clearwater and Salmon rivers.

From Grangeville, follow U.S. Highway 95 southwest across the Camas Prairie, where in both prehistoric and historic times Nez Perce and other Native Americans regularly gathered to dig the nutritious bulbs of the camas, a native plant of the lily family. Camas played an important role in the diet of members of the Lewis and Clark expedition, too, when they traveled through the region.

From the summit of legendary **White Bird Hill** you will, in very short order, lose more than half a mile of elevation. The "new" highway, completed in 1975, connects in 7 miles the same two points that the zippering old road took 14 miles to connect. The old Whitebird Hill road, which you'll see to the east, is noteworthy in that it was a crucial link in the only road within Idaho that joins the capital city of Boise with the northern reaches of the state. The road was finished in 1921, but not paved until 1938.

On the way down the steep, newer road you'll see a pull-out for the **White Bird Battlefield** component of Nez Perce National Historical Park, which comprises more than three dozen sites distributed over four states. It was here on White Bird Hill, on June 17, 1877, that the inaugural skirmish of the Nez Perce War flared. (For more information on the Nez Perce trek *see* Big Hole National Battlefield, Seeing Glacier-Gold

Country and History, Yellowstone-Teton Country. For a brochure describing the entire park, call the Nez Perce National Historical Park headquarters in Spalding, Idaho, at 208–843–2261.)

If it is early spring, by the time you drop into the village of White Bird, located just off the highway, don't be surprised to find the sun shining and flowers blooming—and only moments after you drove through a sideways-blowing snowstorm on White Bird Summit. Between White Bird and Riggins U.S. Highway 95 follows the canyon of the lower Salmon River, which flows opposite the direction you are traveling. Look at a road map of the state and you'll see that at Riggins the river takes a ninety-degree turn northward after cutting through the backcountry heart of Idaho, where it flows through the Frank Church–River of No Return and Gospel Hump wilderness areas.

Riggins is a little burg kept hopping by the river trades. A person living here could refuse to travel any farther than 15 or 20 miles from home, yet experience nearly the full fold of outdoor possibilities: from floating and fishing on the lower canyon of the Salmon, where the summers are hot (the elevation at Riggins is only 1,800 feet); to hiking, horseback riding, camping, and skiing in the Seven Devils Mountains of the Hells Canyon Wilderness. The Seven Devils are spectacular, lake-adorned mountains, some of which reach above 9,000 feet—or more than 7,000 higher than the rivers they lie between, the Snake and the Salmon. For a glimpse at what lies above and beyond the roads, drive southwest from Riggins up gravel Forest/County Road 517, which leaves from the south end of town near the office of the **Hells Canyon National Recreation Area** (telephone 208–628–3916). The road winds for nearly 20 miles up to 8,429-foot **Heavens Gate Lookout**, where you'll earn a 360-degree, four-state panorama that is one of the most impressive vistas accessible by car in the Northern Rockies. Nearby are a couple of Forest Service campgrounds—**Seven Devils** and **Windy Saddle**—and the trailhead for the **Heavens Gate Scenic Trail**.

At Riggins U.S. Highway 95 begins following the Little Salmon River upstream, rapidly ascending through arid canyon country before

Sego lily

poking into stands of conifers and ultimately emerging onto the damper and cooler Meadows Valley north of the town of **New Meadows**. Here you'll see white fences lining river wetlands and brown foothills rimming the agrarian floodplain. The valley is a virtual bowl, completely encircled by mountains. Some of those mountains are heavily timbered, while a fair share of the south-facing slopes remain treeless. The valley is home to large ranches and bright red barns, which sport shiny metal roofs of red, gray, white, brown, or blue that glare in the afternoon sun. As is the case here in the upper valley of the Little Salmon River, a preponderance of metal roofs is often a clue that you are in big-snow country, where they are preferred because they encourage snow to slide off rather than accumulate into roof-threatening loads.

Five miles before reaching New Meadows you will pass the right-hand turn leading a mile to **Zim's Hot Springs**, an island of family-friendly enterprise nestled amid sprawling cattle spreads. In addition to a clean, outdoor warm pool and a hotter soaking pool, Zim's features a campground with electrical hookups and tent sites with shade-giving lean-tos. The big brown main building, built of logs, houses dressing rooms and a recreation room replete with pocket billiards, video games, picnic tables, and a comfy couch hugging the fireplace. On a cool fall or cold winter day the roaring fire is every bit as inviting as are the hot pools out back.

A couple of miles farther along on the main highway you'll pass the right-hand turn onto 45th Parallel Drive (HALFWAY BETWEEN THE EQUATOR AND THE NORTH POLE, states a sign), which leads into the **MeadowCreek Golf & Field Club**. MeadowCreek's lush, rolling eighteen-hole golf course is open to the public at a reasonable greenfee cost. If you'd like to swat at the dimpled ball while visiting the New Meadows–McCall area, this course is recommended over the twenty-seven-hole course in McCall, which has a much less private feel to it and seems often to be torn up and noisy with construction. Activity venues accompanying the golf course at MeadowCreek include a trapshooting range, tennis courts, and a swimming pool. The resort's elegant clubhouse/restaurant/bar is appointed in "neo-hunting lodge," with dark green, brown, and plaid highlights.

New Meadows, population 620, supplanted nearby Meadows as this valley's center of settlement after the Pacific & Idaho Northern Railroad arrived in 1911, bypassing the older town. Although tourism is ever-growing in importance, New Meadows still exists largely to serve the ranching and timbering trades. The town features a few restaurants (German, pizza, or American, take your pick), a historical railroad depot undergoing restoration, a town park with a covered area for picnicking, a Payette National Forest ranger station, and overnight accommodations that include those provided by the attractive **Hartland Inn** motel and 1911 bed and breakfast (telephone 208–347–2114).

At the main junction in New Meadows turn left onto State Highway 55 toward McCall. In 2 miles you'll pass through Meadows, which consists of a scattering of houses and the **Meadows RV Park**, a thirty-seven-space campground located on the east side of the highway. A half mile past there is the left-hand turn to **Packer John's Cabin Park**, site of a replica of the cabin built by John Welch, a pioneer who in the early 1860s packed supplies for prospectors between the Snake River port at Lewiston and the mines in the Boise Basin. The original cabin, whose location was as convenient as anywhere to both north and south Idaho residents, hosted Idaho's first territorial political conventions. Surrounding the modest cabin today are a few dusty campsites.

Continuing toward McCall you will twist through the tight little canyon of Goose Creek and Little Goose Creek, passing the turn to **Last Chance Campground**, a Forest Service site boasting a nearby hot springs. A couple of miles past there you'll encounter the turn to **Brundage Mountain**. The base area for this moderately large ski area is located 4 miles off the highway along paved Forest Road 257. SALMON COUNTRY—HEALTHY RIVERS KEEP 'EM COMING BACK! reads the sign that will greet you shortly after making the turn. In addition to its winter skiing activities, the area is open in summer for mountain biking on trails built specifically for the fat-tire bicycles. The ride to the top can be relatively easy or hard, depending on which trails you use to gain the 1,600 feet of elevation. Or, the ride up can be exceptionally easy, if you opt to ride the chairlift, which runs weekends from Fourth of July weekend through Labor Day.

Road sign outside Donnelly, Idaho

From the ridgetop you are afforded a long-range view encompassing Payette Lake, New Meadows, and, across Hells Canyon of the Snake River, the distant Eagle Cap Wilderness of the Wallowa Mountains in Oregon. From the top you can pick a new trail to return to the Brundage

Mountain base area, or you can loop down the back side of the mountain on the Brundage Mountain Lookout Road and follow Forest Road 451 south, hitting the highway at a point just west of McCall.

Brundage Mountain typically snoozes on summer and fall weekdays, when the deserted mountain-bike trails can double as great hiking trails. Whether you go by foot or by bicycle, a trip to the top is highly recommended: Gardens of wildflowers, ever-changing through the summer, are as gorgeous as the countless dead snags, thick with bent and gnarled branches, are ghostly. Moderately fit individuals should be able to hike to the top and back in three hours.

Three miles before descending into McCall on State Highway 55 you'll pass the **Little Ski Hill**, at whose foot resides the Payette Lakes Ski Club's lodge. Radiating from the small, 405-foot vertical-drop ski hill in winter are as many as 50 kilometers (31 miles) of groomed cross-country trails and several additional ungroomed ski-touring trails. For more than sixty years this community-supported ski area has served as a base for training skiers of all ages in every discipline of the sport—including downhill, cross-country, and jumping—with the ultimate goal of giving townsfolk the precious gift of skiing as a lifetime sport. Not surprisingly, some of America's top skiers have been products of the Payette Lakes Ski Club program.

From the Little Ski Hill you will crest a low pass then continue into **McCall**, where the highway becomes Lake Street. In many regards it appears that McCall, Idaho, and Whitefish, Montana, were fashioned from the same mold. Both communities claim long histories of skiing, traditions that were originally based on volunteer community support that have expanded into large-scale business concerns. Both are tall-timber towns steeped in the ways of the logger and the mill worker, yet today boasting economies less dependent on logs than on tourism: In either town that tall condominium rising against the horizon might occupy the spot where a teepee burner once belched the smoke of burning sawdust.

Both McCall and Whitefish boast large freshwater lakes popular with boaters and other summer recreationists. The two towns' full-time populations are quite close, too, with McCall claiming 2,500 residents and Whitefish 5,000. Both McCall and Whitefish, each the foremost water-and-winter playground in its respective state, even have a microbrewery sitting smack in the middle of downtown.

Winter, spring, summer, or fall, McCall is a fun place to play and/or relax for a few days. In summer, near the tiny, congested heart of downtown, which surrounds the flagship **Hotel McCall**, the skeletal masts of sailboats moored in the town marina bob against a backdrop of black water, blue sky, and dark green masses of mountains. The Salmon River Mountains to the east are salt-and-peppered with light-colored outcrops of the Idaho batholith; standing in contrast to the dark forests surrounding it, the granite glistens in the sun, looking in some spots like patches of left-over snow.

In winter almost everything *is* white with snow, even frozen Payette Lake. Intricately sculpted creatures and structures of snow and ice line the streets of town before, during, and after the very popular **Winter Carnival**, held during the first week of February.

Recommended warm-weather activities in or close to the town of McCall include picnicking at one of several town parks lining the lakefront. The newest is located right downtown. You can grab your own lunch makings at the downtown grocery store or pick up sandwiches at a nearby deli. After lunch you might opt to take a tour of the **McCall Fish Hatchery** (telephone 208–634–2690), located on Mather Road along the North Fork of the Payette. The foremost goal of the hatchery's staff is to help restore populations of chinook salmon to the South Fork of the Salmon River. This potential giant of a fish can grow to over 5 feet long and more than a hundred pounds in weight.

Another option: a tour of the **Smokejumper Base**, one of just a handful of such facilities in the western U.S. Several dozen of the elite corps of Forest Service smokejumpers are stationed each summer at the base, located at the McCall Municipal Airport on Mission Street. Call (208) 634–0390 to schedule a free tour of the facility, where you can learn plenty about the fascinating ways of these intrepid airborne firefighters, who've been parachuting into Western forests since 1939.

WARREN WAGON ROAD TO BURGDORF HOT SPRINGS: A NARRATIVE ACCOUNT

A mile west of the main intersection in downtown McCall, Nancy and I turn north onto **Warren Wagon Road** to begin paralleling the west shore of Payette Lake. Grand conifers, most of them Douglas fir, grow right up to the edge of the road. Homes ranging from quaint log cabins to semi-mansions are settled back in the woods. The timber is so thick that seldom do we catch a glimpse of the lake sparkling through. Occasionally, though, we pass a residence with large grounds where the trees have been cleared or thinned, permitting extended looks at the lake. Its waters glimmer under the slanted rays of early morning sun as if a million diamonds were floating on the surface.

Approximately 4 miles after turning onto Warren Wagon Road we emerge from the forest to drive along a bare-rock cliffside. Sailboats lean

Along Warren Wagon Road, outside McCall

with the wind far out in the middle of the lake, and water skiers carve wet turns up and over the wakes created by the powerful boats pulling them.

In another couple of miles we reach the **North Beach Unit** of Ponderosa State Park, with its boat launch, sand beach, picnicking sites, and canoes for rent. The canoes can be used even by novice paddlers to safely explore this quiet, protected north end of the lake. Passing the right-hand turn onto the gravel Eastside Drive at just over 8 miles, we continue north on the smooth pavement of Warren Wagon Road. Immediately past that junction the terrain turns wilder-looking, less settled. Off to the side of the road meanders a shallow stream, embraced by high alders growing at the base of steep, conifer-forested slopes. Few vehicles share the road with us this morning, other than the occasional loaded log truck headed in the opposite direction on the way to the mill. The multi-wheeled monsters storm through the woods, shattering the quiet and leaving roadside trees waving in their wind for several seconds, long after the trucks have passed from sight.

We zip past several informal campsites, some of them vacant and others occupied by pickup campers or larger recreational vehicles. The living forest, extremely thick and deep green, is interrupted here and there with tall dead trees that look as if they might have been strangled by their own dense mats of branches and foliage. We call them fir ghosts, because that's what they look like.

After 12 miles we enter the Payette National Forest, then, 3 miles later, pass the attractive **Upper Payette Campground**. On the distant shore of the lake we catch our first glimpse of graphic evidence of the awesome forest fires that roared through this country in 1994. Soon we're driving right through the fire zone, where the colorless skeletons of burned trees appear particularly bleak, in contrast to the profusion of bright purple fireweed exploding from the ground below. Similarly, the green slopes higher up on the mountains look all that much greener, thanks to the contrast provided by sweeps of blackened, dead timber.

Above the lake we enter a broad mountain basin teeming with scorched trees. The high slopes and ridges, bejeweled in light gray granite, still hold occasional stands of living trees that were skipped over by the racing conflagration. The for-

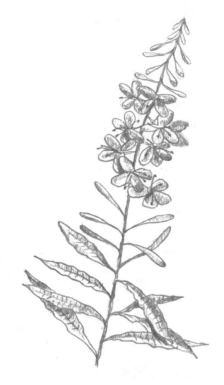

Purple fireweed

est fires really opened up the views. With the ground as green as it is, even in late July, that which the fire left behind appears less ghastly than other burned-over forests we've seen. In fact, the entire setting is quite attractive.

Through this mosaic of light-colored rock, dark green timber, colorful meadows, and scraggly gray-black skeletons, we climb steeply to Secesh Summit, elevation 6,424 feet. The word Secesh (*SEE-sesh*) also belongs to the nearby river whose headwaters drainage we have just entered. The term refers to the Confederate sympathizers known as Secesh Doctrinaries (as in "secessionist"), who came to prospect in the area in the 1860s. Roughly a hundred yards off the road we spot a man and woman picking something— probably huckleberries—and dropping them into red coffee cans. It's obvious that this ridgeline separating the two watersheds served as a natural fireline: We immediately leave the burn behind and descend northward into a uniform forest of living Douglas fir and lodgepole pine.

Thirty miles after leaving McCall we turn left onto gravel Forest Road 246, continue for 2 miles, then pull right into **Burgdorf Hot Springs**. A broad, treeless meadow—probably a great place to spot elk at dawn or dusk—fronts the historic waters. (Warren Wagon Road, which turns to gravel at the junction with Forest Road 246, continues easterly through the Payette National Forest to the outpost of **Warren**, a historic gold-mining town holding a number of intriguing old buildings and a few year-round residents.)

The scattering of weather-worn structures surrounding the pool at Burgdorf makes the place look like a ghost town. It's certainly old enough to qualify as one. Fred Burgdorf was a German immigrant who, alongside hundreds of others, rushed in to the Warren gold diggings in 1864. A year later he staked a claim on a 160-acre homestead encompassing the hot springs, and he quickly set up shop, selling steaks and hot-pot baths to prospectors. Some of those soakers spread the talltale rumor that Fred regularly filtered the water when no one was looking, extracting enough floating gold dust left behind by the miners to make a respectable living. The hot springs resort, which Burgdorf developed in the spirit of the spas he'd visited in his home country, grew into an important social gathering place in the frontier Idaho outback.

Although today Burgdorf does look like a ghost town and is in fact listed on the National Register of Historic Places, it's still a going con-cern. The current owners have poured a substantial amount of money into restoring some of the old buildings, and they plan to continue pouring.

The 50-by-75-foot, log-sided pool is open for soaking daily year-round. A grizzled old fellow who lives and works at the resort sees us eyeing the vacated, sand-bottomed pool. He moseys up and introduces himself, then informs us that as many as 200 soakers can be expected on a midsummer day, with most of them arriving in late afternoon or early evening. Several camping cabins are available to rent, he says. The rustic cabins lack electricity and indoor plumbing, and food and bedding are available only on a bring-yourown basis. There's also a Forest Service campground located just up the road.

Our new friend tells us that the road is generally open to cars from mid-May through late November. In winter Warren Wagon Road is plowed as far north as the North Beach Unit of Ponderosa State Park, and groomed for snowmobiles the remainder of the way to Burgdorf. Folks arrive in winter either on snowmobile or crosscountry skis; having traveled for miles in the frigid air they surely must be ready for a soak in the 104-degree water by the time they get here. (For a fee, the caretakers will shuttle prospective soakers in on snowmobiles from the North Beach Unit.)

The gentleman informs us that Burgdorf closed for several weeks during the big burn of

Remains of 1994 fire outside McCall, Idaho

1994, when fire threatened to consume the resort's historic buildings. But the spirits protected the spot from the flames, he says, as they have on three previous occasions in this century. He also lets us in on this little secret: The 1994 fires could have been quelled when only two days old, but instead they were permitted by the Forest Service to spread. It was all a plot, an end-run, designed to open the doors to additional logging operations in the forest.

We're not so sure about this theory, but we do agree with him that Burgdorf is a great place to hang out.

From Burgdorf Hot Springs we could continue bumping along Forest Road 246 through another 45 miles of backcountry to Riggins, first diving to the Salmon River canyon via the Fall Creek and French Creek drainages. We're concerned, though, that we don't have enough fuel to make that slow, gas-guzzling trip, so we opt to return mostly by the way we came.

Back at the junction 8 miles north of McCall, though, we follow a different route back to town by turning onto Eastside Drive. After skirting the North Beach Primitive Area the road turns to gravel, crosses the lake's inlet, and commences winding along a mix of clear-flowing stream, brackish backwaters, and rugged cliffs. The road brushes the lake's shore after a mile and a half, then climbs through thick forest away from the water. After reclaiming pavement at about 5 miles from the turn, we roll smoothly past a procession of condominiums, fancy homes, and summer camps busy with scouting and church groups.

We arrive at a stop sign at just over 8 miles, where we turn right toward **Ponderosa State Park** rather than immediately turning left to return to McCall. We find that it's a beautiful park, with a campground protected by immense ponderosa pines that provide an almost unbroken blanket of shade. Before parking we motor past a sand volleyball court, where a group of college-age kids appear to be having a great time. We also encounter several small groups of riders on mountain bikes.

Due to the heavy timber cover it is hard to get an overall sense of the setting, but our park map reveals that Ponderosa State Park occupies most of a 1,000-acre peninsula, 2 or 3 miles long, which juts northwestward into Payette Lake and cleaves

Ponderosa pine with ponderosa, larch, fir, and cedar cones

the lake nearly in half. The park is webbed with trails, a pair of them recommended for mountain biking and three others reserved for hikers.

There's also a boat ramp and docks, and a pair of landlocked marshes. According to the brochure, common sightings at Lily Marsh include moose, who are kept company by a host of songbirds and waterfowl. The brochure also informs us that some of the ponderosa pines here are as old as 400 years and reach heights greater than 150 feet.

At the tip of the peninsula we park, grab the backpack we filled with food before departing from McCall this morning, and hike along the short trail leading to Osprey Cliff Overlook. What a fine spot for a picnic it is, overlooking the lake and the mountains beyond. Finally, full and tired, we leave Ponderosa State Park and drive the 2 miles back to McCall, where we repair to our room at the Hotel McCall. After freshening up, we amble over to the **McCall Brewing Company** for the social hour, taking an indirect route that leads us past rows of colorful sailboats and motorboats moored in the town marina.

A DRIVING TOUR FROM McCALL TO THE STANLEY BASIN

Heading south from McCall on State Highway 55, also known as the **Payette River Scenic Byway**, you will traverse a wide prairie containing a mix of subdivisions, ranchettes, and century-old cattle spreads whose owners have thus far resisted the temptation to divide and sell their property. The flats are interrupted here and there by topographical blips of higher ground, rising from Long Valley like islands of timber in a sea of grass. Numerous old barns, sagging and weatherworn from the years, are reminiscent of the tree snags you'll see in the surrounding national forest—something once living and now dead, but still standing. Also like snags, the barns no doubt provide homes for numerous species of birds and small mammals.

At tiny Lake Fork you'll pass the **Lake Fork Mercantile** country store and not a whole lot else; **Donnelly**, 13 miles south of McCall, is a somewhat larger town. In addition to the attractive **Chalet RV Park** the town offers good access to boating and camping at the northern end of immense **Cascade Reservoir**. The still-larger town of **Cascade**, located 16 miles south of Donnelly at the southern end of the reservoir, was named for a falls on the Payette River's north fork

that no longer exists, thanks to the construction of Cascade Dam. The town has a golf course, restaurants, convenience stores, a big lumber mill, the intimate **Creamery Bed & Breakfast** (telephone 208–382–4621) and the **Waters Edge RV Park** (telephone 208–378–4208 or, toll-free in the United States, 800–574–2038), with its inviting sand beach.

The Payette National Forest's **Cascade Ranger District** (telephone 208–382–4271) occupies a modern building sporting an unmissable roof of reflective green metal. There you can get the scoop on another backcountry motor trip, one of the best and favorites in the state. From Cascade the route heads east to **Warm Lake** then north to **Yellow Pine** and, finally, west back to State Highway 55 at McCall. A major draw bringing motorists to this loop is the wealth of hot springs around Warm Lake, including the unique **Molly's Tubs**, a collection of actual bathtubs holding natural hot water fed to the tubs by hose.

Yellow Pine is another of those way-out-there Idaho settlements—like Warren, Atlanta, Dixie, and a scattering of others—that could and probably should be a ghost town, but somehow continues plugging along, if not thriving, despite its remote location. Yellow Pine's full-time population is around forty. That number expands roughly thirtyfold on the first weekend of August, when contestants and spectactors blow into town for the **Yellow Pine Harmonica Fest**.

Back along State Highway 55, after climbing for a few miles away from the North Fork of the Payette River, which flows into and out of the Cascade Reservoir, you'll regain the river near Smiths Ferry, a riverside community composed of a host of neat vacation cabins. **Cougar Mountain Lodge** (telephone 208–375–4455), a cross-country ski center in winter, serves as the settlement's centerpiece.

From Smiths Ferry to a point several miles south, near Banks, you will parallel one of the most revered, feared, and consistently wild stretches of Class V white water in the United States. Kayakers—experts only, one hopes—come from near and far to challenge the frothy torrent as it dances and stair-steps its way south below the walls of a pinched canyon. If it is summer, pull off the road at a wide spot, get out of the car, and stand next to the river with your camera for awhile. Chances are you'll soon see some colorful kayakers come bobbing and teetering past in the watery tantrum, looking remarkably calm and in control as they paddle and shift their weight to keep their crafts' bottom sides down and bows pointed downstream.

About 7 miles south of Smiths Ferry you'll pass **Big Eddy**, a small Forest Service campground located along one of the rare flat-water stretches of this part of the river. In another 3.5 miles is **Swinging Bridge Campground**. More than likely, as you descend along the river amid thinning stands of timber, the temperature outside is rising. The canyon continually gets deeper, too, as the river digs itself ever further into the stone bowels of the earth.

Banks, settled deep in the river canyon, is located at the confluence of the Payette River's south fork and north fork. Downstream from this point it is known simply as the Payette River. The **Bear Valley River Co.,** located at the Banks Store & Cafe turn-off, is a good bet for an outfitted river trip on one of the mellower stretches of the forks of the Payette (mellow relative to the Smiths Ferry to Banks section, anyway). Don't miss wiggling your toes in the sand of the outstanding beach fronting the river just south of town.

A pretty and potentially rewarding side trip from Banks can take you east up the South Fork to mountain-surrounded **Garden Valley** and/or to **Crouch**, home to the **Longhorn Saloon & Restaurant** (telephone 208–462–3108). The good steakhouse has been dishing up supper to the public for more than half a century. Forest Road 698 going north from Crouch follows the Payette's middle fork, providing access to several Boise National Forest campgrounds and undeveloped hot springs, as well as to Forest Road 671, which leads to the privately run **Silver Creek Plunge** (telephone 208–344–8688).

If you don't mind missing **Idaho City**, you can avoid a long gravel stretch by continuing east on the Banks-Lowman Highway past Garden Valley, joining the narrative below at the town of Lowman. On this route you'll find an amazing epicurean surprise, provided you find it open: **Danskin Station** (telephone 208–462–3884), located 10 miles east of Garden Valley and open Friday through Sunday only.

It was on the river this road parallels, the South Fork of the Payette, that Dr. Walt Blackadar, a world-renowned kayaker from Salmon City, Idaho, lost his life in May 1978. Blackadar, who pioneered wild rivers in Alaska and elsewhere, was also a devoted conservationist. He was instrumental in the setting aside of some of Idaho's finest wildlands, including portions of the River of No Return Wilderness. After drowning on the South Fork, Blackadar's family received permission to bury him at the long-closed pioneer cemetery at Garden Valley; he was the last Idaho pioneer to be laid to rest there.

Back along State Highway 55 heading south and nearing **Horseshoe Bend**, you'll follow the main Payette through a dry canyon flanked by grassy slopes that are only occasionally punctuated green with ponderosa pine. It feels as though you're exiting the mountains and entering the desert; and you are, but it's a short-lived low-country reprieve. Log trucks are common along this stretch—often burdened with sticks so fat that just seven or eight of them make a load—thundering down the highway and out of the mountains on the way to the mill. You might also see a railroad train come braking down out of the forests to the north, hauling wood chips in box cars and dimensional lumber on flatbeds. And you're sure to encounter "funhog rigs" going into and out of the mountains, too. Just count the toys gracing some of these Subaru Outbacks, Jeep Cherokees, and other auto models: They appear to have strapped, clamped, and tied to their exteriors as many mountain bikes, kayaks, sailboards, and other recreational toys as the owners could possibly find room for.

Horseshoe Bend and the farm fields encircling it are an oasis of green framed by baked-brown hills slanting toward the timbered flanks of higher mountains. Here the Payette River bends west like . . . well, like a horseshoe to take aim at its confluence with the Snake River near the town of Payette. After crossing the river in Horseshoe Bend, rather than continuing south toward Boise, turn east onto Harris Creek Road. Here you'll begin tracing the route of an 1864 toll road that led from the west of Idaho into the gold-mining reaches of the Boise Basin. The byway generally carries very little traffic, with one notable exception: more logging trucks. So, be sure to hug the right side of the road, particularly on blind corners.

In less than a mile the road turns to gravel, as it continues up a bone-dry canyon. As you gain elevation, though, you also gain vegetation, including fat cottonwoods that thrive beside the creek bed. After 8 miles you'll have gained enough elevation to re-enter a forest of pine. Occasional informal camping spots can be found along the duration of the climb. At 14 miles, after cresting the watershed divide, you'll start down, enjoying long-range views across the approaching valley.

Eight miles beyond the summit the road surface temporarily turns to pavement, where it skirts the site of the old Starr Ranch. As explained on an interpretive sign at the site, the Philip Ranft family, which purchased the ranch in 1874, became known throughout the region for the hotly contested horse races they staged. At its apex the ranch boasted a hotel, dance hall, saloon, sawmill, and several other buildings. Today, however, one lone structure remains, and most of it has been either reclaimed by vegetation or devoured by decay.

Shortly past there gravel resumes, and in another mile and a half you'll arrive at a junction. A right-hand turn leads along the Centerville Road (Forest Road 307) to **Idaho City**, where you'll ultimately want to go, First, though, the mile-long spur leading left to **Placerville** is definitely worth investigating.

Boise Basin Mercantile, Placerville, Idaho

The old mining town, established in 1862, is still home to several residents. Placerville contains a handful of turn-of-the-century homes, as well as old commercial facilities, including the Boise Basin Mercantile and the Magnolia Saloon, now a lawn-fronted museum. A covered picnic shelter resides nearby. In contrast to Idaho City—which, like many Rocky Mountain mining towns, appears to have grown in whichever direction it pleased—Placerville has a planned appearance, with a town square and neat structures raised at right angles to one another. Similar to Idaho City, though, Placerville owns an intriguing pioneer cemetery just outside of town.

Return to the junction and drive toward Idaho City on the Centerville Road, regaining pavement at a point just over 3 miles from the junction. A little stream meanders through this dry valley, the former haunt of gold prospectors, as evidenced by scattered tailings piles. A small ensemble of homes signifies **Centerville**, whose name reflects its location halfway between Placerville and Idaho City. Here you'll pass the left-hand turn to Pioneerville, then cross Grimes Creek and begin climbing. The road, which yet again reverts to gravel, winds up and down, crossing several drainages and ridges before encountering the outskirts of Idaho City, which you'll reach after driving 12 miles from the Centerville Road junction.

Just prior to entering the main part of town, turn right onto Buena Vista Road and wind for a mile on dirt through woods to the haunting, yet fascinating **Boise County Pioneer Cemetery**. Although an estimated 3,000 are buried here, only approximately 300 of the graves hold the remains of identified individuals; "Unknown" is a word you'll commonly see etched in stone. It's startling how many of the graves are occupied by infants who died either at birth or before marking their first birthday—graphic evidence of just how very difficult life must have been on the nineteenth-century western frontier. Grief and dashed dreams seem to hang like a fog over the graveyard, even on a sunny summer day.

Idaho City was founded in October 1862 after gold was struck in the Boise Basin, and the town quickly became the focus of one of the richest gold strikes in U.S. history. The creaky old settlement still hasn't given up the ghost; in fact, it remains the seat of Boise County (not by beating out Boise, though—the capital city doubles as the seat of Ada County). Things have slowed dramatically since the mid-1860s, when Idaho City boasted more than 6,000 residents—very few of whom were women—making it the most populous metropolis in the territory. Gold production ceased in 1942 with the onset of World War II, and today the town is home to roughly 5 percent of the number it claimed during its heyday.

Idaho City and the nearby countryside have that timeworn, dusty feel so typical of one-time mountain boomtowns. You can walk on a wooden boardwalk through downtown, where plenty of false-fronted businesses line the streets. The names of many are as evocative of days gone by as are the old buildings they occupy: the **Boise Basin Mercantile** (the oldest general store in the state), the **Miners Exchange Saloon**, **Calamity's Cafe**, and **Double J Western Wear**. Another building you can visit is the **St. Joseph's Catholic Church**, built in 1867. (Interestingly, back at the hilly Boise County Pioneer Cemetery it was Catholics who early on claimed the highest ground available.) In Idaho City you can even take a hands-on class in gold-panning.

The history-packed **Boise Basin Museum** is housed in the old 1867 post office at the corner of Wall and Montgomery; behind it is a pleasant park with plentiful shade provided by pine trees. The nearby **Idaho City Hotel** (telephone 208–392–4290), like Idaho City in general, has

seen better days. But still, many decades after opening its doors, it greets overnight guests.

At the **Idaho City Ranger District** (telephone 208–392–6681) you can pick up a copy of the Boise National Forest visitor map. Acquiring the map—a valuable addition to your navigational and sight-seeing tools even if you intend to stick to the primary highways—is highly recommended before setting out on any gravel-road side trips, such as the one leading to Atlanta described below.

From Idaho City travel northeastward on State Highway 21, the **Ponderosa Pine Scenic Byway**. Not far from town look high on the ridgetop against the horizon to the south, and you may catch a glimpse of the **Thorn Creek Butte Lookout**. Lookout towers such as this once graced dozens of high peaks throughout the forests of the Northern Rockies; some 800, in fact, in the mountains of Montana and northern Idaho alone. Most were prefabricated, carried by mules to the mountaintops and assembled by Civilian Conservation Corps crews during the 1930s. Human spotters would reside in the lookouts during the summer and fall fire seasons, calling in to their Forest Service supervisors reports of any smoke or fires they detected from their long-range, 360-degree perspectives.

The importance of lookouts rapidly diminished in the 1950s and 1960s, as their role was assumed by spotter planes and vehicles traveling the ever-growing network of roads penetrating the

An Idaho City "shopping mall"

national forests. Many lookouts were destroyed by the agency that had built them, with the Forest Service regarding them in their retired roles as attractive nuisances. Today the historical relevance of fire lookouts is far more appreciated but, unfortunately, by the time enlightenment arrived, only a small percentage of the lookouts remained standing. Of those that do, just a fraction still house spotters during the fire season. Some double—or serve exclusively—as overnight accommodations. The lookout towers can be tough to get to, often necessitating a bumpy ride in a truck and/or a rigorous uphill hike, and the lodgings are primitive. But these mountaintop perches afford views that would be the envy of any four-star luxury hotel. (For leads or details you can contact any of the national forest offices listed in this book.)

Nine miles out of Idaho City you'll pass **Ten Mile Campground**, a Forest Service site, then **Bad Bear Campground** a bit farther up the road. Over the ensuing miles you'll also pass a trio of Idaho State "Park N' Ski Areas"; the first, **Whoop-um-up Creek**, is on the right at a point 17 miles from Idaho City. The next, **Gold Fork**, is 3 miles north of Whoop-um-up and the next, **Banner Ridge**, another 3 miles-plus from there. Radiating from these areas are trails that in winter are designated for cross-country skiing. Some of the trails are machine groomed; others go ungroomed and feature (if you're lucky) skied-in tracks. Because the area is so close to Boise, Idaho's largest city, it attracts hordes of skinny-ski enthusiasts on winter weekends.

The narrow highway winds through a canyon whose close slopes are heavy with ponderosa pine. Also known as yellow pine, this long-needled tree grows tall with thick, gnarled branches, and when mature its broad trunk is covered with a distinctive, rich russet bark that is furled with darker creases. By the time you approach Mores Creek Summit several miles up the road, you'll note that the forest has changed to one composed predominantly of Douglas fir. Whereas ponderosa pine thrives in the warm, relatively dry foothills, Douglas fir grows better when conditions are somewhat damper and cooler. Despite its name, the Douglas fir is not a fir at all, nor is it a hemlock, although it resembles both. Rather, it enjoys a genus of its own: *pseudotsuga,* which in Latin means "false hemlock."

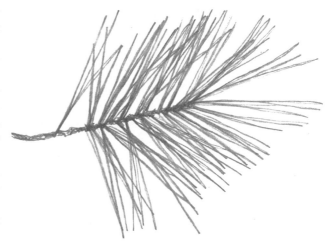

Ponderosa pine needles

About a mile past Whoop-um-up Creek you'll pass the turn to **Atlanta**, a settlement resembling its Georgia counterpart somewhere between very little and not at all. Atlanta is located approximately 40 miles south down a series of dusty dirt roads that turn harrowingly narrow in places—definitely no Peachtree Road. Despite that, they'll lead you past the site of the Boise National Forest's **Robert E. Lee Campground**. The old mining town sits amid dramatic surroundings along the Middle Fork of the Boise River, in close proximity to the south end of the Sawtooth Wilderness Area. As in the Secesh River country outside McCall, nineteenth-century Confederate influence was strong here: Confederate miners, having heard rumors of General Hood's defeat of Sherman's army in the Battle of Atlanta, honored the event by naming this area's primary gold-bearing lode "Atlanta." As it turned out, Sherman was the victorious general. No matter; confident, perhaps, that the South would rise again, the miners stuck with the name and later passed it along to the town that grew around the mineral vein.

A handful of year-round residents hang on today in tiny Atlanta, which draws backpackers in summer, hunters in fall, and hot springs buffs the year around, thanks to a pair of undeveloped springs: **Atlanta Hot Springs** and the more private **Chattanooga Hot Springs**. But the most surprising find of all is the **Greene Valley Resort** (telephone 208–864–2168 or, toll-free in the United States, 800–864–2168), a lavish and spendy eighteen-room inn centered on a 500-acre estate just outside of town. Think of it as the Tara of Atlanta, Idaho.

Back on State Highway 21, after passing the Gold Fork and the Banner Ridge Park N' Ski Areas, at a point 24 miles from Idaho City you will see your first evidence of the giant 1989 Lowman fire. Several pull-outs over the next few miles feature interpretive signs explaining the factors leading up to the fire, as well as changes the fires have wrought. Here, as throughout the Northern Rockies, a century of intense fire-suppression efforts had permitted huge quantities of deadfall fuels to build. In 1989 a low-snowfall winter in the Boise National Forest was followed by an exceptionally hot and dry summer, a summer that also experienced an overabundance of dry lightning storms. The Forest Service reported that during that July alone, lightning ignited 157 fires in the Boise National Forest, 36 of them occurring in one twenty-four-hour period.

A number of smaller wildfires joined forces and ultimately raged across seventy-two square miles of the national forest. They took with them not only vast acreages of timber, but more than two dozen homes and other structures in the settlement of Lowman. More than 2,000 firefighters from throughout the West poured in, some of them working more than a month trying to contain the beast, which burned from July 26 through August 30.

The highway climbs rapidly, passing beneath steep avalanche chutes that each winter have passing motorists holding their breath. After cresting Mores Creek Summit, elevation 6,118 feet, you will begin a steep descent, winding amid dry mountain slopes covered with standing snags, former living trees that were killed by the fire. It is a jumbled, topsy-turvy, deeply dissected terrain, and negotiating it in a car may not be enjoyable for those prone to suffering travel sickness. For others, though, it should be great fun.

Thirty-four miles after leaving Idaho City you'll drop in alongside the South Fork of the Payette River, where the western portion of **Lowman** is situated. The **South Fork Store** here has a minimal supply of groceries, along with gas pumps, a state liquor store, and cabins and RV sites for rent. The **Lowman Stage Stop** grocery store is also found nearby. State Highway 21

swings eastward at this point to follow the South Fork upstream and take aim at the river's high-mountain origins.

Heading out of town first you will pass the **Mountain View Campground** (Boise National Forest), then the **Lowman Ranger District** (telephone 208–259–3361). The forest fire obviously burned very intensely here, through what surely was a beautiful, timbered canyon prior to the burn. Evidence remaining from the wildfire includes denuded hillsides; structureless building foundations, some with river-rock fireplaces still standing; and extensive gullying and erosion on the slopes above town. The severe erosion resulted not only from the dearth of vegetation, but also from the scorched and baked soils left behind by the fires. The heat effectively sealed the ground, causing water to run across the surface instead of allowing it to soak in.

Pass the **New Haven Lodge**, which includes RV hookups, then the **Kirkham Campground**, a Forest Service site where you'll also find a roadside hot springs. Another Forest Service site, **Helende Campground**, is on the right at a point 9 miles from where you entered Lowman. After passing through a small rural housing settlement at about 12 miles, you'll soon begin seeing occasional patches of unburned timber. Progressively the mosaic pattern leans toward the living and—presto!—within a couple of miles more the road runs through virtually unburned forest.

Nineteen miles from Lowman you'll pass **Bonneville Campground**, which also has an associated hot springs nearby. At 21 miles a right-hand turn off the highway leads for 6 miles up the South Fork to **Grandjean**, home to the venerable **Sawtooth Lodge** (telephone 208–259–3331) and not much else. The lodge, which was established in 1927 and has been in the hands of the Lockett family since 1954, is perched at the edge of the Sawtooth Wilderness Area, within access of the Idaho State Centennial Trail. The lodge includes a restaurant, log-cabin rentals, a campground, and a natural warm-water pool. **Sawtooth Wilderness Outfitters** operates their business out of here, offering guided horseback outings into the Sawtooth backcountry ranging in duration from an hour to several days.

Back at its junction with the road to Grandjean, State Highway 21 begins climbing away from the South Fork toward Banner Summit. Striking views of the distant Sawtooth Range emerge as you gain elevation. Here again, as on Mores Creek Summit, even in summer you can see graphic evidence of the winter snowslides that are so common on the surrounding slopes, with many long, narrow patches of former forest having been swept clean by avalanching snow.

At Banner Summit, elevation 7,056 feet, you will enter the **Challis National Forest**; then, a mile later, pass the left-hand turn onto Forest Road 100, which leads a couple of miles to **Bull Trout Lake** and a scattering of smaller lakes. Where you round **Cape Horn**, swinging from a northeasterly to southeasterly direction, have a look at the Forest Service map and you'll see that you're less than a mile's drive north to the southern extremity of the Frank Church–River of No Return Wilderness.

The change in terrain is dramatic as you leave behind the steep, timbered canyons of western

Idaho and roll into the big sky ranching country of central Idaho. You'll pass through broad meadows lined with the buck-and-rail fences that are one of the defining characteristics of the big spread of country lying ahead, known variously as the Sawtooth Valley, Stanley Basin, and upper Salmon River Valley. The fences, typically built four logs high, seem to zigzag everywhere across the flatter parts of the landscape. With the area's bounty of skinny, straight-standing lodgepole pine, it's easy to understand why this is the fence style of choice.

Between 42 and 52 miles after leaving Lowman you'll pass a series of Forest Service campgrounds, including three encompassed by the Sawtooth National Recreation Area, entered 6 miles after rounding Cape Horn. Big views of the high Sawtooths are there for the taking. At 54 miles is the right-hand turn to spectacular **Stanley Lake**, popular with anglers and boaters. The lake is about a mile outside the Sawtooth Wilderness

Lodgepole pine fence, Stanley Basin

Area, so powerboats are permitted. Three Forest Service campgrounds hug the lake, and a good trail leads hikers to nearby destinations such as the impressive **Bridalveil Falls**. Not far from Stanley Lake is where John Stanley and his prospecting compadres struck gold in 1863. This precipitated the relatively early settling of the Stanley Basin, which is graced by some of the oldest cattle spreads in the Northern Rockies.

Back on the main highway, 2 miles before reaching Stanley you'll pass the turn to **Iron Creek Campground**, which lies 3 miles southwest off the highway. Here you will find the trailhead for the hike to **Sawtooth Lake**. The trail rapidly ascends from slopes wrapped in pungent sage to cool pine forest, entering the Sawtooth Wilderness Area and coinciding for a short distance with the well-worn Alpine Way Trail. Startling, 250-foot-deep Sawtooth Lake, with its glorious backdrop of 10,190-foot Mt. Regan, is the reward for 5 miles of hiking, the final stretch of it over a steep trail carved from solid rock. The hike makes for a good long day outing, or it can serve as the first stage of a longer backpacking expedition leading into the lake-riddled heart of the Sawtooth Range.

On to **Stanley,** population seventy-one, a Hollywood-perfect little cow town nestled in a valley encircled by the serrated high Sawtooths and a rippling of mellower mountains. All things considered, it's a spectacular vision with few rivals.

Stanley consists largely of a smattering of small log and log-frame cabins. It's a bit hard to decipher where town and country part ways; cows and horses—and the fences setting off their pastures—seem not to yield to the town limits. Stanley maintains a low buzz of visitors in summer, when it's the primary staging area for guided float trips on the wilderness-embraced Middle Fork of the Salmon River. The settlement becomes an arctic outpost come winter, when the buzz, not always so low, is provided by snowmobiles. The machine serves as an essential mode of travel for many Stanley Basin residents who live off the main highway, as well as a recreational mode of getting about for hundreds of winter visitors.

Regardless of the season, Saturday night in Stanley is something to behold, with "locals" arriving from as far away as Sun Valley to kick up their heels and let down their hair. If the partying

fails to spill out of the **Rod & Gun Club** and other taverns and onto Ace of Diamonds Avenue . . . well, it's a relatively boring Saturday night in Stanley.

FROM STANLEY TO REDFISH LAKE: A NARRATIVE ACCOUNT

Pulling into Stanley, Nancy and I see that a trio of related enterprises dominates both sides of the highway just west of the town's main intersection: **Mountain Village Lodge**, **Mountain Village Restaurant**, and **Mountain Village Mercantile**. At this intersection three designated scenic byways collide—as if visitors need to be reminded that the place is scenic!—each branching out in its own direction: the Ponderosa Pine Scenic Byway, which we leave at this point; the **Salmon River Scenic Byway**, which heads east then north; and the **Sawtooth Scenic Byway**, leading southeasterly along State Highway 75 over Galena Summit before dropping into the valley of the Big Wood River.

At the intersection, rather than immediately turning south toward Galena Summit and Sun Valley, we turn left toward Lower Stanley, pulling in alongside the Salmon River. Here the famous river is a high-mountain meanderer, a glistening of water waltzing across polished cobbles at a low gradient. It's a mere whisper of what it becomes downstream, as the Salmon gathers ever more water and steepens its descent to transform into the storming River of No Return. On this hot summer day, rather than seeing kayakers buried deep in bottomless troughs of white water—which is what we typically associate with the Salmon—we pass a dozen or so kids riding inflated inner tubes, lazily bobbing along in the chilly waters toward Lower Stanley.

To our right we pass the alluring **Salmon River Lodge**, which sports some tremendously inviting waterfront picnic tables. On the opposite side of the road is the equally attractive **Stanley Museum**. The good pioneer museum occupies the small but stately old Stanley Ranger Station, a classic building of log construction that is stained dark brown and has white chinking filling the gaps between the logs. It's an agreeable look, we've noticed, that seems to be *the* look for buildings throughout this high valley. The common, though by no means universal, architectural trend lends the basin the feel of a national park or one gigantic dude ranch.

When the Challis National Forest was established in 1908, a ranger station was built at the site where the museum is located today. A new station was built south of town in the early 1970s, so the existing station—added to the complex here in the early 1930s—was transformed into this museum of the Sawtooth Interpretive and Historical Association.

A sign in front of the museum informs us that in September of 1824, explorer/trapper Alexander Ross and his Hudson's Bay Company companions passed through the Stanley Basin. Ross later wrote that in this area the party had:

> *observed at some distance the appearance of a ploughed field, and riding up towards it, found a large piece of ground more than four acres in extent, dug up and turned over. On getting to the spot, we observed no less than nine black and grizzly bears at work, rooting away.*

The bears apparently were digging for camas and wild onions. Today plenty of black bears remain in the mountains ringing the basin, but the grizzly is a memory. (Stay tuned, however: Grizzly reintroduction has been proposed for the Idaho side of the Bitterroot Mountains and elsewhere in east-central Idaho. If it happens—there's plenty of resistance to the proposal—the big bears may one day again roam over the mountains and foothills ringing Stanley Basin.)

After passing through Lower Stanley, a conglomeration of log-cabin houses, motels, and eclectic enterprises offering river trips, outdoor clothing, mountain bike and snowmobile rentals, espresso, and other items and services, we continue east on State Highway 75, a leg of the Salmon River Scenic Byway. On the edge of town we pass the left-hand turn onto Nip and Tuck Creek Road, which made up part of a fun, 14-mile mountain bike outing that I recall riding a decade ago.

Outside Lower Stanley the road immediately begins twisting between canyon walls, leaving behind the wide-open spaces and far-ranging views. To our right, thick timber stands face north; to the left, sagebrush dominates on the south-facing slopes. Riffles in the river begin to

hinting at what the Salmon will become many miles downstream. We see a sign informing passersby that the river here is closed to wading after mid-August, to protect any spawning chinook salmon that might be in the waters.

Approximately 3.5 miles from Stanley we pass a small, unsigned hot springs whose waters feed through a pipe into the river; someone has constructed a small rock pool to capture the hot waters. In another mile we pass the **Salmon River Campground**, a Sawtooth National Recreation Area site. Then, in short succession, we pass **Riverside**, **Mormon Bend** and **Basin Creek** campgrounds. Wispy clouds on this cool August morning toy with the treetops surrounding the broad opening occupied by the fourth campground.

Twelve miles east of Stanley, between mile markers 201 and 202, we arrive at our first destination of the day, **Sunbeam Hot Springs**. To our delight it looks as if we'll have the riverside pools, which are located just below but beyond sight of the highway, to ourselves this morning. A sturdy stone, doorless bathhouse stands above the springs. A sign tells us that it was built in 1937 by

Old bathhouse, Sunbeam Hot Springs, east of Stanley, Idaho

the Civilian Conservation Corps, that army of men who performed so many good public works in the 1930s, leaving behind a legacy of mountain roads and trails and stout structures.

From the bathhouse a short trail leads us steeply down to the banks of the Salmon. We find several small, makeshift pools that have been built and maintained by previous visitors, fashioned by forming rings of various-sized river cobbles. Their success rates vary; one is too hot and a couple of others, which permit too much river water to seep in, are not hot enough. We find, though, that by shoring up the one in the middle we can make the temperature just about perfect. Once properly submerged, we also find it easy to manipulate and fine-tune the water temperature a few degrees one way or the other, simply by adding or removing a cobble here or there.

This is probably the most favorable time of summer to visit, we decide. During spring and earlier summer the river's water would be higher with snowmelt run-off, so the pools would be flooded and cold. We guess that winter would be the very best time for a visit, though. Sitting and soaking in nature's own bathtub, with steam rising and the clear waters of the Salmon, one of the world's wildest and most beautiful rivers, glimmering past at just below eye level . . . well, we begin to think we're getting an early glimpse of Heaven.

All good things must end, however, and after an hour's soak we need to get back on the road. East up the road about a mile is Sunbeam Village, where the Yankee Fork of the Salmon River enters the main Salmon. The **Land of the Yankee Fork**, between Sunbeam and Challis, is one of Idaho's most important and best-interpreted historic areas. We're not going to investigate it today, however; instead we plan to backtrack to Stanley then head south toward Sun Valley. We'll save the Yankee Fork country for a later adventure, when we'll visit it on a day trip from Challis.

Driving south from Stanley up the Sawtooth Valley along State Highway 75, we enter the heart of the **Sawtooth National Recreation Area** (SNRA). Excepting the lack of crowds and heavy traffic, the entire setting reminds us a great deal of Jackson Hole. This "hole," or valley, is narrower than its Wyoming counterpart, but the high, craggy peaks of the Sawtooth Range—their shad-

ed alpine cirques in early August still packed with last winter's snow—rival the ragged Tetons for their rugged beauty. To our left the less imposing White Clouds slope away from arid, sagebrush-covered foothillls, whose shadier recesses teem with aspen and Douglas fir—much like the setting of the Gros Ventre Range, the mountains defining the eastern rim of Jackson Hole.

Through the middle of it all runs the Salmon, looking like a smaller version of the Snake River as it meanders through Jackson Hole. (Indeed, the two rivers become one along the border of Idaho and northeast Oregon, where the Snake, the bigger of the two, wins the name game. The river remains the Snake until it joins the Columbia.) Finally, as if putting a few finishing touches on nature's work, as in Jackson Hole, weather-worn barns, outbuildings, and corrals add more than a dash of Old West to the Sawtooth Valley.

As Nancy drives, I read from a pamphlet that we picked up at the visitor-information center in Stanley. We learn that the 756,000-acre SNRA covers all or part of four mountain ranges: the Sawtooths, White Clouds, Boulders, and Smokies. Established in 1972, the national recreation area encompasses forty peaks exceeding 10,000 feet in elevation, and, remarkably, more than 1,000 high-mountain lakes, ranging from tiny to very big. The SNRA forms the roof of Idaho: Four major rivers—the Salmon, Boise, Big Wood, and South Fork of the Payette—all rise here, before dropping away in different directions of the compass.

Precipitously steep though they are, we find that the Sawtooths are quite easy to penetrate, thanks to numerous deep, U-shaped valleys gouged thousands of years ago by glaciers. In several of the valleys large lakes hide behind high moraines that reach down from the mountains. Foremost among these is **Redfish Lake**, 4 miles long and less than a half mile wide.

Four miles south of Stanley, just past the left-hand turn to **Sunny Gulch Campground**, we turn right toward that flagship lake, first skirting Little Redfish Lake before arriving at the smaller lake's big brother. If the Sawtooth Valley is the Jackson Hole of Sun Valley–Salmon Country, we decide, then Redfish Lake is its Jackson Lake. Here we even find crowds reminiscent of those that we've been part of on warm summer days in

Redfish Lake, Sawtooth Mountains

Jackson Hole. These crowds—and the glaring lack of them elsewhere in the area—make us better understand the local resistance to turning the SNRA into a national park. It's a suggestion that pops up on occasion but, despite the fact that the natural beauty befits the designation, seems always to be quickly quelled.

We learn from the visitor's brochure that the SNRA offers sanctuary for countless wildlife species. None is more intriguing than the *anadromous* sockeye and chinook salmon that spend the better part of their lives in the Pacific Ocean, but begin and end those lives here in the freshwater of Idaho's high country. The Salmon-Snake-Columbia rivers system is the fishes' 900-mile highway to and from the ocean, but that highway has become increasingly difficult to negotiate with the construction of more and more hydroelectric dams. Intensified commercial-fishing efforts far downstream have also contributed to reductions in the numbers of fish.

Thousands of spawning sockeyes once made the journey to their birthing waters here, turning the outlet waters of Redfish Lake red, and giving the lake its name. Horseback riders are said to have thrown rocks into the water before crossing, in order to scatter the fish and clear the way for their mounts. Redfish Lake remains the only known body of water in Idaho where the Snake River sockeye salmon, an endangered species, continues spawning, but few if any fish successfully make the trip from the Pacific in a given year. Other nearby headwaters of the Salmon provide vital habitat for the Snake River chinook salmon, also listed as endangered under the Federal Endangered Species Act.

We pass the right-hand turn to **Redfish Lake Lodge**, then drive past numerous campgrounds, picnic grounds, boat-launch areas, and even a private horseback riding concession, before reaching the end of the road near **Sockeye Campground**. We choose to set up camp at a site here, feeling fortunate even to have located a vacant spot.

After setting up our tent, we hop on our mountain bikes and pedal back the way we came, turning in to the **Redfish Visitor Center**. The center is closed on Monday and Tuesday; since today is Monday, we're out of luck. They don't close the scenery, however, so we follow a short trail leading behind the center to an outstanding viewpoint overlooking Redfish Lake. Steep, timbered slopes enclose the lake, which is alive with canoeists, anglers, swimmers, and watercraft of both motorized and non-motorized varieties. Jutting skyward near the distant head of the lake is the timeless presence of massive **Mt. Heyburn**.

Back on our bikes, we continue spinning down the smooth blacktop road. Just past Little Redfish Lake, immediately before arriving back at the main highway, we turn right onto Forest Road 210, also called the **Decker Flat Road**. Instantly the swarms of people and cars disappear, and we have the dirt road to ourselves . . . except for the sandhill crane that starts running along beside us, just yards away, and keeps going for nearly a half mile. We can't determine if she's chasing us, we're chasing her, or she's just joining in for the fun of it.

The rustic road more or less parallels State Highway 75, but along the opposite, west side of the Salmon River. The road is a joy to bicycle, although the surface is occasionally covered with a fine, dusty powder. We ride out about 6 miles before stopping in a clearing atop a low bench above the river. The White Clouds rise dramatically to the east, and the Smoky Mountains loom to the south.

Our stomachs tell us suppertime is nearing, so, although we could continue riding south and emerge at the highway in another 5 miles or so, then use the main highway to complete a loop, we opt to turn around . . . but not before having a second weird wildlife encounter (Nancy says it must have something to do with the alignment of the moon and stars): Sixty or 70 yards ahead we see a coyote standing smack in the middle of a group of eight horses. He's looking around, as if he doesn't know what to do next. We figure he probably *doesn't* know, in his outnumbered and outsized predicament.

Back at the campsite the scent and snapping of burning pine blends with the clamor of kids having a great time, making us feel like we're kids, too, worry-free at summer camp. Crowds can actually be fun, we agree; it all depends on one's attitude. Sleep comes easily after a delicious, if not so nutritious, meal of flame-blackened hot dogs, spicy baked beans, and s'mores.

Continuing through the SNRA, to Galena Summit and the Big Wood River Valley

Back on the main highway, at a point 1.5 miles south of the road leading to Redfish Lake you'll reach the right-hand turn to the **Sawtooth Fish Hatchery**. At the hatchery's visitor center you can learn about efforts by fisheries biologists aimed at bolstering populations of the Snake River salmon and steelhead trout. Another 3.5 miles south up the main highway from the hatchery is the road leading to the resplendent **Idaho Rocky Mountain Ranch** (telephone 208–774–3544). Drive in, at

least to have a look, by following the pole-fence-bordered access road as it bumps eastward for half a mile across sage flats.

Built in the 1930s, the ranch originally was known as the Idaho Rocky Mountain Club, when it operated as a private, by-invitation retreat. Today the duplex cabins and four lodge rooms are available to rent by the public in summer, while in winter the ranch runs at a reduced level, with several cabins available for cross-country ski escapes. The rustic main lodge, with its roof of cedar shakes, is surrounded by a procession of cabins, all stained dark brown and boasting river-rock fireplaces. The buildings nestle at the foot of a forested slope that is dotted rust-orange with beetle-killed pines. Atop a lodgepole pine flagpole waves a big American flag, flapping in the breeze above a small pond. Horseback-riding and hiking trails begin virtually at the doorstep of the lodge, from there winding high into the White Cloud Mountains. Guests even enjoy a private hot springs. All in all, it's a bucolic and captivating scene, straight out of an earlier era in the West.

South of here on the highway things turn even less populated—in regard to humans, anyway; there *are* abundant populations of cows and sheep. Even on an ideal summer afternoon you may find that you have the road practically to yourself. A mile and a half from the turn to Idaho Rocky Mountain Ranch you'll zip past the spot in the road known as Obsidian, where **Sessions Lodge** (telephone 208–774–3366) operates as a combination convenience store, motel, cafe, RV park, and real estate office. A couple of miles south of Obsidian you'll pass the left-hand turn onto **Fisher Creek Road** (Forest Road 132). One of the most popular mountain-bike trail rides in the SNRA–Sun Valley area—in fact, in all the Northern Rockies—is the loop fashioned by riding up Fisher Creek Road, down Williams Creek Trail #104, then back to the beginning via the highway. Don't miss it if you've got the time, energy, and appropriate two-wheeled vehicles in tow. Much like the paved Going-to-the-Sun Road in Montana—although most of the Fisher-Williams loop is unpaved—many cyclists would tell you this is *the* classic ride to pick if you do only one ride in Idaho.

As you continue southward, to the west rise the Sawtooths, a pack of peaks and pinnacles

Indian paintbrush and elephant head

marked by steep, talus-strewn slopes forming the walls of pronounced U-shaped valleys. The mountains' lower flanks are generally shrouded in timber; the higher up you look, though, the more they become a symphony of snow, ice, and rock. Lying east of the road are the White Clouds, real mountains by anyone's measure, yet gentler and less imposing than the aptly named Sawtooths.

Just over 7 miles south of Obsidian you'll encounter the turn onto the bumpy dirt road leading westward to **Pettit Lake**; then, approximately 3 miles farther, the paved road leading to **Alturas Lake**. Respectively, Pettit and Alturas are the third and second largest lakes in the SNRA, trailing only Redfish Lake. Both lakes are located approximately 2 miles off the highway, each brims with water bluer than blue, and both include recreation sites and trailheads with trails leading into the 217,000-acre Sawtooth Wilderness, which is legally penetrable only on foot, horseback, or skis.

After passing Busterback Ranch, formerly one of the finest cross-country ski ranches in the Rockies (it no longer serves as a ski ranch), you will level your sights at the notch in the Boulder Mountains called **Galena Summit**. Before begin-

ning the climb, pull in at **Smiley Creek Lodge**, which is pretty much all there is to the modern "town" of Sawtooth City. The lodge (telephone 208–774–3547) is a good place to grab an afternoon sandwich or to spend the night camping in the RV park . . . or in a rented tipi. You can also ask at the lodge for directions to the pair of nearby Forest Service roads leading to the historic sites of **Sawtooth City** and **Vienna**. Both were active gold- and silver-mining centers during the 1880s. Little remains of either now, though, and only by really stretching your imagination can you picture Vienna, home to 800 people, the estimated population at the town's zenith in the mid-1880s.

To see the Salmon River at nearly its tiniest, where you can hop over it without getting your feet wet (assuming you avoid the spring runoff), immediately before commencing the climb toward Galena Summit turn south onto Forest Road 215 and follow it for three miles to the **Chemeketan** recreation site. Beyond there the road continues tracing the rudiments of the River of No Return for another couple of miles, but it rapidly devolves into a four-wheel-drive road.

State Highway 75, meanwhile, spirals up and up, topping out at 8,701-foot Galena Summit. Before reaching the summit pull into the wide parking area on the right marking the Galena Overlook, where you'll spot some rest rooms, and savor one last look back at the Sawtooth Range and into the valley of the upper Salmon River, lying some 2,000 feet below. It's an incredible panorama.

Beyond this point you will lose the hindsight views but quickly reap equally wonderful vistas to the south, first of the Boulder Mountains and then of the far-reaching Big Wood River Valley. In the late-afternoon light of summer the sagebrush clumps covering the lower slopes of the Boulders often appear as incandescent bursts of velvety green. In the shallow depressions that trap greater amounts of moisture grow grasses of brighter green, while aspens thrive in the dampest draws. Those lower, grassy swales slope upward, ever more steeply, to meet rocky peaks holding only narrow bands of timber; the highest reaches, demonstrative of their geology, are apparently void of vegetation altogether. In contrast, the north slopes of the Smoky Mountains to the right are more heavily and uniformly forested in pine and Douglas fir.

At the southeastern foot of the pass you'll go by **Galena Lodge** (telephone 208–726–4010), which serves gourmet lunches year-round and supper at certain times of the year. But the real specialty of the house is cross-country skiing: The lodge regularly grooms an extensive network of trails in winter that traverse SNRA lands, for both the ski-skating and classic kick-and-glide techniques. The annual **Boulder Mountain Tour**, held here early in February, is the most popular all-comers cross-country ski competition in the three-state Northern Rockies region. Nearly a thousand participants, ranging from experts to casual ski tourists, flock in to enjoy one of the best-groomed and most beautiful courses in the world. The tour begins on the trails at Galena and finishes 30 kilometers (18.5 miles) away, near the SNRA headquarters. The course, while generally losing elevation, winds up into, then back out of, several drainages on the west side of the highway, so plenty of sweat is earned by skiing all over the course, regardless of how cold the weather may be.

Sun Valley is widely known as the West's preeminent downhill ski resort. Less known is that this one-day event—and winter-long opportunities at venues including Galena Lodge, Sun Valley Nordic Center, the Wood River Trails, the Lake Creek trail system, and others—make the greater Sun Valley area also the foremost *cross-country* skiing mecca west of the Mississippi River.

You'll pass several Forest Service campgrounds over the ensuing miles, including **Boulder View**, **Easley,** and **Wood River**. There's also an abundance of dispersed, undeveloped campsites along the way. **Easley Hot Springs**, owned and operated by the Idaho Baptist Convention but open to the public, is located off the highway to the west, just past the campground of the same name.

Thanks to the protection afforded these lands by national forest designation, you may find it difficult to believe that you are only 10 or 12 miles from lavish and heralded Sun Valley. As if to magnify this apparent paradox, don't be surprised to spot a sheep camp erected somewhere off the road, settled between the highway and the ranges in the sage-filled distance. The size of the industry has dwindled in recent decades, but the SNRA–Sun Valley region remains prime sheep-raising country. The vestigial, Old West vision

that you will see consists of a canvas- or tin-covered wagon with large wheels, surrounded by a large herd of woolly beasts. Nearby you may see the sheepherder, who's probably of South American or Basque origin, along with his horses or mules and wiry, well-trained dogs.

South of the **North Fork Campground**, 8 miles north of downtown Ketchum, you'll see the SNRA headquarters on the left. The visitor center has a good selection of books and maps, along with displays on the area's flora and fauna.

Just past the SNRA headquarters you will leave the national forest and immediately be greeted by some of the neo-Western mansions for which Sun Valley is known. Initially the slopes above remain almost as empty as those in the adjoining national forest, while the lower benches and the valley bottom progressively hold more, and larger, homes the closer to town you travel. Ahead and to the right you can't miss seeing the ski runs carved on the face of Bald Mountain, the immense ski area that rarely is out of view anywhere you go in the Ketchum–Sun Valley area. Baldy appears deceptively small from this perspective, from which only a fraction of its runs can be seen.

Now, just a few words about this area's potentially confusing place-name terminology. The entire area is casually referred to as **Sun Valley**, but it's not quite accurate to do so. The first town you'll drive into is **Ketchum**, the historic mining settlement originally known as Leadville that predates the Sun Valley Resort by more than fifty years. Sun Valley, now a town unto itself, is located a mile east of Ketchum. Bald Mountain, the ski area often thought of and referred to as "Sun Valley," is actually closer to Ketchum than to Sun Valley. However, the Sun Valley Resort owns Bald Mountain. The resort also owns the much smaller Dollar Mountain, which is situated in close proximity to Sun Valley. Then there are the **Warm Springs** and **Elkhorn** areas . . .

Confused yet? Okay, it *is* easier simply to call the whole affair Sun Valley.

About a mile before rolling into downtown Ketchum, you'll pass the right-hand turn leading into **Adams Gulch**, an area of Sawtooth National Forest lands that offers top-notch, close-to-town hiking and mountain biking. Beyond there, as you near Ketchum on the highway, in summer you'll begin seeing fit-looking cyclists, walkers, and in-line skaters moving in both directions along the immensely popular **Wood River Trail**.

Given its history, it is fitting that this ribbon of blacktop, which extends south some 18 miles to the town of Bellevue, has become a primary artery of recreational travel. The trail follows the right-of-way of the old Wood River Branch of the Oregon Short Line, a subsidiary of the Union Pacific Railroad. It was the existence of this branch line that made the Ketchum area readily accessible by late in the nineteenth century, and which later helped convince Averell Harriman, chairman of the board of the Union Pacific, that this was *the* location to build his dream resort. Several other mountainous areas in the West were considered, then ruled out, including Aspen, Colorado, and the west slope of the Tetons outside Victor, Idaho—which occupies another high valley accessed in those days by an Oregon Short Line spur.

In addition to the primary Wood River Trail, adjoining recreational paths circle through the Sun Valley and Elkhorn resorts and shoot eastward up Trail Creek. Winter or summer, you should not miss the opportunity of traveling these trails by one self-propelled mode or another.

A Day at the Sun Valley Resort: A Narrative Account

Driving into downtown Ketchum at noon on a cloudless day in August, Nancy and I are surprised by the intensity of the sun's heat. Our previous trips to the area have fallen either in winter or autumn. Every time we visit, regardless of the season, it seems that we're pleasantly taken aback by Ketchum's friendly, small-town feel and its general lack of pretense. Like most people, we tend to associate Sun Valley with mink stoles and movie stars, but in general the resort area is actually quite casual and laid-back—although fancier options certainly are available to those looking for them.

Today, as a matter of fact, we see absolutely no fur coats on the sidewalks of Ketchum. But the temperature in the mid-eighties probably has something to do with that. At the stoplight at the main downtown junction we turn east onto Sun Valley Road and drive a mile to the Sun Valley town-limits greeting sign (INCORPORATED 1947;

POPULATION 660). Immediately we pull into the large parking lot fronting the **Sun Valley Lodge**, then get out and walk inside to register and procure directions to our condominium. A doorman, conspicuous in his crisp maroon uniform, holds the door open for us and other summer visitors similarly outfitted in shorts and T-shirts.

The lobby of the Sun Valley Lodge is elegant, distinguished. Dark leather chairs rest on a light brown carpeting accentuated with beefy, dark-brown geometric patterns. The hardwood paneling and wainscoting is richly stained chocolate brown. In glass trophy cases against the wall reside items such as historic Harriman Cups, which are the trophies awarded at Sun Valley's earliest ski races, and original editions of books written by Averell Harriman in his role as a U.S. statesman. Elsewhere in the large lobby our attention is drawn to Western art and to deep-seated couches sporting bright floral patterns. It seems that we detect as many different European languages being spoken as we do various dialects of English.

Before registering we spend a full half hour strolling through the main hallway extending from the lobby toward a wing of rooms. Here, in a nutshell, recorded in black-and-white photographs, is the compelling history of six decades of skiing at Sun Valley. This central-Idaho outpost never has been the easiest place in the world to get to, yet a lot of rich and famous people have managed to make the journey. The photos help to cement my impression that Sun Valley—more than Mammoth Mountain, more than Stowe, more than Aspen—truly is the grande dame of U.S. ski resorts.

Photos hanging in the hallway include those of luminaries such as Gary Cooper, Clark Gable, Claudette Colbert, and Lucille Ball, who is pictured alongside little Lucie and Desi Jr. And the list continues, a veritable "Who's Who" of celebrity skiers: Ernest Hemingway, Ray Milland, Harry S Truman. Over there is Marilyn Monroe, Louis Armstrong, Robert Kennedy. Here's Ricky Nelson, and the legendary mountain man and skier Dick Durrance, winner of the inaugural Harriman Cup in the late 1930s. There's the Shah of Iran, for goodness' sake.

Some celebrities are shown skiing, while others are ice skating or simply posing in the snow. From the occasional shot of ski tracks cut in the powder, it is obvious that slopeside grooming was neither the science nor the priority in the early days that it is today. The skier of yore, even Hollywood, political, and industrial bigwigs, made tracks in whatever fell from the sky. Today's visitor to Sun Valley, in contrast, expects the slopes to be groomed and buffed to polished perfection. And they almost always are.

After signing in at the massive registration desk, we drive over to our room in the nearby Wildflower Condominiums, haul in our luggage, and vow to devote the rest of the afternoon to investigating the Sun Valley Resort on foot.

To begin our sojourn we walk over to the **Sun Valley Inn**, where we enter another large lobby, but one that is slightly more intimate than that of the venerable Sun Valley Lodge. The ceilings of the inn's lobby are lower, and the whole setting feels a bit more modern, although the appointments are similarly dark and refined. Incongruously, on this hot August afternoon a fire roars in the open gas fireplace. A large photo on the wall, entitled "Picard Fashions for the 1947 Ski Season," depicts a pair of wispy fashion models decked out in white ruffled shirts and dark baggy pants. One sports a hat with an extraordinarily long bill, and both girls wear leather lace-up ski boots, which are locked into bear-trap bindings attached to ponderous wooden skis that look as if they weigh as much as the skiers wearing them.

Log home, Sun Valley

We discover—and it is not by happenstance, we realize—that one could never leave the grounds of the Sun Valley Resort, yet enjoy an extraordinarily well-rounded vacation without even sampling all the possibilities at hand. Visitors can golf on a course that regularly makes lists of America's top courses. Tennis, swimming, and ice skating are additional options, and pedal-boat rentals are available at the resort's large pond. The selection of bars and restaurants ranges from cafeteria-style to black-tie affairs. In winter visitors can cross-country ski on expertly groomed trails or, in summer, cycle or in-line skate along hard-surfaced trails, to destinations that include the resort's **Trail Creek Cabin**. Other options include shopping, bowling, and attending the Opera House, which shows first-run movies every evening.

We find that in summer, though, one of the most appealing activities is simply hanging around on the grounds, relaxing and people-watching. The landscaped maze of footpaths, streams, and ponds holding ducks, geese, and swans, encourages such inactivity. Flowers bloom everywhere, and shade is provided by large spruce, aspen, and willow trees. Baggage/client carts zip about in every direction, operated by polite young and not-so-young wait staff who are determined to see that guests needn't go to the trouble of transporting their own luggage.

We amble over to the indoor skating arena, where we discover the cold air on this hot afternoon feels wonderful. Teenage skaters dressed in leotards, sweaters, and gloves zip around, perfecting their dips, twirls, and hand posturing. Then Brian Orser, a two-time Olympic Winter Games silver medalist set to perform in the arena this evening, appears on the ice for a warm-up. Pens, magazines, programs, and napkins materialize from thin air and point at Mr. Orser, who suddenly is surrounded by skaters-turned-autograph hounds; young kids gone nuts, transformed from models of possessed perfection into screaming maniacs.

Chilled, we walk back into the afternoon heat. Between the indoor skating rink and the Sun Valley Lodge we find nestled an outdoor rink, running full blast even on this sweltering day. A dark net screen, billowing downward like rain clouds and flapping in the breeze, protects the ice from the hottest rays of the sun. Still, the cost of the energy used to keep the ice frozen must be astronomical.

We seat ourselves on the veranda behind the Lodge, which in summer serves as an outdoor bar/restaurant. A canvas canopy keeps the sun away. What a great place it is to enjoy a cold drink. The high-pitched whine of the ice-polishing Zamboni mixes with the summer chatter of relaxed, happy visitors. It seems strange, seeing and smelling gladiolus blooming in planter boxes along the edge of the porch, with a frozen ice rink only yards away.

The instant the Zamboni leaves the ice a flood of skinny little girls, some looking as young as four or five, pours onto the rink. They begin looping around in counterclockwise fashion, free skating and holding their arms and hands extended in the positions familiar to anyone who has watched figure skating. Grinning parents on the perimeter point video cameras at their always beautiful but suddenly, and uncharacteristically poised progeny. Recorded music—we know it must have a name but we recognize it as the theme music from the VISA commercial—blares through rink-side speakers, and the young skaters do their best to move in time. An older and obviously more experienced skater helps one aspiring young Nancy Kerrigan to assume the correct pose while gliding on one skate. With one hand the older girl pulls up on the little skater's backward extended left leg, while pushing with the other hand down on her upper back. We hope they don't crash in this entangled position.

Next stop: the summer art fair under way a couple of hundred yards away. Fifty or sixty canvas-topped booths, displaying and offering for sale all sorts of first-class artwork, are arranged in several rows covering an acre or two of the Sun Valley Resort's soccer fields. We inspect realistic wildlife paintings, handsome and intricately fashioned chairs and couches of lodgepole pine logs, "wearable art" composed of all sorts and colors of fabrics, exceptional jewelry ranging from that made of found objects to hand-crafted gold and silver necklaces adorned with gemstones, wood and metal sculptures, elaborate children's toys, and much, much more. Hundreds of people are looking, but only a handful appear to be buying. As for us, we have neither enough cash in our wallets nor room in our car for most of what is available. But it sure is fun to look at.

Five o'clock approaches, time to head over to the Opera House to catch today's free screening of *Sun Valley Serenade*. The classic 1941 Hollywood film stars Sonja Henie, John Payne, and Milton Berle, with great tunes provided by the Glenn Miller Orchestra. The movie, which shows daily the year around, depicts an earlier but altogether familiar Sun Valley, filled with happy, well-to-do, fashionable playboys and playgirls. It is still easy to imagine oneself—even if one lacks the requisite looks, money, and/or attitude—as one of these smiling 1940s, Sun Valley bon vivants. And that surely is one of the irresistible draws of this, the premier winter and summer resort in the Northern Rockies.

After a light supper at **Konditorei**, we take an evening stroll up the paved bicycle path paralleling Trail Creek. Once east of the golf course we're immediately back into deserted rural surroundings. We really like this about the Sun Valley area: Largely because of the protection afforded by close-in national forest lands, "urban sprawl" is concentrated to patches and ribbons, such as that lining the Wood River corridor.

As is almost always the case here, where high desert meets the mountains to form the unique Sun Valley landscape, Bald Mountain looms above it all. It's a constant reminder, even in these summer dog days, that skiing is what motors Sun Valley, where the sun always shines, the powder is always dry, and the cold winter winds are always kept at bay by the embracing hills. Or almost always, anyway.

Before turning around we walk the several yards off the path leading down to the **Ernest Hemingway Memorial**, tucked along the bank of Trail Creek in a grove of trees. Hemingway, one of Sun Valley's best-known regulars, loved to hunt, fish, and drink with his fellow luminaries and his earthy Idaho comrades in and around the Big Wood River Valley. He first arrived at the invitation of Averell Harriman in 1939. On that trip he toiled mornings to wrap up the manuscript of *For Whom the Bell Tolls*, a wartime story of love set in Spain, while holed up in Room 206 of the Sun Valley Lodge. Hemingway, who died by his own hand in the Wood River Valley in 1961, is buried in the Ketchum cemetery, and some of his descendants still live in the area.

Hemingway Memorial

The words inscribed on his monument were written by Hemingway as a eulogy for a friend, but they certainly must apply to him . . . as well as to hundreds of others who have learned to love the magic and beauty of this special place called Sun Valley:

> *Best of all he loved the fall,*
> *The leaves yellow on the cottonwoods*
> *Leaves floating on the trout streams*
> *And above the hills*
> *   the high blue windless skies . . .*
> *Now he will be part of them forever.*

From Sun Valley to Craters of the Moon National Monument

Before leaving Sun Valley—or *as* you leave—be sure to drive on Dollar Road over the low divide leading to the Elkhorn Resort area. The resort's scenic, tough golf course, another nationally top-rated course, snakes alongside the road. Dollar Road links up with Elkhorn Road, which meets State Highway 75 at a point just south of Ketchum.

Heading south on the potentially very busy highway, you'll pass through historic Hailey, home to the **Blaine County Museum**, located at Galena and Main. Hailey might appear to exist only to provide a place for those "regular people" working in Sun Valley with lower-cost housing than is available closer to the resort. To an extent that is true. But the town is undergoing constant polishing and coming into its own, in a renewal effort fueled largely by movie stars Bruce Willis and wife Demi Moore. Hot spots include the **Sun Valley Brewing Company** and the hip **Liberty Theatre** movie house. Great hiking, mountain biking, and ski touring opportunities can be found close to Hailey, too. And, as if not to be outdone by Sun Valley, which boasted Ernest Hemingway as a part-time resident, Hailey even claims its own literary heavyweight: poet Ezra Pound, who was born in Hailey in 1885, during the height of the mining boom. However, Pound, who was arrested for treason during World War II, is not universally loved in the area as Hemingway appears to be. Local feelings for him seem to run the gamut, from adoration to ambivalence to detestation.

Continuing south, you'll come to **Bellevue**, passing **Valley Market**, one of the great grocery stores of the West. Bellevue is also home to some antiques shops, the **Bellevue Bistro**, and the log cabin accommodations of the **Come On Inn**, whose slogan, "Sleep Like a Log," continues the pun-ism. On arriving at the intersection 10 miles south of Bellevue, turn east onto U.S. Highway 20. Prior to reaching the spot in the road called **Picabo** (*peek-a-boo*), you'll pass the right-hand turn leading into the headquarters and small visitor center of the **Silver Creek Preserve** (telephone 208–788–2203).

Silver Creek is a name that sends chills down the spines of fly-fishers everywhere. The stream flows over polished pebbles and mats of moss amid desiccated desert and flooded farm fields, providing a clashing and stunning wetlands contrast. It is as beautiful as any mountain stream, a beauty that is magnified by the drab landscape framing it. Brown and rainbow trout, large and plentiful—but learned and wily—feed and thrive on summerlong hatches of clear-winged mayflies. These are the hallmarks of this crystal-clear creek, which, because it is fed by artesian springs, maintains a constant 52-degree temperature the year around—perfect for trout and the bugs on which they dine. Fishing at the preserve, which encompasses only part of the 15-mile length of Silver Creek, is catch-and-release only, and limited to

Silver Creek, near Picabo, Idaho

barbless dry flies. Also living on or around the creek are some 150 bird species and a number of small mammals, including beaver and fox.

The preserve, maintained and managed by the Nature Conservancy, was garnered and saved from development in a deal negotiated largely by Ernest Hemingway's son, Jack, when he was head of the Idaho Fish and Game Commission in the mid-1970s. A lifelong fishing fanatic, Jack Hemingway is said to be the only U.S. serviceman who parachuted during World War II into occupied France with a fly rod among his packed-along necessities.

Near Picabo—source of the name of champion skier Picabo Street, who hails from nearby Triumph—you'll begin seeing evidence of the young basaltic lava flows that reach their crescendo at **Craters of the Moon National Monument**. The Craters of the Moon lava flows, which cover an area far more vast than the eighty-three square miles composing the national monument, range from a youthful 15,000 to an infantile 2,000 years old.

When Oregon Trail travelers following Goodale's Cutoff—as well as the Indians, explorers, and traders who preceded and followed them—encountered these vast lava flows, they found them strange and impressive. But for the most part they probably couldn't wait to leave the hot, unforgiving lavascape behind. The area did not come to the general attention of the U.S. public until 1924, when an article regarding it appeared in *National Geographic Magazine*.

"For several years I had listened to stories told by fur trappers of the strange things they had seen while ranging in this region," wrote author Robert Limbert of Boise, Idaho. "Some of these accounts seemed beyond belief." So in the early 1920s Limbert undertook a trio of expeditions to see for himself the vast spread of frozen lava, an area so unusual that Limbert could scarcely believe it had almost entirely escaped notice.

The colorful Limbert was a part-time taxidermist and furrier and part-time amateur wrestler and quick-draw specialist. He once challenged Al Capone to a shoot-out at ten paces, but the gangster apparently refused the invitation. Limbert's detailed descriptions of this region, which enraptured him with its eerie brand of beauty, in *National Geographic* and other magazines led to the area being held in protection by the federal government. Under the auspices of the Antiquities Act a rudimentary national monument was designated in 1924, "to preserve the unusual and weird volcanic formations." Since then the park's acreage has been bolstered.

In the *National Geographic* article, Limbert referred to the area in question as the Craters of the Moon, and the name stuck. It's a bit of a misnomer in light of what we know now; that is, most of the moon's craters were created by crashing meteorites rather than by volcanic explosions. Maybe it's not that bad a name after all, however: NASA sent their second crew of moon-bound astronauts to train at Craters of the Moon, hoping to prepare them for walking about in an altogether alien and potentially disorienting landscape.

Craters of the Moon National Monument

From the visitor center, located south of the highway at a point 32 miles northeast of Picabo, you can strike out on a 7-mile loop drive through the center of the monument. The drive encompasses sites such as **Devils Orchard**, a scattering of lava fragments rising above an ocean of cinders; the **Inferno Cone** and **Spatter Cones** areas, where you'll garner vivid glimpses of the Great Rift, that crack in the earth responsible for this topsy-turvy table of blackened terrain; and the **Cave Area**, where a half-mile-long trail leads to several cave-like lava tubes.

For those really wanting to immerse themselves in the lavascape, a pair of short trails penetrate the unroaded, 68-square-mile Craters of the Moon Wilderness, providing access to miles of untrailed, cross-country exploring. The sweltering heat of summer can be relentless, but spring and fall can be wonderful times to visit. For details and information on safety precautions, backcountry-use permits, and other particulars, check in at the visitor center (telephone 208–527–3257), which opens year-round at 8:00 A.M., closing at 6:00 P.M. in summer and 4:30 P.M. the rest of the year. Camping is available at the monument's campground, situated just south of the visitor center.

The Upper Salmon and Big Lost River Valleys

At least a couple of things contribute to make Arco, located 19 miles northeast of Craters of the Moon National Monument, noteworthy. One is the cliffs rising above town to the east, their sides adorned with dozens of painted-on dates, evidently memorializing every graduating class since at least 1925. The other, and the feature that really makes this settlement stand out: In 1955 Arco became the first town in the world to be powered by atomic energy. The lights ran for only an hour or two on electricity generated at the National Reactor Testing Station located in the Arco desert southeast of town, but served its purpose, providing evidence of the peacetime possibilities of the atom.

From Arco head northwest on U.S. Highway 93, up the Big Lost River Valley toward the cattle-ranching and recreation center of Mackay. En route you'll pass through tiny Moore and—on the outside chance you're packing along your hang glider—the right-hand turn to the **King Mountain Launch Site**.

Highlights in Mackay (*MACK-ee*) include the **Bear Bottom Inn** restaurant-motel-gift shop (telephone 208–588–2483), the small but interesting **Lost Rivers Museum**, **Amy Lou's Steakhouse** (telephone 208–588–9903), and the **River Park Golf Course & RV Campground** (telephone 208–588–2296), the perfect getaway for roughing-it duffers. At the **Lost River Ranger District** (telephone 208–588–2224), located at 716 West Custer, you can obtain information on the abundance of hiking trails and other recreational opportunities awaiting in the White Knob Mountains, which lie in close proximity to town on the southwest, as well as in the high Lost River Range to the north.

The population of Mackay ordinarily numbers around 500, but that roughly doubles on the second weekend in August, when the annual **White Knob Challenge** mountain-bike race loops into and back out of the nearby White Knobs. Many of the racers, who range from novices to experts, arrive from the Sun Valley area via the largely gravel back-door route—up Trail Creek from Sun Valley, that is, then over Trail Creek Summit and down the valleys of Summit Creek and the Big Lost River. This makes for an outstanding drive in its own right, even if you're not among those aiming for the starting line of a tough mountain-biking competition.

A public campground, wrapped in rather plain-brown surroundings, is located on **Mackay Reservoir**, about 5 miles northwest of town. The reservoir is created by a dam backing up the waters of the Big Lost, a river known during the fur-trading days as Godin's River. The name came from the trapper said to have "discovered" the river in 1823. Native Americans undoubtedly knew of the river earlier, but their lack of English or French record-keeping precluded their being credited with the discovery. The river's name was later changed by area farmers, for the fact that the river literally becomes lost south of the town of Howe, after disappearing into the

Borah Peak earthquake escarpment

honeycombed basalt of the Snake River aquifer. The waters re-emerge, magically and beautifully, more than 100 miles to the southwest at Thousand Springs near Hagerman.

After passing the left-hand turn toward Sun Valley at a point 15 miles from Mackay, you'll leave the Big Lost River and begin climbing gradually toward Willow Creek Summit. The impressive peaks of the Lost Rivers, such as 12,228-foot **Leatherman Peak**, hang high and near on the right. Soon you will pass a sign marking the turn to the Borah Peak fault scarp, situated 2.5 miles east of the highway on a good gravel road. The escarpment, which clearly shows where and to what extent the earth fractured in the October 1983 Borah Peak earthquake, runs along the base of the Lost Rivers for some 20 miles, but this is one of the most readily accessible viewpoints.

On the opposite, west side of the highway along Thousand Springs Creek sprawls the 1,500-acre **Chilly Slough Wetlands Conservation Area**, one of a rare remaining high-desert, spring-fed wetlands. Canoeing, wildlife viewing, fishing, and bird hunting are the most popular pursuits here, although "popular" is a relative term: You might have the place pretty much to yourself on any given day. Access to the remote northern end of the conservation area is via a county road going west at a point three-quarters of a mile north of milepost 132. For additional information call the Salmon Field Office of the Bureau of Land Management at (208) 756–5400.

From Willow Creek Summit you'll descend along Warm Springs Creek, through the dramatic slot of **Grandview Canyon**, where erosion has exposed a knob of ancient dolomite laid down some 400 million years ago. Approaching **Challis**, you'll pass the right-hand turn onto Hot Springs Road, which in 4.5 miles leads to **Challis Hot Springs and Campground** (telephone 208–879–4442). The springs has been in commercial operation since the early mining days.

Although plenty of water escapes from the ground at the hot springs and the Salmon River flows past Challis, there's not much water forthcoming from the sky in this arid basin. With an annual precipitation of less than 8 inches, Challis occupies one of the driest spots in the Northern Rockies.

Before getting into the small heart of downtown, stop in at the **Land of the Yankee Fork Visitor Center**, located near the junction of U.S. Highway 93 and State Highway 75. At the attractive gray facility, designed to echo the look of a slope-side mill, a slide show and exhibits will orient you to the fascinating Yankee Fork Mining District, which you can explore up close and personal by traveling on the **Custer Motorway Adventure Road**. If you do intend to drive the route, ask at the visitor center (telephone 208–879–5244) about current road conditions and also request the self-guiding brochure describing the tour. The facility is open daily Memorial Day through September from 8:00

A.M. to 6:00 P.M. and 9:00 A.M. to 5:00 P.M. Monday through Friday the rest of the year.

Challis began life in 1876 as a center to supply the nearby mountain mines, with freight first hauled here by horse-drawn wagons from the Union Pacific railhead in Corinne, Utah. The town still serves primarily as a supply center for miners and ranchers, but recreation is constantly gaining ground in importance compared to those more traditional industries. Challis is one of those towns just big enough, it seems, that everybody living there knows everybody else. So—particularly if the car you're driving wears Idaho plates—don't be surprised if almost everyone you see waves "hello." It may be because they're extra-friendly, or it may be that they just do it from habit, or as a precaution: It's safer to wave at someone they don't readily recognize than to chance being branded unfriendly by someone they do know. Whichever it is really doesn't matter; you'll get a real friendly feeling in Challis.

The community includes a handful of restaurants and motels. Under development at this writing is the **Central Idaho Museum for Regional History**, located at the junction of Main Street and U.S. Highway 93. A pleasant park sits adjacent to the facility. At the upper end of Main Street, which slopes steeply to the west toward the flank of the Salmon River Mountains, on the left you'll see the nine-hole **Challis Golf Course**. The course's connecting fairways contribute an oddly shaped splash of green that snakes through a treeless setting embraced by crinkled, brown hills.

If you'd like to tour the Custer Motorway, after topping off your gas tank and stocking up on food and water, continue west on Main Street, which becomes Forest Road 070. The road between Challis and Custer City is winding and narrow in places, and not recommended for low-clearance cars, motor homes, or trailers. The road is generally open June through September. Forest Service campgrounds along the way offer overnight options to those outfitted for camping.

Originally constructed in 1879 as a toll road linking Challis and Bonanza City, the road was upgraded by the Civilian Conservation Corps in the 1930s, then re-named the Custer Motorway. Sites you'll see along the mountainous way include the log remains of Tollgate Station, the Custer Cemetery, the old ore bin of the General Custer Mill, and the historic remains of Custer City, where a self-guided walking tour can be taken. A little way farther down the road is the **Yankee Fork Dredge**, a floating gold dredge that is the last known of its elephantine breed still inhabiting the hills of Idaho. The beast was operational intermittently from 1940 until 1952, when it ran out of riverbed to rip up. Tours of the dredge, considered a fascinating piece of lore by some and an eyesore by others, are offered by the Yankee Fork Gold Dredge Association (telephone 208–879–5244). The

Land of the Yankee Fork Visitor Center

nonprofit group works in partnership with the Forest Service, which received the dredge as a donation from its previous owner, potato magnate J. R. Simplot.

After skirting the remains of the mining and CCC camps at **Bonanza City**, the road meets State Highway 75 at **Sunbeam Village**, where you'll find a store and the **Sunbeam Dam Interpretive Site**. The Sunbeam Consolidated Gold Mining Company built a dam on the Salmon River near here in 1910, for the purpose of generating power for the Sunbeam Mine, which was located north up the Yankee Fork at Jordan Creek. The dam was breached in 1934, to re-allow Salmon the river to flow downstream unhindered, and salmon the fish to swim upstream to their spawning beds. (Sunbeam Hot Springs, described in From Stanley to Redfish Lake: A Narrative Account, is situated about a mile west of the highway junction.)

Drive east on the highway back toward Challis, located a total of 55 miles from Sunbeam. In 1.5 miles you'll pass the bridge crossing the river to **O'Brien Campground**. Six miles from there you'll pass the popular and historic **Torrey's Burnt Creek Inn** (telephone toll-free, 888–838–2313), with its RV park, cafe, log rental cabins on the river, guided kayak and raft trips, and antiques store/trading post. A few miles farther along on the left you'll see the **Yankee Fork Ranger Station** of the Challis National Forest; then, 4 miles east of Clayton you'll pass the **East Fork Recreation Area**. Zigzagging "roads," heading to high mining claims and quarries, can be seen crawling up the surrounding steep, talus-strewn mountainsides. Simply looking at and imagining an attempt at negotiating some of these precipitous tracks can give a person sweaty palms.

Gradually, as you head east, the nature of the Salmon River Canyon changes. By the time you're half way to Challis the river has transformed from a forest-embraced mountain stream to a river flowing through a dry, timberless canyon. On re-approaching Challis, after passing the **Bayhorse Recreation Site**, major scree slopes slant down from the mountains, and a wall of rock rises like ramparts on the left above an area of rural homes. A half mile before reclaiming the main junction and the Land of the Yankee Fork Visitor Center, on the left you'll see a modest marker describing a bison jump once worked here by Shoshone Indians.

From Challis to Salmon

U.S. Highway 93 between Challis and Salmon, part of the Salmon River Scenic Byway, earns my vote as *the* classic head-'em-off-at-the-pass drive in the Northern Rockies. It's a countryside dominated by badlands, crumbling cliffs, occasional and incongruous riverside stands of ponderosa pine, deserted cabins once occupied by hardscrabble ranch families, and bright green hayfields marking current ranching operations.

Driving north out of Challis you'll see colorful volcanic cliffs on the opposite side of river, rising sharply like a mangled row of bad teeth to point toward the timbered tips of higher peaks. Below here the valley of the Salmon spreads out, before tapering again in a few miles. Eighteen miles from Challis you'll pass the Ellis post office and the road going right toward **May**, home of the **Darkhorse Cafe and Saloon** (telephone 208–876–4416). This road heads through basin-and-range country, up the valley of the Pahsimeroi River then down the valley of the Little Lost River as it cuts between the Lemhi and Lost River ranges. There's not a lot to see along this drive—which emerges to the south at the town of Howe—other than hawks, pronghorns, empty country, and stark, stunning mountains.

Continuing north, the jaws of the Salmon River canyon repeatedly open wider, where feeder canyons meet the main valley, then close again. As the elevation drops the temperature rises, and so does the water level of the river. Approximately 36 miles from Challis you'll pass the concentration of rural homes known as **Elk Bend**, where there's also a bar-cafe and the **Salmon River Campground & RV Park** (telephone 208–894–4549). Ask any local and he or she can probably tell you how to find the nearby, undeveloped **Elk Bend Hot Springs**. Five miles farther along is the left turn onto the road crossing the river and leading the 2 miles to the sumptuously rustic **Twin Peaks Ranch** (telephone 208–894–2290), one of the best and longest-running dude ranches in Idaho.

Cross the 45th parallel at 45 miles then, 1.5 miles farther, on the left you'll see the **Greyhouse Inn** (telephone 208–756–3968 or, toll-free in the United States, 800–348–8097), a bed and breakfast occupying an attractive 1894 Victorian house, which in summer is surrounded by beds of blooming flowers. Closer to Salmon you'll begin seeing picturesque ranchettes abutting rocky canyons that are like doors opening on the mountains. You'll pass the left-hand turn to **Williams Lake**, a sparkling beauty located 10 miles off the highway that is nestled in the Salmon River Mountains and home to the **Williams Lake Resort** (telephone 208–756–2007). A mile beyond that turn you'll see the road going right to **Salmon Hot Springs** (telephone 208–756–4449), a decidedly one-of-a-kind commercial operation located about 3 miles off the highway.

As you enter the outskirts of **Salmon**, known also as Salmon City, on the right you'll see the headquarters for the Salmon and Challis national forests (telephone 208–756–4226) and, immediately past that, the district office of the Bureau of Land Management (telephone 208–756–5400). Delve into the scores of maps and other resources available at these two offices and you could find a lifetime's worth of recreational opportunities, and then some. Among the many possibilities are several Forest Service rental cabins perched in the surrounding mountains.

Salmon, population between 3,000 and 4,000, is the essential timber town/ranching town–turning recreational outpost. It's a busy and attractive, but functional town with few frills or boutiques; a swatch of grass and trees backed by foothills of green or brown or white, depending on the season, and the high crags of the Bitterroot Range. The river giving the town its name runs through the middle of it all, and a nice town park lines its banks.

Salmon serves as the primary junction for Salmon River float trips: It's the nearest settlement of any consequence to both the take-out point for wild Middle Fork floats and the put-in for Main Fork floats. Salmon also claims a good golf course and big city park, both located a mile south on State Highway 28 from the highway junction at the south end of town.

Drives out of Salmon offering access to great camping, hiking, mountain-biking, fishing, and other recreational opportunities include the one that begins by going 21 miles north along U.S. Highway 93 to **North Fork**. Here you'll find services including a motel, general store, campground, state liquor store, and the **North Fork Ranger Station** of the Salmon National Forest.

Until you reach North Fork, the Salmon River somehow seems to be skirting around the Salmon River Mountains, but here it turns west to dive headlong into them. Forest Road 030, which begins as a quiet paved road following the Salmon, can make for a beautiful bike ride as well as a great car trip. You'll pass the **Deadwater Picnic Ground**, then a Salmon National Forest Helitack Base, with its incongruous tree-surrounded house, smooth lawn, and ever-ready helicopter. Indian Creek Road takes off to the right near here, leading in 3 miles to the **Indian Creek Guest Ranch** (telephone 208–394–2126), a full-service guest ranch once owned by the late actor Burgess Meredith.

The pavement ends at **Shoup**, 17 miles out, but you can continue past there on gravel for more then 20 miles. First you'll come to Cache Bar, where Middle Fork floaters return to land, and then to Corn Creek, the put-in location for Riggins-bound Main Fork boaters. Here, located on the opposite side of the river from the road, is **Salmon River Lodge**, which rents rooms and serves all three meals of the day. The enterprise (telephone 208–756–6622 or, toll-free in the United States, 800–635–4717) shuttles arrivees across the river in a jet boat.

Backcountry drives branching off from Forest Road 030 include the rough-and-tumble outing leading north into Montana's Bitterroot Valley, via Painted Rocks Lake; and one going in the opposite direction, which leaves the wilds just north of Challis. A few year-round residents along the latter route, which follows Forest Road 055 up Panther Creek then down Morgan Creek, are some of the only folks in America to have their winter mail regularly delivered by a snowmobile-straddling postman. For the northerly route, you'll want to have both the Salmon National Forest and Bitterroot National Forest visitor maps on hand; for the drive to Challis, just the Salmon map will suffice.

Back at North Fork, U.S. Highway 93 continues 15 miles north along the North Fork of the

Salmon to Lost Trail Pass and Lost Trail Powder Mountain, that small ski area that boasts high-caliber snow and is shared by Idaho and Montana. On the way there you'll see the **100 Acre Wood Bed & Breakfast** (telephone 208-865-2165), the settlement of **Gibbonsville**, and the Salmon National Forest's **Twin Creek Campground**.

If from Salmon you would prefer to head toward Yellowstone rather than into Montana, drive southeast on State Highway 28 through the high, lonesome sweeps of the Lemhi River and Birch Creek valleys. Twenty miles south of Salmon, at **Tendoy**, you can make a side loop on the gravel and dirt **Lewis and Clark Back Country Byway**. The byway visits Lemhi Pass, where Lewis and Clark first stepped from the east to the west side of the Continental Divide. State Highway 28 meets State Highway 33 at a point 136 miles southeast of Salmon, in the potato-farming town of Mud Lake. Not far from there is where Sun Valley–Salmon Country, Yellowstone-Teton Country, and Glacier-Gold country share a common point.

⌇⌇⌇ Staying There

The McCall and the Stanley Basin–Sun Valley areas are the two most logical locations to use as bases while exploring Sun Valley–Salmon Country. Each is centrally located within its respective province of the region, and both resort areas offer a slate of lodging, dining, and recreational/leisure opportunities. This doesn't mean, of course, that you should avoid spending time in some of the more outlying areas; in fact, many of the region's brightest gems are hidden far back in the hills. Many of these more isolated enterprises are mentioned in the text of Seeing Sun Valley–Salmon Country.

As throughout the Northern Rockies, room rates can vary dramatically between the high and low seasons. Autumn in particular can be a spectacular, uncrowded, and relatively inexpensive time to tour Sun Valley–Salmon Country.

McCall

LODGING

In McCall

1920 House Bed & Breakfast. 143 East Lake Street. Three comfortable, antiques-appointed guest rooms occupying a beautifully renovated house that on the outside looks rather plain. Gourmet breakfasts and afternoon refreshments are part of the deal. Convenient location near the heart of town. Telephone: (208) 634–4661. Moderate.

Best Western McCall. 415 3rd Street (State Highway 55). Quality motel featuring a fitness center, heated indoor pool and spa, microwaves and refrigerators in some rooms, and a bright green roof that is hard to miss. Telephone: (208) 634–6300 or, toll-free in the United States, (800) 528–1234. Moderate.

Brundage Bungalows. 308 West Lake Street. Simple, but cute self-contained cabins with microwaves and cable TV. The largest, a duplex cabin, can sleep ten or more. Telephone: (208) 634–8573. Inexpensive to moderate.

Hotel McCall. 1101 North Third Street. This hotel, located next to the historic town depot and overlooking Payette Lake, is at the hub of downtown McCall. It opened for business in 1904 and, although it fell into disrepair for a spell, recent renovations have brought the hostelry back to, if not beyond, its original splendor. The comfortable hotel offers an irresistible mix, combining the intimacy of a bed and breakfast with many of the amenities of a modern motel. Most of the twenty-two rooms, which range from basic to lavish, include baths and feature televisions and telephones. In the morning, in the hallway outside their rooms, guests are greeted with freshly brewed coffee and a newspaper. Other classy touches include antique writing tables gracing the upstairs hallway, stocked with plenty of the hotel's attractive stationery. A well-rounded breakfast, wine in the afternoon, and before-bedtime cookies and milk are included in the package. Telephone: (208) 634–8105. Inexpensive to very expensive.

Hotel McCall

Northwest Passage Bed & Breakfast. Located off Boydston Street at 201 Rio Vista Boulevard. The 1938 Hollywood epic *Northwest Passage*, starring Spencer Tracy and Robert Young, was filmed in and around McCall. As incredible as it sounds, MGM Studios built this large place to house the cast and crew. Today, with its combination of guest rooms and guest apartment with a kitchen, the lodge can accommodate individuals, couples, and groups as large as twenty-two, during any season of the year. Telephone: (208) 634–5349 or, toll-free in the United States, (800) 597–6658. Moderate.

Shore Lodge. 501 West Lake Street. Full-service resort motel on the banks of Payette Lake, featuring tennis and racquetball, fitness center, pool and spa, private beach, and a lakeside lounge and restaurant. Telephone: (208) 634–2244 or, toll-free in the United States, (800) 657–6464. Moderate to very expensive.

Super 8 Lodge. Franchise motel relatively new to McCall located on State Highway 55 South. Amenities include a toast and juice bar and a hot tub, and some rooms include kitchenettes and whirlpools. Telephone: (208) 634–4637 or, toll-free in the United States, (800) 800–8000. Moderate.

Vacation Rentals. A host of homes, cabins, and condominiums are available to rent in the McCall area, on either a short- or long-term basis. One example of dozens: **Villa de la Verde**, a comfortable home overlooking the ninth fairway of the town golf course. The villa boasts three bedrooms and two baths, dining and living rooms, two wood-burning fireplaces, a hot tub, and a deck outside the master bedroom. Call Sharlie's Property Management at (208) 634–3830, McCall Vacations at (208) 634–7056, or Accommodation Services at (208) 634–7766. (Sharlie, by the way, is the name of the Payette Lake monster.)

Out of McCall

Bear Creek Lodge. Located five miles north of McCall, just off State Highway 55 at mile marker 149. This new lodge, located close to the turn to Brundage Mountain (but on the opposite side of the highway), offers lodge rooms with fireplaces, and duplex-style cabins featuring immense beds and in-room jet tubs. A large buffet breakfast is served each morning, and dinner is available in Bear Creek's gourmet restaurant. Telephone: (208) 634–3551 or, toll-free in the United States, (888) 634–2327. Expensive to very expensive.

The Creamery Bed & Breakfast. Located on Main Street in Cascade, 30 miles south of McCall. Quaint country-style bed and breakfast, with ready access to Cascade Reservoir. Morning brings a hearty farm breakfast. Telephone: (208) 382–4621 or, toll-free in the United States, (800) 725–9006. Inexpensive to moderate.

CAMPGROUNDS AND RV PARKS

Private

Golden RV Park. 204 North 3rd Street in McCall. Full-service campground in a convenient location. Telephone: (208) 634–5389.

McCall Campground. Large campground located just south of town off State Highway 55. Store, laundry, showers, and playground. Telephone: (208) 634–5165.

Meadows RV Park. Situated in Meadows, 8 miles northwest of McCall. Big camp with plenty of large RV sites and tent sites. Telephone: (208) 347–2325 or, toll-free in the United States, (800) 603–2325.

Zim's Hot Springs. *See* Hot Springs.

U.S. Forest Service

The public lands surrounding McCall encompass a large number of campgrounds. In many cases, campers must be willing to negotiate miles of gravel roads to reach them, but the rewards are usually worth the effort. Call the Payette National Forest supervisor's office in McCall at (208) 634–0400 for information on the many additional campgrounds in the region, and to check on the current status of water availability at the campground you're heading to.

Lake Fork. Located 9 miles east of McCall on Lick Creek Road.

Last Chance. Located 7 miles northwest of McCall on State Highway 55, then 2 miles east on dirt. Relatively large campground with primitive hot springs pool nearby.

Upper Payette Lake. Situated on the shores of Upper Payette Lake, 16 miles north of McCall on Warren Wagon Road. In addition to single sites, includes group sites available by reservation.

Ponderosa. On the Secesh River, 31 miles northeast of McCall on Lick Creek Road.

Big Creek Airstrip. Located 86 miles northeast of McCall on Big Creek Road. A drive to this campground, perched at the edge of the Frank Church–River of No Return Wilderness, will give you some idea of the vast scope of the central-Idaho backcountry. The drive leads past several examples of the airstrips common to that backcountry.

Logging truck, Warren Wagon Road, McCall, Idaho

Burgdorf. Thirty miles north of McCall on Warren Wagon Road, then 2 miles northwest on Forest Road 246. Adjacent to the commercially run Burgdorf Hot Springs.

Grouse. Located next to Goose Lake, north of State Highway 55 on Brundage Mountain Road.

Hazard Lake. Twenty-two miles north of State Highway 55 on Brundage Mountain Road. Set in beautiful, wilderness-like surroundings.

Cold Spring. On Lost Valley Reservoir, west of New Meadows on U.S. Highway 95 and forest roads. Relatively large and popular campground.

STATE PARK

Ponderosa State Park. Beautiful state park located just outside of McCall, with 138-site campground. Swimming, boating, horseshoes, volleyball, nature hikes, and mountain biking are a few of the recreational opportunities at hand. Telephone: (208) 634–2164.

FOOD

Chez Jean-Claude Restaurant. Located in the Hotel McCall (but independently operated). Telephone: (208) 634–5440. Outstanding Continental-style cuisine served in comfortable surroundings. (How does Blackberry-Brandy Salmon sound, for instance?) Outdoor seating available in summer. Dinner only. Moderate to expensive.

Harvest Moon Market & Delicatessen. 1133 East Lake Street. Telephone: (208) 634–5578. Specialty food items, and freshly made breads, muffins, and other baked goods. Also specializes in soups, salads, and espresso and whole-bean coffee.

Lardo's Restaurant & Saloon. Located across from the Shore Lodge on Lake Street. Telephone: (208) 634–8191. Earthy hangout serving good steaks and Italian food. Lunch and dinner. Inexpensive to moderate.

Romano's Ristorante. In the Yacht Club Building at 203 East Lake Street. Telephone: (208) 634–4396. Italian and American food served in upbeat surroundings, with a great view of Payette Lake. Patio dining is available in summer. Also located here is the Yacht Club Lounge, a fun nightspot with pocket billiards, darts, and entertainment on weekends. Dinner only. Inexpensive to moderate.

Shore Lodge. Lake Street. Telephone: (208) 634–2244. Good food and outstanding lake views. Dinner menu in the Narrows Restaurant, which features a full bar, includes beef, seafood, and wild game. Breakfast, lunch, and dinner. Inexpensive to expensive.

Si Bueno. Located south of town, across from the airport. Telephone: (208) 634–2128. Serving south-of-the-border-style fare and also specializing in seafood and steaks. Locally heralded margaritas and daquiris are mixed in Rodrigo's Cantina. Lunch and dinner. Inexpensive to moderate.

Smoky Mountain Pizza & Pasta. Across from Shore Lodge at 504 West Lake Street. Telephone: (208) 634–7185. Family-oriented pizza place with game room and eighteen-hole miniature golf course. Lunch and dinner. Inexpensive.

MICROBREWERIES

McCall Brewing Company. Located downtown at 807 North 3rd (State Highway 55). Telephone: (208) 634–2333. Decent brews, crafted on-site, can be savored solo or utilized to wash down the daily lunch and dinner specials served here. The upper deck is one of the hottest spots in town on a summer's afternoon, both literally and figuratively. Food and beer to go, as well.

BICYCLING

Brundage Mountain. On summer weekends between the Fourth of July and Labor Day the lifts run at Brundage, offering rides not only to humans but also to their bicycles. From the top of the mountain trails built specifically for fat-tire fun lead mountain bikers back to the base. Serious cyclists, who believe that riding the lift is cheating, can also feel free to pedal *up* the mountain.

Gravity Sports. 503 Pine Street. As the name indicates, this business focuses on self- and gravity-propelled sports, including mountain biking— but also kayaking, hiking, and climbing. Good source for rentals and where-to-go information. Telephone: (208) 634–8530.

Home Town Sports. Across from the Shore Lodge on Lake Street. Full-service outdoor shop offering rentals. Can provide information regarding the best places to go for road and mountain biking, which include Bear Basin, Warren Wagon Road, East Fork of the Lake Fork Trail, and Ponderosa State Park's Huckleberry Bay Trail. Telephone: (208) 634–2302.

FAIRS, FESTIVALS, AND EVENTS

McCall Folk Music Festival. Held in late July at the University of Idaho Field Campus, near Ponderosa State Park. Three days of evening concerts featuring the sounds of bluegrass, folk, blues, and world beat. For information call the McCall Folklore Society at (208) 634–8432.

Payette Lakes Fine Arts & Crafts Faire. Anything from furniture to food and from leather goods to landscape paintings can be found at this popular event, which draws more than a hundred vendors from throughout Idaho and the Northwest. Held in mid-August in McCall's Fairway Park. For information call SK Productions at (208) 922–4384.

Payette Lakes Ski Marathon. Twenty-five and 50-kilometer (15.5-mile and 31-mile) freestyle cross-country ski races, beginning and ending at the Payette Lakes Ski Club lodge at the Little Ski Hill. Date varies; sometimes held in January and other years in February. For information call (208) 634–2040.

Winter Carnival. This ten-day event, held in late January and early February, includes parades and fireworks, a snowman-building contest for kids, a Mardi Gras Snowflake Ball, sled-dog and snowmobile races, beard and hairy leg competitions, and the flagship Idaho State Snow Sculpting Championships. For information call the Chamber of Commerce at (208) 634–7631.

FISHING

T. Avery Fly Fishing Outfitters. This McCall-based company guides outings, including fly-in wilderness trips, on area alpine lakes and rivers. Specializes in both trout and smallmouth bass fishing. Telephone: (208) 634–3010.

HIKING

Any direction you turn in the McCall area, good hiking trails beckon. Some of the more popular areas: Goose Creek Falls, Upper Hazard Lake, Boulder Lake, and the Twenty-Mile Trail. Visit one of the outdoor shops in town or call the McCall Ranger District at (208) 634–0400 for maps and more information.

HORSEBACK RIDING

Ya-Hoo Corrals. Located 3 miles off State Highway 55 on Warren Wagon Road. Guided trail rides and sunset barbecue rides. Telephone: (208) 634–3360 or, toll-free in the United States, (800) 562–5772.

Epley's Whitewater Adventures. River-running operation that also rents horses in the McCall area. Telephone: (208) 634–5173 or, toll-free in the United States, (800) 233–1813.

HOT SPRINGS

Burgdorf Hot Springs. Located 32 miles north of McCall on Warren Wagon Road and Forest Road 246. Historic commercial hot springs open year-round but accessible only by snowmobile or skis in winter. Primitive cabins available for rent. (For a more complete description *see* Warren Wagon Road to Burgdorf Hot Springs: A Narrative Account, in Seeing Sun Valley–Salmon Country.)

Zim's Hot Springs. Four miles north of New Meadows on State Highway 55. Family-oriented operation with full-service RV and tenting park, snack bar, and recreation room. Telephone: (208) 347–2686.

Burgdorf Hot Springs, outside McCall, Idaho

RIVER FLOATING

Epley's Whitewater Adventures. Specializes in Salmon River trips, ranging from a half-day to five days in duration. Telephone: (208) 634–5173 or, toll-free in the United States, (800) 233–1813.

Salmon River Experience. Another reputable outfitter, this one working out of Riggins. Telephone: (208) 882–2385 or, toll-free in the United States, (800) 892–9223.

SKIING

Both **Home Town Sports** and **Gravity Sports** (*see* Bicycling) rent, sell, and service alpine and cross-country skis, and sell the necessary accoutrements. **Mountain Cycle & Snowboard** (telephone 208–634–6333), located at 212 North 3rd Street, is a specialty shop catering to shredders.

Brundage Mountain. Located 8 miles north of McCall. The relaxed atmosphere of the day lodge, along with the absence of slopeside overnight facilities, belies the fact that skiers and snowboarders face first-class snow sliding on hopping off the lift at Brundage Mountain. Numerous runs leading through high-quality Rocky Mountain snow will bring them back to the base, located 1,800 vertical feet below the summit. Brundage, which works

particularly hard to attract family groups, features a day-care center (accepting kids as young as six weeks) and an extensive learn-to-ski program for children. Come summer, the mountain opens weekends for mountain biking, hiking, and sightseeing. Several events here bring the summer Idaho hills alive with the sound of music, and the lodge and its services are available in summer for weddings, reunions, and other gatherings. Telephone: (208) 634–4151 or, toll-free in the United States, (800) 888–7544.

Little Ski Hill. Located 3 miles north of McCall on State Highway 55. A small, community-run ski area, whose delightful little base lodge might make you wonder if you've stepped back in time fifty years, and have you looking for your wooden skis and woolen ski pants. The center boasts a small, 405-vertical-foot downhill slope, and approximately 50 kilometers (31 miles) of groomed cross-country trails, maintained through a partnership involving the Payette Lakes Ski Club, the Boise Cascade company, and private landowners. Telephone: (208) 634–5691.

Ponderosa State Park. Trails, mostly over gentle terrain, are groomed here in winter for cross-country skiers. The one-mile Northern Lights Trail is lighted for night skiing. Telephone: (208) 634–2164.

OTHER ACTIVITIES

Boat Rentals. Harry's Dry Dock & Sports Marina, with two locations, 1300 Lake Street and 315 North Third Street, rents various types of crafts and motors designed to power you into Payette Lake. Telephone: (208) 634–8605.

Canoe Rentals. Silver Pig Enterprises, located during summers on the west side of North Beach. The poetically named company rents canoes and kayaks for use in the designated no-wake zone at the north end of Payette Lake and on the upper North Fork of the Payette River. Telephone: (208) 634–4562.

Flightseeing. That's what it's called by McCall Air Taxi, which offers not only day sightseeing tours, but also wilderness drops/pickups, and transfers to and from Boise and other cities with airports. Telephone: Toll-free in the United States, (800) 992–6559.

North Fork, Payette River

Golf. Golfers can practice their unique brand of self-abuse either at the twenty-seven-hole McCall Golf Course (telephone 208–634–7200) or at the lavish MeadowCreek Golf & Field Club (telephone 208–347–2555 or, toll-free in the United States, 800–847–2558), located in the hushed valley north of New Meadows. MeadowCreek, which offers additional recreational opportunities such as tennis and swimming, teams up with McCall's Shore Lodge to offer special golf packages in summer. There is also a nine-hole course in Cascade, located 30 miles south of McCall; its telephone number is (208) 382–4835.

Parasailing. McCall Parasail, located at 615 3rd Street, contends it's so easy—flying 600 feet above Payette Lake, that is—that "anyone can do it, without ever getting wet!" The enterprise also rents jet skis, sailboards, and sailboats. Telephone: (208) 634–4646.

Scenic Drives. There may be no staging area in the Northern Rockies offering more opportunities for backcountry drives than McCall. Pick up the Payette National Forest visitor map at the McCall Ranger District, pore over it, and you'll begin to get the picture. Staff on duty at the station can offer tips on the best drives in regard to the time of the year (wildflowers, best chances to spot wildlife, etc.) Some of these gravel-road excursions, which typically are quite well signed, can be done in a day; others require two or more days. Regardless of the duration, make sure before setting out that you have a full tank of gas, a spare tire and the tools to change a flat, and plenty of food and water. And be constantly vigilant for approaching logging trucks! Among the many possible destinations: Warm Lake, Yellow Pine, Big Creek, Riggins via Burgdorf, and the South Fork of the Salmon via Lick Creek.

Snowmobiling. Medley Sports, located at 809 3rd Street, is a complete sporting goods store that rents snowmobiles as well as other recreational tools. Telephone: (208) 634–2216.

SHOPPING

Antique Boutique. Located along State Highway 55, a block north of the airport. Telephone: (208)

634–7400. Offers a good selection of furniture, cut glass, lamps, porcelain, china, and other collectibles.

Granny's Attic. In the Village Square, at 104 North Third. Telephone: (208) 634–5313. Everything for the quilter, including fabric, needles, and classes.

Mountain Monkey Business. 501 Pine Street, near downtown and across from Legacy Park. Telephone: (208) 634–8268. Unique store offering a blend of fine gift items, jewelry, and sportswear. Authorized Birkenstock dealer. Anyone should be able to find *something* here they didn't know they needed. If you need a mountain-sized lift, the Mountain Java espresso-and-coffee store is located in an annex of Mountain Monkey Business.

Paul's Market. Located in downtown McCall. Telephone: (208) 634–8166. A fairly ordinary grocery store, except that they offer a good selection of high-quality Filson outdoor wear.

Visions in Art. 305 Park Street, in the Park Street Plaza. Telephone: (208) 634–3021. Cooperative selling art primarily by local and regional artists. Also sponsors two or three arts-and-crafts fairs during the year.

TELEPHONE NUMBERS

McCall Area Chamber of Commerce and Visitor's Bureau. (208) 634–7631. Office is located off Lake Street at 1001 State Street. Also here is the Central Idaho Interpretive Museum & Visitor Center. (For historic-tour information call 208–634–4497.)

McCall Ranger District. Lake and Mission streets. (208) 634–0400.

Ponderosa State Park. (208) 634–2164.

Salmon River Chamber of Commerce (Riggins), (208) 628–3778.

Air Service: The best way to get to McCall from outside the region is to fly to Boise and rent a car (Boise is about two hours south by car). For information on charter flights from other airports to the small McCall Airport, call McCall Air Taxi (telephone toll-free, 800–992–6559) or Pioneer Air Service (telephone 208–634–5445). Pioneer Air Service does rent cars, including four-by-fours, at the McCall Airport.

Stanley Basin

LODGING

Mountain Village Resort. Located adjacent to the main intersection in Stanley. Sixty-room motel with associated restaurant and service station/mercantile, spanning both sides of State Highway 21. The motel features its own enclosed natural hot spring. Popular spot with the snowmobile crowd in winter. Telephone: (208) 774–3661 or, toll-free in the United States, (800) 843–5475. Moderate to expensive.

Idaho Rocky Mountain Ranch. Located east off State Highway 75, 9 miles south of Stanley. This is one of the Idaho's most heralded, historic, and picturesque guest ranches, with more than sixty years of practice in the art of pleasing clients. When it opened in the 1930s as the Idaho Rocky Mountain Club, the ranch was a private, by-invitation-only getaway. Today the cabins and rooms in the grand old lodge are available to rent by the public in summer, with both bed-and-breakfast and bed-and-breakfast-and-supper options. The evening meal often includes entrees with a local twist, such as trout or lamb. Horseback-riding and hiking trails beginning at the lodge wind their way high into the White Cloud Mountains, and additional leisure options include volleyball, horseshoes, fishing, and a hot pool. Cross-country skiing doesn't get much better than it does in a Sawtooth Valley winter, when some of the cabins at Idaho Rocky Mountain Ranch remain available to rent. Telephone: (208) 774–3544. Moderate to very expensive.

Redfish Lake Lodge. Found 4 miles south of Stanley, then 2 miles west of State Highway 75. This historic, bustling resort nestled on the shore of Redfish Lake is the Sawtooth National Recreation Area's epicenter of activity. The lodge has managed to maintain its rustic disposition for seven decades.

Cabins, rooms in the 1929 lodge, and motel rooms are all available, and the resort also features a lounge and restaurant, grocery with fishing supplies, and boats and horses for rent. The *Lady of the Lake* pontoon carries guests on excursions of mountain-ringed Redfish Lake. Telephone: (208) 774–3536. Inexpensive to very expensive.

Salmon River Lodge. Located on the opposite side of the Salmon from the highway, between Stanley and Lower Stanley. The attractive cabins, some of which have kitchenettes, sit on a wide-open floodplain meadow facing the Sawtooths, practically within spitting distance of the mellow river. Very beautiful spot. Telephone: (208) 774–3422. Moderate.

Sawtooth Hotel. On Ace of Diamonds Avenue in Stanley. In 1983 Nancy and I stayed here after spending Christmas Eve and Christmas nights in a snow cave, which we excavated up nearby Fisher Creek. Consequently, my initial recollection was that the Sawtooth Hotel is a rather sumptuous place. It was a *lot* warmer than the snow cave. Actually, though, it's a funky old hotel, built in 1931 and featuring a pair of shared baths. Private-bath motel rooms are found out back, too. The hotel serves good breakfasts and lunches, along with a selection of espresso drinks. Telephone: (208) 774–9947. Very inexpensive to inexpensive.

Smiley Creek Lodge. Located near the northwestern foot of Galena Summit, 23 miles south of Stanley. Low-key, full-service resort, with overnighting options that include an RV park, cabins, lodge rooms, and a pair of clean, nicely furnished tipis. With its quiet, central location, Smiley Creek is a good choice for those who would like to explore both Stanley Basin and the Sun Valley area without changing overnight locations. The lodge restaurant serves three meals per day, including a chuck wagon dinner, and there's a convenience store for stocking up on supplies. Great mountain biking, hiking, and snowmobiling begin right out the door. (Syndicated humorist Dave Barry wrote a piece about his snowmobiling experiences here.) There's even an airstrip next to the lodge, for those who would rather fly than drive in. Telephone: (208) 774–3547. Inexpensive to moderate.

Triangle C Ranch. At the west end of Stanley off State Highway 21. Unsurpassed views of the Sawtooth Mountains can be relished from the porch of your own log cabin, some of which feature kitchenettes. Outside, picnic tables and a large fire pit are available for guests' use. Triangle C can also arrange float trips on the Main Fork and the Middle Fork of the Salmon, as well as lake-fishing excursions in the high Sawtooths during late summer. Telephone: (208) 774–2266 or, toll-free in the United States, (800) 303–6258. Inexpensive to expensive.

CAMPGROUNDS AND RV PARKS

Private

Camp Stanley. An unusual brand of camping—especially suitable for reunions and retreats, although they also welcome individuals and couples—run by the folks who operate the Mystic Saddle Ranch. Camp Stanley includes wall tents, tent cabins, portable toilets, bunk beds, and a propane barbecue and fully equipped camp kitchen. There's also a volleyball court and horseshoe pit on the grounds. For information on event planning and reservations, call (208) 774–3591.

Elk Mountain RV Resort & Cafe. Four miles west of Stanley. Friendly and scenic spot to camp with good food, to boot. Telephone: (208) 774–2202 (or 805-934-1919 in winter, when the resort is closed).

U.S. Forest Service

See map of the Sawtooth NRA for more precise locations. Call the SNRA headquarters at 208–727–5000 for additional campground infor-

Irrigation system, Stanley Basin

mation or 800–280–CAMP (2267) to make reservations at those campgrounds marked with an asterisk (*).

Stanley Lake Area: Stanley Lake, Lakeview, Inlet "A," Inlet "B," *Elk Creek, *Sheep Trail, *Trap Creek, Iron Creek.

Redfish Lake Area: Sunny Gulch, Chinook Bay, Mountain View, *Point, *Glacier View, Redfish Outlet, Sockeye, Mt. Heyburn.

Alturas Lake Area: Smokey Bear, North Shore, Alturas Inlet.

Salmon River Canyon: Salmon River, Riverside, Mormon Bend, Basin Creek, Upper O'Brien, Lower O'Brien, Holman Creek.

Wood River Valley (south of Galena Pass, nearing Sun Valley): *Easley, Boulder View, Wood River, North Fork.

BICYCLING

Although bicycles are prohibited in the Sawtooth Wilderness, as they are in all federally designated wilderness areas, that leaves plenty of great trails and roads in the SNRA open to explore by fat-tire bike. Among the many popular outings are the Fisher Creek–Williams Creek loop near Obsidian, the Nip and Tuck loop out of Stanley, and Forest Road 215, which leads along the highest reaches of the Salmon River. For more details, contact the SNRA headquarters.

FISHING

McCoy's Tackle & Gift Shop. Located across from the post office on Ace of Diamonds Avenue in Stanley. The fishing in the lakes and streams of the SNRA can be fantastic, and at McCoy's you can pick up whatever gear you need, as well as learn how to match the catch of the morning or evening. Telephone: (208) 774–3377.

HORSEBACK RIDING

Redfish Lake Corrals. Situated smack in the middle of all the activity surrounding Redfish

Lake, this business offers horseback outings to spectacular destinations such as Sawtooth and Hell Roaring lakes, ranging in duration from an hour to a full day or longer. The stable's meat-and-potatoes overnight trip is a loop encompassing eleven high lakes. Telephone: (208) 774–3311 (or call Mystic Saddle Ranch at 208–774–3591).

HOT SPRINGS

Sunbeam Hot Springs. Riverside springs emptying into the Salmon at a point 12 miles east of Stanley. Do-it-yourself temperature control consists of mixing cold river water and hot, 170-degree water by altering existing or fabricating new river-cobble dams and other sorts of diversions. The first whites known to soak at Sunbeam were Alexander Ross and his fellow Hudson's Bay Company trappers, who came across the springs in the fall of 1824. The old bathhouse still located at the site was built by the Civilian Conservation Corps in the 1930s.

RIVER FLOATING

Middle Fork River Expeditions. Located in Stanley on State Highway 21. Specializes in multi-day trips on the wild Middle Fork, and in preparing gourmet backcountry meals for clients to enjoy at day's end. Telephone: (208) 774–3659 or, toll-free in the United States, (800) 801–5146.

Sawtooth Rentals. Located on State Highway 75 in Stanley. This business rents rafts, which clients utilize to float themselves down a beautiful but gentle 8-mile stretch of the Salmon River. Sawtooth Rentals can provide all the accessories needed for floating, from wet suits to coolers, and the business also rents mountain bikes. Telephone: (208) 774–3409 or, toll-free in the United States, (800) 284–3185.

SNOWMOBILING

Many miles of groomed snowmobile trails—including the Highway to Heaven Trail, linking Stanley and Lowman—branch out across and beyond the Stanley Basin in winter. Among the places you can rent snowmobiles is **Smiley Creek Lodge**, which also makes a good base for a winter visit to the Stanley Basin. Sawooth Rentals (see above) also rents snowmobiles.

OTHER ACTIVITIES

Hiking. Hundreds of miles of hiking trails web the backcountry of the SNRA. You can go it alone or sign on with an outfitter, such as **Sawtooth Wilderness Outfitters** (telephone 208–462–3416 or 259–3408), whose pack horses will permit you to move unencumbered and live in relative comfort in the mountains. The company operates out of the Sawtooth Lodge in Grandjean. (*See* A Driving Tour from McCall to the Stanley Basin in Seeing Sun Valley–Salmon Country.) Recommended day outings in the SNRA include the tough 10-mile round-trip hikes to Sawtooth Lake and to Hell Roaring Lake; and, on the other side of the valley, in the surprisingly spectacular White Clouds, the easier jaunt to Fourth of July Lake on Trail #109. For more information call the SNRA headquarters.

Mountaineering. Sawtooth Mountain Guides (telephone 208–774–3324) is a Stanley-based outfitter offering guided treks, winter backcountry/hut skiing, and technical ascents of Mt. Heyburn, the Elephant's Perch, and other area peaks and pinnacles. More distant destinations include the City of Rocks, located in the extreme south of Idaho, south of Burley.

Scenic Flights. Stanley Air Taxi, located at the Stanley Airport, provides rides in high-wing Cessna craft, offering clients a bird's-eye view of the SNRA's peaks and valleys. In addition to day flights, arrangements can be made for drop-off and pickup for hunting trips, river running, and overnights at backcountry lodgings. Telephone: (208) 774–2276 or, toll-free in the United States, (800) 225–2236.

Skiing. The backcountry skiing found in the Sawtooths and White Clouds is unsurpassed in the Northern Rockies, which is to say in the United States. Sawtooth Mountain Guides (see mountaineering above) is among the outfitters offering guide services. Also, the SNRA periodically grooms ski trails in the areas of Park Creek and Alturas Lake. Telephone: (208) 727–5000.

TELEPHONE NUMBERS

Sawooth National Recreation Area headquarters. (208) 727–5000.

Redfish Visitor Center. (208) 774–3376.

Stanley Ranger District, Sawtooth National Forest. (208) 774–3000.

Stanley-Sawtooth Chamber of Commerce. (208) 774–3411 or, toll-free in the United States, (800) 878–7950.

Sun Valley

LODGING

In Ketchum/Sun Valley

Best Western Christiania Motor Lodge. 651 Sun Valley Road in Ketchum. Several room styles, some including fireplace and/or microwave and small refrigerators. Continental breakfast and use of the year-round hot tub facilities are included. Telephone: (208) 726–3351 or, toll-free in the United States, (800) 535–3241. Moderate to expensive.

Clarion Inn of Sun Valley. Located at 600 North Main in Ketchum. Sixty-room motel also featuring Jack's Appaloosa Restaurant. Telephone: (208) 726–5900 or, toll-free in the United States, (800) 262–4833. Moderate to expensive.

Elkhorn Resort. Located on 280 acres along Elkhorn Road, southeast of the Sun Valley Resort. Self-contained resort including outstanding golf course designed by Robert Trent Jones Jr., tennis, bike trails, 132-room lodge, several dozen condominiums, and full conference facilities. Resort restaurants include the **Plaza Grill**, **Tequila Joe's**, and **Jesse's**, a steak and seafood dinner club. Telephone: (208) 622–4511 or, toll-free in the United States, (800) 355–4676. Expensive to very expensive.

Heidelberg Inn. Located on Warm Springs Road out of Ketchum, midway between the Warm Springs and River Run ski lifts. Spacious rooms, some with kitchenettes and fireplaces, and complimentary continental breakfast and hot spiced wine for après-ski. Indoor spa and sauna. Telephone: (208) 726–5361 or, toll-free in the United States, (800) 284–4863. Moderate to very expensive.

Idaho Country Inn Bed and Breakfast. Located at 134 Latigo Lane, just northeast of downtown Ketchum off Saddle Road. Ten rooms—each uniquely appointed in a theme relating to Idaho's past or present—include the Wagon Days Room, the Audubon Room, and the Willow Room. Unlike many B&Bs, all rooms at this modern facility include televisions, telephones, refrigerators, and private baths. Telephone: (208) 726–1019 or, toll-free in the United States, (800) 250–8341. Very expensive.

Ketchum Korral. 310 South Main Street in Ketchum. Eight rustic log cabins for rent, with stone fireplaces and complete kitchen facilities. Each cabin has a private patio. Telephone: (208) 726–3510 or, toll-free in the United States, (800) 657–2657. Moderate to expensive.

Knob Hill Inn. 960 North Main Street in Ketchum. European-style inn and restaurant, featuring twenty-four rooms with marble bathrooms and other niceties. Options include suites with wet bar and fireplace, and the inn includes a sunroom with lap pool and Jacuzzi. Also on-site are an espresso cafe and the Felix gourmet restaurant. Telephone: (208) 726–8010 or, toll-free in the United States, (800) 526–8010. Very expensive.

Lift Tower Lodge. Located on the south edge of Ketchum at 703 South Main Street. Relatively modest and inexpensive motel by Sun Valley standards, boasting a hard-to-miss, 1939-era ski-lift tower out front. Owned and operated by skiers who know what a lot of skiers want: a clean room at a reasonable price, with just a few of the necessary amenities, such as an outdoor Jacuzzi and in-room refrigerator. Telephone: (208) 726–5163 or, toll-free in the United States, (800) 462–8646. Inexpensive to moderate.

Pinnacle Inn. Situated at the base of Bald Mountain, close to the Warm Springs lift. Suites are available here—replete with kitchen, fireplace, and individual bedrooms—as are somewhat pared-down rooms. Telephone: (208) 726–5700 or, toll-free in the United States, (800) 255–3391. Expensive to very expensive.

Premier Properties. Property-management agency offering an extensive and varied array of vacation homes and condominiums for rent. Telephone: (208) 727–4000 or, toll-free in the United States, (800) 374–1569. Prices vary widely.

River Street Inn. 100 River Street West in Ketchum. Modern bed-and-breakfast–style accommodations featuring large suites, walk-in showers, and Japanese soaking tubs. Six of the nine rooms front whispering Trail Creek; the others look out on Baldy. Telephone: (208) 726–3611 or, toll-free in the United States, (800) 954–8585. Very expensive.

Sun Valley Resort. This is the place to stay if you go to Sun Valley only once and want to do it up right; the Sun Valley Resort is simply one of the world's great resorts for families, couples, or singles. Includes the venerable and lavish Sun Valley Lodge, the Sun Valley Inn, and several choices of condominiums and cottages, including the Harriman Cottage, which rents for around $800 a night. Also features golf, skating, swimming, child-care facilities, movies, trap and skeet shooting, bowling, indoor exercise facilities, tennis, cross-country skiing, and a full-service pedestrian village with numerous shops and restaurants. Among the restaurants found at the resort are the **Lodge Dining Room**, **Gretchen's Restaurant**, **Trail Creek Cabin**, **Ram Restaurant and Bar**, **Konditorei**, **Duchin Bar & Lounge**, and **Continental Cafeteria**. Telephone: (208) 622–4111 or, toll-free in the United States, (800) 786–8259. Expensive to very expensive.

Tamarack Lodge. Corner of Sun Valley Road and Walnut Avenue. European-flair lodgings within easy walking distance of all downtown Ketchum shops and restaurants. The large rooms feature open-beam ceilings and balconies with mountain views. Lodge also has an indoor pool and Jacuzzi. Telephone: (208) 726–3344 or, toll-free in the United States, (800) 521–5379. Expensive to very expensive.

Out of Ketchum/Sun Valley

Povey Pensione. Located at 128 West Bullion in Hailey. Traditional bed-and-breakfast accommodations occupying a circa 1890 home that was built by an emigrant carpenter from Liverpool, England . . . and made over from head to heels by the current proprietors. Four rooms with two shared baths, along with a comfortable parlor shared by all guests. Telephone: (208) 788–4682. Moderate.

Wild Horse Creek Ranch. Located on the east slope of the Pioneer Mountains, accessible from Sun Valley in summer and fall by driving 21 miles over Trail Creek Summit. (Year-round access is available via the town of Mackay.) Accommodations in lodge or bunkhouse rooms or, for the kids, in tipis. Guests are encouraged to use all the facilities in the sumptuous new ranch house. In spring and summer, trail rides into the surrounding mountains are offered, and in fall the ranch specializes in guided big-game hunts, while in winter sleigh rides, cross-country skiing, and snowmobiling are among the popular outdoor pursuits. Telephone: (208) 588–2575. Expensive to very expensive.

CAMPGROUNDS AND RV PARKS

Private

Sun Valley RV Resort. Located west off State Highway 75, about a mile south of downtown Ketchum. Full-service campground with store, pool, mini-golf, Jacuzzi, shaded tent sites, bike rentals, and instant access to the Wood River Trails. Open year-round. Telephone: (208) 726–3429.

U.S. Forest Service

Call the Ketchum Ranger District at 208–622–5371 for more information; also see additional listings under Stanley Basin campgrounds, Wood River Valley.

Sawmill. Located approximately 12 miles east up Forest Road 118, which leaves State Highway 75 between Ketchum and Hailey. En route to the campground you'll pass through tiny Triumph,

former hometown of Picabo Street, the American ski champ.

Two campgrounds—**Wolftone** and **Bridge**—are located west up Forest Road 097, which leaves State Highway 75 at a point 2 miles north of Hailey. Three additional campgrounds are situated along Trail Creek on the backroad route to Mackay: **Boundary**, a Sawtooth National Forest campground, is located approximately 2 miles northeast of Sun Valley Resort; **Park Creek**, 11 miles from Sun Valley, and **Phi Kappa**, located 14 miles out, are both on the east side of Trail Creek Pass and within the Challis National Forest.

FOOD

Ketchum–Sun Valley is one of those places where the dining opportunities are so plentiful and varied that it's tough to know where to begin grazing. These listings represent roughly 10 percent of the options. (Others are mentioned within the descriptions of the Sun Valley and Elkhorn resorts and under the Bald Mountain description.)

Log truck, Idaho City

Buffalo Cafe. 320 East Avenue North in Ketchum. Telephone: (208) 726–9795. A favorite of locals, serving breakfast all day, as well as daily soup and sandwich specials and buffalo burgers. Breakfast and lunch. Inexpensive.

Cafe at the Brewery. 202 North Main in Hailey. Telephone: (208) 788–0805. "Pub grub" served in the sudsy setting of the Sun Valley Brewing Company. The menu includes homemade pot pies, homemade bratwurst, and soups, salads, sandwiches, pizzas, and more. Lunch and dinner. Inexpensive.

Desperado's. Corner of Fourth and Washington in Ketchum. Telephone: (208) 726–3068. Good Mexican fare, with no lard used in anything and only canola oil used for frying. Four styles of freshly prepared salsa; pleasant outdoor seating in summer. Lunch and dinner. Inexpensive to moderate.

Irving's Red Hots. Located on the northeast corner of 4th and Main, across from visitor center. Chicago-style hot dogs served out of a tiny dispensary. This is one of those enterprises that helps Ketchum maintain a degree of regular-folk ambience.

Ketchum Grill. East Avenue and Fifth Street in Ketchum. Telephone: (208) 726–4660. Idaho-American cuisine, including daily fish specials, mini-pizzas, and soup and bread specials. A couple of samples from the dinner menu: Idaho lamb shank with grilled roast garlic polenta, and braised Richfield rabbit with lemon. Housed in the old Ed Williams home, circa 1885; shaded outdoor seating available in summer. Dinner only. Moderate to expensive.

The Kitchen. Second and Main in downtown Ketchum. Telephone: (208) 726–3856. Longtime breakfast favorite for locals and visitors. Breakfast and lunch. Inexpensive.

Michel's Christiania Restaurant and Olympic Bar. Located in Ketchum on Sun Valley Road. Telephone: (208) 726–3388. Exquisite French cuisine served nightly includes specials such as sauteed ruby Idaho trout with toasted hazelnuts and cream, and venison chops with ginger cran-berries and red wine sauce. The elegant, ski-chalet atmosphere is not surprising, considering that the proprietor, Michel Rudigoz, is a former coach of the U.S. Women's Ski Team. The Olympic Bar, in addition to its full bar, offers a lighter menu for diners. Dinner only. Expensive.

Pioneer Saloon. 308 North Main in Ketchum. Telephone: (208) 726–3139. Ketchum stronghold serving legendary Pioneer Burgers, as well as prime rib and other beef cuts, chicken, and seafood. Dinner only. Inexpensive to expensive.

Sawtooth Club. Main Street in Ketchum. Telephone: (208) 726–5233. A favorite for good times and great food, the Sawtooth Club's specialty is mesquite-grilled seafood, steaks, lamb, and poultry. Consistently voted a top favorite in locals' polls. Outstanding Western bar, too. Dinner only. Expensive.

Stock Pot. Located at Fourth and Main in Ketchum. Telephone: (208) 726–7733. Fresh food, served fast in a casual but cool atmosphere. Excellent choice of soups, salads, and sandwiches, as well as daily dinner specials. Lunch and dinner. Inexpensive.

Sushi on Second. 260 Second Street in Ketchum. Telephone: (208) 726–5181. Diners can find options other than steak, Mexican food, and pizzas in the Sun Valley area, as evidenced by this Japanese-food restaurant. Booths, sushi bar, and a private tatami room are all available, as are premium *sakes* and a broad selection of microbrews. Dinner only. Moderate to expensive.

Warm Springs Ranch Restaurant. Located west of Ketchum on Warm Springs Road. Telephone: (208) 726–2609. Good choice for a fine dinner, with traditional steak, lamb, chicken, and seafood the house specialties. Don't miss having a look at the large trout swimming in the pond beside the entrance deck. Dinner only. Moderate to expensive.

Whiskey Jacques. 209 Main Street in Ketchum. Telephone: (208) 726–5297. Another old reliable downtown Ketchum restaurant and nightclub, specializing in hand-thrown pizzas and calzones. Live bands on most nights. Dinner only. Inexpensive to moderate.

BICYCLING
(Also see Sporting Goods)

Sun Valley Singletrack. Offers half- and full-day mountain bike tours, mostly in the Smokies, to destinations that include high-mountain meadows and natural hot springs. Rentals available. Telephone: (208) 622–8687.

Trail Quest. This school, directed by seasoned mountain-bike racers, can teach handling and efficiency skills to cyclists of any level. Additional information covers nutrition, bike sizing, maintenance and repair, and other aspects of the sport. The company offers special group programs aimed at youth and women, and private lessons are also available. Telephone: (208) 726–7401.

FAIRS, FESTIVALS, AND EVENTS

Hardly a weekend goes by without some sort of festival in the Sun Valley area. For a complete schedule, call the Chamber of Commerce, toll-free at (800) 634–3347.

Boulder Mountain Tour. Largest cross-country ski race in the Northern Rockies, with more than 700 participating annually. Set for the first Saturday of February, the tour begins at Galena Lodge and ends 30 kilometers (18.6 miles) later, near the SNRA headquarters. Telephone: toll-free, (800) 634–3347.

Ketchum Wagon Days. Labor Day weekend. Festivities include the Big Hitch Parade—billed as the largest non-motorized parade in the West—in which Ketchum's trademark tall, narrow ore wagons (their wheels are more than 5 feet high) roll through downtown, along with dozens of other buggies, carriages, carts, and buckboards. Telephone: (208) 726–3423.

Sun Valley Arts & Crafts Festival. Held for three days in early August at the Sun Valley Resort. High-quality original artwork is displayed and offered for sale at this show. Telephone: (208) 726–9491.

Sun Valley Ice Show. Takes place Saturday evenings between June and September at the Sun Valley Resort. The series, which includes a buffet dinner on the Lodge Terrace, draws the biggest names in figure skating. Past performers have included Elvis Stojko, Oksana Baiul, and Kristi Yamaguchi. Telephone: (208) 622–2231.

FISHING

Bill Mason Outfitters. Located in the Sun Valley Mall. Offers instruction in fly-fishing, including classes specially tailored to kids, held at a stocked trout pond. Outings include angling on a private stretch of the Big Wood River, and spring steelhead fishing on the Salmon. Telephone: (208) 622–9305.

Silver Creek Outfitters. 500 North Main Street. One of the premier sporting enterprises in the Northern Rockies, offering an extensive array of fly-fishing and bird-hunting gear, along with clothing and other accessories. Silver Creek, which occupies a beautiful new log building in downtown Ketchum, takes its name from the renowned springfed creek located 25 miles south, near the settlement of Picabo. The business proffers guided fly-fishing trips on Silver Creek, the Big Wood and Big Lost rivers, and other waters of the region (including winter outings on the Big Wood). Also offers "Fly-Fishing 101" classes on Wednesdays and Thursdays during the summer. Telephone: (208) 726–5282 or, toll-free in the United States, (800) 732–5687.

Sun Valley Rivers Company. Various-length trips on the Salmon's Middle Fork, all originating in Stanley and most focusing on fly-fishing. Telephone: (208) 774–3444.

GOLF

The greater Sun Valley area boasts four courses open to the public. These include the high-end, top-rated eighteen-hole **Sun Valley Golf Course** (telephone 208–622–2251) and **Elkhorn Golf Club** (telephone 208–622–3300), both of which charge in the neighborhood of $100 for green fees (includes the use of a cart). The other two, both nine-holers, are **Bigwood Golf Club** (telephone 208–726–4024) and **Warm Springs Golf Course** (telephone 208–726–3715). Green fees at these two range from $20 to $25 for nine holes and $30 to $35 for eighteen.

HIKING

Travel in any direction off the main highway running through the Big Wood River Valley, and soon you will stumble across a hiking trail. For leads and maps, visit the SNRA headquarters, located 8 miles north of Ketchum. For hikes close to Ketchum and Sun Valley, try the Fox Creek area trails (the trailhead is located on the opposite side of the highway from SNRA headquarters), the Adams Gulch trails (just northwest of Ketchum), or the Trail Creek area trails. These include a loop off Corral Creek that can incorporate an overnight at the **Pioneer Cabin**, built by the Union Pacific Railroad in 1937 as a backcountry skiing hut. Others in the Trail Creek area include the Aspen Loop, Proctor Mountain, and Trail Creek trails. Businesses offering guided hikes include Bill Mason Outfitters (telephone 208–622–9305), which leads hikes in the Smoky, Boulder, and Pioneer mountains.

HORSEBACK RIDING

Galena Stage Stop Corrals. Opposite Galena Lodge, 24 miles north of Ketchum on State Highway 75. Sure-footed horses haul their riders along old mining and logging trails in the scenic and historic Galena area. Outings range in duration from ninety minutes to all day. Telephone: (208) 726–1735.

MUSEUMS

Ketchum–Sun Valley Heritage and Ski Museum. Located at the corner of First Street and Washington Avenue in Ketchum. Permanent and changing exhibits focus on subjects of local interest, including skiing (obviously), Ernest Hemingway, the Civilian Conservation Corps, trappers and traders, mining, the Hollywood connection, prehistory, and fishing. Open seven days a week from 1:00 to 5:00 P.M. Telephone: (208) 726–8118.

Ore Wagon Museum. Next to the Ketchum Grill on the corner of East Avenue and Fifth Street. This is where they keep the big beasts known as "big hitch" ore wagons, which you can take a gander at by pressing your nose against the glass of the door—or up close, if you happen to find someone working in the storage barn.

RIVER FLOATING

Ketchum Kayak School. Located in the Ski Tek business at 191 Sun Valley Road, behind the Ketchum post office. Offers personal instruction in kayak technique, including rolling, river reading, and paddling skills. Telephone: (208) 726–7503.

Payette River Company. 401 Lewis Street in Ketchum. This outfit, one component of a larger company called Far and Away Adventures, specializes in trips on the spectacular South Fork of the Payette. One-day outings or multi-day trips encompassing the three main gorges of the river: Grandjean, Canyon, and Staircase. Telephone: (208) 726–2288 or, toll-free in the United States, (800) 232–8588.

Middle Fork River Tours, Inc. Company headquartered in Ketchum that offers luxury wilderness trips on the Salmon's Middle Fork, with three-, four-, and six-day options. Telephone: (208) 726–5666 or, toll-free in the United States, (800) 445–9738.

SKIING

Bald Mountain. This is by far the bigger of the Sun Valley Resort's two ski "hills." The statistics are impressive: thirteen lifts—including seven high-speed quads, four triples, and two doubles—servicing sixty-four runs distributed over more than 2,000 skiable acres. The longest run is 3 miles and the total vertical drop is 3,400 feet. Baldy's slopes offer something for all levels of skiers, with 38 percent rated Easiest, 45 percent More Difficult, and 17 percent Most Difficult, and extensive snow-making ensures consistently good conditions. Snowboarding is permitted on most of the mountain. Ski shops are found at each of the two base areas of Warm Springs and River

Run, and slopeside restaurants include **Lookout**, located on top of Baldy; **River Run**, located at River Run Plaza; **Seattle Ridge Lodge**, nestled atop Baldy on the crest of Seattle Ridge (it's the most elegant on-slope option); and **Warm Springs Day Lodge**, serving gourmet and continental cuisine at its Warm Springs base area location. Telephone: toll-free in the United States, (800) 786–8259. For the snow report call (208) 622–2093 or, toll-free in the United States, (800) 635–4150.

Dollar Mountain. This small beginners hill, located in close proximity to the Sun Valley Resort, features a 628-foot vertical drop and five lifts servicing thirteen runs. This is where the heralded Sun Valley ski school, directed by Rainer Kolb, teaches most of their neophytes how to stop and turn on the boards. Telephone: (208) 622–2231.

Galena Lodge. At the base of Galena Pass, 24 miles north of Ketchum. Facility owned by the community and operated by the Blaine County Recreation District. Fifty kilometers (31 miles) of exquisitely groomed trails radiate from a historic day lodge, with lessons, equipment rentals, and overnight rentals of ski-in huts/yurts all available. Fifteen kilometers of trails are open to dogs. (The trend of pup-friendly ski trails began in Sun Valley and is spreading to other areas of the country. In Sun Valley, dog owners can even procure season passes for their hounds for the North Valley trails, which include those at Galena.) Breakfast, lunch, and after-ski snacks are available. Also offers terrific mountain biking and hiking come summer. Telephone: (208) 726–4010.

North Valley and Wood River Trails. Cross-country trails maintained and regularly groomed by the Blaine County Recreation District include Galena (see above), as well as **Prairie Creek**, **Billy's Bridge**, **North Fork**, **Lake Creek**, the **Boulder Mountain Trail**, and the 18 miles of the **Wood River Trails**. In all, these encompass some 145 kilometers, or 90 miles, of groomed trails. Telephone: (208) 726–6662.

Sun Valley Heli*Ski. 260 First Avenue North in Ketchum. For thirty years providing whirlybird lifts to backcountry powder hideaways for skiers of all levels of proficiency, from experts to neophytes. This Forest Service permittee has access to 750 square miles encompassing parts of three mountain ranges. Guide-to-guest ratio of one to four; the guides—including one with the irresistible name of Bozo Cardozo—combine more than 100 years of experience. Telephone: (208) 622–3108 or, toll-free in the United States, (800) 872–3108.

Sun Valley Nordic Center. Full-service Nordic center featuring 40 kilometers (25 miles) of Pisten Bully groomed trails for skating and classic skiing. The trails radiate from the golf course pro shop around the Sun Valley Resort and up past the Hemingway Memorial to historic Trail Creek Cabin, which serves as a warming center in winter. Lessons, rentals, and a special "children's terrain garden" are all part of the scene. Telephone: (208) 622–2250 or, toll-free in the United States, (800) 786–8259.

SPORTING GOODS

Ketchum–Sun Valley boasts several first-class businesses specializing in self- and gravity-propelled sports, where—depending on the season—you can rent or buy bicycles, in-line skates, Nordic skis, river-running craft and accessories, backpacking gear, and more. These include **The Elephant's Perch**, located on Sun Valley Road in Ketchum (telephone 208–726–3497); **Backwoods Mountain Sports**, located in Ketchum near the intersection of Main Street and Warm Springs Road (telephone 208–726–8818); and **Sturtevants**, located on Main Street in Ketchum (telephone 208–726–4501) and Main Street in Hailey (telephone 208–788–7847).

WINTER TOURS

Sun Valley Sled Dog Adventures. Hailey-based business offering hound-powered tours through the winterscapes of the Sun Valley outback. Trips range from ninety minutes to overnight. Telephone: (208) 788–3522.

Trail Creek Cabin Dinner Sleigh Ride. Sleighs leave the Sun Valley Inn at 6:00, 7:00, 8:00, and 9:00 P.M. throughout the winter. Dinner is served in the rough-hewn Trail Creek Cabin, which has been standing alongside Trail Creek since 1937. The facility specializes in barbecued ribs, with optional entrees including prime rib and Idaho trout. Entertainment is provided. Reservations required. Telephone: (208) 622–2135.

OTHER ACTIVITIES

Soaring. Sun Valley Soaring offers glider rides in summer and winter, ranging from short rides over Bald Mountain to longer excursions in the surrounding mountains. It's a beautiful and quiet way to get a bird's-eye view of the Sun Valley area. It's relatively safe, too: According to FAA statistics, the company asserts, soaring is as safe as flying in a commercial airliner. Telephone: (208) 788–3054.

Sun Valley Paragliding. 260 First Avenue North in Ketchum. For a real thrill, if soaring is too ho-hum, fly off Bald Mountain and over the Sun Valley landscape in the company of a certified tandem paraglider pilot. No experience necessary. Telephone: (208) 726–3332.

Solavie Day Spa & Salon. 511 Leadville Avenue. Massage, heat wraps, exfoliation, yoga sessions, steam therapy, acupuncture, dream analysis, and all sorts of other interesting activities and procedures can be arranged at this Ketchum establishment. Telephone: (208) 726–7211.

SHOPPING

Antiques & Country Pine. 620 Sun Valley Road, in Ketchum's Walnut Avenue Mall. Telephone: (208) 622–7551. Fine European and native antiques and reproductions, along with various and unusual home accessories.

Atkinsons' Market. At Giacobbi Square, Fourth and Leadville, downtown Ketchum. Telephone: (208) 726–5668. No mere supermarket, this provider of foodstuffs is the place to be seen filling your grocery cart while in the Sun Valley area. Includes extensive lines of wine and gourmet foods, as well as more commonplace food items. Delivery available.

Chapter One Bookstore. Located in a nineteenth-century bank building on Main Street in Ketchum. Telephone: (208) 726–5425. Good selection of books, magazines, newspapers, and greeting cards at this enterprise that's been running for a quarter century.

Chic Hippies. 518 Leadville Avenue. Telephone: (208) 726–2402. Statement-making, consigned women's clothing, both used and unworn, as well as art, furniture, and collectibles for sale.

Galleria Shops. Located at Leadville Avenue and Fourth Street, kitty-corner from Giacobbi Square. Several good shops are located within this complex, including **No Place Like Home**, the **Sports Connection**, and the **Galleria Wine & Espresso Bar**. What really shines here, though, are the nicest public rest rooms in downtown Ketchum.

Idaho Country Store. Next to the Circle K in Ketchum at 531 North Main. Telephone: (208) 726–4949. Country-style gifts and souvenirs, including quilts, birdhouses, pottery, and toys.

Jane's Holiday House. 180 North Main in Ketchum. Telephone: (208) 726–4170. Christmas shop with decorations and collectibles galore.

Ketchum Kitchens. Located in Giacobbi Square. Telephone: (208) 726–1989. Everything for the cooking room, from basics to frills: cookbooks, cutlery, glassware, and gizmos. Several other businesses are located inside the Giacobbi complex, including **Chicken Lipps**, a specialty children's store.

Moss on cattle chute, outside New Meadows, Idaho

Silverado Western Wear. 371 North Main in Ketchum. Telephone: (208) 726–9019. Purveyors of both traditional Western wear and the fancy sorts of leather-fringed, silver-adorned duds and accessories you thought were worn only by models in magazines—but which, in fact, some daring folks in places such as Sun Valley and Santa Fe do wear in public.

Sun Valley Wine Company. 360 North Leadville Avenue, above the Ketchum liquor store. Telephone: (208) 726–2442. Enormous selection of wines, some with price tags to match and others more moderately priced. Changing selections of wines and beers are served by the glass on the spot, or are available by the bottle or case. Also includes a daily menu specializing in soups, salads, and appetizers.

Toneri Art Gallery. 400 Sun Valley Road in Ketchum. Telephone: (208) 726–5639. One of more than two dozen galleries in Sun Valley–Ketchum, Toneri specializes in Lynn Toneri's dreamy, super-realistic watercolors.

Irresistible images of Bald Mountain and other local scenes can be found.

TELEPHONE NUMBERS

Sun Valley/Ketchum Chamber of Commerce. Visitor center at 4th and Main in downtown Ketchum. (208) 726–3423 or, toll-free in the United States, (800) 634–3347.

Ketchum Ranger District. 206 Sun Valley Road. (208) 622–5371. For the twenty-four-hour Avalanche & Weather Information line call (208) 788–1200 extension 8027.

Sawtooth National Recreation Area. 8 miles north of Ketchum on State Highway 75. (208) 727–5000.

Friedman Memorial Airport, (208) 788–4956. Located a mile south of Hailey. Served by Horizon Air via Seattle, connecting with Alaska Airlines flights; and by SkyWest Airlines from Salt Lake City.

Car Rentals. Rentals are available in the area; however, one of the most popular ways to get to and around Sun Valley is to rent a car at the Boise airport, where most of the major franchises maintain offices.

Public Transportation. Ketchum Area Rapid Transit (KART), (208) 726–7140. Provides free transportation throughout the area, linking Sun Valley Resort, Elkhorn Resort, Ketchum, and Bald and Dollar mountains.

Sun Valley Express, toll-free (800) 634–6539. Makes six daily trips in ten-passenger vans between Sun Valley and the Boise airport, which is served by major airlines including United, Southwest, Northwest, and Delta.

Sun Valley Stages, toll-free (800) 574–8661. Makes one daily trip between Boise and Sun Valley in forty-passenger motorcoaches.

Practical Hints

Planning Your Trip

Peak travel times in the Northern Rockies are mid-June through mid-September and, in those areas where snow is an attraction, Thanksgiving through early April. Make reservations in advance at these times of year if you know your itinerary and are choosy about accommodations. Whether making reservations in advance or on the spot, don't neglect to ask about discounts if you're a member of AAA, AARP, or another organization that may qualify you for a reduced room rate.

In some locations, such as Missoula, Cody, and Craters of the Moon National Monument, midsummer temperatures can reach into the high 90s and even occasionally top 100. Rarely does it not cool off at night, though. Moreover, even in what technically is known as spring and summer, you can find just about any season you want (or don't want!) somewhere in the Northern Rockies. Any day of the year, even during the height of the brief alpine summer, it can snow at the highest elevations, including much of Glacier and Yellowstone national parks. So, regardless of what month the calendar says it is, pack warm.

The off-seasons of April–May and mid-September through late October can be outstanding times to travel in the Northern Rockies. You'll avoid the crowds and often reap the secondary dividends of reduced room rates and deals on meals. In spring you won't be able to explore the high country, unless you travel by an over-snow means, but the lower valleys can be very pleasant at that time of year. The low country will often be green and sprouting flowers, while the high mountains remain buried under many feet of snow. (Note, however, that particularly in the northernmost areas covered, in places such as Whitefish, May and June are often very wet months.) By the time the brief summer finally reaches the high alpine country, fall is just around the corner. Autumn is growing as a favorite time for touring throughout the region, as more people discover the often warm and sunny days, cool nights, and colorful displays of fall foliage.

As is true throughout the Rocky Mountain West, **dress** is generally very casual in the Northern Rockies; even in some of the best restaurants don't be surprised to see folks wearing blue jeans and sneakers or battered cowboy boots. Items to bring that you might forget, clothing and otherwise, include binoculars, sunglasses, sturdy walking or hiking shoes, a rucksack, plastic water bottles, and a brimmed hat. Essential items that you can pick up just about anywhere, but which you may prefer to pack along from home, include sunscreen, lip balm with sunscreen, mosquito repellent, and film for your camera.

The following telephone numbers and, for the growing legion of Internet users, Web sites can lead to dozens of additional phone numbers and linking Web sites. The latter can be particularly helpful for tracking down accommodations.

Longhorns on porch

STATE TRAVEL AGENCIES

Wyoming Tourist Information,
http://www.state.wy.us/commerce/tourism/index.htm; telephone: toll-free in the United States,
(800) 225–5996.

Travel Montana,
http://www.travel.mt.gov; telephone: (406)
444–2654 or, toll-free in the United States (800)
847–4868.

Idaho Travel Council, http://www.visitid.org;
telephone: toll-free in the United States, (800)
847–4843 or (800) 635–7820.

Tourism Regions (for Web links check the sites
listed under State Travel Agencies)

Yellowstone Country, Montana, telephone: (406)
446–1005 or, toll-free in the United States,
(800) 736–5276.

Glacier Country, Montana, telephone: (406)
756–7128 or, toll-free in the United States,
(800) 338–5072.

Gold West Country, Montana, telephone: (406)
846–1943 or, toll-free in the United States,
(800) 879–1159.

Central Idaho Rockies, telephone: (208)
726–3423 or, toll-free in the United States,
(800) 634–3347.

CHAMBERS OF COMMERCE/VISITOR BUREAUS

Jackson Hole Chamber of Commerce,
http://www.jacksonhole.com; telephone: (307)
733–3316 (central reservations toll-free in the
United States, 800–443–6931).

Cody Country Visitors Council,
http://www.codychamber.org; telephone: (307)
587–2297.

Red Lodge Chamber of Commerce, http://www.net/redlodge; telephone: (406) 446–1718.

Livingston Area Chamber of Commerce, telephone: (406) 222–0850.

Bozeman Area Chamber of Commerce, http://www.avicom.net/bozchmbr/; telephone: (406) 586–5421 or, toll-free in the United States, (800) 228–4224.

Big Sky Chamber of Commerce, telephone: (406) 995–3000 or, toll-free in the United States, (800) 943–4111.

Teton Valley Chamber of Commerce, http://www.pdt.net/tetonvalley/; telephone: (208) 354–2500 or, toll-free in the United States, (800) 827–4433.

Bitterroot Valley Chamber of Commerce, http://www.bvchamber.com; telephone: (406) 363–2400.

Missoula Chamber of Commerce, telephone, (406) 543–6623 or, toll-free in the United States, (800) 526–3465. (Web site under development.)

Whitefish Chamber of Commerce, http://www.whitefishmt.com; telephone: (406) 862–3501.

Helena Area Chamber of Commerce, telephone: (406) 442–4120 or, toll-free in the United States, (800) 743–5362. (Web site under development.)

Butte Chamber of Commerce, http://www.butteinfo.org; telephone: (406) 723–3177 or, toll-free in the United States, (800) 735–6814.

McCall Area Chamber of Commerce, telephone: (208) 634–7631.

Stanley Chamber of Commerce, telephone: (208) 774–3411.

Sun Valley–Ketchum Chamber of Commerce, http://www.visitsunvalley.com; telephone: (208)

726–3423 or, toll-free in the United States, (800) 634–3347.

Mackay Chamber of Commerce, telephone: (208) 588–2274.

Challis Area Chamber of Commerce, telephone: (208) 879–2771.

Salmon Valley Chamber of Commerce, telephone: (208) 756–2100.

DESTINATION SKI RESORTS

Jackson Hole Mountain Resort, http://www.jacksonhole.com/ski; telephone: (307) 733–2292 or, toll-free in the United States, (888) 333–7766.

Red Lodge Mountain, http://www.montana.net/rlmresort; telephone: (406) 446–3604 or, toll-free in the United States, (800) 444–8977.

Bridger Bowl, http://www.bridgerbowl.com; telephone (406) 586–2389 or, toll-free in the United States, (800) 223–9609.

Big Sky Ski & Summer Resort, http://www.bigskyresort.com; telephone: (406) 995–5000 or, toll-free in the United States, (800) 548–4486.

Grand Targhee Ski & Summer Resort, http://www.grandtarghee.com; telephone: (307) 353–2300 or, toll-free in the United States, (800) 827–4433.

The Big Mountain Ski & Summer Resort, http://www.bigmtn.com/resort; telephone: (406) 862–1900 or, toll-free in the United States, (800) 858–3913.

Brundage Mountain, http://www.brundage.com; telephone: (208) 634–4151 or, toll-free in the United States, (800) 888–7544.

Sun Valley Resort, http://www.sunvalley.com; telephone: toll-free in the United States, (800) 786–8259.

Being There

The wide-open spaces common in the Northern Rockies are what many people come to experience. It's important to always remember, though, that wide-open spaces means that services are few and far between. You won't find a gas station, restaurant, or latte stand every 10 or 20 miles along most of the roads in this region, even the major highways. Plan accordingly: Always keep an eye on that gas gauge and carry plenty of picnic supplies in case you don't find a restaurant as soon as you'd hoped.

If you don't like the **weather** you find in the Northern Rockies, either wait around half an hour for the weather to change, or travel to a different altitude at once. In general, for each 1,000-foot gain in elevation, the temperature drops three degrees Fahrenheit, all other factors being equal. Moreover, storms often pile up against the mountains, leaving the valleys below enjoying sunshine and dry weather. As you can see by the chart that follows, the elevation range within the region covered by this book is extreme—from the high point, the 13,772-foot tip of the Grand Teton (which, admittedly, not many readers will visit), to 1,593 feet at White Bird, Idaho, which is located near the lower Salmon River, not far from where it empties into the Snake River. (That river, by the way, in a neat piece of poetic geographic justice, carries snowmelt from the Grand Teton.)

Although it is not as big a concern as it is in Colorado, where the Rockies reach their pinnacle, **altitude** nevertheless is a factor to consider when traveling in the Northern Rockies. Some individuals are prone to altitude sickness, suffering symptoms at elevations as low as 6,000 feet, while others seem little affected by it. Reduced atmospheric pressure and lower oxygen supply can cause symptoms that include headache, dizziness, nausea, and impaired mental faculties. Extreme cases, which usually occur at elevations above 12,000 feet, can result in fluid buildup in the lungs. If the subject is not quickly treated or taken to a lower elevation, death can result. The best strategy if you'll be going to the region's highest elevations is to acclimatize gradually, spending a day or two at 1,000-foot increments at elevations above 8,000 feet before climbing higher. Staying adequately hydrated and eating a nutritious diet rich in carbohydrates will also help.

DRIVING

Whether driving your own car or a rental car (franchise locations are listed in the Staying There sections), you should be sure to carry along a number of items. This is particularly true if you intend to explore some of the off-pavement routes described in this book, but even many of the region's paved roads traverse areas that are remote and deserted by most people's standards.

Be sure before leaving home, or when picking up your rental car, that your tires have good tread; that the car's engine, air-conditioner, and heater are in top working condition; and that the radiator is filled with the correct level of antifreeze-coolant. You should check to see that you have a spare tire in good condition, along with all the tools necessary to change a flat. You also should have the know-how to change a flat, which you may end up doing under the most trying of conditions (i.e., rain, snow, wind . . .).

When leaving your car at a trailhead or parking area, leave valuables out of sight. A **windshield screen** to keep out the hot afternoon sun is a good idea, too, and so is a **flashlight**, for those times of the day when the sun is not out. A **spare key** held in a magnetic case and attached somewhere to the car's frame can potentially save a great deal of pain and suffering.

Always keep on hand in your car a couple of gallons of **water** and other drinks, advisably stored in an ice-filled cooler.

In winter, carry **spare warm clothes**, a **sleeping bag**, **tire chains** (practice putting them on to ensure that they fit!), a compact but stout **shovel**, a **window scraper**, and a coffee can containing **emergency food** and a **candle and matches**. In a pinch the candle can be burned in the empty can to provide a heat source. If you get trapped in severe weather, park a safe distance off the road and stay with your vehicle. If forced to stop by the weather or for any other reason, never leave the car running; even then, with the engine shut off, keep a pair of opposing windows cracked open to permit the flow of fresh air.

Sample Altitudes in the Northern Rockies

Place	Feet above Sea Level
Jackson, Wyoming	6,209
Grand Teton summit	13,772
Dunraven Pass, Yellowstone National Park	8,859
Cody, Wyoming	5,016
Beartooth Pass, Wyoming	10,947
Bozeman, Montana	4,795
Mammoth Hot Springs, Yellowstone National Park	6,239
Missoula, Montana	3,210
Whitefish, Montana	3,037
Logan Pass, Glacier National Park	6,646
Butte, Montana	5,767
White Bird, Idaho	1,593
McCall, Idaho	5,020
Galena Summit, Idaho	8,701
Sun Valley, Idaho	5,920
Salmon, Idaho	4,004

More times than he cares to admit, the author—after forgetting to turn off his lights or after sliding into a snow-filled ditch—has been very happy that he has had the foresight to pack along **jumper cables** and a **tow strap**. Even if you never need them yourself, both of these items can make you the hero of the day, because it's not at all uncommon in winter to encounter other motorists in need of a battery jump or a tow.

If you're not accustomed to driving on steep mountain roads, remember when descending to shift into a lower gear, permitting the high-revving engine to help slow the car so you don't end up overusing the brakes. On snow, ice, or slick mud surfaces, pump your brakes repeatedly rather than stamping on them. If you begin to slide, turn the steering wheel in the direction opposite the slide. These measures take practice to become comfortable with; if you're not experienced at driving on snow and ice, the best

thing to do is to find a vacant, snow-covered parking lot and practice there before going into the real world.

Driving laws in the Northern Rockies for the most part are quite similar to those in other states of the Union. The most notable exception is in Montana, where at this writing the daytime speed limit in most rural areas on state and federal highways is "reasonable and prudent." As countless ticketed motorists have learned in recent years, though, driving reasonably and prudently is not the same as going as fast as you want, whenever and wherever you want.

As throughout the United States, law enforcement is cracking down on motorists who drink and drive, with an attitude of near-zero tolerance. The tri-state Wyoming-Idaho-Montana region may own an image of still being the lawless, wild West—but don't try telling that to the state trooper or, later, to the judge.

Sheepherder's wagon, Stanley Basin

A final word of caution: Especially around dawn and dusk, be aware that **deer** or other large animals may be sharing the road with you. This can be extremely dangerous, for both the animals and the occupants of your car. Slow down at these times of day, particularly if the road is wet or snow-covered.

ROAD CONDITIONS PHONE NUMBERS

Wyoming Road & Travel Report: (307) 733–9966.
Montana State Road Report: toll-free, (800) 226–7623.
Idaho Statewide Transportation Information: (208) 336–6600.

HITTING THE TRAIL

Some of the very best the Northern Rockies has to offer can be found only by investigating where the region's trails lead. On many hiking trails outside the wilderness areas and national parks, expect to encounter mountain bikers and even motorized trail bikes and all-terrain vehicles (ATVs). Both within and outside the wilderness areas you'll also meet horseback riders. Indeed, you may choose to sample one or more of these activities yourself. To help ensure that all trail users remain as happy as possible, it's important

that everyone familiarize themselves with the accepted trail etiquette, and to abide by the recommended "yield hierarchy."

In general, hikers should yield trail to equestrians, because horses are often easily spooked. Mountain bicyclists should yield trail to both hikers and equestrians, while for safety's sake pretty much everyone should get off the trail if they hear an ATV approaching. Mechanized recreationists—ATV, trail-bike, snowmobile, and mountain-bike riders, in particular—should respect slower-moving trail users by checking their speed. The International Mountain Bicycling Association's **Rules of the Trail**, while written specifically for mountain bicyclists, can apply to all trail users riding machines, whether or not the machines have an engine:

1. Ride on open trails only.
2. Leave no trace.
3. Control your bicycle (trail bike, snowmobile . . .)
4. Always yield trail.
5. Never spook animals.
6. Plan ahead.

When on the trail, regardless of the mode by which you are exploring it, stay on the designated tread. Never cut switchbacks or make your own trail. Keep your kids and pets in tow, both to protect them and to prevent them from disturbing other trail users. (In the national parks dogs are either not permitted or required to be leashed, depending on where you are.)

A few potential hazards associated with backcountry travel do exist that you should be aware of. The brief discussions to follow only scratch the surface; you can obtain more detailed information at your local library or at a Forest Service or National Park Service office.

In general, **rattlesnakes** are not a concern in the Northern Rockies, although at some of the lower elevations (usually below 6,000 feet) they may occasionally be seen. In the mornings and evenings the snakes can sometimes be found on rocky southern exposures, where the rocks continue holding some of the previous day's heat. If scrambling around places such as this, avoid putting your hand or foot in a place that you haven't first checked with your eyes. During the hottest part of the day snakes seek out cooler places, such as caves and old mine dugouts. Take related precautions if exploring such areas, which, of course, have other dangers associated with them, too.

Certain other biting creatures are much more common than rattlesnakes in the Northern Rockies. The bane of the region's mountains and meadows, as it is in many other wet areas of the country, is the **mosquito**. Hundreds of the little bloodsuckers can turn an otherwise beautiful outing into a nightmare, particularly if you've forgotten your repellent. Studies have shown that repellents containing DEET are most effective in warding off the insects. Covering yourself with lightweight, long pants and shirt, even if it's warm outside, will help some, too; avoid wearing clothes that are red, though, which apparently attracts mosquitoes.

Wood ticks are another bug to watch out for. They thrive generally from early spring until the summer dries out, usually inhabiting brushy areas and even sagebrush-covered slopes, where they hang out awaiting warm-blooded passersby. Some ticks carry potentially serious diseases, such as Rocky Mountain spotted fever and Lyme disease, so try to avoid allowing them to dig in. Thoroughly check yourself and your children immediately after traveling through potentially tick-rich terrain, and the chances are you'll find any ticks before they burrow in. If you find a tick embedded, grab it with a pair of tweezers close to its head, and pull with steady motion. Disinfect the spot, and if you think you may have left part of the tick embedded, it is a good idea to see a doctor.

Most folks' wildlife worries hinge around animals substantially larger than ticks and mosquitoes. The two most dangerous mammals common in the Northern Rockies are **bears** and **mountain lions**. The big cats in particular have been increasing in number in recent years, even as more and more humans build houses and otherwise intrude into the lions' traditional foothills and canyon habitats. An encounter with either a bear or a mountain lion is a potentially lethal situation.

Black bears, although by no means entirely innocent of attacks on humans, tend to be less aggressive than grizzly bears. Grizzlies are most abundant, and most dangerous, in Glacier and Yellowstone national parks and the wilderness areas adjacent to the parks. Usually bears, whether black or grizzly, will run off if they hear you coming; it is when you come upon one and surprise it—particularly if it is a mother with cubs—that the bear may turn aggressive. Make a great deal of noise when hiking in bear country by singing, yelling, and rattling bear bells attached to your pack or belt, particularly in wooded areas and other places where long-range visibility is limited. A growing number of wildlife specialists are recommending that hikers and other recreationists carry a pressurized canister of **pepper spray**, and keep it in a holster where it can be quickly drawn. The spray has been found effective in repelling grizzlies, but one must know how to safely and correctly use it for it to work. Most outfitting stores in the Northern Rockies sell pepper spray, and sales staff typically can provide instructions on using it.

Mountain lions, also known as cougars, have been known to stalk and kill humans as a food source. Although you should in no case attempt to run from either a cougar or a grizzly bear, if you are attacked the recommended behaviors are precisely the opposite: If attacked by a grizzly bear—if you can't chase it off with a shot of pepper spray first—"play dead" by dropping to the ground, lifting your legs to your chest, and clasping your hands over the back of your neck. If attacked by a lion you'll want to do just the opposite: "Look big" and wave your arms, throw rocks at or beat the animal with a stick, and make a lot of loud, fierce-sounding noise.

Bears and other animals are attracted by odors. When camping in bear country keep your camp squeaky-clean and store all odorous items, including food and toiletries, in your car at night. If backpacking, put the items in a stuff sack and hang it from a high tree branch, at least 10 feet above the ground and 4 feet away from the tree's trunk. The farther from your tent, the better. In no case should you ever keep food in your tent at night. Menstruating females may want to avoid camping in bear country altogether.

These things said, rest assured that the chances of being attacked by a ferocious animal are very slim, particularly if you check first with National Park Service or Forest Service personnel to find if the area you plan to visit has a recent record of animal encounters. If it does, the personnel may suggest other places for you to go.

Elk

Weather-related concerns for outdoors enthusiasts include **lightning storms**, potential killers that are very common in the Northern Rockies in summer. Getting caught in one of these slam-bammers can put the fear of Thor in you, even if you come out of it unscathed. Avoid in particular exposed ridgetops when conditions are ripe for the buildup of thunderheads; morning and evening are generally better times to climb that ridge than afternoon is. If you get trapped in a lightning storm, avoid solitary trees, open areas, and the bases and edges of cliffs. Heavily timbered areas offer a relative degree of safety, as do areas beneath or between big rocks in a boulder field.

Hypothermia, a plummeting of the body's core temperature, is the leading killer of those involved in outdoor activities. Wet, windy conditions when the temperature is in the thirties or forties—very common in the Northern Rockies in spring and summer—are optimal for hypothermia. To avoid it, dress in layers, adding or removing a layer as required to stay warm but prevent overheating. Overheating results in sweating, which will dampen your clothes and cause dehydration, both of which can exacerbate the prob-

lem. For the first layer, wear a light "wicking" material, such as polypropylene, directly against your skin.

Heat exhaustion and **heat stroke** can be concerns during the hot days of summer, particularly at the lower elevations. Cover yourself with lightweight and light-colored cotton or cotton-blend clothing, wear a wide-brimmed hat, and use sunscreen on any skin left exposed. Drink more water than you think you need, and take rest breaks in the shade often to allow your body temperature to lower.

You should pack along plenty of **water** whenever you head out on a trail outing, along with one of the compact **water filtering pumps** that are widely available in outdoor stores. The new generation of filters, which start at around $50, can make some of the most disgusting-looking water potable. Be sure that the pump you buy has pores tiny enough to filter out the cysts of *Giardia lamblia*, a one-celled organism that thrives in cold water. Even the seemingly purest of mountain streams may contain giardia, which, if ingested, can cause the severe and often long-lived intestinal illness known as giardiasis.

Big-game hunting season is something to be aware of if you visit the Northern Rockies in the fall. In one or another of the three states, hunters will be stalking elk, deer, and other big-game animals from September through November. Inquire at the local Forest Service office about the hunting season; if it is under way in that area, dress in blaze orange if going into the woods. Forest Service personnel should also be able to recommend public areas that are off-limits to hunting, or at least areas less frequented by hunters. Hunting is illegal in Yellowstone and Glacier national parks, while highly controlled elk hunts are occasionally held in Grand Teton National Park.

Skiing and/or **snowmobiling** is what brings most wintertime leisure seekers to the Northern Rockies. Too much of a good thing—snow, that is—can sometimes make the activities dangerous. Each winter you hear reports of snowmobilers, cross-country skiers, and/or snowshoers being killed in **avalanches** in Wyoming, Montana, and Idaho. If you plan to head into avalanche-prone backcountry in winter, you should learn the basics of snow behavior, either through a book or a class, and each person in your party should be equipped with avalanche equipment, including a transceiver, shovel, and probe poles. In ski/snowmobile country, many Forest Service districts have snow rangers on staff. Before heading out check with them at the ranger station to find out the current avalanche conditions, as well as the weather forecast for the time you will be in the field. Be prepared to change plans if the weather forecast is unfavorable.

Avalanches occur at alpine ski areas, too, but when conditions are ripe the ski patrol typically sets off slides with dynamite or cannon shells before the lifts open. It is not unheard of for ski areas in the Northern Rockies to close during particularly fierce storms or periods of intense cold, when the wind and low visibility or the cold makes things too dangerous. Pack along a deck of cards or a good book, in case you're forced to sit out a storm during your visit to Jackson Hole, The Big Mountain, or other ski area.

WILDLIFE VIEWING

One of the major draws in Yellowstone and Glacier national parks, as well as at countless places outside the parks, are the wild animals that are so abundant in the Northern Rockies. The paramount rule of watching wildlife is to get "close" only with binoculars. Getting physically close can be dangerous for the viewer, particularly in the case of big beasts like bears, moose, and bison. It can also be hazardous for the viewee.

For birds and mammals, you know you're too close if the animals stop feeding, if they stand from a resting position, or, obviously, if they turn and walk, run, or fly away. Getting too close to animals can put tremendous stress on them. It can result in

mothers and young becoming separated, it can distract animals from nearby predators, or it can scare birds from their unhatched eggs. Especially in winter, because of the cold and the dearth of food, animals need to conserve all the energy they can. To approach too close on foot, skis, or snowmobile can contribute to that animal's death, if you force them to run and needlessly use up a portion of their valuable energy reserves.

Bison, one of the most popular and easily viewed animals in Yellowstone National Park and parts of Montana, are also one of the most dangerous. They can literally weigh a ton and, although they often appear docile, can quickly turn aggressive. Many visitors in Yellowstone have been gored by bison. Keep a lot of ground between you and a bison.

Special Tips for Foreign Visitors and Others

GROUND TRANSPORTATION

Good public transportation is available within a few of the region's largest cities, such as Missoula, and also around the concentrated resort areas like Jackson Hole, Whitefish, and Sun Valley. Concerning travel by train, the only places in the region served by Amtrak, the quasi-federal rail service, are Whitefish, West Glacier, and East Glacier. Bus travel, unfortunately, seems to be a universally unpleasant experience in the United States. Nevertheless, you might like to know that

Teton Range

Greyhound Bus Lines (telephone toll-free, 800–231–2222) serves cities in Montana along the east–west Interstate 90 corridor, and Rimrock Stages (telephone toll-free, 800–255–6755) links Idaho Falls, Idaho, with points north, including Butte, Missoula, and Kalispell.

Other than that, largely owing to the small, dispersed population of the region, public ground transportation is not well developed in the Northern Rockies. Renting a car is often the most inexpensive and convenient way to get around. Rental cars, including four-wheel-drive vehicles, can be obtained relatively cheaply in the United States. You'll find that most rental cars in this country are equipped with air conditioning, automatic transmission, and AM-FM radio. (Incidentally, the author's very favorite station in the tri-state area is KUWR FM, Wyoming Public Radio out of Laramie, found toward the left end of the dial throughout Wyoming and parts of southern Montana and eastern Idaho. Don't miss dialing in if you're in the area.) If you'll be doing a lot of driving, it is usually more economical to rent from a company that offers unlimited mileage, so inquire at another company if the first one contacted does not offer that option. Most companies require that drivers be at least twenty-five years of age, and all require that you have a valid driver's license and a major credit card for security. If your driver's license is not printed in English, inquire through your travel agent about obtaining an international driver's license.

If you're a member of an automobile club in your country, ask if they have a benefits-exchange program with the American Automobile Association (telephone, toll-free in the United States, 800–222–4357), which offers towing and other emergency road services.

Distances on maps and highway signs in the United States are indicated in miles. If you are accustomed to thinking metric, you can convert miles to kilometers by multiplying the miles by 1.61. The same goes for miles per hour: If the posted speed limit is 75 m.p.h., multiply by 1.61 to find that the kilometers per hour equivalent is 120 k.p.h. Speedometers on many cars sold in the United States indicate both miles and kilometers per hour.

KEEPING TIME

The entire region covered in this book is within the Mountain Time Zone, with the exception of the short stretch between Lolo Pass and Riggins, Idaho (*see* Sun Valley–Salmon Country), which is in the Pacific Time Zone. Pacific Time is always an hour earlier than Mountain Time. All of the region observes Daylight Savings Time, which is in effect from the first Sunday in April until the last Saturday in October. Standard Time, when the clocks are set back an hour, is observed the rest of the year.

ODDS AND ENDS

A 15 percent tip—a little less for poor service, a little more for exceptional—is generally expected by wait staff at restaurants. No tipping is expected at fast-food restaurants; at other establishments, such as coffee shops, where you order over a counter, you will often see a jar for tips, which the staff shares. Tipping is optional at places such as this.

You may want to purchase traveler's checks in U.S. dollars at your bank in your home country before leaving on a trip to the United States. You can also use your VISA card or MasterCard for most purchases. Virtually all motels and hotels in the Northern Rockies accept credit cards, and so do many bed-and-breakfast establishments. Most restaurants other than fast-food outlets also take plastic.

The legal drinking age is twenty-one in Wyoming, Idaho, and Montana. In Idaho and Montana, beer and wine can be purchased in grocery stores, while hard liquor is available only in licensed liquor stores. In Wyoming, all alcoholic beverages are available only through licensed liquor stores, which are more abundant in that state than in the other two.

Montana has no state sales tax, although a few of the individual communities charge a "resort tax." Wyoming and Idaho both have excise state sales taxes in the neighborhood of 5 percent.

If you are a smoker, ask in public establishments before smoking. Many restaurants and bars in the United States have banned smoking, and more are expected to do so in the future.

If you are camping and in need of a shower, you won't find one at most public campgrounds, such as those in the national parks and national forests. Plan to stay instead at one of the private campgrounds listed in the Staying There sections. Private campgrounds tend to be more expensive, and they offer a greater number of services to match. Don't stay exclusively at private grounds, however, since some of the most pleasant campgrounds in the Northern Rockies are found on public lands.

⎯⎯⎯⎯⎯⋀⋀⋀⋀⋀ Bibliography

Yellowstone-Teton Country

GENERAL DESCRIPTION AND TRAVEL

Burt, Nathaniel. *Wyoming*. Oakland, Calif.: Compass American Guides, 1990.

Maturi, Mary Buckingham and Richard J. *Wyoming: Off the Beaten Path*. Old Saybrook, Conn.: The Globe Pequot Press, 1996.

Pitcher, Don. *Wyoming Handbook*. Chico, Calif.: Moon Publications, 1993.

Scofield, Susan C., and Jeremy C. Schmidt. *The Inn at Old Faithful*. Crowsnest Associates, 1979.

HISTORICAL/CULTURAL

Alter, Cecil J. *Jim Bridger*. Norman: University of Oklahoma Press, 1962; original edition, 1925.

Bartlett, Richard A. *Yellowstone: A Wilderness Besieged*. Tucson: University of Arizona Press, 1985.

Betts, Robert B. *Along the Ramparts of the Tetons: The Saga of Jackson Hole, Wyoming*. Boulder: University Press of Colorado, 1978.

Burt, Nathaniel. *Jackson Hole Journal*. Norman: University of Oklahoma Press, 1983.

Blevins, Winfred. *Roadside History of Yellowstone Park*. Missoula: Mountain Press Publishing Company, 1989.

Calkins, Frank. *Jackson Hole*. New York: Alfred A. Knopf, Inc., 1973.

Cheney, Thomas Edward. *Voices from the Bottom of the Bowl: A Folk History of Teton Valley Idaho, from 1823–1952*. Salt Lake City: University of Utah Press, 1991.

Chittenden, Hiram Martin. *The Yellowstone National Park*. Norman: University of Oklahoma Press, 1964; original edition, 1895.

Foster, Mike. *Strange Genius: The Life of Ferdinand Vandeveer Hayden*. Boulder, Colo.: Roberts Rinehart Publishers, 1994.

Haines, Aubrey L. *Journal of a Trapper: Osborne Russell*. Lincoln: University of Nebraska Press, 1955.

Haines, Aubrey L. *The Yellowstone Story:* Volumes One and Two. Yellowstone National Park: Yellowstone Library and Museum Association, 1977.

Harris, Burton. *John Colter, His Years in the Rockies*. Lincoln: Bison Books, University of Nebraska Press, 1993.

Hough, Donald. *The Cocktail Hour in Jackson Hole*. Worland, Wyo.: High Plains Publishing Company, Inc. Originally published 1951. A light, literary look at an earlier day in Jackson Hole.

Irving, Washington. *The Adventures of Captain Bonneville.* Portland, Ore.: Binfords & Mort, 1954; original edition, 1837.

James, H. L. *Scenic Driving The Beartooth Highway.* Helena: Falcon Press, 1997.

Janetski, Joel. C. *Indians of Yellowstone National Park.* Salt Lake City: University of Utah Press, 1987.

Larsen, T. A. *History of Wyoming.* Lincoln: University of Nebraska Press, 1978.

Lovell, Edith Haroldsen. *Benjamin Bonneville, Soldier of the American Frontier.* Bountiful, Utah: Horizon Publishers, 1992.

Moulton, Candy Vyvey. *Legacy of the Tetons: Homesteading in Jackson Hole.* Boise: Tamarack Books, Inc., 1994.

National Park Service. *Grand Teton: Official National Park Handbook.* U.S. Department of the Interior, 1984.

Reed, Mary, and Keith C. Peterson. *Harriman.* Boise: Idaho Department of Parks and Recreation, 1981.

Saylor, David J. *Jackson Hole, Wyoming: In the Shadow of the Tetons.* Norman: University of Oklahoma Press, 1970.

Schreier, Carl, ed. *Yellowstone: Selected Photographs, 1870–1960.* Moose, Wyo.: Homestead Publishing, 1989.

Schullery, Paul. *Searching for Yellowstone.* New York: Houghton Mifflin Company, 1997. A look both back and forward on Yellowstone's 125th birthday, written by a longtime park ranger and historian.

Thompson, Edith M. Schultz, and William Leigh Thompson. *Beaver Dick: The Honor and the Heartbreak.* Laramie: Jelm Mountain Press, 1982.

Trenholm, Virginia Cole, and Maurine Carley. *The Shoshonis: Sentinels of the Rockies.* Norman: University of Oklahoma Press, 1964.

Urbanek, Mae. *Wyoming Place Names.* Missoula: Mountain Press Publishing Company, 1988.

Whittlesey, Lee H. *Yellowstone Place Names.* Helena: Montana Historical Society Press, 1988.

Yellowstone Assocation. *Yellowstone: The Official Guide to Touring America's First National Park.* The Yellowstone Association, 1997.

NATURAL HISTORY AND GEOLOGY

Brooks, Charles E. *The Henry's Fork.* New York: Lyons & Burford, 1986.

Bryan, Scott T. *The Geysers of Yellowstone.* Boulder: Colorado Associated University Press, 1979.

Lumbering activity

Carrighar, Sally. *One Day at Teton Marsh*. Lincoln: University of Nebraska Press, 1979. Classic natural-history account involving moose, beaver, and countless other critters.

Clark, Tim W. *Ecology of Jackson Hole, Wyoming: A Primer*. Salt Lake City: Paragon Press, 1981.

Clark, Tim W., and Mark R. Stromberg. *Mammals in Wyoming*. Lawrence: University of Kansas Museum of Natural History, 1987.

Craighead, Frank J. *Track of the Grizzly*. San Francisco: Sierra Club Books, 1979. The story of grizzly bears in Yellowstone as told by a longtime bear-research scientist.

Fritz, William J. *Roadside Geology of the Yellowstone Country*. Missoula: Mountain Press Publishing Company, 1985.

Good, John M., and Kenneth L. Pierce. *Interpreting the Landscape: Recent and Ongoing Geology of Grand Teton & Yellowstone National Parks*. Moose, Wyo.: Grand Teton National History Association, 1996.

Largeson, David R., and Darwin R. Spearing. *Roadside Geology of Wyoming*. Missoula: Mountain Press Publishing Company, 1988.

Love, J. D., and John C. Reed Jr. *Creation of the Teton Landscape: The Geologic Story of Grand Teton National Park*. Moose, Wyo.: Grand Teton Natural History Association, 1971.

McEneaney, Terry. *Birds of Yellowstone*. Boulder, Colo.: Roberts Rinehart Publishers, 1988.

McPhee, John. *Rising from the Plains*. New York: Farrar, Straus, Giroux, 1986. McPhee makes geology come to life in this account, based largely on the work of J. D. Love, the dean of Wyoming rock.

Murie, Margaret and Olaus. *Wapiti Wilderness*. Boulder: Colorado Associated University Press, 1985.

Raynes, Bert. *Birds of Grand Teton National Park and the Surrounding Area*. Moose, Wyo.: Grand Teton Natural History Association, 1984.

Wuerthner, George. *Yellowstone and the Fires of Change*. Salt Lake City: Haggis House Publications, 1988.

RECREATION AND NAVIGATION

Adventure Cycling Assocation, *Mountain Biking in the Jackson Hole Area*: Adventure Cycling Association, 1994. Full-color, waterproof map produced by Missoula-based nonprofit organization.

Bach, Orville, *Hiking the Yellowstone Backcountry*. San Francisco: Sierra Club Books, 1979.

DeLorme Mapping. *Wyoming Atlas & Gazetteer*. Freeport, Maine: DeLorme Mapping.

Hunger, Bill. *Hiker's Guide to Wyoming*. Helena: Falcon Press, 1992.

Marschall, Mark C. *Yellowstone Trails: A Hiking Guide*. Yellowstone National Park, Wyo.: Yellowstone Association, 1990.

Turiano, Thomas. *Teton Skiing: A History & Guide to the Teton Range*. Moose, Wyo.: Homestead Publishing, 1995.

LITERATURE

Erlich, Gretel. *Heart Mountain*. New York: Viking Penguin, 1988. Novel based on the World War II Japanese relocation camp outside Cody.

Erlich, Gretel. *The Solace of Open Spaces*. New York: Viking Penguin, 1985.

Krakel, Dean II. *Downriver: A Yellowstone Journey*. San Francisco: Sierra Club Books, 1987.

Glacier-Gold Country

GENERAL DESCRIPTION AND TRAVEL

Gildart, R. C., ed. *Glacier Country: Montana's Glacier National Park*. Montana Geographic Series. Helena: Montana Magazine, 1986.

Gildart, R. C. *Montana's Flathead Country*. Montana Geographic Series. Helena: Montana Magazine, 1986.

McCoy, Michael. *Montana: Off the Beaten Path.* Old Saybrook, Conn.: Globe Pequot Press, 1996.

McRae, W. C., and Judy Jewell. *Montana Handbook.* Chico, Calif.: Moon Publications, 1992.

Tirrell, Norma. *Montana.* Oakland, Calif.: Compass American Guides, 1991.

HISTORICAL/CULTURAL

Barsness, Larry. *Gold Camp: Alder Gulch and Virginia City, Montana.* New York: Hastings House, 1962.

Buchholtz, C. W. *Man in Glacier.* West Glacier: Glacier Natural History Association, 1976.

Cheff, Bud. *Indian Tales and Grizzly Tales.* Stevensville, Mont.: Stonydale Press, 1994.

Cheney, Roberta Carkeek. *Names on the Face of Montana.* Missoula: Mountain Press Publishing Company, 1983.

Clark, Ella E., and Margot Edmonds. *Sacagawea of the Lewis and Clark Expedition.* Berkeley: University of California Press, 1979.

Crutchfield, James A. *It Happened in Montana.* Helena: Falcon Press, 1992.

Dimsdale, Thomas J. *The Vigilantes of Montana.* Norman: University of Oklahoma Press edition, 1966.

Ewers, John C. *The Blackfeet: Raiders on the Northwestern Plains.* Norman: University of Oklahoma Press, 1958.

Grinnell, George Bird. *Blackfoot Lodge Tales: The Story of a Prairie People.* Lincoln: Bison Books, University of Nebraska Press edition, 1962.

Hart, Jeff. *Montana: Native Plants and Early Peoples.* Helena: Montana Historical Society, 1976.

Holterman, J. *Place Names of Glacier/Waterton National Parks.* West Glacier: Glacier Natural History Association, 1985.

Howard, Joseph Kinsey. *Montana: High, Wide, and Handsome.* Lincoln: University of Nebraska Press, 1943.

Johnson, Dorothy M. *When You and I Were Young, Whitefish.* Missoula: Mountain Press Publishing Company, 1982.

Malone, Michael P., and Richard B. Roeder. *Montana: A History of Two Centuries.* Seattle: University of Washington, 1976.

Phillips, Paul C., ed. *Forty Years on the Frontier: As seen in the Journals and Reminiscences of Granville Stuart.* Glendale, Calif.: The Arthur H. Clark Company, 1957.

Spence, Clark C. *Montana: A History.* New York: W. W. Norton & Company, 1978.

Stuart, Granville. *Pioneering in Montana: The Making of a State, 1864–1867.* Lincoln: Bison Books, University of Nebraska Press, 1977; original edition, 1925.

Toole, K. Ross. *Montana: An Uncommon Land.* Norman: University of Oklahoma Press, 1959.

West, Carroll Van. *A Traveler's Companion to Montana History.* Helena: Montana Historical Society Press, 1986.

NATURAL HISTORY AND GEOLOGY

Alt, David, and Donald W. Hyndman. *Roadside Geology of Montana.* Missoula: Mountain Press Publishing Company, 1986.

Fischer, Carol and Hank. *Montana Wildlife Viewing Guide.* Helena: Falcon Press, 1990.

Horner, John R., and James Gorman. *Digging Dinosaurs.* New York: Harper Collins, 1990.

Lopez, B. H. *Of Wolves and Men.* New York: Charles Scribner's Sons, 1978.

McEneaney, Terry. *Birder's Guide to Montana.* Helena: Falcon Press, 1993.

Rockwell, David. *Glacier National Park: A Natural History Guide.* Boston: Houghton Mifflin Company, 1995.

Shaw, Richard J. and Danny On. *Plants of Waterton-Glacier National Parks and the Northern Rockies.* Missoula: Mountain Press Publishing Company, 1979.

RECREATION AND NAVIGATION

Cogswell, Ted. *Montana Golf Guide.* Great Falls: Self-published, 1985.

DeLorme Mapping. *Montana Atlas & Gazetteer.* Freeport, Maine: DeLorme Mapping, 1994.

Fischer, Hank. *Floater's Guide to Montana.* Helena: Falcon Press, 1986.

Glacier Natural History Association. *Hiker's Guide to Glacier National Park.* West Glacier: Glacier Natural History Association, 1978.

Glacier Natural History Association. *Short Hikes and Strolls in Glacier National Park.* West Glacier: Glacier Natural History Association, 1978.

Kirkendall, Tom, and Vicky Spring. *Glacier National Park and Waterton Lakes National Park: A Complete Recreation Guide.* Seattle: The Mountaineers, 1994.

Rudner, Ruth. *Bitterroot to Beartooth.* San Francisco: Sierra Club Books, 1985. Hiking guide focusing on the southwest part of the state.

Sample, Michael S. *Angler's Guide to Montana.* Helena: Falcon Press, 1984.

Schneider, Bill. *Hiker's Guide to Montana.* Helena: Falcon Press, 1990.

LITERATURE

Bass, Rick. *The Ninemile Wolves.* Livingston, Mont.: Clark City Press, 1992.

Duncan, Dayton. *Out West: American Journey Along the Lewis and Clark Trail.* New York: Penguin Books, 1987. Great narrative covering Duncan's driving odyssey along the historic trail.

Garcia, Andrew. *Tough Trip Through Paradise.* Sausalito, Calif.: Comstock Editions, 1967.

Guthrie, A. B. *The Big Sky.* Boston: Houghton Mifflin Company, 1947.

Kittredge, William, and Annick Smith, eds. *The Last Best Place.* Helena: Montana Historical Society Press, 1988. Classic volume of more than 1,000 pages, containing stories and essays ranging from Native American tales to cowpoke poetry.

Walker, Mildred. *Winter Wheat.* Lincoln: University of Nebraska Press, 1992; original edition, 1944.

MAGAZINES

Big Sky Journal. Spring Creek Publishing, Inc., Bozeman, Mont. Quarterly focusing on Montana's people and outdoors, with a literary bent.

Montana Magazine. American & World Geographic Publishing, Helena. General-interest bi-monthly magazine extolling the beauty and diversity of the Big Sky State in words and photos.

Montana Outdoors. Montana Department of Fish, Wildlife and Parks, Helena.

Sun Valley–Salmon Country

GENERAL DESCRIPTION AND TRAVEL

Conley, Cort. *Idaho for the Curious.* Cambridge, Idaho: Backeddy Books, 1982. Exhaustive, 700-page road-traveler's guide overflowing with historical facts, photos, and statistics.

Fanselow, Julie. *Idaho: Off the Beaten Path.* Old Saybrook, Conn.: The Globe Pequot Press, 1998.

Gnass, Jeff. *Idaho: Magnificent Wilderness.* Englewood, Colo.: Westcliffe Publishers, 1988. Photo-filled coffee-table book.

Root, Don. *Idaho Handbook.* Chico, Calif.: Moon Publications, 1997.

HISTORICAL/CULTURAL

Arrington, Leonard J. *History of Idaho:* Volume 1. Moscow: University of Idaho Press, 1994.

Dan Bailey's Fly Shop, Livingston, Montana

Boone, Lalia. *Idaho Place Names: A Geographical Dictionary.* Moscow: University of Idaho Press, 1988.

d'Easum, Dick. *Sawtooth Tales.* Caldwell, Idaho: Caxton Printers, 1977.

Derig, Betty. *Roadside History of Idaho.* Missoula: Mountain Press Publishing Company, 1996.

Linkhart, Luther. *Sawtooth National Recreation Area.* Berkeley, Calif.: Wilderness Press, 1988.

Madson, Brigham D. *Northern Shoshoni.* Caldwell: Caxton Printers, 1980.

Madson, Brigham D. *The Lemhi: Sacajawea's People.* Caldwell: Caxton Printers, 1979.

National Park Service: *Craters of the Moon: Official National Park Handbook.* Washington, D.C.: U.S. Department of the Interior, 1991.

National Park Service. *Nez Perce Country: A Handbook for Nez Perce National Historical Park.* Washington, D.C.: U.S. Department of the Interior, 1983.

O'Reilly, Betty. *The Magic of McCall.* Boise: Lithocraft, 1989.

Peterson, F. Ross. *Idaho: A Bicentennial History.* New York: W. W. Norton & Company, Inc., 1976.

Peterson, Harold. *The Last of the Mountain Men.* New York: Scribners, 1969. The story of Sylvan Hart, a.k.a. Buckskin Billy, a twentieth-century mountain man who lived along the Salmon River.

Schwantes, Carlos A. *In Mountain Shadows: A History of Idaho.* Lincoln: University of Nebraska Press, 1991. Outstanding historic overview of the Gem State.

Watters, Ron. *Never Turn Back: The Life of Whitewater Pioneer Walt Blackadar*. Pocatello: The Great Rift Press, 1994.

Welch, Julia Conway. *The Magruder Murders: Coping with Violence on the Idaho Frontier*. Eagle Point, Ore.: Self-published, 1991.

Williamson, Darcy, and Steven Shephard. *Salmon River Legends and Campfire Cuisine*. Bend, Ore.: Maverick Publications, 1988. Tales, tall tales, and campfire recipes compiled by longtime Salmon River guides.

Taylor, Dorice. *Sun Valley*. New Haven, Conn.: Eastern Press, 1980.

Yarber, Esther. *Stanley-Sawtooth Country*. Salt Lake City: Publishers Press, 1976.

Natural History and Geology

Alt, David, and Donald W. Hyndman. *Roadside Geology of Idaho*. Missoula: Mountain Press Publishing Company, 1993.

Carpenter, Leslie Benjamin. *Idaho Wildlife Viewing Guide*. Helena: Falcon Press, 1990.

Johnson, Frederic D. *Wild Trees of Idaho*. Moscow, Idaho: University of Idaho Press, 1994.

Recreation and Navigation

Carrey, John, and Cort Conley. *The Middle Fork: A Guide*. Cambridge: Backeddy Books, 1992. Guide to the Middle Fork of the Salmon River.

Carrey, John, and Cort Conley. *River of No Return*. Cambridge: Backeddy Books, 1978.

DeLorme Mapping. *Idaho Atlas & Gazetteer*. Freeport, Maine: DeLorme Mapping, 1992.

Fuller, Margaret. *Trails of the Frank Church–River of No Return Wilderness*. Edmonds, Wash.: Signpost Books, 1987.

Fuller, Margaret. *Trails of the Sawtooth & White Cloud Mountains*. Edmonds, Wash.: Signpost Books, 1988.

Hollingshead, Ann, and Gloria Moore. *Day Hiking Near Sun Valley*. Sun Valley, Ida.: Gentian Press, 1995.

Maughan, Ralph and Jackie Johnson Maughan. *Hiker's Guide to Idaho*. Helena: Falcon Press, 1990.

MacMillan, Daniel. *Golfing in Idaho*. Carnation, Wash.: MAC Productions, 1993.

Stone, Lynne. *Adventures in Idaho's Sawtooth Country*. Seattle: The Mountaineers, 1990. Details hiking trails and mountain-bike rides.

Watson, Lewis, ed. *Idaho's Top 30 Fishing Waters*. Rupert, Idaho: Idaho Outdoor Digest, 1989.

Literature

McCunn, Rathanne Lum. *Thousand Pieces of Gold*. New York: Dell Publishing Company, 1981. The story of folk hero Polly Bemis, a Chinese girl who came (as Lalu Nathoy) as a slave to Warren around 1870 and was ostensibly won by husband Charlie Bemis in a poker game.

Studebaker, William, and Rick Ardinger, eds. *Where the Morning Light's Still Blue: Personal Essays About Idaho*. Moscow, Idaho: University of Idaho Press: 1994.

Magazines

Idaho Yesterday. Idaho State Historical Society, Boise. Quarterly publication.

Sun Valley Magazine. Wood River Publishing, Inc., Hailey, Idaho. Slick, thick magazine published two times a year. Tucked amid the real estate and fashion ads are occasional articles of substance.

Regional

GENERAL DESCRIPTIVE AND TRAVEL

Wilfong, Cheryl. *Following the Nez Perce Trail.* Corvallis: Oregon State University Press, 1990.

HISTORICAL/CULTURAL

Brown, Mark H. *The Flight of the Nez Perce.* New York: Capricorn Books, 1971.

DeVoto, Bernard. *Across the Wide Missouri.* New York: Houghton Mifflin, 1947. Classic on the early fur trade in the Rocky Mountains.

DeVoto, Bernard, ed. *The Journals of Lewis and Clark.* Boston: Houghton Mifflin Company, 1953.

Frison, George C. *Prehistoric Hunters of the High Plains.* New York: Academic Press, 1978.

Guth, Richard, and Stan B. Cohen. *A Pictorial History of the U.S. Forest Service, Northern Region, 1891–1945.* Missoula: Pictorial Histories Publishing, 1991.

Josephy, Alvin M. *The Nez Perce Indians and the Opening of the Northwest.* Lincoln: University of Nebraska Press, 1971.

Morgan, Dale L. *Jedediah Smith and the Opening of the West.* Lincoln: University of Nebraska Press, 1953.

Morgan, Ted. *A Shovel of Stars: The Making of the American West—1800 to the Present.* New York: Simon & Schuster, 1995.

Parker, Rev. Samuel. *Journal of an Exploring Tour.* Moscow: University of Idaho Press, 1990. Reprint of account of pioneer missionary's travels in the Northern Rockies in the nineteenth century.

Russell, Osborne. *Journal of a Trapper.* Lincoln: University of Nebraska Press edition, 1965.

Sunder, John E. *Bill Sublette, Mountain Man.* Norman: University of Oklahoma Press, 1959.

Cabin, Pacerville, Idaho

NATURAL HISTORY AND GEOLOGY

Alt, David, and Donald W. Hyndman. *Northwest Exposures: A Geologic Story of the Northwest.* Missoula: Mountain Press Publishing Company, 1995.

Arno, Stephen, and Ramona P. Hammerly. *Timberline: Arctic and Mountain Forest Frontiers.* Seattle: The Mountaineers, 1984.

Chronic, Halka. *Pages of Stone: Geology of Western National Parks and Monuments,* Vol. 1: Rocky Mountains and Western Great Plains. Seattle: The Mountaineers, 1984.

Crittenden, Mabel. *Trees of the West.* Millbrae, Calif.: Celestial Arts, 1977.

Cutright, Paul Russell. *Lewis and Clark: Pioneer Naturalists.* Lincoln: University of Nebraska Press, 1969.

Perry, John, and Jane Greverus Perry. *The Sierra Club Guide to the Natural Areas of Idaho, Montana, and Wyoming.* San Francisco: Sierra Club Books, 1988.

RECREATION

Spring, Ira, Harvey Manning, and Vicky Spring. *Hiking the Great Northwest.* Seattle: The Mountaineers, 1991.

Wilkerson, M.D., James, ed. *Medicine for Mountaineering.* Seattle: The Mountaineers, 1992.

LITERATURE

Maclean, Norman. *A River Runs Through It and Other Stories.* Chicago: University of Chicago Press, 1976. In addition to his acclaimed novella concerning the interrelatedness of family, fly-fishing, and spirituality, Maclean relates a humorous tale about a summer spent working for the U.S. Forest Service in the Bitterroot Mountains of Idaho and Montana.

McMurtry, Larry. *Lonesome Dove.* New York: Pocket Books, 1985. Classic tale of a cattle drive, beginning in Texas and leading through Wyoming and Montana.

MAGAZINES

Montana: The Magazine of Western History. Montana Historical Society, Helena, Mont. Written by professional and amateur historians, this is the best in-depth historical periodical in the region. Contains articles concerning Montana and the Northern Rockies/Great Plains in general.

Index

Boldface numerals indicate pages on which illustrations appear.

A-1 Campground, 92
Absarokee, Montana, 66
Abyss Pool, **52**
Adams Gulch, 270
Adventure Cycling Association, 166
Adventures in Mexico and the Rocky Mountains, (Ruxton), 138
Albright Visitor Center, 68
All Pro Rental Agency, 212
All Star Collectibles, 227
Allentown, Montana, 172
Alpenhof Lodge, 90
Alpine House Bed & Breakfast, The, 88
Alpinglow Inn, 212
altitudes and altitude sickness, 306, 307
Alturas Lake Area Campgrounds, 292
Alturas Lake, 269
American Computer Museum, 80
Amy Lou's Steak House, 277
Anaconda Smelter Stack, 197
Anaconda, Montana, 197
Angler's Inn, 88
Angler's Roost Campground, 203
Anna's Oven, 201
Annapurna Properties, 212
Antique Boutique, 289
Antiques & Country Pine, 300
Antiques on Broadway, 227
Apgar Campground, 217
Apgar Village Lodge, 214
Apgar Village, 181
Apollinaris Springs Picnic Area, 71
Appleton Inn, 223
Archie Bray Foundation, 191
Arlee Pow Wow, 172
Arlee, Montana, 172
Art Museum of Missoula, 166
Artists' Paint Pots, 72
Arts Chateau, 194
Ashton, Idaho, 86
Ashton-Flagg Road, 86
Aspen Acres, Idaho, 86
Astoria Hot Springs, 97
Atherton Creek Campground, 93

Atkinsons' Market, 300
Atlanta Hot Springs, 261
Atlanta, Idaho, 261–62
Audubon Society, 146
Augusta, Montana, 190
Avalanche Campground, 184
Avalanche Creek Campground, 217
avalanches, 310–11
Averill's Flathead Lake Lodge, 210–11
Azteca, 107

Backcountry (bicycling tours), 108
Backcountry Bike & Boards, 201
Backwoods Mountain Sports, 299
Bad Bear Campground, 261
Bad Marriage Mountains, 187
Bagels on Broadway, 206
Baker's Hole Campground, 77, 113
Bald Mountain (skiing), 298
Bangtail Bicycles, 108
Banks, Idaho, 258
Bannack State Park Campground, 201
Bannack State Park, 154
Bannack, Montana, gold strike, 142
Banner Ridge, Park N' Ski Area, 261
Barker-Ewing Jackson Hole River Trips, 97
Barrister, The, 223
Base Camp, The, 224
Bashore Resort Motel, 211
Basin Canyon Campground, 226
Basin Creek Campground, 265
Basin, Montana, 192
Battleridge Campground, 107
Baxter Hotel, 80
Baxter, The, 107
Bay Point Estates, 212
Bayhorse Recreation Site, 280
Bear Bottom Inn, 277
Bear Canyon RV Park & Campground, 105–6
Bear Creek Guest Ranch, 188
Bear Creek Lodge, 284
Bear Valley River Co., 258
Bears Oil & Roots, 248
bears, 309

Beartooth Butte, 64
Beartooth Lake, 64
Beartooth National Scenic Byway, 63
Beaver Creek Campground, 113
Beaver Creek Canyon, 190
Beaver Dam Campground, 197
beaver-fur trade, 138
Beaverhead County Museum, 154
Beaverhead National Forest Recreational Cabins, 199–200
Beaverhead National Forest, 158
Beavertail Hill Campground, 206
Belgrade, Montana, 81
Bellevue Bistro, 275
Bellevue, Idaho, 275
Belly River Campground, 186, 217
Benton, Thomas Hart, 140
Berkeley Pit, 193, **193**
Bernice's Bakery, 206
Beryl Spring, 72
Best Western Buck's T-4 Lodge, 104
Best Western Christiania Motor Lodge, 293
Best Western City Center, 105
Best Western Colonial Inn, 223
Best Western Copper King Park Hotel, 225
Best Western Executive Inn, 204
Best Western Hamilton Inn, 202
Best Western McCall, 283
Best Western Paradise Inn, 199
Best Western Rocky Mountain Lodge, 212
bicycling: in Bozeman, Montana, 108; in Butte,
    Montana, 227; in Dillon, Montana, 201; in Helena,
    Montana, 224; in Jackson Hole, Wyoming 96; in
    McCall, Idaho, 286–87; in Stanley, Idaho, 292; in
    Sun Valley, Idaho, 299; in Teton Valley, 118; in West
    Yellowstone, Montana, 113; in Whitefish, Montana,
    218; in Yankee Jim Canyon, 69–71; in Yellowstone
    National Park, 102; on Pioneer Mountains National
    Scenic Byway, 155–57; in Missoula, Montana, 207
Big Creek Airstrip Campground, 285
Big Creek Campground, 216
Big Eddy Campground, 258
Big Hole Crossing Restaurant, 201
Big Hole Crossing, 158
Big Hole National Battlefield, 154, 159; Nez Perce
    camp, **159**
Big Hole River Valley (the Big Hole), Montana: gold
    strike, 142, **142**; sights, 150, 154–58, 159–61; lodging,
    campgrounds, food, activities. See Dillon, Montana
Big Horn Galleries, 104
Big Ignace, 140
Big Larch, 168
Big Lost River Valley, 277
Big Mountain Environmental Education Center, 177
Big Mountain Ski & Summer Resort, The, 212, 220
Big Mountain, The, 176
Big Sheep Creek Back Country Byway, 153
Big Sky Carvers Outlet Gallery, 82
Big Sky Ski & Summer Resort, 79, 109
Big Sky, Montana, 79; lodging, campgrounds, food,
    activities. See Bozeman
Big Sky, The, (Guthrie), 123

Big Springs Campground, 113
Big Springs Campground, 84
Big Springs, Idaho, 84–85
Big Timber, Montana, 66
Big Wood River Valley, 268
Bigfork Festival of the Arts, 211
Bigfork Inn, 211
Bigfork Rental Agency, 211
Bigfork Summer Playhouse, 175, 211
Bigfork, Montana, 175; festivals, events, and theater, 211;
    food, 211; golf, 211; lodging, 210–11; tours, 212
Bigwood Golf Club, 297
Bill Cody's Ranch Resort, 59
Bill Mason Outfitters, 297
Billy's Burgers, 93
Birchwood Hostel, 204
Bird Woman Falls Overlook, 185
birding, 110
Bison Creek Ranch Bed & Breakfast, 188
Bitterroot Valley, sites, 159, 161–64; lodging, campgrounds
    and RV parks, food, activities. See Hamilton, Montana
Black Bear Campground, 203
Black Butte Trail, 77
Blackfeet Indians, 137, 148; smallpox epidemic, 140
Blackfoot-Clearwater Game Refuge, 168
Blacktail Butte, 45
Blaine County Museum, 275
Blodgett Canyon Campground, 203
Blodgett Canyon, 162
Blood Indian Forest Reserve, 186
Bob Marshall Wilderness Area, 169, 190
Bob Scriver Musuem of Montana Wildlife, 188
Bohart Ranch Cross-Country Ski Center, 110
Boiling River, 68
Boise Basin Mercantile, **259**, 260
Boise Basin Museum, 260
Boise County Pioneer Cemetery, 259
Bonner Park, 167
Bonneville Campground, 262
Bonneville, Bejamin Louis Eulaliede, 25–27
Book Peddler, The, 115
Boone and Crockett Club, 146
Borah Peak, earthquake of 1959, 234
Boulder Hot Springs, 192
Boulder Mountain Tour, 270, 297
Boulder View Campground, 270
Boulder, Montana, 192
Boundary Campground, 295
Bowman Lake Campground, 217
Bowman Lake, 179
Bozeman Hotel, 80
Bozeman KOA, 106
Bozeman Trail, 66
Bozeman Vistor Center, Downtown, 80
Bozeman, Montana, 77, 80–81; airport, 111; bicycling,
    108; campgrounds and RV parks, 105–7; fairs, festi-
    vals, and events, 109; fishing, 108–9; food, 107; golf,
    109; horseback riding, 109; lodging, 104–5; micro-
    breweries, 108; Montana State University, 80;
    Museum of the Rockies, 81; sites, 80–81; other activi-
    ties, 110; river floating, 109; shopping, 110–11; ski-

ing, 109–10; telephone numbers, 111; tours, 110
Breakfast Shoppe, The 116
Bridalveil Falls, 264
Bridge Bay Marina and Campground, 53
Bridge Campground, 295
Bridge, The, 206
Bridger Bowl Ski Area, 100
Bridger Creek Canyon, 25
Bridger Creek Golf Course, 109
Bridger, Jim, 24–25; *Jim Bridger*, (Alter), 24
Broad Axe Lodge, 161, 202
Broadway Bookstore, 64
Brooks Lake Lodge, 45
Browning, Montana, 188
Brundage Bungalows, 283
Brundage Mountain, 251, 286; skiing, 288
Bubba's Bar-B-Que, 94
Buck's T-4, 107
Buckin' Horse Bunkhouse, 66
Buckskin Billy, 233
Bud & Shirley's Restaurant, 162
Bud Lilly's Trout Shop, 114
Buffalo Bill (William F. Cody), 59, 60–62
Buffalo Bill Historical Center, 60–62; events, 61
Buffalo Bill State Park Campground, 103
Buffalo Bill State Park, 59
Buffalo Cafe, 217, 296
Buffalo Hill Golf Club, 219
Buffalo Ranch, 57
buffalo, fur-trade, 138–39
Bull Trout Lake, 263
Bungalow, The, 190
Bunnery, The, 94
Burgdorf Campground, 286
Burgdorf Hot Springs, 253, 255, 287, **288**
Burl Inn, 102
Burlington Northern Depot, **221**
Butte Copper Co., 227
Butte, Montana, 193; bicycling, 226; Boulder batholith, 236; campgrounds and RV parks, 225–26; fairs, festivals, and events, 227; food, 226; hot springs, 227; lodging, 225; shopping, 227; sights, 191, 193–98; skiing, 227; skyline, **196**; telephone numbers, 228; theater, 227–228; tours, 228
Butte–Silver Bow Chamber of Commerce Visitor Center, 194

Cabin Creek Campground, 93, 113
Cadillac Grille, 94
Cafe at the Brewery, 296
Cafe Kandahar, 217
Calamity's Cafe, 260
Calico Italian Restaurant, 94
Camas Prairie, 249
Camp Creek Inn B&B Guest Ranch, 203
Camp Creek Inn B&B, 160
Camp Stanley, 291
Camp Tuffit, 175
Campgrounds: overview of types, xix; for U.S. Forest Service reservations, xix
Campgrounds and RV parks: in Bozeman, Montana,

105–6; in Cody, Wyoming, 103; in Dillon, Montana, 200–201; in Hamilton, Montana, 203; in Helena, Montana, 223; in Jackson Hole, Wyoming, 93–94; in McCall, Idaho, 285–86; in Missoula, Montana, 205–6; in Stanley, Idaho, 291–92; in Sun Valley, Idaho, 295; in Teton Valley, 116; in West Yellowstone, Montana, 113; in Whitefish, Montana, 216–17; in Yellowstone National Park, 102; in Butte, Montana, 226
Campus Inn, 204
Canada, 186–87
Cantina la Cocina, 203
Canyon Ferry Lake Campground, 223
Canyon Ferry Lake, 192
Canyon Hotel, 74
Canyon Lodge Cabins, 101
Canyon Village, 55
Cape Horn, 263
Caras Park, 165
Carbon County Historical Museum, 65
Carousel for Missoula, A, 166
Carriage House Bistro, 223
Casa Sanchez, 107
Cascade Ranger District, 257
Cascade Reservoir, 257
Cascade, Idaho, 257
Catlin, George, 27
Cecil's Fine Foods, 68
Centennial Inn, 199
Centennial Mountains, 150
Centennial Valley, Montana, 150; sights, 150–53
Centerville, Idaho, 259
Central Idaho Museum for Regional History, 279
Chalet RV Park, 257
Challenger Inn, origins, 245
Challis Golf Course, 279
Challis Hot Springs and Campground, 278
Challis National Forest, 263
Challis, Idaho, 278–80
Chambers of commerce/visitor bureas, 304–5
Chapel House Bed & Breakfast, 102
Chapel of the Sacred Heart, 45
Chapel of the Transfiguration, 48
Chapter One Bookstore, 300
Charles Waters Campground, 164, 203
Chatham Fine Art, 67
Chattanooga Hot Springs, 261
Chemeketan Recreation Area, 269
Chez Jean-Claude Restaurant, 286
Chic Hippies, 300
Chicken Lipps, 300
Chico Hot Springs, Montana, 67–68
Chief Cameahwait, 136, 240
Chief Joseph Pass, 160
Chief Joseph Scenic Highway, 62–63
Chief Joseph, 30, 159; surrender, 32
Chief Looking Glass Campground, 206
Chief Mountain International Highway, 186
Chilly Slough Wetlands Conservation Area, 278
chinook, 129
Chisholm Campgrounds, 107
Choteau, Montana, 189

Christmas in Montana, 115
Cinnabar General Store, 68
Clarion Inn of Sun Valley, 293
Clark Canyon Reservoir Campground, 201
Clark Canyon Reservoir, 153
Clark, William, 134–37, 240
Clay Butte Lookout, 64
Clearwater Canoe Trail, 169–70
Clearwater Crossing, 168
Clearwater Junction, 168
Cody Guest Houses, 102
Cody Nite Rodeo, 103
Cody Rodeo Company, 104
Cody, William F. See Buffalo Bill
Cody, Wyoming, 58, 59; campgrounds and RV parks,
    103; Buffalo Bill Historical Center, 60; Buffalo Bill
    State Park, 59; fairs, festivals, and events, 61, 103;
    food, 103; guest and dude ranches, 102; lodging,
    102–3; shopping, 103; telephone numbers, 104
Cold Spring Campground, 286
Coldwater Creek (retail), 100
Colter Bay Campground, 93
Colter Bay Nature Trail, 49
Colter Bay Village, 49, 91
Colter Bay, **91**
Colter, John, 138; birthplace, 22; discovery of
    Yellowstone, 3; Lewis and Clark Expedition, 22
Columbia Falls, 180
Come On Inn, 275
Comfort Inn, 111, 199, 202, 212, 225
Comida, La, 103
Conover's Trading Post, 158
Conrad Mansion, 175
Continental Cafeteria, 294
Cooke City, Montana, 58
Copper King Mansion, 194, **195**, 225
Corps of Discovery. See Lewis and Clark Expedition
Corwin Springs, Montana, 68
Cottonwood Hills Golf Course, 109
Cougar Mountain Lodge, 257
Country Bookshelf, 110
Cowan, George, 31–32
Cowboy songs and range ballads, 61
Cowboy Village Resort at Togwotee, 89, 90
Coyote Roadhouse, 211
Crandell Campground, 217
Craters of the Moon National Monument, 276–77, **276**;
    Cave Area, 277; Devils Orchard, 277; geology, 238;
    Inferno Cone, 277; Spatter Cones, 277
Creamery Bed & Breakfast, The, 257, 284
Creekside Inn, 205
Creston Country Inn Bed & Breakfast, 211
Creston Fish Hatchery, 175
Creston Motel, 199
Crossed Sabres Ranch, 59, 102
Crouch, Idaho, 258
Crow Indians, 138–39
Crown of the Continent, 148
Crystal Park Picnic Area, 156
Cunningham Cabin Historic Site, 45
Curley's Broiler, 206

Curtis Canyon Campground, 93
Curtis Canyon, 42
Custer Motorway Adventure Road, 278–79
Cut Bank Campground, 187, 217

Dalton's Big Sky Stables, 109
Daly Mansion, 162–63
Dan Bailey's Fly Shop, **319**
Dances With Wolves, 172
Danny On National Recreation Trail, 177
Danskin Station, 258
Darby Historic Center of the Forest Service, 162
Darby Trading Post, 162
Darby, Montana, 162
Dark Horse Books, 118
Darkhorse Cafe and Saloon, 280
Darwin Ranch, 92
David T. Vernon Indian Arts Collection, 49
Davis, "Uncle Jack," 33
Davy Jackson Inn, 89
Days Inn, 103
Days of Yore, 224
Dead Indian Campground, 63
Deadwater Picnic Ground, 281
Debris L.T.D., 227
Decker Flat Road, 267
Deer Crossing Bed & Breakfast, 203
Depot, The, 206
Desperado's, 296
destination ski resorts, 305
Devil's Slide, 69, **70**
Devil Creek Campground, 188
DeVoto Memorial Grove, 246
Diamond "P" Ranch, 114
Diamond Hitch Outfitters, 201
Diamond K Chuckwagon, 217
Dickey Bridge Recreation Area, 158
dike, 47
Dillon KOA, 200
Dillon, Montana, 153; bicycling, 201; campgrounds and
    RV parks, 200–201; fishing, 201; food, 201; horse-
    back riding, 201; hot springs, 202; lodging, 199–200;
    shopping, 202; skiing, 202; telephone numbers, 202
Discovery Basin, 198, 227
Dog Sled Adventures, 220
Dollar Mountain (skiing), 299
Donnelly, Idaho, 257
Donut Seed, 227
Doreen's Family Restaurant, 226
Dornans', 48
Double Arrow, 168
Double J Western Wear, 260
Doug Allard's Flathead Indian Museum, 172
Driggs, Don Carlos, 35
Driggs, Idaho, 87
Driving, 306–8
Dublin Gulch Antiques, 227
Duchin Bar & Lounge, 294
Duck Inn, 212
Dumas Old Time Photography Antique Mall, 194, 227
Dunraven Pass, 56

Eagle's Store, 74, 115
Eagle Bend Golf Club, 219
Eagle Fishing Charters, 174
Easley Campground, 270
Easley Hot Springs, 270
East Fork Recreation Area, 280
East Glacier Park, 188
Ecosystems, Glacier National Park, 127–33
Edelweiss, 107
Edgerton, Sidney, 145
Egg Mountain, 189
Ekstrom's Stage Station Campground, 205
Elephant's Perch, The, 299
Elephant Head Lodge, 59, 102
Elk Bend Hot Springs, 280
Elk Bend, Idaho, 280
Elk City Ranger District, 249
Elk City Wagon Road, 249
Elk City, Idaho, 249
Elk Mountain RV Resort & Cafe, 291
Elk Park, 72
Elk Ridge, 65
Elkhorn Golf Club, 297
Elkhorn Hot Springs, 156, 202
Elkhorn Resort, 293
Elkhorn RV Ranch, 205
Elkhorn, Montana, 192
Emily A. Bed and Breakfast, 209
Emma Matilda, 49
Ennis, Montana, 197
Epley's Whitewater Adventures, 288
Ernest Hemingway Memorial, 274, **274**
Essex, Montana, 189
Ezra Pound, 275

Fairfield Inn by Marriott, 81, 105
Fairmont Hot Springs Resort, 227
Fairy Lake Campground, 107
Federation of Fly Fishers, 67
Fighting Bear Antiques, 100
Finley Point Campground, 174
Firehole Ranch, 111
Fish Creek Campground, 179, 217
Fish Technology Center, 109
Fishaus, 204
Fisher Creek Road, 268
Fishing Bridge, 53
Fishing Bridge, Wyoming, 58
fishing: in Bozeman, Montana, 108–9; in Dillon,
    Montana, 201; in Hamilton, Montana, 204; in Helena,
    Montana, 224; in McCall, Idaho, 287; in Missoula,
    Montana, 208; in Stanley, Idaho, 292; in Sun Valley,
    Idaho, 297; in West Yellowstone, Montana, 113
Fishtail, Montana, 66
Flagg Ranch Resort, 50, 93
Flat Creek Motel, 89
Flathead Indians, 137, 140–41; reservation, 171
Flathead Lake, 174
Flathead Music Festival, 219
Flathead National Forest Rental Cabins, 212
Flathead Valley Golf Association, 219

Flathead, Montana, 170, 171–75
Food for Thought, 206
For Whom the Bell Tolls, (Hemingway), 274
Forest Davis Freight & Carriage Co., 174
Fort Benton, founding, 140
Fort Remon, founding, 138
Fort Yellowstone, 68
Fountain Paint Pots, 72
Four Corners, 80
Four Winds Trading Post, 172
4-B's, 206
Frank Church–River of No Return Wilderness, 231
Fred's Mesquite Grill, 107, **108**
Freddy's Feed & Read, 209
Free Enterprise Health Mine, The, 192
Freeheel & Wheel, 114
Frontier Anglers, 201
Frontier Montana Museum, 190

Galena Lodge, 270; skiing, 299
Galena Stage Stop Corrals, 298
Galena Summit, 268, 269
Gallatin County Pioneer Museum, 81
Gallatin Gateway Inn, 80, 105
Gallatin Gateway, 80
Gallatin National Forest Recreational Cabins, 105
Gallatin Petrified Forest, 71
Gallatin River, **78**; naming of, 136
Gallatin Riverguides, 108
Galleria Shops, Sun Valley, 300
Galleria Wine & Espresso Bar, 300
Garden Valley, 258
Garden Wall Inn, 177, 212
Gardiner, Montana, 68
Garnet Ghost Town, 168
Garnet Range Road, 168
Gates of the Mountains Recreation Area, 190
Gatiss Gardens, 175
geology: aa, 238; Absaroka breccias, 8; arêtes, 128;
    asthenosphere, 234–35; basement rocks, 10; basin and
    range faulting, 237; Borah Peak earthquake, 234;
    Boulder batholith, 236; breccia, 8; Central Idaho,
    234–39; cirques, 10, 128; cone geysers, 13; Craters of
    the Moon National Monument, 238; Cretaceous
    rocks, 127–28; extrusive igneous rock, 7; faults, 9–10;
    folded range, 10; Fountain geysers, 13; geothermal
    features, 13; glacial erratics, 156–57; Glacial Lake
    Missoula, 132–33; glacial outwash, 11; Glacier
    National Park, 127–33; glaciers, 127–29; gneisses, 10;
    Great Rift, 238; hanging valleys, 128; horns, 10, 128;
    Idaho batholith, 235; kettles, 11; lateral moraines, 11;
    lithospheric plates, 234; magma, 6; Missoula Valley,
    132–33; mylonite, 235; obsidian, 7; Old Faithful, 13;
    pahoehoe, 238; plate tectonics, 234; Precambrian rock
    formations, 127–28, **128**; resurgent caldera, 6; resur-
    gent domes, 7; rift zone, 238; Sawtooth Mountains,
    238–39; schists, 10; Seven Devils, 235; temperature
    inversions, 129; terminal moraines, 11; thermal man-
    tle plume, 7; thrust faults, 235; trench, 235; U-shaped
    valleys, 128; Washburn Range, 8; weather, 128–29;
    welded tuff, 8; Yellowstone's Central Plateau, 8;

Yellowstone Caldera, 7; Yellowstone volcanoes, 6–7; Yellowstone–Teton Country, 6–14
Georgetown Lake, 198
Geyser Whitewater Expeditions, 109
Ghost Town Hall of Fame, 190
Gibbon Falls Picnic Area, 72
Gibbon Falls, 72
Gibbonsville, Idaho, 282
Gibson Reservoir, 190
glacial erratics, 156–57
Glacial Lake Missoula, geology, 132–33
Glacier Cyclery, 218
Glacier Gateway Rodeo, 220
Glacier Maze, 180
Glacier National Park, 179, 180–86; bill signed into law, 148; ecosystems, 127–33; Going-to-the-Sun Road, 181–86; Lake McDonald, **179**, 182; lodging, campgrounds and RV parks, food, and activities. *See* Whitefish, Montana; Many Glacier area, 186; number of visitors, 124; Triple Divide Peak, 186; weather, 128–29; West Glacier, 180–81; wildlife, 127, 130, 132
Glacier Park Lodge, 188, 215
Glacier View Golf Club, 180
Glacier View Turnout, 45
Glacier-Gold Country, 121–26
glaciers: Glacier Lake Missoula, 132–33; Glacier National Park, 127–29
Glen's Cafe, 164
Gnose Mercantile, 158
Goat Haunt Ranger Station, 187
Goat Lick, 189
Going-to-the-Sun (Natos'i At'apoo) Sun Tours, 221
Going-to-the-Sun Peak, 186
Going-to-the-Sun Road, 148, 181–86
Gold Fork Park N' Ski Area, 261
Gold: panning, 224; robbers, 142–43; strikes, 141–44; in Idaho, 241–42, 243
Golden Eagle Lodge, 104
Golden Gate, 71
Golden Pheasant, The, 206
Golden RV Park, 285
Goldsmith's Inn, 205
golfing: in Bozeman, Montana; 109; in Jackson Hole, Wyoming; 99; in McCall, Idaho, 289; in Missoula, Montana, 208; in Sun Valley, Idaho, 298; in Teton Valley, 118; in Whitefish, Montana, 219
Governor's Cup, 224
Granary, The, 87, 94
Grand Hotel, 66
Grand Loop, 51
Grand Targhee Ski & Summer Resort, 87, 117, **118**
Grand Teton Lodge Company, 90
Grand Teton Music Festival, 96
Grand Teton National Park (GTNP), 39, 42; auto and foot tour, 42–50; bicycling, 96; Grand Teton, 43; Middle Teton, 43; Mormon Row, 34–35; South Teton, 43
Grand Teton Park KOA, 93
Grand Teton, 43; first photos, 28; first summited, 28–29; origin of name, 29–30
Grand Valley Lodging, 115

Grandjean, Idaho, 262
Grandview Canyon, 278
Grandview Point Trail, 55
Grangeville, Idaho, 249
Granit Mountain Mine Memorial, 194
Granite Creek Campground, 93
Granite Hot Springs, 97
Granite Park Chalet, 183
Granny's Attic, 290
Grant Village, 52, 101
Grant-Kohrs Ranch National Historic Site, 190
Grasshopper Inn, 156
Grassy Lake Roard, 50
Gravelly Range, 151
Gravity Sports, 286, 288
Great Bear Wilderness Area, 169
Great Divide Cyclery, 224, 227
Great Divide Ski Area, 224
Great Divide, The, (Dunraven), 36
Great Harvest Bread Company, 107
Great Montana Adventure Company, The, 221
Great Norther Brewing Company, 218, **218**
Great Northern Bar & Grill, 217
Great Northern Railroad locomotive, **147**
Great Northern Railroad, 147
Great Northern Whitewater, 220
Great Rocky Mountain Toy Company, 110
Greater Yellowstone Ecosystem (GYE), 3
Greek Creek Campground, 107
Greene Valley Resort, 261
Greenough Park, 167
Gregson Fairmont Hot Springs, 197
Gretchen's Restaurant, 294
Grey Wolf Retreat, 112
Greyhouse Inn, 281
Grinnell Glacier Overlook, 184
Grinnell, George Bird, 146–47, 148
Grizzly Bar, 66
Grizzly Discovery Center, 74
Grizzly Hackle, 208
Grizzly Outfitters, 108
Grizzly RV Park, 113
Gros Ventre Campgrounds, 44
Gros Ventre Mountains, 44
Gros Ventre River, 44
Gros Ventre Slide Geological Area, 44
Gros Ventre Wilderness, 44
Grouse Campground, 286
Grouse Mountain Lodge, 213
guest and dude ranches, 92, 102
Guleke, Harry, 243–44
Gun Barrel Steak and Game House, The, 94
Gunsight Lake, 186
Gunsight Pass–Sperry Chalet Trail, 183
Gusher Pizza and Sandwich Shoppe, 113

H & J Saloon and Cafe, 158
Hamilton Golf Club, 162
Hamilton, Montana, 162; campgrounds and RV parks, 203; fishing, 204; food, 203–4; hot springs, 204; lodging, 202–3; skiing, 204; telephone numbers, 204

Hamilton: A Public House, The, 203
Hanging Gardens, 185
Hargrave Cattle & Guest Ranch, 213
Harriman State Park, 85
Harriman, Averell W., 244–45
Hartland Inn, 251
Harvest Moon Market & Delicatessen, 286
Hatchet Campground, 93
Hauser Lake, 192
Hayden Valley, **54**, 55
Hayden, Dr. Ferdinand Vandiveer, 27–28; Hayden's
    Survey, 28; Second Hayden Survey, 28
Hazard Lake Campground, 286
Heart Six Ranch, 92
heat exhaustion and heat stroke, 310
Heaven's Gate Lookout, 250
Heaven's Gate Scenic Trail, 250
Heavy Runner Peak, 186
Heidelberg Inn, 293
Helena Campground and RV Park, 223
Helena, Montana: bicycling, 224; campgrounds and RV
    parks, 223; fairs, festivals, and events, 224; fishing,
    224; food, 223–24; founding, 143–44; lodging,
    222–23; shopping, 224–25; sights, 191–93; skiing,
    224; telephone numbers, 225
Helende Campground, 262
Hell's Canyon National Recreation Area, 250
Hell's Canyon, depth, 231
Hellgate Canyon, 164
Hellroaring Saloon and Eatery, 217
Hemingway, Ernest, 232, 274; Memorial, **274**; *For
    Whom the Bell Tolls, 274*
Hermitage Point, 49
Hibernation House, 212
Hibernation Station, 112
Hidden Lake Overlook, 186
Hidden Lake Trail, 185
Hide Out Leather Apparel, 100
High Mountain Heli-Skiing, 98
Highlands Golf Club, 167, 208
Highline Trail, 184
hiking: in Bozeman, Montana, 110; in McCall, Idaho,
    287; in Stanley, Idaho, 293; in Sun Valley, Idaho, 298;
    in Teton Valley, 118; in Whitefish, Montana, 219
Hildreth Livestock Ranch, 200
Historical Museum at Fort Missoula, 167
Historical Walking Tour (Whitefish, Montana), 221
Hob Nob Cafe, 206
Hogan Cabin, 160
Holiday Inn Missoula Parkside, 205
Holiday Inn, Bozeman, 105
Holland Lake Lodge, 209
Holter Lake, 192
Holter Museum of Art, 191
Holton's of Helena, 224
Home Town Sports, 287, 288
Homo sapiens, first appearance of in Yellowstone-Teton
    region, 15
Hood Creek Campgrounds, 107
Hoodoos, The, 71
Hornet Peak Lookout, 178

Hornet Peak, 178
Horse Sweat Pass, 248
horseback riding: in Bozeman, Montana, 109; in Dillon,
    Montana, 201; in Jackson Hole, Wyoming, 97; in
    McCall, Idaho, 287; in Stanley, Idaho, 292; in Sun
    Valley, Idaho, 298; in West Yellowstone, Montana,
    113; in Whitefish, Montana, 219
Horseshoe Bend, Idaho, 258–59
hot springs: in Butte, Montana, 227; in Dillon,
    Montana, 202; in Hamilton, Montana, 204; in Idaho,
    233; in Jackson Hole, Wyoming, 97; in McCall,
    Idaho, 287; in Missoula, Montana, 208; in Stanley,
    Idaho, 292
Hotel McCall, 253, 283, **284**
Howard, General Oliver Otis, 30
Hubbard's Ponderosa Lodge, 205
Huff House Inn Bed and Breakfast, 89
Hungry Horse Dam Visitor Center, 180
Hungry Horse News, **180**
Hunter Peak Campground, 63
hunting season, 310
Huntley Lodge and Shoshone Condominium Hotel, 104
hypothermia, 310

Idaho City Hotel, 260
Idaho City Ranger District, 260
Idaho City, Idaho, 259–60
Idaho Country Inn Bed and Breakfast, 294
Idaho Country Store, 300
Idaho Organic Act, 242–43
Idaho Rocky Mountain Ranch, 268, 290
Idaho State Centennial Trail, 247
Idaho Territory, 242–43
Indian Creek Guest Ranch, 281
Indian Post Office, 248
Inn at Jackson Hole, The, 91
Inn at Old Faithful, **72,** 72–74
Inside North Fork Road, 179
Inspiration Point, 47
International Chorale Festival, 207
International Wildlife Film Festival, 207
Irish Times Pub, 195
Irma Grill, The, 103
Irma, The, 59, 103
Iron Creek Campground, 264
Iroquois Indians, 140
Irving's Red Hots, 296
Irving, Washington, 25–27
Island Lake Campground, 64
Island Park Lodge, 85
Island Park, Idaho, **36**, 83; Sawtell Peak, 83; lodging,
    campgrounds, food, activities. *See* West Yellowstone
Izaak Walton Inn, 189, 214

Jackson Glacier Overlook, 186
Jackson Hole Historical Society & Museum, 41
Jackson Hole Iditerod Sled Dog Tours, 98
Jackson Hole Kayak School, 97
Jackson Hole Mountain Resort, 97
Jackson Hole Pub & Brewery, 95
Jackson Hole Trail Rides, 97

Jackson Hole, Wyoming, 39–42; bicycling, 96; camp-grounds and RV parks, 92–94; fairs, festivals, and events, 96–97; food, 93–95; horseback riding, 96; hot springs, 97; lodging, 88–93; microbreweries, 95–96; other activities, 99–100; river floating, 97; shopping, 100; skiing, 97–98; telephone numbers, 100–101; winter tours, 98–99
Jackson Hot Springs Lodge, 202
Jackson Hot Springs, 158
Jackson Lake Dam, 45
Jackson Lake Lodge, 49, 90
Jackson Lake, 49
Jackson, David E., 24
Jackson, Montana, 158
Jackson, Town Square, **40**
Jackson, William Henry, 27; first photos of Grand Teton, 28
Jackson, Wyoming, 39–42, 83. *See also* Jackson Hole
Jacob's Island Park Ranch, 112
Jane's Holiday House, 300
Jedediah's House of Sourdough, 94
Jefferson River, naming of, 136
Jellystone RV Park, 205
Jenny Lake Campground, 93
Jenny Lake Lodge, 47, 90
Jenny Lake, origins of name, 35
Jenny Leigh's, 94
Jerry Johnson Hot Springs, 247
Jesse's, 293
Jesuits, 140–41
Jewel Basin Hiking Area, 175
Jim Bridger Motor Court, 68
Joe's Pastry Shop, 193, 226
John Bozeman's Bistro, 107
John D. Rockefeller Jr. Parkway Campground, 93
John L. Clarke Western Art Gallery and Memorial Museum, 188
Johnson Saddlery, 202
Johnson, John ("Liver Eatin'"), 62; cabin of, **65**
Jorgenson's Holiday Motel, 223
Jumping Rainbow Ranch, 67

K-Bar-Z Guest Ranch, 63
Kalispell, Montana, 175
Kandahar Lodge, 212
Kelly Warm Springs, 45
Ketchum Grill, 296
Ketchum Kayak School, 298
Ketchum Kitchens, 300
Ketchum Korral, 294
Ketchum Wagon Days, 297
Ketchum, Idaho, 270, origins, 244
Ketchum-Sun Valley Heritage and Ski Museum, 298
kettles, 46
Kibler and Kirch, 65
Kim Williams Nature Trail, 165
King Mountain Launch Site, 277
King Ranch Golf Course, 208
Kinta Lake Campground, 217
Kintla Lake, 179
Kirkham Campground, 262

Kirkpatrick Custom Hat Company, 158, 202
Kitchen, The, 296
Knob Hill Inn, 294
Knotty Pine, 116
KOA Butte Campground, 226
KOA El-Mar Kampground, 205
KOA Kampground, 103
Konditorei, 274, 294
krummholz, 131
KwaTaqNuk Resort, 174

La Salle R.V. Park & Campground, 216
La Trattoria Italian Restaurant, 203
La Villa Montana, 213
Ladysmith Campground, 226
Lake Butte Overlook, 58
Lake Creek Campground, 63
Lake Fork Campground, 285
Lake Fork Mercantile, 257
Lake Lodge Cabins, 101
Lake Mary Ronan, 174
Lake McDonald Lodge Complex, 182–83, 215
Lake McDonald, 182, **179**
Lake Village, 53
Lake Yellowstone Hotel & Cabins, 53, 101
Lakeside, Montana, 175
Lakeview, 151, 152
Lamar Valley, 56
Lame Duck Chinese Restaurant, 94
Land of Magic Dinner Club, 82
Land of the Yankee Fork Visitor Center, 278, **279**
Land of the Yankee Fork, 266
Langford, Nathaniel P., 27, 37; Washburn-Doane-Langford Expedition, 27
Langhor Campgrounds, 107
Larchmont Golf Course, 208
Lardo's Restaurant & Saloon, 286
Last Chance Campground, 251, 285
Last Chance Gulch (Helena), 192; gold strike, 143
Last Chance Tour Train, 192
Last of the Mountain Men, The, 233
Latter-day Saints, 33–35; arrival in Jackson Hole, 33–34; at Fort Lehmi, Idaho, 241; in Franklin, Idaho, 241; Mormon Row, 34–35
Leaf and Bean, The, 81
Leatherman Peak, 278
Lee Creek Campground, 206
Lee Metcalf National Wildlife Refuge, 163
LeHardy Rapids, 54
Lehrkind Mansion Bed & Breakfast, 105, **106**
Leigh Lake, origins of name, 35
Leigh, Richard ("Beaver Dick"), 35; death, 35; Hayden Survey of 1872, 35; Jenny Lake, 35; Leigh Lake, 35
Les Mason Park, 178, 222
Lewis & Clark Campground, 206
Lewis & Clark Diorama, 154
Lewis & Clark, 159; Expedition, 22, 134–37, 240–41, 246; *Map of Lewis and Clark's Track Across the Western Portion of North America From from the Mississippi to the Pacific,* (Clark), 23
Lewis and Clark Caverns State Park, 197

Lewis and Clark Highway, 246
*Lewis and Clark Meeting the Flathead Indians at Ross'
   Hole,* (Russell), 137
Lewis and Clark National Historic Trail, 155
Lewis Lake Campground, 52
Lewis, Meriwether, 134–37, 240
Lewiston, Idaho, origins, 242
Liberty Theatre, 275
Lick Creek Campground, 203
Lift Tower Lodge, 294
Linda Vista Golf Course, 208
Lindley House Bed & Breakfast, 105
Lindley Park, 81
Lion's Den Campground, 196
Little Bear Lake, 64
Little Joe, 157
Little Ski Hill, 252, 288
Livingston Bar and Grill, 67
Livingston Depot Center, 67
Livingston, Montana, 65, 67
Lizard Creek Campground, 50, 93
Lochsa Historical Ranger Station, 248
Lochsa Lodge, 248
Lochsa Selway Outback, 246
Loco's Burrito Bus, 206
Lodge at Jackson Hole, The, 89
Lodge at Potosoi, The, 197
Lodge Dining Room, 294
Lodgepole Campground, 157
Logging Creek Campground, 217
Lolo Hot Springs Resort, 164
Lolo Hot Springs, 208
Lolo Motorway, 248
Lolo Pass Winter Sports Area, 209
Lolo Pass, 164, 246
Lolo Trail, 247
Lolo, Montana, 164
Lone Mountain Ranch, 104, 110
Lone Wolf Saloon, 162
Lonesomehurst Campground, 113
Longhorn Saloon & Grill, Dillon, 201
Longhorn Saloon & Restaurant, Banks, 258
Loon's Echo Resort and Fish Farm, 213
Lost Creek Ranch, 92
Lost Creek State Park, 198
Lost Horizon Dinner Club, 116
Lost River Ranger District, 277
Lost Rivers Museum, 277
Lost Trail Hot Springs Resort, 204
Lost Trail Hot Springs, 160
Lost Trail Powder Mountain, 160, 204
Louisiana Territory, 134
Lower Geyser Basin, 72
Lower Two Medicine, 188
Lowman Ranger District, 262
Lowman Stage Shop, 262
Lowman, Idaho, 262
Lubrecht State Experimental Forest, 168
Ludlow, Captain William, 37
Lunch in the Park, 165
Lydia's Supper Club, 226

M&S Meats, 175
Ma Barnes Country Market, 156
MacDonald Pass (skiing), 224
MacDonald Pass Campground, 223
Mackay Reservoir, 277
Mackay, Idaho, 277
MacKenzie River Pizza Co., 107, 206
Mad Dog Ranch Cabins, 92
Mad Wolf Mountains, 187
Madison Arm Campground and Resort, 77, 113
Madison Buffalo Jump State Park, 82–83
Madison Canyon Earthquake Area, 77
Madison Crossing (retail), 115
Madison Junction, 72
Madison River Outfitters, 114
Madison River, naming of, 136
Magruder Corridor, 249, origins of name, 243
Magruder Massacre, 243
Magruder, Lloyd, 243
Mai Wah, 194
Main Stop Gallery of Original Art, 227
Mammoth Hot Springs Hotel and Cabins, 101
Mammoth Hot Springs, 71
Mammoth Hot Springs, Wyoming, 67, 68
Mangy Moose Emporium, 100
Many Glacier Campground, 217
Many Glacier Hotel, 215-16
Many Glacier, 186
Marias Pass, 188
Marias River, naming of, 137
Marina Cay Resort, 211
Marshall Mountain (skiing), 208
Maverick Mountain RV Park, 200-201
Maverick Mountain, 156, 202
Maxwell's, 103
May Creek Campground, 160
McCall Brewing Company, 257, 286
McCall Campground, 285
McCall Fish Hatchery, 253
McCall Fold Music Festival, 287
McCall, Idaho, 246, 252–53, 257; bicycling, 286–87;
   campgrounds and RV parks, 285–86; fairs, festivals,
   and events, 287; fire, **255**; fishing, 287; food, 286;
   hiking, 287; horseback riding, 287; hot springs, 287;
   lodging, 283–84; microbreweries, 286; other activi-
   ties, 289; river floating, 288; shopping, 289–290; ski-
   ing, 288; telephone numbers, 290
McCoy's Tackle & Gift Shop, 292
Meadow Creek Gold & Field Club, 251
Meadow Lake Golf Resort, 219
Meadow Lake, 180, 213
Meadows RV Park, 251, 285
Medicine Tree, 161
Melrose, Montana, **200**
Menors Ferry, 48
Merry Piglets, 95
Mesa Falls Scenic Byway, 85
Michel's Christiania Restaurant and Olympic Bar, 296
Middle Fork Clearwater Wild and Scenic River, 247
Middle Fork River Expeditions, 292
Middle Fork River Tours, Inc., 298

Middle Teton, 43
Midway Geyser Basin, 72
Mike's Eats, 116, **117**
Mike Harris Campground, 116
Million Dollar Cowboy Bar, 42
Million Dollar Cowboy Steakhouse, 95
Miner Lake Campground, 201
Miner Lake, 158
Mineral Museum, 194
Miners Exchange Saloon, 260
mining, 193–96; lead and silver, 244
Miracle of America Museum, 174
Mission Mountain Country Club, 173
Mission Mountain Winery, 175
Mission Mountains Wilderness, 169
Mission Mountains, 172
Mission Valley, Montana, 170–71
missionaries, 241
Missoula Children's Theatre, 210
Missoula Pendleton Shop, 209
Missoula Valley, geology, 132–33
Missoula, Montana, 164–67, 168, 170; bicycling, 207;
    campgrounds and RV parks, 205–6; development,
    123, 126; fairs, festivals, and events, 207–8; fishing,
    208; food, 206–7; golf, 208; hot springs, 208; lodg-
    ing, 204–5; shopping, 209–10; skiing, 208–9; tele-
    phone numbers, 210; theater, 210
Missouri Headwaters State Park, 83
Molly's Tubs, 257
Monida, Montana, 152
Montana Candy Emporium, 65
Montana Coffee Traders, 177, 217
Montana Historical Society, 191
Montana Law Enforcement Museum, 190
Montana Raft Company, 220
Montana Shakespeare in the Park, 109
Montana Snowbowl, 209
Montana State University, 80
Montana Territory, passage of bill, 145
Montana Traditional Jazz Festival, 224
Montana Trails Gallery, 111
Montana Travel Planner, 199
Montana Troutfitters, 108
Montana Woolen Shop, 80
Montana, statehood, 145–46
Monte Dolack Gallery, 209
Moose Creek Flat Campground, 107
Moose Head Ranch, 92
Moose Junction, 45
Moran Junction, 45
Mormon Bend Campground, 265
Mormon Gulch Campground, 226
Mormon Row, 34–35; *Shane,* 34–35; *Spencer's Mountain,*
    35
Morrison Jeep Trail, 64
Mortimer Gulch National Recreation Trail, 190
mosquitos, 309
Motel 6, in Helena, 223; in Jackson Hole, 89
Mother Lode Theater, 227–28
Mount Brown Lookout Trail, 183
Mount Fleecer, 197

Mount Haggin Nordic Ski Area, 227
Mount Haggin Recreation Area, 158
Mount Helena, Montana, 192
Mount Moran, 43
Mount Owen, 43
Mount Sentinel, 164
Mount St. John, 43
Mount Washburn, 56
mountain biking, in Yankee Jim Canyon, 69–71
Mountain Cycle & Snowboard, 288
mountain elevations, 124
Mountain Glory Coffee House, 204
Mountain High Pizza Pie, 95
mountain lions, 309
Mountain Monkey Business, 290
Mountain Timbers Wilderness Lodge, 214
Mountain View Campground, 262
Mountain Village Lodge, 264
Mountain Village Mercantile, 264
Mountain Village Resort, 290
Mountain Village Restaurant, 264
Mountaineering Outfitters, 119
Mt. Heyburn, 267
Mud Volcano, 54
Murray Hotel, 67
Museum of the National Park Ranger, 71
Museum of the Plains Indian, 188
Museum of the Rockies, 81
Museum of the Yellowstone, 74
Mustard Seed, The, 207
MV *International,* 187

Nancy P's Baking Company, 113
National Bison Range, 173
National Elk Refuge, 41–42, **41**, 98
National Geographic IMAX Theatre, 74
National Parks Postcard and Antique Show, 109
National Wildlife Art Museum, 41
Native Americans, 125
Natural Bridge Bike and Hike Trail, 53
Nelson's Spring Creek Ranch, 67
New Haven Lodge, 262
New Meadows, Idaho, 251
Nez Perce Indians, 30, 242; Chief Joseph, 30, 32; reser-
    vation, 249; treaties 30
Nez Perce Motel, 158
Nine Mile House, 170
Ninemile Remount Depot, 170–71
Ninepipe National Wildlife Refuge, 172
1920 House Bed & Breakfast, 283
No Place Like Home, 300
No Sweat Cafe, 223
Nora's Fish Creek Inn, 95
Norris Camground, 71
Norris Geyser Basin Museum, 72
Norris Geyser Basin, 71
Norris, Philetus W., 37
Norris, Wyoming, 67
North American Indian Days, 188
North Beach Unit, Ponderosa State Park, 254
North Fork Campground, 270

North Fork Hostel and Square Peg Ranch, 178, 214
North Fork Ranger Station, 281
North Fork, Idaho, 281
North Fork, Montana, lodging, campgrounds and RV parks, food, and activities. *See* Whitefish, Montana
North Forty Resort, 213
North Rim Drive, 55
North Valley and Wood River Trails (skiing), 299
North Van Houten, 158
Northern Lights Saloon, 179, 217
Northern Lights Trading Company, 111
Northern Pines Golf Club, 219
Northern Rockies Natural History (tours), 110
Northwest Passage Bed & Breakfast, 284

O'Brien Campground, 280
O'Duachain Country Inn, 211
Obsidian Cliff, 71
Old Butte, 196–98
Old Faithful Geyser, 72, 67, 71
Old Faithful Inn, 101
Old Faithful Snow Lodge and Old Faithful Lodge Cabins, 101
Old Montana Prison, 190
Old North Trail, 146
Old Number 1, 194
Old Post Pub, The, 207
Old Town Cafe, 114
Old Trail Museum, 190
Old West Cinema Gallery and Gifts, 202
Old Works Golf Course, 197
Olive Glenn Golf & Country Club, 103
On Broadway, 223
100 Acre Wood Bed & Breakfast, 282
Open Road Bicycles & Nordic Equipment, 207
Ore Wagon Museum, 298
Oregon Short Line Restaurant, 114
Original Governor's Mansion, 191
Orofino, Idaho, 249
Otto Brothers' Brewing Company, 87, 95
Our Lady of the Rockies Bus Tours, 228
Outpost Campground, 205
outwash plain, 46
Overlook Stream, Glacier National Park, **181**
Owen, William O., 28–29, 33
Owl Cocktail Lounge, 67
Oxford, The, 207

Pablo, Montana, 173
Packer John's Cabin Park, 251
Pahaska Tepee, 59, 102
Pahaska-Sunlight Trail, 59
Painted Buffalo Inn, 89
Painted Rocks Reservoir, 161
Painted Rocks State Park Campground, 203
Painted Rocks State Park, 162
Painter's Store, 63
Palisades Campground, 65–66
Papa's & Granny's Guest House, 66
Parade Rest Guest Ranch, 114
Paradise Valley, Montana, 67

Park Avenue Bakery, 223
Park Cafe, Glacier National Park, 186
Park Creek Campground, 295
Park Lake Campground, 223
Park Plaza Hotel, 223
Parkway Inn Best Western, 89
Parrot Confectionery, The, 192, 225
Patagonia Outlet Store, 153, 202
Pattee Canyon Recreation Area, 209
Paul's Market, 290
Paul's Pancake Parlor & Cafe, 207
Payette Lakes Fine Arts & Crafts Fair, 287
Payette Lakes Ski Marathon, 287
Payette River Company, 298
Payette River Scenic Byway, 257
peak travel times, 303
Pekin Noodle Parlor, 226
People's Center, The, 173
Perugia, 207
Peterson, Harold, 233
Petit Lake, 269
Petunia's by Cindy Owings, 111
Phi Kappa Campground, 295
Pickle Barrel, 107
Pierre's Playhouse, 118
Pine Butte Guest Ranch, 189
Pine Butte Swamp Reserve, 189
Pine Creek Campground, 116
Pine Creek, 67
Pines Motel and Guest Haus, 115
Pinnacle Inn, 294
Pioneer Cabin, 298
Pioneer Mountains National Scenic Byway Campgrounds, 201
Pioneer Mountains National Scenic Byway, 155–57
Pioneer Saloon, 296
Pipestone Mountaineering, Inc., 227
Pishkun Reservoir, 190
Placerville, Idaho, 259
Placid Lake, 168
Plaza Grill, 293–94
Plummer, Henry, 143
Pointer Scenic Cruises, 212
Polaris, Montana, 156
Pole, Pedal, Paddle, 96
Polebridge Mercantile, 179, 222
Polebridge, Montana, 177–79
Pollard Hotel, 65
Polson, Montana, 174
Polson-Flathead Historical Museum, 174
Ponderosa Campground, 103, 285
Ponderosa Pine Scenic Byway, 260
Ponderosa State Park, 256; campground, 286; skiing, 288
Pony, Montana, 197
Poor Richard's News, 111
Pork Chop John's, 226
Port Polson Princess, 174
Potomac Country Store, 168
Povey Pensione, 295
Powell Ranger District, 247
Powell, Idaho, 247

Prairie Rose (retail), 104
Premier Properties, 294
Prince of Wales Hotel, 187, 216

Quake Lake, 77
Quality Inn Pine Lodge, 213–14
Quartz Creek Campground, 179, 217
Quinn's Paradise Resort, 173

Race to the Sky Sled Dog Race, 224
radiocarbon dating, 16
Rainbow Point Campground, 113
Rainbow Ranch Lodge, 104
Ram Restaurant and Bar, 294
Ranch Kitchen, The, 68
Rancho Los Arcos, 226
Range The, (restaurant), 95
Rattlesnake National Recreation Area and Wilderness, 166
rattlesnakes, 308–9
Raynolds Mountain, 185
Red Cliff Campground, 106
Red Lion Wyoming Inn, 90
Red Lodge Ski Mountain Resort, 65
Red Lodge, Montana, 58, 64, 65–66
Red Meadow Lake Campground, 216
Red Meadow Lake, 178
Red Rick Ranch, 92
Red River Hot Springs, 249
Red Rock Inn, 200
Red Rock Lakes National Wildlife Refuge, 151
Red Rock Pass, 150
Redfish Lake Area Campgrounds, 292
Redfish Lake Corrals, 292
Redfish Lake Lodge, 267, 290
Redfish Lake, 264, 266–67, **267**
Redfish Visitor Center, 267
Reeder's Alley, 192
Rendezvous Ski Tours & Guest House, 117
Rendezvous Trail System, 114
Riddle Lake, 52
Ride the Reds, 222
Riggins, Idaho, 250
Rising Sun Campground, 186, 217
Rising Sun Motor Inn, 216
River Park Gold Course & RV Campground, 277
River Runs Through It, A, (Maclean), 77, 132
River Street Inn, 294
Riverside Campground, 265
Riverside Park, 174
RJ Cain and Company Outfitters, 108
road conditions, 308
Road Kill Cafe, 67
Roaring Mountain, 71
Robert E. Lee Campground, 261
Rock Creek Resort, 65
Rock Creek Testicle Festival, 208
Rockin' Rudy's, 165, 209
Rocky Knob Lodge, 161
Rocky Mountain Elk Foundation, 165
Rod & Gun Club, 264

rodeos, in Cody, Wyoming, 103; in Whitefish, Montana, 220
Romano's Ristorante, 286
Ronan, Montana, 173
Roosevelt Arch, 69
Roosevelt Lodge Cabins, 56, 101
Roscoe, Montana, 66
Rose's Cantina, 158
Ross' Hole, origins, 137
Roundup, The, (retail), 100
RU Outside, 119
Running Eagle Falls, 188
Rush's Lakeview Guest Ranch, 200

Sacajawea, 136
Sacajawea Inn, 83
Salmon Hot Springs, 281
Salmon Lake State Park, 168
Salmon River Campground & RV Park, 265, 280
Salmon River Canyon Campgrounds, 292
Salmon River Experience, 288
Salmon River Lodge, 264, 281, 291
Salmon River Scenic Byway, 264
Salmon River, 231; first commercial use, 243–44
Salmon, Idaho, 280, 281–82
Sanders Bed and Breakfast, 191, 223
Sawmill Campground, 295
Sawtell Peak, 84
Sawtell Resort, 84
Sawtooth City, Idaho, 269
Sawtooth Club, 296
Sawtooth Fish Hatchery, 268
Sawtooth Hotel, 291
Sawtooth Lake, 264
Sawtooth Lodge, 262
Sawtooth Mountains, geology, 238–39
Sawtooth National Recreation Area (SNRA), 266, 268
Sawtooth Rentals, 292
Sawtooth Scenic Byway, 264
Sawtooth Wilderness Outfitters, 262, 293
Scapegoat Wilderness Area, 169
Schoolhouse and Teacherage Bed and Breakfast, 170
Scott Bed & Breakfast Inn, 225
Seattle Ridge Lodge, 299
Seeley Creek Trails, 209
Seeley Lake, Montana, 168
Seeley-Swan Valley, 168–70
Selway Falls, 249
Selway-Bitterroot Wilderness, 162
Sessions Lodge, 268
Seven Devils Campground, 250
Seven Devils, geology, 235
Shack, The, 165, 207
Shadow's Keep, 167, 207
Shambo Station, 151
Shane, 34–35
Sheepeater Cliffs, 71
Sheepeaters, 20–21
Shore Lodge, 284, 286
Shoshone Indians, 136, 240
Shoshone Lodge, 102

Shoshone National Forest, 59
Shoup, George, 242
Shoup, Idaho, 281
Si Bueno, 286
Signal Mountain Campground, 93
Signal Mountain Lodge, 45
Signal Mountain, 46
Silver Creek Outfitters, 297
Silver Creek Plunge, 258
Silver Creek Preserve, 275, **275**
Silver Gate, Montana, 58
Silverado Western Wear, 301
skiing: in Big Sky, Montana, 79; in Bozeman, Montana,
    109; in Butte, Montana, 227; in Dillon, Montana,
    202; in Hamilton, Montana, 204; in Helena,
    Montana, 224; in Jackson Hole, Wyoming, 97–98; in
    McCall, Idaho, 288; in Missoula, Montana, 208–9; in
    Stanley, Idaho, 293; in Sun Valley, Idaho, 298–99; in
    Teton Valley, 117; in West Yellowstone, Montana,
    75–77, 113; in Whitefish, Montana, 220
Skinny Skis, 98
Sleeping Indian formation, 87
Sleepy Hollow, 112
Slough Creek Campground, 57
Smiley Creek Lodge, 269, 292
Smith & Chandler, 115
Smokejumper Base, 253
Smokejumper Trail, 165
Smokejumpers Base and Aerial Fire Depot Visitor
    Center, 165
Smoky Mountain Pizza & Pasta, 286
Snake River Grill, 95
Snake River Overlook, 45
Snake River, 231
Snow King Mountain, 97
Snow King Resort, 89
Snow King Stables, 97
Sockeye Campground, 267
Soda Butte, 58
Solavie Day Spa & Salon, 300
Solitude Cabin Dinner Sleigh Rides, 99
Someplace Else, 227
Somers, Montana, 175
South Fork Store, 262
South Jenny Lake, 47
South Teton, 43
South Van Houten, 158
Spanish Peaks Brewery and Italian Cafe, 80, 108
Specimen Creek Trail, 77
Specimen Ridge, 57
Spencer's Mountain, 35
Sperry Chalet, 183
Sports Connection, 300
Sportsman Motel, 202
Sprague Creek Campground, 182, 217
Spring Creek (resort), 91
Spring Creek Camp and Trout Ranch, 66
Spring Creek Sleigh Rides, 99
Spring Creek Touring Center, 98
Spring Gulch Campground, 161, 203
Spud Drive-In, 118

Spur Ranch Log Cabins, 92
St. Helena Cathedral, 192
St. Ignatius Mission, 172
St. Joseph's Catholic Church, Idaho City, Idaho, 260
St. Mary's Mission, 163
St. Mary's Motel & RV Park, 203
St. Mary Campground, 186, 217
St. Mary Village, Montana, 186, 187
St. Patrick's Day, 227
Stage Coach Inn, 84, 112, 114
Stanley Basin, 257
Stanley Lake Area Campgrounds, 292
Stanley Lake, 263
Stanley Museum, 264
Stanley, Idaho, 264–65; bicycling, 290–92; campgrounds
    and RV parks, 291–92; fishing, 292; horseback riding,
    292; hot springs, 292; lodging, 290–91; other attrac-
    tions, 293; river floating, 292; snowmobiling,
    292–93; telephone numbers, 293
State travel agencies, 304
Steak Out Restaurant, 66
Steamboat Geyser, 71
Stevensville, Montana, 163
Stock Pot, 296
Stonehouse Restaurant, 223
stratified sites, 16
Streamside Anglers, 208
Stringed Instrument Division, 210
Stumptown Historical Museum, 177
Sturtevants, 299
Sula Ranger Station, 160
Sula Store and Campground, 160, 203
Summit Campground, 188
Sun River Wildlife Management Area, 190
Sun Valley Arts & Crafts Festival, 297
Sun Valley Brewing Company, 275
Sun Valley Golf Course, 297
Sun Valley Heli Ski, 299
Sun Valley Ice Show, 297
Sun Valley Inn, 272
Sun Valley Lodge, 271–72; origins, 245
Sun Valley Nordic Center, 299
Sun Valley Paragliding, 300
Sun Valley Resort, 271–77, 294
Sun Valley Rivers Company, 297
Sun Valley RV Resort, 295
Sun Valley–Salmon Country, 229–33
Sun Valley Serenade, 274
Sun Valley Singletrack, 297
Sun Valley Sled Dog Adventures, 299–300
Sun Valley Soaring, 300
Sun Valley Wine Company, 301
Sun Valley, Idaho, 270–77; bicycling, 297; campgrounds
    and RV parks, 295; fairs, festivals, and events, 297;
    fishing, 297; food, 295–97; golf, 297–98; hiking,
    298; horseback riding, 298; lodging, 293–95; muse-
    ums, 298; origins, 244–45; other activities, 300; river
    floating, 298; shopping, 300–301; skiing, 298–99;
    sporting goods, 299; telephone numbers, 301–2; win-
    ter tours, 299–300
Sunbeam Dam Interpretive Site, 280

Sunbeam Hot Springs, 265–66, **265**, 292
Sunbeam Village, Idaho, 280
Sundance Lodge, 158
Sunlight Ranger Station, 63
Sunny Gulch Campground, 266
Sunrise Campground, 106
Super 8 Motel, 89, 103, 116, 199, 225, 284
Sushi on Second, 296
Swan Creek Campground, 107
Swan Lake Flat, 71
Swan Range, 169
Swan River Inn Cafe and Dinner House, 211
Sweet Pea Festival, 109
Sweetwater Grill, 95
Swift Reservoir, 189
Swiftcurrent Motor Inn, 216
Swinging Bridge Campground, 258
Sylvan Hart ("Buckskin Billy"), 233
Syringa, Idaho, 249

T. Avery Fly Fishing Outfitters, 287
T. Charbonneau's Trading Company, 111
Taggart Lake, 48
Tally Lake Campground, 216
talus, 132
Tamarack Lodge, 294
Teewinot Mountain, 43
Ten Mile Campground, 261
Tendoy, Idaho, 282
Tequila Joe's, 293–94
Teton Canyon Campground, 116
Teton Cyclery, 96
Teton Mountain Bike Tours, 96
Teton National Park, lodging, campgrounds, food,
    activities. *See* Jackson Hole
Teton Pass, 98, 189
Teton Pines, 91, 98
Teton Range, **29**, **47**, **311**
Teton Science School, 45
Teton Tepee Lodge, 116
Teton Valley Campground, 116
Teton Valley, campgrounds and RV parks, 116; food,
    116; history, 35; lodging, 115–16; other activities,
    118; shopping, 118; skiing, 117; telephone numbers,
    119; theater, 118; winter tours, 117
Theodore Roosevelt Ranch, 189
Thomas Nygard Gallery, 111
Thorn Creek Butte lookout, 260
Three Bear Lodge, 112
Three Bear Restaurant, 114
Three Forks, Montana, 83
Three Rivers Resort, 248
Threemile Campground, 59
320 Guest Ranch, 104
ticks, 309
time zones, 312
Tom Miner Campground, 71
Toneri Art Gallery, 301
Tony's Pizza & Pasta, 116
Top of the World Store & Motel, 64
Torrey's Burnt Creek Inn, 280

Towe Ford Museum, 198
Tower Fall, 56; columnar basalt, **57**
Tower-Roosevelt, 56
Townsite Campground, 217
Trail Creek Cabin, 273, 294; Dinner Sleigh Ride, 300
Trail Creek Campground, 116
Trail of the Cedars, 184
Trail Quest, 297
Trail Town, 62
Trailside Americana Fine Art Gallery, 100
Trapper Peak, Bitterroot Range, **161**
travel suggestions: altitudes, 306, 307; avalanches, 310;
    clothing, 303; driving, 306–8; for foreigners, 311–12;
    health, 308–10; hiking, 308; hunting season, 310;
    peak travel times, 303; time zones, 312; weather, 306;
    wildlife viewing, 311
Travels With Charley, (Steinbeck), 123
Triangle C Ranch, 291
Triangle X Ranch 92; float trips, 97
Triple Divide Pass, 187
Triple Divide Peak, 186
Troutfitters, 158
Truby's, 217
Tuchuck Campground, 216
Tupelo Grille, 218
Turpin Meadow Ranch, 92
Twin Bear Gift Shop, 115
Twin Bridges, Montana, 197
Twin Creek Cabins, 92
Twin Creek Campground, 282
Twin Lakes Campground, 201
Twin Peaks Ranch, 280
Two Medicine Campground, 217
Two Medicine Lakes, 188
Two Medicine River Outfitters, 219
Two Ocean Lakes, 49

U.S. High Altitude Sports Center, 196
Union Club Car, 167
Union Pacific Railroad, 244–45
University Golf Course, 208
Upper and Lower Mammoth Terraces, 68
Upper Geyser Basin, 72
Upper Lake Campground, 151
Upper McDonald Falls, 184
Upper Mesa Falls, 85
Upper Payette Lake Campground, 254, 285
Upper Salmon River Valley, 277
Upper Waterton Lake, 187
Upper Whitefish Lake, 178
Uptown Cafe, 226

Valley Market, 275
Valley View at Henry's Lake, 113
Victor Emporium, 117
Victoria Joy's Bed & Breakfast and Tea House, 225
Vienna, Idaho, 269
Village Greens Golf, 219
Village Inn, 214
Virginia City, Montana, 197
Virginian Lodge, The, 89

Virginian RV Park, 93
Visions in Art, 290
Vista Grande, 95
Voices From the Bottom of the Bowl, (Cheney), 35
Voss Inn, 105

Wagon Wheel Campground, 93
Walking Stick Tours, 110
Wapiti Valley, 59
Warm Lake, Idaho, 257
Warm River Campground, 85
Warm Springs Day Lodge, 299
Warm Springs Golf Course, 297–98
Warm Springs Ranch Restaurant, 296
Warm Springs, Idaho. *See* Sun Valley
Warren Wagon Road, 253–57, **253**
Warren, Idaho, 255
Watchable Wildlife Refuge, The, 163
Waters Edge RV Park, 257
Waterton Lakes National Park, Alberta, Canada, 149, 186
Waterton Townsite, Alberta, Canada, 186
Waterton-Glacier International Peace Park, 149, 186
Wayfarers Campground, 174
weather, 306
Weeping Wall, 185
Weir Creek Hot Springs, 247
West Fork Meadows Ranch, 162, 203
West Glacier, Montana, 180–81
West Thumb Geyser Basin, 52
West Thumb, 52
West Yellowstone Conference Hotel, 112
West Yellowstone, Montana, 74–77, 83; bicycling, 114; campgrounds and RV parks, 113; fishing, 114; food, 113–14; lodging, 111–13; Rendezvous Trails, **76**; sites, 74–75; skiing, 75–77; shopping, 115; skiing, 114; telephone numbers, 115; winter tours, 115
Western Design Conference, 103
Western Montana College, 153
Western Montana Fair, 208
Whiskey Jacques, 296
White Bird Battlefield, 250
White Bird Hill, 250
White Knob Challenge, 27
Whitefish Arts Festival, 219
Whitefish KOA, 216
Whitefish Lake Golf Club, 219
Whitefish Lake Lodge Resort, 214
Whitefish Lake Restaurant, 218
Whitefish Lake Run, 219
Whitefish Lake State Park Campground, 216
Whitefish Lake, 175
Whitefish Property Management, 214
Whitefish, Montana, 175, 179; bicycling, 218; campgrounds and RV parks, 216–17; fairs, festivals, and events, 219; food, 217–18; golf, 219; hiking, 219; horseback riding, 219; lodging, 212–16; microbreweries, 218; river floating, 220; rodeo, 220; shopping, 222; skiing, 220; telephone numbers, 222; tours, 220–22; water sports, 222
Whitehouse Campground, 226

Whoop-um-up Creek Park N' Ski Area, 261
Wild Goose Island, 186
Wild Horse Creek Ranch, 295
Wild Horse Island, 174
Wilderness Motel, 162
wildlife, 125, 311
Williams Lake Resort, 281
Williams Lake, 281
Willow Campground, 157
Willow Creek Inn, 83
Wilson, Elijah N. ("Uncle Nick"), 34
Wilson, Sylvester, 33–34
Windbag Saloon and Grill, 223
Windy Saddle Campground, 250
Winona Lake, 179
winter carnivals, 219, 253, 287
Winternational Sports Festival, 227
Wisdom Ranger Station, 158
Wisdom, Montana, 158
Wise River Club, 157
Wise River, Montana, 157, 158
Wolftone Campground, 295
Wood River Trail, 271
Wood River Valley campgrounds, 292
World Museum of Mining & Hell Roarin' Gulch, 194
Wort Hotel, 90
Wyoming Buffalo Company, 104

Ya-Hoo Corrals, 287
Yankee Fork Dredge, 279
Yankee Fork Ranger Station, 280
Yellow Bay Campground, 174
Yellow Pine Harmonica Fest, 257
Yellow Pine, Idaho, 257
Yellowstone Inn Bed & Breakfast, 68
Yellowstone Jazz Festival, 103
Yellowstone Lake, 53
Yellowstone National Park: Albright Visitor Center, 68; bicycling, 102; campgrounds and RV parks, 102; fire, 51; first automobile, 36; first bicycle tour, 33; first national park, 28; first photos, 27; first roads, 36; Fort Yellowstone, 68; Grand Loop, 51; Hayden's surveys, 28; headquarters, 68; lodging, 101–2; number of visitors, 4; Old Faithful Geyser, 72; origins of name, 30; George Catlin, 27; Roosevelt Arch, 69; Roosevelt, Theodore, 38; sights, 50–59, 68–76; telephone numbers, 102; under various superintendents, 37–38;
Yellowstone National Park, The, (Chittenden), 38
Yellowstone Raft Company, 68
Yellowstone Story, The, (Haines), 25
Yellowstone Townhouses, 113
Yellowstone-Teton Country, introduction, 1–5
Yesterday's Calf-A, 153, 201
Yodeler Motel, 65
Yostmark Mountain Equipment, 119
Young Men and Fire, (Maclean), 190

Zim's Hot Springs Campground, 285
Zim's Hot Springs, 251, 287

About the Author

Michael McCoy is a travel writer who hails from Teton Valley, Idaho. He holds degrees in anthropology and zoology and is the author of *The Wild West* and *Montana Off the Beaten Path*, both published by The Globe Pequot Press.